Tl
in Ireland, Sco

In Memoriam

Giovanni B. Andretta, S.J. (1901–1997)
William V. Bangert, S.J. (1911–1985)
James P. Bradley, S.J. (1927–2010)
Joseph T. Browne, S.J. (1926–2009)
James A.P. Byrne, S.J. (1915–2004)
Philip Caraman, S.J. (1911–1998)
Thomas H. Clancy, S.J. (1923–2009)
Donald T. Clifford, S.J (1929–2009)
Gabriel Codina Mir, S.J. (1933–2008)
William M. Davish, S.J. (1913–2002)
Joseph K. Drane, S.J. (1909–1990)
Francis O. Edwards, S.J. (1922–2006)
Edward P. Ennis, S.J. (1919–1992)
T. Geoffrey Holt, S.J. (1912–2009)
Hugh A. Kennedy, S.J. (1918–2009)

Walter P. Krolikowski, S.J. (1923–2007)
Michael Kyne, S.J. (1929–1989)
Albert J. Loomie, S.J. (1922–2002)
László Lukács, S.J. (1910–1998)
Daniel J. McGuire, S.J. (1919–1997)
Frederick P. Manion, S.J. (1916–1985)
D. Bradley Murray, S.J. (1922–2003)
Allen P. Novotny, S.J. (1952–2010)
Charles E. O'Neill, S.J. (1927–2009)
László Polgár, S.J. (1920–2001)
William A. Ryan, S.J. (1914–2009)
Michael J. Smith, S.J. (1915–1990)
David M. Stanley, S.J. (1914–1996)
Hugo Storni, S.J. (1922–2008)
Frederick Turner, S.J. (1910–2001)

Acts 3:6

The Society of Jesus in Ireland, Scotland, and England, 1589–1597
Building the Faith of Saint Peter upon the King of Spain's Monarchy

THOMAS M. MCCOOG, S.J.
Fordham University, USA

LONDON AND NEW YORK

First published 2012 by Ashgate Publishing

Published 2016 by Routledge
2 Park Square, Milton Park, Abingdon, Oxon OX14 4RN
711 Third Avenue, New york, Ny 10017, USA

First issued in paperback 2017

Routledge is an imprint of the Taylor & Francis Group, an informa business

Copyright © Thomas M. McCoog, S.J. 2012

Thomas M. McCoog, S.J. has asserted his moral right under the Copyright, Designs and Patents Act, 1988, to be identified as the author of this work.

All rights reserved. No part of this book may be reprinted or reproduced or utilised in any form or by any electronic, mechanical, or other means, now known or hereafter invented, including photocopying and recording, or in any information storage or retrieval system, without permission in writing from the publishers.

Notice:
Product or corporate names may be trademarks or registered trademarks, and are used only for identification and explanation without intent to infringe.

British Library Cataloguing in Publication Data
McCoog, Thomas M.
  The Society of Jesus in Ireland, Scotland, and England, 1589-97 : building the faith Saint Peter upon the King of Spain's monarchy. -- (Catholic Christendom, 1300-1700)
  1. Jesuits--Ireland--History--16th century. 2. Jesuits--Scotland--History--16th century. 3. Jesuits--England--History--16th century. 4. Catholic Church--Great Britain--History--16th century. 5. Great Britain--Foreign relations--1558-1603. 6. Spain--Foreign relations--1556-1598. 7. Great Britain--Foreign relations--Spain. 8. Spain--Foreign relations--Great Britain. 9. Great Britain--Church history--16th century. 10. Great Britain--History--Elizabeth, 1558-1603.
  I. Title II. Series
  271.5'3041'09031-dc22

Library of Congress Cataloging-in-Publication Data
McCoog, Thomas M.
  The Society of Jesus in Ireland, Scotland, and England, 1589-97 : building the faith of Saint Peter upon the King of Spain's monarchy / Thomas McCoog.
    p. cm.
  Includes bibliographical references and index.
  ISBN 978-1-4094-3772-7 (hardcover)
  1. Jesuits-Ireland--History--16th century. 2. Jesuits--Scotland--History--16th century. 3. Jesuits--England--History--16th century. 4. Ireland--Church history--16th century. 5. Scotland--Church history--16th century. 6. England--Church history--16th century. I. Title.
  BX3719.M33 2011
  271'.5304109031--dc23
                                                                    2011022329

ISBN 13: 978-1-138-11112-7 (pbk)
ISBN 13: 978-1-4094-3772-7 (hbk)

Contents

Series Editor's Preface		*vii*
Publishers' Note		*ix*
Preface		*xi*
Abbreviations		*xiii*
Introduction		1
1	The "Cradle of Nascent Catholicity": Life on the Mission, 1589–1593	15
2	"Schools of Sedition": Catholic Exiles on the Continent, 1589–1593	95
3	"Lurking Papists": Treasons, Plots, Conspiracies, and Martyrdoms, 1594–1595	143
4	"No Union of Hearts": Catholic Exiles on the Continent, 1594–1595	205
5	"Growen Odious to the World": Conflict and Discord on the English Mission, 1596–1597	275
6	"Leagues of Unquiet and Subversive Spirits": Continental Struggles, 1596–1597	335
Conclusion: "Good Newes from Fraunce"		407
Bibliography		419
Index		449

Series Editor's Preface

The still-usual emphasis on medieval (or Catholic) and reformation (or Protestant) religious history has meant neglect of the middle ground, both chronological and ideological. As a result, continuities between the middle ages and early modern Europe have been overlooked in favor of emphasis on radical discontinuities. Further, especially in the later period, the identification of "reformation" with various kinds of Protestantism means that the vitality and creativity of the established church, whether in its Roman or local manifestations, has been left out of account. In the last few years, an upsurge of interest in the history of traditional (or catholic) religion makes these inadequacies in received scholarship even more glaring and in need of systematic correction. The series will attempt this by covering all varieties of religious behavior, broadly interpreted, not just (or even especially) traditional institutional and doctrinal church history. It will to the maximum degree possible be interdisciplinary, comparative and global, as well as non-confessional. The goal is to understand religion, primarily of the "Catholic" variety, as a broadly human phenomenon, rather than as a privileged mode of access to superhuman realms, even implicitly.

The period covered, 1300–1700, embraces the moment which saw an almost complete transformation of the place of religion in the life of Europeans, whether considered as a system of beliefs, as an institution, or as a set of social and cultural practices. In 1300, vast numbers of Europeans, from the pope down, fully expected Jesus's return and the beginning of His reign on earth. By 1700, very few Europeans, of whatever level of education, would have subscribed to such chiliastic beliefs. Pierre Bayle's notorious sarcasms about signs and portents are not idiosyncratic. Likewise, in 1300 the vast majority of Europeans probably regarded the pope as their spiritual head; the institution he headed was probably the most tightly integrated and effective bureaucracy in Europe. Most Europeans were at least nominally Christian, and the pope had at least nominal knowledge of that fact. The papacy, as an institution, played a central role in high politics, and the clergy in general formed an integral part of most governments, whether central or local. By 1700, Europe was divided into a myriad of different religious allegiances, and even those areas officially subordinate to the pope were both more nominally Catholic in belief (despite colossal efforts at imposing uniformity) and also in allegiance than they had been four hundred years earlier. The pope had become only one political factor, and not one of the first rank. The clergy, for its part, had virtually disappeared from secular governments as well as losing much of its local authority. The stage was set for the Enlightenment.

Thomas F. Mayer,
Augustana College

Publishers' Note

This volume is a co-publication between Ashgate Publishing and the Jesuit Historical Institute.

As well as being part of Ashgate's *Catholic Christendom, 1300–1700* monograph series, it is the 73rd volume in the Jesuit Historical Institute's series *Bibliotheca Instituti Historici Societatis Iesu*.

LONDON AND NEW YORK

Institutum Historicum Societatis Iesu

Preface

In the summer of 1989, if I remember correctly, I drafted a proposal for a four-volume history of the English Province of the Society of Jesus. I intended to cover the reigns of Elizabeth I and James I (1558–1625) in one volume; a second volume would continue to the "Glorious Revolution" (1625–1688). I approached Eamon Duffy and Peter L'Estrange, S.J., as possible authors for the third and fourth volumes. Both were reluctant to commit. Dr Duffy was in the process of leaving the eighteenth century as he researched what would become *The Stripping of the Altars* (New Haven/London, 1992); Father L' Estrange was completing his doctoral thesis on nineteenth century English Jesuits. I abandoned the project in favor of a monograph on Elizabethan/Jacobean England. That turned into an enterprise far greater than I had originally anticipated. *The Society of Jesus in Ireland, Scotland, and England 1541–1588: "Our Way of Proceeding?"* (Leiden, 1996) appeared 15 years ago. Editorial duties as director of publications of the Institutum Historicum Societatis Iesu in Rome from 2000 to 2010 slowed progress on its sequel. Ten years of commuting between my post in Rome and my position in London as archivist of the British Province of the Society of Jesus meant, however, that I had continual access to the two most important archives for any study of the English Jesuits during that period.

In this volume as in its predecessor, my perspective is decidedly Jesuit not simply because of my membership in that religious order, but principally because the Archivum Romanum Societatis Iesu (ARSI) serves as the archival base of my research. With the exception of the Anglia codices and the Collectanea, formerly deposited at Stonyhurst College, Lancashire, but transferred to the Archivum Britannicum Societatis Iesu (ABSI) a decade ago, the provincial archives hold few contemporary documents. But the ABSI does possess an amazing collection of transcripts, photocopies, microfilms, and now DVDs of material from other archives, a collection compiled over the years by historians such as John Hungerford Pollen, S.J., Leo Hicks, S.J., Francis Edwards, S.J., and Penelope Renold, often in connection with The Cause of the English Martyrs. In many cases they or an amanuensis provided fairly literal English translations. Later translations by Joseph K. Drane, S.J., James A.P. Byrne, S.J., and Antonio Maldonado, S.J., augmented the collection. I have used their translations but usually after some re-working, I have compared transcripts with original documents unless, as in a few cases, I did not have access to the original. I then cite only the transcript. Regarding dating, unless the documents themselves specify otherwise, I assume that documents written in the three kingdoms were dated in the "old style," and those on the continent, "new style." I understand the year for both, however, as beginning on 1 January and not 25 March.

I accumulated many debts during this period of gestation. Ginevra Crosignani, Peter Davidson, Peter Harris, John LaRocca, S.J., Robert Miola, Hiram Morgan, and Michael Questier have been especially helpful. More than once I accepted their advice. Joseph De Cock, S.J., Marek Inglot, S.J., Robert Danieluk, S.J., José Antonio Yoldi, S.J., Mauro Brunello, of ARSI; James F.X. Pratt, S.J., Nicoletta Basilotta, Caterina Talloru, Stephen Fernando, Francisco de Borja Medina, S.J., Mark A. Lewis, S.J., and László Szilas, S.J., of the former Institutum Historicum Societatis Iesu; Brian MacCuarta, S.J., and Paul Oberholzer, S.J., of the restructured Institutum; James Hodkinson, S.J., Anna Edwards, and Mihaela Repina of ABSI, facilitated my research. I am grateful to Monsignor Michael Kujacz, rector of the Royal and Pontifical English College of St Alban, Valladolid, for allowing me to reproduce the painting used on the cover. Dermot Preston, S.J., Michael Holman, S.J., David Smolira, S.J., and James Crampsey, S.J., the four provincials of the British Province under whom I have worked, provided much needed encouragement. Joaquín Barrero, S.J., superior of Curia Generalizia in Rome, did everything within his considerable powers, to improve conditions for research. The indefatigable Ms Andrea Campana prevented many embarrassing errors through her careful proofreading and indexing. I thank Joseph M. McShane, S.J., president, John J. Cecero, S.J., rector, and the Jesuit community of Fordham University, for providing a perfect environment for the completion of this work. Finally I dedicate this work to 30 deceased Jesuit friends and colleagues, who played significant roles in my vocation as a Jesuit and my life as an historian.

Abbreviations

AAW	London, Archives of the Archdiocese of Westminster
ABSI	London, Archivum Britannicum Societatis Iesu
AHSI	*Archivum Historicum Societatis Iesu*
ARCR	*The Contemporary Printed Literature of the English Counter-Reformation between 1558 and 1640*. Eds. A.F. Allison and D.M. Rogers. 2 vols Aldershot: Scolar Press, 1989–1994.
ARSI	Archivum Romanum Societatis Iesu
ASV	Vatican City, Archivio segreto vaticano
BIHSI	Bibliotheca Instituti Historici Societatis Iesu
BL	London, British Library
CRS	Catholic Record Society
CSPD	*Calendar of State Papers, Domestic Series of the Reigns of Edward VI ...* Eds. Robert Lemon et al. 12 vols London, 1857–1872.
CSP Foreign	*Calendar of State Papers Foreign Series of the Reign of Elizabeth*. Eds. Joseph Stevenson et al. 23 vols in 26 parts. London, 1863–1950.
CSP Simancas	*Calendar of letters and papers ... preserved principally in the archives of Simancas*. Ed. Martin A.S. Hume. 4 vols London, 1892–1899.
CSP Scotland	*Calendar of the State Papers relating to Scotland, and Mary, Queen of Scots, 1547–1603 ...* Eds. Joseph Bain et al. 13 vols in 14 parts. London, 1898–1969.
ed.	editor
edn.	edition
fol. (fols)	folio, folios
HMC	Historical Manuscript Commission
IJA	Dublin, Irish Jesuit Archives
IT	London, Inner Temple
MHSI	Monumenta Historica Societatis Iesu

MSS	Manuscripts
num.(s)	numbers
para. (s)	paragraph(s)
pp.	page, pages
SP	State Papers
STC	A *Short Title Catalogue of Books Printed in England, Scotland, and Ireland and of English Books Printed Abroad, 1475–1640*. Eds. A.W. Pollard and G.R. Redgrave. 2nd edn. Revised and enlarged W.A. Jackson, F.S. Ferguson and Katherine F. Pantzer. 3 vols London: The Bibliographical Society, 1986–1991.
TNA	Kew, The National Archives
vol. (vols)	volume, volumes

Introduction

In a circular letter dated April 9, 1588 and addressed to Jesuit provincials in Italy, Claudio Acquaviva, Superior General of the Society of Jesus, recommended prayers for the *impresa* then being prepared by King Philip II of Spain. This enterprise against England, he wrote, was of the utmost importance for the Roman Catholic Church, its defense and exultation. Thus Jesuit fathers and brothers should pray for its success. Jesuits had done so in the past; now they should pray with even more fervor because Philip himself and Enrique de Guzmán, Count of Olivares and Spanish ambassador in Rome, had specifically asked Jesuits in those locales for spiritual assistance. Acquaviva therefore directed that provincials ensure some Masses and prayers were said weekly in each college and house.[1]

Contemporary historians persistently remind us that Ignatius Loyola and his companions did not establish the Society of Jesus to counteract the Protestant Reformation. Yet decisions made by Loyola quickly launched the new order as Counter-Reformation *par excellence*. In 1550, 10 years after the foundation of the Society, Pope Julius III approved a revision in the order's foundational document. Pope Paul III's earlier bull of approval, *Regimini militantis ecclesiae*, defined the Society's purpose as "the propagation of the faith and the progress of souls in Christian life and doctrine." *Exposcit debitum*, Julius III's bull of 1550 adjusted "propagation of the faith" to "the defense and propagation of the faith."[2] Albeit slight linguistically, the alteration witnesses a change of mentality. We may justifiably argue the appropriate historical label for the religious sixteenth-century, or the date in which the Catholic Reformation became the Counter-Reformation, or, indeed, the identity of the first Counter-Reformation pope.[3] But historians concur there was a change. Regardless of its spiritual origins, the Society of Jesus in the eyes of its enemies, Catholic and Protestant, and in the evolving self-understanding of its members, quickly engaged Protestants and heretics on educational, social and theological fronts.[4] The interpretation of pivotal moments in

---

[1] ARSI, Instit. 40, fol. 104ʳ.

[2] See John W. O'Malley, S.J., *The First Jesuits* (Cambridge, Mass., 1993), pp. 4–5.

[3] See John W. O'Malley, S.J., *Trent and All That. Renaming Catholicism in the Early Modern Era* (Cambridge, Mass., 2000); Elisabeth G. Gleason, "Who Was the First Counter-Reformation Pope?," *Catholic Historical Review*, 81 (1995): pp. 173–84.

[4] See Oskar Garstein, *Rome and the Counter-Reformation in Scandinavia Jesuit Educational Strategy 1553–1622* (Leiden, 1992) for the role of Jesuit colleges in papal

the Spiritual Exercises, for example, the two standards, the call of the king, lord/vassal relationship,[5] became more and more militaristic: soldiers united under the banner of Christ in battle against evil.[6] The ever-prudent Everard Mercurian, Acquaviva's predecessor as superior general, commented on each Jesuit's responsibility to help his neighbor grow towards perfection. For this reason, Mercurian argued, "at the end of the Exercises some rules are given for thinking with the orthodox Church in mind and work, particularly in these times of ours, so that we can directly oppose the heresies of our day."[7] Jesuits, Mercurian elucidated, aid "others to their salvation and eternal blessedness, as has been stated regarding the Spiritual Exercises—so that in this way greater knowledge of our Lord may be had in every circumstance and action of ours, and the name of God be more greatly glorified."[8] In an exhortation to Jesuits at the Roman College in 1574, he described the Society's spirituality "in terms of a collective crusade against evil." The Society of Jesus was, he said, an army on a "glorious expedition" to tear souls "from the tyrannical power of the devil and ... [bring] them back to their Creator, Maker, and Redeemer, Jesus Christ our Lord."[9]

Much recent historiography of the Society of Jesus concerns the implementation of the principles of the Ignatian Spiritual Exercises and other foundational documents of the Society's Institute, specifically congregational decrees, rules, ordinances. For the Society of Jesus, "Institute" means "the way they lived and worked, and they thus include in the term all the official documents of the order." Practically synonymous

---

Counter-Reformation policy; and Anita Mancia, "La controversia con i protestanti e i programmi degli studi teologici nella Compagnia di Gesù 1547–1599," *AHSI*, 54 (1985): pp. 3–43, 209–66; Francesco C. Cesareo, "The Jesuit Colleges in Rome under Everard Mercurian," in *The Mercurian Project: Forming Jesuit Culture 1573–1580*, (ed.) Thomas M. McCoog, S.J. (Rome/St Louis, 2004), pp. 607–44; Thomas M. McCoog, S.J., "'Replant the Uprooted Trunk of the Tree of Faith': The Society of Jesus and Continental Colleges for Religious Exiles," forthcoming, for curriculum.

[5] See for example Robert L. Schmitt, S.J., "The Christ-Experience and Relationship Fostered in the Spiritual Exercises of St Ignatius of Loyola," *Studies in the Spirituality of Jesuits*, 6/5 (1974): pp. 217–55.

[6] See Peter Schineller, S.J., "From an Ascetical Spirituality of the *Exercises* to the Apostolic Spirituality of the *Constitutions*: Laborers in the Lord's Vineyard," in *Ite inflammate omnia*, (ed.) Thomas M. McCoog, S.J. (Rome, 2010), pp. 85–108.

[7] "Short Instructions on Giving the Exercises" in *On Giving the Spiritual Exercises: The Early Jesuit Manuscript Directories and the Official Directory of 1599*, (ed.) Martin E. Palmer, S.J. (St Louis, 1996), p. 104.

[8] "Counsels of Father Everard Mercurian to Fabio de Fabi," in Palmer, *On Giving the Spiritual Exercises*, pp. 114–15.

[9] See Philip Endean, S.J., "'The Original Line of Our Father Ignatius': Mercurian and the Spirituality of the Exercises," in McCoog, *Mercurian Project*, p. 43.

with "Institute," is the cherished expression "our way of proceeding" (*noster modus procedendi, nuestro modo de proceder, nostro modo di procedere*).[10] Earlier Jesuit historians, generally members of the same Society, presented the Society as born quasi-Venusian from the mind and heart of Ignatius. Now more critical historians have exposed this interpretation's apologetical and controversial roots, and demonstrate the evolution of a distinctive Jesuit "way of proceeding." John W. O'Malley, S.J. argues that the Jesuit "way of proceeding" was more or less stabilized by 1565, the death of Diego Laínez, the second superior general of the order. Post-1565 changes, according to O'Malley, "moved almost inexorably and ever more definitively into modalities characteristic of the Counter Reformation as such."[11] No matter how inexorable the progress may have been, the path was not without difficulties.

Nearly 40 years ago John Bossy commented on the type of history then being written by and about English Catholics, specifically David Mathew's *Catholicism in England. The Portrait of a Minority: Its Culture and Tradition* (London, 1936; 2nd edn., 1948). Such a volume, aimed primarily at a Catholic audience, "was also likely to sustain the inherited conviction of outsiders that a Catholic community was a foreign body with which—even if they were historians, perhaps especially if they were historians—they were not required to bother."[12] Fortunately the situation has changed. Scholars have discovered post-Reformation English Catholicism. (We cannot call it a revival because there was nothing to revive.) Many would agree, in theory if not in practice, with Ethan Sagan that:

> many of the fundamental issues of English history cannot be adequately understood without taking into account a Catholic perspective, while many of the fundamental issues of Catholic historiography cannot be understood in isolation from the rest of English society.[13]

As English Catholics struggled against marginalization, they, to use Michael Questier's distinction, displayed a coherence, a self-identity,

---

[10] O'Malley, *First Jesuits*, p. 8.

[11] O'Malley, *First Jesuits*, p. 368. See also his introduction to *The Jesuits II, Cultures, Sciences, and the Arts, 1540–1773*, (eds.) John W. O'Malley, S.J., Gauvin Alexander Bailey, Steven J. Harris and T. Frank Kennedy, S.J. (Toronto, 2006), pp. xxiii–xxxvi.

[12] John Bossy, *The English Catholic Community 1570–1850* (New York, 1976), p. 2.

[13] Ethan Shagan (ed.), *Catholics and the "Protestant Nation." Religious Politics and Identity in Early Modern England* (Manchester, 2005), p. 2.

without permanent harmony.[14] And the lack of harmony becomes ever more evident as the century ends.

In *The Society of Jesus in Ireland, Scotland, and England 1541–1588 "Our Way of Proceeding?*,[15] I explored the flexibility of the "Institute" and the nature of Jesuit Counter-Reformation involvement as the Jesuits adapted to precarious situations within the British Isles and Ireland. Mindful of Hugh Trevor-Roper's lament that Jesuit historians too often employed a principle of "distorting background"[16] by excluding compromising or embarrassing details, I set Jesuit activity within early modern cultural, diplomatic and political history not just of Ireland, Scotland and England but of the continent. I stress again that my principal focus is England, but the new British historiography has opened our eyes to the importance of the interplay of events within the three kingdoms, and the dangers of considering one kingdom in isolation. The same arguments can be advanced for continental affairs. European monarchs tracked events in England. As France's religious wars morphed into a dynastic struggle, Spain consolidated its position as the major Catholic power ready to intervene, to effect a regime change if necessary, for the good of Catholicism and of Spain. King Philip II refashioned a crusader mentality inherited from his great-grandparents Ferdinand and Isabella, into a "messianic imperialism," a "messianic vision."[17] The three kingdoms of Ireland, Scotland and England provided an ideal situation for the implementation of the vision.

Jesuit involvement in the three kingdoms predated the actual foundation of the Society of Jesus: Ignatius Loyola begged alms in England, possibly in London, in 1531. Two of his first companions, Alfonso Salmerón and Paschase Broët, stopped at the court of King James V of Scotland, on their diplomatic mission to Irish ecclesiastical and secular leaders then in rebellion against England's King Henry VIII in 1541–42. Reginald, Cardinal Pole kindly rejected Loyola's offer of Jesuit assistance during the brief restoration of Catholicism under Queen Mary Tudor (1553–58)

---

[14] Micheal Questier, *Catholicism and Community in Early Modern England. Politics, Aristocratic Patronage and Religion, c. 1550–1640* (Cambridge, 2006), p. xii.

[15] (Leiden, 1996). The following paragraphs summarize the book.

[16] Hugh Trevor-Roper, "Twice-Martyred: The English Jesuits and Their Historians," in *Historical Essays* (London, 1957), pp. 113–18.

[17] See Geoffrey Parker, *The Grand Strategy of Philip II* (New Haven/London, 1998), pp. 93–109; "The Place of Tudor England in the Messianic Vision of Philip II of Spain," *Transactions of the Royal Historical Society*, 6th series 12 (200): pp. 167–221. Messianic imperialism in brief, was Philip's "direct mandate [from God] to uphold the Catholic faith at almost all times and in almost all places" (*Grand Strategy*, p. 93). The first biography of Philip proclaimed his motto as *Suma ratio pro Religione* (Religion is the highest priority) (*Grand Strategy*, p. 95).

and her husband Philip of Spain. Pope Pius IV employed the Dutch Jesuit Nicolas da Gouda on a mission to Scotland and the Irish Jesuit David Wolfe to Ireland in the 1560s. The former concluded Scottish Catholicism could only be saved if Mary, Queen of Scots, married a strong Catholic prince, perhaps Philip II himself. Until then, and only after Mary had secured a firmer hold on the throne, there would be no Jesuit mission. By May 1568, Mary was under house arrest in England and her infant son James in the custody of a staunch Protestant regent.

As David Wolfe nominated suitable candidates for Irish bishoprics and travelled throughout the island, often in association with opponents of English authority, two Jesuits operated a small school in and around Limerick. One, an Englishman William Good, consistently bemoaned living conditions, the impossibility of religious life in these circumstances. His lamentations and increased enforcement of anti-Catholic legislation because of Pope Pius V's excommunication of Queen Elizabeth with *Regnans in Excelsis*, resulted in a recall of Jesuits from Ireland in 1570. After a period in prison, Wolfe crossed to the continent in 1573 to seek Spanish aid for a revolt against England. Apparently his involvement with the rebellion ended in his dismissal from the Jesuits circa 1577. Jesuit contact with England was intermittent during the first 20 years of Elizabeth's rule: the Spanish Jesuit Pedro de Ribadeneira observed the religious transition after the death of Queen Mary 1558; William Good passed through England in 1564; Thomas Woodhouse, a secular priest, professed himself a Jesuit on the eve of his execution in 1573. Thomas King, the only Jesuit actually sent to England, went for reasons of health in 1564. The Society remained on the fringe of Catholic activity within the three kingdoms until it reluctantly assumed administration of the English College, Rome, in 1579.

In the 1570s Mercurian replied to William Allen's periodic requests for Jesuit assistance in England with promises of prayers. Mercurian feared friction between secular clergy and Jesuits in the absence of a Catholic hierarchy. Having received frequent complaints from Good during his stay in Ireland, the general doubted whether conditions in England allowed a proper style of religious life. Moreover, he feared the English government would misinterpret a Jesuit mission as a political enterprise. In 1579 he finally conceded permission for a Jesuit mission to England in the expectation that some form of religious tolerance would follow the queen's marriage to François Valois, Duke of Anjou. In April of 1580 Robert Parsons, Edmund Campion and Ralph Emerson set off from Rome with considerable fanfare, a small part of a much larger band. Prior to their departure, Parsons and Campion met Pope Gregory XIII. To their specific question about Pius V's excommunication, Gregory replied that, conditions being as they were [*rebus sic stantibus*], Catholics were not obliged to obey it under pain of sin or excommunication.[18] Perhaps Mercurian hoped the inclusion of the Marian bishop Thomas Goldwell, sometime Bishop of St Asaph, would prevent any clerical friction. The general's instructions stressed the spiritual nature of the mission and exhorted Jesuits to live their religious lives as well as they could. News of a Spanish-Papal military expedition to Ireland raised English fears and tightened security.[19] Support among the queen's councillors for the Anjou marriage collapsed. Meanwhile Parsons and Campion preached on sensitive subjects to large congregations as they travelled secretly throughout the realm. Recusancy, they argued, was the only acceptable Catholic response to the government's demands for religious conformity, and attendance at Protestant services demonstrated acceptance of heresy rather than political loyalty. The premature dissemination of Campion's so-called "brag," an *apologia* for his mission in England intended for release after his capture, intensified the search for the Jesuits, whose protests that the mission was spiritual, were dismissed as specious. What Catholics saw as reconciliation to the Roman Church, the government regarded as treason, and issued severe legislation accordingly. Henceforth all recusants must conform at least once a month, and anyone reconciled to the Church of Rome became guilty of high treason, as did the reconciler. Penalties against both saying and attending Mass were increased. Campion was captured in July 1581 and executed on December 1. Parsons escaped to the continent, to the protection of the Guises, the defenders of orthodoxy in religiously conflicted France. Parsons, William Allen, and Henry, Duke of Guise, negotiated various plans for the overthrow of Elizabeth and the liberation of Mary, Queen of Scots. The Throckmorton Plot of 1583/84, the first of a number of conspiracies involving Spain, real, imagined, fabricated or manipulated, alerted English subjects to Catholic designs. In 1584 Parliament passed an Act to protect the queen; an Act against Jesuits and seminary priests, proclaiming as traitors all such who remained within the kingdom 40 days after its enactment, immediately followed. Parliament asserted that not only did Jesuits deny the spiritual authority of the queen but also that they recognized the authority of a foreign prince, the pope, engaged in conspiracies against her.

---

[18] See Ginevra Crosignani, Thomas M. McCoog, S.J. and Michael Questier, (eds.), with the assistance of Peter Holmes, *Recusancy and Conformity in Early Modern England* (Toronto/Rome, 2010), pp. 90–100.

[19] See Alexandra Walsham, "'This Newe Army of Satan': The Jesuit Mission and the Formation of Public opinion in Elizabethan England," in *Modern Panics, the Media and the Law in Early Modern England*, (eds.) David Lemmings and Clare Walker (Basingstoke, 2009), pp. 41–62.

Persecution raised doubts about the mission's future. Claudio Acquaviva had periodic misgivings. As one of Mercurian's advisors, he had argued in favor of a mission. Now he too wondered whether continual Jesuit involvement posed not only threats to the Jesuits themselves, but to the lay men and women who supported them. More than once Parsons and Allen convinced Acquaviva not to abandon the mission.

Campion and Parsons constructed a network of safe houses, often with residential chaplains, among the members and friends of the Vaux family of Harrowden. William Weston, arriving in September 1584, established a fund purse to support the clergy. The network expanded further with the arrival of more Jesuits. William Weston was arrested in London in early August 1586, and remained in prison until 1603. Henry Garnet succeeded him as superior. In London Robert Southwell revived the important mission of the written word. Unlike Parsons, who had used his clandestine press to denounce occasional conformity and Campion's opponents in 1580–81, Southwell wrote spiritual treatises to console and strengthen frightened believers.

The Jesuit mission in Ireland ended in late 1581 with the collapse of the Baltinglass rebellion and the defeat of the Spanish-Papal expeditionary force. In Scotland the few Jesuits associated with Catholic nobles, and operated in shires under their influence. But throughout the three kingdoms, the Jesuit missions tested the flexibility of the early Society. The Jesuit "way of proceeding" adapted to the precarious situations of the three kingdoms and would continue to do so as the number of Jesuits on the mission increased. Mercurian had worried about the effects of persecution and clandestine operations on religious life. Once the hopes of a French marriage vanished and the government responded to the high-profile activities of the first Jesuits with more severe legislation, Mercurian most likely would have cancelled the mission if he had lived. Even his more adventuresome successor Claudio Acquaviva hesitated. But by 1588 the English mission's future was more secure.

Mercurian had also feared that the government would spin Jesuits as political activists. Intimations and rumors of Catholic intervention provided grounds for the crown's fears, and Parsons did play a significant role in the diplomacy surrounding the formation of leagues and coalitions to overthrow Elizabeth. Philip II was involved in all negotiations; Spain's ascendancy eventually caused a serious rift among English Catholic exiles. Parsons and the Scottish Jesuit William Crichton participated in high-level discussions about her deposition. Parsons may even have heard about a proposal to assassinate her as he and Allen prepared official rationales and propaganda for the one implemented design: the Spanish Armada of 1588. Shortly after its failure, Parsons departed Rome for Spain to make sure that Philip II did not forget England amidst his dynastic involvement with France.

Waging Counter-Reformation war brought Jesuits into closer contact with popes, kings, princes, dukes and bishops. As the Society solicited their friendship as benefactors for colleges,[20] it initially wanted little if any involvement at court.[21] But these benefactors turned more and more to Jesuits for advice and assistance. Could the Society aid its benefactors without involvement in works and ministries deemed inappropriate for religious men? Mercurian had worried that Wolfe's association with the Fitzgerald rebellion conflicted with the Society's Institute. As Acquaviva explored new possibilities, some Jesuits feared the political involvement of Parsons and others compromised the Society. Jesuit association with Scottish Catholic earls, Hugh O'Neill, Earl of Tyrone, and the king of Spain, each deemed actually or potentially dangerous by the English crown, challenged traditional understandings of the "things of Caesar and the things of God."

In his excellent survey of Jesuit political thought, Harro Höpfl points out that the "point at which the spiritual and the temporal, religion and statecraft, most obviously coincided and as often as not collided, was the issue of heresy."[22] "The Society of Jesus," Höpfl explains:

> recognised from its inception that an engagement with the world of secular rulers was inescapable. Most Jesuits in most places and at most times had nothing to do with "matters of state." They neither sought nor welcomed political prominence. But the Society's more hysterical opponents accused it of liking nothing better than interfering in politics. The Society's apologists for their part just as routinely proclaimed that the Society's own articles of association sternly prohibited any political meddling.[23]

Almost from its foundation the Society of Jesus stood accused of meddling in political, secular affairs. Sabina Pavone explains that many now classic anti-Jesuit treatises, were actually written by former members of the Society and reflect intra-Jesuit disputes and tensions. Arguably the most infamous, the *Monita secreta*, was written by a Polish ex-Jesuit circa 1614 to reveal to the world already suspicious of Jesuit machinations, an alleged

---

[20] See Olwen Hufton, "Every Tub on its Own Bottom: Funding a Jesuit College in Early Modern Europe," in O'Malley, *Jesuits II*, pp. 5–23.

[21] On the role of Jesuits at court, see Dennis Flynn, "Jasper Heywood and the German Usury Controversy," in McCoog, *Mercurian Project*, pp. 185–208.

[22] Harro Höpfl, *Jesuit Political Thought. The Society of Jesus and the State, c. 1540–1630* (Cambridge, 2004), p. 3.

[23] Höpfl, *Jesuit Political Thought*, p. 1.

secret document demonstrating clearly and definitively the Society of Jesus as a small but diabolically astute force which exploited the sacrament of confession and spiritual direction for their political ends.[24] Although rules of behavior were formulated for Jesuits serving in the sensitive role as royal confessor, fears of Jesuit exploitation of the role persisted.[25] Individual Jesuits serving as confessors and advisors to nobility and royalty wielded considerable influence, but did it harmonize with Jesuit principles? It is not coincidental that as Jesuit philosophers and theologians expounded the Thomistic indirect power of the papacy, provincial congregations debated the nature and extent of political engagement as unbecoming to religious and contrary to "our way of proceeding."

To many English subjects Robert Parsons typified the political Jesuit. Alarmed by recent congregational decrees, he astutely observed that religious and political issues were so intertwined in England that one could not treat the former without touching on the latter. Anxious lest he violate the decrees, he requested a dispensation from Acquaviva. The general did not grant one because Parsons did not need one. Together they implemented the principles of the indirect power of the papacy: as long as a Jesuit worked for the greater glory of God and not the advancement of any one nation or dynasty, he avoided involvement in political matters. The sacred must guide the secular. Jesuits could, apparently, do more than simply pray for the *impresa* as Acquaviva had recommended in 1588.

Bill Shankly, the legendary coach of Liverpool Football Club, allegedly said "Some people believe football is a matter of life and death, I am very disappointed with that attitude. I can assure you it is much, much more important than that." So too was the question of "occasional conformity" for Catholics. Refusal could result in poverty and, perhaps, execution; participation could mean mortal sin and eternal damnation. The political activities of Elizabethan England are played out against a backdrop of eternity. Protestants and Catholics agreed that "*extra ecclesiasm nulla salus*" (outside the Church there is no salvation) but differed, of course, on which denomination was the Church in question. In his monograph on early modern Dutch Catholicism, Charles H. Parker stresses this point:

> Men and women in the sixteenth and seventeenth centuries did not regard heresy, idolatry, or apostasy as religious choices; rather they understood them as plagues of the soul, seductions of the devil, and portals to hell. Paradoxically they believed that the religious choices they did make would free them from

---

[24] See Sabina Pavone, *The Wily Jesuits and the Monita Secreta. The Forged Secret Instructions of the Jesuits. Myth and Reality* (St Louis, 2005), pp. 8–9.

[25] See Robert Bireley, S.J., *The Jesuits and the Thirty Years War. Kings, Courts, and Confessors* (Cambridge, 2003) for an exposition of the complex problem of royal confessors.

these terrors. Since all confessional groups regarded themselves as the true body of Christ, each denomination necessarily considered all others as sectarian, schismatic, heretical, or idolatrous.[26]

Toleration was not the norm; in the sixteenth-century it was at best extolled as expedient by the *politiques* to the disgust of most Jesuits. As Benjamin J. Kaplan observes, toleration was an "embarrassment."[27] The persistence of popery with its magical rituals and superstitious devotions, from a Protestant perspective, or the admission of heresy with its debasement of sacraments and iconoclastic destruction, from a Catholic one, threatened the body politic. The presence of religious dissenters might provoke a wrathful God to punish such shortsightedness. God held, as Kaplan rightly points out, "entire communities to account for the behavior of its members."[28] As outsiders within the walls, dissenters were often perceived as a potential fifth column. Pastoral responsibilities of ecclesiastical and secular elites demanded an appropriate social discipline. Religious dissenters were a cancer that could infect the entire body. Without discipline weaker individuals could succumb to temptation and consequent damnation. The presence of a non-conforming minority posed a risk for the entire society, natural and supernatural threats so great that their demonization is understandable.[29]

In a thoughtful introduction to *Salvation at Stake*, Brad S. Gregory warns historians against contemporary approaches that do injustice to early modern self-understanding by reducing them to post-modern categories. "We are left with starkly different interpretations of the reformers," Gregory rightly claims. "Fundamentally were they social control ideologues who imposed their constructions on an oppressed populace, or conscientious pastors who strove to rattle the complacent out of their deadly spiritual stupor?"[30] I follow Gregory's lead by adhering to the second.

In *Providence in Early Modern England*,[31] Alexandra Walsham demonstrates the prevalence of the conviction of God's intervention in

---

[26] Charles Parker, *Faith on the Margins: Catholics and Catholicism in the Dutch Golden Age* (Cambridge, Mass., 2008), p. 6.

[27] Benjamin Kaplan, *Divided by Faith. Religious Conflict and the Practice of Toleration in Early Modern Europe* (Cambridge, Mass., 2007), p. 143.

[28] Kaplan, *Divided by Faith*, p. 55. See also pp. 75, 100, 114–15.

[29] See Kaplan, *Divided by Faith*, pp. 34–42.

[30] Brad Gregory, *Salvation at Stake. Christian Martyrdom in Early Modern Europe* (Cambridge, Mass./London, 1999), p. 14. See also his "Can We 'See Things Their Way'? Should We Try," in *Seeing Things Their Way: Intellectual History and the Return of Religion*, (eds.) Alister Chapman, John Coffey, and Brad S. Gregory (Notre Dame, 2009), pp. 24–45.

[31] (Oxford, 1999). See also Clodagh Tait, "'The Vengeance of God': Reporting the Violent Deaths of Persecutors in Early Modern Ireland," in *Age of Atrocity: Violence and*

human affairs. Contrary to earlier insistence that this theological position was restricted to a minority of "hot" Protestants, Walsham elucidates how providentialism permeated all aspects of English society from popular print to pulpit polemics. With care, scrutiny and proper instruction, Christians could discern God's favor or displeasure in natural and preternatural incidents and events. If the latter, with care, scrutiny and proper instruction Christians could also correct the situation. The presence of heterodox Christians remained a persistent irritant. Christians could recall Abraham's intercession in favor of Sodom. Aware of their grievous sin, the Lord said "I will go down now, and see whether they have done altogether according to the cry of it, which is come unto me; and if not, I will know." "Wilt thou also destroy the righteous with the wicked? Peradventure there be fifty righteous within the city: wilt thou also destroy and not spare the place for the fifty righteous that are therein?" Thirty? Ten? This familiar passage ends: "And the LORD went his way, as soon as he had left communing with Abraham: and Abraham returned unto his place" (Genesis 18: 16–33, King James's Version). But all did not end well. In the next chapter the Lord did indeed destroy Sodom and Gomorrah; only Lot and his family were saved. God's punishment of such communities warned of dire consequences for the toleration of sin. The Elizabethan Archbishop Edwin Sandys condemned such tolerance as complicity: "The evil which others do buy our sufferance is ours ... We do it when we suffer it to be done."[32] To prevent a fate similar to Sodom and Gomorrah, confessional groups urged political authorities to destroy non-conformists and dissenters.

Elizabethan preachers decried the vestiges of papist beliefs and practices that lurked, ignored or de facto tolerated, in corners of the realm. Until all traces of Roman Catholicism were eradicated, England's relationship with the divine teetered on the precipice. Preachers may rejoice in the blessings bestowed by God on Elizabethan England, but nothing guaranteed their continuation.[33] Marvels and prodigies, tempests and earthquakes warned of future catastrophic vengeance. The minorities too pondered their options in their confrontation with a state that impeded their eternal salvation. French Huguenots, the monarchomachs, justified active resistance to King Henry III, especially after the St Bartholomew's Day Massacre in 1572. The Allen/Parsons faction among English Catholics worked for the removal of Elizabeth as the only remedy to persecution in this world and possible

---

Political Conflict in Early Modern Ireland, (eds.) David Edwards, Pádriag Lenihan, and Clodagh Tait (Dublin, 2007), pp. 130–53, for an exposition of divine punishment inflicted on ruthless persecutors.

[32] Cited in Kaplan, *Divided by Faith*, p. 70.
[33] See Walsham, "'This Newe Army of Satan,'" p. 52.

damnation in the next. They continued their campaign, undeterred by the disaster of the Armada.

The formation of distinct communities of religious exiles and the foundation of colleges and seminaries on the continent made post-1588 English Catholicism increasingly bipolar. Consequently the following chapters, at the risk of some confusion and repetition, will oscillate between events within the three kingdoms, and developments on the continent, in a chronological narrative. Within England occasional conformity remained the defining issue;[34] within Ireland the gradual identification of "faith and fatherland" as espoused by O'Neill divided Catholics; Scottish Catholics seemed unsure whether they should follow the Catholic earls or collaborate with James VI. Within all three the question of a Catholic candidate for the English throne assumed increasingly greater importance. Preservation of domestic Catholicism depended on the formation of qualified clergy at the seminaries, all of which depended financially on Spain and/or the Papacy, and, with the qualified exemption of the English College in Douai, intellectually and spiritually on the Society of Jesus. What little ecclesiastical organization existed within England was provided by the Jesuits.[35] William, Cardinal Allen remained at the papal court despite periodic Spanish suggestions that he establish residence in Belgium with subsequent loss of English influence in Rome. Parsons patrolled arguably the more important court of Philip II. Surprisingly little correspondence between Parsons and Allen remains. Jesuits exercised considerable influence on all aspects of the mission, an influence not always deemed benign. After the death of Allen in 1594 complaints of Jesuit domination of the mission, and of their subservience to Spanish interests, became more frequent and more vociferous. Christopher Bagshaw, admittedly a partisan observer, claimed that Jesuits "by their writings, their Sermons, and by all their indevors labored to perswade all Catholicks, that the King of *Spayne* and our faith are so linked together … [that without Spain] the Catholick religion will be utterly extinguished and perish." He accused Jesuits of "building the faith of Saint *Peter* and his successors upon the King of *Spaynes* Monarchie."[36] Bagshaw and others exploited the popular anti-Spanish "Black Legend" in their conflict with Jesuits through their

---

[34] See Crosignani, *Recusancy and Conformity*.

[35] Interestingly around the same time comparable problems regarding ecclesiastical organization irritated Jesuit relations with the secular clergy in Holland. See Parker, *Faith on the Margins*. For comparative studies of Catholic communities in both countries, see Benjamin J. Kaplan, Bob Moore, Henk van Nierop and Judith Pollmann, (eds.), *Catholic Communities in Protestant States. Britain and the Netherlands c. 1570–1720* (Manchester, 2009).

[36] Christopher Bagshaw, *A sparing discoverie of our English Iesuits* (n.p. [London], 1601), ARCR, vol. 2, num. 38, STC 25126, pp. 7–8.

identification of the Society of Jesus with the aggressive policies of the Spanish monarchy.[37] Demands from some secular clergy that Jesuits be removed from the administration of the colleges and from the mission itself, found a more receptive audience in Rome as a pro-French, anti-Spanish papacy pondered a Stuart succession. Less than a decade after he had departed for Spain, Parsons returned to Rome to defend English Jesuits and prevent their sacrifice. Even his enemies would admit there were few as qualified for the task.

By 1589 two generations had passed since the Elizabethan settlement had replaced Marian Catholicism. Eamon Duffy observes:

> By the end of the 1570s, whatever the instincts and nostalgia of their seniors, a generation was growing up which had known nothing else [but the Established Church], which believed the Pope to be Antichrist, the Mass a mummery, which did not look back to the Catholic past as their own, but another country, another world.[38]

That generation was now grown. Some Catholics nonetheless refused to acknowledge England's permanent departure from the Roman fold. Catholicism could still be restored through Elizabeth's violent replacement or through the careful cultivation of her successor. Others insisted on some form of accommodation with the government. Disagreement on these and other matters simmered within the community for years before a public explosion in the 1590s.

---

[37] On the "Black Legend," see William S. Maltby, *The Black Legend in England: The Development of anti-Spanish Sentiment, 1558–1660* (Durham, N.C., 1971). On the identification of the Society of Jesus with Spain, see Peter Burke, "The Black Legend of the Jesuits: An Essay in the History of Social Stereotypes," in *Christianity and Community in the West. Essays for John Bossy*, (ed.) Simon Ditchfield (Aldershot, 2001), pp. 175–77.

[38] Eamon Duffy, *The Stripping of the Altars: Traditional Religion in England 1400–1580* (New Haven/London, 1992), p. 593.

CHAPTER 1

The "Cradle of Nascent Catholicity": Life on the Mission, 1589–1593

Introduction

In 1588 the Established Church promulgated official prayers to beg divine assistance for a kingdom ever fearful of Spanish invasion. Assembled Christians beseeched the Lord to protect his people as he had once aided Abraham, Joshua, and David, and to grant similar success and victory to their armies. They prayed that God would abate the fury of their enemies who:

> either of malice or ignorance do persecute them who put their trust in thee, and hate us, but also ... molify their hard hearts ... open their blinded eyes, and ... lighten their ignorant minds, that they may see and understand, and truly turn to thee, and embrace thy holy word, and unfeignedly be converted unto thy Son Jesus Christ, the only Saviour of the world, and believe and love his Gospel, and so eternally be saved. Finally, that all Christian realms, and specially this Realm of England, may by thy defence and protection enjoy perfect peace, quietness, and security, and that all desire to be called and accounted Christians may answer in deed and life to be good and godly a name ...[1]

Prayers and sermons exhorted true Englishmen to the defense of the realm. Queen Elizabeth proclaimed to her troops at Tilbury that "under God" she had placed her trust in the loyal hearts and goodwill of her subjects. For them, her kingdom and her God, she was willing to lay down her life but instead predicted "a famous victory over thes enimyes of my god,

---

[1] William Keatinge Clay, (ed.), *Liturgical Services. Liturgies and Occasional Forms of Prayers set forth in the Reign of Queen Elizabeth* (Cambridge, 1847), p. 616. See also pp. 614, 617, 624–25. Compare Ben Lowe's re-interpretation of such prayers as a petition not for victory but for an end to all fighting because "peace is the Christian's true and primary obligation" ("Religious Wars and the 'Common Peace': Anglican Anti-War Sentiment in Elizabethan England," *Albion*, 28 [1996]: pp. 415–35).

and of my kyngdom."² And a famous victory it was, commemorated by portraits, poems and prayers:

> O Noble England
> fall down upon thy knee
> And praise thy God with thankful heart
> which still maintaineth thee.
> The foreign forces
> that seek thy utter spoil
> Shall then through his especial grace
> be brought to shameful spoil.
> With mighty power
> they come unto our coast:
> To overrun our country quite,
> they make their brags and boast.
> In strength of men
> they set their only stay:
> But we upon the Lord our God
> will put our trust alway.³

God had demonstrated his favor.⁴ The kingdom celebrated its delivery from the Spanish threat with great ceremony in London at St Paul's Cathedral on November 24, 1588. Seated in the window of a friend's house in Ludgate Circus, Henry Garnet, one of two Jesuits, Robert Southwell was the second, who remained outside an English prison, watched the spectacle.⁵ Unfortunately, from an English perspective, dangers remained. Not only did the threat of a Spanish attack continue, but domestic peace was not forthcoming.

In mid October, approximately one month before the service in St Paul's, the first Martin Marprelate tract unleashed a new attack on the Established Church. A series of clandestine pamphlets in 1588 and 1589

---

² Two versions of the oration are appendices to Janet M. Green, "'I My Self': Queen Elizabeth I's Oration at Tilbury Camp," *Sixteenth Century Journal*, 28 (1997): p. 443. See also Susan Frye, "The Myth of Elizabeth at Tilbury," *Sixteenth Century Journal*, 23 (1992): pp. 95–114.

³ See Bertrand T. Whitehead, *Brags and Boasts: Propaganda in the Year of the Armada* (Stroud, 1994), p. 95.

⁴ See Alexandra Walsham, *Providence in Early Modern England* (Oxford, 1999), pp. 245–66.

⁵ Garnet's report can be found in his letter to Claudio Acquaviva, London 5 December 1588, ARSI, Fondo Gesuitico 651/624. See also Thomas M. McCoog, S.J., *The Society of Jesus in Ireland, Scotland, and England 1541–1588: 'Our Way of Proceeding?'* (Leiden, 1996), pp. 257–58.

assailed episcopacy to agitate for the establishment of a Presbyterian style of ecclesiastical government. On February 9, 1589 Richard Bancroft rebutted Marprelate's charges in his sermon at Paul's Cross; the sermon was published the following month. A royal proclamation on the 13th ordered that anyone possessing any of the "sundry schismatical and seditious books, deflamatory libels, and other fanatastical writings ... containing in them doctrine very erroneous and other matters notoriously untrue and slanderous to the state, and against the godly reformation of religion and government ecclesiastical established by law and so quietly of long time continued ..." turn them over to the local ordinary for destruction. Moreover similar publications were forbidden under pain of punishment.[6]

The Martin Marprelate controversy has striking similarities to the popular uproar surrounding the circulation of the "Brag" and the *Rationes decem* of Edmund Campion in 1580–81.[7] In both cases secret presses printed controversial literature embarrassing to the government. In both cases authors and publishers sought to move a discussion of specific sensitive issues out of cabinet chambers and corridors of power into a more public sphere.[8] Subsequent sermons and proclamations denounced the authors as seditious agitators bent on the destruction of the "godly reformation of religion" so well established. Like Roman Catholics, Presbyterians were labelled disloyal subjects whose demand for alteration undermined good government.[9] The Established Church now waged a two-front war. Prayers that all English subjects might "jointly all together in one godly concord and unity, and with one consonant heart and mind,

---

[6] Paul L. Hughes and James F. Larkin, C.S.V., (eds.), *Tudor Royal Proclamations* (3 vols, New Haven, 1964–1969), vol. 3, pp. 34–35. On Marprelate and the subsequent controversy see Patrick Collinson, *The Elizabethan Puritan Movement* (London, 1967); Leland H. Carlson, *Martin Marprelate, Gentleman: Master Job Throckmorton Laid Open in His Colors* (San Marino, California, 1981), Patrick Collinson, "Ecclesiastical Vitriol: Religious Satire in the 1590s and the Invention of Puritanism," in *The Reign of Elizabeth I: Court and Culture in the Last Decade*, (ed.) John Guy (Cambridge, 1995), pp. 150–70; and Peter Milward, S.J., *Religious Controversies of the Elizabethan Age: A Survey of Printed Sources* (London, 1977), pp. 86–93.

[7] On this see McCoog, *Society of Jesus*, pp. 152–54 and Thomas M. McCoog, S.J., "'Playing the Champion': The Role of Disputation in the Jesuit Mission," in *The Reckoned Expense: Edmund Campion and the English Jesuits. Essays in Celebration of the First Centenary of Campion Hall, Oxford (1896–1996)*, (ed.) Thomas M. McCoog, S.J. 2nd edn. (Rome, 2007), pp. 139–63.

[8] See Peter Lake and Michael Questier, "Puritans, Papists, and the 'Public Sphere' in Early Modern England: The Edmund Campion Affair in Context," *Journal of Modern History*, 72 (2000): pp. 587–627.

[9] Joseph Black, "The Rhetoric of Reaction: The Martin Marprelate Tracts (1588–89), Anti-Martinism, and the Uses of Print in Early Modern England," *Sixteenth Century Journal*, 28 (1997): pp. 707–25, especially pp. 711–12.

may render unto thee all laud and praise,"[10] did not end religious division. The Presbyterian challenge was louder and audacious; Roman Catholic recusancy was more muted but equally steadfast. Neither would be controlled by prayer alone.

"Winter of the Soul": The State of Catholics in England

Father General Everard Mercurian had consistently rejected appeals from William Allen, the de facto superior of English Catholics, for Jesuit involvement in the mission. In late 1579 Mercurian finally agreed perhaps in the expectation that the government would grant some form of religious toleration as it negotiated an anti-Spanish marital alliance with France. In April of 1580, three Jesuits, Robert Parsons, Edmund Campion and Ralph Emerson, accompanied other ecclesiastics and laymen on their journey to England. But instead of tolerance the party encountered increased vigilance and more severe persecution due to the collapse of the negotiations and the arrival of a Spanish-Papal expeditionary force in Ireland. By the summer of 1581 Parsons had escaped to France and Campion had been captured and would be executed the following December. If Mercurian had lived, most likely he would have aborted the mission. However Claudio Acquaviva, a fervent supporter of the mission, had been elected Mercurian's successor in February of 1581. Nonetheless, despite his initial enthusiasm, Acquaviva considered the mission's closure or suspension as the government cracked down on Catholics because of their involvement, real and imagined, in plots and conspiracies against Elizabeth and in favor of her imprisoned cousin Mary, Queen of Scots. Parsons's agitation secured the mission's future.[11]

Robert Southwell and Henry Garnet, superior of the English mission after William Weston's capture in 1586, lamented the Armada's horrific consequences on English Catholics. According to Southwell, the English now directed their hatred of the Spanish towards Catholics. Discouraged by the prospects of renewed attacks, Southwell feared the "winter of the soul" and urged Acquaviva to pray that flowers would return again in spring.[12] Garnet corroborated Southwell's report: Catholics now endured

---

[10] Clay, *Liturgical Services*, p. 616.

[11] See McCoog, *The Society of Jesus in Ireland, Scotland, and England*, pp. 129–77, and Thomas M. McCoog, S.J., "The English Jesuit Mission and the French Match, 1579–1581," *Catholic Historical Review*, 87 (2001): pp. 185–213 for more detail.

[12] See Southwell's letters to Acquaviva, July 10, 1588, August 31, 1588, December 28, 1588, ARSI, Fondo Gesuitico 651/648 (published in Thomas M. McCoog, S.J., "The Letters of Robert Southwell, S.J.," *AHSI*, 63 [1994]: pp. 112–17, 121–23).

the wrath of the government as the Israelites once suffered under the Egyptians. Some executions were scheduled; others expected to be arrested. Indeed "nearly all of us can be said to be in prison because we dare not go around the city but at night and on urgent business."[13] Was Southwell aware of Parsons's role in the political discussions surrounding the Armada? Can we read an implicit criticism of such activities in the poet's lament?

Originally scheduled to convene on November 12, 1588, Parliament was prorogued until February 4, 1589. Sir Christopher Hatton's opening speech arguably typified national popular sentiment more than irenic liturgical prayers. Enumerating the various crimes committed against a Virgin Queen and an innocent country by Pope Sixtus V "that wolfish bloodsucker" and King Philip II "that insatiable tyrant," Hatton castigated those English subjects, especially "of all the villanous traitors that I thinke this lande ever bred or brought up, that wicked priest, that shamelesse atheiste and bloodie [William] Cardinal Allen, he in deede excelleth," who sought to overthrow the queen and destroy the Established Church. The Church of England, as it was constituted, "maie iustlie be compared to anie church which hath bene established in anie countrie it is agreable with the scriptures, with the most auncient generall councells, with the practise of the primitive church, and with the iudgements of all the olde and learned fathers." England must remain vigilant because its enemies prepared another attack: "Our duties towards God, hir Majestie, and our countrie, doth require all this at your handes."[14]

Despite the power and fury of Hatton's opening address, Parliament did not pass new penal legislation. Indeed the renewed Presbyterian challenge dominated the proceedings. The Presbyterians addressed a petition to Queen Elizabeth in which they urged that she "unburthen the realme of a heavy yoke of divers unecessary and penall Lawes" by rescinding said laws until Parliament revoked them. Denying all charges of treason and disclaiming any desire to legislate new religious laws, the anonymous author desired "a preaching ministery ... [to] all the people of your kingdome [so that they] may be taught to obey and serve your Highnes, not with eye service, but from the hart in the feare of the Lord, who only seeing the heart, can discerne hipocrasie, and will publish the least conceipt that may rise to the contrary." Without the introduction of

---

[13] Garnet to Acquaviva, London October 29, 1588, same to same, November 24, 1588, ARSI, Fondo Gesuitico 651/624.

[14] Hatton's speech can be found in T.E. Hartley, (ed.), *Proceedings in the Parliaments of Elizabeth I* (3 vols, Leicester, 1981–1995), vol. 2, pp. 414–24. For an account of this Parliament see J.E. Neale, *Elizabeth I and Her Parliaments* (2 vols, London, 1953–1957), vol. 2, pp. 193–239.

this remedy, popery would seduce more subjects who would then follow Jesuits and seminary priests with disastrous consequences.[15] Despite such petitions, the old religious laws remained on the books, vigorously enforced whenever there were rumors of invasion.

A new set of prayers "necessary for the present time and state" was introduced in 1590. Thanking God for "a peaceable princess and a gracious Queen" and for his providence that has saved her from "sundry great perils and dangers," the prayer asked that the queen's and God's enemies, who were the same, be converted "if it be thy will: make them to see the madness and wickedness of their enterprise and that they do but kick against the prick: to the end they may give over the pursuit of their bad cause, abstain from shedding Christian blood, and in time kiss thy Son in humility, whom they in pride have hitherto so unadvisedly impugned." If, however, they persisted in their malice, the congregation prayed that they be confounded.[16] Fear of invasion not only prompted new liturgical services but provided understandable motivation for intensified persecution. William Cecil, Lord Burghley, again terrified by the threat posed by recusant gentry, decided on new measures, one of which was their re-imprisonment. Scribbled in haste as he was departing for prison in Ely, Sir Thomas Tresham repudiated Burghley's contention that Catholics were of questionable loyalty by reminding him of their allegiance in the Armada crisis of 1588.[17] Tresham and other recusant gentry remained in prison until October after which they were often subject to house arrest.[18]

On January 16, 1590 Southwell reported that "the condition of Catholic recusants here is the same as usual, deplorable and full of fears and dangers; more especially since our adversaries have looked for wars. As many of ours as are in chains, rejoice and are comforted in their prisons; and they that are at liberty, set not their hearts upon it, nor expect it to be of long continuance." Perhaps, he wondered, "The field of the Church had to be watered with, as it were, these spring rains [the blood of martyrs] that she might rejoice in such drops as she sprouts forth. We also,

---

[15] See Hartley, *Proceedings*, vol. 2, pp. 486–89. Compare the supplication of John Stubbs in which he touched on many of the same issues. He resented that opponents of bishops were treated as fellow-travellers with "Jesuites, recusantes, rebelles, and traytors" and abhorred "all traytors and all sedicious persones" (pp. 490–92).

[16] Clay, *Liturgical Services*, pp. 644–45.

[17] Sir Thomas Tresham to Archbishop John Whitgift and Privy Council, 25 March 1590, BL, Add. MSS 39,828, fols 139^r–142^v. On Tresham's loyalty see Sandeep Kaushik, "Resistance, Loyalty and Recusant Politics: Sir Thomas Tresham and the Elizabethan State," *Midland History*, 21 (1996): pp. 37–79.

[18] For Burghley's introduction of new measures against recusants and for his Catholic policy in general, see William Richardson, "The Religious Policy of the Cecils 1588–1598" (unpublished D.Phil. thesis: Oxford University, 1994), pp. 126–39.

like hirelings, unless we happen to be unworthy of so great an honour, look for the time when our day comes."[19] Two months later Southwell commented on the ongoing persecution: "We are still tossed in the midst of dangers, and indeed in no small peril; from which nevertheless we have been hitherto delivered by the grace of God."[20] Garnet too reported that Catholics continued to bear witness to their faith despite persecution:

> if this witness does not lie hidden in darkness and remain enclosed in what amounts to a prison, it does not stir either the pity or admiration of pious souls. But for sure the spreading flame cannot long be contained without bursting out and showing itself, nor can the virtue and devotion of the children of our Holy Mother Church long be obscured so as not to express itself at length, and like a glowing lantern placed upon the lampstand, shed grateful light upon those who are in the house of Christ.

The government seized upon any threat of invasion to justify the terror:

> It is we who are hauled before the magistrates, we who are subject to questioning, we who are tortured and torn apart, we who are not plotting but hiding at home, giving ourselves to prayer and devotions, we who are beaten about the head unless we swear that we will support the queen in a war, however unjust, unless we affirm that there is no authority in the pope to excommunicate or depose the queen, and that in any case we will take up arms against him.[21]

Garnet barely concealed his anger. The militant Catholic policy pursued by exiles on the continent increased burdens endured by recusants within the kingdom. Moreover any chance that Spain would follow up the ill-fated Armada diminished because of King Philip II's increased involvement in a struggle to prevent the succession of the Huguenot Henry of Navarre to the French throne.[22]

---

[19] Southwell to [Acquaviva or Alfonso Agazzari], January 16, 1590, ARSI, Fondo Gesuitico 651/648 (published in McCoog, "Southwell," pp. 123–24 and partially translated in Henry Foley, S.J., *Records of the English Province of the Society of Jesus* [7 vols in 8 parts, Roehampton/London, 1877–1884] vol. 1, p. 324).

[20] Southwell to [Acquaviva or Agazzari], March 8, 1590 (published in John Hungerford Pollen, S.J., (ed.), *Unpublished Documents Relating to the English Martyrs (1584–1603)* [London, 1908], pp. 330–32 and translated in Foley, *Records*, vol. 1, pp. 325–26).

[21] Garnet to Acquaviva, May 25, 1590, ARSI, Fondo Gesuitico 651/624. In his letter to Acquaviva on May 1, 1589, Garnet recounted the trial of one such victim: Philip Howard, Earl of Arundel (ARSI, Fondo Gesuitico 651/624).

[22] See McCoog, *Society of Jesus*, pp. 259–64.

Initial successes of the Catholic League and their Spanish allies resulted in direct English military support for Henry in the autumn of 1589.[23] Prayers "for the good success of the French King, against the enemies of God's true religion and his State" and "for the prosperity of the French King and his nobility, assailed by a multitude of notorious rebels that are supported and waged by great forces of foreigns" were introduced in 1590. A second prayer expressed English anxieties:

> O most mighty God, the only protector of all Kings and Kingdoms, we thy humble servants do here with one hear, and one voice, call upon thy heavenly grace, for the prosperous estate of all faithful Christian Princes, and namely at this time, that it would please thee of they merciful goodness to protect by thy favour, and arm with thine own strength, the most Christian King, the French King, against the rebellious conspirations of his rebellious subjects, and against the mighty violence of such foreign forces, as do join themselves with these rebels, with intention not only to deprive him most unjustly of his kingdom, but finally to exercise their tyranny against our Sovereign Lady, and this her Kingdom and people, and against all other, that do profess the Gospel of thy only Son our Saviour Jesus Christ.[24]

Since everyone knew the identity of the "foreign forces," their names were discreetly avoided.[25] Such circumspection ended with the proclamations of the following year.

Fears that Roman Catholics would aid future Spanish intervention in England received confirmation after the apprehension of secular priests John Fixer and John Cecil at Dover around May of 1591.[26] Protesting their opposition to Robert Parsons's pro-Spanish policies, both made damaging accusations in their statements. Using the alias of John Snowden, Cecil claimed that Parsons delegated him to inform English Catholics that

---

[23] See Wallace T. MacCaffrey, *Elizabeth I: War and Politics 1588–1603* (Princeton, 1992), pp. 137–49 for the English expeditionary force under the leadership of Peregrine Bertie, Baron Willoughby d'Eresby.

[24] Clay, *Liturgical Services*, pp. 647–53, especially 652.

[25] Much Protestant propaganda was published in English translation to arouse English sentiments and to obtain English involvement. See Lisa Ferraro Parmelee, *Good Newes from Fraunce: French Anti-League Propaganda in Late Elizabethan England* (Rochester, N.Y., 1996) *passim*.

[26] On them see Godfrey Anstruther, O.P., *The Seminary Priests* (4 vols, Ware/Durham/Great Wakering, 1968–1977), vol. 1, pp. 63–68, 118. On Fixer, see Patrick McGrath, "Apostate and Naughty Priests in England under Elizabeth I," in *Opening the Scrolls: Essays in Honour of Godfrey Anstruther*, (ed.) Dominic Aidan Bellenger, O.S.B. (Bath, 1987), p. 73. Anstruther noted that the usually perspicacious Parsons only slowly realized Cecil's duplicity. About Cecil also see McGrath, "Apostate and Naughty Priests," pp. 71–72.

Spain was not interested in the conquest of England but simply in "the reformation of religion." Cecil, moreover, was to ascertain who would support a Spanish invasion. Parsons allegedly suggested that he inflate the number to mislead Spain into believing:

> that the number of their favourites were great and their hands and hearts ready when they should see an Army on foot to stand with them and in truth this is the only bait the Card. [Allen] and Persons feed the King withal that the Catholics in England are his and they depend all upon the direction of them 2 which are capital enemies not only of the present state but of the Catholics themselves in England, for in respect of their practices abroad poor men suffer here at home.

During his stay in England, Cecil was to seek a meeting with Ferdinando Stanley, Lord Strange, and to encourage Catholics to support his candidacy as Elizabeth's successor.[27] John Fixer, alias Thomas Wilson, repeated these charges in his statement.[28] Fixer explained that love of country and opposition to foreign invasion motivated his return. Believing Lord Burghley's claim that he would not "persecute or trouble no man for matter of conscience where it is not intermeddled with affairs of estate,"[29] Fixer and Cecil promised that they would not fulfill Parsons's instruction to work for a Spanish invasion but instead would do all they could to lay "blocks and blockhouses in their way." Cecil, in turn, asked Burghley if "he would have the name and memory of Catholiques utterly exterpated or no" and if English Catholics could "have eny indulte in matters of conscyence givinge securitye of theyre fydelitye, as they have in Germany and fraunce"? He recommended that Burghley add "one stringe moore" to his bow and follow the example of King Henry IV by employing moderate Catholics to counteract the extremists. Moreover Cecil suggested that the Confraternity of the Rosary—and he had authorization from the Dominican general to establish a chapter presumably for the laity—be erected whose priest members would behave "in habite conformable to theyre vocation, and take some othe not to heare or suffer any practise

---

[27] Statement of John Cecil to William Cecil, Lord Burghley, May 21, 1591,TNA, SP 12/238/160.

[28] John Fixer to [William Cecil, Lord Burghley], [May 21, 1591], TNA, SP 12/238/162. On Cecil and Fixer see Christopher Devlin, S.J., *The Life of Robert Southwell Poet and Martyr* (London, 1956), pp. 226–30, Albert J. Loomie, S.J., *The Spanish Elizabethans: The English Exiles at the Court of Philip II* (New York, 1963), pp. 73–74, and Francis Edwards, S.J., *Robert Persons: The Biography of an Elizabethan Jesuit (1546–1610)* (St Louis, 1995), pp. 144–48.

[29] Cecil made these assertions in *The execution of justice in England* (London, 1583), STC 4902, 4903. See also McCoog, *Society of Jesus*, p. 215, especially n. 153.

of treason, or deale in matter of state, or with suche that deale with foren princes in matters of state, and to have some one ruler amongest them that shoulde be wholy dependente uppon your Lordship ..."[30]

After the failure of the Armada, Burghley wrote *The copie of a letter sent out of England to don Bernardin Mendoza* under the name of the recently martyred Richard Leigh. He cited the many Catholics who had offered to fight for England as evidence that persecution in England was for treason and not for religion. He argued that Catholics should not only repudiate their attachment to Spain, but abandon dependence on force. Instead Catholics should encourage sound teaching and virtuous example. For that only learned and temperate priests should be sent on the mission.[31] Joel Hurstfield considered the publication "an ingenious piece of propaganda designed to drive a wedge between the Jesuit missionaries and the main body of English Catholics." According to Hurstfield, Burghley considered English Catholics to be loyal "as indeed Armada year **had** [emphasis Hurstfield's] shown, and, if the Jesuit spearhead were broken, internal religious peace would be in sight." Burghley was "groping towards some find of *modus vivendi* with Catholics."[32] Not surprisingly Burghley's reply satisfied Cecil and Fixer: all three hoped the elimination of the Jesuits would improve the condition of Catholics within the kingdom. According to John Hungerford Pollen, S.J., there "seems to be good reason for suspecting that many of the accusations enumerated in the proclamation of 18 October ... were due to the disloyal and treacherous statements of this man [Cecil]."[33]

Two royal proclamations dated October 18 were promulgated in late 1591. The first thanked God that Queen Elizabeth has reigned 33 years despite persistent, unjustified attempts by Philip II, King of Spain, to topple her. Now aided by his Milanese "vassal" Pope Gregory XIV,[34] Philip has invaded France "a kingdom that hath been always a maintainer of that Church in all their oppressions." In colleges founded in Spanish territories under "certain principal seditious heads, being unnatural subjects of our kingdom (but yet very base of birth)," Philip has gathered together

---

[30] The questions addressed to Cecil and Fixer can be found in TNA, SP 12/238/165. Fixer's reply is SP 12/238/166; Cecil's SP 12/238/167, 168. Cecil merits further study if only to ascertain his sincerity.

[31] (London, 1588), *STC* 15412, pp. 3–5, 9, 13, 33–34.

[32] Joel Hurstfield, "Church and State, 1558–1612: The Task of the Cecils," in *Studies in Church History II*, (ed.) G.J. Cuming (London, 1965), p. 135.

[33] Pollen, *Unpublished Documents*, p. 199.

[34] Ironically Gregory XIV, who reigned from December 5, 1590 to October 16, 1591, had died before the proclamation was promulgated. According to J.N.D. Kelly, the conclave that elected him was "notorious for factional intrigues and brutal intervention by the Spanish government" (*The Oxford Dictionary of Popes* [Oxford, 1986], pp. 273–74).

"dissolute young men" to "be instructed in school points of sedition, and from thence to be secretly and by stealth conveyed into our dominions with ample authority from Rome to move, stir up, and persuade as many of our subjects as they dare deal withal to renounce their natural allegiance due to us and our crown,[35] and upon hope of a Spanish invasion to be enriched and endowed with the possessions and dignities of our other good subjects."[36] To achieve their goal these priests used oaths, sacraments and indulgences. Among other strategies to frustrate Spanish ambitions, for example diligent preaching from godly ministers who lived exemplary lives, the proclamation established commissions in every shire, city and port to examine suspicious persons "to discover these venomous vipers [the priests] or to chase them away from the realm."[37]

The second proclamation detailed the questions to be asked by the commissioners. With the assistance of local clergy and justices of the peace, the commissioners compiled lists of recusants and reputed receivers of priests. These lists were not to be made public. If the commission found "probable and good cause," it should summon anyone on the list for examination. The proclamation stressed that the commission was not to "press any person to answer to any questions of their conscience otherwise than to cause them [to] answer whether they do usually come to the church, and why they do not ... " If the commissioners concluded that the suspect was a "willful recusant," they should question him about his allegiance to Queen Elizabeth, his attachment either to the Spanish king or the pope, and his possible support of any Jesuit or seminary priest. If suspected of Roman or Spanish sympathies, they were to be asked under

---

[35] In a speech to students in Oxford in 1592, Elizabeth marvelled at their devotion to her: "Your love for me is of such a kind as has never been known or heard of in the memory of man. Love of this nature is not possessed by parents, it happens not among friends, no, not even among lovers, whose fortune does not always include fidelity, as experience teaches. it is such love as neither persuasion, nor threats nor curses can destroy. Time has no power over it. Time, which eats away iron and wears away the rocks, cannot sever this love of yours. It is of this your services consist, and they are of such kind that I would think they would be eternal, if only I were to be eternal" (quoted in Christopher Haigh, *Elizabeth I* [London, 1988], p. 154). Even granted the hyperbole and arrogance, the devotion expected by Elizabeth had no room for rivals.

[36] In 1567 Jerónimo Ruiz del Portillo, appointed first provincial of Peru the following year, proposed to Francis Borgia, then superior general of the Jesuits, that Jesuits be sent to Peru instead of Florida as long as a war was waging in the latter. The reason for his proposal was: "For ours [Jesuits] do not go to conquer, but to evangelise." It has been suggested that this slogan would be equally appropriate for the Spanish support of the English colleges (see Francisco de Borja de Medina, S.J., "Jesuitas en la Armada contra Inglaterra (1588)," *AHSI*, 58 [1989]: p. 28). That may indeed reflect the mentality of the Society of Jesus regarding the colleges, but Philip seems to have hoped that evangelization would aid conquest.

[37] Hughes and Larkin, *Tudor Royal Proclamations*, vol. 3, pp. 86–93.

oath if they would furnish "assistance to the forces of the pope or King of Spain when they shall happen to invade this realm."[38]

Francis Edwards, S.J., the foremost contemporary apologist for Robert Parsons, admitted somewhat grudgingly that Elizabeth and her ministers were justified in their efforts to ascertain the identities of those who would favor a Spanish invasion. However, he continued, they did not try to distinguish "recusants who acknowledged only the spiritual authority of the Pope and reserved the right to reject his temporal policies ... [from] those who, like Allen and Persons, were prepared to countenance even foreign invasion to bring relief to their fellow papists." Thus left with no alternative, Allen and Parsons continued their campaign with the only weapons at their disposal.[39] But Burghley would have considered the oath an attempt to separate the sheep from the proverbial goats. The difficulty was finding a formula sensitive to Catholic consciences and acceptable to the government.[40]

In his analysis of Elizabethan and Jacobean recusant legislation, John LaRocca, S.J., argued that the first proclamation was yet another attempt—admittedly more urgent now because of continental developments—to improve a bureaucratic system for gathering names and information only and not for obtaining convictions.[41] The following spring (1592) the Privy Council instructed other commissioners to search for arms in homes of recusants identified as such since 1585. Anything discovered was to be confiscated unless it was required for defense of the household. These arms would be returned as soon as the recusant conformed to the Established Church. Without arms recusants would not be able to provide the military assistance expected by the kingdom's foes.[42]

Catholic newsletters reported an increase of persecution as a result of the proclamations. Two English gentlemen, one of whom was Laurence Mompesson, provided Richard Verstegan with news of current affairs. Verstegan relayed the news to Parsons.[43] Horrible tales about a new

---

[38] Hughes and Larkin, *Tudor Royal Proclamations*, vol. 3, pp. 93–95. On these and similar questions see Patrick McGrath, "The Bloody Questions Reconsidered," *Recusant History*, 20 (1991): pp. 305–19.

[39] Edwards, *Persons*, p. 151.

[40] Interestingly at the very time government officials were drafting the proclamations, a noted Catholic Sir Anthony Browne, Viscount Montague, was entertaining the queen at Cowdray. On his ability to remain Catholic and loyal see Michael Questier, "Loyal to a Fault: Viscount Montague Explains Himself," *Historical Research*, 77 (2004): pp. 225–53.

[41] "English Catholics and the Recusancy Laws 1558–1625: A Study in Religion and Politics (unpublished Ph.D. thesis: Rutgers University, 1977), pp. 148–53.

[42] LaRocca, "English Catholics," p. 145.

[43] There are two versions of this newsletter: an English version (ABSI, Coll B 37) and a Spanish (ABSI, Coll B 41). Both were published in Anthony G. Petti, (ed.), *The Letters and*

"Cecillian Inquisition" circulated. In each parish county commissioners appointed eight men, among whom were the minister, constable and churchwardens, to examine parishioners. Suspects were reported to the commissioners for further examination. Imprisonments and executions followed. In the Spanish account Verstegan concluded that such "a rigorous persecution has never been seen before." In the English account, Verstegan opined that there was not "half so great iniquitie in Sodoma as is now in England, besydes the shedding of innocent blood, which daily crieth for vengeance and may give us most hope of our countries recoverie." The time was now most ripe to remedy definitively the evil suffered by Catholics but, he cautioned, there were among Catholics "divers foxes in lambes' skinnes" with "protections" from Cecil.[44]

Various writers defended Catholics against the proclamations' allegations. Richard Verstegan contributed two works: *A declaration of the true causes of the great troubles*[45] and *An advertisement written to a secretarie of my L. Treasurers*.[46] The first blamed Lord Burghley, the queen's evil counselor, for the current miserable state of the commonwealth. This "sly sicophant," in order to achieve power well beyond his merit, persuaded the queen to embark on her treacherous course especially in regard to religion. In the recent proclamation Cecil sought "to turne

---

Dispatches of Richard Verstegan (c. 1550–1640) (London, 1959), pp. 39–48. Verstegan is an important figure who finally has received some recognition. See Paul Arblaster, *Antwerp & the World: Richard Verstegan and the International Culture of Catholic Reformation* (Leuven/Louvain, 2004).

[44] Petti, *Verstegan Papers*, pp. 47, 40. See also [Robert Southwell (?)] to [Richard Verstegan], [London? December 1591], ABSI, Anglia I, 70 (published in Petti, *Verstegan Papers*, pp. 1–16), Verstegan to Roger Baynes, Antwerp June 6, 1592, ABSI, Coll M 127b (published in Petti, *Verstegan Papers*, p. 49), and "An Ancient Editor's Note Book," in *Troubles of Our Catholic Ancestors as Related by Themselves*, (ed.) John Morris, S.J. (3 vols, London, 1872–1877), vol. 3, pp. 1–59. In a letter from April (?) of 1593, apparently from John Arden, whose brother Robert was a Jesuit, to Lord Burghley, the author reported the uproar occasioned in every Jesuit college by the news of persecution in England, comparable, they claimed, to Nero's (R.B. Wernham, *List and Analysis of State Papers Foreign Series: Elizabeth I* [7 vols, London, 1964–2000], vol. 4, par. 644).

[45] (n.p. [Antwerp?], 1592), *ARCR*, vol. 2, num. 760, *STC* 10005.

[46] (n.p. [Antwerp?], 1592), *ARCR*, vol. 2, num. 757, *STC* 19885. This is an English summary of Robert Parsons, *Elizabethae Angliae Reginae haeresim Calvinianum propugnantis saevissimum in Catholicos sui regni edictum* (Augsburg [vere Antwerp], 1592), *ARCR*, vol. 1, num. 885 (see nos. 886–892 for other editions). Because the charges demanded a rebuttal, Philip subsidized publication of this volume and instructed that it be printed in five European cities. On differences between the replies of Parsons and Verstegan, on the one hand, and those of Southwell and Stapleton see Victor Houliston, "The Lord Treasurer and the Jesuit: Robert Persons's Satirical *Responsio* to the 1591 Proclamation," *Sixteenth Century Journal*, 32 (2001): pp. 383–401; and *Catholic Resistance in Elizabethan England. Robert Persons's Jesuit Polemic, 1580–1610* (Aldershot/Rome, 2007), pp. 47–70.

the hatred which himselfe hathe deserved, upon a few poore Priests and Jesuites, by publishing that they are sent into the realme, to persuade men to assist the King of Spaine in an intended invasion, whereas they are not otherwise sent, but to exercise their priestly office and function, as they go unto the Indies, and other places where the exercise of their religion is also prohibited."[47] Verstegan dismissed Burghley's familiar claim that men were not executed for religion but for treason with the now traditional rejoinder: "Catholikes are offred their lives and liberties, yf they will but go to the Churche: which doubtlesse can-be no satisfaction for any temporall treason, but only for matters of religion."[48] Burghley's machinations have caused not only present and past disturbances but anticipated problems for the future because of his failure to allow the problem of Elizabeth's successor to be resolved. Perhaps a proposal to marry his grandchild to Arabella (or Arbella) Stuart, Verstegan suggested, was an attempt to gain the kingdom for himself.[49] Yet despite his persistent attack on Catholics, they persisted in their faith and they "putteth him in more feare then ever afore."[50] Unless Burghley repented and returned to the bosom of the true Church, he would not escape eternal damnation.

In *An advertisement* Verstegan defended King Philip II, Gregory XIV, Cardinal Allen and Father Parsons against Burghley's calumnies. Regarding the two Englishmen, Verstegan asked "why these two men above others should be so odious to the state of Ingland, seing they never committed anything against them that mighte iustely be imputed to hatred or evill will, but rather have soughte by all meanes their good both temporall, and eternall yf they would see it."[51] The true villain was Burghley himself. Following the example of Roman emperors Burghley has fabricated stories of treason in order to justify persecution of Christians. Like the Roman

---

[47] Verstegan, *Declaration*, p. 42.

[48] Verstegan, *Declaration*, p. 44.

[49] Interestingly English Catholics, perhaps with encouragement from the Elizabethan government, hoped to arrange a marriage between Lady Arabella and Ranuccio Farnese, Prince of Parma. Charles Paget seems to have been involved. As for Allen, he explained to Don Antonio Folch y Cardona, Duke of Sessa and Spanish ambassador in Rome, that he would not work in favor of the marriage until he had assurances that Philip II approved. See Allen's memorials on the subject in Penelope Renold, (ed.), *Letters of William Allen and Richard Barret 1572–1598* (London, 1967), pp. 209–16. Unfortunately her lament "The whole matter has never yet been thoroughly investigated, however, and no connected account of the intrigues exists. The only certainty is that none of them resulted in any benefit to English Catholics, or amelioration of the circumstances of the persecution at home. Allen's suspicions that any such negotiations were, from the English side, insincere, were well justified" (p. 212 n. 1) remains true.

[50] Verstegan, *Declaration*, p. 73.

[51] Verstegan, *An advertisement*, p. 34. Far more dangerous, according to Verstegan, were the "Martinistes or Puritans" (p. 19). See Black, "Rhetoric of Reaction," p. 717.

emperors Burghley's folly would result in his own destruction and in the happiness of those whom he persecuted.[52]

"Most almighty and most merciful, most feared, and best beloved Princesse," the opening words of Robert Southwell's *An humble supplication to her Maiestie*,[53] sounded a totally different tone, a tone similar to that employed by Robert Parsons in the first treatise he secretly published in England, *A brief discours contayning certayne reasons why Catholiques refuse to goe to church* (Doway [*vere* East Ham], 1580).[54] He dedicated the treatise "TO THE MOST HIGHE & MIGHTIE Princese ELIZABETH by the grace of God, Quene of England France and Irland &c." On her he showered compliments and concluded with a prayer: "IESUS Christ, in abundance of mercye, blesse your Maiestye, to whome (as he knoweth) I wyshe as much good as to mine owne soule: perswading my selfe, that all good Catholicks in England do the same."[55] For Parsons and Verstegan, the language of discourse had changed, but Southwell avoided scurrility and attacked no minister. He simply replied eloquently to each of the proclamation's allegations. Far from being "unnaturall subiects," English Catholics were willing to give their lives for the sake of their countrymen:

> ... that to reare the least fallen soule among your Maiesties subiects from a fatall lapse, we are contented to pay our lives for the ransome: how much better should we thinke them bestowed, if so high a pennyworth as your gracious self, or the whole Realme might be the gayne of our deare purchase?[56]

Despite persistent persecution, Catholics remained loyal to their queen. Southwell asked how the Catholics could be labelled seditious unless:

---

[52] Verstegan, *An advertisement*, p. 21. On the "kingdom of the Cecils" see Natalie Mears, "*Regnum Cecilianum*? A Cecilian Perspective of the Court," in *The Reign of Elizabeth I: Court and Culture in the Last Decade*, (ed.) John Guy (Cambridge, 1995), pp. 46–64. Mears concluded that "*Regnum Cecilianum* was a rhetorical device of criticism. It was founded on the paranoia of those who considered that they were at a political disadvantage to the Cecils and to their perceived supporters; it was a term of abuse to define what the Essexians were not; it was certainly not the reality ... The kingdom was still the queen's: the Cecils had been able to entrench themselves into the Court establishment but such strength had always been dependent on the royal will ... " (p. 63). See also Michael A.R. Graves, *Burghley: William Cecil, Lord Burghley* (London, 1998), p. 202.

[53] (n.p. [London], 1595 [*vere* 1600/1]), *ARCR*, vol. 2, num. 717, *STC* 22949.5. More accessible is R.C. Bald's edition (Cambridge, 1953).

[54] *ARCR*, vol. 2, num. 613, *STC* 19394.

[55] *Brief discours*, ‡‡ ii, [‡‡ viii].

[56] Robert Southwell, S.J., *An humble supplication to her Maiestie* (n.p. [London], 1595 [*vere* 1600/1601]), *ARCR*, vol. 2, num. 717, *STC* 22949.5. (ed.) R.C. Bald (Cambridge: Cambridge University Press, 1953), p. 4.

it be accounted Sedition to gather the ruynes of gods afflicted Church, and to have provided Sanctuaries, for persecuted and succourles soules, which forced at home either to live with a goared Conscience, or to lie open to continuall vexations, rather Chose to leave their Cuntry then their Catholique Religion.[57]

Moreover, the Catholic Church taught that "Subiects are bound in Conscience, under paine of forfeiting their right in heaven, and incurring the guilt of eternall torments, to obey the iust Lawes of their Princes; which both the Protestants and Puritanes deny ... "[58] Unlike Protestants who frequently rebelled against Mary Tudor for religious reasons, Catholics have done so only once. Despite their fidelity, it was often claimed that priests conspired to assassinate the queen, an act "Contrary to their Calling." Priests rather entered England:

> to shedd our owne, not to seeke the effusion of others bloud. The weapons of our warrfare are spirituall, not offensive. We carry our desires soe high lifted above soe savage purposes, that we rather hope to make our owne Martyrdomes our steppes to a glorious eternity, then others deaths our purchase of eternall dishonour. And who but men unwillinge to have us thought owners of our right witts, would abuse your Maiesties authority to sooth up soe great unlikelyhoods, sith none can be ignorant, how pernitious it were, both for Priests and all Catholiques to loose the protection of your Highnes, and to forgoe present sureties for uncertaine Changes.[59]

Instead Catholics "rather trust to the softnes of your mercifull hand, and next unto god rest the height of our possibilities in your favour and Clemency, then by any unnaturall violence against gods annoynted seeke the ruyne of our Realme, and draw upon our selves the extreamest of wordly harmes."[60] If there were an invasion, "we doe assure your Maiestie,

---

[57] Southwell, *Humble supplication*, p. 4.

[58] Southwell, *Humble supplication*, p. 16. In a case of conscience from Allen and Parsons it was asked whether Catholics could obey the queen in political matters. The reply was: "The resolution of this case depends rather on the judgement of Catholics in England who know all the facts of the matter well. But it seems to me that although they are perhaps not bound to do so, Catholics may lawfully obey her in everything of a purely political nature which does not involve the persecution of Catholics, at least to avoid worse evils befalling them. The Bull of Pius V [*Regnans in Excelsis*] did not withdraw from Catholics permission to obey the Queen since it did not properly achieve its purpose" (Peter Holmes, (ed.), *Elizabethan Casuistry* [London, 1981], p. 121). See also Ginevra Crosignani, Thomas M. McCoog, S.J., Michael Questier, ed, with the assistance of Peter Holmes, *Recusancy and Conformity in Early Modern England* (Toronto/Rome, 2010), p. 110.

[59] Southwell, *Humble supplication*, p. 32.

[60] Southwell, *Humble supplication*, p. 33.

that what Army soever should come against you, we will rather yeald our brests to be broached by our Cuntrie swords, than use our swords to th' effusion of our Cuntries bloud."[61] Yet the proclamation asserted that Catholics suffered nothing on account of their religion and would not be examined on matters of conscience but simply about church attendance. But what is Catholic recusancy:

> but a meere matter of Conscience? For as there is none soe knowne or usuall a way to distinguish any Religion from other as th'externall Rites and Sacraments peculiar to every one: soe can none more effectually deny his owne, then by making open profession of a contrary Faith, by his assistance and presence at the solemnities and service proper to it. For not only he that denieth Christ in his heart, but he also that denieth or is ashamed of him before men shall in the later day be denied by him before his Angells. And seeing men best iudg of our mynds by our actions, we cannot possibly give any better proofe unto them that we are noe Catholiques, then if we ioyne with protestants in their Churches and service; by which, as by their most certaine and espetiall markes, they themselves are knowne to be of that opinion.[62]

The recent proclamation destroyed the small hope that conditions would improve. Thus Southwell resorted to this supplication to reveal to the queen how unjustly many of her subjects suffered and plead for her mercy.[63]

---

[61] Southwell, *Humble supplication*, p. 35. Here one can hear echoes of a statement attributed to Anthony Browne, Viscount Montague: "That if the Pope himselfe should come in with crosse, key and gospell in his hand, he would be readie with the first to run unto his holines to cast himself downe at his feete to offer his service unto him in all humbleness of hart, and what not to shew himselfe a dutifull childe. But if in steede of comming in solemne procession with crosse, booke, praiers and preaching: he should come in asounding royall march with heralds of armes, with banners of blood displaied, with trumpets, alraum, spikes, harquebuse & men of armes all marshald in rankes set in battell aray: then would be be the firsy man in the field armed at all points, to resist him in the face with al his might and power he were able to make; and what not would he doe to shew himself a dutifull naturalized in an English soile on that behalfe" (William Watson, *A decacordon of ten quodlibeticall questions concerning religion and state* [n.p. (London), 1602], *ARCR*, vol. 2, num. 794, *STC* 25123, p. 177). Attempts to pinpoint this citation have failed, but the sentiment adequately summarizes Montague's position. See Michael C. Questier, *Catholicism and Community in Early Modern England. Politics, Aristocratic Patronage and Religion, c. 1550–1640* (Cambridge, 2006).

[62] Southwell, *Humble supplication*, p. 42.

[63] A comparison of the sentiments expressed in Southwell's work with those of Sir Thomas Tresham would be most interesting. On Tresham's arguments see Sandeep Kaushik, "Resistance, Loyalty and Recusant Politics: Sir Thomas Tresham and the Elizabethan State," *Midland History*, 21 (1996): 37–79.

Southwell's treatise was not published during his lifetime. Philip Caraman, S.J., contended that Henry Garnet forbade the work's publication because he believed the current intensified persecution would end more quickly if Catholics bore it patiently instead of stoking the fire with polemical, controversial works.[64] Moreover he thought that publication would increase the search for Southwell and thus damage the mission. Finally, Caraman remarked, the appearance of a book with such praise of the queen "might lead to further misunderstandings between Catholics at home and abroad."[65] Thus *An humble supplication* circulated in manuscript and did not appear in print until 1600 when opponents of the Society, the so-called Appellants because of their appeal to Rome against the establishment of an archpriest in 1598, used it to discredit Jesuit strategy.[66]

The Appellant clergy rightly discerned an incongruity between Southwell's (and perhaps by inference Garnet's) contribution to the debate and those of his continental colleagues. Observing how out-of-step Southwell was, Peter Holmes questioned the Jesuit's sincerity because the views expressed in *An humble supplication* did not fit the pattern of resistance and compromise, the framework of his investigation of recusant political writings. As evidence of Southwell's acceptance of the more militant Allen/Parsons ideology, Holmes cited his long dispatch to Verstegan from December of 1591.[67] Many of the complaints about the state of the kingdom were repeated by Southwell in *An humble proclamation* and by Verstegan in his works. Southwell did not consider desirable the intervention of any foreign power. Then "if any foreyne power be ready to assalt us (as they pretend the King of Spayne to be), what better opportunitie can be taken then to come to a people dismembred among them selves, dismantled of their chief fences, headlesse and lawlesse?"[68] Holmes, I think, misinterpreted the Jesuit's comment:

---

[64] Other replies to the proclamation were Joseph Creswell, S.J., *Exemplar literarum, missarum, e Germania, ad D. Guilielmum Cecilum, consiliarium regium* (n.p. [Rome], 1592), ARCR, vol. 1, num. 275; and Thomas Stapleton, *Apologia pro Rege Catholico Philippo II* (Constance [vere Antwerp?], 1592), ARCR, vol. 1, num. 1141. See Milward, *Religious Controversies*, pp. 113–14, and P.J. Holmes, "Robert Persons and an Unknown Political Pamphlet of 1593," *Recusant History*, 17 (1985): pp. 341–47. About these books, Arnold Oskar Meyer commented, somewhat cynically, that "the pen, indeed, was the only weapon left to the vanquished since the Spanish guns had been silenced off Gravelines" (*England and the Catholic Church under Queen Elizabeth* [London, 1916], p. 352).

[65] *Henry Garnet (1555–1606) and the Gunpowder Plot* (London, 1964), pp. 141–42. I have not found any documentary evidence for Caraman's argument.

[66] On the writing of the book, see Devlin, *Robert Southwell*, pp. 240–56.

[67] ABSI, Anglia I, 70 (published in Petti, *Verstegan Papers*, pp. 1–16).

[68] Petti, *Verstegan Papers*, p. 15.

Southwell worried about a possible civil war if the queen's succession was disputed. If the question of succession remained unanswered, the possibility of a civil war repelled Southwell. If he had favored foreign intervention, he would have welcomed that possibility.[69] Nonetheless it is fascinating to conjecture where these sentiments would have led Southwell if he had not been captured shortly after the manuscript's completion and executed a few years later.

Richard Verstegan's newsletters to Robert Parsons and Roger Baynes throughout 1592 detailed the effects of the proclamation on English Catholics. In one Warwickshire parish, seven score recusants were reported. In divers shires commissioners forced recusants to attend parish churches. In Chester an unnamed "famous preacher" and a Catholic prisoner debated theological doctrine. As rumors of the sighting of Spanish ships off the Channel Islands circulated, more Catholics were imprisoned in Banbury and Ely. To avoid fines and incarceration some Catholics crossed to Ireland "where for the tyme they are at more quiet than yf they were in England." Among the imprisoned and executed were Nicholas Fox, Edmund Gennings, William Pattenson, Swithin Wells, Robert Grey and Roger Ashton. In late June Robert Southwell was captured.[70] Amidst the furore some Catholics, perhaps decrying the relative comfort enjoyed by their ecclesiastical leaders on the continent as they suffered for their faith in the kingdom, revived the discredited theological position that in such circumstances attendance at Protestant services as a demonstration of loyalty to the queen was acceptable and lawful.[71]

---

[69] See *Resistance and Compromise: The Political Thought of the English Catholics* (Cambridge, 1982), pp. 169–73. See also Arnold Pritchard, *Catholic Loyalism in Elizabethan England* (London, 1979), pp. 67–72. Arnold numbered Southwell "among the precursors of opposition to the program that became widely identified with Allen, Parsons, and the Jesuits" (p. 67).

[70] For information on the persecutions see Verstegan to Parsons, Antwerp March 5, 1592, same to Baynes, Antwerp June 6, 1592, same to same, Antwerp June 27, 1592, same to same, Antwerp August 1, 1592, same to Parsons, Antwerp August 3, 1592, same to same, Antwerp August 6, 1592, same to Baynes, Antwerp August 22, 1592, same to Parsons, Antwerp October 15, 1592, same to same, Antwerp October 18, 1592, same to same, Antwerp October 29, 1592, ABSI, Coll B 37–40, ABSI, Coll M 127a, ABSI, Coll M 127a, ARSI, Anglia 38/II, fols 199ʳ⁻ᵛ, ABSI, Coll B 53–56, ABSI, Coll B 57–58, ABSI, Anglia I, 67, ABSI, Coll B 59–60, ABSI, Anglia I, 69, ABSI, Coll B 61–64 (published in Petti, *Verstegan Papers*, pp. 39–41, 49, 50, 51–52, 57–60, 63– 64, 72–73, 79–80, 83, 86–88); "Life and Death of Edmund Gennings," ABSI, Coll M 186, 187 (published in Pollen, *Unpublished Documents*, pp. 204–207); Anstruther, *Seminary Priests*, vol. 1, pp. 128, 123–24, 270–71.

[71] We shall return to this issue later in this chapter.

On December 12, 1592 William, Cardinal Allen drafted a consolatory letter to English Catholics.[72] Addressing them as "my moste sweete and faithfull coadjutors and true confessors," the cardinal exhorted them to perseverance because the end of their suffering was near:

> the nombers of our bretheren that are to suffer for his truith are nere made up and shortlie to receive, not onlie in the next, but in this worlde, the worthie fruites of theire happie labors. God Almightie and all mercyfull will not suffer longe the rod of the wicked to leay so heavy upon the lott of the just, neither let us be tempted more then by his grace we shalbe able to beare, but will shorten those daies of affliction for the electes sake.[73]

From his position in Rome, Allen was ashamed that he did not share their suffering but such was God's will. Perhaps one day he too would be asked to endure persecution, but in the meanwhile "wee succor you and the cause with prayers, sacryfice, teares, sighes and grones from the bottomes of our hartes and with contynuall instance to God and man for some releife of your miseries."[74] In their suffering, however, they must "teache not nor defende that it is lawfull to communycate with the protestantes in theire praiers or service or conventicles where they meete to mynister their untrue sacramentes; for this is contrarie to the practyse of the churche and the holie Doctors in all ages."[75] Despite this repetition of the now traditional prohibition against frequenting Protestant churches, Allen, nonetheless, asked Catholics to be compassionate and merciful to those who "for meere feare or savinge theire family, wyfe and children from ruyne,"[76] have attended Protestant services. After they had confessed their sins and been absolved, they should be welcomed back no matter how often they fail.

"Founding and Nurturing Domestic Churches"

William Weston, Thomas Metham, and Thomas Pounde were imprisoned in Wisbech Castle, and Ralph Emerson in either the Counter or the Clink

---

[72] Published in Thomas Francis Knox, (ed.), *The Letters and Memorials of William Cardinal Allen (1532–1594)* (London, 1882), pp. 343–46. Copies of this letter can be found in TNA, SP 12/243/80, 81, 82. The letter can also be found in Crosignani, *Recusancy and Conformity*, pp. 260–62.

[73] Knox, *Letters of Allen*, p. 344.

[74] Knox, *Letters of Allen*, p. 344.

[75] Knox, *Letters of Allen*, p. 345.

[76] Knox, *Letters of Allen*, p. 344.

in London.[77] Henry Garnet and Robert Southwell remained at liberty. To assist them Father General Claudio Acquaviva sent William Holt and Joseph Creswell on February 24, 1588. In consultation with Alessandro Farnese, Duke of Parma, the two Jesuits would decide whether to cross to England before or with the Spanish forces. Holt, who had been sent to England in 1581 and had established good relations with King James VI as he worked on the king's behalf in political negotiations on the continent, was scheduled to return to Scotland. Presumably the Jesuits and Parma decided that they should cross with the Armada. After its failure, Holt remained in Belgium as chaplain to English troops in the Spanish army, and Creswell returned to Rome as rector of the English College. John Gerard and Edward Oldcorne, both admitted into the Society on August 15, 1588, were almost immediately dispatched to England. In November they landed in East Anglia.[78]

John Gerard arrived in London in December of 1588; Edward Oldcorne had preceded him. With the assistance of some Catholics, he located Henry Garnet anxious that some mishap lay behind Gerard's absence. For an unspecified period of time, Garnet, Gerard, Oldcorne, and Southwell, who had recently returned from work in the country, discussed tactics, strategies, and perils of life on the mission. Because danger was greater during festivities, the four Jesuits dispersed just before Christmas. Gerard travelled to Grimston, the house of Edward Yelverton, about six miles north-east of King's Lynn. Through his host the Jesuit met many East Anglian gentry. Dressed as a "gentleman of moderate means ... [because it] was thus that I used to go about before I became a Jesuit and I was therefore more at ease in these clothes than I would have been if I had assumed a role that was strange and unfamiliar to me,"[79] Gerard moved freely and safely among Catholics and Protestants, some of whom he reconciled to the Roman Church, despite persecution. In the summer of 1589 Gerard moved to Lawshall, about six miles southeast of Bury St Edmunds. He directed the house's owner, Henry Drury, through the Spiritual Exercises of Ignatius Loyola. Given his brief to the point of non-existent formation as a Jesuit, one wonders how Gerard acquired competence as a spiritual director. At Lawshall he was more easily able "to live the life of a Jesuit, even in the external details of dress and arrangement of time."[80] Under Gerard's guidance Lawshall became an apostolic center, a quasi-retreat

---

[77] Philip Caraman, S.J., (ed.), *William Weston: The Autobiography of an Elizabethan* (London, 1955), pp. 161–62, Foley, *Records*, vol. 3, pp. 32–33.

[78] McCoog, *Society of Jesus*, pp. 253–56.

[79] Philip Caraman, S.J., (ed.), *John Gerard: The Autobiography of an Elizabethan* (London, 1951), pp. 17–18.

[80] Caraman, *John Gerard*, p. 24.

house: among Catholics who made the Exercises were future Jesuits Thomas and John Wiseman, Thomas Everard, and the apostate secular priest Anthony Rouse.[81] During the winter of 1591 Gerard moved again to Braddocks, the home of the Wisemans, situated between Thaxted and Saffron Walden, Essex. Here the danger was so minimal there that he often dined with the family "in clerical dress." He, of course, had a soutane and biretta but Garnet had forbidden Jesuits to wear them outside the chapel for reasons of security.[82] At Braddocks, besides preaching on feast days and Sundays, Gerard instructed the household in meditation, ascetical reading, and the Jesuit practice of examination of conscience.[83] His influence must have been considerable: two daughters entered the Augustinian convent in Louvain; two sons became Jesuits and a third son "distinguished himself in battle against the heretics in the Low Countries."[84] From Braddocks Gerard made occasional trips to Lancashire, his home county, to Stafford, and to the West Riding of Yorkshire, the home of Lady Elizabeth Woodroff, daughter of Thomas Percy, late Earl of Northumberland.[85]

Oldcorne remained in London with Garnet until early spring of 1589 when they departed for the West Midlands. Garnet's principal residence in Warwickshire was the home of Sir Nicholas Throckmorton at Coughton, near Alcester, on the principal road between Warwick and Worcester. Garnet introduced Oldcorne to the different mission stations in that area. Oldcorne remained at Baddesley Clinton after Garnet's return to London.[86] Not far from Baddesley Clinton was Hindlip House, approximately five miles from Worcester. The house belonged to Thomas Habington then a prisoner in the Tower of London. His sister Dorothy was a Protestant "brought up at the Queen's court and there had drunk in heresy so deeply that no one could be found to cure her."[87] Blaming Catholic priests for

---

[81] On the Jesuits Wiseman and Everard see Thomas M. McCoog, S.J., *Monumenta Angliae* (2 vols, Rome, 1992), vol. 2, pp. 299, 534. On Rouse see Anstruther, *Seminary Priests*, vol. 1, pp. 295–96.

[82] Caraman, *John Gerard*, p. 32.

[83] On the importance of the examination of conscience see *The Spiritual Exercises of St Ignatius*, (ed.) Louis J. Puhl, S.J. (Chicago, 1951), pp. 15–24 (nums 24–44), McCoog, *Society of Jesus*, p. 137, and John W. O'Malley, S.J., *The First Jesuits* (Cambridge, Mass., 1993) *passim*.

[84] Caraman, *John Gerard*, p. 30.

[85] On his activities see Caraman, *John Gerard*, pp. 17–40, 48–50.

[86] Michael Hodgetts stated that Oldcorne spent the year at Baddesley Clinton and moved to Hindlip House in 1590 after his conversion of Dorothy Habington (*Secret Hiding Holes* [Dublin, 1989], p. 71). According to Gerard, "On his first arrival in England, he [Oldcorne] stayed with the Superior, as he had no home of his own to go to." See Caraman, *John Gerard*, p. 44.

[87] See Caraman, *John Gerard*, p. 44.

her brother Edward's destruction during the Babington Plot in 1586, she resolved that neither priest nor Papist would be harbored in the house. Her Protestant zeal eventually cooled into a melancholia. Catholic gentlemen and priests, with keeping their identity secret, sought to convince her that her heretical views were the cause of the melancholia. Without yielding on any point she finally asked to converse with someone more learned. Garnet sent Oldcorne. Arguments from Scripture, reason, and authority were fruitless. Finally, according to John Gerard, Oldcorne tried to "cast out the dumb devil by prayer and fasting." On the second day Dorothy wondered how long he could live "as the angels do." After four whole days of fasting, Oldcorne "put her devil to flight." He reconciled Dorothy to the Roman Church and Hindlip House remained the center of Oldcorne's missionary network for 16 years.[88] According to Gerard, Oldcorne was a talented preacher who exercised considerable influence on Catholics in the region. "It is not easy to be believed," Gerard wrote years later:

> how many obstinate heretics he converted, how many weak Catholics he confirmed, how many scholars he sent over to the Seminaries and religious women to monasteries, how many houses he brought to that degree of devotion that he might and did settle Priests in them. Indeed, I may safely say of him, without amplification, that "in illis partibus totas fere fundavit rexitque ecclesias domesticas" [in those parts he founded and nurtured total domestic churches].[89]

Oldcorne became a familiar figure in the area and from the alms of his Catholic supporters he was able to provide much needed assistance to Garnet and the English mission.[90]

We know less about the arrival of John Curry and Richard Holtby.[91] From a cryptic remark in Garnet's letter to Acquaviva on May 1, 1589 about four veterans viz. Garnet, Southwell, Curry and Holtby, we can approximate their arrival in late 1588 or early 1589.[92] Both had worked in England as secular priests before returning to the continent to enter the Society. Now as Jesuits they returned to the regions they knew best: Holtby

---

[88] See Caraman, *John Gerard*, pp. 44–45. See also an account of Oldcorne, apparently written by Thomas Lister, in ABSI, Anglia VI, 54 (published in Foley, *Records*, vol. 4, pp. 213–16).

[89] John Morris, S.J., (ed.), *The Condition of Catholics Under James I: Father Gerard's Narrative of the Gunpowder Plot* (London, 1871), p. 283.

[90] See Caraman, *John Gerard*, pp. 44–48; Caraman, *Henry Garnet*, pp. 91–92; Morris, *Condition of Catholics*, pp. 282–84.

[91] On them see McCoog, *Monumenta Angliae*, vol. 2, pp. 282, 358.

[92] Garnet to Acquaviva, 1 May 1589, ARSI, Fondo Gesuitico 651/624.

worked in the north, using as his base the residence of John Trollope in Thorneley in the diocese of Durham; and Curry in the south-west, in and around Chideock Castle, Dorset.[93]

Garnet and Southwell had painstakingly repaired the missionary system frequently damaged by death and persecution.[94] In late 1588, before the arrival of Gerard and Oldcorne, Garnet complained that the post-Armada persecution harmed the system even more. As more Catholics capitulated to the authorities, all clergy were held suspect. Daily more previously friendly households locked their doors to priests. Consequently many priests therefore wandered the countryside.[95] As a result Garnet deemed it inexpedient to send more secular clergy, but made no comparable restriction on Jesuits.[96] Denial of access to recusant houses made it even more imperative for the clergy to have a house of their own, independent of gentry control. In 1588 Garnet rented a comfortable garden cottage in Finsbury Fields. Here he met incoming priests and arranged their accommodation. Here too he found refuge from his labors. Southwell was originally stationed at Lord Vaux's London home in Hackney. As a result of his friendship with Anne Howard, Countess of Arundel, he moved into one of her properties, most likely within the precincts of the

---

[93] Caraman, *Henry Garnet*, pp. 96–97. See "Father Richard Holtby on Persecution in the North," in Morris, *Troubles*, vol. 3, pp. 113–14.

[94] Regarding the development of the early Jesuit system of missions see Thomas M. McCoog, S.J., "'Sparrows on the Rooftop': 'How We Live Where We Live' in Elizabethan England," in *Spirit, Style, Story. Essays Honoring John W. Padberg, S.J.*, (ed.) Thomas M. Lucas, S.J. (Chicago, 2003), pp. 327–64.

[95] Henry More, S.J., cited the opening and closing paragraphs of a letter attributed by him to Southwell on wandering priests *Historia Provinciae Anglicanae Societatis Iesu* (St Omers, 1660), pp. 188–89. I quote Devlin's English translation: "I am grieved when I hear of your unsettled way of life, the guest of many and at home with none. We are all pilgrims, I know, but not vagabonds; we must risk our lives, but not our destiny. To be a vagabond and fugitive was the Curse of Cain, a sordid punishment to suit his crime. A mind inconstant is like one diseased, twisting and turning always, and finding no resting-place for quiet and holy thoughts ..." (*Robert Southwell*, p. 222).

[96] [Garnet] to [Acquaviva], n.d. [late 1588], ARSI, Fondo Gesuitico 651/624. There may have been another motive for Garnet's recommendation that no more secular priests be sent at this time. In a later letter Garnet complained about the quality of recently ordained priests from Reims: "some have been sent here recently from Reims whom those at Reims scarcely deemed worthy of the priesthood. Yet they are sent here and, seeing that they know not how to rule themselves but rule others, they form a stumbling block" (Garnet to Acquaviva, September 12, 1589, ABSI, Anglia I, 41). Once can find a list of secular priests sent to England in 1589 but I cannot identify any priest as the troublemaker reported by Garnet. For the first see Thomas Francis Knox, (ed.), *The First and Second Diaries of the English College, Douay* (London, 1878), p. 31.

former Augustinian hospital near Bishopsgate in an area now known as Spitalfields. It was here that he set up his printing press.[97]

From the mission's foundation Jesuit secret presses in England produced pamphlets and treatises addressing specific religious and theological issues.[98] Other works, for example Southwell's treatise on equivocation, now lost, and *An humble supplication*, circulated in manuscript. His *A short rule of good life*, written originally for the countess of Arundel and finished shortly before his capture in 1592, was eventually published by Garnet.[99] As he had done in his earlier spiritual writings, Southwell interpreted basic principles of Ignatian spirituality for English laymen and laywomen living in a hostile environment amidst non-Catholics. Such difficulties, however, did not diminish responsibility for leading a godly life and presiding over a godly household. Individuals were placed in this world to serve the Lord and in so doing to save his/her soul. Because men and women were created to serve God "in this life and to enjoy him in the next," "body, mind, time, and labor; and all other affairs" must be directed towards that goal. Building on the "first principle and foundation" from the Spiritual Exercises, Southwell developed its implications in various aspects of everyday life: duty to superiors, neighbors, self; rules for care of children and servants, and a proper daily order. Again following traditional Jesuit practice, Southwell exhorted each to monitor his/her behavior with daily examinations of conscience. Temptations there were aplenty:

> I cannot serve God in this world, nor go about to enjoy him in the next, but that God's enemies and mine will repine and seek to hinder me; which enemies are three: the world, the flesh, and the devil. Wherefore I must resolve myself and set it down as a thing undoubted that my whole life must be a continual combat with these adversaries, whom I must assuredly persuade myself to lie hourly in wait for me to seek their advantage, and that their malice is so unplacable and their hatred against me so rooted in them that I must never look to have one hour secure from their assaults, but that they will from time

---

[97] McCoog, *Society of Jesus*, pp. 236–37, 273–74. Nancy Pollard Brown has argued against the traditional view that Southwell resided in Arundel House and in favor of the Spitalfields house in "Paperchase: The Dissemination of Catholic Texts in Elizabethan England," in *English Manuscript Studies*, (eds.) Peter Beal and Jeremy Griffiths, vol. 1 (Oxford, 1989), p. 123.

[98] See Gerard Kilroy, "Paper, Inke and Penne: The Literary *Memoria* of the Recusant Community," *The Downside Review*, 119 (2001): pp. 95–124 for a discussion of the importance of and circulation of manuscripts.

[99] *A short rule of good life* (n.p, n.d. [London?, 1596–97), ARCR, vol. 2, num. 721, STC 22968.5.

to time, so long as there is breath in my body, still labor to make me forsake and offend God, allure me to their service, and draw me to their damnation.[100]

Southwell soon provided ample witness of his own resolution during his imprisonment.

A reason for Everard Mercurian's hesitation in authorizing a Jesuit mission to England was his fear that demands and dangers would prevent a regular religious life. After he had conceded to the arguments of his consultors, he instructed the first Jesuits to observe as much of the Society's Institute as possible.[101] Hints of that anxiety can be seen in the above-cited references to Gerard's concern for religious dress and daily order. A more important example was the semi-annual meeting of Jesuits, a practice established around the time of Garnet's and Southwell's arrival. During this triduum convened usually around Easter and in the autumn, Jesuits confessed to each other, renewed their religious vows, and discussed procedures. On March 2, 1590 Garnet wrote of a recent meeting. Since the Jesuits spent most of their time separated from their brethren, the meetings were always a source of tremendous joy. They reinforced each other's zeal and revived their Ignatian spirit.[102] Southwell's account was more poetic and more revealing:

> We have altogether, to your great comfort, renewed the vows of our Society, spending some days in mutual exhortations and conferences. "We opened our mouths and drew in the spirit." I seemed to myself to behold the cradle of nascent Catholicity in England, of which we now are sowing the seeds in tears, that others may come to carry the sheaves. Yet we have sung the song of the Lord in a strange land; and in this desert we have sucked honey from the rock, and oil from the hard stone. But this our joy ended in sorrow, and we were dispersed by a sudden alarm; but in the end we escaped with more damage than hurt. I, and another of us, in avoiding Scylla fell into Charybdis; but by

---

[100] For the above exposition I have used Nancy Pollard Brown's edition of the manuscript instead of the later published version (Robert Southwell, S.J., *Two Letters and Short Rules of a Good Life* [Charlottesville, 1973]). The citations can be found on pp. 24–25. On the importance of the written word see Nancy Pollard Brown, "Robert Southwell: The Mission of the Written Word," in McCoog, *Reckoned Expense*, pp. 251–75.

[101] See McCoog, *Society of Jesus*, pp. 132–33, 136–39, 275–78; McCoog, "The English Jesuit Mission and the French Match"; and Thomas M. McCoog, S.J., "'Striking Fear in Heretical Hearts': Mercurian and British Religious Exiles," in *The Mercurian Project: Forming Jesuit Culture 1573–1580*, (ed.) Thomas M. McCoog, S.J. (Rome/St Louis, 2004), pp. 645–73.

[102] Garnet to Acquaviva, March 2, 1590, ABSI, Coll P II 555.

an especial mercy of God we escaped both dangers, and now are at anchor in harbour.[103]

Unfortunately we have no specific details about this close call with the authorities. Despite such dangers the autumn meeting was held in September. By then the number of Jesuits on the mission had increased by two.[104]

For reasons unspecified but probably related to Ignatian spirituality and to the religious structure provided by the Jesuit administration in England, secular priests on the mission were attracted to the Society. In late 1588 Garnet reported that there were five interested clerics: Thomas Harvey (alias Stanney), John Cornelius, John Mush, Ralph Bickley, and Christopher Southworth.[105] All were priests of the "first rank." Garnet was especially eager to receive Stanney but first he needed the general's approval.[106] In April of 1589 Stanney entered the novitiate in Brussels; he returned to England approximately a year later, perhaps with John Nelson.[107] They were the two new Jesuits at the meeting in September of 1590.[108] Yet even before their arrival, Garnet sought a Welsh Jesuit: the first, John Bennet, arrived in late 1590.[109]

Like John Cecil, Garnet wanted to introduce the Confraternity of the Holy Rosary for laymen, and the Sodality of the Blessed Virgin for laywomen. The Dominicans directed the former, but their general could not grant permission to a Jesuit directly. Presumably the Dominican

---

[103] Southwell to [Acquaviva or Agazzari], March 8, 1590, in Pollen, *Unpublished Documents*, pp. 330–32 (translated in Foley, *Records*, vol. 1, pp. 325–26). Caraman identifies the unnamed companion as Garnet (*A Study in Friendship* [Anand, 1991], p. 57).

[104] Garnet to Acquaviva, diocese of Worcester 13 September 1590, ARSI, Fondo Gesuitico 651/624.

[105] On them see Anstruther, *Seminary Priests*, vol. 1, pp. 34–35, 88–89, 240–41, 326–28, 332.

[106] [Garnet] to [Acquaviva], n.d. [late 1588], ARSI, Fondo Gesuitico 651/624.

[107] McCoog, *Monumenta Angliae*, vol. 2, pp. 416, 488.

[108] Because I was not able to identify other novices arriving in 1591, Stanney and Nelson must been the ones about whom Garnet worried so because they lacked adequate formation. What would happen to them, he wondered, thrust into such miserable conditions with so little spiritual formation? Even though he found no faults in the recent arrivals, he feared problems if they were inadvertently separated from their guardians for long periods. See Garnet to Acquaviva, London October 18, 1591, ARSI, Fondo Gesuitico 651/624.

[109] Garnet to Acquaviva, September 12, 1589, ABSI, Anglia I, 41; same to same, March 2, 1590, ABSI, Coll P II 555; Acquaviva to John Bennet, Rome May 11, 1590, ARSI, Franc. 1/I, fol. 323ʳ. On the number of Welsh Jesuits see Thomas M. McCoog, S.J., "The Society of Jesus in Wales; The Welsh in the Society of Jesus: 1561–1625," *The Journal of Welsh Religious History*, 5 (1997): pp. 2–5, 21 n. 18.

general had to work via the Jesuit general.[110] Because the important victory over the Turks at Lepanto in 1571 was popularly attributed to the general recitation of the rosary, there was a resurgence in the confraternity's popularity. Members promised to model their lives on the Virgin Mary and to recite the 15 mysteries of the rosary at least once a week. Perhaps, in the case of England, Catholics hoped that another victory would follow.[111] The Sodality of the Blessed Virgin, on the other hand, was distinctly Jesuit, founded at the Roman College by the Belgian Jan Leunis in 1563. A Jesuit always served as a director.[112] Twice Garnet petitioned Acquaviva. The first request was, apparently, overlooked.[113] The English superior pressed again in 1591.[114]

Is it simply a coincidence that John Cecil and Henry Garnet raised the subject of the confraternity? Were they cooperating on its introduction? Or was Cecil hoping to establish some formal ecclesiastical/religious structure independent of the Jesuits? A few years later Garnet published *The Societie of the Rosary* on his clandestine press to "present therfore unto my moste deare countrey with the same love and affection with which I would if so it pleased God present it my blodd, a singular meane of winning this Virgins favour ... " At the foot of the title page is the antiphon: "*Gaude, Virgo Maria, cunctas hereses sola interemisti in universo mundo*" ("Rejoice, Virgin Mary, since thou alone has crushed all heresies throughout the world").[115]

Despite various difficulties Thomas Stanney managed to leave the kingdom to complete his noviceship on the continent. Others, both secular clergy and laity, wanted to follow his example but for various reasons they were impeded. One unnamed candidate wanted to entrust his estate to the Society in anticipation of his entering the Jesuits but he had been released

---

[110] This Sodality appeared shortly after 1475 as a result of the sermons of the Dominican Alan de Rupe. Its organization remained in the Dominicans whose general had to approve all new chapters. See Herbert Thurston, S.J., "Confraternity of the Holy Rosary" [subsection of the article on "Rosary"], in *Catholic Encyclopedia* (16 vols, New York, 1907–1914), vol. 13, pp. 188–89; Anne Dillon, "Praying by Number: The Confraternity of the Rosary and the English Catholic Community, c. 1580–1700," *History*, 88(2003): pp. 451–71; and Lisa McClain, *Lest We Be Damned. Practical Innovation and Lived Experience among Catholics in Protestant England, 1559–1642* (New York/London, 2004), pp. 81–107. Caraman claims that permission to establish the confraternity had been granted to eleven priests between 1585 and 1586 (*Henry Garnet*, p. 145 n. 3). Would that he had identified them!

[111] On the confraternity see Caraman, *Henry Garnet*, pp. 143–44.

[112] See O'Malley, *First Jesuits*, pp. 197–98.

[113] Garnet to Acquaviva, London August 26, 1587, ARSI, Fondo Gesuitico 651/624.

[114] Garnet to Acquaviva, London October 18, 1591, ARSI, Fondo Gesuitico 651/624.

[115] (n.p. [London], n.d. [1593–94]), *ARCR*, vol. 2, num. 319, *STC* 11617.4, sig. A4. I use Philip Caraman's translation (*Henry Garnet*, p. 144).

from prison on the condition that he would not leave the kingdom. Naturally his assets would be appreciated and useful, but Garnet hesitated accepting a man's estate without guaranteeing his acceptance. Such problems were the motive for Garnet's later proposal that secular priests be allowed to complete their noviceship *in situ*. Two novices, Thomas and John Wiseman, who had made the Spiritual Exercises under John Gerard, had been sent to Oliver Mannaerts, the Belgian provincial, for the novitiate. If the Belgian novitiate could not afford them, Garnet, apparently eager to avoid the bill himself because of his own financial problems,[116] hoped that they would be welcomed at the novitiate in Rome and/or supported by other provinces.[117] They were sent to Rome.

Semi-annual consultations were opportunities to debate different issues as cases of conscience. One practical matter was the possibility of buying Weston's and Emerson's release from prison. In 1588 the subject was first raised regarding Weston. Anne Howard, Countess of Arundel, offered to secure Weston's release and exile by offering a large sum. Weston urged Southwell to dissuade her:

> It seemed to me a dishonourable course–a course particularly alien to the Society, so many of whose members were daily risking their lives for the salvation of souls in so many different parts of the world–for a paltry sum to tarnish in a shamefaced manner the confession of my faith. Also I felt I would not be able to look men straightly and confidently in the face again, if I was branded and marked, as it were, with the stigma of pusillanimous, not to say ignoble, conduct. It was not that I did not shudder at the thought of death, nor prize my freedom. I was very much afraid, and I would have welcomed my liberty gladly and with open arms. But the thought always obsessed me, that it was a despicable method of liberation, particularly unworthy of those times in which so many martyrs had been killed for their faith.[118]

---

[116] Priests outside the Society often looked to Garnet for financial assistance. On November 23, 1591, the imprisoned Eustace White asked Garnet to assist him in his need by collecting monies owed to him (ABSI, Anglia I, 66).

[117] Garnet to Acquaviva, diocese of Worcester September 13, 1590, ARSI, Fondo Gesuitico 651/624; same to same, London October 18, 1591, ARSI, Fondo Gesuitico 651/624; same to same, London February 11, 1592, ARSI, Fondo Gesuitico 651/624; Acquaviva to Mannaerts, Rome May 22, 1592, ARSI, Fl. Belg. 1/I, p. 500. See also Henry Walpole to Joseph Creswell, Brussels August 22, 1591; same to same, Brussels October 17, 1591, ABSI, Anglia I, 58, 64 (published in Augustus Jessop, (ed.), *Lettters of Fa. Henry Walpole, S.J.* [Norwich, 1873], pp. 34–36, 43–44).

[118] Caraman, *William Weston*, pp. 118–19. See also Caraman, *Henry Garnet*, p. 67.

Garnet reported to Acquaviva that it might be possible to ransom both Weston and Emerson.[119] Garnet hesitated because "it would seem a base thing for a pastor [Weston] to flee, and that would be judged a squalid kind of cleanup in which the chains of Christ would be sold at the cost of a counterfeit freedom." Emerson, however, was a different matter. Familiar with Jesuit affairs, he would be extremely useful in England, Scotland, or Ireland. Because he would remain involved on the mission, his release would not be considered "as fleeing the enemy" but as "rising in a new suit of armor."[120] He awaited Acquaviva's decision.

There was not always consensus at the semi-annual conferences. Under interrogation must a priest admit his identity? To protect himself might he deny he was a priest? Some argued that serious sin was committed only when essentials of the faith were denied and one's chosen state of life was not included among them. Others contended that priests were morally obliged to admit their status out of reverence for God's honor. Everyone admitted that the English situation was unique. Because of penal laws, the questions "Are you a priest?" and "Are you a public enemy?" were the same. Nonetheless a priest could not deny his priesthood any more than a Christian his Christianity. Because it was necessary that everyone adhered to the same position, Garnet referred the matter to Acquaviva as final arbiter.[121] The general's reply has not been located.

---

[119] The exchange of John Wells, an imprisoned Englishman in France, for John Leslie, nephew of the bishop, and "the Jesuit Edmondes [Weston]" was discussed in the summer of 1590 (Wernham, *List and Analysis*, vol. 2, paras. 429, 463).

[120] Garnet to Acquaviva, diocese of Worcester September 13, 1590, ARSI, Fondo Gesuitico 651/624. Similar questions were treated in the seminaries. In a case of conscience, it was asked: "Is it lawful for a man to buy off persecution when heretics are about to arrest him or after he has been caught? 'Whether it is lawful, to give money to hereticall Catchepoles, to lett one passe unapprehended?' The persecution which heretics inflict upon Catholics is unjust. It is therefore lawful to buy it off because it is lawful for anyone to buy off unjust persecution in whatever form of temporal ill-treatment it takes. I think, however, that a man who is called to the profession of his faith and ought not to flee, like a priest, cannot buy off persecution inflicted on him. For when he is in this position if his use of bribery is not a denial of faith, it is at least flight, because he does not actually profess the faith by word or deed, and now is the time for confession" (Holmes, *Elizabethan Casuistry*, pp. 51–52). See also Jonathan Wright, "Marian Exiles and the Legitimacy of Flight from Persecution," *Journal of Ecclesiastical History* 52 (2001): pp. 220–43.

[121] In a Douai-Reims case of conscience whether a priest may equivocate or remain silent the reply was: "If they are interrogated by the highest royal officials or their pursuivants and are asked whether they are priests (and they are priests), or are asked whether they are Catholics, they sin mortally if they are silent or equivocate, because they are questioned by these men out of hatred for their religion, in which case everyone is bound to confess his faith" (Holmes, *Elizabethan Casuistry*, p. 54). We shall return to the question of equivocation in Chapter 3.

Two matters treated current practices among some lay Catholics. By long-standing custom, shipwrecked goods, assuming that no one survived the crash, belonged to the Crown. Many Catholics, having been granted royal rights over their maritime estates, possessed such goods without scruple. Some theologians and canon lawyers disputed the English tradition. Garnet offered sound arguments for the validity of England's legal tradition—and thus legitimizing the practice of said Catholics—but, again, referred the question to the general's decision. The second issue was patronage. Many Catholic gentry held the right of patronage to livings now within the Established Church. Could these livings be bought and sold either independently or with the property involved? Garnet preferred to follow the established policy, viz. to permit sale of the right of patronage without papal permission because it was not something spiritual. Marital cases and dispensations from vows demanded much less discussion than the cases of conscience. Garnet and the others wished neither to be out of step with the Christian world in general and the Society in particular, nor did they wish to repudiate established traditions too flippantly.[122] They would accept whatever decision the general made.[123]

Even though, with proper precautions, semi-annual gatherings were possible, constant vigilance was necessary. Southwell narrowly avoided apprehension in 1590. In the spring of 1591 Garnet's cottage in Finsbury Fields was raided.[124] Hugh Sheldon, the cottage's caretaker during Garnet's many absences from London, was disguised as a gardener and was known as "Mr. Gregory."[125] Sheldon looked after the clerical guests. During the winter of 1590–91, Sheldon was employed elsewhere. He returned to London in early spring to prepare for the arrival of Edward Oldcorne who was coming to London to consult a doctor.[126] After Sheldon's but before Oldcorne's arrival, the secular priest James Younger sought assistance at the cottage.[127] Sheldon informed Younger of the dangers of wandering around the city by day, but the priest foolishly thought that it would be

---

[122] For similar cases see Holmes, *Elizabethan Casuistry*, pp. 43–44, 46–48, 96–98, 100–103, 106–107, 114–17.

[123] Garnet to Acquaviva, diocese of Worcester September 13, 1590, ARSI, Fondo Gesuitico 651/624; Caraman, *Henry Garnet*, pp. 116–21. The issue of occasional conformity was not discussed at this meeting although it was the most burning issue.

[124] I follow the account in Garnet's letter to Acquaviva, London March 17, 1593, ABSI, Anglia I, 73.

[125] On Sheldon see McCoog, *Monumenta Angliae*, vol. 2, p. 472 under Seldon. He probably entered earlier than the date recorded there because Garnet referred to him as a lay brother given to him by Oliver Mannaerts.

[126] Earlier in the same letter Garnet said the episode occurred around Pentecost. In 1591 Pentecost fell on May 23.

[127] On Younger see Anstruther, *Seminary Priests*, vol. 1, pp. 391–93.

safe in the area. Upon his return to the cottage a few days later Younger was identified as a seminary priest by a young boy and apprehended. The boy later confessed that he had made a mistake in his identification but nonetheless believed that he had seen the man in Spain. The constable and his posse returned to the cottage to examine it. During the interval Sheldon returned. Claiming that he had no proof that the searchers were not thieves, he refused to admit them. Having secured all the doors, Sheldon hid all compromising material. The constable returned with a magistrate. Defended by his neighbors who explained that Sheldon only used the house during the seasons when the garden needed tending and that he rarely had visitors, Sheldon explained that the priest must have been lost and knocked on his door by mistake. The magistrate asked him when he had last been at church. Sheldon replied on the Lord's Day without, of course, specifying which church. During the subsequent search another priest knocked at the garden gate. Sheldon berated him for his intrusion and the man realized that something was happening. As he tried to make his escape, he was apprehended, examined and imprisoned when he admitted that he had not been to church for 23 years. Sheldon, however, was left at the house. Once everyone had departed and the situation quieted, Sheldon burned the documents. He later eluded the watch left to guard the house and escaped to friends. He feared that one of the captured priests would confess so he did not return to the house.[128] A few weeks later Garnet sent a few men to remove the furniture and the house was left empty.[129]

More serious was the raid during a semi-annual meeting.[130] Garnet had written to Acquaviva at the end of the session, but before the raid. Subsequently he said nothing out of fear of discovery. He did not write about the events until nearly two and a half years later, ostensibly because he feared the letter would be intercepted, and the place and persons recognized. Psychologically it may have been too difficult to relate the events. At an unnamed residence in the country nine Jesuits met from October 14 to 19.[131] Their names were not given in any account but they must have been Garnet, Southwell, Holtby, Curry, Oldcorne, Gerard, Nelson, Stanney, and Bennet. The house belonged to two sisters, Eleanor Brooksby and Anne Vaux, and had been used for an earlier meeting. Shortly

---

[128] Younger did confess. I have not been able to identify the second priest.

[129] A more detailed account of the raid can be found in Caraman, *Henry Garnet*, pp. 122–26.

[130] The two primary sources of information are Garnet's letter to Acquaviva, London March 17, 1593, ABSI, Anglia I, 73, and Caraman, *John Gerard*, pp. 40–43.

[131] Baddesley Clinton is the commonly accepted site (see Caraman, *John Gerard*, p. 264 and Hodgetts, *Secret Hiding Holes*, pp. 65–70) but Nancy Pollard Brown suggests Rowington Hall as a possibility ("Paperchase," p. 137).

before the meeting began, a drunken pursuivant demanded admission. He was kept outside as incriminating evidence was hidden. Angered by the delay he threatened to return with a posse within 10 days. Not knowing whether his threats should be taken seriously and unable to get word to the Jesuits who were on their way, Garnet decided to hold the meeting as scheduled. Having concluded all business Garnet spontaneously warned them at the final dinner that he could not guarantee their safety and that those who wished to leave, could. Four Jesuits (apparently Holtby, Curry, Bennet, and Nelson) left immediately and two secular priests arrived.[132] Shortly before day break on the 19th the house was surrounded. Catholic stable workers repulsed the approaching pursuivants. The constable in charge then sent a request for admission to the mistress of the house, Anne Vaux, with the promise that she would be treated gently. During the delay religious articles were concealed and the priests escaped into hiding holes: the five Jesuits were in a tunnel, ankle deep in water. The search lasted four hours but nothing was found. Fearful of a watch the Jesuits decided that no one would leave immediately. The following day Gerard and Southwell departed; the day after Garnet, Oldcorne and Stanney.[133] The two raids taxed Garnet personally. In the letter written just before the raid, Garnet asked that someone replace him as superior: "… let the race be run under the leadership of someone other than myself." In the following February Garnet was in London while Southwell rested in the country. Because there was no place left to hide as a consequence of the increased dangers after the proclamations of October of 1591, he recommended that Acquaviva not send any more Jesuits.[134] Garnet said very little about the proclamations of 1591 and the consequent persecution.[135] Jesuits continued to do well and performed their ministries effectively. They would "undoubtedly about to gather an abundant harvest when the Lord extends his blessing."[136] The future became less rosy a few months later with the capture of Robert Southwell.

Garnet opened a letter to Acquaviva with a lament on the demise of the almost divine protection recently enjoyed by the Society:

---

[132] Michael Hodgetts suggests that William Warford was one of the secular priests ("The Jesuits at Baddesley Clinton, October 1591," *Worcestershire Recusant*, 24 [1974]: pp. 39–40).

[133] A longer account of the raid can be found in Caraman, *Henry Garnet*, pp. 128–38.

[134] Garnet to Acquaviva, London October 18, 1591; same to same, London February 11, 1592, ARSI, Fondo Gesuitico 651/624.

[135] According to Caraman (*Henry Garnet*, p. 140), Garnet "judged it safer not to discuss the document; probably he feared he might be quoted by the Catholic pamphleteers; possibly also he was disinclined to give his views on a measure which would certainly bring the Queen into odium overseas."

[136] Garnet to Acquaviva, London February 11, 1592, ARSI, Fondo Gesuitico 651/624.

> Now at length, after six years of fair and tranquil sailing, we are beginning to experience the severe gusts of some savage storms. For with our gentle associate snatched by the plunderers, how else can we sail except in a shattered vessel without pilot. This calamity was for us not in the least sudden or unexpected, but one long beforehand planned by our common enemy. We had noticed several months before, in several places at the same time, that antagonisms were being stirred up and inflamed against us all. But what did not prevail with the rest of us, he succeeded in bringing about in one case after several vain efforts. Either God judged the rest of us unworthy of such a trial, or a provident Father wished it so in behalf of the common good.[137]

Southwell's capture affected him deeply: they embarked on the mission together and supported each other throughout the subsequent trials and difficulties. Garnet lost a valued collaborator and a dear friend.

In the annals of recusant hagiography and martyrology, few rival Richard Topcliffe in malevolence. Philip Caraman, S.J., describes Topcliffe as "a Yorkshireman of almost unmitigated evil ... [whose] tortures worse than any hitherto practised on priests lay ahead for those unfortunate enough to fall into his hands."[138] Working primarily in southern England, he wielded power and influence far greater than other pursuivants. Assisted by Richard Young, Justice of the Peace for Middlesex, Topcliffe terrorized Catholics from the early 1590s. In the spring of 1592 the pursuivant's attempt to blackmail John Whitgift, Archbishop of Canterbury, and his almost obscene bragging about his familiarity with the queen nearly led to his downfall.[139] His deeds were often as foul as his words and he seems to have abused and raped Anne Bellamy, daughter of Richard Bellamy whose house at Uxenden was frequented by Southwell and Garnet. She had been imprisoned for religious reasons in January of 1592. In a subsequent scheme to marry the pregnant Anne to Topcliffe's assistant Nicholas Jones, Anne was offered a chance to save her family from persecution by betraying Southwell. The trap was set.

On the feast of St John the Baptist, June 24, 1592, Southwell met Thomas Bellamy, Richard's son, in Fleet Street and set out for Uxenden. They arrived around noon and Mass was celebrated almost immediately. Planning to continue on the next day to meet Garnet, presumably in Worcestershire, Southwell spent the night. In the middle of the night, Topcliffe surrounded the house with a large number of men, and demanded that a certain Cotton (one of Southwell's aliases) be handed over to him. Having carefully

---

[137] ARSI, Fondo Gesuitico 651/624.
[138] *Henry Garnet*, p. 106.
[139] See Verstegan to Parsons, Antwerp n.d. [end of 1592?], ABSI, Anglia I, 68 (published in Petti, *Verstegan Papers*, pp. 97–98).

concealed Southwell, Mary Bellamy, in the absence of her husband, denied that there was anyone there with that name. Topcliffe explained that he knew that the Jesuit was there and that he even knew where he was hiding. If Cotton were not handed over, the pursuivants would destroy the house. Mrs. Bellamy relayed to Southwell what Topcliffe had said and left the next move to the Jesuit. Southwell decided to come out of hiding. As soon as Topcliffe, in the words of Garnet "that butcher (as he certainly is, and I do not think that I exceed the limits of modesty with that word)," saw Southwell, he cried out "Foulest of all the traitors in the kingdom" and sought to run him through with his sword. To the accusations that he was a priest, a traitor and a Jesuit, Southwell replied that Topcliffe had to prove all this and that, in the meanwhile, he was slandered by being called a traitor. According to Garnet, Southwell dissembled to protect his hosts. Topcliffe immediately informed the queen of his prize. Southwell was first taken to Topcliffe's house near Westminster prison, where he was examined and tortured. Attempts to extract useful information from him, failed. According to Garnet's report to Verstegan, Southwell admitted that he was a priest but "true to the Queen and State, free from all treasons, only doing and attending his functions."[140] By the end of the month Southwell had been transferred to the Gatehouse prison. "The news of the capture," Garnet explained to Acquaviva, "travelled straightway throughout the entire city, and with incredible speed throughout the country. Certainly it can not be said how great was the grief of all Catholics; you would have thought that they had all lost a parent."[141]

Fully aware of the ever-present dangers, Garnet was more surprised that Southwell had eluded capture for so long. In his melancholia, the question "why?" plagued Garnet. His attempt to retain religious hope in the face of the loss of Southwell is worth quoting:

> And therefore if, as we hope, this is the work of a compassionate God, and not the just vengeance of a wrathful one, the Catholic cause will receive a more than slight benefit, for even though we cannot not feel the sorrow or the pain, we have been

---

[140] [Garnet] to [Verstegan], London July 26, 1592, ABSI, Coll B 49–51 (published in Foley, *Records*, vol. 1, pp. 352–53 and Petti, *Verstegan Papers*, pp. 67–69).

[141] On Topcliffe and these incidents, see Garnet to Acquaviva, July 16, 1592, ARSI, Fondo Gesuitico 651/624. In a subsequent letter to Acquaviva on October 8, 1592, he referred to earlier letters of August 15 and September 4, in which he gave reports about Southwell (ARSI, Fondo Gesuitico 651/624). Unfortunately these letters have been lost. The news had reached Richard Verstegan in Antwerp by 1 August when he relayed the information to Roger Baynes in Rome (see ARSI, Angl. 38/II, fols 199r-v [published in Petti, *Verstegan Papers*, pp. 51–52]). For more detailed accounts of Southwell's capture see Devlin, *Robert Southwell*, pp. 274–90; Caraman, *Henry Garnet*, pp. 146–52; Caraman, *Study in Friendship*, pp. 59–66.

deprived of our associate, our dearest father assistant. Still, on the other hand, we are refreshed in the awareness that, out of his afflictions and insults, God usually increases his honour, stabilises the Church, and confounds his enemies. And this I see within me as the firmest of hopes, and I take the greatest consolation from the work of this man who never allowed his hopes to be vain ones.[142]

All was in God's hands and there was always the chance that "we might be exposed to the birds of the air"[143] before Acquaviva received the letter.

One slight note of anger could be detected in Garnet's observation that general distrust of Jesuits had increased after the appearance of the Spanish fleet. Priests, and especially Jesuits, were suspected of rallying Catholics to support the Spanish king. Torture was now more common in order to obtain information and names. Because of consequent pain, death was often a release. Nonetheless because all were united in one body torture was bearable:

> Since what is unbearable to one is distributed through the individual members and its severity is diminished. The bond of charity makes the pain light. This is to carry each other's burdens; this is the mutual compassion among members when the weakness of one is strengthened by the strength of the others. It is therefore with this hope that, if at some time we shall be hurled by God's will into those straits, we shall be able to share our torments with others who are willing to bear them.[144]

Of other Jesuits in England, Garnet reported the death of Thomas Metham and the continual imprisonment of Weston, Pounde, and Emerson. Each could be ransomed. In fact each asked to be ransomed, but the decision was Acquaviva's and he might fear that their liberation could give scandal. Meanwhile the Society's work in England would continue and Garnet was grateful that Acquaviva had accepted the candidate Henry Drury into the Society. He was "a devout young man and so educated by his Catholic parents that he brings out of the secular world into religion something of a baptismal garment of innocence which will be adorned with religious pearls."[145] Garnet, meanwhile, thought it best to stay away from London.[146]

---

[142] Garnet to Acquaviva, July 16, 1592, ARSI, Fondo Gesuitico 651/624.

[143] Garnet alludes to the exposure of an executed man's head and four parts on spikes on London Bridge, and at the gates of the city.

[144] Garnet to Acquaviva, July 16, 1592, ARSI, Fondo Gesuitico 651/624.

[145] This was Gerard's second host and spiritual disciple. See McCoog, *Monumenta Angliae*, vol. 2, p. 292 and Foley, *Records*, vol. 7, part 1, p. 211.

[146] According to Nancy Pollard Brown, Garnet went to London as soon as he heard of Southwell's capture presumably to keep informed of all developments ("Paperchase," p. 133). He does not mention his location in his letter of 16 July to Acquaviva, but he signed

Acquaviva commiserated with Garnet's loss and encouraged him in his efforts:

> no one is crowned save he who has striven lawfully and no one attains a glorious prize save he who endures great hardships. I am confident that by this hope our zeal is inflamed and your Lordship's efforts are so bolstered that if aught more bitter should happen, I doubt not that God's grace will always be at hand that all adversity may not only be borne bravely, but also surmounted gloriously.

However, Acquaviva did not alter his views on ransoming Jesuits as a result of Southwell's capture and torture. Primary consideration must be the fear of scandal. Consequently Acquaviva opposed any scheme but he promised to give the matter more prayer and reflection before he made a final decision. Upon return to Rome Acquaviva promised that he would look for a suitable associate to carry on Southwell's work in London.[147]

Acquaviva addressed other issues in early 1593. Garnet had feared that faculties to admit candidates into the Confraternity of the Holy Rosary expired with the death of the one who granted said faculties. In a previous letter Acquaviva denied that such was the case, but promised to discuss the matter with the Dominican general to make sure. The Dominican confirmed Acquaviva's earlier judgment. The two Wiseman brothers had arrived safely at the novitiate in May but unfortunately, John the younger brother, died in early August. Acquaviva gave serious consideration to Garnet's request that another assume the burden of office as the mission's superior but denied it. Because of Garnet's expertise and experience Acquaviva decided "this is a project you must undertake with ready spirit and we all have fond hopes that you will succeed well." Finally, he promised more men once the situation was more tranquil.[148]

The mission limped along as Garnet awaited Southwell's successor. Whoever was named would not have an easy task. Garnet and Southwell had complemented each other well for six years on the mission. They alternated roles to elude capture: each spent a few months in London and then a few months in the country. With no assistant Garnet was obliged to remain in London at considerable risk or to spend his time in the country thus failing to provide aid to the recently arrived priests.

---

his letter of the 26th to Verstegan from London (ABSI, Coll B 49–51 [published in Foley, *Records*, vol. 1, pp. 352–53 and Petti, *Verstegan Papers*, pp. 67–69]).

[147] Acquaviva to Garnet, Mantua October 10, 1592, ARSI, Fl. Belg. 1/I, pp. 507–508.
[148] Acquaviva to Garnet, Rome January 9, 1593, ARSI, Fl. Belg. 1/I, p. 509.

"traffiquing Jesuits, Seminarie preests, and other emissareis of Antichrist": Jesuits in Scotland

James Beaton, Archbishop of Glasgow, pressed Everard Mercurian for a Jesuit mission to Scotland. Mercurian insisted that he would not even consider a mission until he had received a request from either Pope Gregory XIII or Mary, Queen of Scots. Shortly after Mercurian's death his vicar-general Oliver Mannaerts promised the archbishop that he would send two Jesuits, Edmund Hay and James Gordon, after the upcoming general congregation. Acquaviva delayed their departure after his election as superior general in February of 1581. Apparently around this time he solicited the views of the Scottish Jesuit Robert Abercrombie who visited his homeland for a few months in late spring-early summer of 1580. Independently in the summer of 1581, Robert Parsons sent William Watts, a secular priest then working in northern England, to Scotland to ascertain whether English clergy could seek temporary sanctuary there with impunity. Because of the ascendancy of Esmé Stuart, Sieur d'Aubigny (later Duke of Lennox), Watts returned to England with proposals more grand and far-reaching than Parsons's simple request. But by then Parsons was on the continent. The information gathered by Parsons corroborated what Acquaviva had learned from other sources. Thus the general selected William Crichton for the mission; William Holt travelled from England as Parsons's substitute. On March 7, 1582, Crichton and Holt met with Lennox at Dalkeith. Their discussion initiated a series of negotiations, plots and conspiracies for the conversion of James, the rescue of his mother, the deposition of Elizabeth, and the forcible restoration of Roman Catholicism in Scotland, England and Ireland, with foreign military assistance and foreign gold. The fall and banishment of Lennox in January of 1583 portended Scotland's withdrawal from future projects, but the coalition of Scottish Catholic nobles restored some hope.[149]

The Treaty of Berwick signed between England and Scotland on July 5, 1586 apparently secured England's northern frontier and ended the traditional anti-English alliance between France and Scotland. Because of the treaty, Scotland could not become a base for either Guise or Spanish intervention or invasion.[150] Nonetheless Spain still courted either King

---

[149] For a survey of Jesuit activity in Scotland in the sixteenth century and biographical data on Scottish Jesuits of that period, see Thomas M. McCoog, S.J., "'Pray to the Lord of the Harvest': Jesuit Missions to Scotland in the Sixteenth Century," *The Innes Review*, 53 (2002): pp. 127–88.

[150] See Susan Doran, "Loving and Affectionate Cousins? The Relationship between Elizabeth I and James VI of Scotland 1586–1603," in *Tudor England and its Neighbours*, (eds.) Susan Doran and Glenn Richardson (Basingstoke, 2005), pp. 203–34.

James and the Catholic nobility that included George Gordon, earl of Huntly; David Lindsay, earl of Crawford; Francis Hay, earl of Erroll; and John Maxwell, earl of Morton.[151] Protestant nobles such as Francis Stuart, Earl of Bothwell, cherished prospects of a Spanish alliance against England as retaliation for the execution of Mary, Queen of Scots. Attempts by William Chisholm, Bishop of Dunblane, and Jesuits William Crichton and Alexander MacQuhirrie to recruit King James VI to active participation in an invasion, failed. In March of 1588, approximately at the time the embassy met with James, one of the Gordon clan fled to the protection of the earl of Huntly after having committed a murder. Huntly promptly refused a royal order to hand him over; Crawford, Erroll, and Bothwell rallied to his support. For protection James withdrew to Edinburgh, but his opponents did not follow.

Near the end of April, Colonel William Semple[152] and the earl of Morton, sometime Warden of the West Marches initiated a rebellion in southwest Scotland upon their return from Spain. Securing a port as a door for Spanish soldiers was their goal. Demonstrating his new friendship towards Elizabeth, James sent his forces against the insurgents. By the end of June the rebellion had been quashed, and both leaders were in prison. Two months later both escaped.[153] By turning against Catholic leaders, James gave the English government the impression that he had finally ceased his oscillations and sided openly with England in its struggle with Spain. Yet, according to Crichton, Scottish Catholics received and cared for more than 1,000 shipwrecked Spaniards with tacit royal approval.

In a memorial on his mission Crichton claimed that nearly two-thirds of the Scottish people had hoped for the success of the Armada. Indeed they had been prepared to welcome the Spaniards even after the expedition had failed. They, of course, were disappointed that the ships sailed past. To assist shipwrecked soldiers and sailors, Crichton remained in Edinburgh, lodged in a house of William Douglas, Earl of Angus, near Canongate. But

---

[151] On the extent of the Catholic faction see Lord Burghley's memorandum of July 1, 1592 published with annotations in William Forbes-Leith, S.J., (ed.), *Narratives of Scottish Catholics under Mary Stuart and James VI* (Edinburgh, 1885), pp. 361–74.

[152] Sent to Scotland by Philip II in 1588 to solicit James's support in a campaign against Elizabeth, Semple was also provided with a back-up plan: if James could not be swayed, Semple should incite Scottish Catholic nobles against their king. See Glyn Redworth, "Between Four Kingdoms. International Catholicism and Colonel William Semple," in *Irlanda y la Monarquía Hispánica: Kinsale 1601–2001. Guerra, Política, Exilio y Religión.* (eds.) Enrique García Hernán, Miguel Ángel de Bunes, Óscar Recio Morales and Bernardo J. García García (Madrid, 2002), pp. 255–64.

[153] McCoog, *Society of Jesus*, pp. 241–44.

he was obliged to abandon this accommodation and go into hiding once heretics discovered his dealings with the Spanish.[154]

After Morton's revolt, principal Catholics found themselves excluded from court and accused of rebellion. Under pressure, the earl of Huntly, again accepted the Kirk's profession of faith. His conformity, however, did not quell popular fears as most questioned his sincerity. The Kirk did not think that Scotland had survived unscathed as Spanish ships passed its coastland. According to David Calderwood:

> Notwithstanding that the Lord did manifest, the yeere preceeding, by the overthrow of the Spanish Armada, what care he had of his poore kirk in this yle, yitt did the enemeis continue still in their despite and malice: sindrie practising, traffiquing Jesuits, Seminarie preests, and other emissareis of Antichrist, creeping in the countrie, ceassed not to pervert and subvert in diverse parts, namelie, in the North and in the South, wherupon dangerous effects were like to follow.[155]

When the Kirk convened in Edinburgh in January, the ministers petitioned James against interference in their proceedings against the Papists. They wanted to initiate searches for Jesuits and establish commissions to examine the religious convictions of any suspected person. King James agreed.[156]

In late January or early February of 1589, English agents delivered to James intercepted letters from Scottish Catholics to Spanish leaders. The agents contended that said letters revealed the true sentiments of some trusted earls. In a joint letter, the earls of Huntly and of Morton, and Claude, Lord Hamilton had lamented their disappointment to King Philip II that his army had not landed in Scotland. If it had, the army would have encountered no resistance; indeed, with Catholic support, they

---

[154] ARSI, Fondo Gesuitico 651/616. The letter was published in Hubert Chadwick, S.J., "Father William Creichton S.J., and a Recently Discovered Letter (1589)," *AHSI*, 6 (1937): pp. 259–86. See also Francisco de Borja de Medina, S.J., "Intrigues of a Scottish Jesuit at the Spanish Court: William Crichton's Mission to Madrid (1590–1592)," in McCoog, *Reckoned Expense*, pp. 277–325, and "Escocia en la Estrategia de la Empresa de Inglaterra: La Misión del P. William Crichton cerca de Felipe II (1590–1592)," *Revista de Historia Naval*, 17 (1999): pp. 57–59.

[155] Thomas Thomson, (ed.), *Calderwood's History of the Kirk of Scotland* (8 vols, Edinburgh 1842–1849), vol. 5, p. 1. Unless specifically noted, I follow the narrative of Calderwood, Andrew Lang (*A History of Scotland from the Roman Occupation* [4 vols, Edinburgh/London, 1900–1907], vol. 2, pp. 333–51), and more recently, Michael Yellowlees (*"So strange a monster as a Jesuite": The Society of Jesus in Sixteenth-Century Scotland* [Isle of Colonsay, 2003], pp. 117–28).

[156] Thomson, *Calderwood*, vol. 5, p. 1.

would have been able to attack England from the north. Despite all talk and declarations to the contrary, the Armada demonstrated that English Catholics would not provide massive support for a Spanish invasion. Scottish Catholics, they claimed, would provide more trustworthy service in future ventures. In a separate letter to Alessandro Farnese, Duke of Parma, Huntly explained the insincerity of his recent acceptance of Protestantism: if he had not conformed, he would have been forced either to leave the kingdom or to take up arms against Spanish forces. For Scottish Jesuits, Robert Bruce's letter to Parma was extremely damaging.[157] Regarding Jesuits Edmund Hay and William Crichton, who had reconciled the earls of Erroll and Crawford respectively, Bruce wrote that they were "able and wise young lords, and most desirous to advance the Catholick faith, and your enterprises in this Yle."[158] Shortly after the letters were delivered, the Scottish Privy Council banished by name Crichton, Hay, Bruce and others. Hamilton and Huntly were imprisoned; the latter's stay was brief. Erroll remained at large. Each protested innocence of any treason or machinations against the king: they wanted simply to depose James's low-born but powerful chancellor Sir John Maitland. Opposition to Maitland united Catholics with Protestants.[159]

In April Maitland's opponents planned to liberate James from the chancellor's control. Erroll, Huntly, and Crawford gathered their forces in the north for a march on Edinburgh. According to their agreement, Bothwell was to free James and, possibly, slay Maitland. Informed of the conspiracy, James escaped back to Edinburgh; he summoned his loyal subjects to his defense. On the 10th James ordered Maitland's opponents to lay down their arms. At the head of his army James proceeded to Perth where the Catholic allies were assembled. His forces were outnumbered, but James was resolute. At Brig o' Dee the combined forces of Huntly, Crawford and Erroll confronted the king. Erroll wanted to fight; the others were not sure: total defeat and forfeiture would follow a military loss. There was no battle and a compromise was reached. Huntly surrendered to James without loss of title and property. He, Bothwell, and Crawford were found guilty of treason on May 24; their punishment was left to the

---

[157] Bruce was in the entourage of Huntly. Later he was a political agent on the continent, a spy and possibly a double agent.

[158] The letters can be found in Thomson, *Calderwood*, vol. 5, pp. 14–35. The citation treating Crichton and Hay is on p. 25.

[159] Chadwick, "Creichton," p. 278 n. 58. In the descriptive phrase of Wallace T. MacCaffrey, Bothwell was "the rogue male among the Scottish nobility." A Protestant, he changed sides whenever he saw an opportunity for advancement. After the king's marriage, friction between James and Bothwell developed into hostility. His strong hatred of the chancellor drove Bothwell into an alliance with the Catholic earls (*Elizabeth I: War and Politics*, p. 308).

king. Erroll submitted in August. While the Catholic nobles were in prison, Hay and Crichton sailed from the kingdom. By autumn the two Jesuits were on the continent and the Catholic leaders were released from prison. Such leniency angered Elizabeth and encouraged Scottish Catholic exiles. Crichton hoped to return to Scotland although the general advised against it. Instead Crichton pursued Scottish matters at Philip's court in Spain.[160] We shall consider his activities there in the next chapter. For the time being Acquaviva did not want any more Jesuits sent to Scotland.[161] Hay was called to Rome in November of 1589 and was appointed a confessor at St Peter's, Rome. Around the end of March of 1591, Acquaviva appointed him his assistant for Germany.[162] He died in that post on November 4, 1591.[163]

James and Anne of Denmark were married by proxy on August 20, 1589 and Anne set sail for Scotland shortly thereafter. A storm forced her to return to Norway. On October 22, James sailed to Denmark to be with his wife. Maitland, who had opposed the marriage, accompanied him. The royal couple landed at Leith on May 1. Although James made all major decisions with a backward glance at Elizabeth's reaction, the English queen seems to have played a negligible role in his selection of Anne. Indeed, of the two serious contenders for James's hand, Anne of Denmark and Catherine de Bourbon, sister of Henry, Elizabeth probably preferred the latter. Marriage to the sister of the French Huguenot then

---

[160] Acquaviva to Crichton, Rome November 24, 1589, ARSI, Fl. Belg. 1/I, pp. 447–48; same to Oliver Mannaerts, Rome [c. April 15, 1590], ARSI, Fl. Belg. 1/I, p. 458.

[161] Acquaviva to Mannaerts, Rome February 23, 1590, Fl. Belg. 1/I, p. 451.

[162] At the time the Jesuit general had four assistants to advise him on matters related to their assistances of Italy, Spain, France and Germany.

[163] Acquaviva to Crichton, Rome November 24, 1589, ARSI, Fl. Belg. 1/I, pp. 47–48; Rom. 53/I, fol. 152^v; Hist. Soc. 42, fol. 10^r. On the difficulties that preceded Hay's appointment see Burkhart Schneider, S.J., "Der Konflikt zwischen Claudius Aquaviva und Paul Hoffaeus," *AHSI*, 26 (1957): pp. 3–56, 27 (1958): pp. 279–306. After Hay's death Acquaviva would have preferred Odo Pigenat but that was impossible because of his health and the situation in France. James Tyrie was eventually appointed (Acquaviva to Tyrie, Rome February 8, 1592, ARSI, Franc. 1/II, fol. 372^v. See also a letter sent by the general to all communities on February 1, 1592 on the matter (ARSI, Instit. 40, fols 141^{r-v}). Ruth Grant reminds us of Huntly's mixed motives: "One therefore cannot interpret Huntly's correspondence with Spain between 1586 and 1589 solely as Catholic idealism nor as a desire to be in the vanguard of the Counter-Reformation. Huntly's faith certainly was a significant factor, but his over-riding motivation was to shift the balance of power within domestic politics. This shift might have proven favorable to Catholicism; however, that was not at the top of the priorities set by Huntly's party" ("The Brig o' Dee Affair, the sixth Earl of Huntly and the politics of the Counter-Reformation," in *The Reign of James VI*, (eds.) Julian Goodare and Michael Lynch [Edinburgh, 2008], p. 103). Not surprising, Elizabeth increased her subsidies to James to assist him against the Catholic earls. See Julian Goodare, "James VI's English subsidy," in Goodare, *Reign of James VI*, pp. 110–25.

fighting for his right to the throne, would have allied James closely with the Protestant cause and would have involved him in continental religious struggles. In the evaluation of Helen Georgia Stafford, "a marriage with Anne, while it kept him [James] safely within the ranks of Protestants, committed him to no open war against Catholics. Surely Anne was the safer choice."[164] Neither faction could anticipate how the introduction of a Lutheran queen would affect the religious balance of power.

The General Assembly of the Kirk of Scotland assembled in Edinburgh on August 4, 1590. The moderator, Patrick Galloway, asked James to ratify the Kirk's liberties, to provide a sufficient stipend to each church, and to purge the land "of Jesuits, seminarie preests, [and] abusers of the sacrament." In his reply, James claimed that they all knew of his desire to free the kingdom from Papists and Jesuits.[165] In this regard, James's sincerity was always questioned. On September 15, reports that the Jesuit James Gordon could not be apprehended because he had a royal warrant, angered Presbyterians. Despite promises to the General Assembly, James apparently still favored one Jesuit. The following year the General Assembly asked that action be taken against Jesuits, especially Gordon. But nothing was forthcoming.[166] Of the earls who had submitted to the king at Brig o' Dee only Bothwell remained a public problem. Accused of treason and association with witches on April 15, 1591, Bothwell was imprisoned in Edinburgh Castle. He escaped on June 21, and celebrated the event at a dinner in Leith with the earls of Erroll and Morton on the 22nd. Bothwell was denounced as a rebel and "put to the horn" on the 24th. On December 27, Bothwell led a small attack on Holyrood Palace apparently to seize James and Anne. The attackers were repelled. In 1592 James once again was obliged to deal with the unholy alliance between Bothwell and the Catholic earls who, throughout this period, had been secretly negotiating with Spain.

Because there is scant extant correspondence, we know little about the few Jesuits working in Scotland between 1588 and 1591. We do know, however, that they were responsible for reconciling various earls to Catholicism. Appointed superior upon his departure for the mission in July of 1585, Edmund Hay reconciled his kinsman the earl of Erroll. Apparently he worked in the north of Scotland, probably in Erroll's entourage, until

---

[164] *James VI of Scotland and the Throne of England* (New York/London, 1940), p. 52. On the queen's influence on Scottish politics, see Maureen M. Meikle, "A meddlesome princess: Anna of Denmark and Scottish court politics, 1589–1603," in Goodare, *Reign of James VI*, pp. 126–40.

[165] Thomson, *Calderwood*, vol. 5, p. 105.

[166] Thomson, *Calderwood*, vol. 5, pp. 112, 134.

his return to the continent in the summer of 1589.[167] Crichton returned to Scotland in 1587 to convince James to support the Spanish Armada. During his two years, he seems to have worked around Edinburgh. He reconciled the earl of Crawford.[168] John Durie (or Drury) returned to Scotland as Hay's companion in July of 1585. An able controversialist and author of a Latin defense of Edmund Campion against William Whitaker in 1582, he had been on the faculty of the Jesuit college in Angers.[169] With the support of William Maxwell, Lord Herries, Durie worked in the southwest, especially in Dumfries and was responsible for Morton's reconciliation. He died in 1588.[170]

In 1586 Robert Abercrombie and William Ogilvie were sent to Scotland. Abercrombie seems to have worked with John Durie in the southwest. He remained on the mission until, approximately, 1609 when he returned to the Jesuit college in Braunsberg (now Braniewo).[171] William Ogilvie died in Scotland in May of 1594. Between his arrival and death, he made at least one trip to the continent.[172]

Jesuits George Durie (or Drury) and William Murdoch returned to Scotland sometime in 1588. Apparently Murdoch was in and out of Scotland regularly in the early 1590s. Between Scottish ventures, he could be found at the Jesuit college in Pont-à-Mousson.[173] Durie abandoned the

---

[167] McCoog, *Society of Jesus*, p. 211; Medina, "Crichton's Mission," p. 281; Medina, "Escocia en la Estrategia," p. 58; Thomson, *Calderwood*, vol. 5, p. 25.

[168] Chadwick, "Creichton," p. 282 n. 12; Medina, "Crichton's Mission," p. 281; Medina, "Escocia en la Estrategia," p. 58; Thomson, *Calderwood*, vol. 5, p. 25.

[169] *Confutatio responsionis Gulielmi Whitakeri* ... (Paris, 1582), ARCR, vol. 1, num. 334.

[170] Acquaviva to Crichton, Rome February 20, 1589, ARSI, Franc. 1/I, fol. 334ᵛ; McCoog, *Society of Jesus*, pp. 210–11; Chadwick, "Creichton," p. 271 n. 36, p. 273 n. 48, p. 278 n. 1, p. 282 n. 12; Hubert Chadwick, S.J., "A Memoir of Fr. Edmund Hay S.I.," *AHSI*, 8 (1939): p. 79 n. 16 (the original document edited by Chadwick can be found in ARSI, Angl. 42, fols 211ʳ–215ᵛ).

[171] John Hungerford Pollen, S.J., *The Counter-Reformation in Scotland* (London, 1921), pp. 61–62; Chadwick, "Memoir," p. 79 n. 14; ARSI, Angl. 42, fol. 239ʳ; Lith. 6, fol. 9ᵛ.

[172] Pollen, *Counter-Reformation*, p. 62 (I followed his account in *Society of Jesus*, p. 242 n. 68) placed Ogilvie's death in late 1587 or early 1588. His death, however, is recorded as May of 1594 (ARSI, Hist. Soc. 42, fol. 10ᵛ). He is listed as being in Poznań in 1593 (ARSI, Angl. 31/I, fol. 121ʳ).

[173] On Murdoch see John Durkan, "William Murdoch and the Early Jesuit Mission in Scotland," *The Innes Review* 35, (1984): pp. 3–11. Jesuit catalogues list Murdoch in Pont-à-Mousson in 1589, 1590, and 1593 (ARSI, Franc. 10, fols 77ʳ, 137ʳ, 161ʳ; Angl. 31/I, fol. 121ʳ).

Society circa 1594, remained in Scotland with his family, and eventually apostatized.[174]

James Gordon travelled to Scotland with William Crichton in August of 1584. Dutch Calvinists captured both but released Gordon out of fear of his nephew, George Gordon, Earl of Huntly. During his sojourn in Scotland, Gordon worked primarily in the Highlands, but seems to have enjoyed considerable liberty throughout the kingdom because of his nephew. In 1585 he debated George Hay, a noted controversialist, and in February of 1588, he was involved in a disputation with King James on selected topics: invocation of the saints, communion *sub utraque specie*, justification, and predestination. During the five hours, Gordon praised the king's knowledge of Scripture. The two agreed on justification and predestination. But surely, James opined, Gordon's views did not correspond with Roman Catholic doctrine and thus the Jesuit would be reluctant to put his signature to any agreement. But Gordon did sign his name with the contention that all Catholics would do the same. James, however, believed that Gordon "would never more dare to go back to the Jesuits or Papists, or they would burn him for such a confession." Gordon remained in Scotland until late 1593.

"[Catholics] sucked dry and reduced to extreme poverty"

In late 1592 or early 1593 Henry Garnet visited Richard Holtby in northern England, a region then subjected to harsh persecution. According to Garnet, Henry Hastings, Earl of Huntingdon and President of the Council of the North, ruled Yorkshire, Durham and Northumberland with quasi-royal magnificence as if he were a viceroy.[175] He named pursuivants; he gave them authority to summon and arrest any Catholic according to the proclamation of October of 1591. These pursuivants approximated a private army under his direction. So intense was persecution that schismatic nobles, presumably this refers to occasional conformists, were even not spared. Not only were they obliged to deliver their Catholic wives for imprisonment but pursuivants demanded guarantees that they would neither hire Catholic servants nor harbor any Jesuit or seminary priest in their house. Moreover the nobles must attend a service either in the parish church or in their homes to demonstrate their allegiance. Refusal meant prison. Among the women arrested in Yorkshire were Lady Margaret

---

[174] McCoog, "'Pray to the Lord of the Harvest,'" p. 167.

[175] McCoog, *Society of Jesus*, pp. 205, 243; Pollen, *Counter-Reformation*, pp. 50–53, 68–69. The only account of the discussion can be found in *CSP Simancas* (1587–1603), pp. 260–61. On Hastings see McCoog, *Society of Jesus*, p. 110 n. 91.

Constable, wife of Sir Henry Constable; Lady Constable of Everingham; Lady Cholmeley of Whitby; Lady Ursula Cholmeley of Brandesby; and Ladies Grace Babthorpe, Catherine Metham, Catherine Ingleby, and Holtby. In the diocese of Durham, Ladies Lawson of Neson, Anne Killingale and others were arrested. An order from the queen's council obtained the release of Sir Henry Constable's wife, but with tremendous restrictions. Lady Holtby was released through the intervention of her husband who then forcibly conveyed her to Protestant services. So many recusant men and women were apprehended that new prisons were opened in Sheriff Hotton, Knaresborough, Rotheram, Bransby Castle, and two in York. Twice during 1592 Huntingdon visited Durham. At each visit he scattered his pursuivants throughout the countryside to harass Catholics. On the Monday of Holy Week, since Holtby presumably was talking about 1592, on March 20, pursuivants raided the house of John Trollope in Thornley. He, his family, and two maids concealed themselves in a hiding hole. For three days the pursuivants besieged the house, searching everywhere for the occupants. Unable to find the family, the pursuivants looted the house and carried away anything of value.[176]

John Fenwick, one of Huntingdon's most notorious assistants, assembled more than a hundred men for attacks on the Ogles in Dishington, the Rutherfords in Rutchester, and the widow Lawson in Grange. Thomas Rutherford and his wife were apprehended; Mrs. Lawson eluded capture by hiding in an oven with serious consequences for her health. Frightened Catholics deserted their homes to live rough in woods, caves, and holes. The Jesuit John Nelson, his unnamed host and his wife constructed two apartments under an old oak tree.[177] Since all searches took place either at night or in the morning, they only emerged above ground in the afternoon. They lived in this way for six weeks. Others too lived among ruins or underground where their companions were frogs, toads, lizards, and adders. One young woman had to be medicated because she believed that an adder had slipped down her throat while she slept.

What resulted from this persecution, Garnet wondered? According to Holtby, the government was waging war against a few priests and unarmed Catholics. Hunting recusants was the principal concern of all justices, judges, and bishops whose goal was the suppression of Catholics and the eradication of the true faith. More money was expended and more force exerted on their domestic war against Catholicism than in campaigns against foreign enemies. Yet the faith increased daily and shone brightly: the just were winning the kingdom!

---

[176] Richard Holtby often used their residence as his base. See Hodgetts, *Secret Hiding Holes*, pp. 119–21.

[177] See Hodgetts, *Secret Hiding Holes*, pp. 123–25.

Persecution was less intense in other parts of the kingdom more distant from the threat of Scottish Catholic earls; nonetheless there were martyrs.[178] Thomas Portmort was executed in St Paul's churchyard, London, on February 21, 1592. John Lampton was martyred in Newcastle on July 24, 1592. In Winchester in the summer of 1592 laymen James Byrd and John Thomas were executed.[179] A Marian priest named Williams (presumably Richard Williams) who returned to the Roman Church after years as a Protestant minister, was executed.[180] Two other priests, Thomas Clifton and John Brushford, died in prison.[181] These were but a few who confessed their faith. Garnet claimed that equally constant confessors could be found in nearly every parish and town. Indeed, there was no person who has been a Catholic more than a year who has not "either publicly confessed his faith, or has suffered pillaging of his property, or is in perpetual hiding, living as a wanderer or exile, or detained in prison." Catholics expected every type of difficulty and were prepared to endure it. That was their spirit; that was their resolution.[182]

Catholic martyrologies have consistently portrayed the earl of Huntingdon as a bloodthirsty monster. In 1586 an anonymous Catholic referred to him as a tyrant who was "god, king, bishop, president, catchpool, and whatsoever else to annoy the Catholics."[183] Tales of his cruelty flowed from the pen of Richard Holtby and were sent to Rome for wide dissemination.[184] Cruel he may have been, but Michael Questier has clearly shown that his actions were not irrational excess. Ruthless persecution throughout the north must be linked to real fears about Scottish intervention in England by taking advantage of religious differences. Scottish Catholic earls did conspire with Spain regarding

---

[178] Pollen published the section on the martyrs from Garnet's letter in Pollen, *Unpublished Documents*, pp. 228–33.

[179] There is some problem with the dating of Byrd's death. Although this letter was clearly written in March of 1592/93, the traditional date for Byrd's death is March 25, 1593 (Petti, *Verstegan Papers*, p. 23 n. 37). If we date Garnet's letter March 17/27, the Jesuit had an account of Byrd's death two days after it had occurred.

[180] See Verstegan to Roger Baynes, Antwerp June 6, 1592, ABSI, Coll M 127a (published in Petti, *Verstegan Papers*, p. 49).

[181] See Anstruther, *Seminary Priests*, vol. 1, pp. 56–57, 80–81, 204–205, 280–81; Thomas M. McCoog, S.J., (ed.), *English and Welsh Jesuits 1555–1650* (1 vol. in 2 parts, London, 1994–1995), p. 186.

[182] Garnet to Acquaviva, London March 17, 1593, ABSI, Anglia I, 73. Sections on the martyrs of 1592 and 1593 were published, with an English translation, in Pollen, *Unpublished Documents*, pp. 227–33. See also Caraman, *Henry Garnet*, pp. 166–69.

[183] "A Yorkshire Recusant's Relation," in Morris, *Troubles*, vol. 3, p. 65.

[184] See for example other accounts by Richard Holtby, ABSI, Anglia I, 74; Anglia, II, 12 (published in Morris, *Troubles*, vol. 3, pp. 118–219, 221–30).

an invasion of Scotland or England. Involved in their plans if not their intrigues were Charles Nevill, Earl of Westmorland, and Francis Dacre, scions of families that still enjoyed strong support throughout the north. Despite the Treaty of Berwick, England remained vulnerable along the borders, a vulnerability that conspirators, English and Scottish, sought to exploit. The government, on the other hand, sought to remedy the problem by securing the allegiance of northern Catholics, not always as unarmed as Garnet asserted, through conformity. Persecution was the alternative. Considering recusants as potential supporters of a Scottish invasion, the government employed all means to insure that Catholics would not provide any aid. To Huntingdon and his pursuivants protection of the realm was as important a consideration as the preservation of the Established Church. Consequently defeat of the Catholic earls at the Battle of Glenlivet in October of 1594 played a more significant role in the reduction of persecution in the north than the death of Huntingdon in 1595.[185]

After the near disaster at Baddesley Clinton in October of 1591, Garnet hesitated convening all Jesuits at the same time. Instead during 1592 only two or three Jesuits met together. It was not until late January/early February of 1593 that all met. Even then the meeting resulted not from a relaxation in persecution or religious freedom but "to a lull portending still greater severity in laws and penalties," that is, preparations for a new Parliament. New edicts and inquisitions followed a comparable interlude in late 1591. Thus Garnet feared the new Parliament would devise new modes of persecution to re-enforce the old. They were, he claimed, "never sated by bloodshed and persecution of the innocent." They only paused now because they conceived and planned greater atrocities.[186]

Rumors of yet another conspiracy to assassinate Elizabeth circulated in January of 1593. On the 17th John Scudmore, a secular priest, was arrested with an Irishman Hugh Cahill, who immediately accused the priest of having been ordered by Robert Parsons to assassinate Elizabeth.[187] Surprisingly, shortly after his arrest and examination, Scudmore was

---

[185] See Michael Questier, "Practical Antipapistry during the Reign of Elizabeth I," *Journal of British Studies*, 36 (1997): pp. 371–96, and also "The Politics of Religious Conformity and the Accession of James I," *Historical Research*, 71 (1998): pp. 14–30.

[186] Garnet to Acquaviva, London March 17, 1593, ABSI, Anglia I, 73. Verstegan shared Garnet's pessimism about the new Parliament. See his letter to Parsons, Antwerp March 5, 1593, ABSI, Coll B 75 (published in Petti, *Verstegan Papers*, pp. 104–105).

[187] On this plot see Francis Edwards, S.J., *Plots and Plotters in the Reign of Elizabeth I* (Dublin, 2002), pp. 193–204.

released and allowed to leave the kingdom. The question remained whether the new plot would effect new legislation against English Catholics.[188]

Parliament assembled on Monday, February 19, 1593. In his opening speech Sir John Puckering praised Queen Elizabeth's reluctance to convene Parliament frequently unlike her predecessors. Dangers, however, threatened the realm with Rome and Spain as the great enemies, and the queen needed financial support to combat them. Instead of seeing the hand of God in the defeat of the Armada, Philip II persisted in his desire to weaken Elizabeth's realm. His and his allies' armies controlled much of France and only God's assistance to Henry IV prevented Philip from adding France to his empire. More worrisome for England was Philip's occupation of Breton ports, convenient bases for another attempt to invade England. Over the past year Philip's intrigues with Scottish earls nearly resulted in an invasion from the north. The Spanish king "breathed nothing but bloodie revenge, vowyinge as it hath been here confessed by a Jesuyte, that he would spend his candle to the sockett, but he would be revenged and have his will of her."[189] Unfortunately not all threats were outside the realm: "others much nearer, and so much the more dangerous as they lurke *intus et in cute* [inside and outside]." Plots against the queen's life continued. Nearly two months ago an unnamed subject confessed to a proposed attempt on the queen's person and on her place in the hearts of her subjects by persuading them that "her Majestie, neyther is, nor cann be ther lawfull Queene, but standeth accursed and throwen out of the fayth and therby deprived of all the loyaltie and due obedience of her naturall subiectes."[190] Hidden among the populace were the Spanish king's secret intelligencers commissioned to keep him informed of all

---

[188] On May 15, 1593 Garnet informed Acquaviva about a disturbance instigated by a priest who arrived from Rome in August of 1592. He claimed that William Holt entrusted him with an important message for Garnet: papal judgment about the views of Thomas Bell. Although no Jesuit in England was worried about the issue, there was fear of popular reaction if the opinion became public. Garnet did not question the priest's piety but he marvelled that he alone possessed knowledge of the opinion and, thus, wondered about its authenticity (ARSI, Fondo Gesuitico 651/624). Apparently the carrier was Scudmore. See also Garnet's letters to Acquaviva, June 10, 1593, London September 30, 1593, London November 12, 1593, January 3, 1594, ARSI, Fondo Gesuitico 651/624. For more on Scudmore see Anstruther, *Seminary Priests*, vol. 1, pp. 304–305; McGrath, "Apostate and Naughty Priests," p. 58; and Verstegan to Parsons, Antwerp February 18, 1593, ABSI, Coll B 135 (published in Petti, *Verstegan Papers*, p 101, see also p. 102 n. 5). We know that Scudmore's rumor concerned Bell from William Allen's letter to James Tyrie, Rome n.d. [between May and September 1593], ARSI, Fondo Gesuitico 651/594 (published in Renold, *Letters of Allen and Barret*, pp. 231–33).

[189] T.E. Hartley claims that this is a reference to James Younger's confession (*Proceedings*, vol. 3, p. 17 n. 2).

[190] Is this a reference to Hugh Cahill and John Scudmore?

developments within the kingdom. To deal with these perils the queen convened Parliament.[191] Internal security was a concern and, in the words of J.E. Neale, "owing to the nature of the conflict, [that] was primarily a matter of religious conformity."[192]

Garnet explained the bicameral nature of Parliament to Acquaviva. Under the guidance of Lord Burghley and his son Sir Robert Cecil, "hateful to God and men, whom even the vulgar sort ridicule with the name Lord Rebukers of the Upper and Lower House," both houses prepared new bills against Catholics. "An Act for Restraining Recusant Papists to a Fixed Domicile" was introduced in the Upper House on February 24. In his speech Burghley repeated many of Puckering's points regarding Spanish aggression. He was more worried, however, by Spanish and papal efforts to form a party within the realm. He admitted that they had gained a number of supporters who would flock to the invaders in expectation of rewards and honors.[193] The new law sought to restrict the movements of persons suspected of supporting Spain. Obstinate recusants were ordered to remain within five miles of their homes; failure to do so without a license from justices of the peace could result in forfeiting all goods and income. Only submission to the Established Church brought relief from the act. In the formula as forwarded by Garnet the supplicant must profess that "the Bishop of Rome hathe not, nor ought to have, any power or aucthoritie over Her Majestie, or within any Her Majestie's realmes or dominions; and I do promise and protest without any disimulation or any collor, or meanes of dispenceation."[194] Before the bill was passed (35 Eliz c. 1), one substantial change was made: recusant wives were exempt from banishment.[195]

The bill introduced in the Lower House on February 26 had a much more difficult passage. The original bill, "An Act for the reducing of disloyal subjects to their due obedience," varied financial penalties for recusancy according to the wealth of the offenders: anyone failing to submit to the queen before June risked losing all goods and chattels, and two-thirds of the income from their lands. Other clauses deprived recusant wives of their dowries and fined anyone marrying a recusant woman two-thirds of her dowry. Children of recusants were to be removed from their parents and entrusted to others to be raised in the Established Church at

---

[191] Puckering's speech can be found in Hartley, *Proceedings*, vol. 3, pp. 14–19.

[192] Neale, *Elizabeth and Her Parliaments*, vol. 2, p. 280. For his account of this Parliament see pp. 241–323.

[193] Burghley's speech can be found in Hartley, *Proceedings*, vol. 3, pp. 23–27.

[194] Verstegan included a copy of the act in his letter to Parsons, Antwerp [mid-April 1593], ABSI, Coll B 43 (published in *Verstegan Papers*, pp. 121–22).

[195] On the legislation see LaRocca, "English Catholics," pp. 157–60.

their parents' expense. Recusants were deprived of their inheritance; they were incapable of making contracts. Penalties were harsh. Because the act applied to all recusants and not just Catholics, some extreme Protestants opposed it and demanded clauses restricting the act to Popish recusants. On the day that Garnet wrote to Acquaviva, the bill was stuck in committee. Many, according to Anthony Bacon, considered the bill too harsh. Garnet was well aware of protests in the Lower House and reported that some asserted that if Catholics were the way the government described them, it would be better to kill them directly; if, however, they were deemed worthy of life, they should be allowed to live under decent conditions. Garnet quoted Lord Grey,[196] described as a "distinguished although not a very good man," on the bill: "I was under the impression that up to now your purpose was to keep Papists humble and subjected so that they would not be able to raise disturbances; but now that they are sucked dry and reduced to extreme poverty and yet they are still harassed, I see plainly that you are now persecuting religion." Despite such protests Garnet did not doubt that the act would pass into law. Fortunately for recusants the bill did not become law.[197] Garnet attributed the failure to pass the second law to the Lord's defense of his followers against the "craftly ones of this world." But, he wondered, was the victory chimerical? What advantage was the right to buy and sell when recusants were incapable of having anything to buy or sell?[198]

Lord Burghley played a significant role in drafting the legislation against recusants. According to William Richardson, he was the "architect" of such anti-Catholic legislation again because their allegiance was suspect.[199] But, Richardson argued, his failure to steer his preferred version of these laws through Parliament hinted at the growing discrepancy between Burghley's conviction that recusants remained a threat, and the view of the Privy Council and of Parliament that "recusancy was but a persistent nuisance which, at times of military action, required to be neutralised by routine precautionary measures."[200] In brief, his strident pursuit of recusants was

---

[196] Caraman identifies him as Henry Grey of Enville, Stafford (*Henry Garnet*, p. 171 n. 2).

[197] For accounts of its defeat see Neale, *Elizabeth and Her Parliaments*, vol. 2, pp. 280–94, LaRocca, "English Catholics," pp. 155–57. See Verstegan's letters to Parsons, Antwerp [mid-April] 1593, Antwerp [c. mid-April] 1593, Antwerp [c. mid-May] 1593, Antwerp May 27, 1593, ABSI, Coll B 43, 81, 107, 47 (published in Petti, *Verstegan Papers*, pp. 121–23, 126–27, 150–52, 155–56). On November 12, Garnet reported to Acquaviva that, because the second bill was not passed, "our affairs are in no worse state than they had been" (London November 12, 1593, ARSI, Fondo Gesuitico 651/624).

[198] Garnet to Acquaviva, June 10, 1593, ARSI, Fondo Gesuitico 651/624.

[199] Richardson, "Religious Policy," pp. 79–115.

[200] Richardson, "Religious Policy," pp. 182–83.

quickly becoming anachronistic. A less severe, more practical approach was needed. Already some councillors such as Robert Devereux, Earl of Essex, and Burghley's son Robert explored limited tolerance. But Burghley's perspective was shaped by decades of anti-Spanish rhetoric and near hysterical fears of Popish conspiracies and plots. According to Richardson, he would have "*liked* to have believed in the loyalty of the catholic laity but acted with inveterate caution."[201] Regardless of how they tried, Catholics could provide no guarantees that would satisfy Burghley. Robert Cecil and Essex, however, accepted a distinction between private conscience and public behavior. They formed friendships and alliances with Catholics in England, convinced that they posed no internal threat. Catholics abroad were another matter. Both sought to weaken the influence and authority of dangerous exiles, especially Jesuits, and were willing to discuss the possibility of some type of tolerance in England in return for the removal of Jesuits.[202]

"Iudas with a kisse dost thou betray me?": The Problem of Occasional Conformity

Only compliance with the laws provided relief from persecution and penal restrictions. If Catholics attended heretical churches, in the expression of Garnet, they would be freed from the "yoke of slavery." Garnet recounted a story that he had just heard about the queen: Elizabeth claimed that she had perused ancient fathers of the Church who had written in Hebrew, Greek and Latin, and also many modern Spanish and Italian authorities without finding any grounds for the claim that it was unlawful for Catholics to attend Protestant services. The secular priest, Thomas Bell assisted her with the research.[203]

"How much was perpetrated before their [Jesuits and seminary priests] arrival without any awareness of crime!" he informed Acquaviva:

> How much of superstition, deception, filthy oaths against the Roman Pontiff and the religion of Christ was tolerated, even in the cases of those who wished to be considered as Catholic ... For apart from those few whose constancy in those dark times was as admirable as it was rare, there were unnumbered others, Catholic in name, but in fact betrayers of their holy religion and apostates who frequented the churches of the heretics and led their sons and

---

[201] Richardson, "Religious Policy," p. 287.
[202] See Richardson, "Religious Policy," pp. 286–91 for differences between the two Cecils.
[203] Garnet to Acquaviva, London March 17, 1593, ABSI, Anglia I, 73.

whole families into them. It was held a sign of Catholicity if one was the first to enter the church or the last to leave ... And one thought he was healed by these evils, if he were to mix the sacred with the profane, if after these heretical superstitions, he were present at the most solemn sacrifice of the Church, if he were serving both Baal and Christ.

All this changed with the arrival of the seminary priests and Jesuits. Now nothing was more clear to English Catholics than the necessity of confessing Christ publicly and not betraying him by frequenting heretical churches. Now it was known that such attendance was a sacrilege despite any appeal to obedience to the queen as justification. To Garnet, this stiffening of Catholic resolve was a principal fruit of the English mission.[204] Garnet's depiction of an English Catholic consensus on the issue was unduly optimistic. Edmund Campion and Robert Parsons dealt with the problem shortly after their arrival in June of 1580. In the 1560s some Catholics had evaded punishment through passive, non-participatory attendance at liturgical services. Pope Pius V's excommunication of Elizabeth in 1570 complicated the situation. Nonetheless priests such as Alban Langdale argued that Catholics could attend services under certain conditions. The so-called Synod of Southwark in 1580 condemned the practice, and Parsons's first publication in England, *A brief discours contayning certayne reasons why Catholiques refuse to goe to church* (Douai [vere East Ham], 1580), contested its underlying theology. But defenders of the practice were never fully vanquished. Thomas Bell resuscitated the debate in the 1590s.[205]

Sent to England in 1582, Bell narrowly eluded capture a few times throughout the 1580s. Finally apprehended in 1592 he was sent to John Whitgift, Archbishop of Canterbury, because of his offer to conform. He did so by early 1593.[206] According to Garnet, for years Bell had justified the behavior of Church Papists while at the same time professing his allegiance to the Roman Church. Indeed he had circulated various manuscripts in which he espoused and justified his position.[207] But recently, perhaps because he had been warned of Rome's condemnation of his views, he turned himself over to commissioners, abandoned the priesthood,

---

[204] Garnet to Acquaviva, May 25, 1590, ARSI, Fondo Gesuitico 651/624.

[205] For pertinent documents, see Crosignani, *Recusancy and Conformity*.

[206] In a letter to Acquaviva on October 8, 1592, Garnet reported that two unnamed priests had conformed. One clearly was Anthony Tirell; the other may have been Bell (ARSI, Fondo Gesuitico 651/624). On Tirell and Bell see Anstruther, *Seminary Priests*, vol. 1, pp. 29–30, 361–63; McGrath, "Apostate and Naughty Priests," pp. 52–53.

[207] On his views see Holmes, *Resistance and Compromise*, pp. 95–98; and Alexandra Walsham, *Church Papists: Catholicism, Conformity, and Confessional Polemic in Early Modern England* (Woodbridge, 1993), pp. 56–60. Unfortunately Bell's treatises are not extant.

repudiated Rome, and betrayed his friends. In Lancashire, where he had ministered to Catholics for years, he examined recusants thus: "Do you know who I am? No! You say that you do not, you damned accursed rogue! Did you not hear me preach at such and such a place, on such and such a day, at such and such a gathering? Did I not then argue on such and such a point?" Now he boasted that he was never a priest but had simply assumed that identity in order to study their habits. An unnamed councillor, again according to Garnet, judged Bell thus:

> We enquired from Robert Southwell, who is in the Tower of London, his opinion of Bell. He replied that he had never lived with the man on intimate terms, but that he knew and heard much about him, and that he was held to be a man of moderate learning, but excessively addicted to faction. And truly [continued the councillor], we have found it to be so: for the other [Southwell] is nothing if not zealous and devout; but this man [Bell] is engrossed in factions and crammed with malice.

In his last letter to English Catholics, William, Cardinal Allen reminded them that they must neither teach nor defend that it was lawful to attend Protestant services even though he urged them to be compassionate to those who did so. The cardinal consulted divers theologians and petitioned the pope, presumably Clement VIII, for a decision. The pope "expreslie told me that to participate with the protestants either by prayinge with them or cominge to their churches or service or suche like was by no meanes lawfull or dispensable, but added withall, that such as of feare and weakenes or other temporall force or necessitye should do yt ought to be gentlie dealt withall and easily absolved ..."[208] Despite Bell's apostasy, his views remained influential and Garnet sought confirmation of the papal condemnation.[209] "For what could be more grateful to the whole flock," he asked Acquaviva, "than to hear the judgment of its shepherd? Or what so fitted to crush the insolence of certain individuals as the unshakeable decision of Peter?" If

---

[208] Rome December 12, 1592, published in Knox, *Letters of Allen*, p. 345, and Crosignani, *Recusancy and Conformity*, pp. 260–62.

[209] In a letter to Acquaviva on [July 16/26, 1593] (ABSI, Coll P II 597–98), Garnet wrote "Would that a copy of the decree against Bell, of which all Catholics have heard with much approval, were sent us!" Apparently there was no such decree. William Allen explained the situation to James Tyrie: "When the Fathers and the better priests resisted him [Bell], and wrote also from there for him to be restrained by censures, a rumour was started in England that he had been excommunicated publicly by authority of the Pope, though, however, no such thing was attempted, nor did the Pope intend in any way to do it; as I once told the Fathers in a letter" (Allen to Tyrie, Rome n.d. [between May and September 1593], ARSI, Fondo Gesuitico 651/594 (published in Renold, *Letters of Allen and Barret*, pp. 231–33). The source of the rumor was John Scudmore.

Garnet had not known that God permitted scandals and heresies in order to test the elect, he would be ashamed to be a fellow citizen of a country that nurtured such monsters. Yet despite men such as Bell and the earl of Huntingdon, despite proclamation and imprisonments ("London, like a whirlpool, sucks in and casts out of prison Catholics every day"), the Catholic faith remained strong. Every day more joined the Church and few, succumbing to temptations, slipped away. Once the papal condemnation of Bell became public knowledge, Garnet believed they would be fewer still.[210]

Bell's defection did not discredit his position. A recent book, unnamed by Garnet but according to him accepted by schismatics as if it were "sent down from heaven," defended the practice, and encouraged Catholics to attend services. Proponents of recusancy experienced greater difficulty in their arguments with schismatics. In their debates defenders of occasional conformity appealed to Cardinal Allen's recent letter, with a claim that it vindicated their views.[211] They hoped that he would soon declare attendance only a venial sin. Careful consideration must be given to this question, Garnet argued, because the nature and existence of Catholicism depended on the answer. Thus Garnet suggested that Acquaviva request a concise statement that could be easily promulgated in England.[212]

Thomas Bell revived arguments previously proposed by Alban Langdale.[213] He defended Catholic attendance at Protestant services as long as they neither prayed nor received communion, but simply entered the church out of obedience to the queen. Lest such attendance give scandal, Bell suggested that all Catholics make the following declaration before entering:

> Good people, I am come hither not for any liking I have of any sacraments, service or sermons accustomably used in this place, but only to give a sign of my allegiance and due loyalty to my prince.[214]

Bell cited precedents from the Old Testament: Shadrach, Meshach and Abednego attended the dedication of Nebuchadnezzar's idol without worshiping it (Daniel 3) and Jehu's feigned consent to sacrifices to Baal (2

---

[210] Garnet to Acquaviva, London March 17, 1593, ABSI, Anglia I, 73.

[211] It is important to distinguish a consistent condemnation of the practice of frequenting Protestant churches from the consideration with which contrite conformists were handled. The act was a grave sin, but the repentant sinner was forgiven. See the treatment of occasional conformity in Holmes, *Resistance and Compromise*, pp. 99–125, and Holmes, *Elizabethan Casuistry*, *passim*.

[212] June 10, 1593, ARSI, Fondo Gesuitico 651/624.

[213] On Langdale see McCoog, *Society of Jesus*, pp. 144–45, 152–53.

[214] Cited in Holmes, *Resistance and Compromise*, p. 95.

Kings 10). But the most important precedent was Naaman permitted by the prophet Elisha to assist his king at pagan worship (2 Kings 5).[215]

Garnet initiated a campaign against occasional conformity. On April 1, 1593 Richard Verstegan reported the publication of a book "don by a Catholique and bearing the name to be printed at Douay" against Bell and his arguments in favor of occasional conformity.[216] The treatise was Henry Garnet's *An apology against the defence of schisme*.[217] Lamenting that "it is a miserable thing to sinne, so to lose Gods favour: worse to sinne openly, so to give a scandall: more abhominable to defend your sinne, so to refuse repentance: But most horrible, with the filfth of sinne, reproch of scandall, obstinacy of a proude minde erected against God and his holy spirite, to cause directly the fall of a number,"[218] Garnet attacked the alleged facts on which Bell based his case, and his theological interpretation of Scriptural passages. Contrary to Bell's claims, no pope had granted a dispensation to attend heretical services. In fact, because attendance at a Protestant service involved contempt for the Roman Catholic Church, a pope could not grant a dispensation.[219] In the case of Naaman, Garnet distinguished visiting a church from attending a service. Entering a church "when one goeth for to be present at service: and so, that he may worthely seeme to go as others doe, with conformity in religion, or preiudice, or contempt of Catholicke faith and unity: which in one worde we may well terme, an orderly going to hereticall service" was forbidden.[220] However, it was permissible to accompany a prince to a civil or secular service held in a church because "it is not the Church but the service and profession of conformity which is reproved."[221] Attending a service was either a lie or

---

[215] For his justification of conformity see Holmes, *Resistance and Compromise*, pp. 95–97, and Walsham, *Church Papists*, pp. 56–62.

[216] Verstegan to Parsons, Antwerp April 1, 1593, ABSI, Coll B 83–85 (published in Petti, *Verstegan Papers*, pp. 114–15).

[217] (n.p, n.d. [London, 1593]), ARCR, vol. 2, num. 318, STC 11617.2. The title claimed that the author was an "English Divine at Doway." Many of the objections to Bell's position can also be found in an anonymous manuscript, "An answer to a comfortable advertisement," This manuscript was published in Crosignani, *Recusancy and Conformity*, pp. 157–243.

[218] Garnet, *An apology*, p. 4.

[219] Garnet, *An apology*, pp. 9–10.

[220] Garnet, *An apology*, p. 54.

[221] Garnet, *An apology*, p. 57. A case of conscience presented the issue thus: "is it lawful to accompany the Queen to her chapel? In this special case it is further asked whether it is lawful for noblemen and noblewomen who serve the Queen to follow her to church and to sermons to perform some service for her and not in order to listen while they are there. For example, if a noble should carry a sword before the Queen as an honour on an important occasion, or if he should carry books or cushions or such things. It is not easy to condemn such nobles if they only do it out of duty to the Queen. But it would be better if they openly

an act of betrayal, that would always give scandal regardless of how well known one was, and would always expose one to the risk of infection.[222]

Garnet continued his battle with Bell in another volume published the same year, *A treatise of Christian renunciation*, a collection of quotations from the writings of the fathers and the canons of the Church regarding what each believer must be prepared to renounce for the faith.[223] In the preface, Garnet addressed the question of occasional conformity:

> But what do we see in the like? who knoweth not how often the question of going to hereticall Churches hath been tossed in our countrey? And who is ignorant of the generall resolution of all those learned reverend and godly Priests who are and have bene in the same? But what hath happened? Certaine private persons, who have wholly addicted them selves to make them Gods either of their belly and ease, or of the wicked mammon, setting God behind all things which may delight them, will not onely not refourme their pernicious custome of frequenting hereticall conventicles (which were a crime more tolerable) but they refuse also to beleeve that they do amisse: and that which is more hainous and a most high degree of pride, they defend their wickednes: neither content with this, (as though it were no comfort to perish alone) they induce and by all possible meanes allure their frendes and subiectes to the same iniquitie.[224]

But true Christians were prepared to abandon all—family, wealth, and life—for the gospel. Thus, they would not be seduced by the wiles of these men.

The question of attendance was specifically but briefly addressed at the end of the book. Frequenting Protestant churches was an act of betrayal: "Iudas with a kisse dost thou betray me? amongst hereticks dost thou professe me? no other place to professe chastity, but in the bedd of a harlott? no other time to professe innocency, but in condeming an innocent? no place to professe the honour thou owest me, but where thou in highest degree dost dishonour me?"[225] A prior declaration by a conforming Catholic that such attendance stemmed from obedience to

---

implored the Queen to be excused such service on account of their consciences" (Holmes, *Elizabethan Casuistry*, p. 51).

[222] In an interesting aside, Garnet mentioned that he had heard that there was a different custom in Scotland and he exhorted that country to "learne from ours, which hath bene with so many holy labours, and bloody conflictes of moste holy Martyrs, instructed and embrewed" (*An apology*, p. 150). On this question see Hubert Chadwick, S.J., "Crypto-Catholicism, English and Scottish," *The Month*, 178 (1942): pp. 388–401. See also Crosignani, *Recusancy and Conformity*.

[223] (n.p., n.d. [London, 1593]), ARCR, vol. 2, num. 322, STC 11617.8.

[224] Garnet, *Treatise of Christian renunciation*, pp. 13–14.

[225] Garnet, *Treatise of Christian renunciation*, p. 150.

the sovereign was not sufficient because no protestation could make an evil act good. The example of Naaman was dismissed because he was present in a pagan temple but not at a pagan service.[226] As an appendix, Garnet printed "The Declaration of the Fathers of the Councell of Trent" regarding attendance at Protestant services with an English translation.[227] Regardless of consequent difficulties, fathers at the Council argued "that before all humane lawes, the lawes of God, that is the will and pleasure of God is to be preferred. For unto Caesar Christ commaunded us to geve those thinges which are his; but especially unto God, those things which are dew unto him."[228] Needless to say Garnet's treatises did not end the controversy.[229]

Manning the Mission: Candidates for the Society of Jesus

The Confraternity of the Holy Rosary, according to Garnet, proved to be very effective in fortifying the faith of the laity despite recent proclamations and new legislation.[230] However one problem remained: a shortage of Jesuits. Preservation of Catholicism within the kingdom demanded more priests regardless of any difficulties. Somewhat impatiently, Garnet reminded Acquaviva that he still awaited the arrival of two Jesuits.[231] He had been expecting them for months. He wanted, he confided to Acquaviva, more Jesuits but "the number must be increased gradually lest other workers think they are being excluded, others with whom we live in close association, and there is truly no room for envy."[232] There may have been grounds for the suspicions of "other workers": Garnet sought more Jesuits but discouraged sending more secular clergy.

---

[226] Garnet, *Treatise of Christian renunciation*, pp. 151, 152, 156.

[227] Why this declaration was not published earlier, remains unknown.

[228] The declaration has its own pagination. The above quotation can be found on pp. 34–35.

[229] On Bell, Garnet et al., see Alexandra Walsham, "'Yielding to the Extremity of the Time': Conformity, Orthodoxy and the Post-Reformation Catholic Community," in *Conformity and Orthodoxy in the English Church, c. 1560–1660*, (eds.) Peter Lake and Michael Questier (Woodbridge, 2000), pp. 211–36.

[230] The rules for the confraternity, translated by Garnet, circulated in manuscript among the members. The work was later published as *The Societie of the Rosarie*. Another edition appeared a few years later. See *ARCR*, vol. 2, num. 320, *STC* 11617.5.

[231] Garnet to Acquaviva, May 15, 1593, ARSI, Fondo Gesuitico 651/624. He repeated his request for two veteran priests in letters to Acquaviva of June 10, 1593 and [July 16/26, 1593] (ARSI, Fondo Gesuitico 651/624; ABSI, Coll P II 597–98).

[232] Garnet to Acquaviva, London September 30 [1593], ARSI, Fondo Gesuitico 651/624.

Related to a shortage of Jesuits in England was a persistent predicament with the placement and formation of novices.[233] In May Garnet sent to Oliver Mannaerts a superb candidate for the novitiate, the secular priest Edward Walpole: "he is one of excellent dispositions, uncommon in the estimation of Jesuits and, accordingly, with a very brief review of his studies he can return to our ministries because he has those virtues that are required in these times and circumstances." However, Mannaerts had earlier instructed Garnet not to send any more candidates until he had returned from a trip to Rome. So eager was Garnet to have this man within the Society that he sought the Acquaviva's permission to send him to Flanders without delay.[234]

Among secular priests interested in the Society was John Radford "who has led an innocent life since his departure from us and now understood the meaning and the beauty of the family he left."[235] Radford however hesitated and did not re-join the Society until 1607.[236] James Younger had been released from prison in the spring of 1593 and crossed to Douai. Apparently he too had intended to enter the Society in Flanders, but instead he remained in Douai where he took his doctorate. According to Garnet, Younger clung to the "Reimsian rocks" (*"haesit ad scopulos Rhemenses"*).[237] William Warford, who may have been one of the secular priests at Baddesley Clinton and "a man of high character, of more than a little learning, especially if humane letters are considered, and an uncommon example to all inasmuch as he had once been estranged from the Society," deliberated joining. Warford finally petitioned for admission

---

[233] Parsons faced the same problem in Spain. Parsons asked Acquaviva to urge Spanish provincials to accept two or three English candidates. Parsons himself had raised the matter with some provincials who promised to do so but later argued that their provinces could not afford the expense. Parsons was confident that a slight nudge from Acquaviva would bring about the desired result (Madrid December 4, 1593, ARSI, Hisp. 136, fols 163^r–165^v). With or without a nudge from the general, by March of 1594 there were three English novices in the provinces of Castille, Toledo, and Andalusia (Parsons to Acquaviva, Seville May 10, 1594, ARSI, Hisp. 136, fols 316^r–317^v).

[234] Garnet to Acquaviva, May 15, 1593, ARSI, Fondo Gesuitico 651/624. On Walpole see McCoog, *Monumenta Angliae*, vol. 2, p. 519.

[235] In *Monumenta Angliae*, vol. 2, p. 449, I asked whether the John Radford who had entered the Society in 1584 was the same one who joined the Society later. Apparently he was.

[236] Garnet to Acquaviva, May 15, 1593, same to same, London September 30 [1593], same to same London November 12, 1593, ARSI, Fondo Gesuitico 651/624.

[237] Garnet to Acquaviva, London September 30 [1593], same to same London November 12, 1593, ARSI, Fondo Gesuitico 651/624. See Anstruther, *Seminary Priests*, vol. 1, pp. 391–93.

in late September and Garnet promised to send him to the noviceship in the spring. Warford entered the noviceship in Rome in May of 1594.[238]

The secular priest John Cornelius had pronounced a vow to enter the Society and was ready to travel to Flanders to enter the novitiate if ordered to do so. From his base with the Arundels at Chideock Castle, Dorset, Cornelius worked with at least 30 Catholics. He knew them well, and they valued his assistance. His departure for the novitiate would leave them without a priest. Garnet, moreover, worried that the Belgian Jesuits would not accept Cornelius into the noviceship because of physical problems: he still suffered from a rupture endured some years ago. He could preach, study and, indeed, ride so the disability did not curtail his ministry. Garnet needed advice: should Cornelius be released from his vow, or should he be sent to the novitiate despite his essential work in Dorset and the possibility that he may be rejected? Garnet admitted that Cornelius always lived with a Jesuit and would not suffer if his noviceship was postponed or, indeed, he slyly suggested, if he would be allowed to make his first probation in England. Cornelius was eventually "admitted" into the Society shortly before his execution in the summer of 1594.[239]

The English mission depended on the kindness of the Belgian province for the formation of novices. Apparently ordered to do so by Acquaviva, the Belgian provincial accepted a certain number of English candidates. Yet even though the English quota was not full, candidates often found the doors of the novitiate closed to them. In June of 1593 Garnet complained that only one English candidate had been admitted.[240] It was impossible to recall those who had already embarked, and Garnet feared that they would find their entrance barred. Garnet urged Acquaviva to resolve the problem but without any added expense to the mission, which lacked money. In fact, legacies and endowments of English candidates sustained the mission. They wanted to make over to the mission all their monies and estates. Yet Garnet hesitated using their monies regardless of the mission's needs until their acceptance was secure. He prayed that the novices would be well received. Thus much depended on Mannaerts's willingness to take in the English.[241] Interceding on behalf of the English mission, Acquaviva

---

[238] Garnet to Acquaviva, London September 30 [1593], ARSI, Fondo Gesuitico 651/624. On Warford see Anstruther, *Seminary Priests*, vol. 1, p. 370; see McCoog, *Monumenta Angliae*, vol. 2, p. 522.

[239] Garnet to Acquaviva, [July 16/26, 1593], ABSI, Coll P II 597–98; same to same London November 12, 1593, ARSI, Fondo Gesuitico 651/624. On Cornelius see Anstruther, *Seminary Priests*, vol. 1, pp. 88–89; see McCoog, *Monumenta Angliae*, vol. 2, pp. 274–75.

[240] Thomas Everard was admitted on June 3, 1593 (see McCoog, *Monumenta Angliae*, vol. 2, p. 299).

[241] Garnet to Acquaviva, June 10, 1593, ARSI, Fondo Gesuitico 651/624. Acquaviva's concern for novices "cast off by all countries and lacking in resources" was, according to

granted Garnet permission to send all English candidates to Belgium. If, upon their arrival, Mannaerts judged there were too many, he could send them to other provinces.[242] Two other candidates were accepted that summer: Edward Walpole and George Keynes.[243] But even after the Belgian provincial promised to accept English candidates, Garnet was obliged to proceed slowly. Jesuit "rivals" in England, presumably unnamed secular priests, complained that the Society was depriving the mission of too many needed clergy by sending them to foreign noviceships. The fact that withdrawal was only temporary and that the priests returned more qualified for the mission did not silence the critics.[244] Perhaps the best solution would be allowing secular priests to make their novitiate *in situ*.

Developments in the French religious war made the summer of 1593 especially memorable. Henry IV and the Catholic League agreed to a truce in July after he had renounced his Protestant views. Many questioned his sincerity, but Elizabeth feared its repercussions. The English government hoped to take advantage of the truce to restore peaceful relations with Spain through the mediation of the Holy Roman Emperor Rudolph II.[245] By September, Londoners were more concerned with a new plague "snaking" its way through the city. For two months the plague devastated the population, but by late October it was waning: Verstegan reported that only 300 died during the third week of October.[246] One or two Jesuits were sick, coughing up blood from the chest. Unfamiliar with this type of illness,

---

Garnet, a glowing testimony to the general's commitment to the mission.

[242] Rome June 5, 1593, ARSI, Fl. Belg. 1/I, pp. 516–17. See also Acquaviva to Parsons, Rome June 7, 1593, ARSI, Baet. 3/I, p. 119 in which Acquaviva informed Parsons of Garnet's desire to accept 12 candidates. Acquaviva instructed Garnet to send all to Flanders from where they would be sent to different provinces. Presumably this is the agreement to which William Crichton referred when he asked Acquaviva for a similar arrangement for the Scots. See his letter from Antwerp on October 23, 1593, ARSI, Germ. 171, fols 290[r-v].

[243] On Keynes see McCoog, *Monumenta Angliae*, vol. 2, pp. 376–77. In September of 1593 Garnet mentioned that Master Henry Drury, "a man of great innocence, prudence, and integrity, of whom we were hoping the best," apparently died of the plague. Consequently no one would be sent to Flanders until the plague subsided (Garnet to Acquaviva, London September 30 [1593], ARSI, Fondo Gesuitico 651/624).

[244] Garnet to Acquaviva, London November 12, 1593, ARSI, Fondo Gesuitico 651/624.

[245] According to Garnet the former Jesuit Christopher Perkins was sent on the queen's behalf to the emperor (Garnet to Acquaviva, June 10, 1593, ARSI, Fondo Gesuitico 651/624).

[246] Verstegan to Parsons and Sir Francis Englefield, Antwerp September 17, 1593, ABSI, Coll B 127–29; Verstegan to Allen, Antwerp September 25, 1593, ABSI, Coll B 131–32; Verstegan to Parsons, Antwerp [c. late September 1593], ABSI, Coll B 133; same to same, Antwerp November 10, 1593, ABSI, Coll B 143–44; same to same, Antwerp [c. early December 1593], ABSI, Coll B 145–46 (published in Petti, *Verstegan Papers*, pp. 176–78, 182–83, 185, 189–90, 193–94).

Garnet did not think it the plague and asked Acquaviva to question some Italian doctors about the malady because it was unknown in England.[247]

During the first week of November of 1593 Garnet visited the imprisoned priests at Wisbech in Cambridgeshire, described by William Weston as "a general prison for thieves and criminals of every description."[248] By 1593, however, it had become, in the words of Michael Questier and Peter Lake, a "clerical lodging house ... where many priests were gathered together, to which other Catholics could resort and upon which a considerable public attention might intermittently be concentrated."[249] Supported at considerable expense by Catholics, priests in Wisbech lived a style of life that would have shocked their Protestant contemporaries. Although there were periodic searches, sporadic harassment, and the occasional disputation with a visiting Protestant cleric, priests had their own dining room and make-shift chapel where they were generally able to celebrate daily Mass. Weston explained:

> we now set out to model our life on the pattern, as it were, of a college, arranging study classes and every other form of humanistic exercise. Days were fixed for cases of conscience, controversies, Hebrew and Greek classes, disputations and lectures. We also arranged for sermons, not so much for the benefit of outsiders, as to give useful practice to the priests.[250]

Catholics travelled to Wisbech for spiritual direction and the sacraments. Garnet reported to Acquaviva how well he was received by everyone during his visit. Impressed by what he had seen, Garnet referred to Wisbech as a "college of venerable confessors," and celebrated his visit by singing a

---

[247] Garnet to Acquaviva, London November 12, 1593, ARSI, Fondo Gesuitico 651/624.

[248] Caraman, *William Weston*, p. 162.

[249] Peter Lake and Michael Questier, "Prisons, Priests and People," in *England's Long Reformation 1500–1800*, (ed.) Nicholas Tyacke (London, 1998), p. 201. Lake and Questier provide examples of Catholic ministries emanating from different prisons. See also Lisa McClain, "Without Church, Cathedral, or Shrine: The Search for Religious Space among Catholics in England, 1559–1625," *Sixteenth Century Journal*, 33 (2002): pp. 381–99, and *Lest We Be Damned*, pp. 55–79. Robert Parsons admitted to Alfonso Agazzari in 1583 that "by the supreme providence of God it happens that these very priests who are shut up in prisons are sometimes of more use to us there than if they were at liberty. For these men, being always definitely in the same place, make possible the visits of many people who are unable to discover the whereabouts of other priests. Moreover, as they are always in London or other big cities, they are better able to deal with business in those cities than other priests who either have fewer friends in those parts or, having them, do not presume to make use of them with the same boldness as those who are already in prison do, for fear of exposing themselves to danger" (Parsons to Agazzari, Paris August 24, 1583, in Leo Hicks, S.J., (ed.), *Letters and Memorials of Father Robert Persons, S.J.* [London, 1942], p. 179).

[250] Caraman, *William Weston*, p. 167. See pp. 161–77 for details of life at Wisbech.

Solemn High Mass. As a result of his visit, Garnet decided that it would not be fitting to ransom Weston because, without him, the whole college would collapse.[251]

Acquaviva refused Garnet's request that he be relieved of the burdens of office.[252] Garnet begged nonetheless that a Jesuit with the qualifications to be either Garnet's assistant or successor be sent to England. The superior was too well known to reside continually in London without considerable risk.[253] Earlier Garnet had written to Parsons about the need for more men and had asked for Joseph Creswell presumably to serve in this role. If Creswell were willing, Parsons offered to send him.[254] However, after consultation with Acquaviva, Parsons concluded that Creswell was needed as Parsons's assistant in Spain. Instead Henry Walpole was sent.[255] By November Garnet eagerly anticipated the arrival of the Jesuit destined to be Southwell's replacement and, eventually, his successor.[256]

Garnet's joy at the prospect of Walpole's arrival faded quickly. In early January of 1594, he heard an ominous rumor that Walpole and a Flemish coadjutor serving as his guide had been arrested upon landing.[257] By March 10, the rumor had been confirmed; the only error was that Walpole was alone. Fearing that the loss of Walpole so soon after his arrival would deter Acquaviva from sending others, Garnet reminded him that help was still needed and, although danger could not be eliminated, it could be reduced if Jesuits in England were informed in advance of time and place of arrival. Because of an increase in the number of novices, more men were now available for the mission. In fact Garnet had just sent four more novices off to the "designated place" (presumably Belgium): three secular priests and a layman.[258] There were other candidates but for various reasons, one of which was "because there are some who bear it ill that workers

---

[251] Garnet to Acquaviva, London November 12, 1593, ARSI, Fondo Gesuitico 651/624.

[252] Acquaviva to Garnet, Rome January 9, 1593, ARSI, Fl. Belg. 1/I, pp. 509–10.

[253] Garnet to Acquaviva, [July 16/26, 1593], ABSI, Coll P II 597–98.

[254] Parsons to Acquaviva, Valladolid June 16, 1593, ARSI, Hisp. 135, fols 306^r–307^v.

[255] Parsons to Acquaviva, Valladolid August 11, 1593, ARSI, Hisp. 136, fols 14^r–15^v. William Baldwin was summoned to Spain as Walpole's replacement (Acquaviva to Parsons, Rome February 15, 1593, ARSI, Baet. 3/I, p. 100).

[256] Garnet to Acquaviva, London November 12, 1593, ARSI, Fondo Gesuitico 651/624.

[257] Garnet to Acquaviva, January 3, 1594, ARSI, Fondo Gesuitico 651/624.

[258] The priests were William Warford, John Radford, and Joseph Pullen. The layman was Richard Griffith. On Pullen and Griffith see Anstruther, *Seminary Priests*, vol. 1, p. 283; and McCoog, *Monumenta Angliae*, vol. 2, pp. 440–41 (under Polonus), 338 (under Griffidus). John Radford did not depart. In a letter Acquaviva from London on August 9, 1594 (ARSI, Fondo Gesuitico 651/624), Garnet stated he had sent three to the novitiate and the fourth, Radford, was about to embark "when he was forced by an obvious danger to return to us."

are removed from here," Garnet delayed sending them to the novitiate. Somewhat bitterly Garnet dismissed these critics: "if they [the secular priests entering the Society] were to leave England for some life of ease abroad, they would receive the blessing of everyone, but, obviously, it is a great penance to do what one wishes to do!" Nonetheless Garnet did not want to aggravate the problem by removing too many at the same time.[259]

One aspirant who did not depart was John Cornelius. Captured on April 14, 1594 at Chideock Castle, he still longed to enter the Society. In a letter to Garnet, he hoped "that Father Ignatius of happy memory, will number me among his own if I shall ever escape from the broken bolts of this life." In prison he tried to avoid giving scandal. Although he hoped that the tortures would pass, he prayed for the grace to endure them. "May your Reverence fare well, " he wrote, "a thousand times and urge my cause among the fathers so that in this house of correction, if it is possible, I may suddenly emerge a Jesuit and be on my way to heaven."[260] After Cornelius's martyrdom, Garnet explained how much he tried to console the priest, but it was not within his power to accept him into the Society. Before he was executed at Dorchester in July of 1594, he pronounced the religious vows of the Society "before three principal Catholics, charging them to be witnesses and to disclose the fact to us." Using Cornelius as an illustration, Garnet implored Acquaviva that the superior in England be authorized to accept anyone awaiting execution for "thus both they can freely declare that they are Jesuits, and we shall have the assistance of, and be adorned with such great and worthy protectors."[261]

The Strength of the Earls: Catholicism in Scotland

Rumors and suspicions swirled through Edinburgh after Bothwell's failed attempt to kidnap James on December 27, 1591.[262] The following day at a service in the Great Kirk, Patrick Galloway preached on the Lord's deliverance of King James from the plots of his enemies as a miracle. Admonishing the king because of his leniency in dealing with Catholics, he exhorted James to act decisively to prevent further attempts. On January 10, 1592 a royal proclamation declared Bothwell to be a member of the faction that opposed James at Brig o' Dee, and

---

[259] Garnet to Acquaviva, March 10, 1594, ARSI, Fondo Gesuitico 651/624.
[260] Pollen, *Unpublished Documents*, pp. 269–70.
[261] Garnet to Acquaviva, London August 9, 1594, ARSI, Fondo Gesuitico 651/624.
[262] In the narrative I follow Andrew Lang, *History of Scotland*, vol. 2, pp. 355–84, and Thomson, *Calderwood*, vol. 5, pp. 142–294.

promised rewards for his apprehension. James Stuart, Earl of Moray, rumored to be a supporter of Bothwell, fell under suspicion after the attempted kidnaping. Allegedly if Bothwell's coup had been successful, Moray would have conducted James to his remote earldom. Under the guise of ending a feud, the earl of Huntly planned to call on Moray at Donibristle on February 7. Instead Huntly set fire to the house, and killed Moray as he escaped the flames. James was suspected of collusion because his aversion to Moray as an associate of Bothwell was well known. Although a public proclamation on 8 February declared James's innocence, public outcry at Moray's slaughter demanded some action. On March 10, Huntly surrendered and voluntarily entered a prison in Blackness Castle controlled by his supporters. He later slipped away. More concerned with the capture of Bothwell, James deflected attempts by the Kirk to excommunicate Huntly and his supporters by reminding the ministers that they still had not punished Bothwell, who continued to court the Kirk. Bothwell meanwhile defended his conduct in a letter to the ministers of Edinburgh, distributed throughout the city. Two charges were levelled against him: conspiring with foreign powers for the "overthrow of true religioun," and consorting with witches for the destruction of the king. Regarding the former, he protested that he had never dealt with any foreign power regarding any religious change. Instead, he claimed that many nobles angered by the execution of Mary, Queen of Scots had sworn to avenge her death. Prompted by Sir John Maitland, Lord Thirlestane and now Lord Chancellor, several nobles pledged hostility to England and friendship to her enemies. Spanish agents then in Edinburgh sought to use this oath to their own advantage and to secure Scottish support for their schemes. As Maitland gradually became aware that the earl of Huntly and his faction had more influence with Spain and had in fact received more Spanish gold than he himself had, he proclaimed his Protestantism and friendship with England. Regarding the second charge, Bothwell denied accusations made by "deboshed and infamous persons, and poore beggars that have desperatlie renounced their faith and baptisme."[263]

Hatred of Huntly and outrage at the murder of Moray galvanized the General Assembly that convened in Edinburgh on May 21. At its second session, the ministers proposed that the new Parliament abrogate the hated "Black Acts" of 1584 and ratify the liberties of the Kirk, that is, dismantle the episcopal ecclesiastical structure and replace it with a Presbyterian one. Parliament opened on the 29th. Maitland tempered James's original, strong opposition to the Assembly's proposals so bravely defended by ministers in the king's presence. The chancellor convinced the king that royal concessions on ecclesiastical matters would win him support of the

---

[263] Bothwell's letter was published in Thomson, *Calderwood*, vol. 5, pp. 150–56.

ministers in general and specifically in his campaign against Bothwell. In return for a declaration of Bothwell's forfeiture, the Kirk was granted powers of jurisdiction, discipline, and excommunication. Episcopacy fell and a Presbyterian ecclesiastical structure officially installed. If the Kirk was able to exercise its newly recognized powers, Catholics would be imprisoned, exiled, or executed. Bothwell retorted that the parliamentary declaration with another unsuccessful attempt to capture James at Falkland on June 27. Huntly went unpunished, even though his lands were ravaged, to the dismay of Queen Elizabeth who feared his influence, his Catholicism, and his possible intrigues with Spain. Despite her persistent refusal to receive Scottish rebels as fugitives in England, Elizabeth's anxiety that Spanish influence was strong in Huntly's lands resulted in secret negotiations with Bothwell's agents in late summer of 1592.[264]

As Bothwell eluded capture and travelled almost at will throughout Scotland, more rumors of Catholic intrigues stirred up the Protestant ministers. Scottish ministers became more aggressive in their defense of the reformed religion and in their relations with the king. At a meeting with selected ministers on November 17, James refused a request that Alexander, Lord Hume be dismissed from his company because there was no law requiring the king to send him away. He did, however, acknowledge their claims that various unspecified dangers threatened the Kirk and the commonweal. On the following Sunday, the 19th, William Row asserted in his sermon that the king "might be excommunicated, incace of contumacie and disobedience to the will of God."[265] As implicit definers of the "will of God," ministers, therefore, could move against the king whenever they disapproved of his behavior. At the conference ministers decided to proclaim a general fast throughout the country on December 17 and 24 to avert God's punishment then hovering over the kingdom. Among the reasons for the necessity of the fast were the internal implementation of the subversive decrees of the Council of Trent against true religion, and the defection of many to Popery, seduced by the proselytizing activities of Jesuits and seminary priests. From their pulpits ministers raged against the king despite his attempts to mollify them.

The capture of George Kerr on December 27 in the Cumbrae isles by Andrew Knox, a Paisley minister, demonstrated to many the effectiveness of the national fast. Knox and his associates, enthusiastic students from Glasgow University, found on Kerr packets containing letters from Scottish Jesuits James Gordon and Robert Abercrombie, the English secular priest

---

[264] See Helen Georgia Stafford, *James VI of Scotland*, pp. 66–69. On Elizabeth and Bothwell, see Doran, "Loving and Affectionate Cousins," pp. 210–14.

[265] Thomson, *Calderwood*, vol. 5, p. 179.

John Cecil, and eight suspiciously clean sheets of paper, signed by the earls of Angus, Huntly, and Erroll. Unaddressed, the letters were apparently intended for a person of high rank. Also found were seals bearing the coats of arms of the different earls. In themselves the documents proved nothing but under torture Kerr admitted that the "Spanish Blanks" were to be completed by William Crichton and were intended for a new enterprise to restore the Catholic faith in Scotland and to invade England. Here was further evidence that Protestant fears of Catholic collusion with Spain were not without substantiation.

On January 17, 1593, King James announced that the conspirators already in the government's hands, that is, earl of Angus, George Kerr, and David Graham, Laird of Fintry, would be tried. The earls of Huntly and Erroll, and Sir Patrick Gordon, Laird of Auchindoun, were summoned to appear on 5 February to answer charges levelled against them. Instead they fled to their northern strongholds. Elizabeth reminded James that English law excluded from succession anyone who plotted against her and urged him to take action against the Catholic conspirators.[266] As he proceeded to march north against the earls, James complained of English treatment of the Protestant conspirator, the earl of Bothwell. On 13 February Angus escaped from the castle, probably with assistance. On the 15th the Laird of Fintry was executed for treason. On the 17th James started his march towards Aberdeen; he returned to Edinburgh on March 13. About this northern excursion, David Calderwood cynically commented: "little or nothing was done, saving ... that the Erle of Huntlie's hous was randered to his wife, the Erle of Erroll's to his wife."[267]

The General Assembly of the Kirk convened in Dundee on April 24. Protesting the growth of Popery within the realm, commissioners presented five articles to James. Among them were demands that Papists be "punished according to the lawes of God and the realm" and that a "declaratour may be givin against Jesuits, Seminarie preests, and traffiquing Papists, declaring them culpable of treasoun and lese majestie, whereby the recepters of suche persons may be punished according to an act of

---

[266] See McCoog, *Society of Jesus*, pp. 213–14.

[267] Thomson, *Calderwood*, vol. 5, p. 238. Rumors circulated throughout Rome that James had fled perhaps into England after an encounter with the Catholic earls. Informed of these events and of the necessity of providing some aid, the pope replied that he would pray for the earls. Jesuits James Tyrie and John Myrton had believed that neither Spain nor Rome would ever provide assistance to the Scots because they were "so bloody and unconstant amongst themselves that there is no certain hold of their actions." These disturbances, many asserted, did some good insofar as they were a cause of tremendous anxiety for the Elizabethan government. It seemed likely that Philip II would only provide financial and military assistance if it would further his designs on England. See Wernham, *List and Analysis*, vol. 4, para. 681.

parliament ..."[268] No action was taken when Parliament sat in July. On 21 June George Kerr escaped from prison and successfully eluded a feeble attempt at his recapture.[269] But the Catholic earls remained unharmed. Their representatives offered to give satisfaction to the king and the Kirk but without Kerr, there was no case against the earls. On Sunday July 22, John Davidson ranted against the unpunished "arch-traitors ... [who] have not onlie escaped, but in a manner are absolved, in that they have escaped as men against whom no probation could be gottin."[270] On the 24th Bothwell gained entrance to the Palace of Holyrood and surprised the king. With the tacit support of Queen Elizabeth, Bothwell forced certain concessions from James: his opponents would be banished from court; he and his supporters would retire from Edinburgh temporarily; and a full remission of his and his followers' offenses would be remitted at the next Parliament. By mid September, however, James had recovered his freedom and turned against Bothwell and his faction.[271] Meanwhile different synods, tired of James's procrastination, initiated procedures to excommunicate Catholic nobles. In September the synod of Fife excommunicated Angus, Huntly, Erroll, Alexander, Lord Hume, Sir James Chisholm of Cromlix, and Sir Patrick Gordon of Auchindoun.[272] On October 24, the Catholic earls suddenly appeared before the king on the road between Soutra and Fifa. On

---

[268] Thomson, *Calderwood*, vol. 5, p. 241.

[269] Kerr later recanted his confession. Copies of his recantation from ARSI, Angl. 42, fols 75^{r-v} were published in Francis Shearman, "The Spanish Blanks," *The Innes Review*, 3 (1952): pp. 101–103.

[270] Thomson, *Calderwood*, vol. 5, p. 255.

[271] By early December Verstegan had relayed to Parsons rumors that "the King of Scots is become a Catholique and hathe published an edict for liberty of conscyence ... The King is gon into the northe parte, and the ministers prepare, as we heare, under the conduct of the Lord Bothwell, to make force against him: whereunto we must be ayding at least with mony" (ABSI, Coll B 145–46 [published in Petti, *Verstegan Papers*, p. 193]). A more detailed account of Scottish affairs sent from Antwerp on December 15, Verstegan reported that Queen Anne "seemeth to be very well enclyned unto Catholique religion, beeing thereunto partly perswaded by the Lady Huntley, of whome she hathe receaved a Catholique Catechisme in French" (ABSI, Coll B 147–49 [published in Petti, *Verstegan Papers*, pp. 195–96]). Crichton had heard the story earlier. On October 23, 1593 he reported to the general from Antwerp that the king, betrayed by members of his own family and hostile to the Hamilton clan, adhered to the Catholics whom he knew to be most faithful and most powerful. Moreover the queen was hostile to all heretics and favored a Catholic lady [Lady Huntly] who entertained great hopes and expectations (ARSI, Germ. 171, fols 290^{r-v}). On Anne's eventual conversion to Catholicism see Albert J. Loomie, S.J., "King James I's Catholic Consort," *Huntingdon Library Quarterly*, 34 (1971): p. 304; and Thomas M. McCoog, S.J., and Peter Davidson, "Father Robert's Convert: The Private Catholicism of Anne of Denmark," *Times Literary Supplement*, (24 November 2000): pp. 16–17.

[272] Alan R. MacDonald, *The Jacobean Kirk, 1567–1625: Sovereignty, Polity and Liturgy* (Aldershot, 1998), pp. 52–53.

their knees, they protested that they stood accused on the testimony of one man and only after he had been tortured. They claimed that the "Spanish Blanks" concerned money owed them for support of Jesuits in Scotland. Huntly asked that his Jesuit uncle be allowed to leave the kingdom. They asked to be tried: if guilty they would suffer; if innocent they would either satisfy the Kirk or go abroad. The earls mustered their armies to meet the forces of the Kirk in Perth. Forbidding the trial James ordered the earls to wait in Perth. Instead the "Act of Abolition" of November 26 was proposed as a compromise. All charges against the earls were dropped but they were ordered to accept the "true religion," to remain in places named by the sovereign, and no more:

> to practise, traffique, recept, supplee, or have intelligence with Jesuits, Seminarie preests, excommunicated or avowed Papists, but debarre them furth of their bounds and companie; that they sall forbeare, at their table or otherwise, to dispute or suffer disputatioun against the said true religioun, or in favours of the Papisticall religion, damned by God's Word and his Hienesse' lawes; and sall interteane a minister of God's Word in their hous and companie, and be readie to heare him, conferre with him, and be better resolute of doubts by him, against the tyme of their subscribing of the Confession and Articles of the said true religioun ...[273]

By the same date Jesuits James Gordon and William Ogilvie must be sent out of the realm. If, for reasons of conscience, anyone decided by January 1 that he was unable to accept the "true religion," he must go into exile and not return to the kingdom. During their exile they would not been outlawed and their property would not be confiscated. The act was annulled when the earls rejected the terms. On February 19, 1594 as tensions mounted between the Catholic and Protestant factions, Prince Henry was born at Stirling.

Few modern scholars have investigated the "Spanish Blanks." Francis Shearman, whose "The Spanish Blanks" is one of the few exceptions, concluded "there are a number of details in the whole affair which will probably never be explained."[274] Nonetheless, following the example of Leo Hicks, S.J., he absolved Scottish Catholics of plotting a Spanish invasion at the time of the "Blanks" and blamed the Presbyterian party who sought to discredit Catholics by concocting a plot to force the king to move against them.[275] In a later appendix to the original article, Shearman published a

---

[273] Thomson, *Calderwood*, vol. 5, p. 286.
[274] Shearman, "Spanish Blanks," p. 101.
[275] A reason for questioning the authenticity of these negotiations was the presence of John Cecil in Scotland between 1592 and 1594 and his apparent involvement in discussions about Spanish assistance to the Scots. If Cecil had been an instigator in the affair and, thus,

letter from Bishop Pietro Millino to Pope Clement VIII to demonstrate that William Crichton could not be held responsible for devising the plot because he was not in Spain at the time.[276] As we shall see in the next chapter, in the early 1590s Crichton had indeed been in Spain seeking support to restore true religion in Scotland and England by toppling their monarchs. Before Crichton can be exonerated of any responsibility for the affair, further research based on the sturdy foundations laid by Francisco de Borja Medina, S.J., is needed.[277] Likewise further investigation of the role of the earl of Bothwell is essential. Was he simply a "loose cannon"? Crichton numbered him among supporters of the Catholic earls. Favorite of the ministers and apparent ally of Elizabeth, was Bothwell playing a more devious game? Was his role diversionary to prevent the king from noticing a more serious Spanish threat? Finally, what was James's part in these intrigues? How much did he know? Had the king given the earls some sign of approval for their negotiations? According to David Calderwood, Protestant minister John Davidson recorded in his diary that among the intercepted letters was "one to the Prince of Parma, which tuiched the king with knowledge and approbatioun of the traffiquing, and promise of assistance, &c., but that it was not thought expedient to publishe it."[278] Thomas Graves Law identified this missing paper with a document among the Cecil manuscripts at Hatfield House.[279] Written in June of 1592 for John Ogilvie, Laird of Pury, but somehow confiscated by Kerr or his associates, the document weighed the pros and cons for assisting a Spanish invasion of England. James concluded:

> I submit then that, as well in respect of these reasons preceding as also in case it were enterprised and failed, what discouragement and dishonour would it be to all the enterprisers. What cumber to me and my country being next her, for the proverb is certain, the higher and sudener a man climb, the greater and sorer shall his fall be, if his purpose fail; as surely it is likely this shall do, if it be executed so suddenly as is devised; since both the Queen of England is in expectation of it, as also since the help that is looked for of the most part of the countrymen,

---

responsible for accusations about William Crichton, that would explain the vehemence with which the latter denounced the former a few years later.

[276] See "Miscellany," *The Innes Review*, 4 (1953): p. 60. Contra Thomas Graves Law who claimed that "the whole plan seems born of the brain of a dreaming and unpractical priest ..." ("The Spanish Blanks and Catholic Earls, 1592–94," in *Collected Essays and Reviews*, (ed.) P. Hume Brown [Edinburgh, 1904], p. 262). Yellowlees asserts "there is little doubt that it [the plot] was originally the work of William Crichton and had been conceived during his time in Spain" ("*So strange a monster*," pp. 122–23).

[277] See Medina, "Crichton's Mission" and "Escocia en la Estrategia."

[278] Thomson, *Calderwood*, vol. 5, p. 251.

[279] Law, "Spanish Blanks," pp. 268–71.

will be but scarce while their mistress lives; considering also the nature of the Englishmen, which is ready to mislike of their prince, and consequently easily moved to rebel and free-takers-in-hand, but slow to follow forth and execute, and ready to leave off from [the] time they hear their prince's proclamation, as experience has oft times given proof.[280]

The time was not ripe, James concluded, but if, in a month or two once Elizabeth's suspicions had been quelled, it would be possible to negotiate the issue again. If it were executed, James thought that "it would be a far greater honour to him [Philip] and me both."

Until further research on Crichton, Bothwell and James's involvement is forthcoming, cautious circumspection such as that of R.B. Wernham is the best approach to the whole affair:

> It was particularly difficult to assess how much was real and how much was wishful thinking in the plottings of the English exiles, Scottish Catholics, and the Jesuit henchmen of Father Parsons. Elizabeth therefore could not entirely ignore the reports that she might soon be faced with a Catholic invasion across her northern into those parts of England where Catholicism was most widespread and recusancy most common.[281]

Whether an invasion from the north was possible or probable, as long as James connived with or tolerated the Catholic earls, the threat was real. As a result of the policies of the earl of Huntingdon, if the Catholic earls did spearhead an invasion, there would not be a strong welcoming party of English Catholics.

"Left out in the Cold": Jesuit Mission to Ireland

English forces in Ireland had done their job well. Their suppression of recent rebellions left no Irish leader strong enough or eager enough to support a Spanish invasion. Consequently not one pre-Armada scheme included a role for Ireland. After the dispersal of the Armada, shipwrecked Spanish were washed ashore to be slaughtered or executed by English forces.[282] Historians estimate that 3,000 Spaniards were sheltered and

---

[280] Law, "Spanish Blanks," p. 270.

[281] *After the Armada: Elizabethan England and the Struggle for Western Europe 1588–1595* (Oxford, 1984), p. 459.

[282] See Hiram Morgan, "'Slán Dé fút go hoiche': Hugh O'Neill's Murders," in *Age of Atrocity: Violence and Political Conflict in Early Modern Ireland*, (eds.) David Edwards, Pádriag Lenihan and Clodagh Tait (Dublin, 2007), pp. 95–118; Hiram Morgan, "Policy and Propaganda in Hugh O'Neill's Connection with Europe," in *The Ulster Earls and Baroque*

protected in Ulster, succored by leaders such as McWilliam Burke of May, about 500 of whom escaped to Scotland, and that 6,000 were killed in the rest of Ireland. Sources warned the English crown that Hugh O'Neill, Earl of Tyrone, attempted to establish contact with Philip II through the captain of a Spanish vessel shipwrecked on the Irish coast.[283]

Despite the lack of Irish involvement, the English government remained apprehensive. With only a small garrison on the island, and English troops involved on the continent, Ireland remained vulnerable. A general Irish boycott of services of thanksgiving after the Armada, confirmed English suspicions. On paper the Treaty of Berwick had closed the back door to England; there was nothing comparable for the western front. Despite its failure, the Armada demonstrated Spain's capability so English government knew that it must monitor all rumors and all developments to prevent a second attempt. In December of 1588 Sir William Russell relayed to Sir Francis Walsingham and Lord Burghley reports that Sir William Stanley would lead his troops on a Spanish sponsored invasion of Ireland. In August of 1590 tales of mysterious transactions between the Nugents of Devlin and Parma supposedly involved many more. Between 1589 and 1592, the persistence of such rumors led many to argue in favor of more forceful measures to weaken any possible Irish support for an invasion.[284]

Memoranda in 1591/1592 proposed different remedies to curtail the resurgence of Catholicism. One proposal recommended introduction of English penal laws against the laity, especially high financial penalties for non-attendance at the services of the Established Church. Another advocated universal enforcement of the oath of allegiance, and an intensive campaign against Catholic clergy. Queen Elizabeth, however, advised moderation. In 1592 Lord Deputy Sir William Fitzwilliams was instructed to take action against priests active within the Pale and throughout the kingdom.[285] Names of those who harbored such priests were to be published and the charters

---

Europe. Refashioning Irish Identities, 1600–1800, (eds.) Thomas O'Connor and Mary Ann Lyons (Dublin, 2010), pp. 21–23.

[283] See Steven G. Ellis, *Tudor Ireland: Crown, Community and the Conflict of Cultures 1470–1603* (London, 1985), p. 294; Darren McGettigan, *Red Hugh O'Donnell and the Nine Years War* (Dublin, 2005), pp. 44–45; Henry A. Jefferies, *The Irish Church and the Tudor Reformations* (Dublin, 2010), pp. 237, 259, 262.

[284] See William Palmer, *The Problem of Ireland in Tudor Foreign Policy 1485–1603* (Woodbridge, 1994), pp. 120–24. On the small revolts during this period see Cyril Falls, *Elizabeth's Irish Wars* (London, 1996), pp. 170–73.

[285] The government was especially wary of Dermot Creagh, Bishop of Cork and Cloyne, characterized by Miler Magrath, Protestant Archbishop of Cashel, "as one of the most dangerous fellows that ever came" to the island. He was blamed for stiffening the resistance of Catholics. Magrath suspected that many Irish nobles, despite their appearance of duty and loyalty, actually supported Creagh, See Jefferies, *Irish Church*, pp. 252–54, 263–64.

of towns protecting them, investigated. More drastic action, it was feared, would fuel rebellion. The long-postponed foundation of Trinity College, Dublin, in 1592, prepared zealous Protestant clergy to wean their fellow countrymen from popish superstitions and Gaelic barbarism.[286]

Sometime in late 1590 Edmund MacGauran, Archbishop of Armagh, asked Acquaviva for the services of James Archer and another Jesuit to reopen the Jesuit mission.[287] Acquaviva hesitated: before he could authorize a new beginning, he wanted more information. Thus he denied the archbishop's request on January 22, 1591. Archer remained occupied in Flanders.[288] In his eagerness to restore Catholicism Archbishop MacGauran travelled to Spain and Portugal, seeking financial and military assistance for another uprising. Perhaps Acquaviva's fear the Society would become more involved in such military matters was a reason for rejecting the archbishop's request. MacGauran met Philip II in Burgos in September of 1592. With money from Spanish coffers, the archbishop returned to Ireland and convened a meeting of seven northern bishops in December. With Spanish encouragement, bishops and nobles in the north-west united against the English. Several flashpoints followed. In May of 1593, Hugh Maguire, chieftain of Fermanagh and son-in-law of Hugh O'Neill, Earl of Tyrone, resisted English officials who threatened to displace him.[289] In Leitrim, Brian Óg O'Rourke, embittered by the execution of his father Sir Brian O'Rourke in London in 1591, fought the English. Maguire received support from Hugh Roe O'Donnell, Lord of Tyrconnel and chief of the O'Donnells and another son-in-law of Tyrone. Held as hostage in Dublin from 1587 until his escape at Christmas of 1591 to guarantee the good behavior of his father, Hugh Roe was installed as "the O'Donnell" with the abdication of his father, Sir Hugh MacManus O'Donnell, in 1592. On April 8, 1593 Hugh Roe wrote to Maurice FitzGerald, Thomas FitzGerald [Viscount Baltinglas], and other Irishmen in the service of the Spanish king. James O'Hely, Archbishop of Tuam, was his agent. Informing them of his escape from prison and of subsequent eviction of English soldiers quartered in his territory, Hugh Roe begged Spanish aid to prevent an

---

[286] Robert Dudley Edwards, *Church and State in Tudor Ireland* (London, 1935), pp. 274–78; Colm Lennon, *Sixteenth Century Ireland: The Incomplete Conquest* (Dublin, 1994), p. 320.

[287] The government believed that insidious Jesuits were already operating within Ireland with the connivance and support of Irish gentry. See Jefferies, *Irish Church*, p. 256.

[288] Acquaviva to Edmund MacGauran, Rome January 23, 1591, ARSI, Angl. 41, fols 014ʳ⁻ᵛ. See also Thomas J. Morrissey, S.J., *James Archer of Kilkenny: An Elizabethan Jesuit* (Dublin, 1979), pp. 8–9.

[289] MacGauran was killed in one of Maguire's skirmishes on June 23, 1593.

English attempt to return. With Spanish money and more Irish soldiers, Hugh Roe promised to continue his struggle.[290]

The archbishop of Tuam drafted accounts of the Irish uprising in the hope of obtaining Spanish assistance. Detailing the military strength of the O'Donnells, Maguires, O'Rourkes, and several members of the Burke family who supported them, he recommended that O'Neill be contacted. Promise of Spanish help would, the archbishop was certain, prompt him to side publicly with the rebellion: he already provided them with clandestine assistance. If Spain acted quickly, Philip could occupy the kingdom.

Irish lords serving in Spain rallied to the cause.[291] Cornelius O'Mulrian, O.F.M., Bishop of Killaloe, confirmed Tuam's analysis. He encouraged Philip II to take advantage of the rebellion and send an armada to Ireland. Safely secured Ireland would provide an ideal base for operations against England.[292] Maurice FitzGerald, heir to the earl of Desmond, wrote to Philip from Lisbon on September 4, 1593, urging him "to send them [the Irish in rebellion against Elizabeth] succor with the utmost possible speed." The authors asked permission to accompany any force and trusted that "with the divine favour that your Majesty will be victorious, and conquer for yourself the realm of Ireland, and then enter by this means into England ... If promptness be displayed, the Queen must withdraw the contingent she sent to Flanders and France, and there will be fewer Englishmen on the coasts of Spain." O'Hely insisted that O'Neill secretly supported the coalition. Miler Magrath, Protestant Archbishop of Cashel, decried the role of Catholic priests: they strengthened the resolve of the Irish nobility and gentry, and encouraged them to resist English authority to the point of rebellion.[293]

Philip's reaction was sympathetic:

---

[290] *CSP Simancas* (1587–1603), p. 599. Verstegan reported to Parsons on 20 June that O'Donnell and Maguire had captured two towns and expected Spanish support (ABSI, Coll B 117–118 [printed in Petti, *Verstegan Papers*, p. 174]); McGettigan, *Red Hugh O'Donnell*, pp. 59–62; Jefferies, *Irish Church*, p.259.

[291] *CSP Simancas* (1587–1603), pp. 609–11.

[292] O'Mulrian to Philip II, Lisbon September 3, 1593. O'Mulrian's letter was not summarized in the calendar of Spanish papers. I have used John MacErlean's transcript, ABSI, 46/23/8.

[293] *CSP Simancas* (1587–1603), pp. 608–609. See also pp. 611–12 for the report of John Slatimor sent secretly into Ireland by Maurice FitzGerald to encourage the revolt. For more on developments in Ireland see MacCaffrey, *Elizabeth I: War and Politics*, pp. 349–84; Falls, *Elizabeth's Irish Wars*, pp. 171–77; Lennon, *Sixteenth-Century Ireland*, pp. 288–92; Ellis, *Tudor Ireland*, pp. 298–300; Hiram Morgan, *Tyrone's Rebellion* (Woodbridge, 1993), pp. 139–66; Jefferies, *Irish Church*, p. 259–62.

And if what they say is true, it would be a great pity not to help them. What they demand in one of the letters is very much, and would still be so if it were less than it is. You [Juan de Idiáquez] talk to him [archbishop of Tuam], and get to the bottom of it all, and then we will see what is the very smallest aid that will be needed. If it be so small that we can give it, it will be well to help them.[294]

But Spain was too involved in wars in France and the Low Countries to do anything for Ireland. Moreover instead of coordinating their efforts, English, Scottish, and Irish Catholic exiles frustrated each other's requests for Spanish aid in order to advance their own. Only Spanish assistance could galvanize the rebellious factions into a crusade; only Spanish assistance could persuade O'Neill to side openly with the rebels. O'Hely, returning Irish nobles and prospects of immediate assistance vanished when a ship sent on a fact-finding mission sank in the Bay of Biscay. Further assistance was not forthcoming.[295] Maguire meanwhile was defeated by the combined forces of Henry, Marshall Bagenal, and of O'Neill, playing the faithful vassal, near Belleck on October 10, 1593.[296] O'Donnell was in the vicinity but did not intervene. Maguire was forced to flee and his fortress at Enniskillen was captured in early 1594.[297] Wounded at the battle, O'Neill retired to Dungannon, angry at Bagenal's refusal to acknowledge his cooperation and worried about the implications of the extension of English sovereignty in the north.

There was no Jesuit in Ireland to lament the failure of the Spanish Armada. Some Irish Jesuits volunteered for the mission but Acquaviva refused to send them. Richard Pembroke periodically complained of his work in various Jesuit colleges on the continent and asked to be sent to Ireland. Acquaviva informed him on May 2, 1592 that this mission was

---

[294] *CSP Simancas* (1587–1603), pp. 610–11. The secretary replied that everyone urged Philip to write to the earl of Tyrone to persuade him to join the confederacy openly and that Spain would provide some assistance (ibid., p. 611).

[295] Morgan, *Tyrone's Rebellion*, pp. 141–42.

[296] *CSP Simancas* (1587–1603), pp. 610–11. The secretary replied that everyone urged Philip to write to O'Neill. Rumours of O'Neill's support for the Irish insurrection reached England by the end of April. Because there was insufficient evidence to proceed against O'Neill, who naturally protested his innocence of all involvement, the English government commissioned him to move against Maguire to demonstrate his loyalty (Petti, *Verstegan Papers*, p. 167 n. 12). Verstegan relayed to Parsons rumors of O'Neill's participation in a rebellion in northern Ireland on 26 May (ABSI, Coll B 109–112 [printed in Petti, *Verstegan Papers*, pp. 164]).

[297] In Verstegan's report to Parsons on November 23, he wrote "From Ireland we heare that those of the northe are still up. We accompt litle of it, and expect that winter weather will make their voluntary peace" (ABSI, Coll B 145–146 [printed in Petti, *Verstegan Papers*, pp. 193]).

not possible. He would have liked to send Jesuits to Ireland, but he feared the consequences of Jesuits living alone and without a superior.[298] Because of Jesuit missions to England and Scotland, Pembroke found Acquaviva's explanation odd, and wanted to know why only Ireland was "left out in the cold."[299] Pembroke's superiors frequently noted what a difficult subject he was. Thus one can understand Acquaviva's reluctance to send him to Ireland: he did not possess the required spiritual resolution.[300] Pembroke persisted and his rector Emerich Fosler suggested that he be allowed to go to Ireland or be dismissed. Instead Pembroke was summoned to Rome for tertianship, the final chapter of his formation as a Jesuit. He was later sent to Chambéry. A new community and a new province but the complaints against Pembroke remained the same. The college accepted Pembroke at the request of Father Tyrie, but Pembroke remained impossible since his arrival. The general consensus was that no province should be burdened with men such as Pembroke so he was sent back to Acquaviva's care in Rome. Pembroke complained that there was no real work for him in any province and thus wanted to be sent to Ireland. He also pondered a vocation as a Carthusian. Whether he did or not, we do not know, but he was dismissed from the Society on November 29, 1594.[301]

Conclusion

Robert Southwell wrote glowingly about the cradle of a "nascent Catholicity in England" for which they were then sowing seeds in tears. Tears there were a plenty. An effect of the Armada was increased pressure on English Catholics to demonstrate their loyalty. New commissions investigated suspicious persons and harsh penalties were introduced. More vicious pursuivants such as Topcliffe dedicated themselves to the eradication of the popish pest. As long as any Spanish threat remained,

---

[298] Rome May 2, 1592, same to same, Rome May 31, 1592, ARSI, Austr. 1/II, pp. 614, 616.

[299] Pembroke to Acquaviva, Graz May 11, 1592, ARSI, Germ. 170, fols 129^r–130^v.

[300] See Emerich Fosler to Acquaviva, Graz April 5, 1592, ARSI, Germ. 170, fols 100^r–101^v.

[301] ARSI, Rom. 53/II, fol. 188^v; Hist. Soc. 54, fol. 14^r. See Fosler's letter to Diego Jiménez, Graz August 30, 1592, ARSI, Germ. 170, fols 231^v–232^r. For his post-tertianship career see François Bonald to Acquaviva, Chambéry July 4, 1594, ARSI, Gal. 93, fols 197^{r-v}; Pierre Maior to Acquaviva, Chambéry August 16, 1594, ARSI, Gal. 93, fols 237^r–238^v; Bernard Coster to Acquaviva, Chambéry September 11, 1594, ARSI, Gal. 93, fols 265^r–266^v; Bonald to Acquaviva, Chambéry September 18, 1594, ARSI, Gal. 93, fols 272^{r-v}. Pembroke defended his conduct and appealed to be sent to Ireland in his letter to Acquaviva, Milan September 26, 1594, ARSI, Gal. 93, fols 277^r–278^v.

there was little hope of conditions improving. Approximately eight Jesuits remained outside prison at the end of 1592. Increased government vigilance more than once threatened their work. In the raid at Baddesley Clinton the government nearly destroyed the entire mission. By good fortune or divine providence, the Jesuits were not discovered. That close call and the subsequent capture of Robert Southwell left their mark on Henry Garnet, the mission's superior. Eager to remain on the mission, he asked to be replaced as superior. Claudio Acquaviva's reaction was sympathetic but resolute: Garnet was to remain in the post until a replacement arrived. Unfortunately his heir-apparent, Henry Walpole, was captured almost immediately.

Within the persecuted English Catholic clerical community other problems simmered. The issue of "occasional conformity" divided Catholics despite the apostasy of its principal proponent, Thomas Bell. More ambiguous was Garnet's concern that the application of secular clergy to the Society and their subsequent removal from their missions to a Jesuit novitiate on the continent annoyed some Catholics within the kingdom. Garnet did not name the critics so we do not know if they were cleric or lay. Their displeasure, however, worried Garnet enough to propose radical remedies.

England continued to test the Society's rules and regulations. The mission's survival required men and money. There were candidates but their formation was problematic. If candidates were priests, they were needed in England and their transfer resulted in considerable inconvenience and irritation. The general's requirement that novices spend a period of probation in a Jesuit novitiate on the continent frustrated the vocations of many secular priests. Why could not the priests make their noviceship in England? Because the English mission did not have its own novitiate, its candidates both lay and cleric were placed in novitiates of diverse provinces, usually the Belgian. These provinces restricted the number of English candidates. Once candidates entered the novitiates of other provinces, it was not clear that they would always be available for the mission upon the completion of their formation. The issue of Parsons's authority over such English Jesuits had not been resolved. Could he dispose of them as he saw fit or must he obtain the permission of the superior of the province in which they had entered?[302]

Expense was a reason for Garnet's difficulty in placing English candidates. The mission lacked financial resources so Garnet preferred their maintenance to be paid by the host province. A lack of adequate funds plagued not only the mission itself but its continental colleges whose royal pensions were erratically paid. To balance the books the mission relied on

---

[302] The Irish and Scottish missions encountered the same problem.

alms, a reliance that led to conflicts with other Jesuit institutions, especially in Spain, who solicited aid from the same hard-pressed benefactors. We shall return to this issue in the next chapter.

Because of the mission's financial plight, Acquaviva lifted the original restriction against begging. In 1580 Edmund Campion and Robert Parsons were forbidden to solicit or accept alms, unless the need was urgent, and then only from a few close friends. In April of 1585 some friends promised assistance to William Weston but their contributions were not sufficient. Henry Garnet and Robert Southwell were allowed to expand their search for aid. Fortunately for the mission, the Jesuit found generous benefactors.[303] Nonetheless the mission's major source of income was pensions, endowments, and so on, of candidates who wanted to turn their wealth over to the Society upon acceptance. The novice Thomas Wiseman had left a considerable amount of money to the mission when he joined the Society, but Garnet did not wish to touch it until he was sure that Wiseman had been accepted and had persevered. Thus, the problem with placing candidates had financial repercussions on the mission. Once Garnet was confident that Thomas would remain, he hoped that the general would allow him to apply the money to the use of the mission. But possession of money was only a partial solution; its investment remained a problem. Garnet wisely did not consider it safe to retain large amounts in England so, beginning with Wiseman's money, the mission's fund was invested through the college in St Omers.[304]

After the departure of William Crichton and Edmund Hay, three or four Jesuits worked in Scotland.[305] Hay had been the superior; James Gordon, his successor. Despite occasional setbacks the Catholic faction

---

[303] On the finances of the mission, see Thomas M. McCoog, S.J., "'The Slightest Suspicion of Avarice': The Finances of the English Jesuit Mission," *Recusant History*, 19 (1988): pp. 103–23 and McCoog, *Society of Jesus*, pp. 172–73, 236–37.

[304] The ability to preserve property for confiscation and to invest money in England was a problem for all recusants. The gentry found a solution through the clever use of trusts (see, for example, William, Lord Vaux's settlement of his estates in TNA, SP 12/255/66). Further study of the use of trusts is needed. As an introduction see Thomas M. McCoog, S.J., "The Finances of the English Province of the Society of Jesus in the Seventeenth Century: Introduction," *Recusant History*, 18 (1986): pp. 29–33 and Dennis Flynn, *John Donne & the Ancient Catholic Nobility* (Bloomington, Indiana, 1995), pp. 63–64. The mission's need for money, great though it was, did not prevent it from using some of Thomas Wiseman's bequest as dowries for two of his sisters who entered convents in Belgium (Garnet to Acquaviva, January 3, 1594, and London August 15, 1594, ARSI, Fondo Gesuitico 651/624; Holt to Acquaviva, Brussels December 16, 1593, ARSI, Germ. 171, fols 320^{r-v}).

[305] Alexander MacQuhirrie was not a Jesuit when he returned to Scotland with Crichton in 1587. Apparently he returned to the continent and entered the Society as a priest in 1588. His request to return to Scotland in 1591 was denied (Acquaviva to MacQuhirrie, April 6, 1591, ARSI, Franc. 1/I, fol. 364^{r}). He seems to have returned to Scotland in 1592.

remained strong. But the issue was, as always, the king's religious preferences. He dallied with Catholics and forgave rebellious earls because he needed them to balance the power of the Kirk. Yet overly preferential treatment of Huntly and his associates jeopardized Elizabeth's support and undermined James's chances of ascending the English throne. On the other hand complete repudiation of the Scottish Catholic faction could have repercussions on James's acceptability to English Catholics. As Susan Doran points out, James protected Huntly from Elizabeth, and shielded him from the Kirk in order to "maintain control over his own affairs."[306] In his consideration of the advantages and disadvantages of participating in a Spanish invasion, James wrote:

> ... I will deal with the Queen of England, fair and pleasantly for my title to the crown of England, after her decease, which thing if she grant to (as it is not impossible howbeit unlikely) we have then attained our design without stroke of sword.[307]

James shrewdly played England against Spain, Catholics against Protestants, each convinced that it held James's heart. But James's heart was set on the English throne. And he gained it without "stroke of sword."

See Peter J. Shearman, "Father Alexander McQuhirrie, S.J.," *The Innes Review*, 6 (1955): pp. 28–29.

[306] Doran, "Loving and Affectionate Cousins," p. 211.
[307] Law, "Spanish Blanks," pp. 270–71.

CHAPTER 2

"Schools of Sedition": Catholic Exiles on the Continent, 1589–1593

Introduction

Europe, Catholic and Protestant, awaited definite word on the success of the Armada. Rumors circulated that each side had emerged victorious in the most important naval confrontation since the Christian victory over the Turks at Lepanto in 1571. A strong wind assisted the Christians, and the Turks sank beneath the waves, drowning like pharaoh's army in the Red Sea. Both Protestants and Catholics employed a providentialist theology in their interpretation of the battle. Alexandra Walsham has so clearly demonstrated the accuracy of Patrick Collinson's remark that the "difference between their [the Puritans] beliefs about divine activity and those of their neighbours and peers was essentially one of temperature rather than substance."[1] God had not abandoned his creation nor his people. Either directly through miracles or indirectly through natural instruments, he guided and protected his chosen ones. This time, according to subsequent propaganda, a Protestant wind favored the English. Divine intervention raised up the lowly and had cast down the mighty, leaving Catholics to ponder why God had so abandoned their cause. The Spanish Jesuit Pedro de Ribadeneira, who had spent a few months in London at the death of Queen Mary Tudor and the accession of Queen Elizabeth, had confidently proclaimed: "There is not under heaven anyone who can aid them [the English Catholics] except the unconquered Spanish army, sent as help from heaven for the Catholic King, Philip."[2] Ribadeneira justified Spain's invasion of England, but "we are not going on a difficult enterprise, because God our Lord whose cause and most holy faith we defend, will go ahead; and with such a captain we have nothing to fear." Geoffrey Parker points out that for Ribadeneira "God's cause, Philip's cause and Spain's cause [were] as all one."[3] To this list we may add the cause of the Society of Jesus.

---

[1] Walsham, *Providence in Early Modern England* (Oxford, 1999), p. 2.

[2] Cited in Robert Bireley, S.J., *The Counter-Reformation Prince. Anti-Machiavellianism or Catholic Statecraft in Early Modern Europe* (Chapel Hill/London, 1990), p. 113.

[3] G. Parker, *The Grand Strategy of Philip II* (New Haven/London, 1998), p. 96; "The Place of Tudor England in the Messianic Vision of Philip II of Spain," *Transactions of the*

With confidence shattered Ribadeneira later described the Armada as the "greatest disaster to strike Spain in over six hundred years" and pondered why God would permit heresy to flourish.[4] Ribadeneira then argued that defeat would purify His Catholic Majesty "in order to sanctify him and give him a chance to humble himself under God's powerful arm, and to make him acknowledge the very power that God has given him, and to realize how little value his own power has without God." He admonished King Philip II to identify and correct the abuses for which he was being chastised, one of which, Ribadeneira suggested, was the king's complacent failure to act sooner against Elizabeth. Philip himself confided:

> Very soon we shall find ourselves in such a state that we shall wish that we had never been born ... And if God does not send us a miracle (which is what I hope from Him), I hope to die and go to Him before this happens—which is what I pray for, so as not to see so much misfortune and disgrace.

Hoping for the miracle Philip refused to abandon the crusade:

> I could not—and cannot—neglect the war with England and the events in France, because I have a special obligation to God and the world to deal with them. Also, if the heretics prevail (which I hope God will not permit), it might open the door to worse damage and danger, and we shall have war at home.[5]

English Catholics too wondered why God had not secured their victory. Robert Parsons contended God had actually protected English Catholics through the defeat: Spain refused to acknowledge there were Catholics in England and thus would have punished everyone. But God did not wish more suffering on English Catholics "after having suffered as they have done from the heretics." The English Jesuit John Gerard drew practical conclusions: "the going of the Armada and the knowledge thus gained, have produced results that could not have been obtained otherwise; and that means have now been found by which the enterprise may be effected with greater ease and safety." Richard Verstegan, the accepted author of *The copy of a letter lately written by a Spanishe gentleman*,[6] acknowledged the disaster as divine punishment for sin. Nonetheless, he was not discouraged: England's crimes still demanded vengeance and Spain would soon recover. The children of Israel often failed at their first attempt, but they were eventually successful. The Armada was only

---

Royal Historical Society, 6th series 12 (2002): p. 173.

[4] Bireley, *Counter-Reformation Prince*, pp. 113–14.

[5] Cited in Parker, "Place of Tudor England," pp. 208, 209.

[6] ([Antwerp], 1589), *ARCR*, vol. 2, num. 759, *STC* 1038.

a temporary setback. Philip remained convinced that he pursued God's cause: "I was not moved by desire for new kingdoms," he declared, "I am well content with those given me by his divine Majesty. I have consumed my patrimony. The cause is God's and touches the honor of myself and my kingdom." God's cause demanded the defeat of the heretical powers. Philip may have spent his patrimony, but Catholic powers, especially in the Italian peninsula, supported his—and God's—cause.[7]

Before definitive word on the fate of the Armada had reached Rome, Enrique de Guzmán, Count of Olivares and Spanish ambassador to Rome, formulated new roles for Robert Parsons and William, Cardinal Allen. Olivares recommended that the cardinal be assigned to Belgium to advise Alessandro Farnese, Duke of Parma, on future proposals regarding England. Allen could console English Catholics with assurances that Philip II had not and would not abandon them. Parsons should accompany Allen or, if Pope Sixtus V opposed Allen's going, Parsons could be his substitute. Neither man was sent. Allen remained in Rome; Parsons was sent to Spain.[8] On November 5, 1588, Claudio Acquaviva appointed Robert Parsons superior of all Jesuits sent to England, and of all English Jesuits serving as chaplains in the Spanish army. On the same day the general sent Parsons to Spain to keep England on the royal agenda "in accordance with our Institute and without any interference in military matters." From Acquaviva's perspective more important was a sensitive mission entrusted jointly to Parsons and to the Spanish Jesuit José de Acosta: a controversy surrounding relations between Jesuits and the Inquisition in Spain, and Philip's apparent displeasure with the Society. It was Parsons's task to vindicate the Society from royal suspicions and to retain royal interest in England.[9] The Jesuit brother Fabricio Como[10] accompanied Parsons; Acosta most likely preceded them.

The so-called *Memorialista* controversy disturbed the Society of Jesus in Spain since the start of Acquaviva's generalate in 1581. It had its roots in tensions stemming from the administration of Everard Mercurian (1573–1580).[11] The real crisis, however, began in March of 1586 with

---

[7] See Thomas M. McCoog, S.J., *The Society of Jesus in Ireland, Scotland, and England 1541–1588: 'Our Way of Proceeding?'* (Leiden, 1994), pp. 261–62; Robert E. Scully, S.J., "'In the Confident Hope of a Miracle': The Spanish Armada and Religious Mentalities in the Late Sixteenth Century," *Catholic Historical Review*, 89 (2003): pp. 643–70.

[8] See McCoog, *Society of Jesus*, pp. 259–60.

[9] ARSI, Hist. Soc. 61, fols 28^r, 45^v.

[10] On Como see Thomas M. McCoog, S.J., (ed.), *Monumenta Angliae* (2 vols, Rome, 1992), vol. 2, p. 268.

[11] This controversy, for various and sundry reasons, has remained somewhat of a mystery. For the opening salvos during Mercurian's generalate, see Francisco de Borja de Medina, S.J., "Everard Mercurian and Spain: Some Burning Issues," in *The Mercurian*

the involvement of the Inquisition and King Philip II. Four Jesuits, each holding an important position in Jesuit administration, were summoned to Valladolid and arrested by the Inquisition. The Inquisition claimed that they, especially Antonio Marcén, Jesuit provincial of Toledo, had not informed the Inquisition of alleged sexual advances made by a Jesuit confessor on female penitents. The larger issue was the Society's independence from the Inquisition because the Society claimed the privilege of dealing with suspected Jesuit heretics within the Society. Thus the Inquisition demanded copies of all official Jesuit documents from the *Constitutions* to Apostolic Letters. Meanwhile the Inquisition ordered that no Jesuit leave Spain lest a heretic escape its jurisdiction. As the Inquisition proceeded with its examination in secret, Jesuits from the Castile and Toledo provinces sent anonymous memoranda to Philip II and to the Inquisition. Dissatisfied with Acquaviva's style of government, they murmured about the current state of the Society: they found Acquaviva's style too aloof and criticized his centralizing policies. They demanded an official visitation of Spanish provinces, a proposal also favored by the king. A non-Jesuit was preferred for this role. Factions divided Spanish Jesuits: those loyal to Acquaviva resisted any encroachment of traditional Jesuit liberties; his opponents collaborated with the Inquisition.[12]

José de Acosta had returned to Spain in 1587 after a successful sojourn in Peru and Mexico. In December of 1587 and January of 1588, King Philip summoned him to report on different aspects of Spanish administration of these colonies. Because of his knowledge and experience, Acosta gained wide influence with the king, and with other influential figures at court. To discuss similar matters with Pope Sixtus V and Acquaviva, he travelled to Rome in late summer of 1588. He returned to Spain two months later as Acquaviva's personal representative to the Spanish king. The general commissioned him to quiet the discontented Jesuits and to do all he could to satisfy Philip and the Inquisitor General, Gaspar, Cardinal de Quiroga, and to dissuade them from naming a non-Jesuit as canonical visitor.[13]

Probably because of Parsons's good relations with the Spanish king, Acquaviva designated him Acosta's assistant. In instructions to Parsons on October 31, Acquaviva explained the mission: his primary task was to

---

Project: Forming Jesuit Culture, 1573–1580, (ed.) Thomas M. McCoog, S.J. (Rome/St Louis, 2004), pp. 945–66.

[12] See William V. Bangert, S.J., *A History of the Society of Jesus*, revised edn. (St Louis, 1986), pp. 110–11; Stefania Tutino, "Nothing But the Truth? Hermeneutics and Morality in the Doctrines of Equivocation and Mental Reservation in Early Modern Europe," *Renaissance Quarterly*, 64 (2011): pp. 127–28.

[13] On the crisis see Francis Edwards, S.J., *Robert Persons: The Biography of an Elizabethan Jesuit (1546–1610)* (St Louis, 1995), pp. 130–33, and Claudio M. Burgaleta, S.J., *José de Acosta, S.J. (1540–1600): His Life and Thought* (Chicago, 1999), pp. 56–58.

demonstrate the Society's devotion to Philip. Moreover, he would explain how impossible it was for the Society to assist the king in his far-flung empire unless the Inquisition's order forbidding Jesuits from leaving Spain was rescinded. Neither merchants nor soldiers nor other religious orders were under such constraints.[14] In all discussions with the king and his ministers, Parsons must conform to the Society's Institute "without any intervention into military matters." After Acosta had met with the king, Parsons was to deliver a letter to Philip in which Acquaviva proposed candidates for the position of canonical visitor to the Jesuit provinces of Castile and Toledo: Acosta and Diego de Avellaneda. If it pleased Philip, one could be designated visitor to the provinces of Aragon and Andalusia. If Philip did not wish to make the decision, Acosta had the authorization to do so. After he had finished his business in Madrid, Parsons was permitted to depart for Flanders where he would be superior of the English Jesuits working there and supervise Jesuits on the English mission. Finally he was to relay to Philip, Acquaviva's willingness to do whatever the king desired of him personally or of the Society.[15]

Foreign Wars and Dynastic Struggles

Tentative plans for a new armada were drafted almost immediately after the fiasco of 1588. Consistent English harassment of Spanish and Portuguese ports impeded construction. The proposals, however, included a significantly reduced role for Englishmen. Consequently some English Catholic refugees suspected that the Spanish doubted their dedication perhaps as a result of their failure to rebel. They feared that they had become the scapegoat for the Armada's failure. As we noted in the last chapter Scottish earls played on Spanish suspicions of English Catholics by claiming that they would be much more dependable in the event of a new

---

[14] Henry Kamen's comment regarding the Inquisition's attempt to control books printed in and imported into Spain is relevant here: "At no time was the peninsula cut off from the outside world by the decrees of 1558–9, or by any subsequent legislation. Under Habsburg rule the armies of Spain dominated Europe, its ships traversed the Atlantic and Pacific, and its language was the master tongue from central Europe to the Philippines. Tens of thousands of Spaniards went abroad every year, mainly to serve in the armed forces. Cultural and commercial contact with all parts of western Europe, especially the Netherlands and Italy, continued absolutely without interruption" (*The Spanish Inquisition: An Historical Revision* [London, 1997], p. 135). If the Inquisition had its way, Jesuits would be denied such mobility.

[15] ARSI, Tolet. 4, fols 41^r–42^r.

armada. But chances of another armada diminished because of Spanish involvement in France.[16]

Henry, Duke of Guise was assassinated on December 23, 1588 and Louis, Cardinal Guise the following day. On January 7, 1589 an outraged Sorbonne released all French subjects from their loyalty to King Henry III because of his suspected involvement in their murder. Pope Sixtus V threatened to excommunicate Henry, and summoned him to Rome to explain his role in the assassinations. On April 26, Henry III allied with Henry of Navarre against the Guises and the Catholic League. On August 1, 1589 Jacques Clément, a young friar, assassinated Henry III. Before Henry died, he recognized the Protestant Henry of Navarre as his successor. In the subsequent war, the Catholic League with Spanish support initially prevailed. Henry IV might have been the legitimate king, but his cause lacked necessary military resources to resist Catholic progress. Henry IV was fighting for his life, and losing. In August Henry declared that he would refrain from altering anything that would harm the Catholic faith or the Roman Catholic Church, and that he himself would seek instruction "in the said religion by a good, legitimate, and free general national council, so as to follow and observe whatever might be concluded there" in order to gain wider support.[17] Promises of conversion and preservation of Catholicism might have prevented the defection of Henry's Catholic supporters, but he needed money and soldiers to continue the war. For that he turned to England. An expeditionary force under the command of Peregrine Bertie, Baron Willoughby d'Eresby, fortified by prayers offered throughout England and encouraged by anti-League propaganda disseminated throughout the kingdom, provided enough assistance, in the words of R.B. Wernham, "to keep his [Henry's] own cause so much alive between Brittany and the Seine that the threat of his progress to the great League cities, Paris, Rouen, Orléans, as soon to force Mayenne [Charles Guise, Duke of Mayenne] to risk challenging him to battle. English help in men and money during the last three or four months of 1589 did more than a little to make possible Henry IV's famous victory at Ivry in March 1590."[18] The victory at Ivry destroyed the League's army and left its cities vulnerable. By the end of July Paris was under siege: its capitulation and the collapse of the League seemed inevitable. A year earlier the assassination

---

[16] Albert J. Loomie, S.J., "The Armadas and the Catholics of England," *Catholic Historical Review*, 59 (1973): pp. 390–91. See also Henry Kamen, *Philip of Spain* (New Haven/London, 1997), p. 277.

[17] Cited in David Buisseret, *Henry IV* (London, 1984), p. 28.

[18] R.B. Wernham, *After the Armada: Elizabethan England and the Struggle for Western Europe 1588–1595* (Oxford, 1984), p. 180.

of Henry III saved Paris from a comparable threat. This year's savior was Philip II.

Philip had provided considerable financial assistance to the League; in turn they provided enough distraction to prevent Henry III from intervening during the Armada; for example, the League gained control of Paris on May 13, 1588, the "Day of the Barricades." Because of Spanish military involvement in the Netherlands, Philip, however, wanted to avoid direct military contact. On May 9, 1590 Charles, Cardinal Bourbon or, according to the League "King Charles X," the last Catholic claimant, died. Lack of a Catholic alternative to the Protestant Henry on the throne of Spain's traditional enemy prompted Philip to alter his strategy. Even at the risk of abandoning an offensive against the Dutch in a struggle that was not going well for the Spanish, Philip instructed Alessandro Farnese, Duke of Parma, to provide overt military assistance to the League. By the end of August Paris had been saved, but the presence of the infamous Spanish army in France and the real possibility of Spanish occupation of coastal towns stroked English fears.[19] Diplomatically Elizabeth countered active Spanish involvement with attempts to forge an anti-Habsburg coalition in the defense of the national integrity of France in particular, and of Protestantism in general. Militarily she increased assistance to Henry IV but increased English aid did not significantly affect the prospects of the Huguenot king.[20]

England's primary objective was preservation of Henry's cause. His defeat, England feared, would advance the dynastic claims of Philip's daughter, Infanta Isabella Clara Eugenia, to the French throne. With two armies already fighting in France, Parma's in the northeast and Juan d'Aguila's in Brittany, Philip had the military force to make her pretensions real. Spanish armies turned the war against Henry, but attempts to advance the infanta's claims were not as successful.[21] Even though Pope Sixtus V had excommunicated Henry in 1585, he still preferred Henry's conversion

---

[19] In spring of 1591, Sir William Stanley, assisted by Parsons, proposed that his English troops attack and seize Alderney in the Channel Isles. The island could then serve as a base for attacks on England, and as a sanctuary for Spanish ships in the channel. Alderney's strategic importance increased after Elizabeth provided military aid to Henry IV: Spanish possession would threaten the supply lines between England and the troops. Despite the proposal's attractions, nothing was done. See Albert J. Loomie, S.J., *The Spanish Elizabethans: The English Exiles at the Court of Philip II* (New York, 1963), pp. 147–51.

[20] See Wernham, *After the Armada*, pp. 181–206. Interestingly the former Jesuit Christopher Perkins was sent on a diplomatic mission to Denmark and the Baltics in May of 1590 (ibid., pp. 258–59).

[21] See Stuart Carroll, *Martyrs and Murderers. The Guise Family and the Making of Europe* (Oxford, 2009), pp. 298–99.

to a Spanish candidate. To satisfy him Henry need only convert. No conversion, however, would change Philip's mind.

Henry's consistent failure to honor his promise to seek instruction disenchanted his Catholic supporters. If war continued much longer, he risked losing their support. But even with it, Henry could not defeat militarily the Spanish supported Catholic League but, as long as Henry's opponents could not agree on a Catholic contender, he held the upper hand. Meanwhile Philip applied pressure on the pope and threatened schism if he did not acknowledge the infanta's pretensions. Sixtus finally agreed that he would not recognize anyone unacceptable to Philip as French king. On July 19, 1590 Sixtus and Philip drafted an offensive and defensive alliance.[22] Before these agreements could be formulated into a definitive treaty, Sixtus died on August 27.

Spanish influence played a major role in the election of Sixtus's successor Urban VII in September of 1590, but his pontificate did not even last two weeks. The following conclave lasted longer. After two months of "factional intrigues and brutal intervention by the Spanish government," according to J.N.D. Kelly, Gregory XIV, the pope later maligned by the English government as Philip's Milanese vassal, was elected. The new pope supported Spain and the Catholic League, and dispatched an army into France. On March 1, 1591 he renewed Henry's excommunication.[23] English involvement in Brittany meanwhile ended in disaster, and the siege of Rouen, in which English soldiers played a role, was lifted by Parma in the spring of 1592. Afterwards Parma hastened back to the Netherlands to prevent further Dutch successes. He died at Arras on December 6, thus spared dismissal and imprisonment due to his fall from favor over intervention in France at the expense of military campaigns in the Netherlands. Spain might have been on the verge of losing the Netherlands but, perhaps as compensation, the possibility of a Habsburg ruler in France loomed larger.

Negotiations initiated in late 1591 by the duke of Parma and the Catholic League to name a Catholic candidate floundered over France's traditional adherence to Salic Law. In the autumn of 1592, Charles Guise, Duke of Mayenne, authorized the election of delegates to the Estates-General in the cities and towns controlled by the League to deal with the succession. The Estates convened in Paris in January of 1593. Because only a legitimate king could convoke the Estates-General, Henry denounced the assembly and royal armies prevented the attendance of many. Catholic candidates

---

[22] John Lynch, *Spain 1516–1598: From Nation State to World Empire* (Oxford, 1991), pp. 383–84.

[23] On both popes see J.N.D. Kelly, *The Oxford Dictionary of the Popes* (Oxford, 1986), pp. 273–74.

were numerous: the duke of Mayenne himself; Henry, son and heir of the murdered duke of Guise; the Habsburg Archduke Ernst of Austria; and Charles Emmanuel (I), Duke of Savoy. Spanish money attempted to buy votes for a monarch approved by Spain. Lorenzo Suárez de Figueroa, Duke of Feria, insisted that the Spanish infanta be acknowledged as queen of France despite the country's adherence to the Salic Law: she was the eldest daughter of Henry III's sister, Elizabeth, wife of Philip II. The duke suggested that she marry her cousin Archduke Ernst. After some Catholics complained about electing two foreigners to the throne of France, Feria proposed Duke Henry. Spanish demands divided the League. To obtain support for this proposal Parma promised position, money and territory to League members. If the infanta did ascend the French throne, she would reign over a poorer and smaller kingdom. On June 28, Guillaume du Vair, a judge of the Parlement of Paris, defended the Salic Law. He persuaded the court to issue a decree forbidding transfer of the crown to a foreign prince or princess because it violated the fundamental law of the land. Despite the opposition of the duke of Mayenne and his more militant followers, the decree gained the support of many. Despite the presence of Spanish troops and the free distribution of Spanish money, Spain could not control the Estates-General.[24]

Taking advantage of the confusion, Henry IV repeated his intention to receive instruction in the Catholic faith. On July 25, he abjured Calvinism and was formally welcomed back into the Catholic Church at St Denis.[25] That move changed everything. A common desire for a Catholic king had held the League together despite tension over an alternative candidate. After Henry's profession there was no need to violate Salic Law and moderate Catholics swung to Henry's side. According to Mark P. Holt, the king's conversion "effectively pulled the rug out from under the Holy League."[26] Holt reminds us that the infamous evaluation "Paris is worth a Mass," long attributed to Henry was actually League propaganda intended to convince the French people of the king's insincerity. But Holt contends that the assertion that Henry was "unprincipled or cared little for religion" lacked evidence. Undoubtedly prompted by political reasons, Henry converted to end the fighting and to restore order "by reuniting all French men and women under one religion, the Catholic faith of all French

---

[24] R.J. Knecht, *The French Wars of Religion 1559–1598* (London, 1989), pp. 74–75; Wernham, *After the Armada*, pp. 376–77. See also Mark Holt, *The French Wars of Religion 1562–1629* (Cambridge, 1995), pp. 148–49.

[25] On the prelate who received Henry into the Church despite strong papal disapproval, see Frederic J. Baumgartner, "Renaud de Beaune, Politique Prelate," *Sixteenth Century Journal*, 9 (1978): pp. 99–114.

[26] Holt, *French Wars of Religion*, p. 149.

kings since Clovis."[27] On February 27, 1594 Henry was consecrated and crowned at Chartres: Reims, the traditional site of French coronations, was still controlled by the League. By the end of March he was in control of Paris and by the end of the year most of the major League towns in northern France had submitted. Concessions to Catholics threatened to drive Huguenots to rebellion, but Henry was able to retain their support in an all-out war with Spain, declared in January of 1595.[28]

Elizabeth reacted angrily to the news of Henry's conversion, but she continued her support in the struggle against Philip. English forces remained on the continent until February of 1595 when Sir John Norris's troops were recalled from Brittany after the Spanish threat to Brest had been removed.[29] By that time, Henry's grasp on the throne was secure. In the following September, Pope Clement VIII resisted Spanish pressure and absolved Henry from excommunication.

During Spain's preoccupation with France, the rebellious United Provinces declared themselves the Dutch Republic on July 25, 1590. The duke of Parma's involvement in France allowed the Dutch to consolidate their hold. Parma's pleas that Philip open negotiations with the Dutch went unheeded because of the king's refusal to consider any religious toleration. After Parma's death at Arras on December 3, 1592, both Peter Ernest, Count of Mansfelt, and Don Pedro Enríquez de Azevedo, Count of Fuentes, claimed to be his legitimate successor. Near anarchy followed as each issued contradictory orders to the same forces. At the same time the loyal provinces refused to pay higher taxes that subsidized a war in France instead of suppressing the Dutch rebellion. Consequently Spanish authorities in the Low Countries concluded a truce with Henry IV on July 13, 1593 that lasted until April of 1594.[30] During the truce, Henry was reconciled to the Roman Church, was crowned, and captured Paris. Administrative incompetence prevented the Spanish forces from reversing the tide of Dutch successes. To end the chaos in Brussels, Philip appointed his nephew Archduke Ernst Governor-General in January of 1594. The situation had deteriorated so badly that the archduke was unable to reverse it: Spanish troops mutinied and the Dutch captured the last royalist

---

[27] Holt, *French Wars of Religion*, p. 153.

[28] Holt, *French Wars of Religion*, pp. 158–62.

[29] R.B. Wernham, *The Return of the Armadas: The Last Years of the Elizabethan War against Spain 1595–1603* (Oxford, 1994), p. 22.

[30] Around the same time, feeble attempts were made to reach some type of understanding between Spanish authorities in Brussels and England. The intended goal was the establishment of an independent Netherlands freed from Spanish domination. A factor in their failure was the discovery of the Lopez plot to assassinate Elizabeth in 1594. See Wallace T. MacCaffrey, *Elizabeth I: War and Politics 1588–1603* (Princeton, 1992), pp 193–95.

stronghold in the north, Groningen, on July 23, 1594. After the archduke's death in February of 1595, the count of Fuentes governed until the arrival of another royal nephew, Archduke Albert, in January of 1596. To the shock and dismay of the Dutch, English, and French, the count halted Dutch advances and, on the second front, defeated the French in a few battles.[31]

Working as chaplains in Parma's army were the English Jesuit Henry Walpole[32] and the Irish Jesuit James Archer. Both began their ministries in expectation of a military expedition against Elizabeth.[33] Both still waited, at times impatiently. Walpole wanted to work in the mission but Acquaviva advised him to wait.[34] Archer may have entertained similar ideas but the Jesuit mission in Ireland had been suspended. Edmund MacGauran, Archbishop of Armagh, asked Acquaviva to revive the mission, a request denied by the general on January 23, 1591.[35]

"Dens and receptacles": Continental Colleges and Seminaries

Despite Acquaviva's explicit instructions, Parsons had an audience with King Philip before Acosta. The meeting on February 6, 1589 lasted two hours. Both Parsons and Acosta argued against any violation of the Society's Institute and against the appointment of a non-Jesuit as visitor. Both complained about restrictions preventing Spanish Jesuits from leaving the kingdom. At least as regards the visitor, their arguments swayed Philip who decided that Acquaviva could nominate Jesuits for the office. From the lists carried by both Jesuits, Acosta was named visitor of the provinces of Andalusia and Aragon; Gil González Dávila for Toledo and Castile, and Pedro Fonseca for Portugal.[36] During his interview with Philip, Parsons treated various matters concerning English Catholics. The assassination

---

[31] Peter Limm, *The Dutch Revolt 1559–1648* (London, 1989), pp. 61–64. See also Geoffrey Parker, *The Dutch Revolt* (London, 1977), pp. 228–31.

[32] On Walpole see McCoog, *Monumenta Angliae*, vol. 2, p. 519.

[33] On work of chaplains see McCoog, *Society of Jesus*, p. 254 n. 115. On the considerable influence exerted on the soldiers by the chaplains see Gráinne Henry, "The Emerging Identity of an Irish Military Group in the Spanish Netherlands, 1586–1610," in *Religion, Conflict and Coexistence in Ireland: Essays Presented to Monsignor Patrick J. Corish*, (eds.) R.V. Comerford, Mary Cullen, Jacqueline R. Hill and Colm Lennon (Dublin, 1990), pp. 53–77.

[34] Acquaviva to Walpole, Rome September 14, 1591, ARSI, Fl. Belg. 1/I, p. 487.

[35] Acquaviva to Edmund MacGauran, Rome January 23, 1591, ARSI, Angl. 41, fols 014r–v.

[36] Edwards, *Robert Persons*, pp. 136–37; Burgaleta, *José de Acosta*, p. 58. Unfortunately Parsons's letters to Acquaviva immediately after the interview have not survived.

of Henry, Duke of Guise, and the intensification of hostilities in France had already closed the English College in Eu, and threatened the English College founded originally in Douai but currently protected by the Guises in Reims.[37] Financially stretched, Philip, nonetheless, promised a grant of 3,000 ducats for the survival of the college.[38] Such concessions were a testimony to the king's fondness for Parsons and/or the Jesuit's diplomatic skills.

According to Henry More, first historian of the English Province, Richard Barret, President of the English College, would have preferred an even larger pension, but Parsons explained that a totally new venture would have a better chance of gaining royal support than a request for more alms to Reims. Since the college currently supported more students that it could afford, Parsons suggested that Barret send to Spain 10 or so seminarians, whom the Jesuit hoped to place with bishops and Spanish families favorably disposed to English Catholics.[39] On May 8, 1589, Barret sent Henry Floyd, John Blackfan, and John Bosville, who, despite numerous dangers and adventures, eventually reached Valladolid.[40] Two weeks later Dr Thomas Stillington, John Fixer, and Thomas Lovelace, who were assigned to be their professors, followed.[41] They joined three English priests already in Valladolid: William Cowling, Gerard Clibburn, and Francis Lockwood.[42] Two other students passing through Valladolid on their way to the English College in Rome, Henry Sherrat and John Gillibrand, decided to stay.[43] Initially all attended lectures at the Jesuit college as they awaited arrival of their own teachers. Their poor financial state improved with the arrival of another student, John Cecil, the same

---

[37] McCoog, *Society of Jesus*, p. 264.

[38] In a letter to Parsons from Rome on June 12, 1589, Acquaviva rejoiced in the selection of the visitors, especially Acosta who was a prudent and virtuous man (ARSI, Tolet. 4, fols 53ᵛ–55ᵛ). We shall return to this letter at the end of the chapter. Originally Philip had suggested Jeronimo Manrique, Bishop of Cartagena (Guenter Lewy, "The Struggle for Constitutional Government in the Early Years of the Society of Jesus," *Church History*, 29 [1960]: p. 148). John Lynch (*Spain 1516–1598*, p. 368) claimed that Philip had chosen Acosta instead of Manrique. On later complications see Edwards, *Robert Persons*, pp. 137–38.

[39] Henry More, S.J., *The Elizabethan Jesuits*, (ed.) Francis Edwards, S.J (London, 1981), p. 204.

[40] On Barret and the three students see Godfrey Anstruther, O.P, *The Seminary Priests* (4 vols, Ware/Durham/Great Wakering, 1968–1977), vol. 1, pp. 24–25, 39, 44–45, 120, and McCoog, *Monumenta Angliae*, vol. 2, pp. 236–37, 314.

[41] See Anstruther, *Seminary Priests*, vol. 1, pp. 214, 335 for more on Stillington and Lovelace.

[42] See Anstruther, *Seminary Priests*, vol. 1, pp. 80, 91–92, 211.

[43] See Anstruther, *Seminary Priests*, vol. 1, p. 310. I could not find any more information on Gillibrand.

John Cecil who negotiated with William Cecil, Lord Burghley in 1591, who secured the patronage of Don Alfonso de Quiñones, a wealthy Spaniard.

Unfortunately the foundation of the English College in Valladolid was not as straightforward as presented by the traditional narrative. If Parsons had written to Barret, the letter is no longer extant. The three priests already in Valladolid, that is, Cowling, Clibburn and Lockwood, had been sent from Douai to England in November of 1588. Because wars in France and the Netherlands disrupted the usual route to England, the journey from Rome or Douai/Reims to England now passed through Spain.[44] Presumably the three were awaiting an opportunity to continue their journey. The students and professors sent to Valladolid in May of 1589 were apparently not intended to be the basis of a new college. With the death of Henry, Duke of Guise, wars, and the possibility of a Protestant king in France, the administration of the English College might have been searching for an alternative location. If Philip was to be their principal benefactor and protector, situating the college in Spain, now the major access road to England, would be more convenient. Valladolid was Spain's third largest city, a center through which all travellers to the northern ports passed. The university was strong with recently endowed chairs, and a flourishing Jesuit college. Since 1587 there were more than a dozen English and Irish students at the university. Before a definite decision could be made, general reaction to the presence of more English students had to be gauged. With Sir Francis Drake and Sir John Norris raiding Spanish ports and attacking Lisbon,[45] Spaniards might not have welcomed English students with open arms. The arrest and imprisonment of the first three students because of suspicions that they were spies for Drake were not an auspicious start.

The students lodged near the Convent of Santa Clara under the dual charge of the abbot of the collegiate church, the town's ecclesiastical superior, and the rector of the Jesuit college. The abbot hesitated: he was not eager to supervise students from a heretical country and he was reluctant to work with Jesuits currently under investigation from the Spanish Inquisition. To quell such anxieties Philip insisted that prospective students produce documentation of their date and place of birth, profession, and status as Catholics. Obtained perhaps through the intercession of Parsons, an order-in-council of July 22 granted the students the right to beg alms throughout the kingdom for four years. In November, Cowling and Clibburn received permission to beg alms within Portugal for

---

[44] See John Bossy, "Rome and the Elizabethan Catholics: A Question of Geography," *Historical Journal*, 7 (1964): pp. 135–42.

[45] See Harry Kelsey, *Sir Francis Drake: The Queen's Pirate* (New Haven/London, 1998), pp. 341–64.

four years. The Duchess of Feria, neé Jane Dormer, Sir Francis Englefield,[46] and other friends at court provided money for Parsons's immediate needs, and Don Francisco de Reynosa and Don Alfonso de Quiñones continued to assist the students.[47]

Apparently Jesuit involvement in the Spanish educational project was part of the original plan.[48] On May 14, 1589, Father Acquaviva granted permission to Richard Gibbons, Charles Tancard, and William Flack to travel to Spain.[49] Gibbons continued to Lisbon, where he served as confessor for the English; Tancard completed his theology at Alcalá; and Flack became minister at Valladolid.[50] A month later Parsons asked Joseph Creswell, rector of the English College in Rome, to send students to Spain.[51] By September the new foundation was off to a shaky start as Parsons prepared to depart for Madrid to discuss the seminary with the king in hope of securing greater royal assistance. Three months later Parsons notified Creswell that he had received only 100 crowns from the king for approximately 20 persons. Since the new foundation lacked any laws or constitutions, Parsons asked Creswell to forward an authenticated copy of the constitutions of the English College. He hoped that they could serve as a model and that William, Cardinal Allen be appointed to some supervisory role over both seminaries. Over the next year Parsons shuttled

---

[46] On them see Loomie, *Spanish Elizabethans*, pp. 14–51, 94–128.

[47] On the foundation of the college see Leo Hicks, S.J., "Father Persons, S.J., and the Seminaries in Spain," *The Month*, 157 (1931): pp. 410–417, 497–99; More, *Elizabethan Jesuits*, pp. 203–206; [John Blackfan, S.J.], *Annales Collegii S. Albani in oppido Valesoleti*, (ed.) John H. Pollen, S.J. (Roehampton, 1899); Peter E.B. Harris, (ed.), *The Blackfan Annals. Los Anales de Blackfan* (Valladolid, 2008); Michael E. Williams, *St Alban's College, Valladolid* (London, 1986), pp. 4–7; Edwards, *Robert Persons*, pp. 138–40; Javier Burrieza Sánchez, *Valladlid, tierras y caminos de jesuitas. Presencia de la Compañía de Jesús en la provincia de Valladolid, 1545–1767* (Valladolid, 2007), pp. 209–35.

[48] Even before final approval, dispatches were being sent to England, proclaiming the royal foundation of the new seminary. See the dispatch of June 23/July 3, *CSP Foreign* (January–July 1589), p. 338.

[49] ARSI, Hist. Soc. 61, fol. 47^r.

[50] See Parsons to Creswell, Valladolid 14 September 1589, ABSI, Coll P II 484 (published in John Hungerford Pollen, S.J., (ed.), "Fr. Robert Persons, S.J.–Annals of the English College at Seville, with Accounts of other Foundations at Valladolid, St Lucar, Lisbon and St Omers," in *Miscellanea IX* [London, 1914], p. 20). On them see McCoog, *Monumenta Anglia*, vol. 2, pp. 311, 328–29, 500.

[51] Parsons to Creswell, June 24, 1589, same to same, Madrid July 22, 1589, ABSI, Coll P II 479 (published in Pollen, "Annals of the English College," p. 19). On August 26, 1589 Creswell had complained to the general about the college's poor finances (ARSI, Fondo Gesuitico 651/615). That may have been a reason behind Parsons's suggestion.

between Madrid and Valladolid, obtaining privileges for the foundation and seeking more financial assistance.[52]

Spanish fears of a significant English presence in Valladolid haunted the college during its first months. The Inquisitor, Juan Vigil de Quiñones, objected to English students out of fear they would disseminate heretical doctrines as the Lutherans had done 30 years earlier. Similarly municipal authorities had some qualms that English spies would infiltrate the students and disrupt Spanish life. Not even the king's requirement of proper documentation satisfied them. As a reply to such complaints, Parsons circulated a small pamphlet recounting the successful work of English colleges in preventing the total eradication of Catholicism, and the consequent attempts by the English government to destroy these seminaries.[53] The authorities resolved the difficulty with the appointment of Don Alfonso de Mendoza, abbot of the collegiate church, to examine all students upon their arrival. Parsons cleared the final hurdle when he argued against a proposal that the new English college be combined with the small foundation that the town had already established for Irish seminarians.[54] Probably, as Leo Hicks, S.J., has argued, Parsons recalled an earlier conflict at the English College in Rome when two nationalities were compelled to share limited resources and, thus, opposed a joint foundation and eventually obtained a separate institution.

Despite Acquaviva's fears that the college was off to a bad start, it was taking root: a daily order had been established, a distinctive college dress designed, alms collected and benefactors found.[55] All that was needed was a rector. When Parsons returned to Valladolid in October after a trip

---

[52] Parsons to Creswell, Valladolid September 14, 1589, same to same, Toledo December 9, 1589, same to same, Madrid January 7, 1590, same to same, Valladolid June 24, 1590, same to same, Valladolid July 22, 1590, same to same, Valladolid July 23, 1590, same to same, Valladolid August 20, 1590, ABSI, Coll P II 484, 498, 500 (published in Pollen, "Annals of the English College," pp. 20–22). On a dispute with the Brethren of the Hospital of Sts Cosmas and Damian regarding accommodation for the English students in 1589, see Parsons to Don Juan Ruiz de Velasco, Valladolid 5 August 1589, ABSI, 46/12/3, fols 82–85.

[53] I have not seen a copy of *Información qua de le Padre Personio ... acerca del Seminario en Valladolid* (1589), and I rely on Williams's citation (*English College, Valladolid*, pp. 7–8).

[54] In a report to William Cecil, Lord Burghley on March 5/15, 1591, an unidentified informant did not know if the college would be for English and Irish or restricted to the English (TNA, SP 78/23/286).

[55] Canon Edwin Henson suggested that another trait common to the English colleges had already appeared in the first months: a division among the students into pro- and anti-Jesuit factions (*Registers of the English College at Valladolid, 1589–1862* [London, 1930], p. xiii). Williams, however, does not mention any friction at this time in his more extensive history.

to Madrid, he brought with him the college's first rector,[56] the Spanish Jesuit Bartolomé de Sicilia.[57] His term lasted only a month before the king recalled him to Madrid where he initiated a project that eventually brought him notoriety, dismissal from the Society, and more threats to Jesuits in Spain: a collection of alms throughout all Spanish churches for the needs of the state. Pedro de Guzmán replaced him on November 26. English Jesuits Richard Gibbons, recalled from Lisbon, and William Flack assisted him in the administration. By the end of 1589 there were 20 members of the college and, despite some successful begging tours, Parsons was still petitioning the king to increase his pension. By July of 1591, when Parsons returned to Valladolid, the seminary numbered 60. Later that summer a mysterious epidemic swept through the college. Juan López de Manzano, the college's rector, became ill and withdrew to the professed house to recuperate. Parsons withdrew to the College of San Ambrosio. Eleven died. The epidemic ended as mysteriously as it began and life returned to normal in the autumn.[58]

The English royal proclamation of October 18, 1591 bestowed unwanted notoriety upon the new foundation. In Rome and Spain, the proclamation claimed, numerous "dissolute young men, who have partly for lack of living, partly for crimes committed, become fugitives, rebels, and traitors" are instructed in "points of sedition" to advance Spanish ambitions in England. Traitors called these "dens and receptacles" "seminaries and colleges of Jesuits" and they assured Philip II of greater success on his next attempted invasion.[59] The uncommonly harsh language about another monarch and the quasi-apocalyptic depiction of Spanish foreign policy galvanized support around Philip and the college. More benefactors provided assistance. Indeed, even in England the proclamation

---

[56] To my knowledge no regulation stipulated that the rector must be a Spaniard. It seems that Parsons, well aware of the tensions within the Society and of the fears regarding the English in Valladolid, requested a Spaniard and, indeed, one who was a close friend of the king.

[57] For a short biography of this controversial figure see Henson, *English College, Valladolid*, pp. xvii–xviii, n.

[58] Acquaviva to Parsons, Rome October 2, 1589, ARSI, Tolet 5/I, fols 85ᵛ–86ʳ; Parsons to Creswell, Toledo December 9, 1589, same to same, Valladolid July 23, 1590, same to same, Valladolid November 12, 1590, same to same, Escorial July 17, 1591, ABSI, Coll P I–II 305, 498, 500 (published in Pollen, "Annals of the English College," pp. 20– 22); Henson, *English College, Valladolid*, p. xvii; Hicks, "Persons and the Spanish Seminaries," pp. 499–503; Williams, *St Alban's College, Valladolid*, pp. 8–9, 261; Edwards, *Robert Persons*, pp. 139–42, 150–51.

[59] Paul L. Hughes and James F. Larkin, C.S.V., (eds.), *Tudor Royal Proclamations* (3 vols, New Haven, 1964–1969), vol. 3, p. 88.

had unforeseen consequences: some new students testified that their desire to see the college was aroused by the proclamation.[60]

With new gifts and further assistance from Don Alfonso de Quiñones, the college purchased its first residence. Shortly thereafter, it expanded by acquiring a neighboring house with a connecting garden. On it a church and sacristy were built. As the college grew, the time seemed ripe to petition the pope for the same privileges earlier granted to the English Colleges in Douai and in Rome. In July of 1591, Philip II instructed his ambassador to Rome to ask for papal blessing. Approval was delayed because of deaths in rapid succession of Gregory XIV and Innocent IX.[61] Pope Clement VIII[62] finally issued a bull of confirmation on April 25, 1592. Because the college was supported by alms, generous donations from benefactors such as de Quiñones and de Reynosa, and royal promises and not subsidized by the papacy, it was not pontifical in the technical sense.[63] Nonetheless, the college was placed under the immediate protection of the Holy See. Its government was delegated to the Society of Jesus, but Cardinal Allen held ultimate authority.[64]

The foundation of a third English college on the continent raised the always delicate issue of authority. Proper coordination of curriculum, students, and missions at colleges in Reims, Rome and now Valladolid, demanded someone with a measure of jurisdiction over them. Parsons

---

[60] Loomie, *Spanish Elizabethans*, p. 190; Edwards, *Robert Persons*, pp. 151–52.

[61] Elected on October 29, 1591, Innocent IX reigned until December 30. He continued the pro-Spanish policies of Gregory XIV and supported the Catholic League in France even though he reduced assistance for financial reasons. See Kelly, *Popes*, pp. 274–75.

[62] A zealous reformer Clement was elected on January 30, 1592. During a pontificate that lasted twelve years, he struggled to free the papacy from Spanish domination. See Kelly, *Popes*, pp. 275–76. Clement had been cardinal protector of the English College in Rome while Parsons was rector. After Creswell's arrival in Spain, he told Parsons that the pope had fond memories of his experience with the college and a special love for Parsons's efforts for the reconversion of England. This report prompted Parsons to write to the pope. Because Creswell would discuss the matters at great length in an audience, Parsons did not deem it necessary to relate much about the importance of the work and progress of the English seminaries and "of the great hope which we have of the speedy reduction of England" (Parsons to Clement VIII, Seville December 1, 1592, Archivio segreto vaticano, Borghese, serie III.124.g.2, fols 3^{r-v}).

[63] Hicks, "Persons and the Spanish Seminaries," pp. 503–506; Henson, *English College, Valladolid*, p. xviii; Williams, *St Alban's College, Valladolid*, pp. 11–12.

[64] Allen was not very involved in the foundation of the college. Indeed, he did not express his gratitude to Philip until July 10, 1591 when he wrote from Rome: "I have come to know that besides the innumerable benefits by which, during so protracted an exile in so many different places, you have protected and supported me and my afflicted people, you have with your customary liberality recently allowed to be founded and aided in Valladolid a college for the English similar to those in Rheims and Rome" (published in Penelope Renold, (ed.), *Letters of William Allen and Richard Barret 1572–1598* [London, 1967], p. 206).

hoped that Allen would assume jurisdiction over all English colleges.[65] Allen did assume authority over the English College in Valladolid similar to that of cardinal protector at the English College in Rome.[66] A year earlier, on September 18, 1591, Pope Gregory XIV had appointed Cardinal Allen prefect of the English mission, and had instructed English Catholics to obey him.[67] Allen's position at Valladolid was in keeping with that office. At the time of the confirmation, the rector was Rodrigo de Cabredo, the fourth Spaniard to hold the office and a man described by Parsons as "most affectionate to our nation"[68] and William Flack was minister.[69] Shortly after confirmation, on August 3, 1592, Philip II, accompanied by Infante Philip and Infanta Isabella, paid an official visit to the college. At their entrance, a young student likened Philip to the royal saints of the Old Testament. Special concern was shown to Abdias's statement to Elias: "Have you heard perchaunce … what I did in tymes past when Iezabel the Wicked Queene did persecute and slea the Prophets of God almighty, how I did save a hundred of their lives together, by hyding fyftie in one cave, and fyftie in an other, and feeding them with bread and water?" The comparison was extensively drawn: Philip succored English Catholics persecuted at home and sheltered them not in caves but towns and cities, maintaining them on more than bread and water. Later in the proceedings 10 students delivered short orations on the opening verse of Psalm 72, "God, give your justice to the king, your own righteousness to the royal

---

[65] Parsons to Creswell, Toledo December 9, 1589, ABSI, Coll P II 498 (published in Pollen, "Annals of the English College," p. 20).

[66] Allen never became cardinal protector of England. Cardinals protector were curial officials specifically designated to act on behalf of a specific country, college or religious order in the transaction of business in Rome. Many of their powers and responsibilities were taken over by the Congregation *de Propaganda Fide* created on June 6, 1622. See John Hungerford Pollen, S.J., "The Origin of the Appellant Controversy, 1598," *The Month*, 125 (1915): p. 462.

[67] The bull of appointment was published in Thomas Francis Knox, (ed.), *The Letters and Memorials of William Cardinal Allen (1532–1594)* (London, 1882), pp. 335–36. Allen had been nominated archbishop of Malines by Philip II on November 10, 1589 but, for various reasons including Allen's own work in Rome and deaths of various popes, he never assumed the position; by March 30, 1593 Philip had a new candidate (see Knox, *Letters of Allen*, pp. cxv–cxvii, 347–48, 436–37). Parsons knew of the nomination and in a letter to Creswell, from Madrid on January 7, 1590, hoped that by now Allen had been confirmed (ABSI, Coll P II 498 [published in Pollen, "Annals of the English College," p. 21]). See also Allen's letter to Philip, Rome October 5, 1591, and his report to Don Antonio Folch y Cardona, Duke of Sessa, Spain's ambassador in Rome, [mid 1592?] in Renold, *Letters of Allen and Barret*, pp. 207–208, 222–29.

[68] Parsons to Creswell, Valladolid July 23, 1590, ABSI, Coll P II 500 (published in Pollen, "Annals of the English College," p. 21).

[69] Hicks, "Persons and the Spanish Seminaries," pp. 503–506; Henson, *English College, Valladolid*, p. xviii; Williams, *St Alban's College, Valladolid*, pp. 11–12.

son" in Hebrew, Greek, Latin, English, Scots, Welsh, Spanish, French, Italian, and Flemish.[70] The king's delight at the reception and the work of the college rendered him even more benevolent for Parsons's next request.

Hopes for the establishment of a second seminary in Spain were entertained as early as 1590. In late 1589 William Warford[71] and John Cecil travelled through Andalusia, begging alms for the new seminary. Upon their return they told Parsons how well they were treated and how much they were given in Seville. Many urged Parsons to follow up their visit with a trip to Seville in hope of founding a second college there. Because of other projects and responsibilities, he did not, however, visit Seville until late 1590 when he escorted the first missionaries from the English College in Valladolid on the first leg of the journey to England.[72] During his sojourn, he considered establishing another college but decided it was wiser to secure the Valladolid foundation before he embarked on a new venture.[73]

While Parsons was in Seville, he visited Puerto de Santa Maria near Cadiz to minister to English captives working in the Spanish galleys. He provided religious instruction and received many into the Catholic Church. How sincere such conversions were, it was impossible to judge. Spanish authorities, however, were skeptical and consequently were reluctant to free converts and to accept them in the king's service. It was known that some, once freed, fled Spain and returned to England.[74] Concern for English

---

[70] An account of this visit can be found in [Robert Parsons], *A relation of the King of Spaines receiving in Valladolid, and in the Inglish College of the same towne, in August last part of this yere. 1592* (n.p. [Valladolid?], 1592) *ARCR*, vol. 2, num. 634, *STC* 19412.5, especially p. 30. A Spanish translation appeared at the same time, see *ARCR*, vol. 1, num. 899 for full information. For a summary see Hicks, "Persons and the Spanish Seminaries," pp. 144–46. Parsons's account along with a published Spanish version and the epigrams composed to honor the visit have been collected in *The Fruits of Exile. Los Frutos del Exilio*, (eds.) Berta Cano Echevarría and Ana Sáez Hidalgo (Valladolid, 2009).

[71] On Warford see Anstruther, *Seminary Priests*, vol. 1, p. 370; McCoog, *Monumenta Angliae*, vol. 2, p. 522.

[72] He had, however, mentioned the possibility of an earlier visit to the general. See Acquaviva's letter to Parsons, Rome June 20, 1591, ARSI, Baet. 3/I, fols 3^{r~v}.

[73] "Annales seminarii seu Collegii Anglorum Hispalensis ab anno 1591," ABSI, Coll P II 344–49 (published in Pollen, "Annals of the English College," pp. 1–3); Hicks, "Persons and the Spanish Seminaries," pp. 28–29.

[74] Hicks, "Persons and the Spanish Seminaries," pp. 29–30; Edwards, *Robert Persons*, p. 145. Parsons discussed the significance of this work in an important letter to Don Juan de Idiáquez, Seville April 4, 1591, ABSI, Coll P I 246–47 (published in Knox, *Letters of Allen*, pp. 329–32). We shall return to this letter later in this chapter. On Parsons's work for English converts and his intercession with the Inquisition in behalf of captured English see Albert J. Loomie, S.J., "Religion and Elizabethan Commerce with Spain," *Catholic Historical Review*, 50 (1964): pp. 32–39.

galley slaves along with the necessity of providing accommodation for priests embarking on the English mission, resulted in the establishment of residences at Spanish ports.

In 1517 English merchants had endowed a residence and the Church of St George in the port of San Lucar de Barrameda, at the mouth of the River Guadalquivir. Both deteriorated after England's abandonment of Catholicism and the subsequent tension between the two countries. On his begging tour, John Cecil succeeded in arranging transfer of the property to the priests of the English mission. A public deed of April 29, 1591 handed over the house, church, and property for the use of seminary priests. William, Cardinal Allen was given right of patronage, which right he delegated to Parsons. Dr Thomas Stillington was appointed provost of the church. In 1593, Parsons was instrumental in the establishment of a similar residence in Lisbon. Proposals for a third, in Puerto de Santa Maria, were never implemented.[75]

Jesuits in Seville placed unanticipated barriers to the establishment of another English seminary. The problem was Bartolomé de Sicilia, the first rector of the English College in Valladolid. In his zeal to assist the financially strapped Spanish monarchy, he travelled through Spain, collecting alms. The tactics he employed in Seville at the end of 1591, according to the superior of the professed house there, angered everyone. Because of his strong-arm methods, Jesuits in Seville did not react enthusiastically to news that other Jesuits would be shortly arriving in their city to solicit alms for the establishment of an English seminary. Spanish Jesuits asked Acquaviva to recommend to Parsons that he postpone the seminary. It was at this point in the seminary's erection that Philip visited the English College in Valladolid. So impressed was he that Parsons judged the time ripe to approach him about another institution in Seville. Furnished with letters of recommendation from the king and from various nobles to officials in Seville, Parsons left Valladolid with six students to begin the new college. Despite the recent antics of de Sicilia, civic reception was favorable. Bartholomé Perez, Jesuit provincial of Andalusia, assisted Parsons in his endeavor.[76] Apprehensive that Jesuits in the professed house would consider the arrival of yet more Jesuits dependent on the alms of the faithful as a threat to their support, Parsons suggested that Acquaviva

---

[75] "Annales seminarii seu Collegii Anglorum Hispalensis ab anno 1591," ABSI, Coll P II 344–45 (published in Pollen, "Annals of the English College," pp. 4–6); Hicks, "Persons and the Spanish Seminaries," pp. 30–35. Acquaviva approved the house in San Lucar on 18 March 1591 (ARSI, Baet 2, fol. 141^v). See Loomie, "Religion and Elizabethan Commerce," pp. 39–42, and Williams, *St Alban's College, Valladolid*, pp. 269–73 for a brief history of the San Lucar residence, and Michael Williams, "The Origins of the English College, Lisbon," *Recusant History*, 20 (1991): pp. 478–92 for the activities of the English in Lisbon.

[76] Perez to Acquaviva, Seville December 2, 1592, ARSI, Hisp. 134, fols 327^r–330^v.

stress the groundlessness of such fears: alms collected by the professed house in Valladolid had, in fact, increased after the establishment of the English College there.[77] Acquaviva thus instructed them not to impede the new foundation by word or deed.[78] The list of benefactors to the new college included Rodrigo, Cardinal de Castro, Archbishop of Seville, who had accompanied Philip II to England nearly 40 years earlier; Rodrigo Ponce de Léon, Duke of Arcos; Francisco de Zuñiga y Sotomayor, Duke of Béjar; Antonio Fernández de Córdoba y Cardona, Duke of Sessa; Pedro Fernández de Córdoba y Figueroa, Marquis of Priego; Antonio de Guzmán y Sotomayor, Marquis of Ayamonte, and less noted but equally generous local clergy and laity. The college opened on November 25, 1592 with 14 students at a temporary residence in the Plaza de San Lorenzo.[79] Francesco de Peralta was the first rector. A Spanish Jesuit, Juan de Munnez, was the students' confessor; two Englishmen, Charles Tancard[80] and Joseph Creswell, were appointed minister and procurator respectively. Pope Clement VIII confirmed the Seville seminary on May 15, 1594 in a bull almost identical to that confirming Valladolid. The new college was placed

---

[77] According to the Society's *Constitutions*, professed houses were forbidden fixed revenues, that is guaranteed sources of income, and relied totally on the collection of alms for their support and sustenance. See Ignatius of Loyola, *The Constitutions of the Society of Jesus*, (ed.) George E. Ganss, S.J. (St Louis, 1970), nums 555–561, pp. 253–55,

[78] Acquaviva to Parsons, Rome October 27, 1592, ARSI, Cast. 6, fol. 137ᵛ; Acquaviva to Perez, Rome September 28 and October 27, 1592, ARSI, Cast. 6, fol. 137ᵛ; Acquaviva to Estebal de Hoseda and Melchior de Castro, Rome October 26, 1592, ARSI, Baet. 3/I, pp. 84–85; Acquaviva to Parsons, Rome February 19, 1593, ARSI, Baet. 3/I, p. 100. Nonetheless this issue surfaced regularly as we shall see.

[79] An account of the foundation of Spanish seminaries was the basis of Parsons's *Newes from Spayne and Holland* (n.p. [Antwerp], 1593) *ARCR*, vol. 2, num. 632, STC 22994. This author ominously ended this work with a promise to write a discourse regarding the succession to the English throne. According to Victor Houliston, this work marked a shift from Parsons's interest in armed intervention to the possibility of a Catholic succession ("The Lord Treasurer and the Jesuit: Robert Persons's Satirical *Responsio* to the 1591 Proclamation," *Sixteenth Century Journal*, 32 [2001]: pp. 383–401; *Catholic Resistance in Elizabethan England. Robert Persons's Jesuit Polemic, 1580–1610* [Aldershot/Rome, 2007], pp. 47–70). See also Houliston's "The Hare and the Drum: Robert Persons's Writings on the English Succession, 1593–6," *Renaissance Studies*, 14 (2000): pp. 235–50, and his *Catholic Resistance*, pp. 71–92. For a personal account of the early history of the college in Seville, see the letter from John Price to Parsons, March 1, 1610, ABSI, Anglia III, 99 (published in M.A. Tierney, (ed.) *Dodd's Church History of England* [5 vols, London, 1839–1843], vol. 2, pp. ccclxxvi–ccclxxviii). For a description of the official opening celebrations on the feast of St Thomas of Canterbury (29 December) 1592 see Martin Murphy, (ed.), *St Gregory's College, Seville, 1592–1767* (London, 1992), pp. 6–7. For the college's history see Murphy's work and Francisco de Borja de Medina, S.J., "El Colegio Inglés de San Gregorio Magno de Sevilla (Notas y comentarios)," *Archivo Teológico Granadino*, 62 (1999): pp. 77–105.

[80] Acquaviva transferred him from Cadiz to Seville on March 16, 1592 (ARSI, Baet 3/I, fol. 28ʳ).

under the immediate protection of the Holy See with its government committed to the Society and with Cardinal Allen in his role of quasi-protector.[81]

As superior of English Jesuits, Parsons coordinated activities in England, Netherlands, Spain and Rome. He selected men for the mission, and found places for the English novices in the Jesuit novitiates throughout the continent. Because of his good relations with Philip, he was not only an habitual supplicant for alms for English religious exiles and institutions, but also the general's agent in the ongoing intra-Jesuit conflict The work expected of him—and the work that he actually accomplished—was astonishing. Aware that Parsons needed an assistant, Acquaviva seized this perfect opportunity to remove Creswell as rector of the English College, Rome where he had not been very successful. Jesuit involvement with England began with the administration of the English College in spring of 1579. Tension between Welsh and English seminarians, and disagreement over the very nature of the establishment resulted in Pope Gregory XIII's insistence that the Jesuits take charge. Everard Mercurian could not deny the papal will. But the problems did not end with the arrival of the Jesuits. Creswell's apparent inability to ignore certain defects, and his employment of spies and sentinels to watch over the students, created domestic tension.[82]

---

[81] ARSI, Fondo Gesuitico 1606/6/3/1–3; "Annales seminarii seu Collegii Anglorum Hispalensis ab anno 1591," ABSI, Coll P II 344–49 (published in Pollen, "Annals of the English College," pp. 6–10); More, *Elizabethan Jesuits*, pp. 208–11; Hicks, "Persons and the Spanish Seminaries," pp. 143–52; Murphy, *St Gregory's College, Seville*, pp. 6–7. On the college's curriculum see Michael Williams, "The Ascetic Tradition and the English College at Valladolid," in *Monks, Hermits and the Ascetic Tradition*, (ed.) W.J. Sheils (Oxford, 1985), pp. 275–83.

[82] Williams says nothing about the quality of Creswell's government. Acquaviva complained to Parsons on July 9, 1591 that there was not as much unity at the English College as he would have liked. After consultation with Allen, responsibility for the unrest seemed to be Creswell's so Acquaviva decided it expedient to replace him with William Holt (ARSI, Hisp. 74, fol. 31ʳ). On July 27, 1591 Parsons wrote to Creswell from Valladolid: "I am sorry to see your troubles there with those ungrateful youths. I doubt whether division of chambers brought in by this occasion, will remedy the matter, or no–for all signes of diffidence make Englishmen more distrusters and canvassers, as you know, &–and therefore my opinion is that plain and confident dealing with them, and letting passe all things already don, is the best way of ending this matter,–& assure yourself that many defects must be winked att, and not pursued in a multitude; and for spyeries and sentinels–is the way to marr all &–" (ABSI, Coll P I 305 [published in Pollen, "Annals of the English College," pp. 22–23]). Cardinal Allen explained to Philip II on April 24, 1592 that "by order of his superiors and at my request" Creswell was going to Spain where he will afford some relief to Parsons in his negotiations (see Renold, *Letters of Allen and Barret*, pp. 218–20). On July 15, 1593 Parsons wrote to Acquaviva from Valladolid that Creswell was a great help: he was reliable and religious, and had a special talent for business "greater, perhaps, than for dealing with boys in a college" (ARSI, Hisp. 135, fol. 372ʳ). A year later, from Marchena on May 12, 1594, Parsons however acknowledged that Spanish rectors found Creswell difficult

Muzio Vitelleschi, a future superior general of the Society, succeeded Creswell on April 16, 1592.[83] Creswell was sent to Spain and appointed procurator at the new college in Seville.[84] He assumed his post as Parsons's assistant in Madrid a year later.[85] Acquaviva preferred Parsons to remain in Madrid but realized that care of the seminaries required travel. In his approval of Creswell, Acquaviva stressed that he was to solicit Parsons's opinion on everything and to follow it. Proper subordination was important not just for the successful execution of any project but to demonstrate to Spanish ministers that there was "unity of mind and action."[86]

Acquaviva planned a complete reorganization of the English Jesuits on the continent. Creswell moved to Spain to assist Parsons; William Holt was to leave Flanders to succeed Creswell as rector of the English College, and Henry Walpole was to relinquish his chaplaincy in the duke of Parma's army to take over Holt's work. Holt, however, remained in Brussels because Acquaviva and Parsons decided that his work there was too important to abandon for the English College in Rome. Thus Acquaviva appointed Vitelleschi. With the general's approval, Parsons requested Walpole for one of the new seminaries in Spain, and the Irish Jesuit James Archer, currently a chaplain with Walpole, to work for Philip II's foundation of an Irish College at Salamanca. In late autumn of 1592, Walpole and Archer travelled to Calais and then to Spain.[87]

The Irish Colleges

England was not alone in its attempt to establish colleges in the Iberian Peninsula. In September of 1589 Claudio Acquaviva sent the Irish Jesuit

---

to take and the Jesuits doubted "that they could put up with Fr. Creswell unless I were here" (ARSI, Hisp. 136, fols 318^r–319^v). Originally, as we noted above, Acquaviva hoped to replace Creswell with William Holt but it was decided that Holt's work in Flanders was too important.

[83] ARSI, Angl. 37, fol. 142^v.

[84] Creswell received Acquaviva's permission to go to Castile on April 29, 1592 (ARSI, Hist. Soc. 61, fol. 48^r) and must have departed almost immediately because the general wrote to him in Genoa on 20 June about his work with Parsons (ARSI, Med. 21/II, fol. 387^v).

[85] Hicks, "Persons and the Spanish Seminaries," pp. 148–49. On Creswell's efforts to raise money for the seminaries see Loomie, *Spanish Elizabethans*, pp. 202–207.

[86] Acquaviva to Parsons, Rome March 14, 1594, ARSI, Tolet. 5/II, fol. 330^v; same to same, Rome March 14, 1594, ARSI, Tolet. 5/II, fol. 330^r.

[87] Acquaviva to Parsons, Rome July 9, 1591, ARSI, Hisp. 74, fol. 31^r; Olivier Mannaerts to Acquaviva, Douai August 27, 1592, ARSI, Germ. 170, fols 229^r–230^v; Acquaviva to Mannaerts, Rome September 5, 1592, ARSI, Fl. Belg. 1/I, pp. 505–506; Parsons to Acquaviva, Valladolid July 15, 1593, ARSI, Hisp. 135, fols 372^r–374^v.

John Howling to Parsons in Spain. Seven students from the English College in Rome accompanied him.[88] Although the general's letters said nothing about Lisbon, Howling was there by 1590, perhaps as a replacement for Richard Gibbons on his departure for Valladolid.[89] Residing at the Church of Saõ Roque, Howling ministered to Irish and English sailors and merchants. At the time numerous poor Irish students who had travelled to the continent in search of financial assistance for their seminary studies, ordination, and eventual return to Ireland, resided in Lisbon. Howling provided what support he could, but alms collected only satisfied some immediate needs. By June of 1592, 24 students resided in a small house, surviving on an income estimated sufficient for the support of 12. On June 6, 1592, Walter French described the great poverty of the college but the students at least were now dressed "like collegians, brave cloaks and threadbare purses."[90] Probably because Irish and English students begged alms from the same prospective benefactors, there were occasional conflicts between them. Searching for a definitive solution, Howling turned to Sir Francis Englefield for advice. Unless adequate sources of income were found, tension between seminarians would remain and similar conflicts would periodically occur. Pedro Fonseca, Jesuit visitor to the Portuguese province, assisted Howling in securing royal approval. Despite its poverty the Irish College in Lisbon was founded officially on February 1, 1593. Even though António Fernandez Ximenes, a wealthy nobleman, endowed chairs of theology, the college's finances were not as secure as Howling would have liked. Despite his work Howling did not become the college's first superior. Indeed the Society of Jesus did not assume administration of the college until 1605.[91]

---

[88] Acquaviva to Simone Arpe, Rome September 1, 1589, same to same, Rome September 30, 1589, same to John Howling, Rome September 30, 1589, ARSI, Med. 21/II, fols 264ᵛ, 267ᵛ. Because Parsons paid the travelling expenses, the English Jesuit might have requested Howling for the Anglo-Irish establishment in Valladolid. Once it was decided that the college would be restricted to English seminarians, Howling would have been free to assume another post in Lisbon.

[89] ARSI, Lus. 44/I, fol. 25ᵛ.

[90] See John Howling to Robert, Lord Queensford, Lisbon May 21, 1592, same to Patrick Sinot, Lisbon May 21, 1592, same to Thomas Strong, Bishop of Ossory, Lisbon May 26, 1592, Walter French to Thomas Strong, Lisbon, June 6, 1592, same to John Sinot, Lisbon June 8, 1592, BL, Lans. 71, n. 49.

[91] Prionsias Ó Fionnagáin, S.J., *The Jesuit Missions to Ireland in the Sixteenth Century* (n.p., n.d. [privately printed]), pp. 43–44; Prionsias Ó Fionnagáin, S.J., *Irish Jesuits 1598–1773* (n.p., n.d. [privately printed]), pp. 79–80; Williams, "Origins of the English College, Lisbon," p. 482. According to the 1630 will of the college's original benefactor, any attempt to remove the Society from the college's administration, would result in the entire bequest passing to the Jesuits. If, however, the Society abandoned the administration, assets would pass first to the archbishop of Lisbon and then to the Dominican provincial in Portugal (Williams, "Origins of the English College, Lisbon," p. 490 n. 27). See also Patricia O'

In 1582 another Irish priest, Thomas White, had settled in Valladolid, where he found Irish students with neither the financial means to continue their studies, nor the linguistic ability to beg successfully.[92] White gathered them together into one community and, through his work and his appeals, received donations barely adequate for their support. With the establishment of the English College of St Alban and Parsons's refusal to consider amalgamation with the Irish, prospects for White and his fellow countrymen were bleak. During Philip II's visit to Valladolid, White, though the intercession of Parsons, appealed to the king for assistance. Philip granted him money to meet his immediate needs, and promised to endow a college on the condition that it was established in Salamanca and not in Valladolid. An unnamed Irish gentleman at Philip's court asked the king to place the new college under the direction of the Society of Jesus.[93] Philip agreed. On August 2, 1592 Philip recommended to the city officials in Salamanca that "all good men" be charitable to the Irish students since they were "strangers and poor, and for the service of God have left their own native country." A house was prepared and Philip promised them an annual stipend of 500 ducats. The first vice-rector, who would serve under the rector of the local Jesuit college, was James Archer. Thomas White, meanwhile, prepared to enter the Jesuit novitiate.[94]

In January of 1593 Henry Walpole and James Archer arrived in Seville where they met Parsons who introduced them to the royal court in Madrid. Parsons's introduction was invaluable because, in the words of Thomas J. Morrissey, S.J.: "There was no one better equipped than Persons to instruct him on the establishment of a seminary, on the kinds of public relations

---

Connell, "The Early-Modern Irish College Network in Iberia, 1590–1800," in *The Irish in Europe, 1580–1815*, (ed.) Thomas O'Connor (Dublin, 2001), pp. 62–63; Patricia O' Connell, *The Irish College at Lisbon 1590–1834* (Dublin, 2001), pp. 22–29; and Ana Castro Santamaria and Nieves Rupérez Almajano, "The Real Colegio de San Patricio de Nobles Irlandeses of Salamanca: Its Buildings and Properties, 1592–1768," in *The Ulster Earls and Baroque Europe. Refashioning Irish Identities, 1600–1800*, (eds.) Thomas O'Connor and Mary Ann Lyons (Dublin, 2010), pp. 223–41.

[92] For these students and their requests, see Amalio Huarte, "Petitions of Irish Students in the University of Salamanca, 1574–1591," *Archivium Hibernicum*, 4 (1915): pp. 96–130.

[93] José de Acosta seems to have been influential in the king's decision that the new college be situated in Salamanca and not in Valladolid. It seems too that the new college was originally to be governed by non-Jesuits but somehow under the direction of the Society of Jesus. See Acquaviva to Acosta, Rome August 31, 1592, ARSI, Cast. 6, fol. 129^v.

[94] Thomas J. Morrissey, S.J., *James Archer of Kilkenny: An Elizabethan Jesuit* (Dublin, 1979), pp. 12–14, and "The Irish Student Diaspora in the Sixteenth Century and the Early Years of the Irish College at Salamanca," *Recusant History*, 14 (1978): pp. 245–46. For names of the first students in the College see Denis J. O'Doherty, "Students of the Irish College Salamanca (1595–1619)," *Archivium Hibernicum*, 2 (1913): pp. 1–26. See also O'Connell, "Early-Modern Irish College Network," pp. 54–55.

required in Spain to win financial support, or, indeed, in the ways and means of cultivating royal favour, an almost necessary requirement for survival if one's work depended on a royal stipend." Around the end of the month Archer travelled to Salamanca to assume his post as vice-rector and Walpole to Valladolid.[95]

On January 22, 1593, John Howling wrote a detailed account of the state of Ireland to Acquaviva. During his three years in Lisbon he worked with English, Irish, and Scots. Not technically heretics, many, nonetheless, had abandoned religious devotions and practices. Because of the efforts of different Jesuits, some have been reconciled. In certain sections of Ireland persecution lingered. More ominous to Howling was recent royal permission to establish a college in Dublin (Trinity College) to teach "heresy" and to train Irish ministers for the Established Church. More students now fled to the continent. Consequently the work of Irish colleges was even more important. At the time there were 30 students at the Irish College in Lisbon and many local clergy had formed a confraternity dedicated to St Patrick to assist the Irish. Many students hoped to enter the Society; indeed, some had vowed to do so. All in all, Howling concluded, the conversion of Ireland would depend on the Society of Jesus and he urged that these candidates be accepted because "our language is difficult."[96] Implied was the hope that Acquaviva would re-found a Jesuit mission so that Irish recruits could practice their difficult tongue!

"Returning with the Fleet": Crichton and the Invasion of Britain

William Crichton apparently remained in the Low Countries or northern France after his departure from Scotland in late summer of 1589. By the following summer, however, he was on the road to Spain to negotiate support for the Catholic earls. Tertian fever interrupted his journey at Genoa in August, but he eventually arrived in Madrid around the beginning of November and remained there until August of 1592.[97] The Catholic earls apparently had designated him their agent. Unless he had

---

[95] Morrissey, "Irish College at Salamanca," p. 247.

[96] Howling to Acquaviva, Lisbon 22 January 1593, ARSI, Lus. 72, fols 27ʳ–28ᵛ.

[97] I follow the narrative as related in Francisco de Borja de Medina, S.J., "Intrigues of a Scottish Jesuit at the Spanish Court: William Crichton's Mission to Madrid (1590–1592)," in *The Reckoned Expense: Edmund Campion and the Early English Jesuits. Essays in Celebration of the First Centenary of Campion Hall, Oxford*, (ed.) Thomas M. McCoog, S.J., 2nd edn. (Rome, 2007), pp. 277–325. and "Escocia en la Estrategia de la Empresa de Inglaterra: La Misión del P. William Crichton cerca de Felipe II (1590–1592)," *Revista de Historia Naval*, 17 (1999): pp. 57–59. See also Michael Yellowlees, "*So strange a monster*

some credentials to act in the name of the earls, it seems unlikely that Crichton would have had Acquaviva's qualified approval throughout the negotiations, and that he would have received such a warm royal reception upon his arrival in Madrid. Philip received Crichton's proposals favorably. To further negotiations, the king recommended that Crichton, or some other Jesuit, return to Scotland. Acquaviva, however, would not approve Crichton's journey. Convinced that it would be impossible to prevent the English government from discovering a clandestine Jesuit mission, Acquaviva feared disastrous consequences for any Jesuit, and especially for Crichton, if he was captured, because of his previous stay in the Tower of London and his promise upon his release that he could not return to England or Scotland.[98] The general preferred that no Jesuit go to Scotland unless he went openly with an armada;[99] as an alternative he recommended Robert Bruce who travelled to Flanders after the Brig O' Dee affair.[100]

Crichton persisted despite Acquaviva's disapproval. In February of 1591 he again requested permission to further Philip's (or in the coded language "Ruberto Hiberno") projects. Acquaviva still opposed the trip: Crichton's presence in Scotland, he again contended, would arouse suspicions and could cause more harm than good. Instead he recommended that Crichton send instructions, either verbal or written, to an agent in Scotland qualified to treat the matter[101] In subsequent letters

---

as a Jesuite": *The Society of Jesus in Sixteenth-Century Scotland* (Isle of Colonsay, 2003), pp. 117–28.

[98] See McCoog, *Society of Jesus*, p. 242 n. 68.

[99] Behind Acquaviva's concern that Crichton was so well known that his very presence would arouse English suspicions, may lurk another reason for the general's reluctance to sanction Crichton's active participation. In the early 1580s both Parsons and Crichton shuttled between various parties in an attempt to forge an alliance against England. Concerned that such diplomatic activity was outside the scope of the Society's Institute, Acquaviva tried to curtail their activity. On this see McCoog, *Society of Jesus*, pp. 178–223, 278–80.

[100] Acquaviva to Crichton, Rome August 25, 1590, ARSI, Med. 21/II, fol. 308^v; same to same, Rome December 24, 1590, ARSI, Tolet. 4, fol. 79^v; same to Oliver Mannaerts, Rome c. April 15, 1590, ARSI, Fl. Belg. 1/I, p. 458.

[101] Acquaviva to Crichton, Rome 16 March 1591, ARSI, Med. 20, fol. 024^v. The cipher used in this correspondence, "N.R.P.-Creytton 1590," can be found in ARSI, Fondo Gesuitico 678/21/4. As Acquaviva explained to Gil González Dávila on April 16: "Father Hay says that in no way does it serve the king's interests if Crichton returned to Scotland, unless he returned with the fleet, because he is well known and, without doubt, his presence would do harm" (ARSI, Tolet. 5/I, fol. 182^r).

Acquaviva finally conceded Crichton could travel if it benefited the project.[102] Now royal insistence kept Crichton at court.[103]

Perhaps as a result of Acquaviva's refusal to allow Crichton to play a major role in subsequent negotiations, Philip II invited David Graham, Laird of Fintry, to court in November of 1591 in order to discuss the Scottish situation and to negotiate on behalf of the Catholic earls. Fintry was a nephew of James Beaton, Archbishop of Glasgow, and a frequent participant in English and Scottish Catholic negotiations and intrigues. Crichton respected Finty and greatly anticipated his arrival. But Fintry never replied to the invitation and the subsequent delay disturbed Crichton's plans. Until Fintry arrived, Crichton hesitated leaving for Rome to discuss the enterprise with Acquaviva. Philip wanted him to remain, but the king's persistent inactivity regarding the enterprise annoyed Crichton. Everything, he complained, moved so slowly at court that the Jesuit doubted that anything would ever be done. He observed that England challenged Spain on various fronts: Flanders, France, the West Indies. Instead of wasting forces and finances on these battles, Crichton argued, Philip would be better advised if he dealt with the principal problem: Elizabeth. Like a spider, the queen spun her web in different parts of Philip's house. He could clean the house room by room and dust away the webs, but as long as the spider remained, the webs would re-appear. Instead Philip should concentrate on the destruction of the spider.[104] Crichton wondered whether the king possessed the will necessary to deal with the spider.

Crichton's prognosis improved within a few months. Francis Dacre, brother and heir of Leonard, Lord Dacre, had escaped to Scotland in September of 1589. In early 1592 he arrived in Madrid with even more proposals for Spanish intervention in Scotland, and subsequent invasion of England. He and his retainers would play a role in both.[105] Crichton added his voice to Dacre's: almost all the nobles in Scotland, the Jesuit explained, adhered to Catholicism and were devoted to the Spanish king. They would gladly give their lives to restore Catholicism and to revenge the death of their beloved Mary, Queen of Scots. Moreover in the north of

---

[102] Acquaviva to Crichton, Rome October 1, 1591, ARSI, Tolet. 4, fols 90^{r-v}. Acquaviva suggested that Crichton pass through Rome on his way to Flanders to discuss the matter with Edmund Hay (Acquaviva to Crichton, Rome June 11, 1591, ARSI, Tolet. 4, fol. 85^v; same to same, Rome November 25, 1591, ARSI, Tolet. 4, fols 95^v–96^r).

[103] See Acquaviva to Crichton, Rome June 11, 1591, ARSI, Tolet. 4, fol. 85^v; and authorization for Crichton to travel to Lower Germany, Rome June 7, 1591, ARSI, Hist. Soc. 61, fol. 47^v.

[104] Crichton to Acquaviva, Madrid February 1, 1592, ARSI, Tolet. 37a, fols 212^r–213^v (published in Medina, "Crichton's Mission," pp. 310–11; and "Escocia en la Estrategia," p. 92).

[105] It is not clear whether Dacre's appearance had anything to do with the request for Fintry. He may have been sent as a substitute.

England along the Scottish borders, there were, as the earl of Huntingdon suspected, many Catholics who would rally to support Philip. Dacre and Crichton insisted the enterprise be launched as soon as possible. The Scottish nobles were poised to seize King James,[106] and to turn over their sons and castles to Philip II as collateral. To educate these sons and other Scots, Crichton proposed the establishment of a Scots College in Douai.

Crichton hoped that Robert Parsons and William, Cardinal Allen would assist him in his negotiations with Philip. Allen had inestimable influence with English Catholics. If he could be persuaded of the beneficial consequences of the union of the kingdoms of England and Scotland under Philip, he could galvanize even more support for the cause. Crichton had discussed the matter with Parsons, but the English Jesuit opposed any enterprise originating in Scotland. So obstinate was Parsons to any such plans that many, according to Crichton, believed that he and Allen simply intended to use Spanish military power of Spain to bring down the heretical regime. Once that had been accomplished, the cardinal and the Jesuit would install a king of their own choosing. Crichton did not identify their alleged candidate. Perhaps they were exploring different candidates. In May of 1591, the secular priest John Cecil claimed that he had been instructed to seek a meeting with Ferdinando Stanley, Lord Strange. Allen himself was familiar with secret negotiations involving the marriage of Arabella Stuart to Ranuccio Farnese, Prince of Parma. Because Parsons exercised considerable influence especially in Spain, Crichton doubted that Philip would accept any proposal without his endorsement. Thus, Crichton begged Acquaviva to moderate Parsons's views through the intercession of Allen.[107]

In a memorial apparently addressed to Don Juan de Idiáquez, King Philip's secretary, Crichton weighed the advantages and disadvantages of selecting England or Scotland as the enterprise's destination. Two principal arguments in favor of an English landing were location and resources. Obviously a successful enterprise required the capture of London. Progress to the capital from Scotland would be long and arduous whereas London was a short distance from the south coast. Moreover the English countryside was rich in food and victuals necessary to support the invading army. Scotland, on the other hand, was poor in comparison. But the availability

---

[106] Colonel William Semple had proposed something similar in 1589. See Glyn Redworth, "Between Four Kingdoms. International Catholicism and Colonel William Semple," in *Irlanda y la Monarquía Hispánica: Kinsale 1601–2001. Guerra, Política, Exilio y Religión*, (eds.) Enrique García Hernán, Miguel Ángel de Bunes, Óscar Recio Morales and Bernardo J. García García (Madrid, 2002), pp. 255–64.

[107] On the dispute between Parsons and Crichton over the succession to the English throne, see Thomas M. McCoog, S.J., "Harmony Disrupted: Robert Parsons, S.J., William Crichton, S.J., and the Question of Queen Elizabeth's Successor, 1581–1603," *AHSI*, 73 (2004): pp. 149–220.

of various ports of entry argued in favor of Scotland. English ports were well fortified and controlled by Spain's enemies. In Scotland thousands of soldiers were ready to secure a designated area and Crichton suggested a few possibilities along the Clyde and in Lothian. With such a large number of Scots willing to assist, Crichton did not anticipate any major problem. Scotland certainly was a considerable distance from London. The march would be long but with a pacified Scotland behind the forces, progress would be less dangerous. Moreover a considerable number of English Catholics resided in the northern part of the kingdom. Their numbers, especially the retainers of Charles Nevill, Earl of Westmorland, and Francis Dacre, would augment the Spanish-Scottish army as it moved south. Because England expected an invasion to be along the southern coast, most of the kingdom's soldiers were stationed there. An invasion from the north would catch them unprepared. Food and other victuals needed were more plentiful in the south of England but they were outside the control of Catholic supporters whereas Scottish Catholics would place their more limited supplies under Spanish control.[108] Unfortunately we do not know what Parsons's objections to this proposal were aside from a general dislike of depending on Scottish support because of rapid political changes and subsequent political realignments in the northern kingdom.

Curiously in light of Crichton's earlier and later support for King James's candidacy, at this time he did not propose a Stuart dynasty. He believed the only ruler capable of guaranteeing the restoration of Catholicism in both kingdoms was Philip II. As he explained to Acquaviva:

> if the Catholic king were to be the king, not only would he be able to maintain faith and justice and defend the inhabitants against enemies, but he would also, by making sure of the resources of both kingdoms on behalf of the inhabitants, not draining them out of the country, enable our countrymen to share in his great ventures, honours, wide-spread empire and wealth.

Weighing the advantages and disadvantages of launching an enterprise via Scotland at this time, Crichton argued the time was ripe. Catholics in England and Scotland suffered intensive persecution and looked to Spain for succor. If Spain did not provide immediate relief, they might look elsewhere for assistance. And Spain was in a position to act. Spanish armies controlled the Netherlands and occupied some French ports on the channel. Spain simply required approval from the pope. If the pope

---

[108] ARSI, Angl. 42, fols 32^{r-v} (published in Medina, "Escocia en la Estrategia," pp. 103–105; Medina, "Crichton's Mission," pp. 306–309).

declared James and Elizabeth excommunicated and deposed as cruel and obstinate heretics, Spain would have the necessary legitimation. If the papacy provided Spain with a right to the Scottish and English crowns, Philip had the power necessary to implement the decision.[109]

Related to Crichton's 1592 schemes are a few documents that Father Medina did not include in his analysis. In an important letter written on February 24, 1592, not addressed but endorsed simply "DI," probably Don Juan de Idiáquez, Crichton explained in more detail proposals for King James's capture. The captain of Edinburgh Castle, Sir James Hume, had offered his services to King Philip in a letter of December 18, 1591. He specifically mentioned that he was willing to abduct the Scottish king and deliver him to whomever Philip designated and, at the same time, to relinquish control of the castle to the same person. This castle, Crichton informed his correspondent, dominated the city and was one day's journey from England, on a river capable of sheltering an armada. The cost would be minimal. Moreover, Crichton considered Hume an honest man capable of executing what he promised.

Two years earlier, Crichton reminded the secretary, Philip was offered a castle at Berwick. Approximately the same time, Lord Dacre (presumably Leonard, brother of the above mentioned Francis Dacre) offered his castle in Carlisle. With these three castles under their control, Spanish forces could invade England from the north with no difficulty. To execute this strategy successfully, three things were required: competent sailors and pilots to transport soldiers "because of their absence the last armada was lost"; an agreement with specific English and Scottish nobles without whose assistance an invasion would be difficult if not impossible; and the affection of the people without which the country could not be held. Philip already had Lord Dacre in his service and it would be easy to acquire support of other nobles. To gain the people's affection, Crichton recommended seeking support of James Beaton, Archbishop of Glasgow, "a man famous in Scotland and respected by all"; a generous gift to all nobles who entered the Spanish king's service; and consistent support for Jesuit missions in England and Scotland that sought to win the people to Christ and to the service of the Spanish king.[110]

In a related document Crichton repeated many of the same arguments pro and con intervention via Scotland. Such an intervention would be the

---

[109] Three important documents for Crichton's proposals are his letters to Acquaviva, Madrid April 6,1592, Madrid April 7, 1592, and his "pros and cons" for the enterprise of March of 1592, ARSI, Tolet. 37a, fols 214ʳ–215ᵛ, 216ʳ–217ᵛ, 218ʳ–219ᵛ (published in Medina, "Crichton's Mission," pp. 311–18, and "Escocia en la Estrategia," pp. 93–97, 106–108). The quotation comes from the letter of April 6. I have used Medina's translation.
[110] ARSI, Angl. 30/I, fols 93ʳ–94ᵛ.

panacea that re-established Catholicism in England, Scotland and Ireland, that recovered Flanders for the Spanish crown; that terminated English piracy and, thus, guaranteed safe commerce between Spain and the West Indies; that prevented the accession of Henry of Navarre to the French throne; that eventually led to the total eradication of heresy. But the opportunity must be seized. Regardless of the victor, once the war ended, the French king would oppose a Spanish attack on England and Scotland. If the Guises emerged victorious, they would throw France's weight behind James because of familial affection; if Navarre won, he would oppose all Spanish ventures out of hatred. Because the entire expedition would last only five or six months, Crichton argued, Spain need not withdraw from France. The expedition would be brief because pro-Spanish Scottish nobles would hand over the ports where the armada could disembark. Moreover there would be between 20,000 and 30,000 Scottish soldiers, both Catholic and Protestant, to assist Spain. Catholics aided the invasion in the hope of restoring the old faith; heretics to avenge the cruel and unjust execution of Mary Stuart. Once James had been captured, the opposition would lack a leader. Three things only were needed: a leader agreeable to the people such as Ernst, Archduke of Austria, and a valiant captain such as Don Alonso de Vargas; experienced soldiers to supplement English and Scottish forces; and money.[111]

On March 5, 1592 James Tyrie, formerly the French provincial Odo Pigenat's delegate for Scottish affairs and currently Acquaviva's assistant for Germany (an assistancy that included France, England, Scotland, and the Low Countries),[112] evaluated Crichton's proposals either at the request of Crichton himself or as advisor to Acquaviva. Spanish claims to the English and Scottish thrones especially interested him. Excluding heretics who, *ipso facto*, had no right of succession to any throne, the two Spanish princesses Isabella and Catharina, and the sons of Charles II, Duke of Lorraine, as heirs of Anne of Brittany, were Elizabeth's rightful successors. However, neither the princesses nor the House of Lorraine possessed the necessary military power to enact their pretensions. Therefore, Tyrie argued, the king of Spain could advance his own claim to the thrones of England and Scotland. To corroborate his title to the English throne, Philip could cite Pope Pius V's excommunication and deposition of Elizabeth in 1570 and subsequent papal approval of Spanish ventures against her. Philip's claim to Scotland, rooted in his being named as heir in Mary Stuart's will, would be greatly strengthened if a papal statement excommunicated and deposed James. To assist

---

[111] ARSI, Angl. 30/I, fols 86^r–87^v.

[112] On Tyrie's authority over the Scottish mission see McCoog, *Society of Jesus*, pp. 209–11.

Spanish claims to Scotland, various Scottish lords promised aid and offered their sons as security. Unless Philip acted quickly, Tyrie feared that Scottish and English Catholics would abandon Spain and approach the duke of Lorraine with an explanation of his son's hereditary right to the thrones. If the duke was unable to provide military and financial assistance requested by the Scottish nobles, they would then turn to Ferdinand I, Duke of Florence. Consequently action must be taken immediately. Capture of the king was the first step. Once that was accomplished, Francis Stuart, Earl of Bothwell, and others would accuse him of various crimes, most serious of which were consent to the murder of his mother and an alliance with her murderer Elizabeth. After James had been condemned and placed under a secure guard, Bothwell would proclaim the king of Spain the realm's protector. To prevent unnecessary opposition, possibly from the Protestant Bothwell, Tyrie recommended that nothing be said about the exclusion of heresy during the early stages of the enterprise. After the enterprise had progressed significantly, Philip's role as protector would be announced and the total prohibition of heresy proclaimed.[113]

On May 23, 1592, Crichton lamented that he encountered good will and encouraging words in Madrid, but no action.[114] Regardless of the feasibility of Crichton's projects, he proposed them at the worst possible time. The duke of Parma was involved in a two-fronted conflict: intervention in France to assist the Catholic League, and the ongoing struggle against the Dutch rebels. In February of 1592 Henry of Navarre retaliated by supporting an invasion of northern Aragon. Philip had his hands full. Moreover between the death of Pope Sixtus V (August 27, 1590) and the election of Clement VIII (January 30, 1592) three popes briefly sat on the papal throne. Thus the papal cooperation needed and demanded by Spain was thus not forthcoming. Crichton left Spain in the autumn of 1592 with his mission unaccomplished.[115] He reached Rome in November and departed for Flanders the following January, having been

---

[113] ARSI, Angl. 30/I, fols 90^r–91^v.

[114] Crichton to Acquaviva, Madrid May 23, 1592, ARSI, Tolet. 37a, fols 220^r–221^v (published in Medina, "Crichton's Mission," p. 319; and "Escocia en la Estrategia," p. 98).

[115] In a letter of introduction to Pope Clement VIII written in Madrid on August 3, 1592, Pietro Millino, papal nuncio in Spain, recommended Crichton as one well informed of developments in Scotland and England. During his months in Madrid, he had discussed with King Philip different proposals for the restoration of Catholicism in these kingdoms. Because of Spain's involvement in France and Flanders, nothing was done (Archivio segreto vaticano, Spagna 40, fol. 18^r [published in Medina, "Escocia en la Estrategia," p. 100; Medina, "Crichton's Mission, p. 321]).

appointed superior of the Scottish mission.[116] By April he was in Douai pursuing a pet project: a Scottish college.[117]

Scottish machinations did not go unnoticed. Spies relayed their reports to English court, and Elizabeth warned James of proposals involving Spanish forces landing in south-east and south-west Scotland in order to capture the king and restore Catholicism. James dismissed these reports as fantasies of Jesuits and religious exiles. But the stories were given added weight by the confiscation of letters during the last week of 1592: the "Spanish Blanks" affair.

Crichton monitored all developments in Scotland. Upon his arrival in Flanders, he was more favorably disposed to the Stuart King, perhaps as a result of Spanish reluctance to accept any of his proposals.[118] Supported by Queen Elizabeth, Scottish Protestants exploited the discovery of the "Spanish Blanks" to push for stronger measures against Catholics. Thus, there was little hope for Scottish Catholics unless assistance was provided—and Spanish aid did not appear to be forthcoming despite the encouraging news that continued to emanate from Scotland. An unnamed Scottish candidate for the Society, most likely Thomas Abercrombie,[119] promised to establish a network of reliable informers on his return to Scotland to tidy up his affairs before entering the novitiate.[120] News supplied by these informers was even more encouraging. Regardless of James's possible involvement in the affair, as we saw in the last chapter, Protestant demands following upon the discovery of the "Blanks" so upset the balance of power that the king moved closer to the Catholic earls. By October Crichton was more optimistic. Betrayed by his own family and his closest relatives, James had escaped from their control and, according to Crichton, had now allied himself with the Catholic earls. Moreover, Queen Anne shunned heretics and consistently showed favor to Catholic noblewomen. Mindful perhaps of the example of Henry IV of France, Crichton no longer argued in favor

---

[116] Acquaviva announced Crichton's appointment in a letter to Oliver Mannaerts on January 26, and to Clément Dupuy on February 25 (ARSI, Fl. Belg. 1/I, pp. 510–11; Franc. 1/II, fols 385^r–86^v). From the letter to Dupuy it seems that James Gordon (the younger of Lesmore), who had entered the Society in Paris on September 29, 1573 (ARSI, Aquit. 9/I, fol. 101^v) was acting superior after the departure of Tyrie for Rome.

[117] Letters patent for his trip to Flanders were dated January 13, 1593, ARSI, Hist. Soc. 61, fol. 48^v.

[118] On Spanish reluctance see R.B. Wernham, *List and Analysis of State Papers Foreign Series: Elizabeth I* (7 vols, London, 1964–2000), vol. 4, para. 681.

[119] See McCoog, *Monumenta Angliae*, vol. 2, pp. 204–205.

[120] Crichton to Acquaviva, Douai April 21, 1593, ARSI, Germ. 171, fols 136^{r-v}.

of a Spanish monarch in England and Scotland. Henceforth James remained his candidate.[121]

At the request of some Scottish Jesuits, Giovani Battista Castelli, Bishop of Rimini and nuncio to France, recommended the Scottish youth William Ogilvie to Tolomeo Galli, Cardinal of Como, on February 7, 1582. Ogilvie had considerable promise and the nuncio wondered if he could enter the English College as a student. If the cardinal considered it odd that a Scot seek admission into a college established for English seminarians, the nuncio explained that Scotland and England were one island as if that geographical fact resolved the issue! Ogilvie was not admitted; instead he joined the Jesuits.[122]

The case of Ogilvie highlights a problem for Scottish Catholics: the lack of a college and/or seminary on the continent. Scottish Jesuits administered a seminary founded in Paris in 1580 but relocated to Pont-à-Mousson in 1581. Mary, Queen of Scots, James Beaton, Archbishop of Glasgow, and, possibly, John Leslie, Bishop of Ross, provided the endowment. The college moved to Pont-à-Mousson in affiliation with the university founded there in 1574 by Charles Guise, Cardinal of Lorraine, to combat heresy. He placed the university under the administration of the Society in 1580. In 1581 Pope Gregory XIII added to the endowment an annual pension for 15 years. With the stipulation that Irish students be admitted, Gregory increased his pension in 1584. By the start of 1585 there were 36 Scottish and 7 Irish seminarians. With the execution of Mary, Queen of Scots, the college lost its royal pension. Around the same time Pope Sixtus V reduced the papal pension. Plague added to the college's problems. In 1588 James Tyrie was superior of 20 Scottish and 9 Irish students. Despite his efforts, ruin was imminent. In late 1589 Lazario Visconti, Jesuit procurator for the seminaries, died. Acquaviva appointed Giovanni Hieronimo Gazi to the post. On November 12, 1589 Acquaviva instructed Jean Bleuse, Jesuit rector of Pont-à-Mousson, to send Gazi a *mandatum* so that he could serve the university in general and the Scottish-Irish College in particular. The *mandatum* would authorize him to collect revenues. Income was low and debts high. The college finally closed at the end of the academic year 1589–90.[123] After his return from the congregation of procurators in Rome

---

[121] Crichton to Acquaviva, Antwerp October 23, 1593, ARSI, Germ. 171, fols 290^{r-v} (published in Medina, "Crichton's Mission," pp. 321–22.

[122] Castelli to Como, Paris February 7, 1582, in *Correspondance du Nonce en France Giovanni Battista Castelli (1581–1583)*, (ed.) Robert Toupin, S.J. (Rome/Paris, 1967), p. 263. Ogilvie entered the Society in Rome September 8/18, 1583 (ARSI, Rom. 169, fol. 17^r; ARSI, Rom. 171A, fol. 90^r).

[123] Acquaviva to Jean Bleuse, Rome November 13, 1589, ARSI, Franc. 1/II, fols 344^{r-v}; Auguste Carayon, S.J., *Documents Inédits Concernant la Compagnie de Jésus* (23 parts in 14 vols, Poitiers, 1863–1886), part 22, pp. 274–78; McCoog, *Society of Jesus*, pp. 219, 264;

in November of 1591,[124] Tyrie was sent to Pont-à-Mousson perhaps as an attempt to save the institution.[125] His stay was brief: in February of 1592 he was summoned to Rome to become the general's assistant. But by then the institution was saved and Crichton assumed direction of it and the mission itself in early 1593.

In his negotiations with Philip, Crichton sought to establish a Scottish college for the sons of the Catholic nobles. Presumably this would not be a new foundation but the continuation of the Scottish-Irish College. Acquaviva supported this project enthusiastically and on June 10, 1591, he informed the Belgian provincial Oliver Mannaerts that Crichton would be sent to Flanders to work with the Society's seminaries.[126] Because of pressing negotiations in Spain, including funding for the Jesuit mission to Scotland, Crichton postponed the college's foundation in July of 1592.[127] By April 21, 1593 Crichton reported that the four students in the college now situated in Douai were doing well, but financial problems remained. He hoped that Tyrie's and the general's efforts to obtain more papal subsidies would be successful. Besides seeking papal aid, Acquaviva recommended the college and its needs to the Belgian vice-provincial, Jean d'Heur. By October, Crichton was optimistic that Spanish subsidies would be increased.[128] As 1593 ended the college had weathered a financial storm and was relatively secure and stabile.

"Reducing disloyal subjects to obedience": The Foundation of the College of St Omers

Continued military involvement in France stretched Spanish resources and drained what little money the treasury held. Nonetheless Robert Parsons successfully begged Philip to endow and support English colleges and seminaries. On March 22, 1593 he informed Acquaviva that he had finally

---

Hubert Chadwick, S.J., "The Scots College, Douai, 1580–1613," *English Historical Review*, 56 (1941): p. 580; and Medina, "Escocia en la Estrategia," pp. 85–86.

[124] A congregation of procurators was generally held in Rome every three years to advise the superior general on the necessity of a general congregation. Each province held a provincial congregation to discuss that issue and any other concerns, and elected a procurator.

[125] Acquaviva to James Tyrie, Rome April 6, 1591, ARSI, Franc. 1/II, fols 364^{r-v}.

[126] Acquaviva to Mannaerts, Rome June 10, 1591, ARSI, Fl. Belg. 1/I, pp. 473–74.

[127] Crichton to Acquaviva, Madrid July 18, 1592, ARSI, Tolet. 37a, fols 225^r–226^v (published in Medina, "Crichton's Mission," pp. 320–21; and "Escocia en la Estrategia," p. 99).

[128] Crichton to Acquaviva, Douai April 21, 1593, ARSI, Germ. 171, fols 136^r–137^v; same to same, Antwerp October 23, 1593, ARSI, Germ. 171, fols 290^r–91^v; Acquaviva to Jean d'Heur, Rome August 21, 1593, Fl. Belg. 1/I, p. 521.

received letters-patent authorizing payment of monies promised by Philip to support the new colleges in Valladolid and Seville. Moreover the king contributed a further 1920 ducats to maintain 16 boys at a new seminary to be founded at St Omers in the Spanish Netherlands.[129]

Contrary to assertions of some earlier historians, Leo Hicks, S.J., has demonstrated quite clearly the English College established at St Omers was a new foundation and not a continuation of an earlier college in Eu, a Guise foundation and a victim of the French religious wars. Proposals for the transfer of this college were abandoned for various reasons and a new project initiated.[130] The immediate cause was new legislation against recusants proposed in Parliament in February of 1593. Among clauses designed to reduce "disloyal subjects to obedience" was the injunction that children be taken from recusant parents at the age of seven and placed in Protestant households. There they would be raised in the Established Church at their parents' expense. William Cecil, Lord Burghley, counselled the queen, "you [Elizabeth] shall under colour of education, have them [the children] as hostages of their parents' fidelities, that have power in England, and by this their number will be quickly lessened" once the proposal was approved.[131] Outraged by the proposed legislation Parsons broached the possibility of another Spanish-sponsored college intended for English Catholic boys whose faith would be threatened by the new legislation.[132] Philip approved an annual subsidy of 1,920 ducats and promised further assistance if the number of students exceeded 16. St Omers was selected as the site of the new venture because of its proximity to Calais, Gravelines, and Dunkirk.[133] Like the Spaniards, Flemish authorities worried about the presence of so many Englishmen near the frontier, so the king insisted that

---

[129] ARSI, Hisp. 135, fols 147^r–149^v. In a letter to Pope Clement VIII written from Seville on April 15, 1593, Parsons described the wonderful progress enjoyed by the three new English seminaries (ABSI, Coll P I 327–29).

[130] "The Foundation of the College of St Omers," *AHSI*, 19 (1950): pp. 146–80; see also Hubert Chadwick, S.J., *St Omers to Stonyhurst* (London, 1962), pp. 10–42.

[131] Quoted in Hicks, "St Omers," p. 158.

[132] For an account of the difficulties encountered by a few Catholic boys as they attempted to leave England to study on the continent, see Dom Bede Camm, O.S.B., "The Adventures of Some Church Students in Elizabethan Days," *The Month*, 91 (1898): pp. 375–85.

[133] Regarding a dispute over the site see Parsons to Acquaviva, Valladolid June 16, 1593, ARSI, Hisp. 135, fols 306^r–07^v; same to same, Valladolid July 15, 1593, ARSI, Hisp. 135, fols 372^r–374^v; same to same, Valladolid August 11, 1593, ARSI, Hisp. 136, fols 14^r–15^v; Hicks, "St Omers," pp. 162–63; and Chadwick, *St Omers to Stonyhurst*, pp. 16–17. Cardinal Allen wanted the new college to be situated in Douai in anticipation of the English College's return from Reims (see Acquaviva to Parsons, Rome May 10, 1593, ARSI, Baet. 3/I, p. 115). I do not know how Parsons convinced him that St Omers was a better site.

the Jesuit rector of the college be a Belgian.[134] Parliament did not enact this offensive clause into law, but the college begun at St Omers continues to flourish at Stonyhurst.

Oliver Mannaerts, former German assistant and vicar-general after the death of Everard Mercurian in 1580, was now provincial of Belgium. In the deliberations over a Jesuit mission to England and in subsequent negotiations, Mannaerts consistently favored the Society's efforts there.[135] Perhaps assuming that Mannaerts would endorse the proposed foundation, Parsons sought his approval before his departure for Rome to attend a general congregation. Thus Parsons exhorted Acquaviva to expedite the matter. He recommended Henry Broy and Nicholas Smith be appointed minister and prefect of studies, and William Flack, recently arrived from Spain, spiritual prefect.[136] William Holt could serve as liaison between the college and the royal court in Brussels. Until the arrival of the royal subsidy, Parsons solicited aid from other benefactors and, if needed, he would seek contributions from the other seminaries. All that was required from Mannaerts was a Belgian rector and a lay brother assistant. Because of the work's importance and the support of the king, Mannaerts promised all possible assistance once he had received Acquaviva's permission.[137] Mannaerts nominated Jean Foucart as rector on June 21, 1593;[138] the general gave his approval on July 31, 1593. Because Foucart was serving as assistant to the vice-provincial, Jean d'Heur, who, in turn was acting provincial during Mannaerts's absence in Rome, he was unable to assume office immediately. Until then William Flack was acting superior.[139]

William Flack, who had left San Lucar for St Omers on April 8, 1593, accepted the college's first students as discussions were under way

---

[134] Hicks, "St Omers," pp. 157–62.

[135] See McCoog, *Society of Jesus*, pp. 132–33.

[136] On Broy, Flack, and Smith see McCoog, *Monumenta Angliae*, vol. 2, pp. 251, 311, 480.

[137] From Toledo on March 22, 1593 Parsons suggested "should all else fail, it seems to me that the other seminaries would have to contribute to the support of this one, for it is destined to be the source of supply for them all, in as much as it will send them subjects to study philosophy with them" (ARSI, Hisp. 135, fol. 147^r). See also same to same, Seville April 19, 1593, ARSI, Hisp. 135, fols 187^r–188^v; same to same, Valladolid June 16, 1593, ARSI, Hisp. 135, fols 306^r–307^v; Hicks, "St Omers," pp. 161–62.

[138] On Foucart see McCoog, *Monumenta Angliae*, vol. 2, p. 319.

[139] Mannaerts to Acquaviva, Tournai June 21, 1593, ARSI, Germ. 171, fols 189^{r-v}; Acquaviva to Mannaerts, Rome July 31, 1593, ARSI, Fl. Belg. 1/1, p. 519; Oranus [d'Heur] to Acquaviva, Liège September 22, 1593, ARSI, Germ. 171, fols 273^{r-v}; Parsons to Acquaviva, Valladolid August 11, 1593, ARSI, Hisp. 136, fols 14^r–15^v; Acquaviva to Parsons, Rome August 30, 1593, ARSI, Cast. 6, fols 163^{r-v}; same to same, Rome September 27, 1593, ARSI, Cast. 6, fol. 164^v; Parsons to Acquaviva, Madrid December 4, 1593, ARSI, Hisp. 136, fols 163^r–164^v.

regarding the college's rector. Immediate problems included fear of English spies, and demands from Belgian secular authorities that English students lodge with Belgian students, or in already established student hostels, or with Jesuits who taught at the Belgian college.[140] Once their concerns were assuaged, Flack moved into a small residence with seven students. Rapid increase of students created a new problem: the royal foundation provided for 16 students but within six months there were 19. Again the municipal authorities complained, and only assurances that the royal pension would still be sufficient to support the larger number, silenced them.[141]

As St Omers would often learn, Spanish promises flowed more freely than Spanish money. The pledged support was not forthcoming, and contingency funds, dangerously low. Only the personal intercession of Henry Walpole finally succeeded in obtaining the promised royal grant. In a royal audience before his departure for the English mission, Walpole thanked the king for his consistent generosity towards the English seminaries, and reminded him of the importance of St Omers and its dependence on his aid. Prompted by the comment Philip drafted orders to his ministers on the needs of the college. The king entrusted these letters to Walpole and requested that he proceed to England via Belgium to ensure the problems' resolution. Walpole left for Belgium at the beginning of September.[142] Assisted by William Holt, Henry Walpole delivered the letters. Despite protests from some minor bureaucrats, the Jesuits obtained half the promised money. Philip also ordered city magistrates to find a larger residence closer to the Belgian college. By December a new, larger residence, albeit not the one the English wanted, was found.[143]

Parsons might have anticipated smooth relations between Mannaerts and the English College but Mannaerts's vice-provincial was a different matter. D'Heur repeatedly complained about the number of students, and worried that the new college would be crushed under the burden of a

---

[140] Parsons to Acquaviva, Seville April 19, 1593, ARSI, Hisp. 135, fols 187^r–188^v; same to same, Córdoba March 20, 1594, ARSI, Hisp. 136, fols 249^r–250^v.

[141] Parsons to Acquaviva, Madrid March 10, 1594, ARSI, Hisp. 136, fols 245^r–246^v; Hicks, "St Omers," pp. 165–66; Chadwick, *St Omers to Stonyhurst*, pp. 18–22.

[142] Father General sent William Baldwin as his replacement (Acquaviva to Parsons, Rome February 15, 1593, ARSI, Baet. 3/I, p. 100).

[143] Parsons to Acquaviva, Valladolid August 11, 1593, ARSI, Hisp. 136, fols 14^r–15^v; Walpole to Francisco de Peralta, Escorial August 2, 1593, ABSI, Anglia I, 75 (published in Augustus Jessop, (ed.), *Letters of Fa. Henry Walpole, S.J.* [Norwich, 1873], pp. 45–47); the examinations of Henry Walpole (published in John Hungerford Pollen, S.J., (ed.), *Unpublished Documents Relating to the English Martyrs (1584–1603)* [London, 1908], pp. 235, 248, 251, 253, 254, and 255); Hicks, "St Omers," pp. 166–69. Because of requests from Henry Garnet for more Jesuits in England, Parsons used the authority give him by the general to send Walpole (see the above cited letter of August 11, 1593).

heavy debt. Until the return of Mannaerts, Parsons had no alternative: he had to deal with d'Heur. Intentionally or not, d'Heur created more problems because of his critical, hesitant attitude. Parsons could do nothing to expedite the matter: the precise relationship between the English and the Belgian colleges had not been clearly defined.[144] Although English students would attend classes at the Belgian college, Parsons intended that the English College be separate and independent. However, some Belgians agitated that the English establishment be denied full collegiate status and thus its own rector. Instead they proposed that it be little more than a hostel with a superior entitled "president" subject to the Belgian rector. Parsons insisted that this college, like the ones in Rome and Spain, "have its own special rector and be immediately under the provincial like the other colleges."[145] D'Heur, however, was difficult. Parsons confided to the general:

> has shown himself colder about this business than anyone I have ever seen in my life, always making difficulties and disheartening the people who are there [St Omers]; and in spite of my having written to him so often and told him that there was no obstacle either in the matter of authorization and protection or of the money for its upkeep,–for I would be responsible for procuring both of these, and as a matter of fact, I was in the habit of sending money by every post and I am doing the same at present, although I do not think there will be any shortage,–still, I have not been able so far to put any courage into him.[146]

Parsons hoped that he could hold out until the return of Mannaerts.

---

[144] Acquaviva anticipated such problems. He believed that the Belgians at St Omers would not be happy if the new English college was established as an independent entity. Father general wanted to hear Mannaerts's views before he subjected the English college to the Belgians (Acquaviva to Parsons, Rome April 12, 1583, ARSI, Tolet. 5/1, fol. 292^r). The congregation delayed his reply.

[145] Parsons to Acquaviva, Madrid December 4, 1593, ARSI, Hisp. 136, fols 163^r–164^v; same to same, Córdoba March 20, 1594, ARSI, Hisp. 136, fols 249^r–50^v. In a letter from Madrid on June 16, 1594 Parsons explained that it was essential for the college to have its own rector because it "was the king's intention when founding it, and it is necessary in order to ensure union of hearts and to avoid quarrels" (ARSI, Hisp. 136, fol. 363^r).

[146] Seville April 18, 1594, ARSI, Hisp. 136, fol. 284^r (translated in Hicks, "St Omers," p. 169). On June 16, Parsons complained again to the general that the provincial "has hitherto always acted in a narrow and unenterprising way, giving them [English Jesuits] uncompromising orders to do certain things which might well be let alone or deferred" (ARSI, Hisp. 136, fol. 363^r).

Internal Problems within the Society of Jesus

Acquaviva's successor Father General Muzio Vitelleschi's subsequent decision to destroy correspondence and documentation dealing with the *memorialista* controversy in an attempt to heal the still sensitive wounds, makes it impossible to ascertain Parsons's precise role in the resolution of tension between Philip and the Society of Jesus. We catch only glimpses of Parsons's activity from the few letters that have survived.[147] In a letter of June 12, 1589 Acquaviva told Parsons of his delight that the king accepted José de Acosta and González Dávila as visitors. He praised the former as "more prudent, virtuous and judicious" and he thought that their, his and Acosta's, friendship would be an advantage. Regarding the *"perturbati"* [disturbers] Acquaviva stressed the importance of moderation with due consideration of time and place in the application of medicine (*"andare con temperamento applicando le medicine a tempo et luogo"*). Parsons could use his influence to lift all barriers that hindered a settlement favorable to Acquaviva. Parsons played an important role but, as Acquaviva explained, a defense of truth against such lies would not be difficult. Acquaviva also asked Parsons to persuade Philip to address a letter fulsome of praise for the Society and its Institute to Pope Sixtus V. Several German princes had already done so but more letters were needed to counteract the memorials defaming the general and attacking his governance. Different sources had already informed Acquaviva *"inquieti nostri"* [our disturbers] hoped to forward new memorials to demonstrate that the appointment of visitors had not eliminated any of the abuses plaguing the Society. To prevent further ruin, Philip should be encouraged to silence the malcontents.[148]

José de Acosta and González Dávila toured their respective provinces from 1589 to 1591. Neither had an easy task and both were often attacked by *memorialistas* and by Acquaviva's supporters. Don Francisco de Abreo, a *memorialista* who continued to live in a Jesuit community despite his dismissal from the Society in 1591, levelled charge after charge against Acosta. A Father Lugo provided ammunition for this attack. Some complained of the *pro forma* nature of Acosta's visitation. To them Acosta did not address any problems. On the other hand Acquaviva's supporters groaned that Acosta maligned them. Acosta completed his tour and submitted his report by the end of the summer of 1591. He waited six months for a reply from Acquaviva. Meanwhile nothing was being done. The Inquisition, noting the

---

[147] See for example [Parsons] to [Acquaviva], Madrid June [1592], ARSI, Fondo Gesuitico 651/616 and Acquaviva to Parsons, Rome August 30, 1593, ARSI, Cast. 6, fols 163^{r-v}.

[148] Acquaviva to Parsons, Rome June 12, 1589, ARSI, Tolet. 4, fols 53^v–55^v. The cipher for the code used in this letter can be found in ARSI, Fondo Gesuitico 678/21/2.

lack of any effective change, urged Philip II to name a more competent non-Jesuit visitor. Acosta feared that Acquaviva's slow pace would result in the embarrassing, unwanted intrusion of a non-Jesuit visitor. From mid April of 1592, Acosta was superior of the professed house in Valladolid. During Philip II's visit of Valladolid the following August, during which he received a lavish welcome at the English College, a Spanish minister asked Acosta to embark on a special royal mission: to persuade Pope Clement VIII to convoke a general congregation. Believing a general congregation preferable to a non-Jesuit visitor, Acosta, with the approval of his provincial, set off for Rome. In December of 1592, under pressure from Philip II, Pope Clement VIII ordered Acquaviva to convene a congregation to treat the Society's internal problems. Acquaviva blamed Acosta for this turn of events. By March of 1593 Acquaviva felt so betrayed that he ordered Alonso Sánchez to arrange a meeting with the king in order to discredit Acosta.[149]

Each Jesuit province convened a provincial congregation in 1593 in preparation for the general congregation. Forty Jesuits, some *ex officio* as rectors and provincials and others professed of the fourth vow in order of seniority, attended. Each province sent its provincial along and two delegates. The provincial congregations elected the delegates and proposed *postulata*, issues or topics for discussion and resolution.[150]

At the French provincial congregation in January of 1593, a complaint, variations of which would echo throughout other congregations was first heard. The fathers asked that the general congregation find a "method ... to prevent ours from thrusting themselves in any way into the business of princes and the making of wars. For experience has taught that up to this time evil has resulted and such behaviour has even given offense to many princes."[151] A *postulatum* of the Roman provincial assembly in May urged that the general congregation find some way to prevent Jesuits from involving themselves in public affairs pertaining to altering the state or the kingdom or to the government thereof.[152] In the same month, Jesuits in Belgium asked the general congregation "to consider what means can be taken to keep ours, whether living in colleges or

---

[149] I follow Burgaleta's interpretation as opposed to the traditional account of Antonio Astráin, S.J., who argued that Acosta turned against Acquaviva out of pique because he was not appointed provincial. See *José de Acosta*, pp. 60–63, 127–31.

[150] On the complicated diversity of grades within the Society of Jesus, see Ladislaus Lukács, S.J., "De graduum diversitate inter sacerdotes in Societate Iesu," *AHSI*, 37 (1968): pp. 237–316. An English summary can be found in Ignatius of Loyola, *Constitutions*, pp. 349–56. On congregations see *Constitutions*, nums 679, 682, 692, 755, 782, pp. 294–95, 299, 315–16, 321–22.

[151] ARSI, Congr. 46, fol. 160ᵛ.

[152] ARSI, Congr. 45, fol. 6ʳ.

employed in the courts of princes, from adhering to princes, as we learn that very many are doing, to the great loss of their spiritual advancement and discipline."[153] Again in the province of Lyons, the fathers asked that the congregation:

> consider some way by which it would be less easy for ours to insinuate themselves into the goodwill and familiarity of princes, whether of the Church or secular, in order that in turn they may by that intimacy wrest what they want from superiors; for example, to approach princes again and again; to be present with them ordinarily or at least too much; to be engaged by them in matters not very much in keeping with our Institute; to live, to teach, to preach in one place rather than another; to perform this rather than that office; and other matters of this sort. Especially since in this way the avenue can easily lie open to ambition and to chasing after positions of dignity.[154]

In November, the Venetian provincial congregation asked: "Whereas it seems good that ours be in no way allowed to thrust themselves not only by deed but even by word into what relates to the temporal rule and government of states and empires, to the end that secular princes and republics may at last put an end to the opinion about us formed long ago and greatly strengthened in recent times to the great loss of spiritual good."[155] The province of Aquitaine drafted an important variation in June. It asked some inquiry be made into those who, by their silence, aided the cause of the *politici* or *politiques*.[156] Interestingly none of the Spanish provinces raised the issue. Nonetheless, prompted by these *postulata* the general congregation passed two decrees forbidding Jesuit involvement in secular affairs.[157] It has been suggested that the decrees of the general congregation were specifically directed against Robert Parsons.[158] However, Parsons was not mentioned in any of the *postulata*. More likely, concern for Jesuit involvement in secular and political affairs stemmed, on the one hand, from the religious wars in France and, on the

---

[153] ARSI, Congr. 46, fols 276ʳ, 283ʳ.

[154] ARSI, Congr. 46, fol. 173ʳ.

[155] ARSI, Congr. 45, fol. 57ᵛ.

[156] ARSI, Congr. 46, fols 184ᵛ, 185ᵛ. Pedro de Ribadeneira labeled *politiques* "ministers of Satan" because they placed political concerns ahead of religious ones (Bireley, *Counter-Reformation Prince*, p. 119).

[157] John W. Padberg, S.J., Martin D. O'Keefe, S.J. and John L. McCarthy, S.J., (eds.), *For Matters of Greater Moment: The First Thirty Jesuit General Congregations* (St Louis, 1994), decrees 47–48, p. 200.

[158] See, for example, Adrian Morley, *The Catholic Subjects of Elizabeth I* (London, 1978), p. 125.

other, from the support provided by Philip II to Spanish Jesuits in their conflict with Acquaviva. We shall return to this congregation and the decrees in question in Chapter 4.

Conclusion

In his instructions of 1588, Acquaviva permitted Parsons to depart for Flanders upon completion of his work in Spain. He never made the journey perhaps because Spain became the gateway to England and the king, the porter. English, Irish, and Scottish Catholics independently and/or collectively looked to Philip for financial and/or military assistance. He endowed their seminaries and considered their proposals for invasions. Parsons successfully obtained an increase in the pension to the English College in Douai and royal support for new foundations at Valladolid, and St Omers. Irish colleges in Lisbon and Salamanca benefited from the royal purse. William Crichton sought Spanish funds for a Scottish College during his stay in Madrid. Parsons concluded agreements with Spanish provincials to place at least two English Jesuits in their provinces, presumably without expense to the mission.[159] Apparently around spring of 1589 Parsons and/or Acquaviva abandoned plans for centering the English mission in Flanders in favor of Spain. This placed even greater burdens on Parsons. Acquaviva worried about Parsons's health and admonished him in 1589 that he must not allow various projects, albeit important to the Society and to England, to weaken him. Father General promised him an assistant. For the short term he hoped to obtain a Spaniard; for the long term, he had written to the Austrian provincial to request William Brakenbury but before the letter was posted, the general discovered that Brakenbury had in fact died.[160] A month later Acquaviva asked Gonzalo de Avila to assign someone to Parsons.[161] The difficulty was eventually resolved with the reorganization of the mission and the arrival of Creswell in 1593.

With the foundation of three new colleges, a new administrative structure for the mission's governance evolved gradually. The two colleges in Spain and the English College in Rome, were administered but not owned by the Society. Papal bulls had named Cardinal Allen overseer of the Spanish seminaries with Parsons as his delegate. Parsons, thus, had

---

[159] Parsons to Creswell, Alcalá April 28, 1589, ABSI, Coll P II 479 (published in Pollen, "Annals of the English College," pp. 18–19).

[160] Acquaviva to Parsons, Rome April 17, 1589, ARSI, Tolet. 5/I, fols 58ʳ⁻ᵛ. On Brakenbury see McCoog, *Monumenta Angliae*, vol. 2, p. 243 (under Brakenburius).

[161] Acquaviva to Gonzalo de Avila, Rome May 15, 1589, ARSI, Tolet. 5/I, fols 59ᵛ–60ʳ.

powers of presentation and visitation to the chaplaincies of the Church of St George in San Lucar. But Allen held no authority over the English College in St Omers. So with what authority did Parsons intervene in its teething problems? With Foucart's nomination as rector by a Belgian provincial and approved by the general, Parsons's precise authority was, at best, nebulous. As superior of English Jesuits, he negotiated with royal and papal authorities, sent men to new posts in Spain and the Spanish Netherlands,[162] arranged for their acceptance of candidates into the novitiates of different provinces,[163] selected missioners for England,[164] and maintained contact with those already there. But how could this authority be translated into practical terms and how did it fit in with the legitimate constitutional and institutional authority that rectors and provincials held within the Society?

With fewer institutions and men, the Scottish and Irish missions did not encounter comparable organizational problems. With no Jesuits in Ireland, there was no need for someone to coordinate relations between the mission and the Irish colleges. James Archer was vice-rector of the Irish College in Salamanca but his jurisdiction did not extend beyond the college. As superior of the Scottish mission, William Crichton, however,

---

[162] On July 15, 1593 Parsons requested from Acquaviva authority to transfer English Jesuits: "There are some English fathers of the Society in Flanders and others here [Valladolid]," he explained, "whom it would be necessary to move or exchange for the advantage of these seminaries or for their own consolation, and asking therefore if your Paternity would be agreeable that, in cases of urgency and when it was not convenient to await a reply from Rome, we here with the sanction of the fathers provincial here and in Flanders, who would be chiefly concerned in this matter, should have power to summon an individual here or send him there, reporting everything afterwards to your Paternity" (ARSI, Hisp. 135, fol. 372^r). Acquaviva gave permission on August 30 (ARSI, Cast. 6, fols 163^{r-v}). On November 2, Parsons "humbly thank[ed] your paternity for the authority you give me to further this work of ours of the Seminaries by the interchange between this country and Flanders, when necessary, of some of the English members of the Society" (ARSI, Hisp. 136, fol. 107^r). By December 16, Holt had received word that Parsons had been granted this permission (Holt to Acquaviva, Brussels December 16, 1593, ARSI, Germ. 171, fols 320^{r-v}). The authority was restricted to the English working in the seminaries and did not include all Englishmen in the Society. In the letter of November 2, Parsons sought the general's assistance in obtaining the services of Oswald Tesimond who had expressed a desire to work in Spain.

[163] From Seville on May 10, 1594, Parsons wrote to Acquaviva that he had just heard from Henry Garnet that the general had given permission to accept twelve men into the Society and that Garnet was, thus, sending four more to Flanders (ARSI, Hisp. 136, fols 316^{r-v}). It seems, therefore, that the acceptance of men in England into the Society could be done without the approval and knowledge of Parsons.

[164] Parsons received this authority by mid-1593. In a letter to the general from Valladolid on August 11, 1593, regarding sending Henry Walpole to England, Parsons wrote "I judged it necessary to make use of the authority which your paternity had given me to send Henry Walpole" (ARSI, Hisp. 136, fol. 14^r).

supervised the new Scottish College in Douai and oversaw Jesuits working in the kingdom. Placement of Scottish novices was also a concern for him. Because there were a number of Scottish candidates who could not endure the Roman climate, Crichton asked Acquaviva to grant concessions to the Scots similar to those given to the English, that is, that such candidates could enter novitiates outside Rome, specifically in Belgium.[165]

In a letter to Don Juan de Idiáquez from Seville on April 4, 1591, Parsons frankly noted his shock and disappointment over official reaction to the conversion of many English galley slaves. The converts had made an unspecified offer of goodwill "with such love and at such great personal risk and loss" in return for resettlement in England. The offer's rejection would not further the king's interests. To believe that Spain could prevail in England without having supporters within the kingdom was "a very great illusion." An even greater illusion was the conviction that such a faction could develop without conscious effort on the part of Spain. But for reasons Parsons never understood, Spain did not trust English Catholics. The Armada revealed this to the world. Then more than at any other time Philip needed assistance from his English sympathizers; instead they were entirely ignored. No English Catholic, either within or without the kingdom, was taken into the royal confidence even though there were many who had devoted their lives in Philip's service and were eager to help. Rumors circulated—and Parsons knew them to be true—that principal ministers of Spain claimed that they were unaware that there were any Catholics within England. Nor would these ministers believe anyone claiming the contrary. In fact they doubted the sincerity of any Englishman, for example the galley slaves, wishing to convert. God punished Spain for its treatment of English Catholics with the Armada's failure. Unless the ministers corrected this attitude, there was no hope that God would allow "the genuine reformation of that kingdom." Spanish suspicions of foreigners, whether individuals or regiments of soldiers, hindered a successful outcome of the enterprise, and alienated many potential friends.[166] One wonders whether Philip considered his support of so many seminaries as attempts at forming a body of supporters.

Less than a fortnight later, Parsons wrote to Paolo Camillo, Cardinal Sfondrata, recently appointed secretary of state and elevated to the cardinalate on December 19, 1590 by his uncle Pope Gregory XIV. He recalled with joy their meeting in Milan in 1580 as he and Edmund Campion travelled to England. News of the papal election of his uncle raised hopes of English Catholics, hopes intensified by the cardinal's own

---

[165] Crichton to Acquaviva, Antwerp October 23, 1593, ARSI, Germ. 171, fols 290^{r-v}.

[166] ABSI, Coll P I 246–47 (published in Knox, *Letters of Allen*, pp. 329–32). See also Edwards, *Robert Persons*, pp. 145–46.

promotion. Joseph Creswell had shown the cardinal a personal letter from Parsons because of his interest "in the business treated of in that letter." Although Parsons did not disclose the nature of that business, Parsons's reaction to the cardinal's interest was a great hope that "God is going to make great use of your eminence in this great work," a thinly veiled reference to the enterprise. Anyone who has pondered the matter, Parsons argued, would conclude that "the restoration of Christianity throughout the world hangs more on this than on anything else imaginable, seeing that all other remedies save this alone are incapable of curing the root of the evil." Cardinal Allen remained the "cornerstone" of the endeavor; Parsons, on his part, was dispirited by careless methods and missed opportunities. Nonetheless, "we must conform our wills to that of Our Lord, and who knows whether Our Lord has not reserved this matter to be the chief crown of this pontificate." It was general opinion, however, that the enterprise could be executed more easily than some argued. But, if the enterprise was to be successful, it must derive its strength from, and be directed by the Holy See. Collaboration was not sufficient "but all the enthusiasm, push, guidance, and other vital elements must flow from there [Rome] otherwise ... there is small hope."[167] Prospects that Gregory would act as decisively against Elizabeth as he had done when he renewed Henry's excommunication vanished when he died on October 15, 1591.

Acquaviva instructed Parsons to execute all his duties "without any intervention into military matters." That, however, did not prevent Parsons from lobbying for another Spanish attempt to reform the English Church through an invasion, and from disagreeing with Crichton over Scotland's role. Many Jesuits worried that such advice and encouragement was not in keeping with the Society's "way of proceeding." Surely such secular affairs should be left to the laity. For Parsons and Crichton the line separating secular from spiritual was not as clear. Zeal for the restoration of the true faith to their countries and concern for the salvation of their compatriots naturally prompted them to advise and assist anyone who could bring about their goals.

---

[167] Archivio segreto vaticano, Segreteria di Stato, Spagna 38, fols 420^r–421^v.

CHAPTER 3

"Lurking Papists": Treasons, Plots, Conspiracies, and Martyrdoms, 1594–1595

Introduction

Rumors circulated that King Henry IV had initiated secret negotiations with King Philip II despite prior promises to Queen Elizabeth that he would never seek a separate peace. If the rumors were true and if said negotiations were successful, England and Holland would have faced a strong Spanish army and a navy sufficiently recovered from the fiasco of 1588 without French support. With Ireland on the verge of rebellion on the western front, and Scottish Catholic earls plotting an incursion through the back door in the north, England felt justifiably threatened. Catholic propagandists on the continent stirred the pot by accusing Elizabeth of encouraging Turkish attacks on the eastern flank of the Holy Roman Empire. Even Lutherans of Scandinavia, Danzig and the Hanseatic Towns of northern Germany complained about English interference with their trade with the Iberian peninsula. "Unless new policy initiatives were taken," R.B. Wernham summarized England's predicament, "England might find herself faced by the more or less open hostility of almost the whole of Europe."[1] One initiative was a curious attempt to use English Catholic exiles as England extended "peace feelers" to Spain and Rome.

Peace Feelers and Possible Toleration

William, Lord Burghley, and Sir Thomas Heneage employed John Arden, a Chichester Catholic whose brother Robert was a Jesuit,[2] as a spy in Madrid and Rome. In February of 1593 John Arden visited Rome from Venice.

---

[1] R.S. Wernham, "Queen Elizabeth I, the Emperor Rudolph II, and Archduke Ernest, 1593–94," in *Politics and Society in Reformation Europe: Essays for Sir Geoffrey Elton on his Sixty-Fifth Birthday*, (eds.) E.I. Kouri and Tom Scott (New York, 1987), p. 438.

[2] On Robert Arden see Thomas M. McCoog, S.J., (ed.), *Monumenta Angliae* (2 vols, Rome, 1992), vol. 2, pp. 214–15. Interestingly he was dismissed from the Society on November 13, 1593 *post hoc* or *propter hoc*?

Because his brother was not in the city, he called on William, Cardinal Allen.[3] Upon Robert Arden's return to Rome the following month, the two brothers and Cardinal Allen had an audience with Pope Clement VIII at which someone suggested that peace between Spain and England could be restored if Elizabeth named her successor and arranged for his/her marriage to Prince Philip or his sister Infanta Isabella Eugenia, and granted liberty of conscience to her subjects. John Arden relayed the proposals to the queen. By June 18, Arden was back in Venice.[4] In the summer of 1593 an unnamed English privy councillor, perhaps Heneage, approached Allen through Richard Hopkins, the cardinal's agent in Antwerp, regarding a peaceful resolution of the Anglo-Spanish war that would include toleration for Catholics. It is unclear whether this proposal resulted from Arden's letter or was an independent overture. Hopkins relayed the message to Allen in Rome on July 10. Allen's excitement can be noted in his reply.[5] The councillor solicited Allen's views on reasonable conditions necessary for Catholic toleration. Believing that "God himself hath stirred up in their hearts this motion for the saving of that realm from the present fears and dangers and perplexities it is fallen into," Allen was eager to provide some comfort to his afflicted Catholic friends and "also to serve most faithfully and profitably even my very enemies; though otherwise than through these unfortunate differences and debates in religion (our God forgive the author thereof) I know I have none ... " Anxious to work for the good of the commonweal, Allen promised to do whatever he could. However, he demanded some assurance that the agent had authorization for such negotiations. Without such guarantees, Allen would not raise the matter with Pope Clement VIII and Philip II. Once his credentials were established and Allen was informed of the exact nature of the toleration intended by the English government, the cardinal maintained "we may induce his Holiness to take this motion to heart and to proceed carefully,

---

[3] Eamon Duffy is the only historian to touch on this episode in Allen's career ("William, Cardinal Allen, 1532–1594," *Recusant History*, 22 [1995]: p. 287).

[4] R.B. Wernham, *The Return of the Armadas: The Last Years of the Elizabethan War against Spain 1595–1603* (Oxford, 1994), pp. 9–10. See also R.B. Wernham, *List and Analysis of State Papers Foreign Series: Elizabeth I* (7 vols, London, 1964–2000), vol. 4, paras. 638–48, 650. John Arden later warned England of possible trouble in the north: "for certainly the King of Spain had some great matters in hand, though few knew what for certain." There was talk of another armada but no one knew whether it was headed for Flanders, France, England, or Scotland. See Wernham, *List and Analysis*, vol. 5, para. 684.

[5] Wernham, citing Arnold Oskar Meyer, *England and the Catholic Church under Queen Elizabeth* (London, 1916), pp. 359–64, claimed that Allen was "considerably disillusioned by the disaster to the 1588 Armada about the chances of winning England back to the Roman fold by force, by Spanish force" (*Return of the Armadas*, p. 9).

steadily and effectually in the same." In conclusion he begged Hopkins to make it clear to the unnamed agents:

> wishing them if they mean sincerely, as I do faithfully and as before God and my soul for their general and particular good desire it, to send over some one or two of their civil or temporal wise lawyers of catholic inclination, void of passion and partiality, that know how far the state of the realm may comport [with] the exercise of the catholic religion, and how far the Queen and Council can be contented to condescend therein for a firm and stable peace.

Upon the arrival of the lawyers Allen commissioned Hopkins to select Catholic lay and spiritual leaders to discuss the terms with them. The accepted articles should then be forwarded to Allen, who would present them to the pope. Alternatively, with license from the English queen, the participants might prefer to conduct the negotiations in Rome. If so, Allen would obtain protection for them, procure their passports and arrange a papal audience.[6]

Hopkins received Allen's reply on September 11 and forwarded the letter to the Privy Council in England, dispatching it in such a secure way that he was certain of its arrival. In a memorandum sent to Don Antonio Folch y Cardona, fourth Duke of Sessa and Spanish ambassador in Rome, on December 11, 1593, Allen commented that he still had not received a reply. Perhaps, Allen opined, the English government hesitated until as they observed the unfolding of events in France, and the possible effects of the imminent arrival of Archduke Ernst in Brussels.[7] Nonetheless John Arden returned to Rome in the autumn.[8] In another audience with the pope, Arden claimed that Elizabeth hoped that their original proposal would produce beneficial results for all concerned, but she insisted that her subjects in exile, cease writing against her and refrain from further activities directed against her, and that Philip II promise that he would no longer

---

[6] Allen to Hopkins, Rome August 14, 1593, published in Thomas Francis Knox, (ed.), *The Letters and Memorials of William Cardinal Allen (1532–1594)* (London, 1882), pp. 348–51.

[7] Published in Penelope Renold, (ed.), *Letters of William Allen and Richard Barret 1572–1598* (London, 1967), pp. 235–40.

[8] There is some confusion about the precise date. Wernham (*Return of the Armadas*, p. 10) stated that it was in October. Assuming Arden was the unnamed English intelligencer mentioned in Allen's report to the duke of Sessa, he was with the cardinal on 9 November (Renold, *Letters of Allen and Barret*, pp. 236, 238). On this identification see Renold, *Letters of Allen and Barret*, pp. 230 n. 1, 240 n. 4. On Arden's second visit see Wernham, *List and Analysis*, vol. 5, paras 624–29. Arden claimed that, in reply to the question why he had associated so closely with Spain, Allen confessed that books had been written in order to secure the favor of the Spanish king who supported the exiles (para. 625).

disturb her or her dominions. If these conditions were granted, she would not refuse any proposal not detrimental to her state or person.[9] Through Arden, Allen sent a second letter to Queen Elizabeth. Whether this would elicit a reply, Allen did not know. However the cardinal confided to Sessa that he now doubted England's sincerity. England's peace overtures, the cardinal believed, were designed to influence Pope Clement VIII's reaction to Henry IV's conversion: it was more likely that the pope would lift Henry's excommunication and approve his succession if a general peace and toleration for Catholics in England followed. On the other hand, he continued, fear that the continuation of the war would have disastrous consequences for a peaceful succession upon the death of the queen was strong. For this reason the government was eager to reach some accord. Consequently Allen advised Sessa that they proceed cautiously "not to be too trusting, and to suspect always the worst rarely leads a man to be deceived." Moreover, "under the shadow of this negotiation and treating with the English with this hope of peace, his Majesty could cover whatever plan he has for the impresa of England."

Not all Catholic exiles were as enthusiastic about England's peace feelers as Cardinal Allen. Jesuits Joseph Creswell, William Holt, and Robert Parsons, along with Hugh Owen drafted a memorial to Philip II and Archduke Ernst on the English overtures. Albert J. Loomie, S.J., dated the memorial August of 1594 and associated it with a request for a passport for Sir Thomas Wilkes so that he could carry letters to the archduke.[10] It may, however, have been written nearly a year earlier at the very inception of these secret dealings. But, regardless of the date, this memorial contains nothing as positive as Allen's cautious enthusiasm. Indeed, one wonders if the authors knew about Allen's role in Arden's diplomatic strategies, and whether the cardinal would have approved of their opposition. Describing English religious differences and highlighting divisions among the English regarding succession to the throne, the authors argued that "all the resources of the English heretics are used in keeping nearby states of Flanders, France and Scotland in a state of unrest."[11] Hoping to regain Flushing and other Dutch ports, the English did not seriously pursue peace, but simply exploited the discussions to masquerade their efforts and deceive their enemies. Fearful of the strength and influence of Catholic exiles, the government used spies and agents to foment disagreement among them and to discredit their leaders. With few exceptions, all Catholics in England and in exile considered Cardinal

---

[9] Wernham, *Return of the Armadas*, p. 10.

[10] "Fr. Joseph Creswell's *Información* for Philip II and the Archduke Ernest, *ca.* August 1594," *Recusant History*, 22 (1995): pp. 465–81.

[11] Loomie, "Joseph Creswell's *Información*," p. 471.

Allen their spokesman. He commanded the loyalty of the secular clergy educated in the English colleges on the continent, Jesuits, and Catholic lay leaders. Among the exceptions, Charles Paget and Thomas Morgan opposed Allen and his supporters because of their close connections with Spain. Paget, although receiving a Spanish pension, associated with English spies and pursued policies that opposed Spain's best interests, for example the marriage between Lady Arabella Stuart and Ranuccio Farnese, Prince of Parma. Ralph Ligons, William Tresham, Thomas Throckmorton, John Stonor, Anne, Lady Hungerford, and Owen Lewis, Bishop of Cassano, sided with Paget "however none of these is known to be dealing with spies" like Paget.[12] Cardinal Allen or, in his absence, one of his supporters should be involved in any negotiations to unmask any deception perpetrated by the English government or Paget. Finally the authors admonished the king and the archduke to remember Elizabeth's earlier perfidies: the English government could not be trusted.

A more formal exploration of the prospects of peace was the mission of the ex-Jesuit Sir Christopher Perkins (or Parkins)[13] to Holy Roman Emperor Rudolph II in Prague. Perkins defended Elizabeth against accusations of encouraging the Turks, and offered the services of Elizabeth's ambassador in Constantinople, Edward Barton, as mediator in a dispute between the Turks and the Empire. In return for Elizabeth's efforts at mediation, the queen hoped that the emperor would advise the pope and the Spanish king to pursue a peaceful resolution of their war with England, France, and Holland. The imperial response was encouraging: the offer of assistance in Constantinople was accepted; libelous pamphlets attacking Elizabeth were destroyed; and exhortations to peace were to be sent to Philip II. Despite the pleasant words, no action was taken in Constantinople and nothing was said to Philip.[14]

After the arrival of Archduke Ernst in Brussels, Burghley and his son Sir Robert Cecil recommended that the queen send an agent to remind the archduke of his brother's, the emperor's, promises to intercede with Philip.

---

[12] Loomie, "Joseph Creswell's *Información*," p. 475.

[13] On him see McCoog, *Monumenta Angliae*, vol. 2, p. 431 and Thomas M. McCoog, S.J., *The Society of Jesus in Ireland, Scotland, and England 1541–1588: 'Our Way of Proceeding?'* (Leiden, 1996), pp 159, 167 n. 131.

[14] Wernham, *Return of the Armadas*, pp. 10–12; Wernham, "Queen Elizabeth I," pp. 438–40. Richard Verstegan reported Perkins's mission in a letter to Parsons from Antwerp in late June of 1593 (Antwerp, n.d. [c. end of June 1593], ABSI, Coll B 117 [published in Anthony G. Petti, (ed.), *The Letters and Dispatches of Richard Verstegan (c. 1550–1640)* (London, 1959), p. 174]). On 4 June Verstegan reported to Roger Baynes "Mr. Perkins is with the German Diet to defend, where necessary, the conduct of the Queen of England. He has ten servants, and says mass almost every day," ARSI, Angl. 38/II, fol. 195^r (published in Petti, *Verstegan Papers*, p. 211).

In their memorandum they mentioned Barton's work on the emperor's behalf and complained that they had received nothing from the emperor regarding the continuation of these dealings. Nor, they lamented, had the emperor fulfilled his promise to urge Philip II to make peace. The best path to peace was:

> ... to withdraw these foreign forces which the King of Spain maintaineth apparently in his opinion to conquer France and consequently to subdue the Low Countries to a servitude and thereby to have commodity to invade ours as hath been determined of long time by the councillors of Spain. But if these forces may be totally removed and sent into Hungary against the common enemy, then there may be a most certain peace obtained in Christendom.[15]

The possible involvement of Spanish agents in yet another plot to assassinate the queen delayed any action.

Plots and Conspiracies

Robert Devereux, Earl of Essex and now a Privy Councillor, organized a spy network to rival that of the Cecils. Through this network, he claimed to have discovered a plot to poison Elizabeth. The culprit was her Portuguese Jewish physician Dr Rodrigo Lopez who acted with the knowledge and approval of Spanish ministers in Brussels and Philip himself. The Cecils and the queen were initially skeptical of the plot's authenticity, but confessions extracted from Emmanuel Luis Tinoco, Estevan Ferrera da Gama and on February 25, 1594 from Lopez himself, convinced them. Essex presided over Lopez's trial on February 28.[16] All three were scheduled to be executed on April 19, but Elizabeth stayed the warrant: they were eventually executed at Tyburn on June 7. Discovery of this plot along with others to be discussed later allegedly involving Spanish ministers against the queen, affected sending an agent to the archduke. According to Paul Hammer, Essex's successful prosecution of Lopez with its desired, deleterious effects on peace overtures between Spain and England signalled "his arrival as a politician whose views carried genuine weight with Elizabeth."[17]

---

[15] Cited in Wernham, "Queen Elizabeth I," p. 440.

[16] In a report from Antwerp on February 26, Verstegan notified Roger Baynes that Lopez had been racked "upon suspicion to have attempted to poison the Queen," ABSI, Coll M 81a (published in Petti, *Verstegan Papers*, p. 208).

[17] *The Polarisation of Elizabethan Politics: The Political Career of Robert Devereux, 2nd Earl of Essex, 1585–1597* (Cambridge, 1999), p. 138.

Two other plots were discovered in late 1593 or early 1594. The first resulted in the execution of Richard Hesketh on November 29, 1593. A Catholic candidate for the English throne was Ferdinando Stanley, Lord Strange, who succeeded his father Henry as earl of Derby on September 25, 1593. The secular priest John Cecil had earlier admitted that Catholics had an interest in his claims and that he had been sent to England to sound him out. Hesketh arrived in England on September 9, unaware that the earl was near death. According to the received wisdom, Sir William Stanley, a relative who had passed into the service of Spain when he surrendered Deventer in 1587, the Jesuit William Holt and other Catholic exiles sent Hesketh to encourage Lord Strange to claim the English crown upon Elizabeth's death and promised Spanish aid if he did so. Hesketh met Strange on the very day that he became earl of Derby. The earl refused to entertain any such suggestions and turned him over to the proper authorities. On the scaffold, Hesketh denounced Sir William Stanley and others. On April 16, 1594 the earl died violently. Lacking male children he was succeeded by his brother William safely married to one of Lord Burghley's daughters. If the throne passed to the English family with the best claim, the future English king was safely allied with the Cecils.[18]

The second plot followed shortly upon the execution of Lopez. Edmund Yorke, nephew of Sir Rowland Yorke, the military leader who had handed over the Sconce of Zutphen to the Spanish in 1587, had been received into the Roman Church by the Jesuit William Holt. In late spring of 1594 he petitioned Essex to obtain pardons for himself and two friends, Richard Williams and Henry Young, who had served in Sir William Stanley's regiment, so that they could return to England. Yorke contended that he had been refused his uncle's inheritance unless he swore allegiance to Philip II. This he refused to do, preferring to be a poor good subject in England. On July 30, Young, described by Martin A.S. Hume as "a rogue, poor and simple," informed the government of the true intentions of his confreres. According to Young, Yorke's story about his uncle's inheritance was contrived by William Holt as a cover for his treasonous activities. Yorke and Williams intended to stir up a rebellion in northern Wales to support an invasion devised by Sir William Stanley. The two were imprisoned in the Tower. Essex personally interrogated Yorke who confessed that Holt had commissioned him to carry out some vague mission to Scotland. He

---

[18] The only investigations of this plot are Christopher Devlin, S.J., "The Earl and the Alchemist" in *Hamlet's Divinity* (London, 1963), pp. 74–114; and Francis Edwards, S.J., *Plots and Plotters in the Reign of Elizabeth I* (Dublin, 2002), pp. 169–92. See Verstegan to Baynes, Antwerp January 8, 1594 (published in Petti, *Verstegan Papers*, p. 198 and p. 200 n. 4); and Verstegan to Parsons, Antwerp January 13, 1594, ABSI, Coll B 151–54 (published in Petti, *Verstegan Papers*, pp. 203–204) for his account of events.

was less vague about offers made by Young and Williams. He remembered both Young and Williams say that they had offered or were willing to propose to Father Holt that, in return for large sums of money, they were ready to assassinate Elizabeth. Before the assassination, Sir William Stanley would transport his forces to Scotland to seek assistance, presumably from the Catholic earls, to descend upon England to support the candidacy of the earl of Derby as soon as they heard of Elizabeth's death. Over the next month each accused the others of plotting against the government and of conspiring with the queen's enemies. Under torture Williams and Yorke broke and admitted their role in different intrigues fathered and furthered by Stanley, Holt, Charles Paget, William Gifford, and Thomas Worthington.[19] Both were condemned and executed in February of 1595.[20]

Instructed to raise the subject of assassination plots and to provide copies of the conspirators' confessions, Sir Thomas Wilkes asked the archduke to inform Philip of the accusations levelled against him. Moreover he requested that Spanish agents named in the confessions be prevented from leaving the Low Countries and that seven leading Catholic exiles, Stanley, Holt, Owen, Gifford, Paget, Worthington, and Thomas Throckmorton be returned to England for trial as traitors, and that other named exiles be deprived of Spanish pensions and banished from the Low Countries.[21] Unless Philip cleared his name and repudiated the conspirators, Elizabeth would "publish to all the world a just condemnation of him."[22] Archduke Ernst granted the requested passport, but Elizabeth and her ministers found the tone of his reply unsatisfactory especially his insistence that Wilkes treat nothing to Philip's disservice. Uncertain how to interpret that restriction, Elizabeth decided against sending her envoy.[23] In November *A true report of sundry horrible conspiracies to have taken away the life of the queenes maiestie* reviewed the involvement of Philip II, his ministers and Catholic exiles he supported, in the Hesketh, Lopez, and Yorke plots. The king especially was accused of behaving in an unchristian, unprincely, unjust and dishonorable way by supporting such ventures. Elizabeth, on the other hand, pursued her quarrel with Philip according to the moral

---

[19] Martin A.S. Hume, *Treason and Plot: Struggles for Catholic Supremacy in the Last Years of Queen Elizabeth* (London, 1901), pp. 153–61. The citation can be found on p. 154.

[20] Verstegan to Parsons, Antwerp May 25, 1595, ABSI, Anglia II, 3 (published in Petti, *Verstegan Papers*, pp. 238–39; see also p. 240 n. 8). See also Edwards, *Plots and Plotters*, pp. 236–52.

[21] On Gifford and Worthington see Godfrey Anstruther, O.P., *The Seminary Priests* (4 vols, Ware/Durham/Great Wakering, 1968–1977), vol. 1, pp. 132–33, 387–88.

[22] Cited in Wernham, "Queen Elizabeth I," p. 447.

[23] Wernham, *Return of the Armadas*, pp. 11–18; Wernham, "Queen Elizabeth I," pp. 440–49.

principles of war.[24] A French translation was prepared for distribution in France.[25] Attempts to reach a peaceful settlement with Philip thus ended; the more aggressive policy favored by the earl of Essex would now be pursued.

Neither Philip nor his ministers, however, were specifically named in a new "order for prayer and thanksgiving" issued in late 1594. An introductory admonition reminded the reader of the different detestable plots and conspiracies directed against the queen and true religion, originating in Rome, the "seat of the *Beast*," and formulated by "idolatrous *Priests* and *Jesuits* his creatures, the very loathesome *Locusts* that crawl out of the bottomless pit." "Certain *Potentates* of the earth, who do nothing else but serve themselves of that idolatrous *Romish religion*, as of a Mask and stalking-horse, therewith to cover the unsatiable ambition, wherewith they are possessed, of usurping other men's *kingdoms*" further these schemes.[26] After a recitation of the many attempts against the queen's life, prayers of thanksgiving were offered:

> ... for it hath pleased thee, of thine infinite mercy and goodness in *Christ Jesu*, so wonderfully to uphold, deliver and preserve thine *Hand-maid*, our most dread and Sovereign Queen *Elizabeth*, so many and sundry times, from the cruel and bloody treacheries of desperate men, who address themselves to all wickedness, and at this time especialy, wherein her innocent life was shot at by divers wicked designments of blood-thirsty wretches and traitors.[27]

Let those who sought her destruction be ashamed and confounded; let them fall into the pit that they had prepared for England.

Rumors of conspiracies and assassination plots circulated throughout western Europe. The Dutch had arrested a priest from Namur, Michel Renichon, who confessed that Archduke Ernst and his advisors commissioned him to assassinate Count Maurice of Nassau. Pierre Barrière was executed at St Denis in late 1593 because of his plot to stab Henry IV.[28] Barrière's attempt unleashed savage attacks on French Jesuits who, according to their critics, not only consistently sided with the

---

[24] (London, 1594), STC 7603. See also STC 7603.5 for another edition.

[25] *Discours veritable de diverses conspirations contre la vie de la roine* (London, 1594), STC 7580.

[26] William Keatinge Clay, (ed.), *Liturgical Services. Liturgies and Occasional Forms of Prayers set forth in the Reign of Queen Elizabeth* (Cambridge, 1847), p. 655.

[27] Clay, *Liturgical Services*, p. 660.

[28] Wernham, *Return of the Armadas*, pp. 16–17; Wernham, "Queen Elizabeth I," p. 447; Richard Verstegan to Roger Baynes, Antwerp January 8, 1594 (published in Petti, *Verstegan Papers*, p. 198).

Catholic League but also taught the legitimacy of regicide.[29] How many of the conspiracies were real? How many were carefully cultivated by government officials from the many schemes and conspiracies involving Catholic exiles, Spain, Scotland, and candidates for the English throne? How many were simply created for political gain? An answer requires an exhaustive, critical analysis of a characteristic of the administration of the Cecils: the convenient discovery of divers conspiracies.[30] Regarding the Lopez plot, R.B. Wernham explained:

> The Queen, the Cecils, and most of the other Councillors were at first sceptical about the Earl's claims and historians have generally remained doubtful about Lopez's guilt. Indeed, it is difficult not to see the affair as a neatly timed countermining by the warlike Earl [of Essex] of the Cecils' readiness to explore pacific alternatives to continued war (perhaps almost single-handed) against Spain.[31]

Penry Williams agreed that the "truth of the matter was less important to competing politicians than the advantage to be won from it,"[32] but he accepted Professor David S. Katz's interpretation:

> What has been consistently misunderstood by modern historians is that it is not necessary to establish that Roderigo Lopez actually plotted to poison the queen, that he procured the materials and set about working to a secret plan. By the terms of the treason laws then current, Lopez's secret contacts with the Spanish Crown and his numerous discussions about the possibility of poisoning the queen were more than enough to hang him many times over.[33]

---

[29] See Roland Mousnier, *The Assassination of Henry IV: The Tyrannicide Problem & the Consolidation of the French Absolute Monarchy in the Early 17th Century* (London, 1973), pp. 215–17.

[30] Francis Edwards, S.J., has attempted this in his trilogy: the previously cited *Plots and Plotters*; and *The Succession, Bye and Main Plots of 1601–1603* (Dublin, 2006) and *The Enigma of Gunpowder Plot, 1605. The Third Solution* (Dublin, 2008).

[31] Wernham, *Return of the Armadas*, p. 13. Wallace T. MacCaffrey supports this: "It is not altogether easy to understand this episode. The initial intention was obviously to throw out a peace feeler to a new ruler who might be expected to be detachable from Spanish control. It was queered by the discovery of the plot, which impugned the King of Spain" (*Elizabeth I: War and Politics 1588–1603* [Princeton, 1992], pp. 194–95). Interestingly P.E.J. Hammer claims that during this period Essex was interested in promoting toleration for those Catholics who declared their loyalty to the queen and aversion to Spain. See "An Elizabethan Spy Who Came in from the Cold: The Return of Anthony Standen to England in 1593," *Historical Research*, 65 (1992): pp. 290–91.

[32] Penry Williams, *The Later Tudors: England 1547–1603* (Oxford, 1995), p. 347.

[33] David Katz, *The Jews in the History of England 1485–1850* (Oxford, 1994), p. 106. For a contrary conclusion, see Edwards, *Plots and Plotters*, pp. 205–35.

Real or not, persistent belief in Spanish conspiracies against Elizabeth and fears that civil war would result from a disputed succession destroyed any chance of a peaceful solution. Threats and plots raised the sensitive issue of succession. If an assassin were successful in England, who would ascend to the throne? Would the Spanish king advance his claims in England as forcibly as he was doing in France? Rumors of conspiracies filled the air. With the Spaniard safely lodged across the channel, "Blanks" in Scotland, and with an always volatile Ireland, the rumors were credible. Catholics remained the enemy and the government dealt with them in the customary way.

The Plight of Henry Walpole, S.J.

Sent on the English mission to replace Robert Southwell as Henry Garnet's assistant and perhaps his successor as superior, Henry Walpole was captured shortly after his arrival.[34] Henry, his brother Thomas and Edward Lingham,[35] boarded a ship in Dunkerque. English southern ports were closed to foreign vessels because of fear of plague. Rough weather made the voyage even more difficult and longer. Finally they landed on December 4 near Flamborough Head. Passing through the village, they inquired after a local family, the Constables. Sir Henry was in London and his wife in bed, ill. However their servants provided the visitors with some refreshment before they continued on their way to Bridlington where they purchased horses to ride to Kilham. The local sheriff acting on information provided by a Scots prisoner on the same French ship, arrested them during the night. The prisoner, put ashore a few days earlier in order to raise money for his ransom, immediately alerted the authorities of the arrival of the three. They were sent to different prisons. Two days later, the Scotsman identified Henry Walpole then confined to prison in York. He remained there until February 25 1594. The first Jesuit to be captured by Henry Hastings, Earl of Huntingdon, Walpole was a prize periodically put on display in disputation. Over an unspecified period, Walpole discussed theological doctrine, for example justification, Scripture and tradition, the

---

[34] Garnet to Acquaviva, London June 20, 1595, ARSI, Fondo Gesuitico 651/624. A copy can be found in ARSI, Angl. 31/I, fols 93ʳ–106ᵛ. Henry More, S.J., used the letter extensively in his history of the province (*The Elizabethan Jesuits*, (ed.) Francis Edwards, S.J [London, 1981], pp. 254–77) as did Philip Caraman, S.J., in *Henry Garnet (1555–1606) and the Gunpowder Plot* (London, 1964), pp. 178–81. Whenever one of the above mentioned summaries diverged from the original letter, I have followed the letter.

[35] Thomas Walpole and Edward Lingham served in Sir William Stanley's regiment (Augustus Jessop, *One Generation of a Norfolk House: A Contribution to Elizabethan History*, 3rd edn., revised [London, 1913], p. 257).

Antichrist, and religious practice, for example veneration of saints with local ecclesiastics, Dr John Favour, William Hardesty, Dr John Bennet, a Mr King, William Goodwin, and Thomas Bell. Hardesty and Bell were renegade Catholic priests.[36] The discussion with Bell (according to Walpole, Bell "who latelie out from us at the dore did now endevoire to get in to deceive me, by the window thus") is the most interesting. For argument's sake Walpole denied the validity of the ministers' orders. Bell retorted that their orders were eventually derived from Catholic orders. "You derive all from Cranmire here and from Luther and Calvin who had both ther orders from us Catholiks?" Walpole asked. Bell agreed; Walpole countered that consequently their orders were either the same or different. Contrary to some of the other theologians, Bell argued that they were the same. If the orders were the same, Walpole asked "how can yt be treason, or trespasse in me to take the same orders that you have"? The orders were the same, Bell continued, but Catholics had added other practices such as "Ointinge, shavinge, and such." "Alas is that treason," was Walpole's rejoinder.[37]

Richard Holtby, principal Jesuit in the north of England, established contact with Walpole by letter, sections of which were later incorporated into Garnet's letter to Acquaviva. He explained to Holtby the nature of the discussions he had with Protestant ministers, an account of which he had composed for the earl of Huntingdon along with an address "in which I warned all to guard themselves from false prophets and to listen to the Church, the spouse, the kingdom, the house, the inheritance, the city, of Christ." Because some disputants complained that he had not recorded their words properly, Walpole demanded that any future dispute be held before witnesses. Although he considered himself "the most unlearned priest" in the Society of Jesus, he judged that his discussions and writings against them could only have beneficial effect.

Richard Topcliffe was dispatched to York to help Huntingdon extract damaging information from the captives. Despite Topcliffe's methods, he

---

[36] Garnet mentioned that two of the ministers who debated Walpole were former Catholic priests but he did not identify them. By examining the names of the disputants and comparing them with Godfrey Anstruther's list, Hardesty and Bell were the only possibilities. Bell's teaching on occasional conformity before his departure from the Roman Church and his apostasy were discussed in the first chapter. On Hardesty see Anstruther, *Seminary Priests*, vol. 1, p. 148, and Patrick McGrath, "Apostate and Naughty Priests in England under Elizabeth I," in *Opening the Scrolls: Essays in Catholic History in Honour of Godfrey Anstruther*, (ed.) Dominic Aidan Bellenger, O.S.B. (Bath, 1987), p. 57. In a letter to Creswell on November 7, 1590, Walpole reported rumors of Hardesty's apostasy: he had published "articles scarce sound, shewing himself a cynic and schismatic" (ABSI, Anglia I, 51 [published in Augustus Jessop, (ed.), *Letters of Fa. Henry Walpole, S.J.* (Norwich, 1873), p. 19]).

[37] TNA, SP 12/248/51 (published as [Henry Foley, S.J., (ed.)], "Two Conferences in the Prison at York with Father Walpole, S.J., An. Dom. 1594. Related by Himself," *Letters and Notices*, 9 [1873]: pp. 46–63).

obtained nothing of value from Henry Walpole who admitted to Richard Holtby:

> In the course of my examinations I gave in writing an account of my whole life abroad, and of my actions and intentions to glorify God and to spread the Catholic faith, for which purpose I had returned here, desiring to convert not only the people but even more the Queen and the nobility. I declared that I would spare no efforts to this end. I refused to answer questions about others except to say where I first met them.

Walpole's steadfastness angered Topcliffe who swore that he would break the Jesuit if given the opportunity to examine him in Bridewell or the Tower of London. Topcliffe hoped Walpole would betray Garnet, but, as with Robert Southwell, the priest hunter was frustrated. Walpole asked Holtby to circulate this account among Jesuits in England and their supporters whose prayers strengthened the prisoner.[38] Walpole admitted that he had worked in Spain for the consolidation of the foundations of the seminaries there, and for the establishment of the new college at St Omers. To the inevitable "Bloody Question" regarding whom he would support if a papally sponsored army invaded England,[39] he replied "that the circumstances then prevailing would necessarily be taken into account, and that I would have recourse to God; I would also seek advice and would think very carefully before embroiling myself in matters of war regardless of who was involved."

In February, shortly before his transfer to London, Walpole had a chance to escape, but he hesitated taking advantage of it without his superior's permission.[40] Holtby was stunned that escape was a real possibility. After having prayed about the matter, Holtby decided that Walpole must not attempt it "because ... it would be a matter of great virtue and merit, and manifestly to the glory of God, if he remained where he was, and I could not see that there was equal glory in flight, but rather flight was a sign of evasion." The flight of a priest would give scandal and tempt subsequent prisoners for their faith. Moreover, if the escape failed, severe punishment would follow. Finally, assuming a successful escape, "a general

---

[38] Thomas Walpole was the only one of the three to reveal anything to the government. He led officials to the spot where his brother buried letters immediately after their arrival in England, and later identified a returned priest (Jessop, *One Generation*, p. 257).

[39] On these questions see Patrick McGrath, "The Bloody Questions Reconsidered," *Recusant History*, 20 (1991): pp. 305–19.

[40] This is recounted by John Blackfan in his history of the English College, Valladolid. See Peter E.B. Harris, (ed.), *The Blackfan Annals. Los Anales de Blackfan* (Valladolid, 2008), pp. 181–83.

search [throughout the country] ... would follow as a consequence not one but many might well fall into their hands, and those, perhaps, weaker and less stable than himself." Exhorting Walpole not to flee the crown being offered, Holtby, nonetheless, left the final decision to him. Walpole accepted Holtby's recommendations, protesting that he had only proposed an escape "to give satisfaction to others." From his perspective:

> This is my Rome and my "*Domine, quo vadis?*" [Lord, where are you going? (John 13:36)]. To tell the truth, I do not see how I could do otherwise than to strive for that reward and recompense towards which we are all running, nor how I could be more usefully employed elsewhere since I have here means to make profession of what I am, and visits also from persons which otherwise I could not have. Wherefore, if I do not hear a contrary voice from heaven, that is the word of Christ in obedience, or some other way: *Ecce me, fiat voluntas de caelo* [Here I am. May your will be done from heaven.].

Although there have been intimations of torture and punishment, Walpole saw little likelihood that the threats would be implemented.

Despite Huntingdon's evil reputation among Catholics, Walpole acknowledged his courteous treatment. The earl provided paper for Walpole, and asked him to explain his faith and his understanding of the Church, papal power, and the nature of the Eucharist. Huntingdon, according to Garnet, was moved tremendously by what he read. So courteous and honorable was the earl that Walpole promised in a letter written on February 11 to cooperate as much as he could "without doing violence to my conscience." To satisfy Huntingdon, Walpole never refused to discuss his faith and to dispute with anyone. But, without books, he was disadvantaged. Therefore he requested a breviary, and the controversial works of Robert Bellarmine and Thomas Stapleton. He would not object to having a copy of Calvin's *Institutes* or some English book with comparable authority among the Protestants. Huntingdon provided paper, writing material, and books, presumably the requested titles although Garnet did not specify any. Two treatises, one entitled "Guard yourselves against false prophets," and the other on the invocation of saints, followed. Walpole's transfer to London prevented further works.

On January 18, Huntingdon forwarded a series of questions regarding Walpole's formation as a Jesuit, his work on the continent, and his associates. After a summary of his 12 years on the continent, he explained that he rarely had contact with non-Jesuits during his formation. Afterwards his contact was, for the most part, restricted to students at the colleges. Generally the only exceptions were his visits to the sick and the imprisoned, or when he served as a translator. Regardless of site or occupation, all his activities were directed towards "the greater glory of God and the good of my neighbour, to which end I have used all the means at my disposal, being on the watch for every opportunity of doing everybody I could some good, or offering some possible comfort." Walpole dedicated his life to bringing all persons to God: he worked to reconcile Protestants to the true faith, to comfort the depressed, and to end hostility. His approach was simple:

> My reason was always fitted to the temperament of him with whom I reasons, always with the intention and desire of bringing him to a higher level in the service of God. All this in such a way that I have without doubt heard much irrelevant discourse, but my intention was always to spread the glory of God and the Catholic faith. To obtain this end I have always considered those means to be the best which are spiritual, gentle, and consonant with the vocation to which God has called me; trying to avoid as far as I could rigour and contentiousness, and willingly embracing everything that tended to the smoothing over of differences at every level. To this end I would willingly occupy myself for all men and women, and by all possible means for the temporal, and at the same time spiritual, good of my beloved country, which, consistently with God's honour, I revere, love, and embrace with the natural affection of one of its most faithful subjects. I prefer it and those who live in it by way of natural love to any other country under the sun, desiring for it all grace, riches, and prosperity.

Walpole provided Huntingdon with answers to all questions but he again refused to name individuals. His conscience forbade that. Begging forgiveness for this refusal, Walpole was ready to do anything else Huntingdon demanded on behalf of England "provided it is consistent with the conscience of a Catholic priest."

On February 25, 1594 Walpole was transferred to the Tower of London where Topcliffe could carry out the threats he had made in York. Under Topcliffe's direction Walpole was tortured during which confessions were extracted from him between April 27 and June 17. Of the ten confessions published in an edition by John Hungerford Pollen, S.J.,[41] four are in Walpole's hand. In the early confessions Walpole repeated much of the information that he had provided Huntingdon in York: he came to England to win the queen's subjects to the Roman Catholic faith but he refused to name any of his contacts. The second was important. In the second examination on May 3, Walpole refused to name a gentleman "for consynes sake (as he sayeth)" and refused to affirm or deny that Braddocks in Essex was one of his destinations. In the third examination on May 18, he again refused to name Catholics in Ireland.[42] He was not as reticent

---

[41] Pollen, *Unpublished Documents Relating to the English Martyrs (1584–1603)* (London, 1908), pp. 244–68.

[42] Pollen, *Unpublished Documents*, p. 250.

about his associates, Jesuits and lay, on the continent possibly because he believed that they were beyond the reach of the English government. He had dealings, it was true, with the king of Spain and had carried letters from him to different Spanish ministers in the Netherlands but these letters concerned only the financial affairs of the new college in St Omers and support of its students. In a conversation Charles Paget had told Walpole about "a peace which he laboured to make for the good of all our nacion."[43] The very prospect excited Walpole and he was eager to help but his imminent departure prevented further discussion. Later in Spain upon hearing rumors of plots and attempts on the life of Elizabeth, Walpole asked Robert Parsons what he thought of such machinations. Parsons replied that as religious men, they "ought to suffer violence but offer none, chiefly to princes."[44] Their methods were persuasion and prayer and Parsons believed that with these alone, the seminaries would eventually effect England's return to the Catholic Church. Apparently Parsons considered his diplomatic activity at court a form of persuasion. Regarding assassination, Walpole ventured his own opinion: he knew that Claudio Acquaviva would dismiss anyone involved in such matters from the Society and that Walpole abhorred "to think thereof, and never did, nor would not move any man thereunto for all the good in the world, Jesus is my witnes."[45] The only instructions Walpole received from Parsons concerned proper submission to his religious superior and his apostolic work in England, that is, ministering the sacraments and winning many to the Catholic faith. On his trip from Belgium to Spain, Sir William Stanley asked him to deliver a memorial to Parsons about the possible conversion of Lord Strange. He also knew about earlier negotiations concerning the marriage of Arabella Stuart and Ranuccio Farnese, Prince of Parma.[46]

Perhaps because of the torture Walpole suffered, the tone and content of his confessions changed after June 18. Upon hearing Sir Francis Englefield blame Catholics in England for not supporting effective means for the restoration of Catholicism, Walpole disliked any suggestion that English Catholics should welcome Spanish armies: "their coming hether by force would not only be the wofull ruine of the commonwealth and my dearest country, but also their example, especially of soldiers, make such as arre of their religion to stagger, because for peace, morall vertue, and good government of the commonwealth, I in my pore iudgement do not know any comparable unto England, not considering religion at

---

[43] Pollen, *Unpublished Documents*, p. 256.
[44] Pollen, *Unpublished Documents*, p. 253.
[45] Pollen, *Unpublished Documents*, p. 253.
[46] Pollen, *Unpublished Documents*, pp. 251–56, 258–62.

all."[47] Walpole was not aware of any immediate threats to the kingdom but he desired to serve the queen in any possible way and to conform to all her laws and "never more be subiect to the ambition of the Pope or any of his adherents."[48] Perhaps as evidence of his sincerity, he told his examiners where he believed Garnet and other Jesuits could be found and the names of certain Catholics known to him. He begged that this statement be concealed until his fate was decided and beseeched all "to take pitye uppon a miserable prisoner and offender" now resolved to do all the queen asked. He promised that he would "never again returne to Popery if her most excellent ma^{tye} my gracious soveraigne will vouchsafe her accustomed clemency upon me."[49] Repudiating the "ambition of the Popes or any of their uniust usurpation over princes and their kingdomes," and ready to conform to the laws of the kingdom, he was willing to go to church and to preach "only such doctrine as my conscience doth tel me and the spirite of God to be manifestly deduced out of the word of God." He would follow the example of learned scholars in the universities in attributing to the queen authority and jurisdiction in spiritual and temporal matters and, through private conference, he would argue with others to do the same. As a result of conferences in York with Protestant ministers, Walpole now realized that the positions of the Established Church differed less from the Roman Church than he had originally thought. General conformity would possibly result if representatives discussed theological doctrine at a free and open assembly. Such unity would comfort all and protect the queen from any foreign intrigues.[50]

Walpole's confessions, especially his willingness to conform by attending church, and his disclosure of the names of Catholics and location of Jesuits, are disturbing. Father Pollen commented that, although the confessions were "extremely clear, their conclusion is somewhat mysterious, but as to the extent of the future Martyr's waverings, and also as to the reason for his instability." On the basis of an examination of Walpole's handwriting Pollen at first believed that the confessions were simply the result of torture but later he decided that "we cannot with certainty affirm that his answers were drawn from him by the pressure of bodily torture." "Dread of future torments, weakness, depression, helplessness, confusion" were more effective.[51] Yet, Pollen noted, his concessions were nuanced: the "popery" to which he swore never to return was papal ambition regarding temporal power and his willingness to serve the queen insofar as it did not prejudice

---

[47] Pollen, *Unpublished Documents*, p. 256.
[48] Pollen, *Unpublished Documents*, p. 257.
[49] Pollen, *Unpublished Documents*, pp. 258, 264.
[50] Pollen, *Unpublished Documents*, pp. 266–67.
[51] Pollen, *Unpublished Documents*, p. 245.

his Catholic faith.[52] Augustus Jessop, Walpole's first modern biographer, was perplexed by the Jesuit's recantations: "The language he [Walpole] uses is not creditable to him, and there are expressions for which I can offer or find no excuse" even if we consider Walpole's qualifier "without prejudice of the Catholic faith, which I ever profess" as an attempt at self-protection. More damaging to Walpole's reputation, Jessop asserted, was his disclosure of names and locations. Here, however, the Jesuit volunteered no information, again, according to Jessop, not previously known to the government.[53] Such an explanation, however, leaves one wondering how a prisoner kept in such close confinement, especially one who had only just arrived in the kingdom, would be so aware of the extent and nature of the government's information about the Catholic community. Moreover even if he did, could any division of his knowledge into what was already known by the government and thus could be disclosed without difficulty, and what was privy to a few whose revelation could have disastrous consequences, resist torture? Shortly after the Second World War with its legacy of false confessions and forgeries, W.F. Rea, S.J., exonerated Walpole of his embarrassing disclosures by arguing that his confessions were not authentic. His argument centered on one passage:

> In the 11 article I had forgotten naming Philopaters booke to meancion y^t it was begunne to be translated and augmented by Sr Francis Englefield who being with Fr. Parsons gave me the residue to prosecute, which I did following too much his humor and stile, for he having spoken unreverently of her Matie and more of some of her councell deceased and the now l. Treasurer, I also called her Matie Bes and suche like as he willed me. . .[54]

The book in question was Parsons's *Elizabethae Angliae Reginae haeresim Calvinianam propugnantis* published under the name of Andreas Philopater.[55] Rea contended that Walpole could not have written this statement because he could not have "translated and augmented Philopater." According to Rea, the English translation was an abridgement done while Parsons and Englefield were in Spain and Holt in Belgium. The volume on which Walpole collaborated was not *An advertisement written to a secretarie of my L. Treasurers*[56] but Parsons's *Newes from Spayne and Holland*.[57] Rea

---

[52] Pollen, *Unpublished Documents*, see e.g. pp. 246, 268.
[53] Jessop, *One Generation*, pp. 287–88.
[54] Pollen, *Unpublished Documents*, p. 265.
[55] (Augsburg [*vere* Antwerp], 1592), *ARCR*, vol. 1, num. 885 (see nums 886–892 for other editions).
[56] (n.p. [Antwerp?], 1592), *ARCR*, vol. 2, num. 757, *STC* 19885.
[57] (n.p. [Antwerp], 1593), *ARCR*, vol. 2, num. 632, *STC* 22994.

argued that Walpole could not have confused a work on which he had labored so energetically with a volume with which he had no association.

Walpole was, it is true, involved in the production of *Newes from Spayne*, but can we be so sure that he did not have a hand in *An advertisement*? Although *An advertisement* is shorter than the Latin original, it is not simply an abridgement as Rea contends. According to David Rogers and Antony Allison, the work "is mainly a summary," mainly but not solely: there is an introductory letter. Moreover the treatment of many Elizabethan privy councillors, especially the lord treasurer, fits Walpole's description and the volume was prepared and published by Richard Verstegan who was in Belgium with Walpole.[58] Walpole's confessions may not be authentic but they cannot be dismissed as forgeries for the reasons alleged by Rea.[59]

A more important question concerns the government's subsequent silence about the confessions. Previous confessions were broadcasted throughout the kingdom, providing excellent material for official religious and political propaganda. But the government said nothing about Walpole. Not even rumors that he had capitulated circulated among the Catholics.[60] Having obtained such damaging disclosures, why did not the government use them? According to Rea, as the government tried to use fake confessions from Robert Southwell to break the resolve of John Gerard so had it earlier attempted to use confessions from Walpole to tempt Southwell. Once this ploy failed, the confessions were forgotten. But this is simple conjecture: there is no evidence that the government ever made such an attempt on Southwell. Pollen's explanation is perhaps closer to the truth. The government paid little attention to Walpole's religious wavering because such oscillation did not interest them. Of more pressing concern were conspiracies and plots. Each month brought the discovery of yet another scheme directed against the queen. What the government wanted,

---

[58] However I was unable to find a reference to "Queen Bess" in either book.

[59] For Rea's argument see "Self-Accusations of Political Prisoners: An Incident in the Reign of Queen Elizabeth," *The Month*, 6 (n.s.) (1951): pp. 269–79, and "The Authorship of 'News from Spayne and Holland' and its Bearing on the Genuineness of the Confessions of the Blessed Henry Walpole, S.J.," *Biographical Studies* (=*Recusant History*), 1 (1951–1952): pp. 220–30.

[60] Because of an ambiguous passage in a letter from Garnet to Parsons on September 6, 1594 (ABSI, Anglia I, 81 [published in Henry Foley, S.J., *Records of the English Province of the Society of Jesus* (7 vols. in 8 parts, Roehampton/London, 1877–1884), vol. 4, pp. 45–48]), it is possible that rumors about Walpole's confessions circulated: "Letters of yours I received none since that which you wrote to meet with Mr. Henry W[alpole]. Wherein I am sorry that I gave you such occasion to dilate of my obscurity. But I assure you that I always wrote as plainly as I could comprehend; and such things as I left out were altogether unknown to me, and as easy to be guessed by you as by me. Neither can we by any means know the circumstances of such matters as come unlooked for, and even as it were by mere chance unto us." Unfortunately the mentioned letters are not extant.

was information about the persons responsible.[61] And that Walpole did not provide. Nonetheless his arrival in England with two former soldiers from Sir William Stanley's regiment and his dealings with Catholic exiles, such as Stanley, Robert Parsons, and William Holt, and Spanish ministers in Belgium, all considered extremely dangerous by the government, were ominous. Walpole associated with them, carried messages from them, and discussed English matters with them. As Michael Questier has shown, rigorous suppression of recusants in northern England had to be linked to fear of Scottish intervention in English politics.[62] References to opponents of the Elizabethan regime and men suspected of plotting the queen's murder and of sending assassins into the kingdom were too frequent to be ignored. Indeed, Walpole's repudiation of Spain might have led the government to worry that he was a supporter of Scotland and thus a potential threat in northern England. Walpole's guilt might have been only by association but that was sufficient given the general hysteria that resulted from the discovery of more plots against Elizabeth. Until the Lenten Assizes of 1595, Walpole remained in the Tower of London not too far from Robert Southwell.[63]

"Hannibal at the Gates": Persecution in England

Despite Walpole's capture, Henry Garnet remained, perhaps unduly, optimistic in early 1594. News of the recent general congregation had reached England and Garnet rejoiced at its successes, presumably Acquaviva's exoneration. On a more personal level, Garnet reported that he had received his mother, who had conformed after her second marriage, into the Roman Church. During the summer of 1593 Garnet had discussed her religious position. On August 15, the Feast of the Assumption, she was reconciled. Now each member of his family was in the Roman Church. Indeed his sister Margaret entered St Ursula's Convent, a convent of the Canonesses Regular of the Lateran, in Louvain. Two years later a second sister, Helen, entered the same convent.[64] Garnet had also welcomed into

---

[61] Pollen, *Unpublished Documents*, p. 246.

[62] See Michael Questier, "Practical Antipapistry during the Reign of Elizabeth I," *Journal of British Studies*, 36 (1997): pp. 371–96 and "The Politics of Religious Conformity and the Accession of James I," *Historical Research*, 71 (1998): pp. 14–30.

[63] Garnet to Acquaviva, March 10, 1594, ARSI, Fondo Gesuitico 651/624.

[64] See his letter to Margaret, October 1, 1593, ABSI, Anglia I, 76 (published in Foley, *Records*, vol. 4, pp. 135–38).

his own house Christina Parsons, Robert's nonagenarian mother, who had been living with her son John, a Protestant minister.[65]

Garnet's optimism was not long lasting. Discovery of various conspiracies to assassinate Elizabeth caused even more heated persecution. Fear of Catholic collusion with Spanish intrigues led to a crack-down throughout the kingdom. Richard Verstegan informed Roger Baynes that persecution was great and it was rumored that many women were executed for harboring priests.[66] John Ingram, sent to London around the same time as Walpole, and John Boste suffered imprisonment and torture in the Tower where they remained in expectation of eventual martyrdom.[67] William Harrington was executed at Tyburn on February 18, 1594.[68] On 15 March Richard Topcliffe skillfully organized and brilliantly executed a raid on known Catholic households in London and the neighboring counties. There was such tumult throughout the city, Garnet reported to Acquaviva, that it was as if Hannibal himself was at the gates or the Spanish fleet in the river Thames.[69] Catholics were routed from their beds and shut into churches as the pursuivants searched their homes. Garnet's former residence in Golden Lane, Holborn was attacked. Concealed there were books, vestments, and other Catholic sacramentals. Garnet was not, but three others including the barber or tailor who managed the house, were not so lucky. The discovery of religious goods clearly demonstrated that the house was a common refuge for priests; Garnet feared the consequences for the captives. Throughout the following week surveillance throughout London was increased and more houses searched. Not long after Easter John Gerard was apprehended.[70]

In early 1594 Garnet acquired a house about "four or five miles from London." Presumably Mrs. Parsons lived here. Garnet and other Jesuits also frequented the London house of William Wiseman, John Gerard's patron, in Lincoln Inn Fields.[71] Gerard gradually realized that the safest

---

[65] Garnet to Acquaviva, March 10, 1594, ARSI, Fondo Gesuitico 651/624.

[66] April 16, 1594, ARSI, Angl. 38/II, fol. 195ʳ (published in Petti, *Verstegan Papers*, p. 210).

[67] On them see Anstruther, *Seminary Priests*, vol. 1, pp. 43–44, 182–84.

[68] See Anstruther, *Seminary Priests*, vol. 1, pp. 149–50. He was briefly in the Society but left for reasons of health.

[69] In his letter to Parsons on September 6, 1594, Garnet compared the commotion to Sir Thomas Wyatt's rebellion, a historical reference that would have meant nothing to Acquaviva (ABSI, Anglia I, 81 [published in Foley, *Records*, vol. 4, p. 46]).

[70] Garnet to Acquaviva, London August 9, 1594, ARSI, Fondo Gesuitico 651/624.

[71] In the narrative regarding Gerard, I follow Garnet to Acquaviva, London August 9, 1594, ARSI, Fondo Gesuitico 651/624; Verstegan to Baynes, Antwerp June 11, 1594, ARSI, Angl. 38/II, fol. 195ᵛ; same to same, Antwerp July 2, 1594, ARSI, Angl. 38/II, fol. 196ʳ; same to same, Antwerp January 21, 1595, ARSI, Angl. 38/II, fol. 193ᵛ (published in Petti,

course for himself and his patrons was to have his own house. Thus Wiseman rented the house in Golden Lane, Clerkenwell, for the Jesuit's use. Gerard was visiting Garnet outside the city but because he had business to attend to, he informed the house's staff that he would return on the 15th. John Frank, one of the Wisemans' servants, betrayed this knowledge to the pursuivants. The capture of another Jesuit so soon after Walpole's apprehension was an exciting prospect. Acting on some unexplained instinct, Henry Garnet urged Gerard to remain another night, dismissing Gerard's insistence that he had pressing work in London. The following morning they learned of the raid. The pursuivants had to be satisfied with William Suffield, a schismatic weaver in Wiseman's service, Richard Fulwood, Garnet's servant,[72] the Catholic musician John Bolt, and John Tarbuck, a Lancashire Catholic. Fulwood was sent to Bridewell prison. All were examined, but no one revealed anything.[73] The following day, purely by chance, William Wiseman stopped by. Instead of finding the expected residents, including Gerard, he discovered members of the posse lurking outside in hope of catching others. Wiseman was taken into custody and imprisoned in the Counter in Wood Street. Gerard meanwhile escaped to Wiseman's country house, Braddocks, to consult with Wiseman's wife and friends regarding their course of action. Early on Easter Monday, April 1, as Gerard and the Wisemans prepared for Mass, justices of the peace arrived with authorization for a search.[74] Taking all incriminating altar materials with him, Gerard concealed himself in a hiding-hole made by Nicholas Owen.[75] Having locked the mistress of the house, her two daughters, and the Catholic servants in different rooms, the pursuivants examined every nook and cranny. After two days the mistress and her Catholic servants were confined locally for further questioning. Unknowingly she revealed Gerard's presence to her servant John Frank, the traitor. For three more

---

Verstegan Papers, pp. 212, 216, 217 and pp. 213 n. 2, 216 n. 2, 218 n. 1) Caraman, *Henry Garnet*, pp. 185–88; John Morris, S.J., (ed.), *The Life of John Gerard, of the Society of Jesus*, 3rd edn. (London, 1881), pp. 135–225; Philip Caraman, S.J., (ed.), *John Gerard: The Autobiography of an Elizabethan* (London, 1951), pp. 54–103, 228–37; More, *Elizabethan Jesuits*, pp. 316–27.

[72] Caraman believed that Fulwood was a Jesuit (*Henry Garnet*, p. 105). If so, I have found no evidence.

[73] See their examinations in TNA, SP 12/248/31, 36, 37, 38, 39, 40, 68, 68i, 68ii, 103 Around the same time Sir Thomas Tresham was examined, see TNA, SP 12/248/44, 45.

[74] The house of Jane Wiseman, William's widowed mother, was raided probably at this time. See Caraman, *John Gerard*, pp. 51–52.

[75] Commonly known as a Jesuit lay brother, I find nothing about Owen in any official Jesuit document (McCoog, *Monumenta Angliae*, vol. 2, p. 423). For more information see Michael Hodgetts's entry in *The Oxford Dictionary of National Biography*, (eds.) H.C.G. Matthew and Brian Harrison (60 vols, Oxford, 2004), vol. 42, pp. 241–42.

days they searched but found nothing. At the end of the fourth day, they decided that Gerard had somehow escaped and departed. Frank remained, his perfidy still unknown. Upon the return of Jane Wiseman, William's wife, and her servants, Gerard emerged from hiding. A few days later he was in London first as a guest of Anne Dacre Howard, Countess of Arundel, and then in a house called "Middleton's" in Holborn as he completed arrangement to rent new accommodation. There, betrayed by the treacherous Frank, Gerard and Owen were captured on April 23.

Examined by a lapsed Catholic, Sir Thomas Egerton, Gerard was asked about seducing loyal subjects from their due allegiance to the queen and meddling in political matters. All Jesuits, he asserted, were forbidden to mix with politics. As for allegiance to the queen, there was no conflict between that due the queen and that due the pope and "the history of England and of all other Christian states shows this." Although Gerard honored the queen and obeyed her in "all that is lawful," he refused to specify names and involve others.[76] Despite Egerton's instructions to treat the prisoner well, Gerard was confined in the Counter in the Poultry. Topcliffe was not as gentle. Neither torture nor a forged confession allegedly from Robert Southwell could break Gerard. Chained in his cell, Gerard made the Spiritual Exercises from memory during the first month of his confinement. In late summer of 1594 a few of Gerard's friends succeeded in obtaining his transfer to a more comfortable prison, the Clink on the south bank of the Thames. There he had much freedom and was a great comfort to Catholics in London.

Gerard considered his transfer to the Clink as a "translation from Purgatory to Paradise."[77] No longer subjected to the bawdy songs of other prisoners, he now heard prayers of Catholics in adjoining cells. Through a hole in the wall he was able to speak with them. Through the same hole an unnamed priest heard his confession and gave him communion. Keys to the cells were so easily obtained that Catholics from his section of the prison were able to gather in his room each day for Mass before the warden made his rounds. In cells near him were the Jesuit Ralph Emerson and the future Jesuit John Lillie.[78] Gerard confessed "for a while I had a quiet and pleasant time" hearing confessions and ministering to other prisoners.[79] During his confinement in the Clink, as a result of bribes, the gaoler left Gerard alone. As a result he was able to set up a chapel in a

---

[76] Caraman, *John Gerard*, p. 67.

[77] Caraman, *John Gerard*, p. 78.

[78] On them see McCoog, *Monumenta Angliae*, vol. 2, pp. 296, 393. Emerson apparently was transferred to Newgate but Gerard's friends hoped to arrange his return. See Garnet to Parsons, September 6, 1594 (ABSI, Anglia I, 81 [published in Foley, *Records*, vol. 4, p. 47]).

[79] Caraman, *John Gerard*, p. 79.

room above his cell and there he conducted six or seven men through the Spiritual Exercises. Even in prison he served as focal point for newly arrived clergy instructed to contact Gerard because he was much easier to find than the more elusive Garnet! With help from friends he provided maintenance and accommodation for the clergy. In charge of a house he established while in prison he placed Anne Line, later to be executed for sheltering priests. At the same time he arranged for young boys to escape to St Omers.

Periodically Gerard was summoned for examination. To these meetings he wore his Jesuit gown and cloak. Once questioned about his dress, the Jesuit replied:

> When I was arrested you called me a courtier ... because I dressed like one to disguise myself and in order to move at my ease among people of rank, without being recognized. Then I told you that I did not like wearing lay clothes, that I would have preferred my proper dress. I have it on now, and you are angry with me. Whether I pipe to you or whether I mourn I cannot please you. You must find some complaint against me.[80]

In the presence of William Wiseman's widowed mother Jane, Topcliffe asked the Jesuit if he recognized her. Denying he recognized her, he reminded Topcliffe that he consistently refused to mention specifically any person or place because that would be against charity and justice. Gerard did, however, admit that he had reconciled many to the Roman Church and regretted that there were not more. To Topcliffe's contention that they would form an army against the queen, Gerard explained that they would be the queen's men because the Roman Church taught "obedience is due to those in authority."[81] On another occasion Topcliffe asked him if he recognized Elizabeth as the true and lawful queen: he did. Topcliffe pressed further with the "Bloody Question": if military force were the only way to re-establish the Roman Church in England, would Gerard support pope or queen? The reply skillfully evaded the issue:

> I am a loyal Catholic and I am a loyal subject of the Queen. If this were to happen, and I do not think it at all likely, I would behave as a loyal Catholic and as a loyal subject.[82]

---

[80] Caraman, *John Gerard*, p. 94.
[81] Caraman, *John Gerard*, p. 95.
[82] Caraman, *John Gerard*, p. 99.

Until his transfer to the Tower of London in April of 1597, Gerard's cell in the Clink was an apostolic center.[83]

By the summer of 1594 Walpole and Gerard joined Southwell, Weston and other Jesuits in different prisons in England. On April 14, the secular priest John Cornelius was captured at Chideock Castle, Dorset, home of Lady Anne Arundel, widow of Sir John Arundel of Lanherne, Cornwall. Sent to London for examination he was returned to Dorchester for trial and was executed on July 3 or 4. Throughout his ministry in England, he begged to enter the Society. Henry Garnet consoled him during his London imprisonment as much as he could while explaining that he did not have the authority to accept candidates. The Jesuit, however, promised to send someone to the continent as soon as possible in order to obtain the required permission.[84] Before Cornelius's execution, he pronounced the three vows of the Society in the presence of three Catholic witnesses, who were instructed to inform Garnet, and proclaimed himself a Jesuit immediately before his death. Citing this example, Garnet beseeched Acquaviva's permission that the Jesuit superior in England be granted the authority to accept clergy and laity into the Society if they were under sentence of death and awaiting execution. They would have the honor to proclaim their Jesuit identity and the Society would benefit from their heavenly intercession.[85]

To protect the queen and to quell popular anxiety aroused by fears for her safety, the government cracked down on Catholics. Rumored involvement of Catholic princes and priests in the various conspiracies discredited Catholics and Jesuits even more. French anti-Jesuit tracts were quickly translated to reveal the secret policies of the nefarious Society. Asserting that the Society was allied with Spain, Antoine Arnauld defended a petition from the University of Paris that the Society be expelled from France. Jesuits, he claimed, worked to weaken France from within by stirring up civil discontent. The principal vow of each Jesuit was obedience to their general, who was always a Spaniard and, Arnauld contended, selected by Philip II, to whom the Society was devoted. From their pulpits they preached the murder of kings. In their schools they taught this doctrine

---

[83] On the use of prisons as apostolic centres, see Peter Lake and Michael Questier, "Prisons, Priests and People," in *England's Long Reformation 1500–1800*, (ed.) Nicholas Tyacke (London, 1998), pp. 195–233.

[84] John Hungerford Pollen included an undated letter from Cornelius to Garnet in *Unpublished Documents*, pp. 269–70 regarding Garnet's decision about his admission into the Society. Verstegan reported his capture to Baynes on June 11, 1594 (ARSI, Angl. 38/II, fol. 195ᵛ [published in Petti, *Verstegan Papers*, p. 212, see also p. 213 n. 1]). Verstegan forwarded a Latin poem to Parsons in late 1595 (ABSI, Anglia II, 13 [published in Petti, *Verstegan Papers*, p. 247]).

[85] London August 9, 1594, ARSI, Fondo Gesuitico 651/624.

and kindled all treason and corrupted the minds of all students. As long as they remained in the kingdom, they would undermine the authority of the French monarchy. Unless they were banished from the realm, the monarchy would not be secure and the life of the king would not be safe.[86]

Such accounts of the Society's activities in France corroborated English fears about Jesuits and demonstrated that England was not unique in its vulnerability. Given the Society's perfidious intentions any action to eradicate their influence and to eliminate their presence within England was justifiable. Any hint of toleration could lead to a civil war comparable to the one France was suffering. Thus the penal laws were more strictly enforced. Searches were frequent; movement was curtailed; all means of persuading "lurking Papists" to disclose their schemes were accepted. Because ports were under closer surveillance, leaving the kingdom was more difficult. In July 11 students about to embark from Chester to the colleges in Spain were arrested. In August two boats containing two women, presumably bound for the Belgian convents, and five boys destined for the college in St Omer, were captured off Gravesend.[87]

Recent developments in England apparently worried Acquaviva. Parsons relayed to Acquaviva what he knew about Jesuit activity in England. He had been informed of Walpole's capture but did not know if he had been martyred. He was confident that he could ransom both Southwell and Weston by exchanging them for other prisoners. Acquaviva worried about the intensification of persecution, but Parsons assured him that few had been executed. God willed that many be captured but few executed. Since the executions of Campion and Cottam in 1581, no Jesuit had been martyred. Thus Acquaviva could continue to send men into England without fearing for their safety.[88]

Despite increased danger and the general's concern for the safety of Jesuits, Garnet revived a request first made by Parsons in 1581.[89] Because they would not be subject to English laws, Garnet asked that some foreign Jesuits, preferably Scots or Italians who could speak English, be sent into the realm. At the moment some Catholics would not approach English Jesuits because of fear of discovery and subsequent persecution.

---

[86] *The arrainement of the whole societie of Jesuites in Fraunce* (London, 1594), STC 779. See also Lisa Ferraro Parmelee, *Good Newes from Fraunce: French Anti-League Propaganda in Late Elizabethan England* (Woodbridge, 1996), pp. 147–50.

[87] Garnet to Parsons, September 6, 1594, ABSI, Anglia I, 81 (published in Foley, *Records*, vol. 4, pp. 45–48).

[88] Seville May 10, 1594, ARSI, Hisp. 136, fols 316^r–317^v.

[89] See McCoog, *Society of Jesus*, pp. 159–60.

Foreign Jesuits would not pose such a threat.[90] Joseph Creswell forwarded Garnet's request in December of 1594.[91] Acquaviva ruled out Italian Jesuits completely because he did not think that anyone unfamiliar with the language (presumably he could not find anyone who spoke English) would be of much assistance to Catholics. Regarding a Scottish or Irish Jesuit, Acquaviva promised to discuss the matter with James Tyrie.[92] Since no foreign Jesuit was sent to England, Tyrie must have argued against it.

In October and early November of 1594, there was a temporary lull as the Elizabethan government debated whether Sir Thomas Wilkes should proceed on his mission to Brussels. The arraignment of Southwell, Walpole and Gerard was postponed, Garnet believed, because of Wilkes's possible departure. A fortnight earlier, perhaps taking advantage of governmental hesitation, the Jesuits in England held their first assembly since the near catastrophe of 1591 at Baddesley Clinton. Unfortunately we know nothing about the agenda save that all were asked to gather historical information and all sent their greetings to Robert Parsons.[93]

All may have gone well at the Jesuit gathering, but dark clouds were forming in East Anglia. Intimations that harmony among the clergy in Wisbech prison, a harmony earlier praised by Garnet, was cracking, reached him. William Weston informed his superior that "things grow worse and worse, with no order and with danger of great scandal." It was still possible, Garnet warned Parsons, to remedy the situation but no one must be blamed for the problems because that would simply acerbate the problem. Proper arrangements must be made to prevent the situation from exploding into a scandal. Delay could be costly.[94]

Buying a King: Jesuits in Scotland

Protestant ministers harangued James for his lenient treatment of the Catholic earls. Since their military strength posed a threat to English security, Queen Elizabeth shared their apprehension: it was always possible that Philip II would seize an opportunity to assist them and together they would invade England through the back door. Consequently the

---

[90] Garnet to Parsons, September 6, 1594, ABSI, Anglia I, 81 (published in Foley, *Records*, vol. 4, p. 48).

[91] Creswell to Acquaviva, Madrid December 3, 1594, ARSI, Hisp. 138, fols 9ʳ⁻ᵛ.

[92] Acquaviva to Creswell, Rome February 5, 1595, ARSI, Tolet. 5/II, fol. 383ᵛ.

[93] Garnet to Parsons, November 19, 1594, ABSI, Anglia I, 82 (published in Foley, *Records*, vol. 4, pp. 48–50).

[94] Garnet to Parsons, September 6, 1594, ABSI, Anglia I, 81 (published in Foley, *Records*, vol. 4, pp. 45–46).

Elizabethan government stirred up Francis Stuart, Earl of Bothwell, and others to counterbalance the power of the earls. To banish the Catholic earls and to avenge James Stuart, Earl of Moray, Bothwell led his forces to invade Edinburgh from the south. As ministers castigated James for his failure to march north to deal with the earls, he retorted that such a move would leave Edinburgh defenseless to Bothwell's forces—a prospect that would have delighted some ministers. In reply to Patrick Galloway's curt comment, James doubted that anyone could accuse him of any grievous crime except that of failing to execute justice against Bothwell. But, he continued:

> ... if yee will assist me against him at this tyme, I promise to persecute the excommunicated lords, so that they sall not be suffered to remaine in anie part of Scotland; and that the guarde sall not be dismissed till it be done. And if the Lord give me victorie over Bothwell, I sall never rest till I passe upon Huntlie and the rest of the excommunicated lords.[95]

Bothwell progressed as far as Leith, but he did not press his advantage. Sermons from ministers such as John Ross who proclaimed the king a "tratour to God, in joyning and shaiking hands with the wicked,"[96] confirmed James's suspicions that the Kirk backed Bothwell and consistently provided theological justification for revolt and, perhaps, assassination.

On May 7, 1594 the General Assembly convened in Edinburgh. In its fourth session the assembly ratified an earlier decision of the Fife synod excommunicating William Douglas, Earl of Angus, George Gordon, Earl of Huntly, and Francis Hay, Earl of Erroll, and their associates, with the exception of the repentant Alexander, Lord Hume, for subverting true religion. Advised by crafty and pernicious Jesuits, said earls conspired against the king and plotted to betray "our native countrie to the cruell and mercilesse Spaniard."[97] On 30 May Parliament declared the estates of Erroll, Huntly, Angus and Sir Patrick Gordon, Laird of Auchindoun, forfeit and James commissioned Archibald Campbell, Earl of Argyll, to pursue them. Some ministers were still not satisfied: fundamentally they

---

[95] Thomas Thomson, (ed.), *Calderwood's History of the Kirk of Scotland* (8 vols, Edinburgh 1842–1849), vol. 4, p. 296. Again unless specifically noted, I follow the narrative of Calderwood (vol. 5, pp. 293–387); Andrew Lang, *A History of Scotland from the Roman Occupation* (4 vols, Edinburgh/London, 1900–1907), vol. 2, pp. 383–400; and Michael Yellowlees, *"So strange a monster as a Jesuite": The Society of Jesus in Sixteenth-Century Scotland* (Isle of Colonsay, 2003), pp. 130–39.

[96] Thomson, *Calderwood*, vol. 5, p. 299.

[97] Thomson, *Calderwood*, vol. 5, p. 310. See pages 310–13 for a detailed list of accusations. See also Alan R. MacDonald, *The Jacobean Kirk, 1567–1625: Sovereignty, Polity and Liturgy* (Aldershot, 1998), pp. 52–58.

did not trust the king. The minister John Davidson compared James to King Charles IX of France who feigned sympathy for the Huguenots but allowed the St Bartholomew's Massacres. Thus they closely monitored James's activities.

The Jesuit James Gordon left Scotland in late 1593, ostensibly in compliance with the orders of the Kirk. News of his safe arrival in Flanders reached Claudio Acquaviva by January 8, 1594.[98] The Scot had business to transact in Rome and Acquaviva granted him the required permission to visit the city. Acquaviva did not specify Gordon's motives in his reply but he did caution him of difficulties he might encounter on the journey. He advised Gordon to discuss the journey with William Crichton and, if they decided that the trip would be useful, Gordon was to dress in nothing more extravagant than the simple cassock common to all Jesuits. The news of recent favorable political developments in Scotland delighted Acquaviva; this news renewed his hope that God's glory could be promoted there.[99]

In Rome Gordon besought the pope to aid the Scottish earls. William Crichton, as we shall see in the next chapter, hoped to convince Spain to intervene. Perhaps as a result of Gordon's news, Crichton now argued that James should be recognized as the most suitable candidate for the English throne. Criticizing those who preferred Henry Stanley, Earl of Derby, as the Catholic candidate, Crichton contended that the earl had neither the means nor the will to press his claims. His death and the refusal of his successor Ferdinando, Lord Strange to present himself as a candidate, left no alternative to James. Confessing that he previously had a very bad opinion of James, Crichton argued that the aid formerly promised the earl of Derby be transferred to James because he now turned to Catholics for assistance, having been deserted by his ministers and Protestant supporters. If Catholics acted swiftly, they could easily gain his approval. He ended his letter with a request that Acquaviva relay this information to the Holy See with an exhortation that someone be sent to Scotland with authorization to negotiate with the earls. Despite a suggestion from an unnamed correspondent in Spain, Crichton did not think it expedient that he himself undertake the negotiations.[100] Whether Acquaviva forwarded

---

[98] Citing a letter written by Crichton in 1605, William Forbes-Leith, S.J., argued that James acting on the advice of his councilors sent Crichton and Gordon to arrange secretly with the pope the proper means for the restoration of Catholicism in Scotland. The king was so moved because of fear of the Kirk (*Narratives of Scottish Catholics under Mary Stuart and James VI* [Edinburgh, 1885], p. 222).

[99] Acquaviva to Gordon Rome January 8, 1594, ARSI, Fl. Belg. 1/I, pp. 523–24; same to Crichton, Rome January 8, 1594, ARSI, Fl. Belg. 1/I, p. 524.

[100] Crichton to Acquaviva, Brussels January 13, 1594 ARSI, Germ. 172, fols 11^r–11a^v (published in Francisco de Borja Medina, S.J., "Intrigues of a Scottish Jesuit at the Spanish Court: William Crichton's Mission to Madrid (1590–1592)," in *The Reckoned Expense:*

the proposal, we do not know, but he did urge Robert Parsons to do all he could to assist Crichton.[101] Again Crichton's efforts failed. In August of 1594, Hugh Owen reported to Ranuccio Farnese, Prince of Parma, that Philip did not have the resources for a new armada. Moreover, Owen doubted that Pope Clement VIII would sanction any undertaking sponsored by Spain. But, a smaller expedition, commanded perhaps by Farnese, might attract Philip.[102]

In an undated memorial to James Tyrie, Gordon, less sure of James's sincerity, argued in favor of the forcible conversion of the king.[103] Although, according to Gordon, James was not firmly committed to any religion, he resisted all arguments in favor of Catholicism because of his Protestant upbringing, and his conviction that adherence to Protestantism safeguarded his position in Scotland and his claim to the English throne. Only the military power of the Scottish Catholic earls could win the king over to Catholicism. Their rebellion—and they could easily justify a revolt—would result in the king's capture and his acceptance of their conditions. If James accepted them, he would be allowed to reign; if not, a Catholic noble would act as regent until he came to his senses. Persistent refusal might lead to his son's succession, but Gordon doubted that would be necessary. The Jesuit recommended that one of James's French relatives be asked to intercede. Since James refused to deal directly with the pope, the same person could serve as an intermediary. If no foreign leader would accept the mission, Gordon recommended James Beaton, Archbishop of Glasgow, duly promoted to the primatial see of St Andrews. Scottish Catholics, however, were not strong enough to resist the English forces that would undoubtedly cross the border to defend him without foreign assistance. Ideally the rebellion should be coordinated with a Spanish attack on England. Now only money was required but it must not be placed in the king's hands because he would only distribute it among his courtiers. Instead the Catholic nobility in general or one Catholic noble in particular should be the recipient: they/he would ensure that it was used for the Catholic cause by purchasing loyalty or hiring mercenaries.

Edmund Campion and the Early English Jesuits. Essays in Celebration of the First Centenary of Campion Hall, Oxford, (ed.) Thomas M. McCoog, S.J., 2nd edn. [Rome, 2007], pp. 322–24; and "Escocia en la Estrategia de la Empresa de Inglaterra: La Misión del P. William Crichton cerca de Felipe II (1590–1592)," *Revista de Historia Naval*, 17 [1999] pp. 89, 101–102).

[101] Rome July 4, 1594, ARSI, Tolet. 5/II, fol. 347^v.

[102] Albert J. Loomie, S.J., "The Armadas and the Catholics of England," *Catholic Historical Review*, 59 (1973): pp. 393–94.

[103] The memorial can be found in ARSI, Angl. 42, fols 26^r–27^r. We can identify Gordon as the author and Tyrie as the recipient from ciphers in Angl. 42, fols 18^r and 22^v.

In Rome Gordon obtained financial support apparently intended for James and not for the Catholic nobles. Armed with a large sum of money from Clement VIII and a promise of a monthly pension if James declared himself a Catholic and granted Catholics his protection, Gordon returned to Scotland in the summer of 1594.[104] Other conditions included placing Prince Henry in Inverness Castle under the custody of Huntly; replacing Sir John Maitland as chancellor with Alexander Seton; naming George, Lord Seton custodian of Edinburgh Castle;[105] finally promising to recall from Flanders all Scots involved in the war against Spain.[106] Dressed as merchants, Gordon and another Scottish Jesuit, William Murdoch, landed safely at Aberdeen on July 16, 1594 even though a Scot boarding the ship recognized Gordon but said nothing out of fear of Gordon's nephew, the earl of Huntly.[107] However a few English secular priests and the papal agent Giovanni Sapiretti were arrested and the money confiscated. Gordon immediately sought his nephew, who, with the earls of Angus and Erroll and the laird of Auchindoun, threatened to burn down the town unless the magistrates released all prisoners into their custody. The Catholic earls then decided the Catholic cause would be better advanced if the money carried by Sapiretti were used wisely by them instead of being forwarded to James. Once they had their hands on the money, they supplied themselves and their followers for the upcoming campaign. Sapiretti retorted that he did not have authority to alter his instructions from Clement VIII: the money was destined for the king upon his conversion. There was no time for discussion or observation of diplomatic niceties as the earl of Argyll's army approached. The impasse was resolved when the Catholic earls and the Jesuits took full responsibility for the decision to spend the money to

---

[104] An anonymous document in *CSP Simancas* (1587–1603) specified the sum as 40,000 ducats with a monthly grant of 10,000 (p. 500). Crichton did not think Gordon the man for the mission because he was easily frustrated and preferred William Chisholm, Bishop of Vaison. Nor was he enthusiastic about Giovanni Sapiretti. See Crichton to James Tyrie, Brussels February 10, 1595, BL, Lans. 96, fols 91ʳ–92ᵛ. These letters were summarized in Wernham, *List and Analysis*, vol. 6, par. 393.

[105] On Alexander Seton and his father George see Maurice Lee, Jr., "King James's Popish Chancellor," in *The Renaissance and Reformation in Scotland: Essays in Honour of Gordon Donaldson*, (eds.) Ian B. Cowan and Duncan Shaw (Edinburgh, 1983), pp. 170–82.

[106] ARSI, Angl. 42, fols 38ʳ–40ᵛ.

[107] Father General informed Murdoch that he was to accompany Gordon on May 22, 1594 (ARSI, Franc. 1/II, fols 393ᵛ–394ʳ). He was, however, not enthusiastic about leaving Pont-à-Mousson (June 19, 1594, ARSI, Gal. 93, fols 177ʳ⁻ᵛ). Acquaviva then allowed John Hay to return to Scotland, presumably as Murdoch's replacement (Acquaviva to Hay, Rome July 6, 1594, ARSI, Lugd. 1, fols 229ʳ⁻ᵛ). Hay did not embark; Murdoch did.

avert a disaster and to make full restitution later. Sapiretti then returned to the continent.[108]

Bothwell's antics added to James's displeasure. The Catholic earls tempted him with their newly acquired wealth.[109] In late summer of 1594 Bothwell allied with the Catholics, but he played no role in the forthcoming battle. The Catholic forces prepared for battle; the Jesuits Gordon and Murdoch heard their confessions and distributed communion. They approached the battle, believing that they were fighting in defense of true religion. On October 3, they defeated the earl of Argyll at the Battle of Glenrinneis (or Glenlivet) with minimal losses.[110] But their success was short-lived: delegating William Douglas, Earl of Morton, his lieutenant for the Borders as protection against Bothwell, James led an army to Aberdeen. Lack of funds allegedly prevented him from doing more than destroying a few castles before his return to Edinburgh in early November. Because of Bothwell's alliance with the Catholics, he lost his support in the Kirk. On February 18, 1595, Bothwell's brother, Hercules Stuart, was hanged. On the same day James finally persuaded the Kirk to excommunicate Bothwell. The Catholic earls remained in the north.[111]

Unaware of recent developments in Scotland, the Jesuit John Myrton accompanied Robert Jones on a trip to the British Isles.[112] Myrton was

---

[108] William Crichton to Claudio Acquaviva, Antwerp November 12, 1594, ARSI, Germ. 173, fols 218^r–219^v; same to same, Carpentras May 6, 1613, ARSI, Angl. 42, fols 259^r–260^v. See also two detailed accounts in *CSP Simancas* (1587–1603), pp. 588–92, 603–606; and letters from Robert Bowes to Lord Burghley, Edinburgh June 17, 1592, *CSP Scotland* (1589–1593), pp. 698–702, and same to same, Edinburgh January 29, 1593, same to same, Edinburgh August 3, 1594, *CSP Scotland* (1593–1595), pp. 33–36, 400–402); John Durkan, "William Murdoch and the Early Jesuit Mission in Scotland," *The Innes Review*, 35 (1984): p. 5. Many of the details regarding Sapiretti come from a report of Innocenzo Malvasia, papal agent in Belgium, which will be considered in greater detail in Chapter 6.

[109] Susan Doran notes James and Elizabeth gradually became aware that Huntly and Bothwell were unreliable associates. See "Loving and Affectionate Cousins? The Relationship between Elizabeth I and James VI of Scotland 1586–1603," in *Tudor England and its Neighbours*, (eds.) Susan Doran and Glenn Richardson (Basingstoke, 2005), pp. 204–205. Well aware of James's need for money, Elizabeth also paid her subsidies lest James seek foreign financial support. See Julian Goodare, "James VI's English subsidy," in *The Reign of James VI*, (eds.) Julian Goodare and Michael Lynch (Edinburgh, 2008), pp. 110–25.

[110] For an account of the battle see William Crichton to Claudio Acquaviva, Brussels May 12, 1595, ARSI, Germ. 174, fols 210^r–211^v. See also Forbes-Leith, *Narratives of Scottish Catholics*, pp. 222–25.

[111] In February Crichton reported that the earls of Huntly, Erroll, Angus and Bothwell were with George Sinclair, Earl of Caithness, awaiting assistance from Spain (Crichton to James Tyrie, Brussels February 10, 1595, BL, Lans. 96, fols 91^r–92^v).

[112] Their letters patent were dated October 11, 1594 (ARSI, Hist. Soc. 61, fol. 49^v). Crichton was slightly skeptical about Myrton because of his esteem for Henry IV: "I feir he sall not obey F. Gordon yat is in Scotland; of me he would have no dependence; sometimes

captured at Leith on March 24, 1595.[113] Letters from the pope to the king were found on him. Upon examination on April 5, Myrton admitted that he was a Jesuit and had been sent to Scotland to encourage James Gordon and the Catholic earls. He was also commissioned to inform them that they had incurred the anger of Monsignor Innocenza Malvasia because of their appropriation and misuse of the money sent for the king. As a result he did not carry money with him but only the nuncio's insistence that they justify their actions before any more was forwarded. His confession confirmed by intercepted letters from the Low Countries informed the government of the intended arrival of more Jesuits and of the common belief that James and many of his retinue were Catholics. Only the lack of money prevented public disclosure of their true faith. To overcome any obstacles, Jesuits highly recommended James Tyrie's nephew, Thomas Tyrie, a confidant of James and of Lord Hume, captain of the royal guard.[114] However on March 19, even before Myrton's arrest, Huntly and his Jesuit uncle had left Aberdeen for the continent. Erroll had fled two days earlier.[115] Both earls promised not to return to Scotland without royal license and not to plot against king or realm during their absence. Their wives continued to enjoy the income from their estates.[116] By the end of April Bothwell followed them to the continent. There he became a Catholic and never returned to Scotland. Angus remained in Scotland. By the beginning of

---

he wold be heir, and not have begonne to say his matings neir supper tyme, and sometime for negligence omitte to saye messe. All yat thinges gevis me feir and matter to suspect evill. Yet yai are bot fondementis of suspicions; he may preve, as I hope he sall, ye honest man, for ye know him best yair. He hes over gud opinion of Navarra and our turbulent Frenchmen, and over greit aversion from Spagnarts and Inglismen, quhilke F. Holt, F. Jonas, and other hes noted heir and tald me. I am sory to wryte zou this malancolie matteres, bot zit ze being in the places ze are, is gud to knaw all" (Crichton to James Tyrie, Brussels February 10, 1595, BL, Lans. 96, fols 91ʳ–92ᵛ).

[113] Crichton claimed that Myrton's life was in danger because the queen of England wanted him executed "for the sole reason that thereby the Pope would lose the whole hope which he had conceived of the King of Scotland" (Crichton to Tyrie, Antwerp June 18, 1595, *CSP Scotland* [1593–1595], pp. 611, 614).

[114] In a letter to Acquaviva, Crichton highly endorsed Tyrie as a faithful, prudent and discreet man who would be able to bring about what was so highly desired (Brussels February 10, 1595, BL, Lans. 96, fols 85ʳ–86ᵛ). Another copy can be found in TNA, SP 77/5, fols 181ʳ⁻ᵛ (summarized in Wernham, *List and Analysis*, vol. 6, par. 393). See also Crichton to Cardinal Cajetan, Brussels February 10, 1595, BL, Lans. 96, fols 83ʳ–84ᵛ (with a copy in TNA, SP 77/5, fols 183ʳ⁻ᵛ [summarized in Wernham, *List and Analysis*, vol. 6, par. 393]). Lord Hume most likely was Sir James Hume.

[115] On Myrton's examination and the instructions he had received from Crichton see *CSP Scotland* (1593–1595), pp. 564–65, 571–73.

[116] The Kirk, not surprisingly, found it practically impossible to exercise discipline over Huntly. See Michael F. Graham, *The Uses of Reform: 'Godly Discipline' and Popular Behaviour in Scotland and Beyond, 1560–1610* (Leiden, 1996), p. 264.

October he was seeking to overturn his excommunication by arranging a conference with representatives of the Kirk.

With the flight of Erroll and Huntly, Angus's possible conformity, and Bothwell's excommunication, relations between James and Elizabeth entered a period of peaceful stability.[117] In fact to many, James seemed to have become a Protestant hero.[118] Yet fear remained. The General Assembly in June of 1595 still urged the forceful extirpation of Roman Catholicism. James, taking advantage of English apprehensions, sought financial subsidies. In a letter to Elizabeth on July 8, 1595 he compared their situations:

> Surelie, madame, if it shall please you to wey it, ye will find we both are but at a truce and not at peax, with the Romishe Spanishe practices. These Spaniolizde rebels of mine, that are fledd the cuntrey are but retired to fetch a greatter fairde, if they may.[119]

James emerged much more secure. With Bothwell banished and Catholic earls in temporary exile, James eliminated two sources of friction with the Kirk. With the departure of the earls, Catholic influence waned and Jesuit presence dwindled. Myrton was freed by order of the king and sent back to the continent.[120] Only Murdoch and Robert Abercrombie remained. But the reinforcements revealed by Myrton were not long in arriving: George Elphinstone and George Christie were sent to Scotland in September of 1595.[121]

---

[117] Doran, "Loving and Affectionate Cousins," p. 216.

[118] From Antwerp on May 25, 1595, Verstegan reported to Parsons that "the ministers in Scotland have gotten the most of the principall Catholique nobillitie oute of the countrie, their landes and provinces so spolyed that scarsly a chicken is left behynde; and therefore the King mighte more easely graunt some of them libertie to enjoye their livings in their absence, for litle enoughe it is lyke to be as some of that nation do reporte" (ABSI, Anglia II, 25 [published in Petti, *Verstegan Papers*, p. 239]).

[119] John Bruce, (ed.), *Letters of Queen Elizabeth and King James VI of Scotland* (London, 1849), p. 111.

[120] He was in Bruges by 1596 (ARSI, Fl. Belg. 43, fol. 29^v).

[121] Originally John Hay was selected as Elphinstone's companion but for reasons unexplained, Christie replaced him. James Gordon hoped to return around the same time but his departure was postponed. Alexander MacQuhirrie, who had left Scotland at an unspecified time, planned to return. See Crichton to Acquaviva, Brussels May 12, 1595, ARSI, Germ. 174, fols 210^r–211^v; Acquaviva to Crichton, Rome September 16, 1595, ARSI, Fl. Belg. 1/I, p. 571; same to Gordon, Rome September 16, 1595, ARSI, Fl. Belg. 1/I, p. 571; same to MacQuhirrie, Rome September 16, 1595, ARSI, Fl. Belg. 1/I, p. 571; same to George Duras, Rome September 16, 1595, ARSI, Fl. Belg. 1/I, pp. 572–73; same to Elphinstone, Rome October 28, 1595, ARSI, Fl. Belg. 1/I, p. 577.

Slow Escalation of Rebellion in Ireland

The conduct of both Hugh Roe O'Donnell and Hugh O'Neill, Earl of Tyrone, after the defeat of Hugh Maguire's revolt in February of 1594, continued to arouse suspicion despite their persistent protests of loyalty.[122] They complained, however, that their loyalty had not reaped appropriate rewards. Among others, Adam Loftus, Lord Chancellor and Archbishop of Dublin, Sir Robert Gardiner, and Sir Anthony St Leger, all known supporters of Tyrone, considered their complaints. They recommended that Maguire be pardoned and that the commissions of Sir Henry Bagenal and Thomas Henshaw, be withdrawn to satisfy O'Neill and O'Donnell. The hated William Fitzwilliams, Lord Deputy of Ireland since 1588, was to be recalled and Bagenal forbidden to move against his enemy and brother-in-law O'Neill. Elizabeth's instructions for the new lord deputy, William Russell, were extremely favorable to the Irish leaders, but by the time he arrived in Ireland in early August of 1594 a new revolt had begun.

O'Donnell joined Maguire in an attack on the Enniskillen fortress in June. O'Neill initially refused to commit himself and considered the act rash. Nonetheless the attack proceeded satisfactorily. Supplemented by Scottish mercenaries, O'Donnell's forces besieged the fortress as Maguire and Cormac O'Neill, Hugh's brother, plotted to ambush English reinforcements. On August 7, Irish forces surprised and repulsed the army of Sir Edward Herbert and Sir Henry Duke at the "Ford of the Biscuits." Nearly a quarter of the English soldiers were either killed or wounded. On August 11, Russell was sworn in as lord deputy and Fitzwilliams departed. On the 15th O'Neill appeared in Dublin to submit to the lord deputy and to offer his assistance in restoring peace. Bagenal, however, had prepared a list of charges against Tyrone, the most serious of which was association of members of O'Neill's family with Archbishop Edmund MacGauran and their involvement in his Spanish-Papal schemes. But Bagenal did not have enough evidence and the new lord deputy permitted O'Neill to leave Dublin. Russell meanwhile relieved the fort at Enniskillen on 30 August.

In 1595 Tyrone moved closer to public association with the rebels perhaps because his desire to govern Ulster alone was frustrated.[123] In

---

[122] I follow the basic narrative in Cyril Falls, *Elizabeth's Irish Wars* (London, 1996), pp. 177–93; Colm Lennon, *Sixteenth Century Ireland: The Incomplete Conquest* (Dublin, 1994), pp. 292–94; Steven G. Ellis, *Tudor Ireland: Crown, Community and the Conflict of Cultures 1470–1603* (London, 1985), pp. 298–302; Hiram Morgan, *Tyrone's Rebellion* (Woodbridge, 1993), pp. 167–98.

[123] Verstegan relayed rumors of Tyrone's preparations for war on March 22, 1595 to Parsons (ABSI, Anglia II, 3 [published in Petti, *Verstegan Papers*, p. 229]). The question of Ireland posed a problem that English Catholic writers could not resolve. Even though they developed theories of resistance that justified rebellion and/or invasion, there was considerable

February of 1595 his illegitimate brother Art MacBaron O'Neill led some of Tyrone's forces in an attack on, and eventual capture of, an English fort on the Blackwater River. In May, O'Donnell, Maguire and Cormac O'Neill recovered Enniskillen and raided Longford. Monaghan castle was the next target. On May 25, Bagenal's forces relieved the castle but on their return to Newry, Tyrone's forces ambushed them at Clontibret. If Tyrone had pressed his advantage, Bagenal's defeat would have been much worse. In early June the English governor of Sligo was murdered by an Irish servant and his Sligo fortress, handed over to O'Donnell. Because of his open involvement in a war against the English government, Tyrone was proclaimed a traitor in June. In September Turlough Luineach O'Neill died. Although it had no effect on his real power, Tyrone went to the traditional site at Tullahogue for his election as chief of the O'Neills.

For different reasons both sides were anxious to secure a truce. England needed more time to complete the transfer of troops from Brittany. O'Neill and O'Donnell realized that complete victory could not be won without Spanish support. Depicting their rebellion in religious terms, they urged Philip II to come to their aid: it was now or never if Spain wanted to restore Catholicism in Ireland. Indeed O'Neill and O'Donnell even offered the kingdom of Ireland to Philip to spur him on. Catholic priests urged the Irish to recusancy, and many obeyed their instructions. Aware of these clandestine negotiations and warned that a Spanish expeditionary force would bring about a "dangerous hazard,"[124] the Elizabethan government pressured O'Neill and O'Donnell. Jumping before they were pushed, on October 18, the two promised to have no further dealings with foreign powers and to be more faithful to the queen. O'Neill explained that he had assumed the title "O'Neill" lest a rival claimed it but he renounced it for the sake of peace. Both sides agreed to a truce until January of 1596, later extended until May.

Aside from James Archer's request that a Jesuit be sent to Ireland to seek financial support for the Irish College in Salamanca from Irish nobles, presumably the Catholic nobles then in rebellion, there was no other reference either to a possible resumption of a mission or to Jesuit involvement with the rebellion despite the desire of some Jesuits such as Richard Pembroke to return home. The Irish leaders whose assistance was sought, were not wealthy and it was unlikely that these same leaders who were seeking support for their rebellion, could afford to support the college. As Irish representatives visited Spain and Rome in their efforts to

---

reluctance to extend that right to the Irish. See Thomas H. Clancy, S.J., "English Catholics and the Papal Deposing Power, 1570–1640," *Recusant History*, 6 (1961): pp. 131–32.

[124] Henry A. Jefferies, *The Irish Church and the Tudor Reformations* (Dublin, 2010), pp. 254–55, 271.

gain foreign support, they frequently asked that some Jesuits be sent to Ireland.[125] But there was another request in Archer's letter to Acquaviva: he also asked permission to visit Rome to discuss with Acquaviva certain matters "which can be done ... for the greater glory of God, but which cannot be suitably committed to writing." Acquaviva denied permission to come to Rome so we do not know what he intended to discuss with the general. But did he hope to establish contact with the Catholic lords? Or did he simply want, as Thomas Morrissey argued, to discuss his current problems with certain Spanish Jesuits.[126]

The Martyrdom of Southwell and Walpole

At his capture on June 24, 1592, Robert Southwell replied to Topcliffe's taunts that he was a priest by demanding proof of the accusation. Discovery of his priesthood not only placed Southwell's life in danger but threatened his hosts. Thus he remained silent. On April 6, 1593, having endured eight months in an "anchorite's cell" in the Tower of London with no visitors save the occasional appearance of the Tower's Lieutenant, Sir Michael Blount, he finally provided the desired information in order to force the government's hand. In a letter to Sir Robert Cecil, he explained the reasons for his silence: protection of his hosts. Now aware that the Bellamy family no longer needed his silence and apprehensive that his refusal to speak would be interpreted as fear, he confessed that he was a Roman Catholic priest and a Jesuit. He returned to England to work for the salvation of his family and friends out of devotion. He could not ignore their plight:

> I was the child of a Christian woman and not the whelp of a tiger; I could not fear, and foresee, and not forewarn; I had not a crueler heart than a damned caitiff, to despise their bodies and souls by whom I received mine. But this was an inveigled zeal, a blind and now abolished faith, a zeal notwithstanding, and a faith it was. And God Almighty is my witness, I came with no other intention into the realm; and as for the blindness thereof, I appeal to the eyes of all antiquity and to the most and happily not to the dimmest of all Christendom,

---

[125] See, for example, "Articuli quidam cum supplicatione Suae Sanctitati nomine Ibernorum exulum proponendi," IJA, MS B.21 (published in Edmund Hogan, S.J., *Ibernia Ignatiana* [Dublin, 1880], pp. 35–37). From internal references to Pope Clement VIII and to the new college in Dublin (Trinity), we can approximate the date of composition.

[126] Archer to Acquaviva, Salamanca August 9, 1594, ARSI, Hisp. 137, fols 115^{r-v}; Thomas J. Morrissey, S.J., *James Archer of Kilkenny: An Elizabethan Jesuit* (Dublin, 1979), pp. 16–17.

who both protest and prove that they have read and seen in this faith the surest and soundest grounds of all human and divine belief.[127]

His faith and vocation were his two most precious possessions. If life could be gained only by abandoning one and forfeiting the other, he preferred a thousand deaths. Mindful that he had become a "suitor" for his own execution by giving evidence against himself, he asked Cecil as one responsible for administration of justice to decide whether he had suffered enough or should be prosecuted in court:

> I have sent you a sharp sword, yet as I suppose, well sheathed—I mean that which you conceive as a capital crime with that which I esteem a reasonable excuse. If it shall please you to draw and to use it, the hand that sent it hath a heart to endure it, if a heart so free from ill meaning to any, and so full of good wishes to Your Honor, must needs offer up all loves in a bloody sacrifice and yield it poor self as a chief portion of the host. If I were born in effect to try the lot which was threatened to Isaac, but not intended, here I have begun with one part of his office, which was to carry the fuel wherein himself was to be the oblation.[128]

The choice was Cecil's: would he play the role of Abraham or the Angel?

According to Garnet, Cecil replied that if Southwell was so eager to be hanged, his wish would be granted.[129] Nonetheless Cecil did nothing and Southwell remained in the Tower. The possibility of Sir Thomas Wilkes's diplomatic mission to Archduke Ernst prevented initiation of any judicial proceedings throughout 1594. Finally on 18 February 1595 the government decided to act: Robert Southwell was transferred from the Tower to a subterranean cell called Limbo in Newgate prison to await his trial.[130]

---

[127] Southwell's letter can be found in *Two Letters and Short Rules of a Good Life*, (ed.) Nancy Pollard Brown (Charlottesville, 1973), pp. 77–85. The quotation is on p. 81.

[128] Southwell, *Two Letters*, pp. 83–84.

[129] Garnet to Acquaviva, March 7, 1595, ARSI, Fondo Gesuitico 651/624 with contemporary copies, ARSI, Angl. 31/I, fols 107^r–109^v; 115^r–116^v.

[130] Garnet's account of Southwell's trial can be found in a letter to Acquaviva, London February 22, 1595, ARSI, Fondo Gesuitico 651/624. There are many copies of this holograph letter, e.g. ABSI, Anglia II, 13. An English translation of the opening paragraphs can be found in Foley, *Records*, vol. 1, pp. 376–77. A full account, written in Italian, was sent on March 7 (Fondo Gesuitico 651/624 with contemporary copies, ARSI, Angl. 31/I, fols 107^r–109^v; 115^r–116^v). A contemporary account of his trial and execution, "A brief discourse of the condemnation and execution of Mr. Robert Southwell, priest of the Society of Jesus," can be found in ABSI, Anglia II, 1 (published in Foley, *Records*, vol. 1, pp. 364–75). See also More,

Southwell was racked 10 times during his years in the Tower of London. Kept under the closest confinement, he had no contact with any Catholics. A generous Catholic and a sympathetic gaoler fitted the cell in Newgate with a bed, fire, and candles. Indeed on his first evening, he was given wine and a good dinner. On the 20th he was taken to Westminster Hall where, in the presence of Sir John Popham, Chief Justice of the King's Bench, Sir Edward Coke, Attorney General, and Richard Topcliffe, he was charged with being a priest and a Jesuit in violation of an "Act against Jesuits, seminary priests, and other like disobedient persons" (27 Eliz. 1 c. 2). For the moment, Southwell's priestly membership in the Society of Jesus did not interest them: plots and conspiracies were their concern.

Popham began the proceedings with a long account of Jesuit treachery, tracing their plots and conspiracies from the Northern Revolt of 1569 through the Babington Plot of 1585 until the more recent attempts by Hesketh, Yorke, and Williams. The queen's life was not safe and the nation was not secure as long as a Jesuit or seminary priest remained at large. The statutes condemned priests and Jesuits for their disloyalty. Southwell was then indicted on three charges: he was a subject of the queen; that he had been ordained priest since the queen's accession; and that he had acted "traitorously and as a false traitor to our said lady the Queen" at Uxenden on July 26, 1592.[131] Denying guilt of any treason, he challenged the legality of the law and asked to be tried by God and his country. He admitted the first charge and his age supported the second. To the third, Southwell contended, he did not commit treason at Uxenden but simply administered the sacraments. But that, Coke replied, was treason according to English law. Because such laws were contrary to the law of God, Southwell countered, they could not be observed. In the ensuing controversy Southwell blamed his poor memory on long confinement and torture. Both Popham and Coke denied knowing anything about torture. Topcliffe demanded proof. Southwell's reply was terse: "Let a woman show her throes!" Topcliffe then tried to justify his treatment of the prisoner but Coke preferred to drop the matter and return to his litany of papal aggression. To the traditional justification of the lawfulness of murdering the queen and subjecting her realm, Southwell had added a novelty that many believed undermined the fabric of civilized society: equivocation.[132] Anne Bellamy Jones was called as a witness. She testified that Southwell

---

Elizabethan Jesuits, pp. 244–54; Christopher Devlin, S.J., *The Life of Robert Southwell Poet and Martyr* (London, 1956), pp. 303–24. My narrative follows these accounts.

[131] "A brief discourse," ABSI, Anglia II, 1 (published in Foley, *Records*, vol. 1, p. 366).

[132] This charge against Southwell, according to Devlin (*Robert Southwell*, pp. 300–302) was the Society's first public association with the doctrine. As we saw in the first chapter, not all Jesuits on the mission agreed on equivocation.

informed her that she could deny under oath that she had seen a priest adding a mental qualifier even though she had in fact seen one. Coke prevented Southwell from demonstrating that equivocation conformed to the Word of God and to civil and canon law by proclaiming that the Jesuit taught perjury was lawful. "Suppose," Southwell proposed:

> that the French King should invade her Majesty, and that she (which God forfend) should by her enemies be enforced to fly to some private house for her safety, where none knew her being, but Mr. Attorney; and that Mr. Attorney's refusal to swear, being thereunto urged, should be a confession of her being in the house (for I suppose that also if Mr. Attorney in this case should be examined and should refuse to swear that he knoweth that her Majesty is not there, with this intention not to tell them), I say, Mr. Attorney were neither her Majesty's good subject nor friend.[133]

Southwell replied to Popham's contention that Coke should refuse to swear by concluding that such silence would condemn his sovereign. Popham and Coke rejected any equivocation because "if this doctrine should be allowed, it would supplant all justice, for we are men and no gods, and can judge but according to their outward actions and sayings and not according to their secret and inward intuitions."[134] Again disruption prevented Southwell from explaining his position. The jury returned a guilty verdict after 15 minutes. Popham pronounced the sentence of hanging, drawing, and quartering to be carried out the following day. On the scaffold he confessed:

> … concerning the Queen's Majesty, God Almighty knoweth that I never meant or intended harm or evil against her; I have daily prayed for her, and yet in this short time in which I have to live, I most humbly and beseech Almighty God for His tender mercy's sake, for His Precious Blood's sake, and for His most glorious Wounds' sake, that he would vouchsafe she may so use those gifts and those graces which God, nature, and fortune hath bestowed upon her, that with them all she may both please and glorify God, advance the happiness of our country, and purchase to herself the preservation and salvation of her body and soul.[135]

---

[133] "A brief discourse," ABSI, Anglia II, 1 (published in Foley, *Records*, vol. 1, p. 369).
[134] "A brief discourse," ABSI, Anglia II, 1 (published in Foley, *Records*, vol. 1, p. 369).
[135] "A brief discourse," ABSI, Anglia II, 1 (published in Foley, *Records*, vol. 1, p. 374).

Protected by the crowd and by Charles Blount, Lord Mountjoy, Southwell was hanged until death. No one cried "Traitor, Traitor" when his head was shown to the people.[136]

The day after Southwell's execution, Garnet confessed that he did:

> not know whether I should grieve or rejoice at this time. My sorrow is that my gentlest and dearest companion has been taken from me. My joy is that he whom I loved so much in the sight of God has been taken up to where he will receive the reward of his labors, rest from his worries, and immense joy in the Lord instead of incredible torments. At this time it is more fitting to rejoice, and for me, your Lordship, and the whole Church to give thanks to God.[137]

Two days after Southwell's martyrdom, Garnet explained the verdict to Acquaviva:

> Behold, now at length I present to his Paternity a lovely flower gathered from his gardens, the sweetest fruit from his tree, a priceless treasure from his bank, silver weighed, tried, and sevenfold purged from earthly dross in the fire; an invincible soldier, a most faithful disciple, and courageous martyr of Christ, Robert Southwell, my former most beloved companion and brother, now my patron, a king reigning together with Christ.[138]

But Southwell was not the only Jesuit victim: Walpole soon followed.

Garnet wrote that Walpole's journey from London to York for the Lenten Assizes in 1595 was a prolonged exercise of mortification.[139] He had no desire to use a bed, preferring bare earth. Upon his incarceration in York, he spent most of the night kneeling on a wooden bench in prayer, or composing English verses to Jesus, Mary, and the angels. By day he disputed with two ministers, Anthony Higgins and someone with the surname of Sander, on justification, perseverance in faith, and Petrine primacy. Higgins apparently lost his fervor and urged that Walpole should be treated with utmost consideration. Each minister, however, urged Walpole to save his life by yielding to the queen on some points:

---

[136] See Verstegan to Baynes, Antwerp June 30, 1595, ABSI, Anglia II, 3 (published in Petti, *Verstegan Papers*, pp. 242–43) for popular reaction to Southwell's execution.

[137] London February 22, 1595, ARSI, Fondo Gesuitico 651/624.

[138] I use Foley's translation (*Records*, vol. 1, p. 376).

[139] Garnet to Acquaviva, London June 20, 1595, ARSI, Fondo Gesuitico 651/624 (copy in ARSI, Angl. 31/I, fols 93ʳ–106ᵛ); More, *Elizabethan Jesuits*, pp. 267–73; Caraman, *Henry Garnet*, pp. 199–202.

he refused. On April 3, the earl of Huntingdon and Francis Beaumont[140] presided over the trial of Walpole and others. Pleading not guilty, Walpole insisted that as a priest he should be tried before ecclesiastical judges. Once that petition was dismissed, Walpole recommended himself to God and his country regarding accusations that he had associated with known English rebels and received financial support from the king of Spain. Not permitted to reply to the charges, Walpole was subjected to Sir John Saville's discourse on Jesuit doctrine and practice. Well educated priests, Jesuits were often employed in all matters "involving politics and treason." Subjection of all nations to the authority of the pope and the exaltation of the Spanish monarchy were known Jesuit goals. Who was responsible for the insurrection in Ireland? Who stirred up troubles within the kingdom? Who schemed against the king of France? Created problems for the king of Scotland? Sowed discord in the Low Countries? Inspired plots against the queen of England? The Society of Jesus! Walpole was a member of that Society. He had consorted with known trouble makers on the continent and refused to reveal names of the men with whom he would work in England. Walpole retorted that he was accused simply because he was a priest and, thus, *ipso facto*, a traitor. But, he continued, priesthood did not make a man a traitor. Certain acts constituted treason and said acts violated his priesthood. Moreover association with specific persons was not treason as long as they did not deal with treasonous matters. Beaumont reminded Walpole that English law required all returning priests to submit to a Justice of the Peace within three days of his arrival. That law did not pertain to him, Walpole countered, because he was captured within 24 hours of landing! Unfamiliar with all English laws because of his residence outside the kingdom, Walpole was willing to obey every one unless it contradicted the law of God. Beaumont summarized the government's case thus:

> You cannot deny that you are a priest and a Jesuit, that you have been with the King of Spain, that you have conferred with our fugitive rebels, with Parsons, Holt, Worthington and many other notable and known enemies, that you came to England with the intention (as you say) of doing good to your country, that is to draw away its subjects from the established religion, that is, as you call it, to the Catholic faith. This is in itself treason.

Walpole's final statement was brief:

---

[140] Francis Beaumont was a church papist who, according to Garnet, sacrificed his faith for his career. His mother's sister Elizabeth married William, Lord Vaux, and was the mother of Henry, Anne, and Eleanor Vaux Brooksby (Caraman, *Henry Garnet*, p. 201 n. 2). Garnet had cared for Beaumont's mother during her final illness. See pp. 201–202 for details.

> Gentlemen, I am a priest. I came to convert my country to the Catholic faith, and to reconcile all from sin to repentance. This I will never deny. These are the duties of my calling. And if you find any other reason which is not bound up with my calling I will ask for no sort of favour.

Regarding the queen, Walpole professed:

> I love her as a most faithful subject, and every day I pray God to bless her with His Holy Spirit, and that He may grant her grace to do as he should in this world so that she may enjoy paradise in the next. And I desire for all here present what I desire for myself, namely the salvation of our souls, and that you may live in the true Catholic faith.

Despite Walpole's protestation, the jury returned a guilty verdict. The following day, April 4, a secular priest Alexander Rawlins, was tried.[141] He too was found guilty. Both were sentenced on the 5th and executed on the 7th.

Why were Southwell and Walpole executed? Traditional confessional historians offered simple explanations: Jesuits were victims of the cruel, bloodthirsty policies of Huntingdon and Topcliffe, on the one hand, or conversely, Jesuits were involved in various plots and conspiracies. Neither explained why some suffered and others remained in prison or were exiled. Since the arrival of Campion and Parsons in 1580, Jesuits exercised their ministry much more publicly than their secular colleagues. They appealed to public opinion by challenging the ecclesiastical establishment.[142] Their secret printing presses produced religious literature aimed at strengthening English Catholic resolve. Their theological writings forbade any compromise with the Established Church. Like the more "hot" Protestants, Jesuits urged Catholics to abandon the Elizabethan Church, to refuse to participate in any service. Thus both Puritans and Jesuits pursued similar policies. But official fear of the Society of Jesus bordered on paranoia because their domestic activities were seen as part of an international programme. Suspicion of Jesuit involvement in plots and their support for regicide were corroborated by news of James Gordon's role in the revolt of the Catholic earls in Scotland and rumors of fanatical Jesuit opposition to Henry IV in France. Confessions of convicted conspirators testified to the part played by Jesuits such as Parsons and Holt. Jesuits were a plague throughout Christendom. But, again, why Southwell and Walpole?

---

[141] On Rawlins see Anstruther, *Seminary Priests*, vol. 1, pp. 285–86.

[142] See Peter Lake and Michael Questier, "Puritans, Papists, and the 'Public Sphere' in Early Modern England: The Edmund Campion Affair in Context," *Journal of Modern History*, 72 (2000): pp. 587–627.

William Weston continued to enjoy relative security in Wisbech and John Gerard developed a thriving ministry in the Clink. Why were Southwell and Walpole singled out for such cruelty?

Consciously or not, each charted his own fate. Walpole admitted association with men abhorred and feared by the English government. He consulted specific Jesuits, Spanish ministers, and the Spanish king. He refused to disclose the persons with whom he was to work in London. Was he another Hesketh sent into England to encourage a Catholic successor to Elizabeth? Was he delivering money like Gordon or making secret arrangements for a Spanish or Scottish invasion? Was he secretly pursuing a pro-Scottish policy? Most definitely not, but his clandestine arrival at a time when the government was more than usually apprehensive in the company of soldiers from the regiment of the hated Stanley, was not fortuitous. His confessions provided more than enough information to justify the government's fears.

Southwell, however, had no contact with the realm's enemies. He was, it is true, a Jesuit and could be condemned for his membership in the Society. But he could not be accused of anything specific. Indeed, his *An humble supplication* proclaimed Catholic loyalty. Nonetheless he became associated with the notorious doctrine of equivocation. We do not know the origin of Southwell's interest in equivocation nor his first defense of the practice. He may have been the Jesuit who defended equivocation at the semi-annual Jesuit meeting in 1590. Around that time he composed a treatise on the practice that had a limited circulation in manuscript. Garnet, however, was so apprehensive about its contents and so restricted its dissemination that he was unable to locate a copy in 1598 and none has since appeared.[143] The introduction of the doctrine of equivocation into Southwell's trial sealed his fate.[144]

---

[143] Nancy Pollard Brown, "Robert Southwell: The Mission of the Written Word," in McCoog, *The Reckoned Expense*, p. 255.

[144] Historians and philosophers have recently rediscovered casuistry and equivocation. Among the important studies are Elliot Rose, *Cases of Conscience: Alternatives Open to Recusants and Puritans under Elizabeth I and James I* (Cambridge, 1975); Peter Holmes, (ed.), *Elizabethan Casuistry* (London, 1981); Peter Holmes, *Resistance and Compromise: The Political Thought of the English Catholics* (Cambridge, 1982); Albert R. Jonsen and Stephen Toulmin, *The Abuse of Casuistry: A History of Moral Reasoning* (Berkeley, 1988); Perez Zagorin, *Ways of Lying: Dissimulation, Persecution, and Conformity in Early Modern Europe* (Cambridge, Mass., 1990); Alexandra Walsham, *Church Papists: Catholicism, Conformity, and Confessional Polemic in Early Modern England* (Woodbridge, 1993); Johann P. Sommerville, "The 'New Art of Lying': Equivocation, Mental Reservation, and Casuistry," in *Conscience and Casuistry in Early Modern Europe*, (ed.) Edmund Leites (Cambridge, 1988), pp. 159–84; Keith Thomas, "Cases of Conscience in Seventeenth-Century England," in *Public Duty and Private Conscience in Seventeenth-Century England: Essays Presented to G.E. Aylmer*, (eds.) John Morrill, Paul Slack and Daniel Woolfe (Oxford, 1993), pp. 29–56;

Despite its close identification with the Society of Jesus and in particular with Southwell and Garnet, equivocation appeared periodically in earlier religious changes during the Tudor Reformations. Dr Edward Crome, a reformer during the reigns of Henry VIII and Mary Tudor, equivocated in his recantations to confuse his examiners. He was not unique: other reformers employed similar tactics to avoid persecution without betraying their faith.[145] Indeed, some theologians, Catholic and Protestant, persuaded others to equivocate to protect their religious beliefs. The case of the Henrician John Forest, a Franciscan Observant of Greenwich, had implications for Southwell's trial.

Arrested in the spring of 1538 on the charge of encouraging sedition in the confessional, Forest admitted that he advised a penitent who had pronounced the oath of supremacy that "he had denied the busshope of Rome by an oth given by his outwarde man but not in thinward man."[146] The distinction between an inner and outer man allowed Forest to propose a form of equivocation to penitents perplexed by a conflict between royal commands and personal beliefs. Because the government realized the significance of the distinction "in exposing the fragility of the popular 'consent' upon which Henry's royal supremacy presented itself as resting," it reacted furiously.[147] Henrician supremacy depended on public acceptance of the royal will as demonstrated by pronouncing the oath. If Forest's distinction remained unchallenged, taking the oath did not signify acceptance. Through equivocation and mental reservation, individuals could mislead interrogators by apparently agreeing to unacceptable doctrines. During his trial Forest explained that he believed the oath he had sworn to be an unlawful one because it violated the law of God. He sought to reconcile his religious beliefs with political obligations by proposing obedience "firste to the kinges highnes by the lawe of god and

---

Andrew Pettegree, "Nicodemism and the English Reformation," in *Marian Protestantism: Six Studies* (Aldershot, 1996), pp. 86–117, Jonathan Wright, "The World's Worst Worm: Conscience and Conformity during the English Reformation," *Sixteenth Century Journal*, 30 (1999): pp. 113–33; Ginevra Crosignani, "*De adeundis ecclesiis protestantium*": Thomas Wright, Robert Parsons, S.J., e il dibattito sul conformismo occasione nell'Inghilterra dell'età moderna (Rome, 2004), Stefania Tutino, "Between Nicodemism and 'Honest' Dissimulation: The Society of Jesus in England," *Historical Research*, 79 (2006): pp. 534–53; and Stefania Tutino, "Nothing But the Truth? Hermeneutics and Morality in the Doctrines of Equivocation and Mental Reservation in Early Modern Europe," *Renaissance Quarterly*, 64 (2011): pp. 115–55.

[145] See Susan Wabuda, "Equivocation and Recantation During the English Reformation: The 'Subtle Shadows' of Dr Edward Crome," *Journal of Ecclesiastical History*, 44 (1993): pp. 224–42.

[146] Cited in Peter Marshall, "Papist as Heretic: The Burning of John Forest, 1538," *Historical Journal*, 41 (1998): p. 362.

[147] Marshall, "Papist as Heretic," p. 362.

the seconde to the busshop of Rome by his rule and profession."[148] The important qualifier was "lawe of god" or, in more conventional terms, "as far as the law of Christ allows," the conditional clause inserted by the Convocation of Canterbury when Henry insisted that he be recognized as Supreme Head of the English Church. Consciously or not the convocation provided justification for equivocation. With priests such as Forest as confessors, the sacrament had the potential to further disaffection with Henrician reforms. Peter Marshall concluded that Forest's case demonstrated "the degree to which conformity to the Henrician settlement could be contorted, conditional, contingent." It revealed "all too clearly how the binding intention of oaths could be casuistically evaded, how loyal subjects might be subverted, or disloyal ones confirmed in their disloyalty by secret persuasions ... "[149] Like its Henrician predecessor, the Elizabethan settlement rested on oaths. To distinguish potential traitors from loyal Catholics, the government drafted the "Bloody Questions" and different oaths of allegiance. The crown trusted the respondent's answers and oath. But through equivocation a Catholic could publicly pronounce allegiance to and support for the queen, and thus remain relatively undisturbed by the government, without internal assent to the propositions. That possibility worried the government.

Southwell revived the issue when he proposed equivocation to Anne Bellamy. If the doctrine became widely known and practiced, the government had no guarantee that oaths pronounced by the outer subject bound the inner. As in the case of Forest, the doctrine's chief proponent was executed to prevent dissemination of a doctrine that would undermine the foundations of society. For Coke the doctrine of equivocation was as subversive as the doctrine of papal jurisdiction over monarchs. Southwell's attempts to explain the use and limits of equivocation were frustrated. Because of subsequent government propaganda, Garnet wrote his own treatise on equivocation in order to clear Southwell's reputation.[150] In it he carefully delineated the traditional conditions for equivocation:

> whansoever that wch outwardly soundeth as a lye in the eares of the hearer, may tend to any dishonour of Almightye God, or to any notable breach of dewetye towardes our neighbour in sowle, bodye, honour, fame, or any exteriour goodes,

---

[148] Cited in Marshall, "Papist as Heretic," p. 365.

[149] "Papist as Heretic," p. 374.

[150] On April 22, 1598, he wrote Parsons that he had written a treatise "to defend Fr. Southwell's assertion which was much wondered at by Catholics and heretics" (ABSI, Coll P II 552). His manuscript was finally edited and published by David Jardine as *A Treatise of Equivocation* (London, 1851) and more recently in Ginevra Crosignani, Thomas M. McCoog, S.J. and Michael Questier, (eds.), with the assistance of Peter Holmes, *Recusancy and Conformity in Early Modern England* (Toronto/Rome, 2010), pp. 298–343.

equivocation, although it may take away the lye wch may seeme to sounde in the wordes, yet can not it hynder but the whole speech is otherwise left in it nature as it would of it selfe be interpreted, although no such equivocall sense were intended. So that if it were hurtfull to any person or dishonourable to God wthout the equivocation, it remayneth so notwthstandinge the equivocation. Wherfore it is manifest that we may not equivocate in matters wch concerne the profession of our faythe, wthout the incurringe of mortall synne.[151]

In the subsequent chapter, Garnet stressed that equivocation was permissible when the examiner was not a lawful superior with authority over the person he questioned. Moreover the examiner must proceed according to a just law. According to Garnet a "judge in the execution of an uniust law is no judge."[152] For these reasons in their examinations Jesuits protested the injustice of the laws and the impropriety of a secular justice exercising jurisdiction of ecclesiastical persons. Despite Garnet's spirited defense of the practice, equivocation quickly become a characteristic of the "evil Jesuit" of myth and legend and another weapon in the government's arsenal against the Society.[153] Throughout the seventeenth-century Jesuits were branded equivocators despite opposition of some Jesuits to the practice. Henceforth there were new grounds for distrusting members of the Society of Jesus. Among the many vices allegedly practiced by Jesuits this was the most damaging because it undermined the Society's credibility. As Johann P. Sommerville summarized the situation: "A Jesuit might swear that he was a loyal and law-abiding citizen. His oaths, however, were unreliable, since it was always possible that they included reservation."[154] Although Garnet feared that both John Gerard and William Weston would be condemned to death and executed, neither was because neither posed

---

[151] Jardine, *Treatise of Equivocation*, pp. 59–60; Crosignani, *Recusancy and Conformity*, pp. 325–26.

[152] Jardine, *Treatise of Equivocation*, p. 69; Crosignani, *Recusancy and Conformity*, p. 329.

[153] See Michael L. Carrafiello, "Robert Parsons and Equivocation, 1606–1610," *Catholic Historical Review*, 79 (1993): pp. 671–80. Carrafiello suggested that Parsons set very precise limitations on the practice of equivocation in order to reach a *modus vivendi* with English Protestants and to obtain some tolerance for Catholics: "Parsons was willing to set aside equivocation in the aftermath of the Gunpowder Plot and never came close to giving a blanket endorsement to the practice in his exchanges with [Thomas] Morton. He believed that his dialogue with Morton represented perhaps the last chance for English Catholics and English Protestants to achieve a measure of stability in their relations" (p. 680). See also his *Robert Parsons and English Catholicism, 1580–1610* (Selinsgrove, 1998), pp. 140–41. Apparently unaware of Southwell's and Garnet's tempered justification of equivocation, Carrafiello attributed too much originality to Parsons's restrictions and thus misinterpreted their purpose.

[154] "'New Art of Lying'," p. 178.

a threat to the established order because of association with the realm's enemies or with the doctrine of equivocation, they escaped execution.[155]

Acquaviva's hesitance about sending more men to England ended quickly. Robert Jones arrived in England sometime before February 22.[156] Before his departure for Wales, Jones conveyed the consoling news that Acquaviva would maintain his support for the mission, despite recent imprisonments, and do everything possible to aid Catholics. Seizing upon this willingness, Garnet urged that William Holt be assigned a supervisory role over English vocations in Belgium. As a result of their contact with Jesuits, many young men and women entered religious life in Belgium. Often lack of a spiritual director with whom they could discuss their progress in their native language, threatened their vocation. Young men and especially young women who abandoned England for Belgian religious houses needed the spiritual conversation and encouragement of someone who spoke their language. For this role he recommended Holt. If the Belgian province did not have the money necessary to subsidize the

---

[155] Garnet to Acquaviva, London May 1, 1595, ARSI, Fondo Gesuitico 651/624. Parsons believed that Gerard's martyrdom was postponed "on account of his belonging to such an important family and his relations being people of influence" (Parsons to Creswell, Seville October 28, 1595, Valladolid, Archivum Collegium Sancti Albani, series II, vol. 1, num. 24).

[156] On October 11, 1594 Jones and John Myrton received permission to travel first to Belgium and then to England and Scotland (ARSI, Hist. Soc. 61, fol. 49^v). On May 10, 1594 Parsons suggested that Jones would be well employed in Spain if the general had nothing for him to do in Rome. Moreover, once he was in Spain, it would be easier to send him to England (Parsons to Acquaviva, Seville May 10, 1594, ARSI, Hisp. 136, fols 316^r–317^v; Acquaviva to Parsons, Rome July 4, 1594, ARSI, Tolet. 5/II, fol. 347^v). There is no evidence that Jones went to England via Spain. Jones (alias Anselmo) wrote his first letter to Acquaviva on February 25 (ARSI, Fondo Gesuitico 651/602). Another letter from London on April 30 (o.s.) was intercepted. It is summarized in Wernham, *List and Analysis*, vol. 6, par. 350. Richard Blount arrived in England in the autumn of 1594. Not yet a Jesuit, he was very favorably disposed towards the Society and wrote a long, complimentary letter to Acquaviva on September 6, shortly after his arrival (ARSI, Hisp. 137, fols 160^{r-v}). In a letter to Acquaviva from Madrid on December 3, 1594 (ARSI, Hisp. 138, fols 10^{r-v}) Creswell included a letter about the Society (presumably this letter) by Blount with the comment that Blount would have joined the Jesuits in Rome if he had not wanted to return to England to convert his parents. From Seville on March 19, 1595, Parsons praised Blount who begged to be admitted into the Society while he was in England. Since Henry Garnet seconded his request, Parsons relayed it to Acquaviva. If the request were not granted, Blount would abandon his work in England to return to Spain to enter the Jesuits (ARSI, Hisp. 138, fols 184^r–185^v). Blount was accepted with the condition that he try for one year to extricate himself so that he could go to the novitiate in Belgium (Acquaviva to Parsons, Rome June 5, 1595, ARSI, Baet. 3/I, p. 220). Blount must have given some money to the Society because Acquaviva was lavish in his gratitude for Blount's generosity (Acquaviva to Creswell, Rome February 13, 1595, ARSI, Tolet. 5/II, fol. 383^v).

required travel, Garnet thought that Holt and/or Parsons would be able to find the money.[157]

A second Jesuit arrived unexpectedly in England sometime in early February. Disguised as an Italian merchant, William Baldwin[158] escorted six boys from Flanders to the English seminary in Seville.[159] From the moment Baldwin donned his custom, he acted out his part. To all he spoke only Italian or Latin. A contrary wind impeded their progress. Fearful of being blown into an English port, the Spanish vessel tried to return to Calais when it was intercepted by an English man-of-war. Feigning ignorance of English, Baldwin successfully deflected any suspicion. Many attempts were made to trip him up but Baldwin eluded them even to the extent of affecting sleep and speaking Italian as if in a dream! Aware that the boys were Catholic and destined for a Catholic college, Charles, Lord Howard of Effingham and Lord Admiral, sought advice. Eventually the boys were assigned to the care of John Whitgift, Archbishop of Canterbury, who placed them in various households for a proper upbringing. Baldwin was sent to Bridewell. Playing upon an officer's hope to obtain ransom money, Baldwin asked to see a Franciscan friar confined in the prison because of a mutual friend. Baldwin arranged to see the friar privately because, as he told the official, "Catholics in England do not like to speak to foreigners nor to acknowledge them unless rather familiar and secret conversation can be held." Baldwin revealed his identity and instructed the friar to get word to Garnet about the Jesuit's disguise and identity. The speed with which Catholics sought to ransom Baldwin aroused suspicions. Before Baldwin was freed, he was obliged to prove his profession and identity. Over the years, Baldwin explained, he resided in many places including Rome and was well known. He suggested that someone ask John Gerard if he ever heard of an Ottaviano Fuscincelli, his official Jesuit alias. Gerard acknowledged knowing the name and that he would probably recognize him if he saw him. Baldwin was thus brought to Gerard's cell. With a gesture Baldwin cautioned silence. Gerard was asked if he remembered the merchant. He replied that he believed that Baldwin was a merchant whom he had met either in Naples or Rome but at that time, he was

---

[157] Garnet to Acquaviva, London February 22, 1595, ARSI, Fondo Gesuitico 651/624.

[158] Robert Parsons summoned Baldwin to Spain to replace Simon Swinburne who found the Spanish climate too difficult (Parsons to Acquaviva, Seville April 18, 1594, ARSI, Hisp. 136, fols 284^r–285^v). Acquaviva sent Baldwin as a replacement for Henry Walpole (Acquaviva to Parsons, Rome April 12, 1593, ARSI, Tolet. 5/I, fol. 292^r).

[159] Twice English ships intercepted vessels transporting students to Seville. The first was in the Irish Sea; the second, the one involving Baldwin, in the channel. The seminary lost twenty students (see Parsons to Acquaviva, Seville May 15, 1595, ARSI, Hisp. 138, fols 264^r–265^v). For the story of the first capture see Bede Camm, O.S.B., "The Adventures of Some Church Students in Elizabethan Days," *The Month*, 91 (1898): pp. 375–85.

dressed differently. Baldwin returned to Newgate a few hours before Southwell's arrival. A ransom of 200 gold pieces was paid and Baldwin was released with a safe-conduct permit from the Admiralty. Generally opposed to ransoming Jesuits, Garnet approved in Baldwin's case because he had been brought to England against his will, and he was not known as a priest but as a merchant. Moreover it was necessary that he be free before his true identity was discovered. Regardless of how Baldwin got to England, Garnet argued that he "was ours by right of possession or by right of ransom" if Acquaviva approved. He could not be sent back to the continent without considerable risk and could be well employed in England.[160]

The Ebbs and Flows of a "College of Confessors" at Wisbech

Three Jesuits, William Weston, Thomas Pounde, and Thomas Metham, were imprisoned in Wisbech Castle.[161] Sometime in the early 1590s discipline in the prison was relaxed considerably, perhaps by the new keeper William Medeley. Henceforth priests moved freely around the castle and its grounds, meet and conversed with visitors even without the presence of any guards. They received a steady stream of visitors, either Catholics or

---

[160] Garnet to Acquaviva, London February 22, 1595, same to same, London May 1, 1595, ARSI, Fondo Gesuitico 651/624. The second letter enclosed a copy of a letter from Baldwin now in ARSI, Angl. 42, fols 69ʳ–70ᵛ. Another account of his capture and liberation can be found in ARSI, Fondo Gesuitico 651/604. See also Foley, *Records*, III, 502–504. See too Verstegan to Parsons, Antwerp March 25, 1595, same to same, Antwerp March 30, 1595, ABSI, Anglia II, 3 (published in Petti, *Verstegan Papers*, pp. 223–30). Anthony G. Petti identified the students as John Copley, William Worthington, John Iverson, Thomas Garnet, James Thompson, and Henry Montpesson (n. 7 pp. 225–26). Parsons thought that the arrival of two Jesuits provided a perfect opportunity to recall Garnet to have a rest although "owing to his [Garnet's] desire for martyrdom, he does not ask it for himself." Because Garnet knew the Jesuits in England better than anyone else, Parsons recommended to Acquaviva that he be allowed to designate his own successor (Parsons to Acquaviva, Seville July 10, 1595, ARSI, Hisp. 138, fols 339ʳ–341ᵛ). Nothing happened. The annual letter from the English College, Valladolid in 1597 summarized Baldwin's account without mentioning his name. See Harris, *Blackfan Annals*, pp. 216–19, 245–47.

[161] The anonymous author of an undated description of Wisbech's prisoners described Weston as "a very daungerous man & especiall accoumpte amongste the papists was sent thether from the Clinke & was suspected to bee a great practiser of treasons." Christopher Bagshaw, according to the same author, "was firste sent to Cambridge to bee conferred withall & so to bee reformed, but hee was very obstinate & doeth very muche harme & mischiefe as is knowen by experience in Staffordshire, hee is a moste daungerous man" (TNA, SP 12/199/91 and published as an appendix in Thomas Graves Law, (ed.), *A Historical Sketch of the Conflicts between Jesuits and Seculars in the Reign of Queen Elizabeth* [London, 1889], pp. 135–37).

those interested in becoming Catholics, to whom they offered instruction and spiritual counsel. Catholics generously donated to the support of the clergy, and years later, in 1599, it was claimed that the young men who had acted as the priests' servants were actually sons of Catholic gentry sent to receive religious instruction. Within the prison priests arranged a daily order of conferences, lectures, and cases of conscience. Thomas Metham, commonly considered the community's spiritual leader, kept the common purse.[162]

The secular priest Dr Christopher Bagshaw, who had abandoned a career in Oxford and was ordained priest in Rome in 1583, was sentenced to Wisbech Castle in 1588. Reputed a difficult character even before his departure from Oxford, he was expelled from the English College in Rome in 1585. On his way to Reims he collected a doctorate in Padua.[163] William Allen refused to allow him to remain in Reims so he was sent immediately to England and was captured almost as soon as he landed in May of 1585. In Wisbech his two closest associates were Thomas Bluet, who assumed control of the common purse after the death of Metham in June of 1592 and, after March of 1595, John Norden.[164]

In November of 1593 Garnet lauded this veritable "college of confessors" where he sang a solemn Mass during his visit. At the time, it will be recalled, Garnet debated whether he should take advantage of an opportunity to ransom Weston. Believing that the entire college would

---

[162] On the history of Wisbech in general and the stirs in particular see Penelope Renold, (ed.), *The Wisbech Stirs (1595–1598)* (London, 1958), pp. xi–xiii; Arnold Pritchard, *Catholic Loyalism in Elizabethan England* (London, 1979), pp. 78–80. In my exposition, I shall follow both. Metham was accepted into the Society in 1579 while he was a prisoner in England. In Father Everard Mercurian's letter of acceptance, May 4, 1579, he recommended that Metham not reveal his Jesuit identity to anyone unless it was necessary (ARSI, Fl. Belg. 2, p. 142). For a description of daily life see Caraman, *William Weston*, pp. 161–77. Christopher Bagshaw contended that Metham regretted his decision: he was a "vertuous learned Priest, who when he was prisoner in the Tower vowed to become a Iesuite; as admiring that calling, because he was not acquainted with their courses: but afterwards at his being in Wisbich, he found by wofull experience that all was not gold that glistered. Sundry times he hath sayd to some of our company, not without teares in his eyes, Keepe this fellow downe asmuch as you can, meaning Fa. Weston: by labouring to be popular, he becometh the ringleader of all mutinies in the house, which in time will breede faction against you. This house will come to utter chame through his folly. I pray God that I dye before it commeth to pass, for I do foresee such a mischiefe" ([Christopher Bagshaw], *A true relation of the faction begun at Wisbich* [n.p. (London) 1601], ARCR, vol. 2, num. 39, STC 1188 [a more accessible edition is in Law's *Historical Sketch of the Conflicts* and the citation can be found on p. 16 there]). See also Lake and Questier, "Prisons, Priests and People."

[163] See Jonathan Woolfson, *Padua and the Tudors: English Students in Italy 1485–1603* (Cambridge, 1998), pp. 209–10.

[164] On the three secular priests see Anstruther, *Seminary Priests*, vol. 1, pp. 13–17, 42, 252–54 and Pritchard, *Catholic Loyalism*, pp. 80–82.

collapse without Weston, Garnet decided against doing so.[165] In light of later developments one wonders if he eventually regretted this decision because less than a year after his visit, the situation had deteriorated so badly that he feared great scandal. No one, Garnet informed Parsons, could be forced to change but if Parsons could resolve the dispute, it would be most appreciated. Aside from allowing anyone who wished to withdraw from common fellowship to do so, Garnet could think of no other remedy.[166]

According to Henry More, Bagshaw and his allies would not attend Scripture readings. Unwilling to accept any regulations, they refused to follow the common order and to participate in any period of study or prayer. Whenever Weston spoke, they heckled him. This clique preferred scenes, quarrels, and drinking bouts. According to Thomas Graves Law, who follows Christopher Bagshaw's explanation, the dispute was sparked by the introduction of a hobby horse with Morris dancers at Christmas.[167] Weston's final withdrawal shortly after Christmas gives some weight to Bagshaw's explanation. But the introduction of such unbecoming frolics seems to have been the proverbial final straw.[168] Weston retired to his own room, refusing to dine with the other prisoners and to associate with the community until moral order was restored.[169] He did this with

---

[165] Garnet to Acquaviva, London November 12, 1593, ARSI, Fondo Gesuitico 651/624.

[166] Garnet to Parsons, September 6, 1594, ABSI, Anglia I, 81 (published in Foley, *Records*, vol. 4, pp. 45–46).

[167] More would not mention the names of the culprits but described them thus: "two men were imprisoned there for the faith who were of a bitter and quarrelsome turn of mind and hostile to our Society. One of them we have frequently pointed out as a jealous man. The other was a certain doctor of medicine. I prefer to suppress their names. Granted that they disagreed with the ways of the Society, and quite frequently attacked it in speech and writing, where their names should now be written is, I think, best left to God's judgement. The curious reader will be able to judge for himself out of the relations from which these things are taken. In any case, it is repugnant to the nature of things not to spare the good reputation of the dead as far as possible. But there two men, untameable by nature and impatient of any discipline, added to their company a third of like temperament from among the older hands. They then began to pour scorn on all existing arrangements" (More, *Elizabethan Jesuits*, p. 186). Weston said nothing about the controversy in his autobiography.

[168] Citing this episode, Ronald Hutton observed that Jesuit offence was "as sign of how in England, as on the Continent, the Counter-Reformation was producing an alteration in the attitudes of some towards the old festivities even as the Reformation had done" (*The Rise and Fall of Merry England: The Ritual Year 1400–1700* [Oxford, 1994], p. 128).

[169] Law, *Historical Sketch of the Conflicts*, p. liv. See Bagshaw, *True relation* in Law's *Historical Sketch of the Conflicts*, p. 18 for the story about the hobby-horse. Mark Tierney blamed the schism entirely on Weston supported by Garnet: "Father Weston, accordingly, was furnished with a plan from Henry Garnet, the superior of their order, then residing in London. At first the proposal was looked upon as a very good expedient, in order to promote virtue and learning among them. But Dr. Windham, Mr. Metham, Mr. Bluet, and others of

his superior's approval. Questioned about his withdrawal, Weston replied that he refused to participate in any communal activity unless there were common rules observed by everyone. Until the promulgation of such rules, he feared accusations of bad example by remaining silent in the face of such behavior. Encouraged by Weston's stand, 18 prisoners drafted rules which they promised to observe. These 22 rules regularized divers aspects of their communal life from insistence on edifying conversation and avoidance of any scandalous behavior, especially regarding women, to presence at communal prayer and exhortations, and the absence of assigned positions at table based on rank.[170] The signers wanted Weston to oversee their execution but he refused by pleading that he was incapable of shouldering such a burden. Moreover as an obedient religious, he could not assume such a position unless he were ordered to do so by his superior. Consequently on February 7, 1595 the priests appealed to Garnet to intercede with Weston.[171]

The new regulations disrupted communal life even before Weston assumed his position of moral leader. The prisoners who preferred not to accept them claimed that they were now ostracized. Weston and his supporters numbered 20 out of the 33 prisoners. Refusal to accept the rules resulted in the isolation of the 13 from all common rooms within the prison. The "college of confessors" was now divided spiritually and geographically. Many years ago, as Garnet explained to Acquaviva,[172] "some very good priests at Wisbech" had asked him to procure from Cardinal Allen some remedy to problems even then spreading throughout the castle. Garnet refused because he did not wish to "delate the defects of others" to Allen and thought that God's grace would effect a better resolution of the difficulty than external interference. Now some priests formulated rules for their common life so that they might live righteously and avoid disgrace from any new scandalous acts. Weston had withdrawn from common life because he "noticed that everything was daily getting worse, as was shown by the abundance of quarrels and uproars when they met together, by scant modesty as table, by drinking parties and the rowdiness

---

the ancient missioners, that were prisoners, apprehending, that this new scheme would be a means of dividing them into parties, and prove prejudicial to the clergy, positively refused to come into the project" (*Dodd's Church History of England* [5 vols, London, 1839–1843], vol. 3, p. 41). Among other things Tierney was not aware that Metham was a Jesuit and was dead by the start of the "Stirs."

[170] There are two copies of the regulations in AAW, V, 7, 8 (published in Renold, *Wisbech Stirs*, pp. 9–11).

[171] There are numerous copies of this letter but the original, without the rules, can be found in ABSI, Anglia II, 2 (published in Renold, *Wisbech Stirs*, pp. 1–2).

[172] July 12, 1595, ABSI, Anglia II, 4 (published in Renold, *Wisbech Stirs*, pp. 55–66). I cite her translation.

of many during public prayers and conferences, by doubts whether very good faith was being observed in the collection and distribution of monies, and what was worst, by suspected familiarity with women."[173] Weston's stand resulted in new rules and a request that he be nominated superior of the group. Garnet granted their petition, after consulting Robert Jones and William Baldwin, but with certain conditions: Weston "should in nowise be held to be a superior, but rather a mouthpiece, who might call the rest together and advise them, or like a Roman soldier assigned in battle to defend the standard, to show others what should be done, by example and not by authority."[174] To demonstrate that Weston did not wish to be considered the community's superior, he abandoned his fixed seat. Moreover Garnet insisted that the entire community punish any violations by special vote and not make Weston responsible. Finally, fearful that the arrangement would antagonize other prisoners, Garnet wanted it clear that the association, and not Weston, was responsible for major decisions. But despite such precautions, Weston's opponents claimed that Jesuits sought to exercise authority over secular clergy. This, they contended, was typical of Jesuit ambition as seen in their expulsion from France. Jesuits as devout adherents of Spain sowed discord wherever possible. Such accusations, Garnet believed, blew the conflict out of proportion.

The new rules bound only the prisoners who willingly accepted them. Thus the others considered themselves by implication judged as less fervent, less pious, and less religious. The rules suggested that anyone who did not accept them was, in the words of Penelope Renold, "living a life which was undisciplined and free from moral restraint."[175] From Christopher Bagshaw's perspective, the rules were based on "idle surmises, uncharitable suspicions, malicious amplified detractions." Moreover Bagshaw interpreted Weston's appointment as "superior" as an attempt by the Society of Jesus to dominate secular clergy and to introduce novel,

---

[173] ABSI, Anglia II, 4 (published in Renold, *Wisbech Stirs*, p. 59).

[174] ABSI, Anglia II, 4 (published in Renold, *Wisbech Stirs*, p. 61). Peter Lake and Michael Questier recently analyzed accusations of immorality in Elizabethan religious debates. Such charges appeared frequently in disputes between Jesuits and secular clergy and reflected fundamentally different ecclesiologies and missionary strategies. See their "Discourses of Vice and Discourses of Virtue: 'Counter-Martyrology' and the Conduct of Intra-Catholic Dispute," in Peter Lake with Michael Questier, *The Antichrist's Lewd Hat: Protestants, Papists and Players in Post-Reformation England* (New Haven, 2002), pp. 281–314.

[175] *Wisbech Stirs*, p. xv. Their conclusion is understandable on the basis of Garnet's letters to Acquaviva.

egalitarian practices such as random seating into an orderly, hierarchical community.[176]

Alban Dolman, a Marian priest, visited Wisbech in March of 1595. On earlier visits he bore alms for the support of the prisoners. This time he attempted to settle the dispute. He failed because he openly sided with Bagshaw's faction and broadcasted news of the dispute throughout the kingdom. He returned in May with the secular priest, John Bavant (or Bavand),[177] who quickly alienated Bagshaw and his supporters because he favored the association. The dispute was spreading and once Garnet allowed Weston to become the association's spokesman, it became even more vicious.[178] Bagshaw complained to Garnet of his involvement in the dispute. Prompted to write because of "the private friendship which I hope holds between us, and of the regard due to the religion we have in common," Bagshaw was astonished that Garnet approved an association without first consulting the others. His approval has furthered a schism that delighted the enemies of the Church and that created a scandal "on such a scale that the like has not been seen since the restoration of the English Church has been set on foot."[179]

Bagshaw persisted in his campaign against the new arrangement. Two weeks before his letter to Garnet, he and Bluet submitted to Weston a list of complaints with demands for their immediate redress. Their grievances included restoration of kitchen instruments and a demand for apologies for slanders against Bagshaw and his associates disseminated by Weston and his allies. A demand that would play an important role in this and all subsequent controversies between Jesuits and secular clergy was Jesuit control of the common purse. Bagshaw insisted that Weston account for all money received for the use of the house.[180]

Garnet denied Jesuit responsibility for the stirs at Wisbech.[181] Even the Society had sponsored the association; he acknowledged no reason for regret. Throughout the history of the Church, he reminded Bagshaw, there have been associations and confraternities. Indeed, even within the same

---

[176] Bagshaw to a certain Norfolk gentleman, [c. late May 1595], AAW, V, 11 (published in Renold, *Wisbech Stirs*, pp. 14–18). For a sympathetic presentation of Bagshaw's position see Pritchard, *Catholic Loyalism*, pp. 86–88.

[177] Bavant had been a friend of Edmund Campion at Oxford. See Anstruther, *Seminary Priests*, vol. 1, p. 27.

[178] See Dolman's letter to Bagshaw, May 20, 1595, AAW, V, 12. Dolman acknowledged the rumor that he was anti-Jesuit, but insisted that he had been so wronged by the Society that any objective judge would decide in his favor.

[179] August 22, 1595, AAW, V, 10 (published in Renold, Wisbech Stirs, pp. 105–108).

[180] August 11, [1595], AAW V, 22 (published in Renold, *Wisbech Stirs*, pp. 86–89).

[181] Garnet to Bagshaw, October 8, 1595, AAW, Anglia IX, 45 (published in Renold, *Wisbech Stirs*, pp. 119–31).

religious order, there was a variety of devotions and practices. If, as was the case at Wisbech, some chose to submit to certain "obligations from a study of virtue, and pursuit of spiritual progress and perfection," this should not anger others because this free association was not intended as a judgment on the activities of the non-members. Garnet considered the association nothing "but an undertaking, whereby some might promote by a rule of life their advancement in doctrine and piety, to the general edification of men, without any contempt for others, without any harm to charity and without casting the least reflection on the esteem due to anyone."[182] The association asked for Weston as superior and he was appointed not as a judge or rector but a "spiritual father to such as desired to be his children."[183] Now it was incumbent on Bagshaw that he do all he could to prove to the outside world that the prisoners remained spiritually united despite their physical separation. Once the Catholic community knew that each group was allowed to live the style of life it selected, all scandal would fade away.

Perhaps as a consequence of Bagshaw's letter, Garnet asked two secular priests, John Mush and Richard Dudley,[184] to arbitrate. All considered Mush friendly towards the Society since his days at the English College in Rome. In fact he had once considered a Jesuit vocation. Mush selected Dudley as a companion because he was Bagshaw's friend. Their mediation began in September at Wisbech. Progress was slow. The initial compromise was accepted by Bagshaw but rejected by Weston allegedly because major decisions required a two-thirds majority. Encouraged by Garnet, Mush and Dudley persisted. Garnet exhorted Bagshaw to "give consideration, as is most becoming to yourself and your profession, to the means and methods whereby you dwell together as brethren, bound to one another in a firm and stable peace." To work for this concord, Garnet commanded Weston "in the name of our Lord Jesus Christ and by virtue of obedience" to apply himself.[185] Once a settlement had been reached, all parties thanked Garnet for his assistance.[186] Common life was restored with careful regulations

---

[182] Garnet to Bagshaw, October 8, 1595, AAW, Anglia IX, 45 (published in Renold, *Wisbech Stirs*, p. 124).

[183] Garnet to Bagshaw, October 8, 1595, AAW, Anglia IX, 45 (published in Renold, *Wisbech Stirs*, p. 125).

[184] On Dudley see Anstruther, *Seminary Priests*, vol. 1, pp. 106–107.

[185] Garnet to Bagshaw, October 22, [1595], AAW, V, 26 with a contemporary translation in V, 27 (published in Renold, *Wisbech Stirs*, pp. 132–37). I have used my own translation. See also Garnet's letter to John Mush on the same day, AAW, V, 28 (published in Renold, *Wisbech Stirs*, pp. 138–40).

[186] Mush and Dudley to Garnet, November 8, [1595], ABSI, Anglia II, 7 (published in Renold, *Wisbech Stirs*, pp. 147–51); Bagshaw to Garnet, November 8, [1595], ABSI, Anglia II, 9 (published in Renold, *Wisbech Stirs*, pp. 152–55); 18 priests to Garnet, November

concerning the common purse, unfounded accusations, and an imposition of punishments against all violators.[187] Public scenes of reconciliation ended the schism.

The one sad note in Garnet's report to Acquaviva on September 6, 1595 was the discord at Wisbech, on which he did not dwell because it was not appropriate that something so distressing be publicized. At the time he was expecting the arrival of Thomas Lister.[188] A meeting of Jesuits on the mission had just concluded and Garnet testified that all, including John Gerard and William Weston in their respective prisons, were doing admirable work.[189] Lister arrived in England in mid October.[190] Within a month, it was evident that Lister's contribution to the mission would not be as anticipated. Garnet confided that Lister's mental state was so unstable that he was entirely unfit for the work in England.[191] In fact, Garnet continued, Lister was almost totally out of his mind: he suffered, it seems, from claustrophobia. A doctor examined him and offered some hope of his eventual recovery. Garnet promised to do all he could but it would be better for all if Lister returned to the continent. Although Garnet again recommended that Jesuit presence in England be increased gradually, he thought that a few of the Jesuits in Belgium such as Richard Gibbons who volunteered for the mission could fill the need for more priests.[192] Garnet could use two or three but he pleaded that no one be sent without the express knowledge and command of the general and/or Parsons. Brothers, however, were of little value in England. For reasons left unexplained by Garnet, brothers would not be admitted into the homes of the nobility because they were laymen. But even if they were admitted, they would not be allowed to exercise any domestic services. Thus they would be forced to spend too much time in idleness, in hostels, and in constant danger of temptation. There were numerous laymen who could provide necessary services.

8, [1595], ABSI, Anglia II, 8 (published in Renold, *Wisbech Stirs*, pp. 156–60); Bagshaw to Garnet, December 4, [1595], ABSI, Anglia II, 11 (published in Renold, *Wisbech Stirs*, pp. 161–64).

[187] For the first set of articles drafted by Mush and Dudley on September 26, 1595 see AAW, Anglia IX, 12 (published in Renold, *Wisbech Stirs*, pp. 112–18). For the final set on November [6], 1595, see AAW, V, 29 and 30 (published in Renold, *Wisbech Stirs*, pp. 141–46).

[188] On Lister see McCoog, *Monumenta Angliae*, vol. 2, pp. 394–95.

[189] ARSI, Fondo Gesuitico 651/624.

[190] His first letter to Acquaviva was written on February 16 (o.s.) 1596, Fondo Gesuitico 651/634.

[191] On January 12, 1595 Acquaviva had written to Lister, who was in Pont-à-Mousson, that he would be sent to England if his health improved. Apparently the general was convinced that he had recovered (ARSI, Gal. 44, fol. 13^v).

[192] On Gibbons see McCoog, *Monumenta Angliae*, vol. 2, pp. 328–29.

Garnet's letter concluded with a baffling passage. After a heartfelt expression of gratitude to Acquaviva for all that he did for the English mission, Garnet asserted that "all posterity will attribute to our Society and especially to your paternity the spark of religion which was kept alive in England, the renewed fervor, and the flame now bursting forth." Lately, he explained, there has been talk of a division between the secular clergy. In fact a few years ago when Cardinal Allen reported that there was a disagreement between secular priests and Jesuits, many objected because Allen could not name one secular priest who had ever injured or been injured by a Jesuit. During his 10 years on the mission, Garnet had only heard of one or two priests estranged from the Society.[193] Was Garnet naive? Or was he trying to minimize tension? At the start of the Jesuit mission to England, Everard Mercurian was apprehensive that the absence of ecclesiastical structure would eventually result in conflict between Jesuits and secular clergy.[194] At Wisbech more than one or two secular priests opposed the Society—and their number was growing.

Conclusion

In a letter of March 16, 1594, Cardinal Allen warned John Mush "to be ware above all things of partialities, differences, dissentions, discorde, aemulation and discontentment of one towards another, of old against yonge, saecular against religiouse, preists against Jesuits." Peace was the gift that Christ left to his disciples and peace was what Allen wished to see reign among the English Catholics.[195] Seven months later on October 16, 1594, Allen died in Rome. Many, like Richard Barret, mourned his passing and wondered about its implications for the mission:

> you can imagine what state of mind we were, how great was our grief, and how many our wretched tears. Oh, how true is what his grieving disciples said to Blessed Martin: "Why do you desert us, Father, and to whom do you leave us desolate; for rapacious wolves are attacking the flock."[196]

But dangers to the mission's unity and cohesion were not simply from without. The peace for which Allen longed and strove, was breaking down.

---

[193] November 6, 1595, ARSI, Fondo Gesuitico 651/624.

[194] See McCoog, *Society of Jesus*, p. 132.

[195] ABSI, Anglia I, 79 (published in Knox, *Letters of Allen*, p. 357).

[196] Barret to Innocenzo Malvasia, nuncio in Belgium, Douai December 3, 1594, in Renold, *Letters of Allen and Barret*, pp. 242–43.

Tensions between Jesuit and secular clergy predated Allen's death. Garnet was aware of some murmuring and thus periodically cautioned a modest increase of Jesuits on the mission lest others become upset. Similarly he argued that the Society must proceed prudently regarding secular priests who wished to enter the Society. Acceptance of too many too quickly and at the overall expense of the mission would cause a problem. Overt conflict erupted after Allen's death with the "Wisbech Stirs." Eamon Duffy notes that Allen's "eirenical nature and passionate concern were exerted to the full in holding together a community increasingly riven by the bitterness of defeat, in particular the ominous gap opening between the secular clergy and his revered Jesuits."[197] Yes, his "revered Jesuits" were under attack. No longer were their policies unanimously accepted. No longer was their presence in England considered an asset. Even if Allen had survived a few more years, it is doubtful that he would have been able to prevent the schism. Factions were too strong; acrimony too bitter; theological and ecclesiastical differences too great. But would Allen have continued to support his "revered Jesuits"?

Shortly after the death of the Jesuit Francisco, Cardinal Toledo, a periodic thorn in the side of Robert Parsons, Alfonso Agazzari, rector of the English College in Rome, remarked to Parsons:

> Certainly, my father, it seems to me a great indication of the divine Majesty, and a great and visible sign of God's love towards the Company, this college, and the cause of England, that when human means fail He almost miraculously interposes His divine hand. So long as Allen walked aright in this matter, in union with and fidelity to the Company, as he used to do, God preserved, prospered and exalted him, but when he began to leave this path, in a moment the thread of his plans and life were cut short together.[198]

"Leaving the path" suggests a parting of ways between Allen and Jesuits. Thomas Francis Knox considered it impossible "to doubt that some divergence of view had arisen between Allen and the Society, and further that this divergence was of a grave character" because of Agazzari's apparent satisfaction at Allen's death.[199] Ignoring the passage completely

---

[197] Duffy, "William, Cardinal Allen," p. 286.

[198] Agazzari to Parsons, Rome September 25, 1596, in Thomas Francis Knox, (ed.), *The First and Second Diaries of the English College, Douay* (London, 1878), pp. 386-89. I use the translation of this passage found on p. xcviii.

[199] Knox, *Douay Diaries*, p. xcviii. Christopher Bagshaw, admittedly a suspect source, claimed Allen questioned Jesuit involvement in the mission from the start: "Cardinall Alane, when the Iesuites first came into England, told sundry of his friends, that certainely they (the sayd Iesuites) would rayse great garboyles in this countrey, by seeking to disgrace secular priests, and to advance themselves above them. He had great experience of the ambition

and by focusing solely on relations between Parsons and Allen, Leo Hicks, S.J., denied there was a breach. He concluded his three-part investigation of relations between Allen and the Society thus:

> Little space is left to speak of the friendship and union that existed between Allen and Persons. Two years after the death of the Cardinal, [William] Holt wrote of them, that they appeared not as two but as one, and that they directed all with such unanimity that there was never the slightest difference of opinion between them. Certainly that is the conviction that is impressed on one by the study of these documents. When the Cardinal lay on his death-bed, he called to him his nephew Thomas Hesketh, and, mastering for a time his grief in silence, told him at length that he knew God was calling him. "From recent letters from Spain," he continued, "I have learnt that Father Persons too is very dangerously ill. Should he also die at this time I clearly perceive that all that we have accomplished so far for the restoration of the Faith in England, working with united minds and forces over so many years, will be threatened with disaster and I fear utterly ruined and brought to naught." Alike in his friendship and in his politics the Cardinal was consistent to the end.[200]

Penelope Renold, following the example of her mentor Leo Hicks, argued that Allen's letters to Acquaviva and Agazzari in her edition "underline afresh Allen's very close relations with the Jesuits throughout his career ... " Nothing in her volume supported the assertion that he and they parted ways towards the end of his life.[201] But the omission of the offending letter, reduction of relations between Allen and the Society to his friendship with Parsons, and publication of earlier letters between Allen and different Jesuits do not solve the problem. Acknowledging the importance of Agazzari's comment to Parsons, John Hungerford Pollen, S.J., argued that it did not justify suspicion that relations between Allen and the Society had deteriorated. Pollen contended that Agazzari's "fears were aroused by some of Allen's entourage," specifically Thomas Throckmorton, whose marriage to one of the cardinal's nieces he reluctantly approved.[202] Throckmorton was notoriously anti-Spanish, so much so that Allen assured his friends William Holt, Sir William Stanley, and Hugh Owen that they had nothing to fear

---

which raigned in many of that societie, and therefore indevoured (as he might conveniently) to repress that humor in our English Iesuites, which kept them within some reasonable compose whilst he lived. But afterwards they heard no sooner of his death. but their insolencie burst foorth as a flame that had bin long suppressed. charging the Cardinall to have bin but a simple man, and of no great worth" (*True relation* in Law's *Historical Sketch of the Conflicts*, pp. 16–17).

[200] Leo Hicks, "Cardinal Allen and the Society," *The Month*, 160 (1932): p. 536.

[201] Renold, *Letters of Allen and Barret*, pp. xvii–xviii.

[202] "Colleges in Spain 1589–95," in his unfinished history of the Jesuits in England, ABSI 46/5A/1B, fols 61–65.

that Throckmorton would influence the cardinal "to runne or folowe anie other course then that which he had alwayes kept ... "[203] On the basis of this letter, Knox concluded that there was no disagreement regarding political matters. But there were other possibilities. Knox suggested that Allen and the Society disagreed over administration of the seminaries and of the mission and cited Joseph Cresswell's unsatisfactory administration of the English College in Rome as an example. But the speed with which he was removed from that post, would not have provided grounds for a lingering dispute.[204] Other possible reasons were reactions to Elizabeth's diplomatic overtures detailed at the start of this chapter. Was Allen annoyed that Cresswell, Holt et al. condemned the peace feelers too quickly while he was eager to follow up any hint? As Allen investigated peace initiatives, Parsons continued to agitate for another armada. Could Allen have been one of the complainers that secular priests were being drained from the mission to enter the Society? Or was Allen annoyed at Henry Garnet's hard-line on occasional conformity?[205] We know that Garnet's dissemination of a rumor of Thomas Bell's excommunication because of his teachings despite Allen's letter that the pope had not done so, displeased the cardinal who was exhorting English Catholics to be sympathetic to the less strong.[206] In the final years of Elizabeth's reign during the archpriest controversy, secular clergy opposed to Jesuits sought to extricate Allen from close identification with the militant policies of Parsons and the Society, who, they charged, misled the innocent cardinal. Eventually towards the end of his life, they asserted, Allen realized what was happening and turned against his former allies. For political reasons the appellants minimalized Allen's participation in political and diplomatic intrigues and fashioned a gullible cardinal easily betrayed.[207] This unauthentic portrait, however, must not lead to the a priori rejection of their claim of a disagreement. Nor must contemporary Jesuit insistence of consistent harmony blind us.

---

[203] Thomas Worthington to Thomas Allen (alias Hesketh), Douai December 18, 1601, in Knox, *Letters of Allen*, p. 396. See also Peter Norris, "Robert Parsons, S.J., (1546–1610) and the Counter Reformation in England: A Study of His Actions within the Context of the Political and Religious Situation of the Times" (unpublished Ph.D. thesis: University of Notre Dame, 1984) p. 195 n. 130.

[204] Knox, *Douay Diaries*, pp. xcix–ci and Chapter 2 above.

[205] See Crosignani, *Recusancy and Conformity*, pp. xxviii–xxix.

[206] Allen to James Tyrie, Rome n.d. [between May and September 1593], ARSI, Fondo Gesuitico 651/594 (published in Renold, *Letters of Allen and Barret*, pp. 231–32).

[207] See Holmes, *Resistance and Compromise*, p. 193.

CHAPTER 4

"No Union of Hearts": Catholic Exiles on the Continent, 1594–1595

Introduction

The French religious wars turned in favor of Henry IV. On March 22, 1594 he entered Paris by the same gate through which Henry III had fled during the "Day of the Barricades" six years earlier. Once there he graciously allowed Spanish troops to depart and banished only the most obstinate leaguers. He demonstrated his new Catholicism by attending Mass at Notre Dame that very morning and by participating in a religious procession a week later. On the 28th, *parlement* and other sovereign courts were re-established; all legislation enacted since December 29, 1588 prejudicial to royal authority was cancelled on the 30th. Henry's sudden triumph affected Jesuits in France. During the final years of the religious wars, French Jesuits generally sided with the Catholic forces. Earlier division into factions supporting the league or the legitimate monarch vanished once the "legitimate" monarch was a Protestant. Even after Henry's acceptance of Catholicism, problems remained. In March of 1594 Claudio Acquaviva instructed French Jesuits to avoid any oath of allegiance to Henry as long as he was under sentence of excommunication out of deference to the Holy See. Consequently stories about the Society's disloyalty circulated as Jesuits were pressured to follow the example of other clergy and take the oath. Jesuit reluctance prompted Antoine Arnauld and others to publish tracts accusing the Society of pursuing pro-Spanish policies. Jesuits were vilified as Spanish agents, conspirators, and assassins. The only remedy was their expulsion. The readiness of many French Jesuits to deflect such criticism by pronouncing the oath angered Claudio Acquaviva:

> I want you to know that you have offended not only Catholics in general but also our own men ... Complaints have reached me from many provinces of different nations ... They regard your offer to take the oath as a dishonor to the Society.[1]

---

[1] Cited in William V. Bangert, S.J., *A History of the Society of Jesus*, revised edn. (St Louis, 1986), p. 121. Two Jesuits irritated by *apologiae* published in defense of French Jesuits (most likely Pierre Barny's *Defenses de ceux du college de Clermont, contre les requeste & plaidoyez eux cy deuant & publiez 1594*), were William Crichton and Jean d'Heur, rector

On December 27, 1594, Jean Chastel, sometime student at the Jesuit College of Clermont, attempted to assassinate Henry.[2] Encouraged by anti-Jesuit polemicists, many saw the hand of the Society in this attempt. Citing this example of Jesuit perfidy, a few days later the *parlement* of Paris ordered Jesuits to leave the city within 3 days, and the region within 15 days. Not every *parlement* followed the Parisian example so the Society was not obliged to leave the kingdom.[3] But the Society's existence in France remained precarious until the Edict of Rouen of September 1, 1603, obtained through the influence of Pierre Coton, S.J., finally lifted the ban. Coton became royal preacher and, in 1608, royal confessor, and he sealed the new friendship between Henry IV and the Society.[4]

On September 17, 1595, Henry frustrated any Spanish aspirations with the conclusion of an agreement with Pope Clement VIII. To the dismay of Philip II and the vestiges of the Catholic League, the pope confirmed Henry's absolution;[5] Henry, in turn, admitted the insufficiency of his prior abjuration, and promised, once he was more secure on the throne, to appoint Catholics to high offices and restore Catholicism in Béarn, and to work for the pope's interests, especially the implementation of the decrees of the Council of Trent and the return of the Jesuits.[6] Many Catholic nobles then submitted to the king. By the spring of 1596 only Philippe-Emmanuel, Duke of Mercoeur, opposed Henry. Huguenot discontent jeopardized prospects of domestic peace. Fearful of the consequences of Henry's appeasement of Catholics, Huguenot assemblies in 1594, 1595 and 1596 demanded legal recognition of their status with guarantees for their

---

in Antwerp. See Acquaviva to d'Heur, Rome January 14, 1595, ARSI, Fl. Belg. 1/I, p. 547; same to Crichton, Rome Fenruary 11, 1595, ARSI, Fl. Belg. 1/I, p. 549. I am grateful to Dr Eric Nelson for information regarding Barny's treatise. See his *The Jesuits and the Monarchy: Catholic Reform and Political Authority in France (1590–1615)* (Aldershot/Rome, 2005) for a thorough investigation of the anti-Jesuit sentiment and the political conditions that led to the Society's banishment.

[2] See Robert Descimon, "Chastel's Attempted Regicide (27 December 1594) and its Subsequent Transformation into an 'Affair,'" in *Politics and Religion in Early Bourbon France*, (eds.) Alison Forrestal and Eric Nelson (Basingstoke, 2009), pp. 86–104.

[3] The Society remained strong in southern France because the *parlements* of Toulouse and Bordeaux refused to register its banishment.

[4] David Buisseret, *Henry IV* (London, 1984), pp. 56–57, 118, 121; Bangert, *History of the Society*, pp. 120–23. The protest of the *parlement* of Paris upon the return of the Jesuits and Henry's reply can be found in Roland Mousnier, *The Assassination of Henry IV: The Tyrannicide Problem & the Consolidation of the French Absolute Monarchy in the Early 17th Century* (London, 1973), pp. 368–74.

[5] See Alain Taillon, "Henri IV and the Papacy after the League," in *Politics and Religion in Early Bourbon France*, (eds.) Alison Forrestal and Eric Nelson (Basingstoke, 2009), pp. 21–41.

[6] I thank Dr Eric Nelson for this clarification.

future. Eager to unite Catholics and Protestants against a common enemy, Henry declared war on Spain. His successes in the south were matched by setbacks in the north. In September of 1596 he regained Lyons, but aided by the duke of Mercoeur, Spain had earlier captured Cambrai and Calais.[7]

Elizabeth shared Huguenot apprehensions about Henry's appeasement of the Catholics. As Henry made his peace with the Roman Church, Elizabeth feared he would abandon her to conclude a separate peace with Spain. In November of 1593 Elizabeth had withdrawn her troops from Normandy; she recalled her forces from Brittany once the Spanish treat to Brest ended with the capture of Fort Crozon in February of 1595. As we saw in the last chapter, English clandestine peace feelers were cancelled after the discovery of alleged Spanish support for various plots against the queen. Despite public outcry, England was not eager to commit more troops in a continental war. Initially English assistance was not needed: in the beginning of 1595 Dutch and French forces rolled back Spanish armies. The death of Archduke Ernst in February of 1595 and the subsequent struggle over leadership of Spanish forces in the Netherlands seemed to ensure that such success would continue. As long as the struggle went well against Spain, Elizabeth could resist Dutch and French requests for military aid and, indeed, press the Dutch to repay earlier expenses. Spain's naval forces, however, remained a threat to English security by aiding Irish rebels or Scottish Catholic earls, or attempting another invasion of the kingdom itself. To prevent a naval attack, the English government increased patrols of the Irish Sea and the English Channel and opted to strike the first blow by capturing Spanish gold on its journey from the New World to Spain. In retaliation for Philip's support of assassination plots, Robert Devereux, Earl of Essex, urged decisive action against Spain. Accordingly on January 29, 1595 the crown approved an ambitious scheme to capture the Isthmus of Panama, a vital link in the movement of gold from Peru to Cuba. Sir Francis Drake and Sir John Hawkins were appointed joint commanders. By the end of July they still had not sailed. Meanwhile four Spanish galleys raided Penzance and neighboring villages on July 24. The English fleet finally sailed from Plymouth on August 28. Failing to capture Puerto Rico, the fleet meandered around the Caribbean, making odd raids on Spanish forts and towns. Hawkins died on November 12. The English ships arrived at Nombre de Dios, the Caribbean port of the isthmus and the principal target of the expedition, in December. Warned of the approach of the English ships, the Spanish evacuated the town. After feeble resistance, the English occupied it on December 27. Attempts to extend their conquest

---

[7] R.J. Knecht, *The French Religious Wars of Religion 1559–1598* (London, 1989), pp. 79–80; Mark Holt, *The French Wars of Religion 1562–1629* (Cambridge, 1995), pp. 159–62.

beyond the port's walls failed. Lacking a clear strategy, the English torched the city on January 5, 1596 and sailed westwards. More important than the lack of military progress was the effect of sickness and disease on the English. Drake fell ill and died on January 28, and Sir Thomas Baskerville assumed control of the expedition. His ships straggled home in the late spring of 1596 with neither booty nor glory to their credit. The whole expedition lost money and was generally considered a failure.[8]

As English ships sailed for the Spanish Main, Spain turned the tide in the Netherlands. Don Pedro Enríquez de Azevedo, Count of Fuentes, led Spanish forces after Archduke Ernst's death. Despite dispatching most of his army to fight the French along the frontier, he turned back a Dutch invasion of the principality of Liège and prevented the Dutch from capturing more cities. By September of 1595 Fuentes captured Doullens and Cambrai, a city held by the French since 1580. Spanish victories continued after the arrival of the new Governor-General Archduke Albert, another nephew, in the Netherlands in early 1596.[9] Spanish triumphs in the Netherlands and English failures in the Caribbean raised serious doubts about England's estrangement from France. Unable to protect itself against the Spanish menace, closer and more menacing after Philip's capture of Calais in April of 1596, England needed Henry despite his religion, and the Dutch despite their debts.

Supervising the Continental Colleges

During the struggle for the French throne, Robert Parsons consistently extracted from Philip promises of financial support for English seminaries and English refugees despite Spanish preoccupation with the possibility of a Protestant France. Given the depleted Spanish treasury and the convoluted Spanish bureaucracy, the translation of promises into hard currency was not easy but Parsons secured enough funding to keep all foundations open and operating. His diplomatic negotiations for a new armada were less successful. Philip's involvement in a war with so many fronts precluded a new venture. With Philip thus distracted any initiative for a second attempt

---

[8] R.B. Wernham, *The Return of the Armadas: The Last Years of the Elizabethan War against Spain 1595–1603* (Oxford, 1994), pp. 21–54. See also Harry Kelsey, *Sir Francis Drake: The Queen's Pirate* (New Haven/London, 1998), pp. 367–91.

[9] Peter Limm, *The Dutch Revolt 1559–1648* (London, 1989), pp. 63–64; Geoffrey Parker, *The Dutch Revolt* (London, 1977), p. 231.

on England must originate in Rome, but a rapid succession of popes and an increasing hostility to Spain made that unlikely.[10]

Robert Parsons visited his new foundations in Spain and supervised their growth on a less than royal progress from college to college. At each he paid homage to benefactors, sought more secure sources of revenue, and arranged for the transfer of students and English Jesuits between the foundations on the Iberian Peninsula and the college in the Spanish Netherlands. Throughout he interceded with Philip II on Claudio Acquaviva's behalf in the Society's "constitutional crisis," and he was involved in the production of one of the most important books of the decade, *A conference about the next succession to the crowne of Ingland*[11] despite frequent bouts of quartan fever, a type of malaria.

Philip's failure to pay the 1,700 ducats promised to the English College in Valladolid resulting in a debt in 1593, did not worry Parsons. The college remained in excellent condition, both spiritually and temporally. On the first Sunday of Advent the college had opened a new refectory large enough to accommodate 100 persons. Parsons attributed much of the success to the rector, Rodrigo de Cabredo, whom students held in high esteem. For unexplained reasons, Parsons feared Acquaviva would appoint him to another position in the province. Arguing that Cabredo was irreplaceable, Parsons contended that his removal would have serious consequences on the college's life and spirit. Expressing his deep gratitude, Parsons repeated how well Cabredo executed his office. He was a young man and, as a result of this experience, he would be an even better servant of the Lord and great administrator in the future. Under his guidance, peace and content reigned in the community and students progressed in learning and virtue. It was not, however, utopia and there were some problems (a few of which involving English Jesuits we shall examine later) especially at the Jesuit College of San Ambrosio where the English seminarians heard lectures. Many worried these problems would migrate to the English College. From the sidelines, Parsons watched San Ambrosio deteriorate as Jesuits there became more dejected and discontented with the college's governance and programme of studies. English students especially disliked the teaching style of a Father Martinez, and had no respect for his approach to Thomist philosophy. Parsons unsuccessfully tried to dissuade them from these convictions. Apparently only force compelled them to attend his classes. Father Antonio de Padilla, whose lectures the students ordinarily praised, was now so occupied with sermons, business affairs and

---

[10] Urban VII reigned less than two weeks in September of 1590. Gregory XIV ruled from December of 1590 to October of 1591. Innocent IX was in office two months (November–December of 1591). The anti-Spanish Clement VIII was elected on January 30, 1592.

[11] (n.p., n.d. [Antwerp, 1594]), *ARCR*, vol. 2, num. 167, *STC* 19398.

other non-academic matters that he was obliged to cancel many classes. Parsons recommended that Martinez be transferred and Padilla freed from other obligations to concentrate on his teaching. Perhaps a change of rector at San Ambrosio would signal improvements. Of the candidates, Luis de la Puente was a learned and holy man, but Parsons doubted that he was qualified to deal with material problems because he was so very reserved and taciturn. Some suggested that Cabredo be transferred from the English College to San Ambrosio, but Parsons hoped that Acquaviva would reject this proposal as he had refused a similar request earlier. Moreover, the translation of Cabredo would upset the English College more than it would profit San Ambrosio. Parsons's apprehensions were soon realized: On December 31 Gonzalo del Río replaced Cabredo as rector of the English College. Because of Cabredo's careful management, the new rector found the college's debt cleared and money in the bank.[12] Around the same time the learned and holy Puente was named rector of San Ambrosio.

Initial reaction to del Río was positive, but the honeymoon did not last long. By May of 1595 Parsons directed very specific complaints to del Río. Lamenting that the outgoing rector had not sufficiently instructed his successor on a style of governance unique to the English seminaries, he urged del Río to discuss all matters with the college's consultors, especially Gaspar Alonso and Charles Tancard,[13] and to accept their advice and not counsel from friends outside the college. Parsons reminded him that the college's daily order and its various procedures were established after much reflection and discussion, and warned him against the understandable reaction of a new rector to change everything. Such behavior was not acceptable in English colleges where Jesuits were simply administrators of a patrimony that did not belong to the Society. Among del Río's more disturbing innovations were forcing servants to eat outside the refectory, altering baking practices, and entertaining too many guests. Allegedly del Río banished servants from the refectory with a comment that not every sort of rascal from the street should dine there. Not all servants were scoundrels, Parsons argued. Indeed not one was; if in the future, one was employed, he could be asked to eat outside! All of this would have been explained to del Río if he had consulted his advisors. Parsons approached Francisco de Peralta in Seville to intervene with del Río. Originally Peralta opposed the custom of servants eating at a third table, but

---

[12] Parsons to Clement VIII, Seville April 15, 1593, ABSI, Coll P I 327; Parsons to Acquaviva, Madrid December 4, 1593, ARSI, Hisp. 136, fols 163^r–65^v; same to same, Madrid June 4 and 16, 1594, ARSI, Hisp. 136, fols 362^r–363^v; same to same, Valladolid, July 12, 1594, ARSI, Hisp. 137, fols 24^r–25^v; Edwin Henson, (ed.), *Registers of the English College at Valladolid, 1589–1862* (London, 1930), p. xix. See Albert J. Loomie, S.J., *The Spanish Elizabethans: The English Exiles at the Court of Philip II* (New York, 1963), p. 212.

[13] On Tancard see Thomas M. McCoog, S.J., (ed.), *Monumenta Angliae* (2 vols, Rome, 1992), vol. 2, p. 500.

now he favored it. Moreover del Río's insistence that English and Spanish servants dine separately aroused suspicion, jealousy, and nationalist factions. The last was especially dangerous since it could spread as an epidemic from servants to staff, and from staff to students. Parsons had experienced firsthand the disastrous consequences when nationalist sentiment gripped a college that accommodated more than one nationality. Constructed a few years earlier at a cost of more than 200 ducats, the bakery saved the college much money and would eventually recover its costs. Indeed, the college in Seville was so impressed by the operation that it considered building its own bakery despite the expense. Regarding the bread, although no students complained about it, the rector could improve its quality as long as he stayed without the college's financial restraints. Even small modifications already made in the amount of flour cost as much as the upkeep of two or three students. Finally, reports of rather lavish entertainment of guests reached Parsons and Acquaviva. Again Parsons reminded del Río that Jesuits must render an account of all expenditure to laymen who controlled the college's patrimony. Reception of guests, therefore, must be restricted. Indeed father general preferred that no guests be entertained in the English Colleges. The college's finances were not as strong as Parsons would have liked. Now he feared the loss of 600 ducats per annum that would follow upon the death of a generous benefactor, Francisco Sarmiento de Mendoza, Bishop of Jaen. To compensate for the loss of that income some economies were essential, but Parsons did not think del Río would take necessary action. The general consensus was that he spent too much on superfluities.[14]

The rector initiated yet another crisis in June of 1595: he and the popular Antonio de Padilla publicly disagreed over a thesis defended by a priest at the college. The ensuing fracas scandalized many inside and outside the community. Unimportant in itself, the dispute demonstrated a lack of harmony. What distressed Parsons even more was the rector's failure to report the incident to him. Parsons's patience with del Río was clearly running out. The root cause of Valladolid's problems, Parsons concluded, was the rector's close friendship with José de Acosta to whom he often turned for advice and guidance. Parsons was certain that Acosta had del Río in his pocket. Acosta supported del Río's repudiation of "modern young theologians" like Francisco Suárez[15] and Luis de Molina, a repudiation

---

[14] Parsons to Acquaviva, Seville March 19, 1595, ARSI, Hisp. 138, fols 184ʳ–185ᵛ; Parsons to Gonzalo del Río, Seville May 12, 1595, Valladolid, Archivum Collegium Sancti Albani, series II, vol. 1, num. 23; same to Acquaviva, Seville May 15, 1595, ARSI, Hisp. 138, fols 264ʳ–265ᵛ; same to same, Seville July 10, 1595, ARSI, Hisp. 138, fols 339ʳ–341ᵛ; Francis Edwards, S.J., *Robert Persons: The Biography of an Elizabethan Jesuit 1546–1610* (St Louis, 1995), pp. 178–79, 181.

[15] On a visit to the English College in Valladolid in late October of 1593, Suárez was so impressed by their facilities that he asked if his books could be published there. According to

that underlay his dispute with Padilla. The controversy aggravated the current strain in relations between Acosta and Parsons: Acosta believed, with some justification, that Parsons had secretly acted against him in events surrounding the Fifth General Congregation. Parsons confessed to Acquaviva:

> I think Father Acosta was a bit suspicious about me in reference to his activities in the past since he said smilingly a few times that I too had had my knife in him. But your paternity knows that it is not so, for I never interfered with his business except to report occasionally, and by no means often, what I learned here and what it was my duty to report.[16]

Parsons believed, however, that amiability would be restored at their next meeting. But the problem of the rector remained: he did not seek advice from his consultors but from someone outside the community to whom he broadcasted all difficulties. By December, Parsons discussed del Río with the Jesuit visitor, García de Alarcón, who agreed that a change was necessary. But it would follow upon the visitor's stay in Valladolid and not before. There he would find, Parsons feared, lack of discipline and strong antipathy, both of which would be remedied through a change of rectors. Indeed, if Cabredo were restored, the change could be made without casting aspersions on del Río: his term could be explained simply as temporary expedience while Cabredo served in another post. In June Acquaviva advised Parsons to tolerate del Río slightly longer to see if there was an improvement. If not, Acquaviva was ready to remove him and appoint a new rector.[17] On January 15, 1596, Acquaviva informed Parsons that he had requested del Río's removal and a more acceptable rector, if possible Cabredo, would be installed.[18]

Parsons, "we for our part having regard both to the merits of the work itself as well as to the person of one who deserves so well of all, and especially of the English nation, are most ready to do for him any charitable service we can and which he asks of us" (Parsons to Acquaviva, Valladolid November 2, 1593, ARSI, Hisp. 136, fols 107ʳ–108ᵛ).

[16] Parsons to Acquaviva, Seville July 10, 1595, ARSI, Hisp. 138, fol. 341ʳ.

[17] Parsons to Acquaviva, Seville July 10, 1595, ARSI, Hisp. 138, fols 339ʳ–341ᵛ; same to same, Madrid December 2 and 9, 1595, ARSI, Hisp. 139, fols 122ʳ–126ᵛ; Acquaviva to Parsons, Rome June 5, 1595, ARSI, Baet. 3/I, p. 220.

[18] Acquaviva to Parsons, Rome January 15, 1596, ARSI, Baet. 3/I, pp. 248–49; same to same, Rome February 11, 1596, ARSI, Cast. 6, fols 237ᵛ–238ʳ. In a letter to Creswell from Valladolid on January 16, 1596, Parsons reported that del Río had departed for Segovia the day before. Parsons was certain that if he had remained for three years, "he would undoubtedly have ruined the college completely. Signs were not wanting that tares were beginning to appear; and if he had been able to gain the adherence of even one individual priest or of a single Spanish or English layman in the house to start a sedition, he would have made trouble for us, having already brought over to his side by means of feasts and

Unlike the college in Valladolid, the English College in Seville did not receive financial assistance directly from the king of Spain, but others befriended the college because of his favor and patronage. In 1593 relations between Spanish and English Jesuits in Seville were extremely good. The Spaniards did everything to assist the English enterprise and for this, Parsons was very grateful. Because of such cordial relations the English College progressed in matters spiritual and temporal. Debts were low and expectations high. The house was convenient and comfortable. Although at the time it was slightly more than half full, arrangements had been made for the acquisition of a neighboring house if expansion was necessary. Peralta was a satisfactory rector, but not as outstanding as Cabredo, and Tancard, an exceptional minister. Nonetheless there was friction between them. Tancard and Joseph Creswell disagreed with the rector over certain unspecified points, but Parsons hoped for reconciliation. Presumably fences were not mended: Tancard was sent to Valladolid and Creswell went to Madrid.[19]

Fearing that the financial stability of the English College was threatened, Parsons hastened to Seville in April of 1594. Armed with royal letters to the council of the city and to its chief magistrate, Pedro Fernández de Córdoba y Figueroa, Marquis of Priego, Parsons asked that their annual donation be increased to 500 ducats. Instead they increased it to 600! Moreover they promised to assist Parsons find even larger quarters. Parsons already had his eyes on a large house near the College of San Hermenegild and the river. Why the quarters praised so highly the previous year were no longer satisfactory, Parsons did not explain. His confidence that the college could acquire this new house was justified because he was certain the king would order it. Hopes to move into the new house by the end of the year were, however, frustrated. Despite royal intervention and increased financial assistance from the city, the college remained very dependent on the charity and generosity of Spanish Jesuits. Both the superior of the professed house, Antonio Cordeses,[20] and the rector of San Hermenegild, Melchior de

---

entertainments some of our officials; but he found no one would take his part." This letter was quoted extensively by Joseph Creswell in his *Responsio ad Calumnias*, ABSI, MSS A.V.9, fol. 254. Christopher Grene noted that Parsons had written to John Cecil from Valladolid on January 20, 1596 about the dissensions at Valladolid. Unfortunately he did not transcribe the letter which is now no longer extant (ABSI, Coll P II 488).

[19] Parsons to Clement VIII, Seville April 15, 1593, ABSI, Coll P I 327; Parsons to Acquaviva, Seville April 19, 1593, ARSI, Hisp. 135, fols 187^r–188^v; same to same, Valladolid June 16, 1593, ARSI, Hisp. 135, fols 306^r–307^v; same to same, Valladolid July 15, 1593, ARSI, Hisp. 135, fols 372^r–373^v; same to same, Madrid December 4, 1593, ARSI, Hisp. 136, fols 163^r–65^v; Edwards, *Robert Persons*, p. 169.

[20] On him see Philip Endean, S.J., "'The Strange Style of Prayer': Mercurian, Cordeses, and Álvarez," in *The Mercurian Project: Forming Jesuit Culture, 1573–1580*, (ed.) Thomas

Castro, were completing their terms. Parsons therefore asked Acquaviva to commend the English College to their successors. If superiors continued to favor the college, other Jesuits would follow. And their kindness has not been without benefit to the Spaniards. The Lord repaid the generosity of the professed house by increasing the amount of alms they collected annually.[21]

Renovations of the new house took more time and money than originally estimated. The total cost was 18,000 ducats. Once completed the college in Seville would be the finest around and would accommodate more than 150 persons, but in May of 1595 there were only 60. There would have been 20 more if English ships had not intercepted two parties of students in the Irish Sea and the English Channel. Parsons expected the increase in alms that usually followed the safe return of the fleet bearing gold and silver from America to cover the extra costs. Accompanied by one or two Seville gentlemen and four students, Parsons begged from the traders. They received so little Parsons was disheartened. But the Lord provided! Some merchants and gentlemen privately pledged sufficient funds to deal with current emergencies and expenditures.[22]

Despite Parsons's increased esteem for Peralta as rector of the English College in Seville, there was the occasional problem. Benefactors sent stipends to the English College for Masses to be said. Previously the rector sent a short note acknowledging receipt and stating that the Masses had been allotted and said by students. He testified that students at the college had said the Masses and in no way suggested that any Jesuit was benefiting from the stipends. Regardless the rector preferred that each student send out his own acknowledgment.[23] This innovation, Parsons believed, would

---

M. McCoog, S.J. (Rome/StLouis, 2004), pp. 351–97.

[21] Parsons to Acquaviva, Seville April 18, 1594, ARSI, Hisp. 136, fols 284^r–285^v; same to same, Marchena May 12, 1594, ARSI, Hisp. 136, fols 318^r–319^v; same to same, Madrid June 4 and 16, 1594, ARSI, Hisp. 136, fols 362^r–363^v; same to same, Valladolid July 12, 1594, Hisp. 137, fols 24^r–25^v; same to same, Valladolid October 2, 1594, ARSI, Hisp. 137, fols 201^r–202^v; same to same, Seville February 20, 1595, ARSI, Hisp. 138, fols 142^r–144^v; Edwards, *Robert Persons*, p. 175.

[22] Parsons to Acquaviva, Seville May 15, 1595, ARSI, Hisp. 138, fols 264^r–265^v; same to same, Seville June 12, 1595, ARSI, Hisp. 138, fols 299^r–301^v; same to Creswell, Seville October 28, 1595, Valladolid, Archivum Collegium Sancti Albani, series II, vol. 1, num. 24; Acquaviva to Parsons, Rome July 31, 1595, ARSI, Baet. 3/I, pp. 228–29.

[23] This matter was discussed at the Fifth General Congregation in 1593–1594: "the congregation finally decided to define or declare nothing favoring either side of the question [whether accepting stipends in compensation for ministries was contrary to the Society's vow of poverty or simply contrary to the *Constitutions*], but rather strongly to commend that all observe with the greatest exactitude that most important constitution, an observance most fundamentally necessary to assure greater edification and the sincerity and purity of our poverty." See John W. Padberg, S.J., Martin D. O'Keefe, S.J. and John L. McCarthy, S.J.,

not be acceptable to the college's friends and he asked Cristobal Méndez, provincial in Andalusia, to restore the former practice.[24]

Partially a result of a spirituality obsessed with death and suffering, and partially a result of the martyrdom of Henry Walpole, one of the college's first students, a penitential fervor permeated the English College in Seville. Two students, Robert Waller and Thomas Egerton, died from excessive mortification in 1595. To obtain the grace of his parents' conversion, the former fasted thrice a week, wore a hair shirt and made frequent and prolonged use of the discipline. The latter drew so much blood from his mortifications that he became consumptive. The seminary stressed rigorous physical and spiritual formation to prepare students for the dangers of the mission, and occasionally, it seems, the fervor of some was excessive.[25]

Parsons celebrated the feast of St George, April 23, 1593, in the newly furnished and restored Church of St George in San Lucar de Barrameda. The house was ample with income from shops adequate to support the priest-in-charge and the chaplains working there. Somehow Parsons convinced the English merchants to convey ownership of land and property to secular clergy. Once that had been done, Parsons drafted rules and guidelines for the priest-in-charge. By December of 1595, he entrusted the task of obtaining papal approval for the transfer to Roger Baynes and John Cecil.[26]

Parsons was not so preoccupied with finances that he neglected English Jesuits serving in the seminaries. Although Parsons depended on provinces making English members available for the work of the mission, he could move Jesuits from college to college with the cooperation of the respective provincials.[27] Convincing provincials to hand over able-bodied men for the mission was not easy. Oswald Tesimond[28] wanted to work in the English

---

(eds.), *For Matters of Greater Moment: The First Thirty Jesuit General Congregations* (St Louis, 1994), p. 194, decree 29.

[24] Parsons to Cristobal Méndez, Seville May 20, 1595, ARSI, Hisp. 138, fols 281^{r-v}.

[25] Martin Murphy, (ed.), *St Gregory's College, Seville, 1592–1767* (London, 1992), pp. 8–9.

[26] Parsons to Acquaviva, Seville May 15, 1595, ARSI, Hisp. 138, fols 264^r–265^v; same to same, Madrid December 2 and 9, 1595, ARSI, Hisp. 139, fols 122^r–126^v; Leo Hicks, S.J., "Father Persons, S.J., and the Seminaries in Spain," *The Month*, 158 (1931): pp. 31–35; Edwards, *Robert Persons*, p. 180.

[27] On July 15, 1593 Parsons requested authorization "in urgent cases and when it was not convenient to await a reply from Rome," to move individual Jesuits between English colleges in Spain and Flanders with the sanction of the provincials involved. The general would be informed afterwards. See Parsons to Acquaviva, Valladolid July 15, 1593, ARSI, Hisp. 135, fols 372^r–373^v. He thanked Acquaviva for the authority in his letter from Valladolid on November 2, 1593 (ARSI, Hisp. 136, fols 107^r–108^v).

[28] On him see McCoog, *Monumenta Angliae*, vol. 2, p. 502.

colleges in Spain after completion of his philosophical studies in Palermo. Parsons wanted him because he needed English Jesuits in both colleges, but he lacked the authority to summon Tesimond. Therefore he asked Acquaviva to do so. To Parsons's delight Acquaviva agreed and Tesimond was sent to Seville to succeed Simon Swinburne. By May of 1595 Tesimond had been transferred to Valladolid.[29]

Once Jesuits were granted to the English mission, Parsons assumed responsibility for their physical, spiritual and psychological problems. Simon Swinburne, minister of the English College in Valladolid,[30] was so affected by the heat that the doctor recommended that he winter in Seville and then abandon Spain for the more favorable Belgian climate. He exchanged places with Charles Tancard, who, as we have seen, was having problems with Father Peralta. In April of 1594 Swinburne continued on to St Omers.[31] Two Italian lay brothers, Fabricio Como and his nephew Ambroglio Ligi,[32] were unhappy in Spain. Como worked at the English College in Seville. Because of an ongoing dispute with a Spanish lay brother, Como grew frustrated and requested his provincial to reassign him. Later he repented writing the letter and asked Parsons to intercede to prevent his return to Italy. Parsons sang Como's virtues. Although he could be pig-headed and demanded great patience from others, he was a good worker and Parsons recommended that the general ignore his transfer request and allow him to stay. His nephew was similarly stubborn and had angrily stormed out of the English College in Valladolid in the autumn of 1593. He later repented and did penance for his rashness. Like his uncle, Ligi

---

[29] Parsons to Acquaviva, Valladolid November 2, 1593, ARSI, Hisp. 136, fols 107^r–108^v; same to same, Madrid December 4, 1593, ARSI, Hisp. 136, fols 163^r–165^v; same to same, Madrid March 10, 1594, ARSI, Hisp. 136, fols 245^r–246^v; same to same, Córdoba March 30, 1594, ARSI, Hisp. 136, fols 249^r–250^v; same to same, Seville May 10, 1594, ARSI, Hisp. 136, fols 316^r–317^v; same to same, Marchena May 12, 1594, ARSI, Hisp. 136, fols 318^r–319^v; same to same, Madrid June 4, 1594, ARSI, Hisp. 136, fols 362^r–363^v; same to same, Valldadolid August 10, 1594, ARSI, Hisp. 137, fols 118^r–119^v; same to same Seville May 15, 1595, ARSI, Hisp. 138, fols 264^r–265^v.

[30] On him see McCoog, *Monumenta Angliae*, vol. 2, pp. 497–98.

[31] Parsons to Acquaviva, Valladolid November 2, 1593, ARSI, Hisp. 136, fols 107^r–108^v; same to same, Madrid December 4, 1593, ARSI, Hisp. 136, fols 163^r–165^v; same to same, Seville April 18, 1594, ARSI, Hisp. 136, fols 284^r–285^v; same to same, Marchena May 12, 1594, ARSI, Hisp. 136, fols 318^r–319^v. In exchange for Swinburne, Parsons asked Oliver Mannaerts, Belgian provincial, to send either William Baldwin or Nicholas Smith. Baldwin was on his way to Spain as Swinburne's replacement when he and the students were seized and taken to England.

[32] On them see McCoog, *Monumenta Angliae*, vol. 2, pp. 268, 393.

was a good worker and Parsons wanted him to stay in Spain. Acquaviva allowed both to remain.[33]

At Valladolid Tancard, Richard Gibbons and Thomas Wright, were sources of discontent.[34] By early 1593 Gibbons, unhappy in Valladolid, asked to return to Lisbon or be reassigned to Rome. Gibbons was very impetuous but, according to Parsons, a good religious nonetheless so he advised Acquaviva not to take much notice of his requests. Father Cabredo knew how to deal with him and, as a result, Gibbons would eventually feel more at home. By the summer he and Cabredo were great friends and Parsons doubted that Gibbons could find a more enjoyable residence. By July of 1594, Gibbons, however, was no longer needed in Valladolid after the arrival of Thomas Wright. Because he was writing on the Pauline epistles, Parsons recommended that he be transferred to Rome where he would have easier access to tomes, especially by Protestants, essential for his research. There too he could discuss his work with others and profit from their advice. Parsons doubted not that some useful employment could be found for him either as English confessor at St Peter's or in the Roman College. Despite Parsons's recommendation, Gibbons remained a troublesome character. His fits of anger became more frequent and increasingly more violent. To alleviate any suspicions or doubts that he was not trusted, Parsons used him as his confessor and allowed him use of his room and books whenever he was absent. To demonstrate his trust, Parsons sent Gibbons a key to a chest, requesting that he extract some papers to forward to Madrid. In his search for the desired document, Gibbons found a letter from Creswell criticizing Tancard. He showed the letter first to Wright and then to Tancard himself who was so upset that he immediately volunteered to work in Germany until Parsons successfully soothed his ego. A more serious incident followed. Cabredo complained to Parsons that the three English Jesuits avoided contact with Spanish Jesuits. In confidential correspondence, Parsons suggested suitable remedies until he could deal with the problem on his next visit. Gibbons, suspecting something, borrowed Cabredo's key to his room ostensibly in order to get a book. Once inside he searched the room. He found the letter in question, copied it, and showed it to Tancard and Wright. They were furious with Cabredo and Parsons but by the time Parsons arrived, their anger had abated. But Gibbons, now a major problem infecting Tancard and Wright, could no longer be tolerated in Valladolid. The rector did not want him to remain because of his mood swings. He recommended that Gibbons

---

[33] Parsons to Acquaviva, Valladolid November 2, 1593, ARSI, Hisp. 136, fols 107ʳ–108ᵛ.

[34] On Gibbons and Wright see McCoog, *Monumenta Angliae*, vol. 2, pp. 328–29, 542–43.

be assigned to a city where he would encounter few English because he was quick to turn them against foreigners, and where few burdens would be placed upon him. Once Gibbons left, Parsons knew that Tancard and Wright would then adjust because their disposition was more mild and more peaceful. Gibbons left Valladolid on August 1, 1594 for Rome where, Parsons hoped, Acquaviva would use Gibbons's significant skills in mathematics, controversial theology, languages, and Scripture. His talents could not be denied but he was so irritable that Parsons beseeched Acquaviva to feign ignorance of all that had occurred in Valladolid. On November 8, 1594 he was sent to Loreto as penitentiary; on May 17, 1595 he was transferred to Louvain.[35]

The Scottish Jesuit George Turnbull had cast doubt on the orthodoxy of some of Thomas Wright's ideas and aroused suspicions about his behavior while Wright was on the theological faculty in Louvain.[36] Apparently Wright considered leaving the Society because of the allegations. Eager to retain Wright because Parsons had something to do with his vocation, he recommended Wright's withdrawal from Louvain. The Society had invested much in Wright and Parsons did not want to lose him. Earlier Parsons had defended Wright and prevented his dismissal in Milan because of prolonged melancholia resulting from conflicts with superiors. Now he advised that Wright be sent to Spain. If problems persisted, Parsons believed that he could be dismissed in Spain quietly because he was not well known. In a later letter Parsons admitted that he had underestimated the gravity of the charges levelled against Wright but, nonetheless, he thought it a great work of piety and "a special favor [to Parsons]" to allow Wright one more chance to reform. Parsons promised that he would reprimand Wright severely and do whatever Acquaviva decided but he appealed "for yet another year, according to the Gospel, 'until I dig around and put in manure ...'" (Luke 13:8).[37]

---

[35] Parsons to Acquaviva, Valladolid June 16, 1593, ARSI, Hisp. 135, fols 306^r–307^v; same to same, Valladolid August 11, 1593, ARSI, Hisp. 136, fols 14^r–15^v; same to same, Valladolid July 12, 1594, ARSI, Hisp. 137, fols 24^r–25^v; same to same, Valladolid August 10, 1594, ARSI, Hisp. 137, fols 118^r–119^v; same to same, Valladolid September 7, 1594, ARSI, Hisp. 137, fols 164^{r-v}; Acquaviva to Parsons, Rome June 7, 1593, ARSI, Baet. 3/I, p. 119; ARSI, Hist. Soc. 61, fol. 49^v.

[36] Acquaviva to Wright, Rome May 1, 1593, ARSI, Fl. Belg. 1/I, p. 515; Wright to Oliver Mannaerts, Louvain May 3, 1593, ARSI, Germ. 171, fols 159^{r-v}; Oliver Mannaerts to Acquaviva, Louvain June 21, 1593, ARSI, Germ. 171, fols 188^{r-v}; William Waringham to François de Fléron, Louvain May 3, 1593, ARSI, Germ. 171, fols 336^{r-v}; Oliver Mannaerts to Acquaviva, Louvain July 4, 1593 ARSI, Germ. 171, fols 195^r–196^v; Acquaviva to Mannaerts, Rome August 28, 1593, ARSI, Fl. Belg. 1/I, p. 521; Acquaviva to Parsons, Rome December 20, 1593, ARSI, Tolet. 5/I, fol. 325^r.

[37] Parsons to Acquaviva, Valladolid July 15, 1593, ARSI, Hisp. 135, fols 372^r–373^v; same to same, Valladolid November 2, 1593, ARSI, Hisp. 136, fols 107^r–108^v; same to same,

Wright lectured on controversial theology after his arrival in late November of 1593. Because of his promise to reform, it seemed that Parsons's gamble worked. All went well until summer of 1594 when his involvement in the disturbances generated by Richard Gibbons angered Cabredo and upset Parsons. On October 2, Parsons confessed that he wished there were a "little more spirituality and interior life" to Wright but acknowledged that such was a gift of the Lord and could not be instilled by human means. Moreover, beginning in late summer, Wright pressed Parsons for permission to return to England for reasons of health. Parsons, Creswell, and Charles Tancard tried to dissuade him but he insisted that mental and physical health would result from a visit. Repeatedly Parsons stressed that he was suffering from delusions and that the risks were much greater than he anticipated. Wright finally concluded that he would no longer lecture on controversial theology and that he would return to England. If he could not do so as a member of the Society of Jesus, he would take a leave of absence from the Society. The decision rested with Acquaviva. If Wright were allowed to go as a member of the Society, he would be delighted. Parsons too would be happy with this solution because of the consolation it would bring to Wright, but he would neither advise that approach nor request it because he did not think Wright suitable for the mission. Dismissal was the alternative although Parsons suggested this dismissal was temporary (a leave of absence) because "in the letters of dismissal [you] can order him never to say in England that he is a member of the Society." As Acquaviva pondered the next move, Wright became more unbearable. By March of 1595 Gaspar Alonso, the college's confessor, protested that Wright's continued presence in the college undermined good governance and religious discipline. That was the final straw. Parsons doubted that Wright could be tolerated much longer and thus dismissed him. Acquaviva always doubted the depth of Wright's vocation and approved of Parsons's decision. Wright was in England by June.[38]

Madrid December 4, 1593, ARSI, Hisp. 136, fols 163^r–165^v.

[38] Parsons to Acquaviva, Valladolid July 12, 1594, ARSI, Hisp. 137, fols 24^r–25^v; same to same, Valladolid July 12, 1594, ARSI, Hisp. 137, fols 26^{r-v}; same to same, Valladolid October 2, 1594, ARSI, Hisp. 137, fols 201^r–202^v; Acquaviva to Parsons, Rome December 19, 1594, ARSI, Tolet. 5/II, fol. 377^r; Acquaviva to Creswell, Rome March 8, 1595, ARSI, Tolet. 5/II, fol. 398^v; Parsons to Acquaviva, Seville March 19, 1595, ARSI, Hisp. 138, fols 184^r–185^v; Acquaviva to Parsons, Rome June 5, 1595, ARSI, Baet. 3/I, p. 220. In a letter that Parsons forwarded to Acquaviva, Wright complained of his dilemma: if he went to England as he wanted, he would be forced to leave the Society (Wright to Parsons, Valladolid February 20, 1595, ARSI, Hisp. 138, fols 147^{r-v}). According to John Ferne, Wright was respected by the Catholics but considered unlearned by Protestants who had discussed religious matters with him (Ferne to Sir Robert Cecil, York October 12, 1595, in *Calendar of the Manuscripts of the Most Hon. the Marquis of Salisbury*, (eds.) S.R. Scargill-Bird et al.

Tension between English and Spanish Jesuits was common. Often problems were simply personal, easily resolved through religious discipline and transfers. Occasionally conflict over money threatened the smooth running of the colleges and the mission itself. The English College in Seville needed extra financing to remain open.[39] So successful was Brother Como's begging that Spanish Jesuits complained to Acquaviva that Como was depriving them of necessary alms. Invited to La Ceresa by some Spanish gentlemen to obtain oil, Como stopped at a few houses frequented by Spanish Jesuits on their begging missions. Apparently he accepted alms, and the customary recipients later complained of his poaching. The Society's Institute required professed houses, such as the one in Seville, to rely on alms for their sustenance. The superior, Pedro Bernal, claimed that the English College was siphoning off much needed revenue. To calm Spanish fears, Parsons promised that Como would no longer solicit alms for the college and that greater care would be taken lest the college approach the professed house's benefactors. Although, as Parsons wrote to the Andalusian provincial, Cristobal Méndez, he was devoted to the work of the college, he was even more devoted to the Society and did not want zeal for the former to result in a financial loss to the latter.[40]

New restrictions on Brother Como did not end the affair. Parsons complained to Acquaviva that "ours of the Society" posed greater problems to English colleges than the Elizabethan government! Despite tremendous care not to accept alms from any benefactors of the professed house, the superior still complained. If the current provincial and superior of the professed house had been in office when the college was founded, Parsons doubted the enterprise would have gotten off the ground. Neither

---

[24 vols, London, 1883–1976], vol. 5, pp. 414–15). Under examination Miles Dawson said that Wright claimed that he had been appointed by his superiors to come to England in order to win souls. Wright later wrote that he had surrendered himself in order to avoid capture. Dawson's examination on October 5, 1596 can be found in Scargill-Bird, *Salisbury* MSS, vol. 6, pp. 431–32. For a favorable interpretation of Wright's subsequent career see Theodore A. Stroud, "Father Thomas Wright: A Test Study for Toleration," *Biographical Studies* (later *Recusant History*), 1 (1952): pp. 189–219 with subsequent additions, Basil FitzGibbon, S.J., "Addition to the Biography of Thomas Wright," pp. 261–62; and David M. Rogers, "A Bibliography of the Published Works of Thomas Wright (1561–1623)," pp. 262–80. Stroud, on the basis of Wright's later works, argued that Spain's role in the restoration of Catholicism in England was the issue that alienated Wright from the Society. Perhaps, but there is no hint of it in the extant correspondence. The most recent study is Ginevra Crosignani, "*De adeundis ecclesiis Protestantium*": *Thomas Wright, Robert Parsons, S.J., e il dibattito sul confirmismo occasionale nell'Inghilterra dell'età moderna* (Roma, 2004).

[39] In the triennial catalogues for 1593, 1597, 1599, and 1603 it is repeated that the college had no stable income but had to rely on alms (ARSI, Baet. 8, fols 103^v, 130^r, 151^v, 188^v).

[40] Seville May 20, 1595, ARSI, Hisp. 138, fols 281^{r-v}.

appreciated the work of the college nor its importance for England. Instead of investigating further both acted on complaints made by lay brothers who knew nothing about the situation. Parsons preferred that Acquaviva not intervene until he himself had tried to resolve the matter with the Spanish superiors. For the moment Parsons simply wanted to keep Acquaviva informed so that he "understand what is going on and with your wonted paternal charity may help us as occasion offers, and have the wheels oiled sometimes where it is required, using your holy prudence and discretion, to the end that they may on and not halt when the difficulties arise, which do so rather from the narrowness of our hearts and affections which we ourselves contract and by which we are mutually straitened, than from the nature of the work itself."[41]

The English seminaries, however, had one important advantage over the Spanish professed houses in their quest for alms: martyrs.[42] In 1582 English seminarians distributed copies of Parsons's *De persecutione Anglicana* among potential benefactors prior to collections to support the English College then at Reims.[43] Similar tactics followed the establishment of English colleges in Spain. Spanish accounts of English martyrs, especially those in some way associated with Spain, flowed from the presses as a spur to generosity, for example Joseph Creswell's, *Historia de la vida y martyrio que padecio en Inglaterra, este año de 1595. P. Henrique Valpopo ... el primer martyr de los seminarios de España* (Madrid, 1596) and Diego de Yepes, *Historia particular de la persecucion de Inglaterra y de los martirios que en ella ha aiudo, desde el año del señor, 1570* (Madrid, 1599).[44] Because of the type of spirituality popular in Seville, a spirituality, in the words of Martin Murphy, that "had always been obsessed with death and suffering, embodied in the images of the agonized Christ and his grieving mother which were ... the centrepieces of the Holy Week processions," accounts of the martyrs were especially appealing and effective.[45] The

---

[41] Parsons to Acquaviva, Seville June 12, 1595, ARSI, Hisp. 138, fols 299r–301v.

[42] On the role of martyrdom in the formation of the seminarians, see Michael E. Williams, "The Ascetic Tradition and the English College at Valladolid," in *Monks, Hermits and the Ascetic Tradition*, (ed.) W.J. Sheils (Oxford, 1985), pp. 275–83, and his "Campion and the English Continental Seminaries," in *The Reckoned Expense: Edmund Campion and the Early English Jesuits. Essays in celebration of the First Centenary of Campion Hall, Oxford (1896–1996)*, (ed.) Thomas M. McCoog, S.J., 2nd edn. (Rome, 2007), pp. 371–87.

[43] See Thomas M McCoog, S.J., "'The Flower of Oxford': The Role of Edmund Campion in Early Recusant Polemics," *Sixteenth Century Journal*, 24 (1993): pp. 908–909.

[44] ARCR, vol. 1, nums. 276, 284. See also nums 1062–1068. Hicks makes the same point about the effective use of the martyrologies ("Persons and the Spanish Seminaries," pp. 27–28).

[45] Murphy, *St Gregory's College*, p. 8.

Spanish Jesuits had nothing comparable and, unless something was done, they risked losing much of their alms to the English.[46]

More and more often Parsons lamented that Spanish Jesuits did not appreciate the importance of the English colleges for the preservation of Catholicism in England. Indeed some protested any alms received for the colleges' support because they believed that anything given to the colleges meant less for their works and sustenance. Undeceiving them was a slow, arduous work but Parsons claimed that he was making progress. Through the intervention of Father Peralta who provided Pedro Bernal with an exact account of the college's finances, the latter now understood how little money was received from benefactors in Seville. Indeed almost everything came from donors who otherwise did not support the Society. He then promised that he would say no more on the subject. Since then Bernal and members of his community along with Jesuits from the College of San Hermenegild visited the English College to the delight of all. Such visits, Parsons hoped, would repair damaged fraternal bonds.[47] Acquaviva finally wrote to Cristobal Méndez about the persistent clashes over begging and recommended that Parsons discuss the matter periodically with the superior of the professed house. There should not be a problem. Nonetheless Acquaviva decreed that henceforth two seminarians should accompany each Jesuit on a begging mission to demonstrate that the money was not being solicited for the Society but for the English College.[48] On this secure basis relations between Spanish and English Jesuits continued to improve in Seville but strife remained elsewhere.

In Valladolid a friend of the former rector, Rodrigo de Cabredo, offered to subsidize one student at the college. His generosity generated suspicions among Spanish Jesuits as rumors and accusations circulated that the college was begging throughout the city. Parsons did not know whether the college's benefactor was a frequent donor but the mutterings against the college and against Cabredo personally affected relations between Spanish and English Jesuits. In fact, of the 4,000 or 5,000 ducats that the Valladolid college spent annually, Parsons estimated that no more than 18 ducats came from the city itself. Although Parsons did not think that Acquaviva would allow such unfounded stories to influence his judgment, it was rumored that these suspicions led to Cabredo's replacement. If so, the college has suffered dearly because of the insinuations: after a long

---

[46] One wonders if the renewed interest in Campion at this time should be seen in this context. See Richard Gibbons to Acquaviva, Valladolid October 6, 1593, ARSI, Hisp. 136, fols 92^{r-v}.

[47] Parsons to Acquaviva, Seville July 10, 1595, ARSI, Hisp. 138, fols 339^r–341^v.

[48] Acquaviva to Parsons, Rome July 29, 1596, ARSI, Baet. 3/I, pp. 278–79. See also Murphy, *St Gregory's College*, p. 23.

interregnum the college received the current incumbent, a man "with little energy and aptitude." As a result there was "no union of hearts" within the college.[49]

As Parsons's assistant in Madrid, Joseph Creswell alienated many Spanish Jesuits. They, of course, considered him a good religious and a man of considerable intelligence, but he held uncommonly peculiar views which he insisted on executing. Parsons did not explain to Acquaviva the exact nature of those views but, as a result, Creswell was extremely unpopular. Indeed, when Parsons was absent, they found him unbearable. Yet the work he did was exceptional, and Parsons wanted him to remain despite his abrasive personality. By March of 1595 Creswell's work had increased to such an extent that he needed a socius. Charged with supervising affairs of Spanish and Belgian colleges, and other matters pertaining to England, Ireland and Scotland, Creswell had much to do. Since provinces were allowed individual procurators to oversee their affairs, Parsons requested that Acquaviva grant Creswell comparable status with his own companion because he attended "to the claims of a kingdom and an entire nation." To settle Spanish reproaches that they were supporting Creswell without his working for them and that they would have another mouth to feed if he was granted an assistant, Parsons recommended that the English mission pay the college in Madrid for Creswell's and his companion's room and board. Acquaviva approved Parsons's recommendation that Creswell be provided with a socius and asked that a brother be named. However, he said nothing about altering Creswell's status.[50] Tension, however, remained.

Suspicion that Joseph Creswell would launch an appeal in Madrid that would deprive the Spanish Jesuits of some financial aid was, according to Parsons, a reason for general opposition to him. Juan García, the college's rector, assigned lay brothers to spy on Creswell to ascertain whether he was in fact collecting any alms. Indeed, he thought that Creswell's very presence deprived the college of benefactions. The tension made Creswell's job more difficult. To add to Creswell's burden, Scottish and Irish agents in Madrid begged assistance from Philip. In all matters involving the British Isles and Ireland, Philip depended on Don Juan de Idiáquez who, in turn, refused to accept reports from anyone personally unknown to him. Consequently Creswell served as an intermediary. Despite consistent requests that Parsons return to Madrid to deal with the matter himself, he

---

[49] Parsons to Acquaviva, Seville June 12, 1595, ARSI, Hisp. 138, fols 299^r–301^v.

[50] Parsons to Acquaviva, Toledo March 22, 1593, ARSI, Hisp. 135, fols 147^r–149^v; same to same, Marchena May 12, 1594, ARSI, Hisp. 136, fols 318^r–319^v; same to same, Valladolid August 10, 1594, ARSI, Hisp. 137, fols 118^r–119^v; same to same, Seville March 19, 1595, ARSI, Hisp. 138, fols 184^r–185^v; Acquaviva to Parsons, Rome March 14, 1594, ARSI, Tolet. 5/II, fols 338^r, 338^v; same to same, Rome June 5, 1595, ARSI, Baet. 3/I, p. 220.

preferred leaving it to Creswell.[51] Earlier adjustments that Creswell should have a lay brother assistant and that their expenses would be underwritten by the mission worked satisfactorily for some time, but problems later re-emerged as his assistant was assigned to tasks in the community. Said lay brother caught between religious obedience to his superior and loyalty to Creswell was so upset that he considered leaving the Society. Parsons consulted different unbiased Spanish Jesuits in the college and he could unearth no reason for such opposition to Creswell. The provincial, González Dávila, was ashamed of the whole controversy but no one could convince some members, including Father García, that Creswell was not depriving the college of a single cent. Nonetheless Parsons directed Creswell to present to the community a regular account of the sources of his income. The only permanent remedy, however, would be Creswell's official recognition as the mission's procurator resident in a Spanish community but independent of it and dependent on the mission itself. His assistant would have a comparable status. Dependent on the mission's superior and financially supported by the mission, the lay brother would only assist the procurator. Unless the mission paid all their expenses and the procurator and his socius were directly dependent on the mission's superior, there would be no peace. That arrangement, Parsons recommended, would remain as long as the mission had affairs to conduct at court. García did not think that a procurator was suitable for a mission so Acquaviva should explain his reasons for the appointment carefully. García was a good man, Parsons believed, but he had an extremely provincial outlook because he had never been outside of Spain.[52]

On a visit to the dreaded Madrid in late November of 1595, Parsons sought royal assistance for French Jesuits. Expelled from France and under attack because of Spanish associations and alleged involvement with assassins, they hoped that Philip II would come to their defense even though this would seem to confirm some of the charges levelled against them. They asked the Castilian provincial González Dávila to intercede in their behalf but he ignored their request because, as Parsons learned from others, he was less than enthusiastic about the project. Such reluctance

---

[51] Parsons admitted that he avoided Madrid as often as possible: "I feel such a repugnance to paying a visit to Madrid that I go there was though it were to purgatory. I feel this way for many reasons but especially because I see the hopeless want and misery of many Englishmen there and hear the clamors of the many who write to me as soon as they discover that I am in the city. Please God, I shall avoid Madrid as much as I can although, at times, it will not be possible without very great injury to the cause in which we are engaged" (Parsons to Acquaviva, Toledo March 22, 1593, ARSI, Hisp. 135, fols 147^r–149^v).

[52] Parsons to Acquaviva, Seville June 12, 1595 ARSI, Hisp. 138, fols 299^r–301^v; same to same, Madrid December 2 and 9, 1595, ARSI, Hisp. 139, fols 122^r–126^v; Acquaviva to Parsons, Rome July 31, 1595, ARSI, Baet. 3/I, pp. 228–29.

to assist fellow Jesuits in need disturbed Parsons who volunteered to raise the issue with the king the following day. Parsons recommended that the provincial approach Philip directly and not deal with any of his secretaries. The provincial and Sebastian Hernandez went to the Prado a few days later but were unable to see the king. Instead they left a letter with Prince Philip and discussed the issue with a few ministers. A few days later Parsons raised the matter in a meeting with the king despite lack of authorization. Immediately he realized that none of the ministers had discussed French needs with the king because they too were lukewarm about the request. So on November 27, 1595, in an audience with Philip, Parsons delineated various reasons why he should be generous to French Jesuits. Such generosity would be so worthy of a great monarch and the Most Catholic King. Philip's reaction was favorable and he asked for a memorial with more information. Meanwhile Parsons pressed for more financial support for the English colleges and received an additional 7,000 ducats to distribute among the colleges and residences to pay their debts. Because of suspicions then current among Spanish Jesuits in Madrid, Parsons did not intend to inform them of the gift. Because he was departing within a few days for Valladolid, Parsons would not be able to urge the king to help the French. Instead he left that in the hands of the provincial.[53]

Spanish disinterest in lobbying for their French colleagues and their persistent suspicions regarding intentions of English Jesuits confirmed Parsons's earlier judgment that many Spaniards were extremely provincial. Some Spanish Jesuits, men such as Gil González Dávila, Bartolomé Perez, and Pedro de Ribadeneira who had lived and worked outside Spain, agreed that Spanish Jesuits generally showed little interest in the affairs of foreign Jesuits. They were good men, Parsons stressed, but because of their myopia, they were a trial to all non-Spaniards. Lacking experience of a world beyond Spanish boundaries, they did not understand it. And they could not love what they did not understand. Parsons admitted that he found greater love and friendship in Spain than anywhere else in his life, but he was not blind to certain flaws. At the suggestion of the above mentioned Spaniards, Parsons mentioned the problem to the general with a recommendation that would foster union within the Society and especially between Spain and Rome: Parsons advised Acquaviva to insist that at least a dozen students from Spain study in Rome. There would, of

---

[53] Parsons to Acquaviva, Madrid December 2 and 9, 1595, ARSI, Hisp. 139, fols 122^r–126^v. Acquaviva thanked Parsons for his intercession in favor of French Jesuits (Rome February 11, 1596, ARSI, Cast. 6, fols 237^v–238^r).

course, be extra expense and some students could become ill and die but the advantages outweighed such disadvantages.[54]

Besides English colleges in Spain, Robert Parsons sought financial assistance for other English foundations. In 1593 William, Cardinal Allen decided the English College should end its exile in Reims and return to Douai. From the end of June, students, faculty and administration moved from Reims. Apparently Allen asked Parsons to remind Philip II that much of the money he had promised the college remained unpaid. Because of sensitive negotiations involving the English Jesuit college in St Omers, Parsons was reluctant to introduce another cause. Thus he postponed interceding in favor of Douai until the end of 1593. But by March of 1594 as a result of Parsons's intervention, Philip II paid the 4,000 crowns that he owed both the college and the nuns in Syon, and increased his grant to the English Jesuit college.[55]

Parsons was enthusiastic about the college at St Omers. Assured by Henry Garnet that there would be enough students to fill the new college, he believed that it would provide an important service to English Catholics and to the other English colleges on the continent. Parsons rejected initial attempts by some Belgian Jesuits to locate the new college in Courtrai instead of St Omers as contrary to the royal will, but he could not resist their insistence that the English college be dependent on the Belgian college in the same city despite his preference that it follow the example of the English colleges in Spain and Rome. Subsequent friction strained relations among the Jesuits and their definitive resolution awaited the return of Oliver Mannaerts from the general congregation in Rome.[56] Parsons persistently reminded Philip II of the college's importance. As a result the king overrode restrictions on the number of students imposed by the city fathers by increasing his pension. Besides financial assistance, Philip recommended to Jean de Vernois, Bishop of St Omers, Archduke

---

[54] Parsons to Acquaviva, Madrid December 2 and 9, 1595, ARSI, Hisp. 139, fols 122^r–126^v.

[55] Thomas Francis Knox, (ed.), *The First and Second Diaries of the English College, Douay* (London, 1878), pp. xci–xcii; Parsons to Acquaviva, Valladolid August 11, 1593, ARSI, Hisp. 136, fols 14^r–15^v; same to same, Madrid March 10, 1594, ARSI, Hisp. 136, fols 245^r–246^v; same to same, Córdoba March 20, 1594, ARSI, Hisp. 136, fols 249^r–250^v; same to same, Madrid June 4 and 16, 1594, ARSI, Hisp. 136, fols 362^r–363^v; "The dispatches which his Majesty hath commanded to be made for the Seminaries of Rhemes and of St Omers and for the Nunns of Sion, 24 febr. 1594," ABSI, Coll P I 248 (published in John Hungerford Pollen, S.J., (ed.), "Fr. Robert Persons, S.J.–Annals of the English College at Seville, with Accounts of other Foundations at Valladolid, St Lucar, Lisbon and St Omers," in *Miscellanea IX* [London, 1914], pp. 23–24).

[56] Parsons to Acquaviva, Valladolid June 16, 1593, ARSI, Hisp. 135, fols 306^r–307^v; same to same Valladolid July 15, 1593, ARSI, Hisp. 135, fols 372^r–373^v; same to same, Madrid December 4, 1593, ARSI, Hisp. 136, fols 163^r–165^v.

Ernst, and the city fathers to provide whatever aid they could to secure the college's foundation and to facilitate its work.[57] Nothing was to impede the college's administration and growth.

As we saw in Chapter 2, Parsons did not find working with Jean d'Heur pleasant: d'Heur was narrow and uncompromising and rarely consulted the English Jesuits before making decisions that affected that nation's concerns. Unlike Spanish provincials who periodically sought advice from their English subjects on matters pertaining to England, d'Heur ignored their expertise. Moreover his insistence that the college be deprived of an independent rector and subject to Christian Dalmer, rector of the Walloon college, was both contrary to the king's intention and detrimental to "union of hearts" within the Society. Parsons petitioned Acquaviva to deal with these issues.[58]

Oliver Mannaerts returned safely to Belgium by early June of 1594. Almost immediately he addressed problems concerning affairs of the English College and, on June 19, drafted regulations to guide relations between the English and Belgian colleges. George Duras, scheduled to succeed Mannaerts as provincial on the 23rd, also approved the proposals. Because of distance between the two colleges Mannaerts permitted the English to celebrate Mass in their domestic chapel so that the boys would not be "compelled to walk in the streets more often than necessary with waste of time and with considerable distraction." Moreover he allowed an English Jesuit to conduct catechism classes for the pupils. To the request that the rector and consultors of the college have the right to determine how many students they would accept, Mannaerts replied that this decision should be left to the Belgian provincial who was encouraged to admit as many students as the college's endowment could afford. To the relief of Parsons, Mannaerts argued that it was common policy that colleges and seminaries administered by Jesuits were not dependent on the rector of the neighboring Jesuit college. Nonetheless the rector of the seminary should consult the rector of the college to prevent any tension or difficulty and not seek the advice of anyone outside the seminary without the rector of the college's knowledge. The rector of the seminary should be accountable to the provincial to whom he would provide financial statements and accounts of daily life. Because the students were "sons of noblemen or very honourable persons," it was asked that they not be beaten or treated like servants with public punishments or penances. Mannaerts agreed that, unless the crime was scandalously public, erring students would be

---

[57] Parsons to Acquaviva, Madrid March 10, 1594, ARSI, Hisp. 136, fols 245^r–246^v; same to same, Córdoba March 20, 1594, ARSI, Hisp. 136, fols 249^r–250^v; same to same, Seville April 18, 1594, ARSI, Hisp. 136, fols 284^r–285^v.

[58] Parsons to Acquaviva, Madrid June 4 and 16, 1594, ARSI, Hisp. 136, fols 362^r–363^v.

punished privately. Finally, Mannaerts granted the request that the English college be governed according to the norms of the English colleges in Rome and Spain "as far as possible."[59] Like most compromises this was not the final word. Mannaerts's regulations were barely implemented when new problems surfaced.

When Nicholas Smith reentered the Society around 1592, he surrendered his books and other possessions to Mannaerts who bestowed them on the Jesuit college in Douai. Smith later inherited a legacy of 300 or 400 ducats from his father. A Catholic uncle who was a doctor in London held the money and promised to send all or some whenever Smith requested it. William Holt had already received an unspecified amount and Smith expected more to be forwarded. However, the English said nothing to the Belgian Jesuits probably because they feared that the Belgians would apply the money to one of their colleges. Because of the financial needs of the English college and because Smith himself spent little time in the Jesuit college in Douai, he wanted to give the money to the English college in St Omers. For that, Smith needed Acquaviva's permission. Earlier Henry Garnet had made a similar request: he had asked that money and estates left in England by Jesuits be applied to the needs of the mission. Until the general made a decision, the English wanted to keep the matter a secret. Permission was granted.[60]

Parsons's authority in St Omers was challenged almost immediately. During the summer of 1594 Jean Foucart, rector of the English college, questioned the right of William Flack and other English priests to read and receive letters to and from Parsons without Foucart's authorization, and had inquired into their financial dealings. Because only procurators and ministers could engage in financial matters, Foucart's concern was justifiable. But in conversations with them, Foucart questioned Parsons's right to be involved in the college's domestic affairs. Presumably Foucart considered their correspondence a violation of the regulations laid down by Mannaerts. Parsons beseeched Acquaviva to explain to Foucart that it was "your pleasure that they should listen to what I have to say by way of assisting that seminary and keeping it united to the seminaries here [Spain], for the greater good of the whole and in order to carry out the intention of the king and of your Paternity."[61]

---

[59] "Primae determinationes R.P. Oliverii Manarei pro seminario Audomarensi," ARSI, Germ. 177, fols 313^{r-v}; Hubert Chadwick, S.J., *St Omers to Stonyhurst* (London, 1962), pp. 30–31.

[60] Parsons to Acquaviva, Madrid December 2 and 9, 1595, ARSI, Hisp. 139, fols 122^r–126^v; Acquaviva to Holt, Rome November 25, 1595, ARSI, Fl. Belg. 1/I, p. 581^a; same to Parsons, Rome February 11, 1596, ARSI, Cast. 6, fols 237^v–238^r.

[61] Parsons to Acquaviva, Valladolid September 7, 1594, ARSI, Hisp. 137, fols 164^{r-v}.

The Fifth General Congregation

A constitutional crisis led to the convocation of the first general congregation in the history of the Society for reasons other than the election of a new general: the Fifth General Congregation (November 3, 1593 – January 18, 1594). We noted in Chapter 2 how long the crisis had simmered in Spain and how Parsons served as Acquaviva's "eyes and ears" at the court of the apparently hostile Philip II who, with the Inquisition, wanted to alter the Society's Institute and threatened to impose a visitor. Pope Sixtus V favored some changes, especially the name of the religious order and he asked Acquaviva to do so because he considered the appropriation of the name "Society of Jesus" a sign of pride. The general was willing to satisfy the pope, but the issue ended with Sixtus's death on August 27, 1590. A year later Pope Gregory XIV confirmed the Society's Institute.[62] But criticisms continued and the combined pressure of Philip II and Clement VIII forced Acquaviva to convoke a congregation despite his deep misgivings and apprehensions.

In Rome Claudio Acquaviva waged a careful campaign to discredit José de Acosta with Philip and Clement. Arguing that he had not been canonically elected, Acquaviva tried to exclude Acosta from the congregation. But Clement ordered that Acosta attend with active and passive voice. According to Claudio Burgaleta, S.J., Acquaviva's defamation marginalized Acosta during his stay in Rome. Acosta was evicted from the professed house and, during the congregation, he was obliged to swear that he had written nothing against the Society's Institute and that he in no way sympathized with the *memorialistas*. Working with Gonzalo Fernández de Córdoba, Duke of Sessa and Spanish ambassador in Rome, and the Jesuit Francisco, Cardinal de Toledo[63] on behalf of Pope Clement VIII, Acosta kept Philip informed of all developments but, at the same time, he did not wish to be seen as the king's lackey. Burgaleta stressed Acosta lacked duplicity when he voted in favor of Acquaviva and opposed the *memorialistas*. Indeed, he resisted the "politically opportune move" and voted according to his convictions. All in all, Burgaleta concluded that Acosta served Philip's interests well and attained many of his own goals. A number of decisions, including a commission to review his generalate and an order to elect new assistants more favorable to Spain, reprimanded Acquaviva. Moreover, Jesuits renounced their privilege to absolve heretics

---

[62] See Bangert, *History of the Society of Jesus*, pp. 99–100. Frequently Jesuits were blamed for Sixtus's death because of his stance on the name of the Society.

[63] Clement created Toledo a cardinal in 1593 on the eve of the congregation in the hope that he would preside over the congregation. Acquaviva, however, dissuaded the pope from this course of action (Bangert, *History of the Society of Jesus*, p. 100).

without informing the Inquisition and the congregation recommended that Jesuits extend to the Inquisition every service possible. Finally the congregation urged Philip not to be misled by false accusations aimed at the destruction of the Society's reputation. Having examined everything as Philip desired, the congregation concluded that such accusations were groundless and the king should "not suffer the Society in his realm, loyal as it is to him, to be harassed in any way by these calumniators."[64] In July of 1594 Acosta resumed his position as superior of the professed house in Valladolid from which position, as we saw earlier, he interfered in the affairs of the English College.

As provincial congregations prepared *postulata* and Acquaviva countered Acosta's influence in Rome, Parsons worked for Acquaviva at the Spanish court. Urged by Gil González Dávila and Alonso Sánchez, Parsons spoke to Philip about the upcoming general congregation in the spring of 1593. He hoped the congregation would bear "good results for the service of God and the general welfare of His poor family" but he feared "some disaffected persons" would use the congregation to create a disturbance by attempting to achieve their goals through irregular means. Since all Jesuits knew well from experience that Philip was their great protector, Parsons urged him to defend the Society now from these men. By defending the Society's freedom, Philip would gain the esteem and affection of all Jesuits who would "return to their countries consoled and encouraged to serve His Majesty and edified by his prudence and compassion in not allowing himself to be influenced by individual grievances of a handful of disaffected men who made trouble in their order."[65] At the same time Parsons appealed to Pope Clement VIII along the same lines. "I greatly rejoice," Parsons wrote from Seville on April 15, 1593, "that God has provided an opportunity for the whole Society to become indebted to your holiness more than to any of your predecessors since it was founded: in as much as it is in your holiness's pontificate that the Society is to hold the first general congregation that it has held in the general's lifetime." This was not only the first but it may be the most important in the Society's history because of the "schemes and machinations of certain persons against her Institute" that was the work of the Devil: "I say the Devil, because in all sincerity

---

[64] Claudio M. Burgaleta, S.J., *José de Acosta, S.J. (1540–1600): His Life and Thought* (Chicago, 1999), pp. 63–67. For the decrees see Padberg et al., *For Matters of Greater Moment*, decrees 18, 21, 28, 55, 64, 73 on pp. 191–94, 206–207, 210, 212–13. For a brief history of the congregation see John W. Padberg, S.J., "The General Congregations of the Society of Jesus: A Brief Survey of Their History," *Studies in the Spirituality of Jesuits*, 6/1–2 (1974): pp. 15–20.

[65] Parsons to Acquaviva, Toledo, March 22, 1593, ARSI, Hisp. 135, fols 147^r–149^v; same to same, Seville April 19, 1593, ARSI, Hisp. 135, fols 187^r–188^v; same to same, Valladolid July 15, 1593, ARSI, Hisp. 135, fols 372^r–373^v.

and before God I declare that in the course of these four years or more that I have been in Spain I have weighed in my mind as best I could and with complete impartiality the aims of some of the dissatisfied members of this Society who are said to be the source of these broils." As a result Parsons concluded that the schemers lacked piety and religious devotion, and were motivated by ambition and jealousy. They also resented being subject to any orders from Rome, persuading some that absolute government from Rome was potentially harmful: "Your holiness can easily see whither this argument leads, and that its inevitable result will be to lead on to more serious things." If the congregation were allowed to operate freely, Parsons was certain that Acquaviva would be vindicated.[66]

Despite his efforts in Acquaviva's favor, Parsons played no official role in preparing for the congregation or at the congregation itself. Invited to participate at the congregation for the Castile province at Medina del Campo, Parsons could not attend because necessary business in Portugal demanded immediate attention.[67] Instead he worked in the wings as a lobbyist. In an audience with Philip on February 6, 1594, Parsons spoke about Jesuit affairs at considerable length and repeated much of his earlier message. News from Rome of the intervention of the duke of Sessa with a memorial demanding radical changes in the Society's Institute caught Parsons by surprise. The congregation unanimously rejected it but many worried that this was simply the first attempt at interference. Yet Parsons remained hopeful, believing that the duke was acting on his own and not on directives from Philip.[68]

On April 16, 1594 Parsons received orders from Acquaviva via Juan de Sigüenza to negotiate with King Philip Acosta's return to Spain. Instead of departing immediately for Madrid as Sigüenza urged, Parsons wrote to Juan de Idiáquez, copies of which letters he forwarded to Acquaviva so that he could advise further action. Meanwhile Parsons promised to pursue whatever policy Acquaviva desired on his next visit to Madrid. Nearly a

---

[66] ABSI, Coll P I 327. This letter was sent with Acquaviva's approval. See Parsons to Acquaviva, Seville April 19, 1593, ARSI, Hisp. 135, fols 187ʳ–188ᵛ.

[67] Parsons to Acquaviva, Seville April 19, 1593, ARSI, Hisp. 135, fols 187ʳ–188ᵛ; ARSI, Congr. 45, fols 271ʳ–272ᵛ. In his reply on August 30, 1593, Acquaviva was reassured by Parsons's willingness to do anything he could to serve the Society. While other fathers attended the general congregation, Acquaviva asked Parsons to go to Philip's court to assist various Spanish Jesuits striving to win the king over to Acquaviva's side (ARSI, Cast. 6, fols 163ʳ⁻ᵛ). On February 2, 1594 Acquaviva repeated his permission for Parsons to discuss Jesuit matters with Philip (ARSI, Hisp. 76, fols 10ʳ⁻ᵛ). For some reason, Francis Edwards suggested that Parsons attended the provincial congregation (*Robert Persons*, p. 159).

[68] Parsons to Acquaviva, Madrid March 10, 1594, ARSI, Hisp. 136, fols 245ʳ–246ᵛ; same to same, Córdoba March 20, 1594, ARSI, Hisp. 136, fols 249ʳ–250ᵛ. See also Bangert, *History of the Society of Jesus*, pp. 100–101.

month later Parsons admitted that he had made the right decision by not departing immediately for Madrid. The matter was well in hand, and Parsons hoped to get to the root of this unspecified problem after discussions with fathers returning from the general congregation.[69] As we have seen, Acosta returned to his post as superior of the professed house in Valladolid. Even though Parsons's letters do not provide details regarding his mission from Acquaviva about Acosta, it seems that Acosta's suspicion that Parsons had opposed him was justified.

By May 12, 1594 Parsons received a copy of the congregational decrees. With the exception of a decree against Jews and *conversos*, he thought that all would be accepted favorably.[70] Long a concern in Spain, the Society had resisted *limpieza de sangre* and refused to deny admission to those who lacked "purity of blood."[71] The Society finally capitulated to Spanish pressure. A reason offered for this reversal was the nationality of many who had opposed Acquaviva: 25 of the 27 "false sons," Jesuits who had signed memorials against the *Constitutions*, were of Jewish or Moorish descent. Nonetheless, Parsons was troubled by the decree. How could we exclude one race of Christians "from the means which our Lord left for our salvation, that is, the religious life?" Parsons predicted the decree would alienate many influential men from the Society and would occasion some internal discord. It would, he believed, be well received at the Spanish court because "it agrees with their humor and with the matter of procedure in the country." Earlier he had advanced many reasons why the Society should not exclude "New Christians"; now he would "turn over a new leaf and seek the best arguments we can to defend what our mother has decided, for that will be the most proper thing to do: sons must submit their judgements to hers."[72]

---

[69] Parsons to Acquaviva, Seville April 18, 1594, ARSI, Hisp. 136, fols 284^r–285^v; same to same, Marchena May 12, 1594, ARSI, Hisp. 136, fols 318^r–319^v; same to same, Seville June 12, 1595, ARSI, Hisp. 138, fols 299^r–301^v.

[70] Padberg et al., *For Matters of Greater Moment*, decree 52, p. 204.

[71] On Jesuits and Jews see James W. Reites, S.J., "St Ignatius of Loyola and the Jews," *Studies in the Spirituality of Jesuits*, 13/4 (1981): pp. 1–48 and Francisco de Borja Medina, S.J., "Ignacio de Loyola y la '*limpieza de sangre*,'" in *Ignacio de Loyola y Su Tiempo*, (ed.) Juan Plazaola, S.J. (Bilbao, n.d. [1992]), pp. 579–615; Robert A. Maryks, "The Jesuit Order as a 'Synagogue of Jews': Discrimination against Jesuits of Jewish Ancestry in the Early History of the Society of Jesus," *AHSI*, 78 [2009]: pp. 339–416; Robert A. Maryks, *The Jesuit Order as a 'Synagogue of Jews': Jesuits of Jewish Ancestry and Purity-of-Blood Laws in the Early Society of Jesus* (Leiden, 2009). On the question of racial purity see Henry Kamen, *Inquisition and Society in Spain in the Sixteenth and Seventeenth Centuries* (London, 1985), pp. 114–33 and *The Spanish Inquisition: An Historical Revision* (London, 1997), pp. 244–47. Many currently are investigating the general topic of Jews and the Society of Jesus. Consult the web page http://www.jewishjesuits.com.

[72] Parsons to Acquaviva, Marchena May 12, 1594, ARSI, Hisp. 136, fols 318^r–319^v.

The congregational decrees forbidding Jesuit involvement in the affairs of princes was of more immediate concern. As a result of many *postulata*, the congregation decreed:

> Because our Society, called forth by the Lord for the spread of the faith and the harvest of souls, can happily attain the end it proposes through the ministries proper to its Institute—spiritual armaments carried under the banner of the cross with benefit to the Church and the edification of our neighbor—that same Society would hinder the achievement of these goals and expose itself to extreme perils if it were to engage in what is secular and belongs to political affairs and the governance of states.[73]

A second decree stated:

> Special attention must be given to this warning: Ours are not to cultivate familiarity with princes to the detriment of spiritual welfare and religious discipline; and they should not become engaged in other secular affairs, even though connected with the particular affairs of relatives, friends, or anyone else, unless perchance in the judgment of superiors charity might occasionally dictate otherwise ... we must take special care that we make the effort to assist our neighbor within the limitations of our Institute.[74]

Parsons protested that he wanted to observe these decrees fully, but:

> it seems that the interests of the Catholic religion in England are so bound up and intermingled with those of the state that one cannot deal with the one without dealing with the other, since there is no government in England except that of the heretics, and everything that we attempt to do for the service of religion is in opposition to their government; and even if we wished to keep matters of religion separate from those of state in theory, in practice it is not possible to deal with the one without bringing in the other.[75]

Consequently Parsons wanted an explanation or dispensation to continue his work.

Many would consider Acquaviva's reply a masterpiece of "Jesuitism." He hoped that Parsons would act so prudently and religiously that a dispensation would be unnecessary. Moreover, Acquaviva doubted that he could easily grant a dispensation regarding a matter that had so upset the Society universal. He did, however, clarify the decree: it did not forbid

---

[73] Padberg et al., *For Matters of Greater Moment*, decree 47, p. 201.
[74] Padberg et al., *For Matters of Greater Moment*, decree 48, p. 201.
[75] Parsons to Acquaviva, Marchena May 12, 1594, ARSI, Hisp. 136, fols 318^r–319^v.

advising rulers on matters pertaining to the service of the Lord even if such matters were mingled with state affairs. The decree forbade Jesuits to "solicit such matters by letter, [and] still less [to] attend to their execution."[76] A few months later, Joseph Creswell asked for a copy of Acquaviva's clarification lest activities of English Jesuits upset Spanish rectors and provincials.[77]

In July of 1593 Parsons recommended that Creswell be sent to the Spanish Netherlands as William Holt's replacement because Holt was a *"persona non grata"* as a result of conflicts with certain unnamed English soldiers and gentleman in Flanders;[78] because of his past associations with Cosme Masi, secretary to the duke of Parma, and because of his unfamiliarity with the Spanish language and protocol. Because he could not effectively advance English concerns, Holt was depressed and eager to leave. He himself suggested Creswell as successor: he spoke Spanish, knew the right people, and had a good business sense. Since Parsons and Creswell had important business to transact with King Philip in September, any move approved by Acquaviva would have to wait until October.[79] The exchange was not made. Instead Parsons designated Creswell his assistant in Madrid, an appointment that resulted in the above discussed difficulties. By January of 1594 Parsons opposed Holt's re-assignment to Spain. Nonetheless Acquaviva had already instructed Holt to depart for Spain as soon as he had heard from Parsons. Acquaviva insisted that his order be obeyed despite a change in Parsons's position. Perhaps reluctantly Parsons acquiesced to the general's will. Even though Holt was "of a somewhat unsociable disposition," Parsons believed that his intelligence and virtue would compensate. Because he could accommodate himself to the views of others, he would serve well in Spain. In light of Holt's reply, however, Acquaviva concluded that he could not be removed from Flanders. Holt was ready to depart, but Secretary Esteban de Ibarra prevented him. Holt suggested that Parsons request from the king a letter detailing the important work that the Jesuit was to undertake in Spain.

---

[76] Acquaviva to Parsons, Rome July 4, 1594, ARSI, Tolet. 5/II, fol. 348ʳ. Oddly Francis Edwards did not mention the general's reply (*Robert Persons*, p. 171). The traditional distinction between religion and statecraft blurred around the issue of heresy, and the role of a royal confessor. On these complicated subjects see Sabina Pavone, *The Wily Jesuits and the Monita Secreta. The Forged Secret Instructions of the Jesuits. Myth and Reality* (St Louis, 2005); Robert Bireley, S.J., *The Counter-Reformation Prince. Anti-Machiavellianism or Catholic Statecraft in Early Modern Europe* (Chapel Hill, 1990); Robert Bireley, S.J., *The Jesuits and the Thirty Years War. Kings, Courts, and Confessors* (Cambridge, 2003).

[77] Creswell to Acquaviva, Madrid December 3, 1594, ARSI, Hisp. 138, fols 9ʳ–10ᵛ. I have not found a copy of the requested clarification.

[78] We shall look at this more closely in Chapter 6.

[79] Parsons to Acquaviva, Valladolid July 15, 1593, ARSI, Hisp. 135, fols 372ʳ–373ᵛ.

That would force Ibarra to allow him to leave. Until such a letter was sent, Holt advised that no action be taken.[80] Holt remained in Flanders until 1598.

Scots and Irish Colleges

The English College in St Omers was not the only college opened in Flanders by religious exiles in the 1590s. On April 5, 1594 Pope Clement VIII approved Tyrie's and William Crichton's relocation of the financially troubled Scots College from Pont-à-Mousson to Douai. Persistent warfare and periodic plague had so often disrupted religious and academic life that Clement concluded the college could no longer remain at Pont-à-Mousson.[81] In Douai the college struggled despite Acquaviva's insisting that Parsons use his influence to obtain support for the seminary, and his committing the college to the care of George Duras, Belgian provincial. For his part, Parsons promised to do what he could because, as he assured Acquaviva, "if I did not have responsibility for these Englishmen, I would assume responsibility for the Scots, nay more so because they are more deserving. However, everything possible shall be done for both."[82] William Crichton was placed in charge of the college but subject to the jurisdiction of the Belgian provincial and, unlike the English College at St Omers, under the rector of the Jesuit College in Douai, François Delapré. Acquaviva exhorted the provincial and the rector to be attentive to the needs of the college and to the formation of the students.[83]

Threats of war forced Crichton to transfer some students to Courtrai: by February of 1595 only philosophers and theologians remained in Douai. Because his work for the college demanded frequent absences from Douai, Crichton appointed the Scottish secular priest-philosopher James Cheyne superior in charge of administrative and financial matters. Crichton spoke highly of him and anticipated that he would strengthen the college's financial foundation despite the opposition he had already

---

[80] Parsons's letter is not extant. We know if it from Acquaviva's reply, Rome March 14, 1594, ARSI, Tolet. 5/II, fol. 330ʳ. See also Parsons to Acquaviva, Marchena May 12, 1594, ARSI, Hisp. 136, fols 318ʳ–319ᵛ; Acquaviva to Parsons, Rome July 4, 1594, ARSI, Tolet. 5/II, fol. 347ᵛ.

[81] A copy of Clement's bull can be found in ABSI, MS.A.II.3 (57). See also ARSI, Angl. 39, fols 109ʳ⁻ᵛ; J.H. Baxter, "The Scots College at Douai," *Scottish Historical Review*, 24 (1927): p. 251. Baxter claimed the college moved in 1592, but 1593 is the more likely year.

[82] Parsons to Acquaviva, Valladolid September 7, 1594, ARSI, Hisp. 137, fols 164ʳ⁻ᵛ. See also Edwards, *Robert Persons*, pp. 174–75.

[83] Crichton to Acquaviva, Antwerp November 12, 1594, ARSI, Germ. 173, fols 218ʳ–219ᵛ; Acquaviva to George Duras, Rome December 17, 1594, ARSI, Fl. Belg. 1/I, pp. 543–44; same to Crichton, Rome December 17, 1594, ARSI, Fl. Belg. 1/I, p. 544.

encountered from Jesuits. Appeals for financial assistance bore fruit.[84] William V, Duke of Bavaria and educated by the Jesuits, donated 300 gold pieces. Jesuits in Milan sponsored a collection for the college; Crichton attributed the small sum not to the lack of generosity but to poor preaching. Merchants in Brussels contributed as did Scottish exiles in Paris.[85] Financial improvement, however, could not resolve all problems. War remained a constant threat. Because French armies were never far away, by June of 1595 Crichton and Acquaviva were pondering another move. In 1596 the seminary moved to Louvain.[86]

A dispute over the college's foundation complicated the matter. Many Irish clergy claimed that the college's papal subsidy required it to support as many Irish as Scottish students. Scots, however, contended that the subsidy stipulated only a small amount for the Irish, and they were extremely reluctant to devote even that meager sum to the education of Irish clergy. The Irish, they argued, had seminaries in Lisbon and Salamanca exclusively for the education of their nationals. In Lisbon, there were nearly 30 students; in Salamanca, 12. On the other hand, Scotland had only one college, and the Scottish mission needed more priests if Catholics hoped to reap a good harvest. If the college was obliged to divert some of its meager finances from the education of Scots, Scotland would not have the workers required. Both nationalities appealed to their cardinals protector, Enrico Caetani for Scotland and Girolamo Mattei for Ireland. The dispute was finally settled in 1596 when the Scots were given full control over the college. Cardinal Caetani ordered that the Irish be excluded from the seminary and imposed a perpetual silence to quell the dispute. It seems, however, that a small part of the endowment was transferred to the Irish College in Salamanca.[87]

---

[84] George Thomson (pseudo.?) published *De antiquitate Christianae religionis apud Scotos* (Rome, 1594), ARCR, vol. 1, num. 1251 as an appeal for aid to the financially troubled institution. This small volume was edited by Henry D.G. Law as "The Antiquity of the Christian Religion Among the Scots, 1594," in *Miscellany of the Scottish History Society, Vol. II* (Edinburgh, 1904), Scottish History Society 44, pp. 117–32.

[85] Crichton to James Tyrie, Brussels February 10, 1595, BL, Lans. 96, fols 91^r–92^v. This letter was summarized in R.B. Wernham, *List and Analysis of State Papers Foreign Series: Elizabeth I* (7 vols, London, 1964–2000), vol. 6, par. 393.

[86] ARSI, Angl. 39, fols 108^r–109^v. Acquaviva had listened to arguments for and against a move to Louvain, and decided to leave the final decision to Crichton after a consultation with the Belgian provincial and James Tyrie (Acquaviva to Crichton, Rome June 3, 1595, ARSI, Fl. Belg. 1/I, p. 558). Since the college remained in Douai for two more years, Crichton must have postponed a move until the wars forced his hand.

[87] See ARSI, Rom. 156/II fols 330^r–334^r; ARSI, Angl. 39, fols 106^{r-v} for pertinent documents.

Besides the consolidation and location of the Scots College, Crichton worried about Scottish candidates to the Society. Acquaviva had instructed Crichton to send suitable candidates to the novitiate in Rome, but, the Scot insisted, many found the Roman climate unbearable. Consequently he asked that the privilege granted to English Jesuits be extended to him, viz. some Scots could be sent to the novitiate in Belgium. By assuring him that there would always be room for suitable candidates Acquaviva quelled Crichton's anxieties even though he did not specify where.[88]

Under the direction of James Archer, the Irish College in Salamanca fostered internal discipline and intellectual standards.[89] Although the educational pace was determined by a seminarian's age, capacity and prior education, the college supervised carefully all activity. Three days after a student's arrival, he made the Ignatian Spiritual Exercises for 8 or 10 days during which his behavior was scrupulously watched. Observance of rules and spirit of prayer were especially noted. After the retreat each seminarian made a profession of faith and promised under oath to become a priest and to return to Ireland to work for the salvation of his countrymen and women. Moreover each promised under oath to obey the college's authorities and to reimburse the college for his education if he neither sought ordination nor returned to Ireland. The college's spiritual regime was strict: daily Mass, half-hour of meditation, and recitation of the rosary and the Office of the Blessed Virgin, a popular Marian supplement to, or substitution for, the Divine Office. The college emphasized strongly Thomist theology and the watchful eye of the Inquisition prevented any divergence. Academic and spiritual demands were intended to weed out unsuitable candidates and to discipline future priests for the discomforts and harsh realities of life on the Irish mission.

More than 6,000 students attended the University of Salamanca in 1593. Colleges, monasteries and convents were scattered around the city. The Castilian province had a professed house dependent on alms and, after 1595, a college. Perhaps mindful of the problems the English Jesuits encountered in Valladolid and Seville, Archer sought to avoid any conflict with his Spanish colleagues. He, of course, was subject to the local Jesuit rector and like Parsons he fostered good relations by insisting that the Irish College not blatantly violate Spanish Jesuit customs and standards.

---

[88] Crichton to Acquaviva, Douai April 21, 1593, ARSI, Germ. 171, fols 136^{r-v}; same to same, Antwerp October 23, 1593, ARSI, Germ. 171, fols 290^r–291^v; Acquaviva to Crichton, Rome January 8, 1594, Fl. Belg. 1/I, p. 524; Crichton to Acquaviva, Antwerp November 12, 1594, ARSI, Germ. 173, fols 218^r–219^v.

[89] I follow Thomas Morrissey, S.J., in his presentation of the spiritual and academic life of the Irish College. See his *James Archer of Kilkenny: An Elizabethan Jesuit* (Dublin, 1979), pp. 13–17 and "The Irish Student Diaspora in the Sixteenth Century and the Early Years of the Irish College at Salamanca," *Recusant History*, 14 (1978): pp. 248–55.

Insufficient funds, however, chilled relations. Protesting the college could not survive on an unreliable royal annuity of 500 ducats, Archer bemoaned his financial problems to Acquaviva. The new English College in St Omers, he pointed out, received nearly four times as much money and only had twice as many students. Yet it too complained of a lack of funds.[90] Unless other sources were found, the college could not continue to exist let alone progress. Having consulted Robert Parsons, Archer suggested that a prudent Jesuit be sent to Ireland to seek alms from principal Irish nobles, whom, he believed, would be very generous. Perhaps, he opined, Pope Clement VIII would grant the college revenues from some ecclesiastical benefices in a diocese for a stated period of time. Archer was certain that he could obtain King Philip's permission if the pope agreed. Moreover, Archer complained, Irish have a stronger claim on papal assistance than English and Scots because as a papal fief, Ireland was part of the Church's patrimony and its natives the pope's subjects.[91] To seek papal assistance, to prevent loss of its share of the papal subsidy to the Scots-Irish College in Douai, and to obtain the same papal concessions granted to the English regarding ordination, Archer wanted to visit Rome. There were also other matters that could not "be suitably committed to writing."[92] Acquaviva refused permission. Archer then requested a Jesuit agent in Rome to oversee Irish business. Because he personally knew no one in Rome with proper qualifications for this position, he could not recommend anyone. This agent could petition the pope for ecclesiastical benefices, and briefs allowing Irish students to be ordained without fulfilling certain canonical requirements. Moreover this agent could argue to prevent loss of Ireland's share of the Douai subsidy. Archer also needed an agent at the Spanish court. Unless the needs of the Irish college were regularly presented to the king, Philip would forget them. Without the king, the college would collapse. Various secretaries warned Archer that he risked losing everything without an agent. Moreover lack of representation at court prevented the Irish College from securing more aid. Recently Gaspar de Quiroga, Cardinal of Toledo, wished to grant alms to both the Irish and the English. Because there was no Irish representative there to receive the grant, the

---

[90] St Omers received 1900 ducats for sixteen students; the Irish College, 500 for nine in 1593 and twelve in 1594 (Morrissey, "Irish College at Salamanca," pp. 251–52).

[91] In an undated supplication addressed to the pope, unnamed Irish exiles asked Clement VIII to restore what Henry VIII violently seized under Clement VII. Although few were infected with heresy, Rome forgot Ireland. The papacy assisted the Scots and the English but gave nothing to the Irish. To withstand the assault of graduates of the recently established Trinity College, Irish Catholicism needed more priests. Therefore they begged Clement to support the Irish College and to re-establish a Jesuit mission to Ireland (IJA, MS B.21 [published in Edmund Hogan, S.J., *Ibernia Ignatiana* (Dublin, 1880), pp. 35–37]).

[92] Archer to Acquaviva, Salamanca August 9, 1594, ARSI, Hisp. 137, fols 115^{r-v}.

Irish College received nothing—and the English obtained 21,000 ducats! Unfortunately Spanish Jesuit assistance was not dependable. Regarding Spanish indifference, Archer's sentiments echoed Parsons's: there would be no Irish College if he had to rely on the Spanish! Thus Archer sought permission to travel to Madrid whenever it was necessary. There he could transact important business such as his request for ecclesiastical revenues. To improve relations with Spanish Jesuits in Salamanca, Archer wanted a Spanish Jesuit assistant. Perhaps through his intercession, the Irish College would find more benefactors. But here Archer had to be careful. The college needed alms, but the Jesuit rector forbade Archer to beg. As in Seville, Jesuits feared that any attempt by the Irish to solicit alms in Salamanca would deprive Spanish Jesuit communities of needed funds of their own.[93]

On March 13, 1595 Acquaviva wrote to Archer and to Gil González Dávila, Castilian provincial. He instructed the latter to provide all possible assistance to Archer and to the college because Ireland was "an isolated nation in need of aid." To Archer, the general explained that the only agent he needed in Rome was James Tyrie who would examine the issue of Ireland's share of the papal subsidy and any other matter referred to him. Any decision about Archer's trips to Madrid was left to González Dávila and Francisco de Porres, provincial of Toledo. He instructed Archer to discuss the matter with them. If Archer were unable to make the journey, he should recommend the business to Joseph Creswell. Indeed, it probably was more diplomatic and less offensive if all matters passed through Creswell's hands. The Castilian provincial promised his assistance and apparently granted his permission because Archer made numerous trips to Madrid throughout 1595.[94]

Negotiating Conversion: James and Scottish Catholics

William Crichton's preoccupation with the Scots College did not prevent him from travelling to Cologne on May 13, 1595 to meet James Gordon and the earls of Huntly and Erroll.[95] All three expected James to proclaim his Catholicism once the means and the opportunity were available and, thus,

---

[93] Archer to Acquaviva, Salamanca December 23, 1594, ARSI, Hisp. 138, fols 36^r–37^v.

[94] Acquaviva to González Dávila, Rome March 13, 1595, ARSI, Cast. 6, fol. 206^v; same to Archer, Rome March 13, 1595, ARSI, Cast. 6, fol. 207^v; González Dávila to Acquaviva, Arevalo May 17, 1595, ARSI, Hisp. 138, fols 271^r–272^v. See also Morrissey, "Irish College at Salamanca," p. 254.

[95] On 12 May Crichton told the general that Father Gordon and the earl of Huntly had sent the Jesuit brother William Martin to summon him to Cologne and that he would depart on the next day (Crichton to Acquaviva, Brussels May 12, 1595, ARSI, Germ. 174, fol. 211^v).

did not anticipate remaining outside the kingdom for long. Among Scottish nobles in the earls' entourage were Crichton's kinsman, Robert Crichton, Lord Sanquhar,[96] and a "106" described by Crichton as "a gem of the first order." Unfortunately no extant cipher lists a "106." Also on the continent was the "Young Laird of Pury Ogilvie," that is John Ogilvie of Pury, to whom some of the letters in the "Spanish Blanks" affair were addressed. All these noblemen sought to make peace between Crichton and Robert Bruce, a Scottish agent/spy in the Low Countries, who, Crichton claimed, had calumniated him and many Scottish Catholic nobles.[97]

Tension between Bruce and Crichton dated almost immediately from Crichton's move to Flanders. Besides operating as a double agent who informed the English government of the activities of Scottish exiles, Bruce resented Crichton's and Gordon's soliciting foreign assistance for the Catholic cause. According to John Myrton, Bruce brought charges against Gordon before Innocenzo Malvasia, papal agent in Brussels, and Archduke Ernst. The nuncio informed Crichton who, in turn, told Myrton before his departure so that he could warn Gordon upon his arrival in Scotland.[98] This may have been the reason that Gordon avoided Flanders and headed for Germany. Bruce complained that the Catholic earls intercepted money intended for the king and used it contrary to the intention of King Philip. Instead of advancing the Catholic cause, the money subsidized military action involving the king's sworn enemy and heretic, the earl of Bothwell. Consequently relations between Philip and James soured, and the Catholic cause suffered a setback. Moreover Gordon's and Crichton's reports questioned the authenticity of Bruce's commission from James to negotiate with Philip's ministers. Bruce asserted that James commissioned him alone to pursue any negotiations and he resented Jesuit interference.[99] Despite the goodwill of the recent arrivals, they did not heal the breach.

Lord Sanquhar returned to Scotland in early summer of 1595 and Pury Ogilvie, claiming to be the ambassador of the king of Scotland,[100] travelled

---

[96] John Cecil ridiculed Crichton's efforts to connect his family with Sanquhar's " ... (as I am credebly informed) you are as neare a kynne as *Powles steepel, to charing crosse* ... " (*A discoverye of the errors committed and iniuryes done to his Ma. off Scotlande* [n.p., n.d. (Paris, 1599)], *ARCR*, vol. 2, num. 129, *STC* 4894. fol. 26r).

[97] Crichton to James Tyrie, Brussels February 10, 1595, BL, Lans. 96, fols 91r–92v; same to same, Antwerp June 18, 1595, *CSP Scotland* (1593–1595), pp. 611–13, 613–15.

[98] On Myrton's examination and the instructions he had received from Crichton see *CSP Scotland* (1593–1595), pp. 564–65, 571–73. On the incident itself, see *supra* Chapter 3.

[99] See the memorials prepared by Crichton for Tyrie, ARSI, Angl. 42, fols 38r–42v; 43r–v. See also Michael Yellowlees, *"So strange a monster as a Jesuite": The Society of Jesus in Sixteenth-Century Scotland* (Isle of Colonsay, 2003), pp. 139–41.

[100] In his article on James Fullerton, David Edwards lamented a "particularly glaring lacuna is the absence of any systematic examination of the role played by special agents and

to Rome in search of assistance. In Flanders Ogilvie met with Malvasia, Charles Paget, William Gifford, and the secretary Ibarra. He continued to Rome with a letter of introduction from King James VI to Owen Lewis, Bishop of Cassano. The king also authorized him to conduct negotiations with the pope. Among other things James requested a red hat for Cassano, and the removal of William Holt from Flanders and Robert Parsons from Spain because of their perceived opposition to the Scottish king. Ogilvie meandered through the Republic of Venice, and the Grand Duchy of Florence, seeking their approval of James's right to the English throne. By the time he arrived in Rome, Cassano had died and Malvasia himself introduced Ogilvie to the pope to whom Ogilvie presented a personal letter from James. Moreover he recommended that Pope Clement VIII send the Scot William Chisholm, Bishop of Vaison, to James's court to confirm his credentials if there was any doubt.[101] Gordon and Crichton, presumably in connection with Ogilvie's mission, requested Acquaviva's permission to travel to Rome, a permission he denied. Acquaviva explained to Crichton that in view of his age and health, he should not embark on an arduous and unnecessary journey.[102]

Ogilvie portrayed James as sympathetic to Catholics, and advanced specific actions, such as James's release of John Myrton from prison,[103] as signs of royal affection. James, therefore, should be supported as Catholic claimant to the English throne and not, as many English argued, one of the Habsburgs. Philip II was, according to Ogilvie, not interested in anything but acquiring another title for his family. The pressure being brought to bear in Rome by English Catholics for the excommunication of James was simply another ploy to present the Habsburgs as the only Catholic contenders. James needed papal support lest the Catholic earls hand over

---

'intelligencers' in negotiating by stealth the progress of King James's claim to the English and Irish thrones with the key figures of both kingdoms" ("Securing the Jacobean Succession: The Secret Career of James Fullerton of Trinity College, Dublin," in *The World of the Galloglass. Kings, Warlords and Warriors in Ireland and Scotland, 1200–1600*, (ed.) Seán Duffy (Dublin, 2007), p. 188. I thank Dr Paul Hammer for this reference.

[101] John Petit to [?], September 21/October 1, 1596, *CSP Scotland* (1595–1597), pp. 320–21. Chisholm performed a similar service in 1587/88. See McCoog, *Society of Jesus*, pp. 242–44.

[102] Acquaviva to Crichton, Rome July 22, 1595, ARSI, Rh. Inf. 3, fol. 82^v; same to Gordon, Rome July 22, 1595, ARSI, Rh. Inf. 3, fol. 82^v. Gordon did in fact travel to Rome and was professor of cases of conscience (or moral theology) at the Roman College between 1595 and 1596 (Riccardo G. Villoslada, S.J., *Storia del Collegio Romano dal suo inizio (1551) alla soppressione della Compagnia di Gesù (1773)* [Rome, 1954], p. 325).

[103] Myrton was in Brussels by late October (Claudio Acquaviva to Myrton, Rome November 11, 1595, ARSI, Fl. Belg. 1/I, p. 581).

Scotland to the king of Spain to the detriment of not only himself, but of Italy, the papacy and all Christendom.[104]

In Rome John Cecil and the Spanish ambassador, Gonzalo Fernández de Córdoba, Duke of Sessa, whom Ogilvie visited at night, questioned Ogilvie's credentials, abilities, and honesty. In conversations with Ibarra and Sessa, Ogilvie allegedly disclosed that his negotiations were in fact an elaborate ruse concocted by James, Queen Elizabeth and King Henry IV. James actually had no intention of becoming a Catholic. Ogilvie, however, wanted to sabotage this scheme. Privately he offered counter-proposals said to be from John Erskine, Earl of Mar and a secret Catholic. Mar offered to deliver some strong castles and James's son Henry into the hands of Philip. Ogilvie claimed to be pursuing two different strategies. Publicly he argued that James was willing to reconcile himself and his kingdom to the Church of Rome, to make peace with the Catholic earls, to sign an offensive and defensive treaty with Spain, to establish permanent ambassadors in Spain and Flanders, to protect all Catholic refugees fleeing from England, to wage war against Elizabeth and to offer his son as security if, in return, Philip promised to support no rival to James's claims to the English throne but work for James's succession, to treat with James henceforth and not his subjects like the Catholic earls, to grant certain trading rights to Scots, and to establish an ambassador in Scotland. Rome was skeptical despite Malvasia's enthusiasm, and a general hope that James would imitate Henry of Navarre.[105]

Cecil disputed the public position taken by Ogilvie. He, Cecil claimed, associated himself with the pro-Scottish party of Charles Paget and William Gifford and "other members of the party of English politicians who follow the King of Scotland [without regard for their Religion]." Ogilvie was not on good terms with the earls and spoke poorly about Scottish Jesuits.[106] James, Cecil explained, "has never shown any sign of wishing

---

[104] For various memoranda regarding these negotiations see *CSP Scotland* (1595–1597), pp. 225–27, 227–29, 230–33 and "Summa de los Memoriales," edited and translated by Thomas Graves Law in "Documents Illustrating Catholic Policy in the Reign of James VI," in *Miscellany of the Scottish History Society. Vol. 1* (Edinburgh, 1893), Scottish History Society 15, pp. 21–40. Robert Bowes, of course, did all he could to stay informed of the developments. On April 18, 1596 he wrote to Lord Burghley that James insisted that he was resisting all offers to join an anti-English alliance. Two months later, on June 8 and 21, Bowes told Burghley of Jesuit efforts to arouse Scottish nobles to work for the overthrow of Elizabeth and of attempts by Spain to purchase assistance for another armada (*CSP Scotland* [1595–1597], pp. 190–93, 239–41, 248–49). Shortly thereafter, Elizabeth wrote to James that she was "as evil treated by my named friend as I could be by my known foe" ([June 24, 1596] *CSP Scotland* [1595–1597], p. 250).

[105] See Law, "Summa de los Memoriales," pp. 34–35.

[106] One wonders if Crichton should be included in this alleged condemnation. As we shall see later, Crichton leapt to Ogilvie's defense.

to become a Catholic, notwithstanding the diligence with which the fathers of the Society, both of the English and of the Scottish nation (and they are many) have laboured."[107] According to Cecil, James's newfound interest in Catholicism was rooted in the publication of the *Book of Succession*. James realized that he needed an alliance with Rome and Spain if he was to ascend the throne. Cecil recommended that Spain and Rome do nothing until James had accepted Catholicism. Ogilvie returned to Spain in late 1596. There he was arrested and imprisoned in Barcelona.

The Scottish earls had their own representatives at Philip's court. Sir Walter Lindsay and Sir Hugh Barclay most likely were the two unnamed Scots mentioned by Robert Parsons in a letter to Acquaviva on 15 May 1595.[108] Barclay and the English secular priest John Cecil bore a commission to Parsons from the Catholic earls and requested the Jesuit's presence in Madrid to assist them in their dealings at court. Parsons, however, was laid up because of problems with his legs. Using this excuse, he resisted every plea to travel to Madrid. Parsons provided letters but would not go personally. "May God give them the success I desire," Parsons confided to Acquaviva, "but I am afraid that the dilatory methods of this court, for our sins, are bound to ruin everything." They had no success.

Parsons's failure to provide any real assistance to Ogilvie probably acerbated already strained relations with Crichton. By May of 1594 Crichton had sided against Holt in a conflict that was unrelated to Holt's battle with Charles Paget and Thomas Morgan—a conflict to which we shall return in a later chapter. Holt and Crichton had been good friends and, although Holt, described first as "of a somewhat unsociable disposition," and then "with his dry disposition," may have provided sufficient grounds for the falling-out, Parsons believed that Crichton's envies and prejudices were the real reason. Crichton complained that English were the recipients of numerous foundations from Philip II while the Scots received nothing. In a letter written to Colonel William Semple,[109] who showed it to Parsons, Crichton lamented that Parsons had successfully obtained a lucrative royal endowment for a seminary established for "poor and undistinguished

---

[107] Law, "Summa de los Memoriales," pp. 36–37.

[108] ARSI, Hisp. 138, fols 264^r–265^v. John Cecil wrote that he went to Spain with Barclay to negotiate Spanish assistance for James. See Godfrey Anstruther, O.P., *The Seminary Priests* (4 vols, Ware/Durham/Great Wakering, 1968–1977), vol. 1, p. 67.

[109] At this time Semple was arguing for a more aggressive naval policy against England and warning Spain of the likelihood of a Stuart succession and a united Great Britain unless Philip prevented it. See Glyn Redworth, "Between Four Kingdoms. International Catholicism and Colonel William Semple," in *Irlanda y la Monarquía Hispánica: Kinsale 1601–2001. Guerra, Política, Exilio y Religión,* (eds.) Enrique García Hernán, Miguel Ángel de Bunes, Óscar Recio Morales and Bernardo J. García García (Madrid, 2002), pp. 255–64. He was allied with Parsons on these two issues.

boys from England." An untrue accusation, Parsons quickly countered, because "the greater number of those who come to St Omers are the sons of gentlemen of very good position." More important was Crichton's allegation that Philip did nothing for "boys from Scotland who were of noble lineage." Recently Parsons had heard from an unnamed Jesuit informant in Flanders that, in reply to a query from Jean de Vernois, Bishop of St Omers—not known for his enthusiastic support of the English College—why the English had so many seminaries and the Scots none, Crichton explained that the English were more successful with their colleges because they "went begging far and wide, but the Scots were more reserved and of a more aristocratic temperament and were not affected with that base spirit." Crichton also reprimanded Parsons, as Parsons heard on the grapevine, for not supporting the Scot's proposals during his Spanish sojourn. These charges Parsons dismissed: "I promise your paternity on my word as a religious that if you yourself had come to Spain, I could not have helped or served you with greater goodwill than I did him in every way I could, putting at his disposal money, my labour, advice and everything else." It was true, however, that Parsons considered Crichton's schemes for "curing the ills of Scotland" to be "not well-founded and impracticable" and consistently told him so. Parsons advised him to abandon such designs and concentrate on founding a Scottish seminary in Flanders. Despite Parsons's advice, Crichton delayed drafting a memorial on the seminary until the day before his departure. Too impatient to wait for a reply or, indeed, to seek travelling expenses, Crichton has since dealt with the matter by letter, "very feeble method to use with people here who are cold and dilatory." Now unable to obtain what he wants Crichton blamed others for his own mistakes.[110] Crichton, apparently, allowed concern over financial woes of the Scots College in Douai to alienate the very Jesuits, that is, Parsons with almost unique access to Philip, whose assistance was essential.

As Parsons considered Crichton's projects for the restoration of Catholicism in Scotland impracticable so too did the Scot murmur about similar attempts by English exiles. In January of 1594 Crichton decried a failed attempt to entice Ferdinando Stanley, Lord Strange and later Earl of Derby, to the Catholic cause by proposing him as their candidate as Elizabeth's successor. Crichton contended that the English should abandon their quest for a Catholic alternative and throw their support behind

---

[110] Parsons to Acquaviva, Marchena May 12, 1594, ARSI, Hisp. 136, fols 318^r–319^v. Despite the conflict between Holt and Crichton, there were rumors in July of 1594 that the two, along with a number of other Jesuits, had departed for Scotland (Sir William Browne to Sir Robert Sydney, July 23, 1594, Charles Lethbridge Kingsford et al., (eds.), *Report on the Manuscripts of Lord D'Isle and Dudley Preserved at Penshurst Place* [6 vols, London, 1925–1966], HMC 77, vol. 2, p. 154).

James.[111] Without becoming involved in the succession issue, Acquaviva consequently urged Robert Parsons to do all he could to assist Crichton.[112] Reports carried by Huntly and Gordon confirmed Crichton's conversion to James's cause. But, as we have seen, Parsons did not provide much assistance. More than likely Crichton would have echoed Pury Ogilvie's complaint. Parsons did not aid the Scots because he did not support James's candidacy. Too often Parsons had heard auspicious accounts of James's imminent conversion. Too often such high expectations were groundless. The extent of Parsons's opposition to James would be demonstrated by the appearance of one of the most controversial works of the decade: R. Doleman's *A conference about the next succession to the crowne of Ingland*.[113] It provided more than ample fuel for their dispute.

A Red Hat for Parsons?

Factions split Scottish Catholic exiles. Robert Bruce fumed over Jesuit involvement. Pury Ogilvie, claiming to act in the king's name, insisted that Parsons and Holt be withdrawn from their positions and recalled to Rome because of their indifference or outright opposition to Scottish interests. Lacking an authoritative spokesman to argue their case in Rome and Madrid, Scottish infighting impeded progress. Disunity too now marked the English Catholic community in exile, but William, Cardinal Allen prevented factions from developing into schisms and thus from harming their common cause. Under him governance of the English mission was a structureless patriarchy in which, according to John Hungerford Pollen, S.J., "Everything and everyone depended on him [Allen] in a sort of happy family way."[114] On November 10, 1589, Philip II nominated Allen

---

[111] Crichton to Acquaviva, Brussels January 13, 1594 ARSI, Germ. 172, fols 11ʳ⁻ᵛ (published in Francisco de Borja Medina, S.J., "Intrigues of a Scottish Jesuit at the Spanish Court: William Crichton's Mission to Madrid (1590–1592)," in *The Reckoned Expense: Edmund Campion and the Early English Jesuits. Essays in Celebration of the First Centenary of Campion Hall, Oxford*, (ed.) Thomas M. McCoog, S.J, 2nd edn. [Rome, 2007], pp. 322–24; and "Escocia en la Estrategia de la Empresa de Inglaterra: La Misión del P. William Crichton cerca de Felipe II (1590–1592)," *Revista de Historia Naval*, 17 [1999]: pp. 101–102). On relations between Parsons and Crichton, see Thomas M. McCoog, S.J., "Harmony Disrupted: Robert Parsons, S.J., William Crichton, S.J., and the Question of Queen Elizabeth's Successor, 1581–1603," *AHSI*, 73 (2004): pp. 149–220.

[112] Rome July 4, 1594, ARSI, Tolet. 5/II, fol. 347ᵛ.

[113] (n.p. [Antwerp], 1594 [1595]), *ARCR*, vol. 2, num. 167, *STC* 19398.

[114] Quoted in Peter Norris, "Robert Parsons, S.J. (1546–1610) and the Counter Reformation in England: A Study of his Actions within the Context of the Political and Religious Situation of the Times" (unpublished Ph.D. thesis: University of Notre Dame, 1984), p. 178.

Archbishop of Malines but a rapid succession of popes and subsequent affairs in Rome prevented him from travelling to Flanders. On March 30, 1593, tired of the delay, Philip nominated Laevinus Torrentius, Bishop of Antwerp, who refused to accept an appointment to such an impecunious see unless he was allowed to retain income from his old bishopric. Thus Philip again turned to Allen. Many worried how Allen's transfer would affect the mission. Parsons believed that the decision should be left to Pope Clement VIII, Enrique de Guzmán, Count of Olivares, the Duke of Sessa, and Allen himself.[115] Nonetheless Parsons discussed the matter with Philip and left court with a clear understanding that Allen's role in Flanders was not restricted to the archbishopric of Malines. The Dowager Empress María[116] strongly favored Allen's reassignment so that he could assist Archduke Ernst "in the affairs of our country and in other business that may arise" and urged that he be sent because of anticipated beneficial consequences. Philip and his council agreed: they referred the matter to Rome where the ambassador would discuss it with the pope and the cardinal.[117] Presumably they hoped that Allen would reconcile the different factions dividing English and Scottish exiles in Belgium, and the divisions among the English themselves.[118] Any hope that Allen would play a more significant role in religious and political matters ended when he died in Rome on October 16. "Two or three days before his death," Olivares reported to Philip:

> when the doctors had quite given him up, he spoke to me alone with great tenderness, saying that what he felt most was that he had come to the end of his life without having been able to fulfil the desire which your Majesty had shown of sending him to Flanders, where perhaps he might have been of some use in helping the good Catholics, whom, though he knew it was unnecessary to recommend them to your Majesty, since you were so careful to protect them, he yet begged me to beseech your Majesty not to abandon; for that he was dying in full confidence that by means of your Majesty's crown that kingdom would one day be reconverted to the obedience of the Holy See; and among other things by which he has shown this confidence which he feels, he has left by will certain chasubles of small value which he had in his chapel to his parish church where he was born, when the people should become Catholics, and that

---

[115] Parsons to Acquaviva, Madrid March 10, 1594, ARSI, Hisp. 136, fols 245ʳ–246ᵛ.

[116] María, Emperor Charles V's oldest daughter, married her cousin Maximilian of Austria in 1548. She was a great patroness of the Jesuits in Vienna. Upon the death of her husband, she returned to Spain. On her relations with the Society see Hugo Rahner, S.J., *Saint Ignatius Loyola: Letters to Women* (Freiburg/London, 1960), pp. 33–34.

[117] Parsons to Acquaviva, Córdoba March 20, 1594, ARSI, Hisp. 136, fols 249ʳ–250ᵛ.

[118] Was Philip's desire to transfer Allen to Flanders in anticipation of another armada?

meanwhile they were to be kept in the chapel of the English college here, in which he ordered that he should be buried.[119]

Apparently Allen died as he had lived for the past decade: a devoted son of Spain.[120] English Catholics, however, lamented his passing for other reasons: according to the secular priest John Pitts: "All we who suffer persecution for the faith still mourn the death of this most excellent man, and as orphans we feel more and more every day that we have lost our common father."[121]

Fathers are hard to replace, but until one could be found certain practical arrangements had to be made. Allen had granted various faculties to priests on their way to serve on the mission so his death had immediate, concrete consequences. Someone had to grant those faculties until another English cardinal was appointed. Richard Barret, president of the English College, Douai, petitioned Owen Lewis, former head of the English Hospice, Rome, currently Bishop of Cassano and executor of Allen's will, to obtain this delegated power for Barret.[122] Cardinal Caetani, cardinal protector of England, granted them to Barret on April 14, 1595.[123]

Three candidates were considered as Allen's successor: Parsons, Lewis, and the aged theologian and sometime Jesuit Thomas Stapleton.[124] Lewis and Parsons were the strongest contenders; both had fervent supporters. Creswell, not surprisingly, argued that Parsons's appointment was essential for the future of the English Church.[125] But not all Jesuits were so enthusiastic. Oliver Mannaerts informed Parsons personally that, given a choice between him and Lewis, Mannaerts preferred the bishop. That decision did not rest on any personal animosity. If Parsons received the red hat,[126] Mannaerts argued, he would be obliged to abandon the important work that he was currently doing for the English Church:

---

[119] Quoted in Thomas Francis Knox, (ed.), *The Letters and Memorials of William Cardinal Allen (1532–1594)* (London, 1882), p. cxix. See also pp. cxv–cxviii and Knox, *Douay Diaries*, pp. lxxxvi–lxxxix.

[120] See *supra* Chapter 3.

[121] Cited in Knox, *Douay Diaries*, p. cii.

[122] Barret to Cassano, Douai December 12, 1594, in Penelope Renold, (ed.), *Letters of William Allen and Richard Barret 1572–1598* (London, 1967), p. 246.

[123] Renold, *Letters of Allen and Barret*, p. 247 note 1.

[124] On Stapleton see McCoog, *Monumenta Angliae*, vol. 2, p. 489.

[125] Creswell to Acquaviva, Madrid December 3, 1594, ARSI, Hisp. 138, fols 9ʳ–10ᵛ.

[126] Francesco Toledo, named a cardinal in 1593, was the only Jesuit to have received the red hat. Parsons would have been the second.

> It would very much better serve your Reverence, England, particular individuals and the seminaries, that you should remain as you are, a plan religious, rather than be promoted to the dignity of cardinal. For in the latter case, you would be much less free than now to maintain contact with all types of Englishmen, understand secret affairs, and prescribe what is necessary for individuals, and those with secret commissions. Neither could you beg alms from rulers, nobles, prelates, ecclesiastics, burgesses and merchants, as a cardinal. As it is, you can do this freely without offence to any, being a private man and covered by religious convention.

The Belgian exhorted Parsons "to give evidence to the whole Society, and the world itself, of your integrity and sincerity towards the same Society."[127] Acquaviva shared Mannaerts's anxieties as some Englishmen in Rome campaigned for Parsons's nomination. Convinced that Parsons was intelligent enough to foresee the difficulties that would follow upon his appointment, Acquaviva promised to do all he could to stop the campaign and asked Parsons as a "good son of the Society" to do the same in Spain.[128]

Until Parsons received Mannaerts's letter, he had considered the very possibility of his promotion ridiculous. Aware now that others including Lorenzo Suárez de Figueroa, Duke of Feria, and Archduke Ernst regarded him as a serious candidate, he sought advice from Jesuits at the English College in Seville. They recommended that he beseech Acquaviva and Jesuits at Philip's court to use their influence to prevent his appointment. Unless the matter got completely out of hand, he deemed it inappropriate to write personally to the king or to his councillors. Parsons did nothing about the rumors at first because he thought it more "a case for a smile and a shrug than resistance." He decided not to react "lest what I said by way of dissipating the smoke be taken as an intention to fan the flame." Only after he had learned that individuals in Madrid, Rome, and Brussels were campaigning in his favor did he realize that he could not remain silent. But he assured Acquaviva "that the very mention of this subject

---

[127] Brussels November 24, 1594, ARSI, Hisp. 139, fols 98^{r-v}. Most of the letter was included in Henry More's history of the English Province (*The Elizabethan Jesuits*, (ed.) Francis Edwards, S.J. [London, 1981], pp. 287–88). I use Edwards's translation. Edwards believed that "Mannaerts's arguments were not all that cogent and one suspects a trace of jealousy in his anxiety to discourage" (*Robert Persons*, p. 177). I think that Mannaerts's fears were rooted in his concern for the Society's Institute than personal resentment. On Jesuits and ecclesiastical promotion see John W. Padberg, S.J., "Ignatius, the Popes, and Realistic Reverence," *Studies in the Spirituality of Jesuits*, 25/3 (1993): pp. 20–28 and Thomas M. McCoog, S.J., "Ignatius Loyola and Reginald Pole: A Reconsideration," *Journal of Ecclesiastical History*, 47 (1996): p. 269.

[128] Acquaviva to Parsons, Rome 16 January 1595, ARSI, Baet. 3/I, p. 192.

has been repugnant to me in the extreme." Agreeing with Mannaerts that his current work with and for the seminaries was essential, he argued that "my work is altogether more useful to my country and countrymen as it is now—supposing it is useful—than it would be after the fashion that some would like to trust upon me."[129] Acquaviva acknowledged that Parsons would serve his country better if he were not elevated and urged him to inform King Philip that he did not support the campaign for his promotion and that he indeed actively opposed it.[130] Parsons, meanwhile, asked Jesuits in Madrid to keep him informed of any action taken to further his cause. He hoped that Acquaviva would "ever find [him] a loyal son of the Society, and far from having any designs in that direction."[131]

Sir Francis Englefield advocated Parsons's promotion. As soon as Parsons became aware of this, he stopped him from further action. After much consultation and prayer, Parsons concluded that "even if the well-being of the whole world depended on my promotion to this dignity which you desire for me ... I could neither wish nor strive directly or indirectly for such a promotion since I am bound by vow not to seek it." Parsons was content with his life and would resist any promotion. But, if an irresistible authority imposed the honor upon him despite his protestations, he hoped there would be sufficient grace to help him shoulder the burden.[132] By June 12 Parsons had persuaded his friends to abandon their campaign and the affair quietly died. According to Parsons, he chose "life in the Society as the means of his salvation and in it alone does he rest content, fearing and turning away from anything else."[133]

With Parsons's withdrawal, Owen Lewis was the obvious candidate despite his Welsh blood. Consecrated Bishop of Cassano on February 3, 1588, he had supporters in Rome and Flanders some of whom, as we shall see, played prominent roles in anti-Jesuit agitation. According to Leo Hicks, S.J., Lewis's adherents—or, more precisely, Parsons's opponents—seized upon the *Book of Succession* to eliminate him as a

---

[129] Parsons to Acquaviva, Seville February 20, 1595, ARSI, Hisp. 138, fols 142^r–144^v. I use Edwards's translation from More, *Elizabethan Jesuits*, pp. 289–90.

[130] Acquaviva to Parsons, Rome April 10, 1595, ARSI, Baet. 3/I, pp. 209–10.

[131] Parsons to Acquaviva, Seville March 19, 1595, ARSI, Hisp. 138, fols 184^r–185^v.

[132] Parsons to Englefield, [Seville] May 10, 1595, cited extensively in More, *Elizabethan Jesuits*, pp. 291–92.

[133] Parsons to Acquaviva, Seville June 12, 1595, ARSI, Hisp. 138, fols 299^r–301^v. Parsons explained to Roger Baynes that he had done everything he could to avoid the elevation and that he wanted his friends to halt their campaign in his favor (Seville January 24, 1596, ARSI, Angl. 38/II, fol. 195^r).

candidate for the red hat by proclaiming the Jesuit's authorship of the controversial work in order to destroy his reputation in Rome.[134] Many flocked to Lewis's support as the only alternative to Jesuit dominance and he probably would have been given the red hat by Pope Clement VIII if death had not removed him from the scene on October 14, 1595.[135] Parsons, apparently, opposed Lewis's promotion. Parsons told Acquaviva that he had asked Camillo Caetani, Patriarch of Alexandria and nuncio in Madrid, on June 10, to grant all powers and honors of the late Cardinal Allen not to Lewis but to the cardinal protector. A day later, Creswell, presumably one of those convinced by Parsons to stop their agitation for his promotion, wrote a similar letter to Cardinal Caetani.[136]

Now the only serious candidate was Stapleton.[137] In 1596 and 1597 Clement VIII summoned Stapleton to Rome with the intention of creating him a cardinal, but arguing age and illness, Stapleton postponed the journey. In late August of 1597, he finally prepared to travel to Rome from Louvain.[138] Because of the pope's strong anti-Spanish sentiments, Clement VIII's preference for Stapleton alarmed Alfonso Agazzari who warned Parsons to reflect on the consequences of Stapleton's elevation: "That matter of Stapleton is of importance; but your Reverence should think it over and try to remedy it by procuring the promotion of some one about whose fidelity to the crown [of Spain] there can be no doubt."[139]

---

[134] Leo Hicks, S.J., "Father Robert Persons, S.J. and *The Book of Succession*," *Recusant History*, 4 (1957): p. 108.

[135] Knox, *Douay Diaries*, pp. ciii–iv.

[136] Godfrey Anstruther, O.P, "The Sega Report," *The Venerabile*, 20 (1961): pp. 209–10.

[137] As we shall see in Chapter 6, other names were proposed by opponents to Spain's domination of English Catholicism.

[138] See his letters to Thomas Harley, Louvain January 20, 1597, and to Parsons, Louvain April 16 and July 6, 1597, in Knox, *Douay Diaries*, pp. 389–93. Further relevant correspondence between Ottavio Mirto Frangipani, Pietro, Cardinal Aldobrandini, and others can be found in *Correspondance d'Ottavio Mirto Frangipani, Premier Nonce de Flandre (1596–1606)*, (eds.) Leon Van der Essen and Armand Louant (4 vols, Rome/Bruxelles/Paris, 1924–1942), vol. 1, pp. 64–65, 84–85, 94, 96–97, 99–101, 107–108, 114–15, 161; vol. 2, pp. 120–21, 179–83, 195–96, 202–203, 232–33, 238, 243–45, 249–51, 254–56, 397–99. Stapleton's letter to Aldobrandini on August 20, 1597 in which he explained why he had not departed for Rome can be found on pp. 430–31.

[139] Agazzari to Parsons, Rome September 25, 1596, published in Knox, *Douay Diaries*, p. 388. I cite the translation on p. civ. Parsons too wondered why Monsignor Malvasia worked so diligently for the elevation of Stapleton: "it is strange to see an Italian so labour for an Englishman as this good prelate doth without interest as it seemeth, except he hope that the good Doctor wil concurre with him in his discourse to gaine England to the Cath. religion by dryving Jesuits from thence" (Parsons to [Thomas Fitzherbert?], Rome September 26, 1597, ABSI, Coll P I 315. In 1591, John Cecil claimed that Stapleton opposed a pro-

Presumably prompted by Agazzari's concern, Parsons twice wrote to Stapleton. Unfortunately neither letter is extant, but we do have Stapleton's replies. In the first he sought to assuage Parsons's fears:

> Nowe, good father, as I desire sincerely to remayne a trew and trusty servant to his Maj. of Spayne, though I hap to live and perhaps to continew in the court of Rome, and as I meane before my departure hence to insinuat so much to his Highness here, so I would wish that some of the counsel aboute his Maj. in Spayne might understand the same; of which point you may consider and deale as you thinke good.[140]

Three months later Stapleton repeated that he would always "remayne a trusty servant to his Maj. of Spayne" and confirmed his esteem for the Society despite the acrimonious dispute at the English College in Rome:

> Not only I never liked, but have allwaies utterly misseliked and condemned such unquiet heads against their superiors and namely against the Socyete, to whom all our countre catholike youths are so highly beholding. And in that sense, especially for the credit and avancement of the Socyete, to which is conjoyned the wealth and avancement of the cath. religion as well abrode as especially at home, you shall allwayes find me.[141]

But, for reasons unknown, Stapleton never made the trip and remained in Louvain where he died on October 12, 1598.[142] No one was appointed and the absence of an English cardinal highlighted the ecclesiastical problems of the Church in England.

"the most pestinent [treatise] that ever was made": *A conference about the next succession*

Concern about succession to the English throne simmered throughout Elizabeth's reign. Certain critical events, for example her brush with death from smallpox in late 1562, the birth of the Scottish Prince James in 1566,

---

Spanish policy. See his list of names in TNA, SP 12/238/181. We shall return to this matter in Chapter 6.

[140] Stapleton to Parsons, Louvain April 16, 1597, published in Knox, *Douay Diaries*, p. 391.

[141] Stapleton to Parsons, Louvain July 6, 1597, published in Knox, *Douay Diaries*, p. 393.

[142] See Knox, *Douay Diaries*, p. civ n. 6 for suggestions that factors more sinister than ill health prevented Stapleton's departure for Rome.

and Mary Stuart's flight into England in 1568 brought the issue to a boil. Repeatedly Parliament asked her to marry and to settle the succession issue, but Elizabeth consistently refused to be pressured.[143] Marriage was her decision, she asserted. Twice discussion of the succession was forbidden by law under penalty of death. The first was in 1571:

> And for the avoiding of contentions and seditions, spreading abroad of titles to the succession of the crown of this realm ... be it enacted, That whatsoever shall hereafter during the life of our said Sovereign Lady, by any book or work printed or written ... affirm at any time before the same be by Act of Parliament of this realm established, ... that any person is or ought to be the right heir and successor to the Queen's Majesty ... except the same be the natural issue of her Majesty's body, or shall ... publish ... any books or scrolls to that effect, ... that he, their abettors [&c.] shall for the first offence suffer imprisonment of one whole year and forfeit half his goods, whereof the same moiety to the Queen's Majesty, the other moiety to him or them that will sue for the same ... in any of the Queen's Majesty's courts; ... and if any shall eftsoons offend therein, they and their abettors [&c.] shall incur the pains and forfeitures which in the Statute of Provision or Praemunire are appointed and limited. (13 Eliz. I c. 1)[144]

Parliament returned to the same theme with another law in 1581:

> ... be it also enacted, That if any person ... during the life of our said Sovereign Lady the Queen's Majesty that now is, either within Her Highness' dominions or without, shall by setting or erecting any figure or by casting of nativities or by calculation or by any prophesying, witchcraft, conjurations, or other like unlawful means whatsoever, seek to know, and shall set forth by express words, deeds or writings, how long her Majesty shall live, or who shall reign a king or queen of this realm of England after her Highness' decease, or else shall advisedly and with a malicious intent against her Highness, utter any manner of direct prophecies to any such intent, or shall maliciously by any words, writing or printing desire the death or deprivation of our Sovereign Lady the Queen's Majesty that now is ... that then every such offense shall be felony, and every offender therein, and also all his aiders [&c], shall be judged as felons and shall suffer pains of death and forfeit as in case of felony is used, without any benefit or clergy or sanctuary. (23 Eliz. I c. 2)[145]

---

[143] On William Cecil's exploration of the Elizabethan succession crisis see Stephen Alford, *The Early Elizabethan Polity: William Cecil and the British Succession Crisis, 1558–1569* (Cambridge, 1998).

[144] G.W. Prothero, (ed.), *Select Statutes and Other Constitutional Documents Illustrative of the Reigns of Elizabeth and James I*, 4th edn. (Oxford, 1946), pp. 59–60.

[145] Prothero, *Select Statutes*, pp. 78–79.

The laws did not silence the presses, but they prevented Parliament from clarifying the issue. With the elimination of Mary Stuart, James was the legitimate successor if Henry VIII's will was disallowed and he did not exclude himself by violating "An Act for provision to be made for the surety of the Queen's most royal person" (27 Eliz. I c. 1) through association in a plot or conspiracy against Elizabeth. Peter Wentworth's attempt to raise the forbidden subject in 1591 with a manuscript "Booke of the heir apparent to the Throne," landed him in trouble.[146] Nonetheless he proposed to address Parliament and to introduce a bill on the same subject. His attempt to do so on February 25, 1593 resulted in his imprisonment in the Tower of London where he remained until his death in 1594.[147]

Unless a second armada succeeded, Catholics pinned their hopes on Elizabeth's successor although they differed on who that should be. In 1572 the anonymous *A treatise of treasons against Q. Elizabeth, and the crowne of England*, commonly attributed to the Scottish Bishop John Leslie, blamed Cecil and Sir Nicholas Bacon for all the kingdom's ills. They sought to tamper with the succession by persuading Elizabeth not to marry, and by attempting to deprive Mary Stuart of her legitimate right to the English throne.[148] Charles Arundel's *The copie of a leter, wryten by a master of arts of Cambridge, to his friend in London*, better known as *Leicester's Commonwealth*, revived the matter in 1584.[149] Behind the scurrilous attack on the earl of Leicester lurked a treatise on the succession. *A treatise of treasons* blamed Cecil and Bacon for the succession crisis; Charles Arundel, himself a victim of the political fallout that followed upon the breakdown of negotiations for a marital alliance between Elizabeth and François, Duke of Anjou, pointed the finger at Leicester.[150] Having destroyed the last possible attempt to secure a peaceful succession,

---

[146] Wentworth to William Cecil, Lord Burghley, September 27, 1591, *CSPD* (1591–1594), p. 107. His *A pithie exhortation to her maiestie for establishing her successor* (Edinburgh, 1598), STC 25245, either the original manuscript mentioned in his letter or a revision, was published after Wentworth's death to establish James's credentials.

[147] T.E. Hartley, (ed.), *Proceedings in the Parliaments of Elizabeth I* (3 vols, Leicester, 1981–1995), vol. 3, pp. 42, 44, 68–69.

[148] Charles Arundel, (n.p. [Louvain], 1572), *ARCR*, vol. 2, num. 502, STC 7601. For a discussion of Leslie's authorship see Thomas H. Clancy, S.J., "A Political Pamphlet: The Treatise of Treasons (1572)," in *Loyola Studies in the Humanities*, (ed.) G. Eberle (New Orleans, 1962), pp. 15–30. For a defense of Leslie's authorship see Peter Holmes, *Resistance and Compromise: The Political Thought of the Elizabethan Catholics* (Cambridge, 1982), pp. 23–26.

[149] (n.p. [Paris?], 1584), *ARCR*, vol. 2, num. 31, STC 5742.9. See Dwight C. Peck's edition, *Leicester's Commonwealth: The Copy of a Letter Written by a Master of Art of Cambridge (1584) and Related Documents* (Athens, Ohio/London, 1985).

[150] See Thomas M. McCoog, S.J., "The English Jesuit Mission and the French Match, 1579–1581," *Catholic Historical Review*, 87 (2001): pp. 185–213.

Leicester dismissed Mary Stuart's rights in favor of Henry Hastings, Earl of Huntingdon, in the pursuit of more sinister goals. At the end of Robert Parsons's *Newes from Spayne and Holland*, the author promised a discourse in the near future regarding succession to the English throne.[151] Even before that volume was published, it generated controversy.

On March 30, 1594 Claudio Acquaviva inquired about a rumor that Parsons had written a tract on the English succession. Although, he conceded that the book might please a few people, he did not think that the majority of the English would relish it. Unable to verify any of the stories, Acquaviva asked whether the rumors were true. He feared that such a volume would offend some princes and nobles, and thus considered it inappropriate that any Jesuit should discuss the subject. Acquaviva might have been especially sensitive to such issues so soon after their discussion at the general congregation. In a matter as controversial as the English succession, he did not believe it possible to keep the author's identity secret despite attempts to do so. The book's appearance would threaten the Society's work. Thus, he preferred its publication aborted. Nonetheless he allowed Parsons to exercise his discretion: if his intervention would result in more harm than good, "it would be better not to do anything."[152] Acquaviva's letter crossed with one from Parsons to him. Among "other matters ... of less importance," Parsons mentioned that he would send the general "the portion of the *Book of Succession* of England which is being translated."[153] At the time he had not realized the treatise's impact.

Despite Acquaviva's leaving the final decision to Parsons, the Englishman interpreted the instruction as an order. Even before the letter's arrival in Madrid on June 4, orders, by whom Parsons did not say, had been sent to the agent in Brussels, presumably Richard Verstegan, to stop the presses, and to maintain secrecy about the manuscript. Until Cardinal Allen had examined the matter and given his approval,[154] the English edition was to be suspended. Nonetheless, "in deference to the duty of obedience and to comply with your paternity's will and pleasure," Parsons repeated the orders. Unfortunately Parsons had no authority over the Spanish version, that is, the second part of the book in which the author examined the

---

[151] (n.p. [Antwerp], 1593), *ARCR*, vol. 2, num. 632, *STC* 22994. On the question of succession in general, see Howard Nenner, *The Right to be King: The Succession to the Crown of England, 1603–1714* (London, 1995).

[152] Acquaviva to Parsons, Rome March 30, 1594, ARSI, Tolet. 5/II, fol. 333ᵛ.

[153] Parsons to Acquaviva, Madrid March 10, 1594, ARSI, Hisp. 136, fols 245ʳ–246ᵛ.

[154] In ARSI, Angl. 37, fol. 21ᵛ, there is a note by Grene on Allen's evaluation: " ... a Censure of Card. Allen touching the book of succession, written by his secretarii (as it seemeth) after the Cardinals death anno 1595 wherein C. Allen is sayd to have much praised the book, and many of his discourses touching this point are here related." Allen's judgment, as recorded by his secretary Roger Baynes, can be found in AAW, Angl. IX, 17.

pretensions of each claimant: Don Juan de Idiáquez had control over it. Yet Philip's secretary promised that he would observe due discretion and secrecy, and not show the manuscript to anyone but Clement VIII and Count Olivares. If Parsons had anticipated Acquaviva's apprehension, he would have acted earlier even though "the matter was not entirely in my control" because of the involvement of three or four others.[155] Each was a man of experience and not one thought that there would be consequences harmful to Catholics. Indeed everyone expected the Catholic cause to benefit from the book's publication. Perhaps Acquaviva would change his mind after reading a Spanish version which Parsons dispatched to him. In the meanwhile Parsons summarized the book to alleviate Acquaviva's fears.

Both parts were written by "learned men" "with all courtesy and impartiality and without prejudice to anyone." The first book discussed prerequisite qualifications for succession and argued that blood relationship was not the only consideration but "other circumstances also especially religion and the worship of God." Such an emphasis was extremely important "in order to prevent Catholics from running blindly after any person who may happen to have a claim to the succession by blood without any other consideration." The second book, "without preferring one claimant to another," examined the pretensions of 5 royal houses, and 10 or 11 candidates who have *prima facie* claims. In the analysis the authors spoke ill of no candidate *in se*. Again such a presentation was essential because the heretics forbade any discussion of the English succession in the hope that by "keeping everyone in darkness," they would be able to force their candidate on the English people. This book would open the eyes of English men and women to the number of available candidates. Regarding James of Scotland, nothing was said against him except that he was a heretic. Because the credentials of each candidate were expounded fairly and objectively, Parsons concluded that the book would "undoubtedly tend to the service of God and the advantage of England, and will give just cause for offence to nobody." If Acquaviva concluded differently, Parsons would do everything in his power to have the book suppressed.[156] Acquaviva replied that, although he found the book "good and necessary," he preferred that Jesuits have nothing to do with its publication.[157]

---

[155] Only Sir Francis Englefield and "another man from Ireland" were mentioned by Parsons. On Englefield and his work for the cause of the English Catholics at the Spanish court see Loomie, *Spanish Elizabethans*, pp. 14–51. The Irishman was Richard Stanihurst (Albert J. Loomie, S.J., "Richard Stanyhurst in Spain: Two Unknown Letters of August 1593," *Huntington Library Quarterly*, 28 [1965]: p. 148).

[156] Parsons to Acquaviva, Madrid June 4 and 16, 1594, ARSI, Hisp. 136, fols 362^r–363^v.

[157] Acquaviva to Parsons, Rome August 1, 1594, ARSI, Cast. 6, fol. 183^r.

Despite Parsons's explication of his role in the book's composition, some historians, for example Mark Tierney, attribute sole authorship to him.[158] Subsequently Leo Hicks, S.J., exonerated Parsons of this accusation.[159] More recently Peter Holmes has revived the issue.[160] His arguments apparently are so convincing that Michael Carrafiello does not even acknowledge any doubt.[161] Parsons might, of course, have lied to Acquaviva, but their friendship makes that possibility unlikely. Until we can clearly demonstrate otherwise, we should give him the benefit of the doubt and follow Anthony Allison and David Rogers: "R. Doleman is a pseudonym masking several authors [including Robert Persons and probably, William Allen, Sir Francis Englefield and Richard Verstegan]."[162]

R. Doleman's *A conference about the next succession to the crowne of Ingland* had an impact far greater than that anticipated by Parsons.[163] Michael Carrafiello astutely observed that the *Book of Succession* was not written "as a political treatise alone ... but as a book of practical instruction to English Catholics."[164] Indeed, the book's political philosophy

---

[158] See *Dodd's Church History of England* (5 vols, London, 1839–1843), vol. 3, pp. 31–35 note.

[159] Hicks, "Persons and *The Book of Succession*," pp. 126–28.

[160] Peter Holmes, "The Authorship and Early Reception of *A Conference about the Next Succession to the Crown of England*," *Historical Journal*, 23 (1980): pp. 415–29.

[161] Michael Carrafiello, *Robert Parsons and English Catholicism, 1580–1610* (Selinsgrove/London, 1998). Carrafiello opened his chapter on the treatise with the simple statement "Robert Parsons wrote his *Conference about the Next Succession to the Crowne of England* (1595) only after substantial and sustained efforts to convert James VI to Catholicism had failed" (p. 33). Harro Höpfl takes Parsons's authorship for granted (*Jesuit Political Thought: The Society of Jesus and the State, c. 1540–1630* [Cambridge, 2005] p. 123).

[162] *ARCR*, vol. 2, p. 40. Victor Houliston concluded that "we can be fairly confident that Persons was responsible both for the rhetorical disposition and the theoretical underpinning of the book" ("The Hare and the Drum: Robert Persons's Writings on the English Succession, 1593–96," *Renaissance Quarterly*, 14 [2000]: p. 237 and *Catholic Resistance in Elizabethan England. Robert Persons's Jesuit Polemic, 1580–1610* [Aldershot/Rome, 2007], pp. 71–92).

[163] On the rejoinders see Peter Milward, S.J., *Religious Controversies of the Elizabethan Age: A Survey of Printed Sources* (Lincoln, Nebraska/London, 1977), pp. 114–16.

[164] Carrafiello, *Parsons and English Catholicism*, p. 55. Carrafiello echoed John Hungerford Pollen's comment: "It was a book written with a purpose–to influence the succession to the crown" ("The Question of Queen Elizabeth's Successor," *The Month*, 101 [1903]: p. 527). For other accounts see Thomas H. Clancy, S.J., *Papist Pamphleteers: The Allen-Persons Party and the Political Thought of the Counter-Reformation in England 1572–1615* (Chicago, 1964), pp. 62–72; Arnold Pritchard, *Catholic Loyalism in Elizabethan England* (London, 1979), pp. 18–27; Holmes, *Resistance and Compromise*, pp. 152–57; Norris, "Parsons and the Counter Reformation in England," pp. 205–208.

was not novel.¹⁶⁵ Its significance, and a major reason for the controversy it generated, resulted from a practical implementation of still revolutionary ideas. Through a consideration of Scripture, historical precedents, laws, coronation oaths, and practices, the lawyers in the book recognized that, although propinquity in blood was the normal way to determine succession, it was frequently disregarded.¹⁶⁶ The most important reason for setting aside the normal procedure was religion:

> Heerof it insueth also that nothing in the world can so iustly exclude an heyre apparent from his succession, as want of religion, nor any cause what so-ever iustifie and cleare the conscience of the commonwealth, or of particuler men, that in this case should resist his entrance, as if they iudge him faulty in this pointe, which is the head of al the rest, and for which al the rest do serve.¹⁶⁷

Moreover, anyone assisting a claimant of a different religion succeed to the throne was guilty of "a most grevous and damnable sinne." Doleman argued that heretical claimants should not simply be deprived of support, but they must be resisted. If faithful subjects did not resist "when it lyeth in my power, by al which I do iustly make my selfe guyltie of all the evills, hurts, miseries and calamities both temporal and spiritual, which afterward by his evel goverment do or may ensew, for that I knowing him to be such a one, did notwithstanding assist his promotion."¹⁶⁸ "Rather than a crafty manoeuver on the part of a scheming Jesuit," Victor Houliston argued, the treatise was intended as "a first step towards a Catholic policy on the succession."¹⁶⁹ To prevent Catholics from knowingly or unknowingly aiding the accession of a heretic, the second part of the *Conference* analyzed the credentials of each claimant according to the criteria delineated in the

---

[165] On the influence of French Catholic League political thought on the *Book of Succession* see Frederic J. Baumgartner, *Radical Reactionaries: The Political Thought of the French Catholic League* (Geneva, 1975), pp. 241–42. The single most important influence was William Rainolds's, *De iusta reipub. Christianae in rrges [sic] impios et haereticos authoritate* (Paris, 1590), ARCR, vol. 1, num. 931. So evident was its influence that William Gifford greeted the *Book of Succession* with the comment: "The first part is generall and stolen quasi ad verbum out of the first three capita of Mr. Reinoldes booke" (cited in Thomas H. Clancy, S.J., "English Catholics and the Papal Deposing Power, 1570–1640," *Recusant History*, 6 [1961–62]: p. 126). For more on Rainolds see Clancy, pp. 123–31 and Baumgartner, pp. 145–60.

[166] In France, political writers faced a similar problem. See Paul Lawrence Rose, "Bodin and the Bourbon Succession to the French Throne, 1583–1594," *Sixteenth Century Journal*, 9 (1978): pp. 75–98.

[167] Doleman, *Conference*, p. 212.

[168] Doleman, *Conference*, pp. 216, 217.

[169] "Hare and the Drum," 240.

first part. Because religious orthodoxy was the most important criterion, serious candidates must be Catholic: the Spanish infanta was only one of several candidates.[170] If she were unwilling or unable to succeed, Doleman advised Philip II that he must secure the crown for the house of Parma or the house of Braganza, or be prepared to become king himself.[171]

Despite Parsons's persistent protestation that the book was an objective evaluation of all claimants, it endorsed the candidate supported consistently by the Allen/Parsons party in letters and memorials since the execution of Mary Stuart.[172] Of the candidates considered in the *Book of Succession*, the authors advanced only a few arguments against the infanta's title. Dwight C. Peck neatly summarized the book's intent: it "advanced the Spanish Infanta's claim through a very subtle process of elimination."[173] On the other hand they went to great length to denigrate James, the front-running candidate. In a letter to Sir Anthony Standen Parsons repeated many of the arguments against James.[174] If, as the English government claimed, Mary Stuart was executed because of her involvement in plots and conspiracies against Elizabeth, the oath and statute of association (27 Eliz. I c. 1) negated James's title because it excluded his mother. James's candidature was also unacceptable because "few either Scotts, English, Danes or others desire the union of both kingdomes but have great cause to abhorre it." Other reasons, that is, his religion ("Puritanisme"), his lack of power, his "extreme ingrate and unnaturall dealing towards his mother," and his treatment of James Douglas, Earl of Morton, and other "friends of his own religion, whome cunningly he sent to the slaughter, when yet he was but a little lyon, and began to learne to catch his prey," made his acceptability to the English doubtful. In reply to unmentioned queries raised by Standen, Parsons believed that it was "enough for a catholik sober man to have any prince admitted by the body of his realme and allowed by the authority of Gods Catholik Church, and that will defende the religion of his old noble

---

[170] Hicks criticized historians because they "have far too easily accepted his [Wiliam Gifford's] view that the book was written to promote the cause of the Infanta and against the claims of James" ("Persons and *The Book of Succession*," p. 116).

[171] Doleman, *Conference*, pp. 263–64.

[172] I find the book slightly more tilted in favor of the Spanish infanta than Houliston who argued that the treatise "promoted not simply one candidature, but a certain frame of mind or mental disposition in the reader" comparable to the indifference espoused in Parsons's *Book of Resolution* ("Hare and the Drum," p. 242).

[173] Peck, *Leicester's Commonwealth*, p. 40.

[174] Parsons's correspondence with Standen then in the service of the earl of Essex is interesting. Francis Edwards commented that Standen had written to Parsons "to draw him out on the forbidden topic" (*Robert Persons*, p. 182), but one wonders if there was more to the correspondence than entrapment.

ancestors." Unless a candidate fulfilled these conditions, he/she should not be favored or accepted.[175]

The book's appearance provoked the wrath of the Elizabethan government for raising the forbidden subject and the indignation of the Scottish faction because of its anti-James and pro-Isabella bias. At the request of Innocenzo Malvasia, papal agent Flanders, Charles Paget and William Gifford obtained a copy of the manuscript by bribing a boy who worked at the press of Richard Verstegan. They recognized Verstegan's handwriting with long corrections and additions by Parsons. Gifford decried the treatise as "the most pestilent that ever was made" and claimed that Malvasia confided to him that Parsons "had ruined himself and that the Pope would detest his behaviour and that he could never have done anything more disgustable to the Pope."[176] Malvasia, sympathetic to the Scottish faction, denounced the book to Rome where it was received unfavorably by many students at the English College. Paget wrote about the book to the English government.[177] In general Cassano's supporters used the volume against Parsons's candidacy. Devoted now to the Scottish cause, William Crichton later joined the attack on the book with his fear that not only would his king be excluded from the English throne but that Catholics in Scotland would suffer as a result.[178]

Discontent at the English College, Rome

After the tumultuous administration of Joseph Creswell, Muzio Vitelleschi's rectorate passed uneventfully. According to Anthony Kenny, Vitelleschi "had governed admirably for two years; he had won the praise of all, and had shown that capacity for ruling men which was later to lead him to the generalship of the Society of Jesus."[179] His successor, Girolamo Fioravanti, was named on May 27, 1594.[180] Described by Kenny as "a pious, kindly man ... the sort of person who would bring sweets to you if you were ill,

---

[175] Madrid September 8, 1595, ABSI, Coll P I 310–311.

[176] Cited in Holmes, *Resistance & Compromise*, p. 194. See also Hicks, "Persons and *The Book of Succession*," p. 107.

[177] "A Proposition of Charles Pagets," *CSPD* (1598–1601), p. 68.

[178] Pollen, "Queen Elizabeth's Successor," pp. 527–32; Hicks, "Persons and *The Book of Succession*," pp. 107–108, 119–26.

[179] Anthony Kenny, "The Inglorious Revolution 1594–1597," *The Venerabile*, 16 (1954): p. 241. I shall follow Kenny's superb presentation. His article, in four parts, can be found in *The Venerabile*, 16 (1954): pp. 240–58; 17 (1955): pp. 7–25; 77–94; 136–55. For a shorter account see Michael E. Williams, *The Venerable English College* (London, 1979), pp. 16–21.

[180] ARSI, Angl. 37, fol. 142ᵛ.

and one of the students' nicknames for him was '*mater*,'"[181] Fioravanti lacked knowledge of English affairs, and experience with the English temperament. Almost immediately, he relaxed significantly the college's discipline; for example, penances became personal matters, executed in the privacy of one's room and not communally in the chapel. Celebrations and feasts, to which the college invited members of the English colony in Rome, became almost commonplace. The festive season climaxed at Carnevale in 1595. The eight days before Ash Wednesday were celebrated with cockfights, seven-course dinners, masked ball for guests, and comedies. Unable to attend the festivities because of illness, Fioravanti was nonetheless described by students as "a model Rector, and the real Father of Englishmen."[182]

Beneath the joyful facade lurked discontent. Collegiate discipline might have been more relaxed, but it was still too rigorous for some. Seminarians recently arrived from Douai complained that the mild regime of Fioravanti was more demanding than that to which they were accustomed. Others taking advantage of the rector's kindness broke the remaining rules. Increasing hostility towards Jesuits encouraged the lack of discipline. Stories about Jesuit plans to dominate the English mission and to use their wider faculties to gain influence with nobility circulated among the students, many of whom were predisposed to believe the accounts. Nationalism also contributed to discontent. Antagonism between English and Welsh nearly 20 years earlier resulted in Jesuit involvement in the college. Although that antagonism lingered, a national pride directed against their country's enemy, Spain, and its supporters, united English and Welsh. Proud of England's achievements against Spain, these students reacted violently against leaders who had harnessed the English Catholic cause to Philip II. The hidden discontent burst forth after the death of Allen.

Despite frequent disagreements, Owen Lewis, Bishop of Cassano, remained Allen's friend. A permanent resident of Rome and well known in papal circles, Lewis was widely expected to be Allen's successor. The campaign initiated by Parsons's friends to have the Jesuit nominated and Lewis excluded, angered the bishop. On March 10, 1595 he explained attempts to block his nomination to Humphrey Ely. Two or three Englishmen, Lewis asserted, were working actively against him: "They say I am an Italian, that I passe not for the Nation, that I am Britannus, and not verus Anglus. That I will never returne into Ingland, if it weare Catholick ... " Lewis wanted such lies refuted. Despite his age, Lewis would abandon his bishopric and worldly honors "and go to serve my

---

[181] Kenny, "Inglorious Revolution," p. 241.
[182] Kenny, "Inglorious Revolution," p. 243.

naturall countrey and countrey men, whom in banishment I have served and loved more than all theis good fellowes."[183] The anti-Jesuit faction in Flanders, especially Paget and Gifford, rallied to Lewis's cause. Sometime in April of 1595 it was decided—by whom it is not known—that support for Lewis's candidacy should be sought among students at the English College where he was known and liked. His popularity received an extra boost as a rumor spread that he would use his influence to cancel an unpopular theological examination. Edward Tempest[184] received Fioravanti's permission to promote the bishop's candidacy for a red hat among college students. Under Tempest's direction, three memorials were drafted: the first asked Pope Clement VIII to grant all Cardinal Allen's faculties to Lewis; the second begged Enrico Caetani, Cardinal Protector, to use his influence with the pope to further Lewis's cause; and the third, addressed to Lewis himself, explained all that the students had done, and that Cardinal Caetani, as a puppet of the Jesuits, could not be trusted. Lewis delivered his memorial to Caetani, who, in turn, reported the whole affair to Father Acquaviva. Tempest and his supporters tried to explain away the problem: they were not anti-Jesuit but opposed only to English Jesuits hostile to Lewis's promotion. Acquaviva recommended that they leave ecclesiastical decisions to proper authorities and return to their studies. Contrary to their hopes, Pope Clement granted all Allen's faculties to Cardinal Caetani, who sub-delegated them to Richard Barret, and not to Bishop Lewis. A quasi-peace followed especially after Fioravanti granted Bishop Lewis's request that the hated examination be cancelled. Ecclesiastical politics still attracted many, but there was no public strife.

Edmund Harewood,[185] minister at the College, considered continuation of clandestine ecclesiastical maneuvers a violation of Acquaviva's decision. As minister, he had the authority to patrol rooms and to monitor unauthorized meetings. He persuaded one of the conspirators, Francis Fowler,[186] to abandon such activity. Students then turned on Harewood, accusing him of sowing discontent among the students with such tactics. Harewood, moreover, aroused suspicion among many students because

---

[183] Quoted in Kenny, "Inglorious Revolution," p. 245.

[184] On him see Anstruther, *Seminary Priests*, vol. 1, pp. 348–49.

[185] On him see McCoog, *Monumenta Angliae*, vol. 2, p. 349.

[186] Fowler entered the English College in 1592 but was never ordained. See Wilfrid Kelly, (ed.), *Liber Ruber Venerabilis Collegii Anglorum de Urbe* (Rome, 1940), p. 87. Henry Bird, a student dismissed from the college during these disputes, described him as "the pretyest youth" and accused Harewood of deriving unnatural satisfaction from disciplining him privately (AAW, V, 112). See Peter Lake and Michael Questier, "Discourses of Vice and Discourses of Virtue: 'Counter-Martyrology' and the Conduct of Intra-Catholic Dispute," in Peter Lake with Michael Questier, *The Antichrist's Lewd Hat: Protestants, Papists and Players in Post-Reformation England* (New Haven, 2002), pp. 281–314.

of a strong rumor that he was enticing seminarians to join the Jesuits.[187] Richard Button, one of the suspicious students, made a veiled reference to this rumor in a sermon in the refectory.[188] Twice Harewood cautioned him. In anger Thomas Hill,[189] an older priest-student, stormed across the room and struck Harewood's name from a house list on the notice board, and walked out. A crowd followed him. Failing in his attempt to restore the minister's name, Fioravanti departed to consult Cardinal Caetani. Hill was expelled the following morning. Students loyal to Hill pledged to defend each other and sent a manifesto to the protector. Cardinal Caetani revoked the expulsion order, but decreed that Hill must restore the minister's name and do a public penance. Both were done.

For a second time there was a false peace. One scheme devised for Lewis's promotion was a demand for an official visitation of the college. Since the bishop of Cassano was one of the college's apostolic visitors, his supporters assumed that the pope would appoint him *ipso facto* to any official visitation. Lewis would thus gain complete control over the college. These new intrigues did not escape Harewood's attention. Now the minister responded with rumors of his own: he spread stories about the moral lapses of some students, lapses that would become public during any visitation. Harewood's allegations inflamed many to outright rebellion. To quell the new outburst, Cardinal Caetani paid a personal visit to the college. At a meeting with the students, their spokesman attacked the general government of the college, complaining about everything from the behavior of the *ripetitori*, to financial mismanagement, to the promotion of the Society of Jesus to the detriment of the college and the mission.[190] Harewood replied to the specific question regarding the morals of students by denying that he had ever said anything.[191] Caetani departed abruptly during the ensuing pandemonium.

A total of 37 of the 44 seminarians protested and assiduously avoided anyone who defended Jesuits. The seven pro-Harewood seminarians, considered spies by the others, were given the cold shoulder whenever they appeared. This treatment affected the college's sacramental life: rebellious students refused to attend community Mass if one of the others presided. After a Jesuit confessor denied absolution until one of the rebellious

---

[187] This was a persistent concern. See Leo Hicks, S.J., "The English College, Rome and Vocations to the Society of Jesus, March, 1579–July, 1595," *AHSI*, 3 (1934): pp. 1–36.

[188] On him see Anstruther, *Seminary Priests*, vol. 1, p. 60.

[189] On him see Anstruther, *Seminary Priests*, vol. 1, pp. 167–68.

[190] A list of complaints from this period can be found in ARSI, Angl. 30/II, fols 335^{r-v}.

[191] Harewood's version of the affair can be found in his letter to Acquaviva, Rome August 21, 1595, ARSI, Fondo Gesuitico 651/626, and the undated, unsigned apologia in ARSI, Angl. 30/II, fols 337^r–338^v.

retracted an insult, the majority boycotted Jesuits and went outside the college to confession. With each violation, probability of an official visitation increased. Finally some students decided to force the issue by requesting a papal audience. Discovering their intentions the evening before the audience, the rector prevented their departure by locking the doors of the college, but they escaped through a small unlocked gate. Cardinal Caetani hastened to the papal palace on the Quirinal and saw the pope before their arrival. Obliged to stand outside in the hot August sun, these students were eventually informed by the cardinal that Pope Clement wanted them to return to their college without fuss. Their ploy, nonetheless, was successful: Clement ordered a visitation to be conducted by Monsignor Bernadino Morra, notary of the Congregation for Bishops and Religious, during the last week of August. His subsequent report was primarily an exhortation to understanding and benevolence.[192] Two students, however, left the college, perhaps under compulsion, and other students demanded an impartial judge to settle disputes between students and Jesuits.[193] Pope Clement VIII, never known as a supporter of the Society of Jesus, declared himself the impartial judge. He removed control of temporal and administrative affairs from the Jesuit general and gave them to the cardinal protector. He installed a second confessor, chosen from the students, and replaced Jesuit *ripetitori* with students. On the other hand, all students who had assembled outside the papal palace, were punished by a fast; one of their leaders was suspended. Pope Clement exhorted both sides to amity and ordered the entire college to make a retreat together. The rebels, albeit temporarily humiliated by the penance, considered this a victory. The rector's attempt to appoint as confessor a student from the pro-Jesuit faction was challenged, so he eventually named Edward Bennett, a leader of the rebellion. Two others were named *ripetitori*: Edward Tempest and Anthony Champney.[194] Shortly thereafter, at the suggestion of Father General Acquaviva, Harewood retired to Sant' Andrea, the Jesuit novitiate, for reasons of health. The issue that sparked the controversy, viz. Lewis's promotion, was also decided but not made public: Clement VIII would name him cardinal at the next opportunity. The rebels apparently won on every issue.

---

[192] Kenny claimed that the report was not extant, but further investigation may reveal that it is a document entitled "Propositiones quaedam considerandae ad Collegii Anglicani statum pertinentes" (ARSI, Angl. 30/II, fols 333ʳ–34ᵛ).

[193] Henry Bird, one of "dismissed" students, wrote the above-cited memorial, most of which can be found in AAW, V, 112. Bird entered the English College in 1592 but was never ordained (Kelly, *Liber Ruber*, p. 87).

[194] On them see Anstruther, *Seminary Priests*, vol. 1, pp. 30–31, 70–71, 348–49.

In April of 1594, Robert Parsons rejoiced that students at the English colleges in Seville and Valladolid were "free from the infection of evil humors" which periodically attacked those in Rome and Reims.[195] Parsons apparently was not aware that these "evil humors" had again manifested themselves until letters from Acquaviva reached him in Spain.[196] Because unnamed Jesuits at the English College promised to inform Parsons of all recent developments, Acquaviva's account was brief. After a papal audience, Clement VIII left the resolution of the problem to Cardinal Caetani and Acquaviva. The general promised to proceed carefully, but he foresaw that it would be necessary to dismiss a few students. His attempt to quell the storm failed and he considered relinquishing administration of the college. But he awaited advice from Parsons and Creswell before he made a final decision.[197]

Understanding Acquaviva's frustration, Parsons was not surprised that the general considered relinquishing the college's governance: "so far the Society has gotten nothing but trouble from and nothing but ingratitude from those who have benefited from it [the Society's administration]." Parsons warned him of the possible consequences. Without the Society, Parsons believed license would take root, and many seminarians would thus be ruined. Moreover there were not sufficient secular clergy with the needed competence. Perhaps the most feared possibility was the encouragement that decision would give to the discontented students who would then become even more defiant. Many would interpret the Society's abandonment of the college as a recognition that it was at fault in the conflict. Finally, without Jesuits the college could become a "perpetual seed bed of license, factions, enmity, and hatred of the Society and of all other seminaries under the Society's control." Parsons suggested a more radical alternative: the de facto closure of the college. So many found the Roman climate difficult, perhaps it was advisable to withdraw all students from Rome, and apply the college's revenues, after an unspecified sum was deducted for maintenance of English priests as chaplains in the church, to seminaries in Flanders where "students could be maintained in greater

---

[195] Parsons to Acquaviva, Seville April 18, 1594, ARSI, Hisp. 136, fols 284ʳ–285ᵛ. He repeated this sentiment in a letter from Marchena on May 12, 1594, ARSI, Hisp. 136, fols 318ʳ–319ᵛ. Regarding Fioravanti, Parsons accepted his appointment and promised to give him "all the consolation and willing collaboration here that we can, and will strive that he gets it in other quarters too so that the burden of office may be less grievous for him" (Parsons to Acquaviva, Valladolid August 10, 1594, ARSI, Hisp. 137, fols 118ʳ–119ᵛ).

[196] Rome July 31, 1595, ARSI, Baet. 3/I, pp. 228–29; Rome October 23, 1595, ARSI, Cast. 6, fol. 232ʳ.

[197] Interestingly priests leaving Spain for the English mission sent a letter to students at the English College, lamenting the dispute and attributing it to the devil (October 2, 1595, ABSI, Coll P II 359).

humility, modesty and native simplicity than in Rome where, it seems, merely from the atmosphere and by reason of visits of so many personages and intercourse with so many people, and from conversing with so many English laymen outside the college, they acquire a spirit of excessive boldness and forwardness..." In conclusion Parsons begged Acquaviva not to abandon the college until other courses of action had been tried. He recommended a new rector:

> a resolute man who will rule them with sweetness and mildness, but with prudence and firmness as well; who will cherish the good ones and chastise the bad. Likewise let him be neither too intimate and familiar with them, nor on the other hand, too finicky in taking notice of trifles, firm however in persevering discipline and above all segregation, cutting them off from all intercourse with externs and with those within the College who are turbulent. Let him show that he is not afraid to punish them or dismiss them when necessary.

Parsons discussed the alterations already made, for example the appointment of three students as *ripetitori*, with Jesuits in Madrid and all disapproved. They concluded that any capitulation would simply result in even more demands. The *ripetitori* should have been chosen from the best students and not from the leaders of the rebellion. Moreover it would not be wise to remove Edward Harewood from the college because of pressure from students. Since Alfonso Agazzari, the college's first Jesuit rector, had returned to Rome, Parsons suggested that he be consulted about any changes.[198]

The Roman "stirs" attracted the attention of Philip II who ordered his ambassador, the duke of Sessa—at Parsons's instigation, as we shall see—to help Acquaviva restore order. Parsons informed Philip's secretary Juan de Idiáquez of the possibility that the Society would abandon the college's government.[199] Supported by Englishmen outside the college, the rebels had so wearied the general that he was ready to make this drastic move. Any hope that dissension would end with Lewis's death vanished: an Irishman Andrew Wyse, calling himself Grand Prior of England, assumed Lewis's role as leader of the faction. Hugh Griffin (or Griffeth), the bishop's nephew,[200] Thomas Throckmorton and others, supported him in his defense of the rebellious students. Without the Society, the college was doomed and, paraphrasing what he had written to Acquaviva, it

---

[198] Parsons to Acquaviva, Madrid December 2 and 9, 1595, ARSI, Hisp. 139, fols 122^r–126^v.

[199] Parsons to [Don Juan de Idiáquez], Madrid December 6, 1595, ABSI, 46/12/3, fols 430^r, 431^r, 432^r.

[200] On him see Anstruther, *Seminary Priests*, vol. 1, pp. 138–39.

would be a "seed bed of license and dissensions, and of enemies of the interests of Spain and his Majesty." This, after all, was one of their goals. If they succeeded, they would attempt something similar in the Spanish seminaries. Prepared to rush to Rome to throw himself at the pope's feet, he concluded upon reflection that a letter from Philip to his ambassador would be more effective. Philip should recommend his ambassador to work for restoration of peace by punishing the turbulent and isolating them from their external supporters, and by encouraging the pope to consult "good and peaceable men" such as Roger Baynes,[201] John Cecil,[202] and Richard Haydock.[203] Philip's non-intervention would jeopardize "his royal interests and all that we are attempting to do for England." Of course, any Spanish intervention in domestic collegiate matters would fan the students' nationalism and corroborate their accusations that the English Jesuits had tied themselves to the Spanish crown.

The arrival of new students for the academic year 1595/96 provided a wonderful opportunity to recruit members for each faction. Flaunting recent successes, the anti-Jesuit students first invited and later threatened seminarians not eager to join their faction. Strife permeated all aspects of collegiate life. Because sermons too often degenerated into tirades, they were discontinued. Serious study was limited. Eventually news about the Roman "stirs" reached England and foreign cities where English Catholic exiles gathered. These stories acerbated already existent tensions as much of Catholic England chose sides.

After the conclusion of Monsignor Morra's official visitation, Father Acquaviva visted the college. He exhorted them to obedience and charity, and afterwards listened to complaints.[204] Spokesmen requested an opportunity to implement Morra's recommendations. Acquaviva agreed and returned to the Gesù. But Acquaviva soon perceived that Monsignor Morra's visitation had little effect on discontented students: secret meetings continued and students still met with sympathetic English laity in Rome. Acquaviva, awaiting Parsons's reply to his suggestion that

---

[201] On January 31, 1596, Parsons wrote Baynes that he was ready to go to move to settle the disturbances and that he had two or three plans for the prevention of future difficulties (ARSI, Angl. 38/II, fol. 194r).

[202] English Jesuits held Cecil in high esteem. Richard Cowling, a consultor and confessor at the college, however, was suspicious: "his [Cecil's] presence profited our cause not a whit, whatever letters you [Creswell] wrote him, he revealed to the rebels and thus forestalled their execution and many quote him against the fathers" (Cowling to Creswell, Rome March 10, 1596, AAW, V, 40). On Cowling see McCoog, *Monumenta Angliae*, vol. 2, pp. 277–78.

[203] On him see Anstruther, *Seminary Priests*, vol. 1, pp. 159–60.

[204] Presumably the undated "Memoriale quietorum ad P. Generalem" (AAW, V, 109) was compiled around this time.

the Society abandon the college's administration, discussed the problem at length with Clement VIII, Cardinal Caetani, and his Jesuit consultors and advisors.[205] One consequence of these deliberations was a decision that outside servants should be hired to act as prefects within the college because the current student prefects were incapable or unwilling to keep discipline.

Students too continued to petition the pope. On October 13, 1595 a delegation travelled to Frascati to appeal to Clement personally, but he refused to alter his earlier decisions.[206] Upon their return to Rome on the 17th, they learned of the deaths of Owen Lewis and Thomas Throckmorton.[207] Two years later Robert Parsons pronounced his judgment on these two men in "An observation of certayne aparent iudgements of almightye God, againste suche as have beene seditious in the Englishe Catholique cause for these nine or ten years past":

> And hetherto God wente softe and fayre with these people, cuttinge off now one and now another of theire heades and winges, thereby to checke and warne them: but when they passed forwardes to kindle and blow that greate and furiouse fyre of sedition in Rome and Flanders at one time, with evydente perill to overthrow our whole cawse, then God begann to lay aboute him more eagerly and cutt off many together. For then died Doctor Lewes the Bishop of Cassano, that was accompted in this affaire *radix peccati* [root of all sin]; and this within three or four dayes sicknes, when moste of all he thoughte and desired to live and bee advanced. And with him died in like haste Mr Thomas Throgmorton, who beinge drawen by Thomas Morganne into this factioun, hadd made himselfe the Bushops principall agente, to gett him the redd capp by tumultes in the English College.[208]

By implication anyone allied with the anti-Jesuit faction could expect similar retribution.

The quiet interlude occasioned by the deaths of Lewis and Throckmorton ended in early November. Before his departure for Apulia on November 1, Cardinal Caetani re-affirmed his decision to impose outsiders as prefects and appointed his deputy as vice-gerent of the college

---

[205] At one of these meetings, a paper on the "English temperament" was circulated. For a summary see Kenny, "Inglorious Revolution," p. 10. The original can be found in ARSI, Rom. 156/II, fols 171^{r-v}.

[206] The petition in Archivio segreto vaticano, Borghese, serie III.124.c., fols 127^r–28^v was probably delivered around this time.

[207] For a sympathetic study of Lewis, see Godfrey Anstruther, O.P, "Owen Lewis," *The Venerabile*, 21 (1962): pp. 274–94.

[208] "The Memoirs of Father Robert Persons," (ed.) John H. Pollen, S.J. in *Miscellanea II* (London, 1906), pp. 207–108.

during his absence.[209] A week or so later, Thomas Hill, Edward Tempest, Robert Fisher, and John Jackson[210] were summoned to the vice-gerent's residence. Fearing that they would be expelled, they refused to go. The vice-gerent then came to the college to proclaim the papal sentence: the four were to be expelled from the college and banished from Rome. As they packed, their supporters gathered extra clothes and positioned themselves at the college's door, determined to depart with their exiled leaders. Only police prevented them from doing so. As news of the expulsion spread through Rome, a former student of the college John Sacheverell,[211] now a Dominican and known as Father William, warned the pope of dangers that could possibly follow the expulsion: if the four students apostatized, they could provide the English government with extremely dangerous data.[212] Clement then revoked the expulsion orders and the four returned to Rome. At an audience with them, Clement promised to re-examine the whole affair. Regardless of Parsons's views on the subject, Acquaviva had had enough. In January of 1596 Acquaviva decided to pull the Society out of the English College. He prepared his arguments for presentation to the pope, but he doubted Clement would approve.[213] Only the pope's refusal prevented him from the implementation of his decision And it was unlikely that the pope would budge until another visitation reviewed the situation. But, Acquaviva maintained, even if the Society continued to administer the college, drastic changes were necessary.[214] Thus the future of Jesuit administration depended on the visitation.

At the end of November Pope Clement named Filippo, Cardinal Sega, Vice-Protector.[215] On the 30th, Sega and Monsignor Morra conducted

---

[209] No one has identified with certainty the vice-gerent. He was either Paolo de' Corti, the Theatine theologian, or Alessandro Ludovisi, later elected Pope Gregory XV (Kenny, "Inglorious Revolution," p. 14 n. 18).

[210] On Jackson see Anstruther, *Seminary Priests*, vol. 1, pp. 186–87.

[211] See Patrick McGrath, "Apostate and Naughty Priests in England under Elizabeth I," in *Opening the Scrolls: Essays in Catholic History in Honour of Godfrey Anstruther*, (ed.) Dominic Aidan Bellenger, O.S.B. (Bath, 1987), pp. 64–65.

[212] Richard Cowling believed that this was the principal reason why Clement was unwilling to punish the rebels (Cowling to Joseph Creswell, Rome March 10, 1596, AAW, V, 40).

[213] Acquaviva to Parsons, Rome January 15, 1596, ARSI, Baet. 3/I, p. 251. The arguments can be found in Archivio segreto vaticano, Borghese, serie III.448a–b, fols 416r–417v.

[214] Acquaviva to Parsons, Rome February 11, 1596, ARSI, Cast. 6, fols 237v–238r.

[215] Sega, passionately pro-Spanish, advocated the conquest of England through military means. He was convinced, in the words of Arnold Pritchard, that "the church is engaged in a war to the death with the English government, a war not less real for being fought largely by spiritual means" *(Catholic Loyalism*, p. 110). Also see Thomas M. McCoog, S.J., *The Society*

another visitation of the college, the second for each. Their original intention to interview each student personally proved to be impractical, so Sega conducted the visitation by writing. Until an official decision was made, Sega instructed seminarians to obey Jesuits, and told Jesuits to allow the students to do whatever they wanted. With the exception of a few defenses,[216] most papers were grudges and complaints directed against Jesuits.[217] Every controversial episode over the previous three years was resurrected. Having examined all accusations, Anthony Kenny reduced them to five general complaints: first, the Society of Jesus aimed to dominate the English mission and used its special faculties to further this goal; second, a select group of students known as "guardian angels" were encouraged to spy on other students; third, the Jesuits treated the college as a novitiate and enticed the best students to join their ranks; fourth, Jesuit disregard of social etiquette, academic rank, and laws of precedence angered many; and finally, the Society's temporal administration of the college worried many. Presented with the accusations, Sega instructed Jesuits to reply. Denying any ambitions regarding England, they claimed that they did their best to instill respect for all priests among the laity. If the laity gave them more alms, the reason was, perhaps, their admiration of the religious life. Because discipline was not a problem in other English colleges run by the Society, the system *in se* was not at fault. Regarding use of favorites, the Jesuits pointed out that leaders of the rebellion currently held most offices. The charge that the Society recruited students was denied and Cardinal Sega was informed that at least one student who wished to join the Society was not accepted. Aside from a few remarks about humility, little was said about the charges regarding precedence. Regarding finances, the Society was willing to reduce the staff and cut a few corners.

As Cardinal Sega prepared his final report,[218] the Society of Jesus employed a favorite, time-honored tactic: various English religious figures testified to their devotion to the Society and to the important work done by it for the sake of England. Letters and testimonials flooded Rome. Dr Thomas Worthington and Dr William Percy defended the Society's style and manner of government and, incidentally, attacked the current administration at Douai. The problems resulted not from incompetent

---

of Jesus in Ireland, Scotland, and England 1541–1588: 'Our Way of Proceeding?' (Leiden, 1996), pp. 115, 116, 188, 189, 224, 225.

[216] One defense of the Society can be found in Archivio segreto vaticano, Borghese, serie II.448.a–b, fols 318^{r-v}.

[217] An example of the complaints can be found in ARSI, Angl. 30/II, fols 345^r–46^v. A list of demands can be found in AAW, V, 113.

[218] Sega's report was published in Henry Foley, S.J., *Records of the English Province of the Society of Jesus* (7 vols in 8 parts, Roehampton/London, 1877–1884), vol. 6, pp. 1–66.

governance but from the "imperfections of the men living there," who were encouraged by others outside the college. Both read different letters and complaints attacking the Society, but they had found little evidence: "we are unable to discover that they committed any mistake in government so grievous or gave any example so bad, as to have given occasion for ills so great." The college's ills resulted from student demands for ever-greater freedom and from their uncontrolled ambition. They lamented the inferior quality of seminarians but "even in the Church of God, the successors of the apostles were not the peers of the apostles." Regarding the college's finances, Worthington and Percy praised Jesuits for the care they consistently exercised in financial matters in Rome, Belgium, England, and Spain. The college remained solvent because of their energy and concern. To remedy the college's problems, they recommended that the obstinate be dismissed and a more strict regime be introduced in Douai.[219]

These memorials influenced the final report delivered by Cardinal Sega on March 14, 1596. In a long, historical introduction, Sega held the English government responsible for using self-seekers such as Owen Lewis and other members of the anti-Jesuit faction to stir up trouble. Because of universal devotion to the Society of Jesus, they would not be removed from the mission, or the college's administration. Instead, discontented seminarians were transferred to Douai. Sega, however, demanded a total reorganization of the college's finances. In early April, Caetani, Acquaviva, Fioravanti, Barret, and Tyrie met to discuss remedies, the most immediate of which was the appointment of a new rector more familiar with English affairs. On May 17, 1596 Alfonso Agazzari returned as rector of the English College.[220] Implementation of other remedies was slow. On May 29, Cardinal Sega died. Cardinal Caetani meanwhile was on a papal mission to Poland. Thus Clement VIII appointed the Spanish Jesuit Francisco, Cardinal Toledo and a known opponent of Claudio Acquaviva, Vice-Protector with immediate jurisdiction over the college.

Toledo acted quickly in favor of the dissident students. Surreptitiously he obtained a papal brief that removed the college from the jurisdiction of any Jesuit provincial and general and placed it immediately under him. Moreover he could dismiss any Jesuit working there and summon any Jesuit he so desired. But the changes did not stop there. Toledo intended to recall all Jesuits from England, and to reform the governance of the English College in Douai with the removal of Richard Barret and his replacement

---

[219] Dr Worthington and Dr Percy to Cardinal Caetani, n.p. [Brussels?] n.d. [1596], printed in Knox, *Douay Diaries*, pp. 368–75. A testimony from Richard Barret and professors at Douai can be found in Renold, *Letters of Allen and Barret*, pp. 256–58. On Percy see Anstruther, *Seminary Priests*, vol. 1, p. 272.

[220] McCoog, *Monumenta Angliae*, vol. 1, p. lxxxiii.

as president by William Gifford. Equally important Toledo planned to steer the college and the mission away from its traditional dependence on Spain in favor of France, and to support the Stuart claimant for the throne of England. Toledo had been instrumental in persuading Clement to lift the excommunication of Henry IV. Like so many in Rome, he hoped he had in James another Henry.[221]

Richard Barret had travelled to Rome in the spring of 1596 to assist in the resolution of the college's problems. Observing the changes made by Toledo, he confessed his fear to Parsons that the rebels' desire that the Society be removed from the college's administration would be granted. In an interview with the pope, Barret explained that the dire consequences of a decision to withdraw the Society. All students "of good conduct and obedient" would leave and only the rebels would remain. In the future no student favorable to the Society would attend the college. The scandal that would follow the departure of good students would be greater than any disruption caused by dismissal of the rebellious. Moreover withdrawal of the Jesuits would affect the Catholics in England for "amid the seizure of their possessions, their imprisonment and other misfortunes which, for Christ and the authority of the Apostolic See they willingly endure, it has been the greatest consolation to them that they have Colleges under the government of the Fathers to which they could send their sons." Thus, speaking for the seminarians, English Catholics, and the martyrs, Barret begged the pope not to permit the Jesuits to leave. In his reply, Clement asked "Do you think that the whole world would perish if the Society relinquished government?" Barret conceded that Clement was better informed about what would happen to the whole world, but he knew what the consequences would be in England. Thus the pope agreed that the Jesuits would remain and warned students not to meddle in the college's government. After the death of Cardinal Toledo on September 14, 1596,[222] Clement appointed Camillo, Cardinal Borghese,[223] Vice-Protector. Barret took advantage of the papal audience to defend William Holt: any stories

---

[221] Robert Chambers's narrative of the disturbances at the English College, ABSI, Anglia II, 45; Agazzari to Parsons, Rome August 27, 1596, AAW, V, 66; [Parsons to Juan de Idiáquez], Rome May 1, 1597, ABSI, Anglia II, 26; [same to same], Rome May 22, 1597, AAW, VI, 36.

[222] Parsons interpreted Toledo's early death as a sign of God's disfavor because he "upon evill information, and preoccupatioun by the factiouse, that hadd promised him among other matters to withdraw all Inglish dependantes from Spaine, whereto at that tyme hee was nothinge devoted, was theire only stay and pillar of the tumultuouse for a time, thoughe hee was so weaire of them in the ende, as hee told dyverse that if hee lived, hee would punish them severely" ("Certayne aparent iudgments," p. 208). Would he have punished them? Or would he have used them in his campaign against Acquaviva?

[223] He would become Pope Paul V.

the pope may have heard about the Jesuit's activities in Belgium were exaggerated and without foundation.[224] Despite Acquaviva's willingness to relinquish control, the Society continued to administer the college. Parsons and his associates emerged victorious from a long and bloody battle, but the wounds were deep and they did not heal. Lasting peace remained a chimera.

Conclusion

Lack of a proper administrative structure troubled the Jesuit mission. Parsons's position as superior was an anomaly without constitutional foundation and dependent on the discretionary power of a general then under attack. The Fifth General Congregation examined Acquaviva's conduct as superior of the Society. Although the generally favorable report did criticize Acquaviva for tending towards favoritism and for being overly tenacious in maintaining his position, it vindicated him of more serious charges. Nonetheless the crisis was not over.[225] Parsons was a favorite and his active intervention in support of Acquaviva antagonized many. Their fates were interwoven and troubles that plagued one would affect the other.

Under Acquaviva's direction, a unique style of governance evolved in the English mission and with English Jesuits. The general gradually granted to Parsons power and authority over individuals and institutions within distinct provinces. Not surprisingly provincials and rectors did not quite understand the nature and extent of Parsons's authority. In September of 1594, Parsons recommended that Acquaviva explain Parsons's authority to Jean Foucart, rector of St Omers. Acquaviva did so on October 24.[226] Cardinal Allen's death on October 16 aggravated the issue by revealing a complicated, constitutional entanglement. As prefect of the mission, Allen had some authority over English Catholic institutions and activities. No one assumed that authority. The establishment of colleges and seminaries either owned or administered by Jesuits from one province or mission, in the territory of another province, with rectors from the host province, created a confusing hierarchical structure within the Society of Jesus. How much authority did the superior of the English mission have in English houses in a foreign province with foreign rectors responsible to foreign

---

[224] Barret to Parsons, Rome September 28, 1596, published in Renold, *Letters of Allen and Barret*, pp. 253–55. See his earlier letter to Parsons, Rome April 10, 1596, published in Tierney/Dodd, *Church History*, vol. 3, pp. lxxiii–lxxv.
[225] Padberg et al., *For Matters of Greater Moment*, p. 11.
[226] ARSI, Cast. 6, fol. 191ʳ.

provincials? Who would mediate any conflict between the interests of the mission and those of the host province? The English often complained that foreign provincials and rectors understood neither English character and temperament, nor the English religious and political situation. With the instructions sent to Foucart, Parsons sought to define his authority vis-à-vis St Omers.[227] Allen's quasi-protector position allowed him to prevent disagreement at any of the English colleges in Spain or Rome from becoming too serious. No one possessed comparable authority after his death. Ongoing problems with Spanish and Belgian Jesuits, and the continuing tension at the English College in Rome convinced Parsons of the need for a more clearly delineated and structured form of government. Although he was superior of the mission with specific responsibilities, he wanted stronger powers. On December 9, 1595, he forwarded a memorial to Acquaviva, a memorial unfortunately no longer extant, that proposed the establishment of a prefecture headed by someone to oversee affairs of English residences and colleges in Spain, and to supervise their rectors. Without a prefect, Parsons believed the seminaries would eventually fail.[228] On February 11, 1596 Acquaviva agreed. If Parsons, Acquaviva continued, left Spain and nominated his successor, Parsons should leave him a copy of the rules which he had already sent to Rome.[229] Nearly two years expired before the prefecture was fully established.[230]

The mission's troubles were not restricted to administration. Conflicts between secular and Jesuit at Wisbech, and between the Jesuit administration and many students at the English College, Rome threatened

---

[227] Unfortunately these instructions are not extant.

[228] In addition to his letter to Acquaviva on December 2 and 9, 1595 (ARSI, Hisp. 139, fols 122^r–126^v), Parsons discussed a prefecture in his letter to Creswell from Valladolid on January 16, 1596 (printed in Joseph Creswell, "Responsio ad Calumnias," ABSI, MSS A.V.9, fol. 259^r). Parsons must have consulted Sir Francis Englefield on the issue because he enclosed a letter to Father Acquaviva in his epistle to Roger Baynes from Madrid on February 24, 1596. He explained the importance of the activities of Fathers Parsons and Holt at Spanish courts in Madrid and Brussels: "it will please him [Acquaviva] to understand that which wee knowe to be moste certain, to wit, howe insufficient the Fathers of straunge nacions be, either to understand the particularities of our Country and Nacion, or to moderate and govern them with fruite and good successe, which hath heatherto apeared whiles they were governed by Fathers of our own Country: And in this respect that it will please his Fatherhode so to establish the creadite and auctorytie of Fa. Parsons here, and of Fa. Holte in Flanders, that their orders and ordinances in governing the persons or affaires of our nacion, be not encountred, altered, nor dissolved by anie Superior Father that be of straunge nacions, withoute the expresse commandement of his Fatherhode, nor before they have participated their intencions and reasons with the said Fathers Parsons and Holte..." (AAW, V, 39).

[229] This rules are no longer extant.

[230] Rome February 11, 1596, ARSI, Cast. 6, fols 237^v–238^r. See Edwards, *Robert Persons*, p. 187.

Jesuit involvement at the college and on the mission. A cease-fire had been proclaimed at both but no one knew how long it would last. As we shall see in Chapter 6, others dissatisfied with English Jesuit solutions targeted William Holt in Brussels. Doleman's *Book of Succession* fuelled tension. Attempts by Acquaviva to halt its publication, failed. Rumors regarding its contents were confirmed with its publication. This volume, according to Thomas H. Clancy, typified a change in the attitude of the Allen/Parsons party. Earlier, Catholic exiles considered papal deposition aided, of course, by foreign invasion as the principal means for securing Catholic succession and the restoration of Catholicism. Now they placed their hope on a careful selection of the best candidate among the possible successors of Elizabeth, a candidate who would secure and protect Catholicism.[231] Neither forged a consensus among Catholics. Implicit preference for a Spanish princess over a Scottish king disturbed former collaborators such William Crichton. Their devotion to the House of Stuart resulted in an uneasy alliance with the Morgan/Paget party.

---

[231] Clancy, *Papist Pamphleteers*, p. 76; Clancy, "English Catholics and the Deposing Power," p. 133.

CHAPTER 5

"Growen Odious to the World": Conflict and Discord on the English Mission, 1596–1597

Introduction

In late October of 1595 an unnamed Englishman who had spent many of his 35 years ministering to imprisoned Catholics in his homeland, arrived in Seville. Originally four students for the seminaries in Spain accompanied him, but two were apprehended in Chester and a third, in Bristol. He carried letters, concealed in buttons, shoes and other secret places, from various prisoners including John Gerard who confided that he expected to be executed in the immediate future. With some justification, however, Robert Parsons believed that Gerard's family connections would save him from that fate. From the unnamed escort Parsons also learned that, although many talked of Sir Francis Drake's naval expedition, more were concerned about the possibility of another armada, the prospect of which terrified Queen Elizabeth. Reaction throughout the kingdom to such rumors was more ambivalent: not only Catholics but many others "who wish for a change" rejoiced at the prospect. Recently 2,000 apprentices had taken up arms against the lord mayor of London. Their demonstration was crushed, and their leaders drawn and quartered. Elizabeth, according to the same source, was currently more lenient to Catholics. Persuaded by Henry IV that reasons of state dictated greater clemency, Elizabeth released many Catholics from prison upon their promise not to leave the country. Parsons intimated that Elizabethan mercy may have had other motives: the Privy Council worried that Spain would exploit the current war in Ireland and/or the unrest in Scotland.[1]

Drake's naval expedition might have been a popular topic of conversation as the remaining ships struggled home under the leadership of Sir Thomas Baskerville, but the mission actually failed to achieve its goals.[2] Perhaps

---

[1] Parsons to Joseph Creswell, Seville October 28, 1595, Valladolid, Archivum Collegium Sancti Albani, series II, vol. 1, num. 24.

[2] I follow R.B. Wernham, *The Return of the Armadas: The Last Years of the Elizabethan War Against Spain 1595–1603* (Oxford, 1994), pp. 55–140 and Wallace T. MacCaffrey, *Elizabeth I: War and Politics 1588–1603* (Princeton, 1992), pp. 113–24. For

anticipating its success, Charles, Lord Howard of Effingham, Lord Admiral (and after 1597 Earl of Nottingham) planned an attack on Spanish ports. With the active support of Robert Devereux, Earl of Essex, and assistance from William Cecil, Lord Burghley and his son Sir Robert Cecil, Howard proposed in November of 1595 an attack to weaken Spain's Atlantic navy and to acquire much needed Spanish gold. To conceal the real objective, officials disseminated different explanations of the fleet's purpose, that is, resist an expected Spanish invasion, supplement English forces in Ireland, and so on. Howard and Essex wanted a large fleet divided into four squadrons under Lord Howard of Effingham, Essex, Sir Walter Raleigh, and Thomas, Lord Howard. The cost of the expedition and involvement of so many sailors and soldiers left Elizabeth with little interest for French schemes of a combined offensive against Spanish forces in Picardy and the Netherlands before the arrival of the new governor-general, Archduke Albert. However, the urgency of French requests for assistance hit home when the archduke's troops laid siege to Calais at dawn on March 30, 1596. On 15 April the city's citadel capitulated. Fearful that more military disasters would follow, French ambassadors increased their pressure on Elizabeth. Without English assistance, they warned, France would have no alternative but to heed Pope Clement VIII's plea to make peace with Spain. Peace with France would free Spain to concentrate on England and Holland, and to provide more support to the rebels in Ireland. The consequent Anglo-French Treaty of Greenwich signed on May 14, united the two kingdoms offensively and defensively against Spain. Moreover it stipulated neither would make peace with Spain without the other's written approval. With the addition of the Dutch Republic on October 21, the treaty expanded into the Triple Alliance.

As Howard and Essex organized their departure, the Cecils legitimized the venture with *A Declaration of the causes moving the Queen's Majesty to prepare and send a Navy to the Seas for Defence of her Realms against the King of Spain's Forces* in French, Italian, Dutch, Spanish, and English.[3] On June 1, the ships departed; on the morning of the 20th before the city's defense could be mobilized, the fleet appeared before Cadiz. As Essex's forces plundered the city, the Spanish set fire to ships laden with goods for the Indies and deprived England of booty that would have easily paid the expenses of the expedition. Despite strong arguments from Essex that he remain in Cadiz with his forces, the lord admiral refused to return to England without him.

---

more information on Cádiz see Paul E.J. Hammer, "New Light on the Cadiz Expedition of 1596," *Historical Research*, 70 (1997): pp. 182–202.

[3] Published in John Strype, *Annals of the Reformation and Establishment of Religion* (4 vols, 2nd edn, London, 1725–1731), vol. 4, pp. 260–62.

Their return in August was not triumphal. Elizabeth reminded them of the expedition's goals: destruction and/or seizure of Spanish ships and provisions; interception of the homeward bound ships from America and the Indies; and the prevention of private despoliation of any cities taken.[4] Because the venture did not even recover its costs, let alone make a profit, she considered it a failure. Essex justified his actions by placing blame on the lord admiral. Political developments in the autumn of 1596 curtailed their conflict. By late September the government received word that a Spanish agent had met in Ireland with Hugh Roe O'Donnell and Hugh O'Neill, Earl of Tyrone. Reports from Spain told how Philip II was so incensed by the sacking of Cadiz that he hastened preparations for a new armada whose size and power was comparable to its 1588 predecessor. No one, however, knew its destination. Did Philip intend to aid O'Donnell and O'Neill? Or Spanish forces in France? The archduke in Calais? The earls in Scotland? Or did he plan to invade England? The actual destination was Ireland with Milford Haven as a second possibility. The Privy Council, having weighed the options, concluded an attack was imminent. With limited resources, the government debated where to deploy them. Lord Burghley recommended that recusants be apprehended and deprived of horses and weapons. Responsibility for the enforcement of these measures was assigned to John Whitgift, Archbishop of Canterbury.

Fears and Disenchantment

Some Catholics wondered whether they could, in good conscience, play an active role in the resistance of Spanish invaders. Sometime after Thomas Wright's arrival in England in June of 1595, he received the patronage of the earl of Essex. As a result, Wright had liberties and privileges denied most other clerics. In 1596, Wright complained to Henry Garnet that Catholics believed he was a Judas because of this singular treatment. Indeed someone had spread malicious rumors about Wright in a letter to Garnet. Wright protested "before Jesus Christ our blessed Ladie and all the court of heaven, that since my comminge into Ingland I have furthered in word and deed, as farr as to me was possible to helpe the Catholiques, and amplifie Catholique religion: and with the grace of God pretend [=intend] to do heerafter." His liberty, much more restricted than his critics thought, was achieved by virtue of his friendship with an unidentified nobleman,

---

[4] A chalice taken from the Jesuit college as booty by a soldier was given to Garnet. If suitable means could be found, he offered to restore it to its rightful owners (Garnet to Acquaviva, December 4, 1596, ARSI, Fondo Gesuitico 651/624).

presumably Essex.[5] Sometime in 1596, at the request of some English Catholics, Wright resolved as a case of conscience whether they could bear arms to defend the kingdom and their queen against a Spanish invasion. He concluded that it was lawful for Catholics to do so. Important in the argumentation was the suspicion that Philip II invaded the kingdom without papal approval not for the restoration of Catholicism but for revenge or some other secular motive. Moreover, even if he had obtained the pope's permission, the pope might have made a mistake—"the pope may err in all those decrees which do not belong to faith and the measures of the universal church"—because he was misinformed. There were better ways of re-establishing Catholicism. If Catholics demonstrated to Elizabeth that they were faithful subjects and she was certain that they would defend her, Wright believed that "so kind a nature, so easy a disposition, so motherly a piety, may at last yield to them the liberty of conscience; as she hath already granted to some."[6]

Elizabeth may have considered the expedition to Cadiz a failure, but the Established Church praised God for its success. Through divine providence, the English navy achieved notable victories on land and sea. Consequently "the insolencies and pride of our Enemies, which sought our conquest and subversion, [was] ... by these late victories notable daunted, repulsed, and abased."[7] Recent victories may have repulsed and abased Spain, but England remained beleaguered. English congregations exhorted God to continue to bless Elizabeth because proud enemies conspired against her. England's salvation depended not on "our bow nor our sword" but on God's "holy hand and outstretched arm." Thus they begged the Lord to rise:

> to our defence, and break the power and counsels of thine and our enemies, and make them like those people that became as chaff before the wind, when

---

[5] ABSI, Anglia II, 20. The letter is not addressed, dated nor signed. It was endorsed by a contemporary hand as Thomas Wright to Garnet, 1596, regarding suspicions against him.

[6] "An licetum sit catholicis in Anglia arma sumere ... " published in John Strype, *Annals of the Reformation and Establishment of Religion*, vol. 3/2, pp. 583–97. The quotations come from pages 589 and 593. According to Christopher Grene, S.J., Parsons wrote to Father Walpole, probably Edward, on November 14, 1596 about "an et quousque liceat Anglis Catholicis bellare pro haereticis contra Hispanos" (ABSI, Coll P II 488). Unfortunately Grene said nothing more about the letter. Most likely this referred to Wright's treatise. See Ginevra Crosignani, "*De adeundis ecclesiis Protestantium*": *Thomas Wright, Robert Parsons, S.J., e il dibattito sul confirmismo occasionale nell'Inghilterra dell'età moderna* (Roma, 2004), pp. 183–89.

[7] William Keatinge Clay, (ed.), *Liturgical Services. Liturgies and Occasional Forms of Prayers set forth in the Reign of Queen Elizabeth* (Cambridge, 1847), p. 668.

they conspired and went out against those whose shield and buckler, whose castle of defence, whose God and Savior thou wast from everlasting.

English victory would demonstrate to the world that it was "thy favour that prospereth, and thy power that overcometh, and thy blessing that preserveth thy Church from hostility and tyranny, and us thy people from destruction."[8] On October 18 a strong gale caught the armada like "chaff before the wind," destroying many ships and killing 2,000 men. Forty-nine of the original 81 ships found sanctuary in northern Spanish ports so damaged that a second attempt was impossible in the near future. Not for the first time—and, indeed, not for the last—a favorable wind effected England's history. Despite this second disaster, Philip II did not abandon hope.[9] Despite this second reprieve, English fears remained.

Four editions of an interesting anti-Spanish tract, *State of English Fugitives under the King of Spaine and his ministers* appeared in 1595 and 1596.[10] In reply to letters from a Catholic friend who was considering abandoning England for Spanish service, the author argued forcibly against such a decision. Drawing on his own experience and citing specific cases of injustice and cruelty against Englishmen in Spanish service, the author addressed his tract to "unexperienced Gentlemen, as are in desire addicted to the Spanish service" and to "credulous Catholikes at home, upon whose ignorance and driftles search into these matters, our practising traitors abroad doo build their chiefest foundations of all their villanies."[11] Considering it his responsibility to remind the English of "the quiet estate they live in, and the manner of her Maiesties most gracious and mercifull government," the author explained the king of Spain's "cruell and inhumane usage of his miserable subiects, his violent abolition and taking awaie of their priviledges, and in fine, the unspeakable bondage, constrained servitude, and pittiful desolation in which they live, or rather despairfully do languish."[12] Spain seduced many English fugitives and later abandoned them once they were no longer needed. According to the author, Sir Rowland Yorke was poisoned by the Spanish. Sir William Stanley's captains later regretted their folly, implored Elizabeth's pardon and returned to England. Each one died shortly thereafter: "If God himself lay it down as one of his blessings, that he will give the righteous long and many happy daies on the earth, surely then the taking of these men away in the best of their yeres by such violent ends, in my iudgement is

---

[8] Clay, *Liturgical Services*, p. 665.

[9] Henry Kamen, *Philip of Spain* (New Haven/London, 1997), p. 308.

[10] STC 15562–65. I cite STC 15565 (London, 1596).

[11] Sir Lewis Lewkner?, *State of English Fugitives under the King of Spaine and his ministers* (London, 1595, 1596), STC 15562–65, p. 2.

[12] Lewkner, *State of English Fugitives*, p. 3.

an apparent argument of his wrath, from which of his divine inestimable mercie, I beseech him to deliver us."[13]

Endless examples of Spanish cruelty in northern France and Flanders could be cited. But England's queen was different: after the Armada she allowed Spanish sailors shipwrecked in Scotland to pass safely to Flanders, well aware that they would augment depleted forces. Given a choice between Philip's malice and Elizabeth's magnanimity, the author marvelled that some English Catholics preferred the former. Leaving discussion of religious profundities to more competent theologians, the author informed Catholics of "the contentment which you might heere receive in free usage of the same, together with the conversation of such other your countrymen as are heere of the same profession and religion."[14] Exile was not bliss. Moreover, faction and discontent thrived among the Catholic exiles.

Four factions "most malitiously opposite one against another, to the great preiudice and slaunder of them all" divided English exiles. The first pretended to be serious political thinkers and great statesmen. The second were totally devoted to the Society of Jesus and served as spies for Jesuits. In general, they were "verie hatefull to the rest, and are dangerous to converse withall, not so much in regard that anie of them are able to do a chips worth of harme, as of their willingness to do it if they were able." The third group, derided by others as "Patriots, which is to saie, lovers and affectors of their Countrie" disagreed with the English Established Church but they loved their country and spoke reverently of their queen. Such "men of greatest temperance and best behaviour" declare that they would be content to live in a poor cottage if they could return to England without violating their religious conscience. The fourth faction were so "utterly voide both of learning, wit, and civilitie" that the others treated them as dunces.[15] The author blamed the second faction for all conspiracies against the queen; Jesuits and their supporters considered England's interests inferior to Spain's. They encouraged Philip's proposals for an invasion, and used his money to train clergy to sow sedition by winning English Catholics to Spain's cause. These fanatics, if pressed why they forsook their rightful monarch for a foreign king, would argue that England's cruel laws against Catholicism justified their treason. But, the author asked his readers, did Catholic exiles "reade, heare, or know of any one king or queen who did with greater mildness or lenitie tollerate or suffer within his or their dominon, a sect of religion opposite to the lawes by him or them established, especially the same having sundrie times made

---

[13] Lewkner, *State of English Fugitives*, p. 32.
[14] Lewkner, *State of English Fugitives*, p. 48.
[15] Lewkner, *State of English Fugitives*, p. 49.

rebellious attempts against their crowne, estate and dignitie."[16] The author confessed that Elizabeth executed seminary priests just as she punished other criminals for their crimes, but she preferred other solutions to the problem. But everyone knew "that the comming of these Seminaries, Priestes, and Iesuites, to reconcile men (as they tearme it) to the obedience of the Romane Church, is directly and absolutely to alienate and divert their mindes from her maiesty, and to incline them to be readie to assist anie enemie either within our without the realme, that shall colour his cause under the pretext of religion."[17] Consequently Elizabeth forbade their entrance into the realm and ordered those already there, to depart. But they did not obey her. Instead of executing all captured priests as traitors Elizabeth mercifully imprisoned and exiled many. Contrary to Philip II's cruel practices in his many kingdoms, Elizabeth did not desire their execution: she was "alwaies readie to receive into grace and favour, those of whome she hath anie hope that they will become good subiectes, and hath, as I have heard, offered (after that by lawe they were condemned) her princely mercie and favour to some of them, if they would have promised to become good subiects."[18] Yet many Catholics believing exile preferable to life in England eventually succumbed to less merciful and more tyrannical leaders: the Society of Jesus.

Since its foundation, according to the treatise, the Society of Jesus accumulated wealth and influence to the detriment of the older religious orders: "There is not anie mans busines but they must have an oare in it: they never plant themselves in anie places but in the middest of goodly cities, where they wring themselves into the fairest palaces, in some of them dispossessing by violence those to whom they are appertained."[19] Their colleges were rich; their churches sumptuous. Not subject to any ordinary, Jesuits were responsible directly to their provincial or their general superior, neither of whom corrected their faults and abuses. As a rule Jesuits, were "proude, ambitious, aspiring, entermedlers in matters of state, men of greate riches and covetous of more, and therefore by no meanes to bee admitted to such as lye at the point of death."[20] Professing to educate children freely and without any reward, Jesuits used their colleges to indoctrinate students and to ingratiate themselves with parents. The author predicted that Jesuits would suffer the fate of the Knights Templar. He warned them that the same punishment awaited them because they have "growen odious to the world, and to none more odious, than to some

---

[16] Lewkner, *State of English Fugitives*, p. 69.
[17] Lewkner, *State of English Fugitives*, p. 70.
[18] Lewkner, *State of English Fugitives*, p. 73.
[19] Lewkner, *State of English Fugitives*, p. 74.
[20] Lewkner, *State of English Fugitives*, p. 75.

of their owne religion, who doo well foresee the scandall and slander that by their behaviour ariseth unto the Romane Church."[21]

Providentially England was spared the hypocrisy of the Jesuits and the cruelty of the Spaniard. Instead of instigating rebellions and committing bellicose campaigns against other kingdoms, England lived in peace and friendship with her neighbors, eager to assist and aid whenever possible. Her queen was "a princely, zealous, and loving mother carefully tendereth, fostereth, and preserveth her subiects by wisdome and fortitude from forreine violences, and by clemencie, religion, and iustice, from inward mischiefes."[22] After years in exile, the author concluded that he could no longer tolerate Spanish policies and Jesuit intrigues. Especially abhorrent were Jesuits who were:

> malicious enemies to her maiestie, and to their owne countrey, vile and pernicious instruments of the Spanish King and his adherents, who daily (as it is manyfest to them that have knowledge and experience of them and their actions) seeke nothing more than the utter ruine, pulling downe, and destruction of her maiestie and their countrey: He therefore that doth thinke to live among these subtile and dangerous people, in any credit or account, let him, as hee worthily doth deserve, be accounted beside his wits, or els as disobedient and traitorous to almightie God, her maiestie, and his countrey.[23]

Once the author realized the true nature of Jesuit machinations, he petitioned the queen to return to his homeland. Elizabeth granted his request; by implication she would allow others to return.

A.W. Pollard and G.R. Redgrave identified the author of this tract as Sir Lewis Lewkner. Albert J. Loomie, S.J., however, claimed the author was Samuel Lewknor who suffered while serving Spain in the Low Countries in the 1580s. Loomie suggested that Lewknor addressed this tract to his cousin about to commit a similar mistake in 1592.[24] But the intended audience was much larger than the author's relations. Lewknor fashioned his personal experiences into propaganda aimed at English Catholics increasingly disenchanted with Spanish policies and Jesuit domination.[25] His comments fuelled real opposition to English Jesuits. Many perceived

---

[21] Lewkner, *State of English Fugitives*, p. 79.

[22] Lewkner, *State of English Fugitives*, pp. 121–22 (*vere* 129–30).

[23] Lewkner, *State of English Fugitives*, p. 135.

[24] Albert J. Loomie, S.J., *The Spanish Elizabethans: The English Exiles at the Court of Philip II* (New York, 1963), pp. 10–11.

[25] According to Peter Holmes, Lewknor's dissatisfaction was evidence of Catholic opposition to "ideas of political resistance prevalent in English Catholic literature at the time" (*Resistance and Compromise: The Political Thought of the Elizabethan Catholics*

their devotion to Spain, their control of Spanish purses, their governance of English seminaries, their administration of the English mission, and their persistent meddling in political matters as pernicious and inevitably detrimental to the Catholic cause. Lewknor noted how Jesuits derided "patriots" who, but for religion, would be Elizabeth's loyal subjects. Jesuits were irredeemable, but "patriots" could be reconciled once their loyalty was assured. Burghley used Lewknor's tract to advertise to Catholics that the government recognized a distinction between loyal Catholics, with whom it could possibly do business, and treasonous Jesuits, the true root and cause of all current religious ills.

On the Back Foot: Jesuits in England

Unaware of the implications of the four editions of *State of English Fugitives*, Henry Garnet did not foresee how the government intended to exploit current tension between Jesuits and secular clergy. However, the resolution of the disputes at Wisbech left him optimistic about prospects of Catholicism in England. In early January of 1596 he spoke of "a warm peace" among all priests in England without doubt "a special fruit of the Spirit." Perhaps as a consequence of such blessed union, the mission progressed daily. Especially impressive was John Gerard's indefatigable ministry in prison: he reconciled many to the Roman Church, arranged for young boys to be sent to St Omers, directed other prisoners, offered Mass, and assisted incoming clergy.[26] With such workers, a large harvest would certainly follow any relaxation of the penal laws. Other Jesuits, all of whom were well, labored as well as they could "insofar as conditions of time and place allow." The execution of Robert Southwell, Henry Walpole and others backfired by arousing popular sympathy for Catholics. Thus, Garnet believed the government considered altering its strategy to exile clergy instead of executing them, the preferred option if the author of *State of English Fugitives* was to be believed. If these rumors were true, Garnet promised to send any Jesuits released first to William Holt in Belgium, and then to Parsons in Spain. But if Acquaviva wanted William Weston sent directly to Rome, Garnet suggested that he contact Holt about the assignment. In an ambiguous passage Garnet reported the presence of

---

[Cambridge, 1982], pp. 175, 253 n. 31). Holmes believed that Lord Burghley realized and exploited the book's propaganda potential.

[26] See Peter Lake and Michael Questier, "Prisons, Priests and People," in *England's Long Reformation 1500–1800*, (ed.) Nicholas Tyacke (London, 1998), pp. 195–233 for an exposition of Catholic use of prisons as apostolic bases.

two Franciscans in England.[27] He wanted them to request certain faculties which could be extended to everyone on the mission. If such a practice was a violation of the Jesuit Institute, Garnet exhorted Acquaviva to inform him immediately because "we will do nothing that is repellant to our Institute or to your reverence's good pleasure." Yet amidst his sanguine account one problem remained: Garnet did not know what to do with Thomas Lister. Because he suffered from claustrophobia, he was unable to endure any confinement within a hiding hole. Unwilling to place a Jesuit with such an affliction with even his closest friends, Garnet kept Lister with him at considerable risk to both. This arrangement angered Lister who complained to Acquaviva. Meanwhile Garnet could do little but pray for a resolution.[28]

By early spring of 1596 everyone, including the erratic Thomas Lister, was well and to Garnet's delight, peace still flourished at Wisbech. However, rumors regarding expulsions apparently lacked foundation. Indeed amidst a resurgence of persecution, Garnet marvelled that he had not been captured. For the first time in his correspondence with Acquaviva, Garnet worried that someone was tampering with his letters. Lost letters did not concern him because they were so ambiguous that there was little danger of discovery. But, for some unexplained reason, he cautioned Acquaviva that a skilled scribe might counterfeit his hand and relay false information. So Acquaviva should be wary of any letter suggesting or arguing a new approach. More immediate and more troubling was a rumor emanating from the continent that Acquaviva seriously considered withdrawing the Society from the English College in Rome because of the current difficulties. As we saw in the last chapter, this rumor was accurate. The very possibility disturbed Garnet: "But why, dearest father, are you deserting us now? Why are you leaving us so desolate?" The disturbances there, he asserted, were not simply the work of the devil but also the handiwork of the English government. Instead of relinquishing control of the college, Acquaviva should ensure the troublemakers were dismissed. In fact it would be more beneficial if the malcontents were returned to England branded as seditious because of their antics than if they were allowed to stay, were ordained, and came back to the mission "in sheep's clothing and stir[ring] up trouble everywhere." Jesuit withdrawal would be a tragic mistake: "In all these years so many illustrious leaders and brave soldiers have been honored to serve under your leadership. Now with

---

[27] John Jones was one of the Franciscans. He worked closely with Jesuits after his arrival in England (Philip Caraman, S.J., *Henry Garnet (1555–1606) and the Gunpowder Plot* [London, 1964], pp. 252–53). I can not identify the second Franciscan.

[28] Garnet to Acquaviva, January 17, 1596, ARSI, Fondo Gesuitico 651/624. See Caraman, *Henry Garnet*, pp. 204–205.

victory in sight, will you change the standard and emblems that have been so happy and auspicious? Now that we, having sailed through turbulent seas under your competent direction, are within sight of port, would you change everything?" Because Acquaviva consistently demonstrated his love and affection for the English people, Garnet doubted that he would make such a rash decision.[29] Did Garnet truly believe that they were "within sight of port?" Or was he simply exaggerating conditions to prevent a negative judgment? Perhaps Garnet interpreted the current lull in clerical executions as a harbinger of happier times despite any renewed persecution. Elizabeth's reign was drawing to a close; perhaps he expected a more tolerant successor.

Slowly other rumors of dissent and discontent made their way to England. By April Garnet learned of even more turbulent division among exiles in Belgium in a letter from William Holt.[30] The superior feared the dissension would eventually implicate priests currently working peacefully in England. Now Jesuits in England who contemplated "night and day nothing but crosses and the rack" were slandered by fellow countrymen "whom the Society embraced with such love and, like a nurse, fostered so long in its bosom." Men who deserved better were now crucified unjustly in Rome and in Belgium by pseudo-friends who acted "like vipers." Garnet did not know the precise nature of the charges because Holt only hinted at the content of the complaints, but he reminded Acquaviva that Henry Vaux, who later pronounced Jesuit vows on his deathbed,[31] rebutted earlier criticism of the Society thus:

> My sisters [Anne Vaux and Eleanor Brooksby], I am grateful indeed to you for telling me this. Now I see the mark of divine goodness stamped on the men of this Order, and the intimate providence of God who has shown them these tokens of this love. Now I have no doubt that he will be propitious to them; that they in time will reap in this kingdom the same fruit from their labours as they have done elsewhere, for they are not excepted here from the injuries they suffer in other countries.[32]

If Garnet knew their precise allegations, he could refute them without difficulty. Perhaps, he opined, their leaders had not yet decided what their

---

[29] London March 13, 1596, ARSI, Fondo Gesuitico 651/624. As far as possible I have used Caraman's English translation. See *Henry Garnet*, pp. 205–207.

[30] We shall look at this in more detail in the next chapter.

[31] See Thomas M. McCoog, S.J., *English and Welsh Jesuits 1555–1650* (1 vol. in 2 parts, London, 1994–1995), pp. 319–20.

[32] London March 13, 1596, ARSI, Fondo Gesuitico 651/624. I use the translation in Caraman, *Henry Garnet*, p. 209.

charges would be! He knew that Acquaviva's patience was being tested by these troubles on so many fronts that he feared the general would withdraw Jesuits from the mission as a consequence. Garnet thus prepared a defense against some common accusations. Lest his apology appeared too spirited and too bitter, Garnet explained that he was both a Jesuit and an Englishman: "as a subject of your paternity and an unworthy son of the Society of Jesus, I ought ... to be patient in the face of alleged calumnies and neither repeat nor write anything unworthy of your reverence and dignity. But as an Englishman, surely I ought not to suffer quietly the barbarity of insolent men, who putting aside divine and human law, and puffed up with lust and a certain self-importance, brought hate and ignominy upon their whole nation."[33]

From the mission's foundation Jesuits adhered to religious discipline and to their Institute and had no reason to feel ashamed in the sight of God for anything. As evidence Garnet submitted the high esteem in which other religious orders held them; the support they had received from all sides; the eagerness of many lay persons to consult Jesuits and to receive the sacraments from them; the desire of many, including secular priests, to join their number; and the requests that the Society take up residence in different houses. Jesuits were attractive because they followed their Institute. The Society's rules were as carefully observed in England as they were in any continental colleges. Even in remote parts of the kingdom Garnet sought to place two Jesuits in close proximity to each other so that they could profit from mutual counsel and frequent visitations.[34] In his own case scarcely a day passed without some Jesuit conferring with him. Garnet stressed the importance of such personal contact for spiritual and emotional well-being. Similarly, despite risks and inconvenience, all Jesuits continued to meet together semi-annually for general confessions, spiritual exhortations, discussions of cases of conscience, and renewal of vows. Even severe persecution did not postpone these meetings beyond seven or eight months. To these gatherings Garnet invited trustworthy and well-known secular priests. Further evidence of the quality of Jesuit life was the godly atmosphere promoted by Jesuits in the households where

---

[33] London April 16, 1596, ARSI, Fondo Gesuitico 651/624. Imperfect copies can be found in ARSI, Angl. 31/I, fols 129^r–132^r; ABSI, Anglia II, 16, and ABSI, Coll P II 567–69. For Caraman's analysis see *Henry Garnet*, pp. 207–20.

[34] Henry Pollard (*vere* James Sharpe) attested to this practice in 1610: "In the house where I lived [in Yorkshire] we were continually two priests, one to serve and order the house at home, the other to help those who are abroad, who especially in any sickness or fear of death would continually send to us for help, that they might die in the estate of God's Church" (ABSI, Anglia III, 100 [printed in John Morris, S.J., (ed.), *The Troubles of Our Catholic Ancestors Related by Themselves* (3 vols, London, 1872–1877), vol. 3, pp. 467–48]).

they resided. Some households were so devout that "only the name [was] lacking for a religious institute." Unwittingly "the sword and torture of one [foe and] the malicious talk and envious eye of another" aided their spiritual progress. God's grace sustained against the first; virtue would confound the lies of the second. Of course, the Jesuits were fallible men and not perfect, but not one Jesuit sent on the mission had done anything scandalous, apostatized,[35] or betrayed any Catholic. Some priests, Garnet admitted, attacked the Jesuits because the Society disapproved of their acceptance of occasional conformity. Some went so far as to attack religious in general. "It was religious priests who in the past," according to Garnet, "made this island illustrious for its faith." Now that the older orders have been suppressed only a few Jesuits and two Franciscans remained. Without religious priests, Garnet, contended, the realm would never be won back to Catholicism. Taking a swipe at some secular clergy, he explained that:

> You can not call it an apostolic vocation when priests come here merely to seek a living or to amass in a short time sufficient money to keep themselves sumptuously in exile for the rest of their life: the [true] vocation is to devote themselves body and soul to God and his Church: to go out in search of the sheep themselves, not of their fleece.[36]

Restricted by a vow of poverty, Jesuits, he assured Acquaviva, did not suffer from this abuse. Henceforth attacks on Jesuit wealth would assume a more important role in controversies with secular clergy whose accusations would echo those in the *State of English Fugitives*.

Garnet continued his defense with an explication of many pious works performed by Jesuits alone. They decided where to reside not out of expectation of money but from a desire for accessibility and apostolic effectiveness. Each Jesuit constantly risked discovery because many flocked to him for direction and sacraments. Frequently secular clergy and lay people remained for a period of time so as not to arouse suspicion. Because Jesuits considered it unfair to expect their hosts to shoulder the financial burden of such visitors, the Society contributed to their support from alms collected elsewhere. Some secular clergy, who were so protective of their accommodation that they treated their residence almost as benefices, prevented others from residing in their districts despite the need for more priests. Jesuits, on the other hand, provided newly arrived priests with fixed abodes and thus established clergy permanently in regions that

---

[35] Presumably Garnet was talking about the Jesuits who had been sent to work in the English mission. That excluded men such as Thomas Langdale and Christopher Perkins.

[36] London April 16, 1596, ARSI, Fondo Gesuitico 651/624. I use the translation in Caraman, *Henry Garnet*, p. 215.

had previously seen a priest only a few times a year. Moreover, Garnet often supported secular clergy between their arrival and their placement. Consequently few secular priests had not benefited from Garnet's generosity over the years. This generosity continued if a priest was assigned to an area too poor to support him. As long as there was money no priest's need was ever neglected.

With money collected, Garnet established a printing press. The press flooded the kingdom with catechetical books such as Peter Canisius's *A summe of Christian doctrine*[37] and pious works such as Garnet's *A treatise of Christian renunciation*[38] until its recent discovery and confiscation. Fortunately no one was captured in the raid and he retained the entire staff as he sought a site for a new press. Garnet employed these lay workers and paid them presumably from the money he collected. One lay worker, the skilled wood-worker Nicholas Owen, hoped to enter the Society eventually. Meanwhile he travelled throughout the kingdom, constructing hiding holes for the protection of priests without charge. If anyone insisted that he accept money, he offered it to his two brothers, one of whom was a priest, in prison for their faith.[39] Other lay workers served as companions and guides to clergy within England, arranged their transport, and conveyed their letters. Still others conducted young men and women across the channel to seminaries and convents, and carried letters and money to exiled Catholics. This important and dangerous work, Garnet admitted, would not be possible without Jesuit involvement because the Society provided an international network of contacts, agents, and procurators who relayed monies and letters to their appropriate destinations. Finally laymen ordinarily collected alms because they had easier access to wealthy Catholics and involvement in temporalities was not proper for clergy. He reassured Acquaviva that he used all money judiciously. In fact, Richard Barret testified that he received more money from Garnet and Robert Southwell than from any former student of his college.

---

[37] N.p., n.d. [London, 1592–96] *ARCR*, vol. 2, num. 333.

[38] N.p., n.d. [London, 1593], *ARCR*, vol. 2, num. 322. For a list of works published by Garnet's first secret press see *ARCR*, vol. 2, p. 225 under "Press no. 8."

[39] According to Anstruther, Nicholas had two brothers who sought ordination. Anstruther asserted that John recanted his Catholicism and conformed to the Established Church in 1588. The second, Walter, died in Valladolid in 1591 (Godfrey Anstruther, O.P., *The Seminary Priests* [4 vols, Ware/Durham/Great Wakering, 1968–1977], vol. 1, pp. 263, 264). The brothers in prison were John, who, according to Michael Hodgetts, recanted his recantation, and Henry, a printer. See Hodgetts's "The Owens of Oxford," *Recusant History*, 24 (1999): pp. 415–30; and Alice Hogge, "Closing the Circle: Nicholas Owen and Walter Owen of Oxford," *Recusant History*, 26 (2002): pp. 291–300.

All money received, whether from alms or from the patrimonies of two Jesuits[40] bestowed on the mission with Acquaviva's approval was distributed fairly.[41] Garnet explained: "I have always conducted myself thus: I have always given preference to major needs over minor ones, and have never put out any money unless before God's grace and my conscience, using the advice of others when possible, the case seemed a necessary one." If such generosity did not satisfy the Society's critics, Garnet would willingly transfer control of the purse to these "men of charity" as long as they allowed Jesuits to live their vows of poverty and not expect Jesuit financial support upon their arrival in England. Now, unfortunately, there was less money available and sacrifices were required. Garnet concluded his financial discussion by asserting that Jesuits did not hide their treasures but used whatever they had to the benefit of Catholics even if that meant they denied themselves clothing, books, or a horse. He called as a witness to Jesuit generosity Thomas Hill, one of the troublemakers at the English College. Before Hill departed for the continent, he lived with John Gerard at the Society's expense. He should be asked about what he had heard and experienced during his sojourn. He may have changed subsequently but the Society's kindness had not!

Jesuits and secular clergy in England, according to Garnet, enjoyed a "serene peace." With the exception of five or six scattered throughout the kingdom, all secular clergy would be insulted by the suggestion that they were hostile to the Society.[42] As evidence he cited a recent incident in Rome. Someone insinuated to an unnamed cardinal that many priests in England opposed the Society and that he carried an open letter on the subject. Pressed to name specific priests, he answered simply that he was

---

[40] Their patrimonies approximated £1,000. Apparently Garnet invested the sum.

[41] In a letter to William Holt (Rome March 23, 1596, ARSI, Fl. Belg. 1/I, pp. 602–603) Acquaviva granted permission to apply the patrimonies of two other Jesuits, Edward Walpole and John Baptist Docking, to the mission. In the same letter Acquaviva recommended that Holt seek Henry Broy for the mission instead of Thomas Everard as Garnet wanted. On them see Thomas M. McCoog, S.J., (ed.) *Monumenta Angliae* (2 vols, Rome, 1992), vol. 2, pp. 251, 290, 299, 519. Docking was later dismissed from the Society and associated with opponents of the English Jesuits during the appellant controversy.

[42] Blackwell wrote to Enrico, Cardinal Caetani: "There are (as I hear) little equal, or altogether ignorant esteemers of our matters, who have not gently whetted the edge of their wit and style and sharpness of their voice against us. They say (but rashly) that we Priests in England are tossed with divers dissensions amongst ourselves and with the Fathers of the Society of Jesus; and, that more freely in lying they may wander, they report the said Fathers to seek no other thing almost amongst us, than by the contempt of the rest of the Priests, greater authority and dominion in the Clergy might daily grow unto them. A heavy accusation, but most full of falsehood" (January 10, 1597, cited in Penelope Renold, (ed.), *The Wisbech Stirs (1595–1598)* [London, 1958], p. 205 n. 3). On Blackwell see Anstruther, *Seminary Priests*, vol. 1, pp. 39–41.

privy to information denied to others. His story varied with his audience and he acted peeved when confronted by English Jesuits in Rome on the reliability of his account. For unexplained reasons, Garnet now thought that the Society had gained this person's favor. Contrary to such allegations, almost half the secular clergy in England offered to place themselves under Garnet's authority with a promise of obedience, but the Jesuit was unwilling to accept the responsibility. Based on letters and meetings with secular clergy, Garnet concluded that "their hearts hoped for nothing but the peace and love of the Holy Spirit."

Garnet explained possible origins of some accusations at the end of his letter.[43] A few years before, a certain priest, unnamed by Garnet but surely John Mush, spent some time in Rome. He spread a rumor around the English College that priests throughout southern England, especially Jesuits, refused assistance to clergy arriving from the continent. He complained that he spent several days at an inn in London on his way from Rome to the north of England and was unable to celebrate Mass on unspecified feasts. His report troubled those about to depart but, upon arrival in England, they found Jesuits so eager to assist that they wondered how such allegations could be believed. Garnet explained the context of Mush's arrival. Because of increased vigilance, hospitality was practically impossible. Garnet met Mush at the inn, arriving in London purely by chance on the same day. Unsure whether he himself would find any accommodation with a Catholic family, Garnet refused to take Mush with him. Instead he committed Mush to the care of a lay Catholic but the priest got lost as he followed the layman through the streets of London. A few days later Garnet found safe accommodation for Mush. Now he was so kindly disposed towards the Jesuits that he urged Garnet to move heaven and earth to dissuade Acquaviva from withdrawing the Society from the administration of the English College: "Let them have regard to the thunderbolts which will fall upon them from such a multitude of other Catholics, men of the highest virtue and consideration, ever joined with us in the closest of unions, if this suit should be carried for settlement to judgment by the majority."[44] Such were the sentiments of a priest once estranged from the Society.

The controversy at Wisbech was another source of stories about the Society. Considering it unnecessary to repeat what he had earlier written to Acquaviva about the disturbances, Garnet added a few new concerns. Although there was still peace between the two groups, Garnet received letters demanding that he order William Weston and his supporters to

---

[43] This section was published in Renold, *Wisbech Stirs*, pp. 164–78. Henceforth all citations are from her translation.

[44] Renold, *Wisbech Stirs*, p. 170.

return to the common order. Other letters complained about individual clergy and specifically about Weston's sources of money and his use of the alms given to him. Garnet avoided becoming too involved out of fear of rekindling the fire, but he and many Catholics concurred with Weston's refusal to name his benefactors. Such demands "bore marks of the handiwork of Cecil and Topcliffe" in their attempts to identify benefactors, and to discover the means employed for the collection and transfer of money. He implored Acquaviva to repeat this to no one because Garnet was loath to do anything that could "disturb the peace we enjoy at present, or ... incur odium for recounting the faults of others."[45]

Garnet hoped the seminarians in Rome envied the fraternal peace in England. The persistence of such recalcitrant students saddened him, but he pitied more the future of "the Church in England, if it is going to have to take men devoured by pride, given over to faction, full of ambition, men freshly come from the supper of the heretics, and what is worse men who have taken their oaths to be heretics, as they proceeded through every step of their academic degrees, and sometimes ministers who have wandered about keeping clear of any form of ecclesiastical discipline, if such are going to be held in esteem here instead of pastors and apostles." Therefore, Garnet begged Acquaviva that he not permit the insolent to emerge victorious. Their shameful acts must be noted and punished. If not they would further discord. They were "the ferment of the Cecils" that would affect the Church in England. These men must not triumph. Therefore, Garnet implored Acquaviva "to love and cherish, with the solicitude which you have always shown, not only us, your sons, but that College of our nation, the nurse of so many of our martyrs."[46]

During the summer of 1596 Garnet was more concerned with a decline in the number of Jesuits on the mission than with slanders on the continent.[47] John Nelson died on July 10/20; John Curry was seriously ill (he died on September 2). Sent to England for reasons of health soon after completing his noviceship, John Percy was arrested in Holland in the spring. He was committed to Bridewell prison in London on April 23.[48] Garnet anticipated that he would soon be released from prison and exiled.

---

[45] Renold, *Wisbech Stirs*, p. 172.

[46] Renold, *Wisbech Stirs*, p. 173.

[47] Garnet to Acquaviva, August 14, 1596, ARSI, Fondo Gesuitico 651/624.

[48] *Calendar of the Manuscripts of the Most Hon. the Marquis of Salisbury*, (eds.) S.R. Scargill-Bird et al. (24 vols, London, 1883–1976), vol. 6, p. 311. On Percy see McCoog, *Monumenta Angliae*, vol. 2, p. 308 under his alias John Fisher. From Bridewell he somehow established contact with John Gerard in the Clink and they exchanged letters. See Philip Caraman, S.J., (ed.), *John Gerard: The Autobiography of an Elizabethan* (London, 1951), p. 146.

If so, Garnet was certain that he would immediately return by way of the same port from which he was exiled! All Jesuits in England planned to assemble for their semi-annual meetings in late August. At the moment, everything was peaceful to Garnet's delight: there was harmony among the clergy and a slackening of persecution.[49] At the congregation Jesuits would choose a procurator to send to Rome to brief father general on conditions within the kingdom and on the state of the mission.[50] Garnet hoped the delegate would be Thomas Lister. Garnet would have liked to have made the trip, but he concluded that he could not leave the mission. On the other hand, he believed that a trip to Rome would improve Lister's health "who was very ill and most likely incurable in this part of the world." Lister was not sent; William Baldwin served as the mission's procurator and departed for Rome in late summer or early autumn. Events at the English College disrupted Baldwin's plans to return to England and by 1597 he was minister there as successor to the controversial Edward Harewood.[51] Meanwhile Lister's state so deteriorated that he was demanding to return to the continent by December of 1596. Garnet concurred: for peace of soul Lister should be assigned to "the quietest possible place." Perhaps a long break would restore his health.[52]

Sometime in the autumn of 1596, Richard Fulwood, one of Garnet's important lay assistants, was captured as he conducted a student to Gravesend for embarkation to Flanders. Imprisoned in Bridewell, he established contact with John Percy and the two planned an escape by using a rope they had secretly obtained. Along with two other priests and six laymen, Percy and Fulwood lowered themselves from a window and scampered away. Percy headed for one of John Gerard's London houses where Anne Line protected him until Garnet could send him north to

---

[49] On November 23, 1596 Richard Verstegan emphasized that persecution had diminished since the publication of the *Book of Succession*. See his letter to Roger Baynes, Antwerp November 23, 1596, ARSI, Angl. 38/II, fol. 201ᵛ (published in Anthony G. Petti, (ed.), *The Letters and Dispatches of Richard Verstegan [c. 1550–1640]* [London, 1959], p. 249).

[50] Ordinarily each province held a congregation every three years to elect a procurator to attend a congregation of procurators in Rome. England was not a province so it was not obliged to comply with this regulation. Presumably at the general's request England was sending an extraordinary procurator. The next full congregation of procurators was scheduled for 1597.

[51] In a letter from Rome on November 9, 1596, Acquaviva told Oliver Mannaerts that he was not to employ Baldwin in any negotiations because he was going back to England (ARSI, Gal. 44, fols 54ᵛ–55ʳ). As late as August of 1597, Garnet expected Baldwin's imminent return (Garnet to Acquaviva, August 20, 1597, ARSI, Fondo Gesuitico 651/624).

[52] Garnet to Acquaviva, December 4, 1596, ARSI, Fondo Gesuitico 651/624. See Caraman, *Henry Garnet*, pp. 221–26.

work with Richard Holtby.[53] Because Acquaviva may have been surprised or indeed shocked by a successful escape from an English prison, Garnet explained that, although some prisons were conducted humanely and prisoners often gave their word that they would not attempt to escape, Bridewell was notoriously "barbarous and reserved chiefly for whores and vagabonds. Catholics were forbidden access to it and there was no communication permitted between prisoners. Here no pledge was given, for no one had the humanity to ask it. This escape, therefore, caused no scandal."[54] Earlier we noted Acquaviva's reluctance to endorse ransoming Jesuit prisoners out of fear of giving scandal. Apparently escapes posed similar problems.

Despite tension between Jesuits and some secular clergy, two secular priests were attracted to the Society: Richard Banks and Ralph Bickley. The former arrived in England in the second half of 1594. Described by Garnet as a "man of tried virtue and ample learning," Banks was especially suited for the mission.[55] There was, however, a minor canonical problem: he had pronounced a secret vow to join the Benedictines. Now he decided that he wanted to remain in England and asked to join the Society. William Baldwin conveyed to Acquaviva all necessary information about him. All that was required now was Acquaviva's approval once the technicality had been resolved. Bickley expressed interest in the Society earlier.[56] Now a prisoner in Wisbech, he supported Weston throughout the recent conflict. A "man of unusual virtue and more than a little learning," Bickley resolved to remain with Weston unless he was obliged to go into exile. Through Joseph Creswell and Parsons, Bickley pleaded for admission into the Society. Since he was so well known to many Jesuits, Garnet argued that he could be accepted in England without any risk.[57]

As more and more rumors reached England about events at the English College Garnet worried about their effect on relations already strained by Wisbech. "Though it should give us cause for joy rather than for sorrow," Garnet began a letter to Acquaviva:

> we here, who have given no cause for such treatment, are being attacked (so we learn) with divers calumnies where you are in the city, which is the mother

---

[53] See also Caraman, *John Gerard*, pp. 146–47.

[54] I use Caraman's translation (*Henry Garnet*, pp. 225–26). Lake and Questier argue that clerical prisoners only sought to escape when they were unable to exercise ministries within the prison ("Prisons, Priests, and People," p. 199). Percy's escape tends to substantiate their judgement.

[55] On him see McCoog, *Monumenta Angliae*, vol. 2, pp. 221–22.

[56] On him see McCoog, *Monumenta Angliae*, vol. 2, 235.

[57] Garnet to Acquaviva, December 4, 1596, ARSI, Fondo Gesuitico 651/624.

and mistress of all the Churches, and this befalls us after so many years spent in labours, watchings and perils for the sake of Christ. Certain it is that hereby we are offered notable opportunity of imitating Christ, our Leader, and of wearing His livery.[58]

Nonetheless, Garnet continued, because our good deeds must be seen both by God and by our fellow men and women, he again provided an account of the dispute's origins in the hope that Acquaviva would pass the information on to Clement VIII lest the pope believe any accusation levelled against English Jesuits. Even if, as critics claimed, there was tension between Jesuits and some clergy that occasionally became acrimonious, why should Jesuits be blamed as instigators? Garnet reiterated his earlier assertion that Jesuits aided and supported secular clergy. At Wisbech 20 clerics separated themselves from the others and established a more appropriately religious daily order. Their opponents were "neither of the very learned or the very good."[59] But after an investigation they abrogated many of their rules in order to live in peace with the others. At no time during the controversy did Jesuits attempt to oppress secular clergy or to oblige them to abide by quasi-monastic rules. Even if it were true, why should the Society of Jesus be held responsible since secular clergy comprised the majority of the 20 who preferred a more orderly life? Why not blame the secular clergy for involving Jesuits in their own internal battles?

Attendance at Protestant services remained a second source of friction. Certain priests continued to defend the practice despite Clement VIII's condemnation in a conversation with Cardinal Allen. Jesuits consistently contested this position. But this could not be cited as an example of Jesuit oppression because if the Society did not refute their arguments, the Catholic cause would suffer severely. Moreover some priests contemplated leaving the Church over this issue. As many as 15 other secular clergy lived scandalously "some by becoming open heretics, others by becoming open schismatics ... others are living in pretended marriage." Jesuits opposed them whenever they taught or wrote heretical doctrines or impugned the good name of the papacy or the Society of Jesus. Even if outspoken opposition to heresy prompted some to label Jesuits oppressors, Garnet would not moderate the attack. Again Garnet stressed how secular clergy in England often turned to the Society in their need. If Jesuits could provide assistance, if they were able to support poor Catholics, if the Society's benefactors who supplied it with alms, and if Jesuit candidates bestowed their patrimonies on the mission, should not the Society's generosity be

---

[58] Garnet to Acquaviva, London December 10, 1596, ABSI, Anglia II, 19 with copies in ABSI, Coll P II 566–67 and ARSI, Angl. 31/I, fols 132^r–133^v (published in Renold, *Wisbech Stirs*, pp. 199–206).

[59] Renold, *Wisbech Stirs*, p. 202.

praised? Instead they accused the Society of seeking material gain to the detriment of secular clergy. Why would they do that? There was no need for Jesuits "to lay up treasure, who come here to practice poverty, and who, if we happen to be sent into exile, have so large a kindred to see to our wants."[60] Jesuits in England were exemplary, Garnet contended. Indeed:

> As things are, forsooth we are afforded scant leisure and opportunity for the oppression of others. How could we find ourselves otherwise, when we live in daily expectation of death, when we keep with God's help ever before our minds, thoughts which may prepare us to endure death bravely for Christ's sake? Assuredly, such thoughts have nothing to do with jealousy, strife, envy, conceit and suchlike states of mind which breed contempt and oppression of others. Rather do they breed humility, love, entire contempt of the world and of worldly honours, which virtues is the main object of religious life to foster.[61]

Troubles there were in England, Garnet agreed, but he concluded with a plea that Acquaviva not add to them by heeding anti-Jesuit critics in Rome and abandoning the English College.

Garnet's letters to Acquaviva intimated that the peace established at Wisbech by an accord of November of 1595 was not holding. Discontent still lurked beneath the surface. Recently stiffer control and tighter regulations reduced visitors and, thus, the alms received by the priests. Enforced poverty was an issue that occasioned bickering between the two groups as Christopher Bagshaw and his associates accused Weston, and Jesuits in general, of hoarding money and diverting in to their own use. The arrival of Robert Fisher from Rome in September of 1596 transformed these quarrels into another public dispute.

Robert Fisher, as we shall see in the next chapter, had been sent as an envoy by students opposed to the Society's administration of the English College to establish contact with the anti-Weston faction in Wisbech. In Belgium he met with Charles Paget and William Gifford. Upon arrival in England, he contacted Christopher Bagshaw at Wisbech and relayed to him instructions from the group in Belgium. Fisher coordinated the activities of three groups united in their opposition to the Jesuits and in their determination to remove the Society from the governance of the seminaries and from the mission in general. For these reasons they promoted dissension, circulated rumors about Jesuits, and negotiated with the English government in hope of gaining tolerance at the expense of the Society. Presumably these were the "patriots" lauded in the *State of*

---

[60] Renold, *Wisbech Stirs*, p. 203.
[61] Renold, *Wisbech Stirs*, p. 204.

English Fugitives. Fisher travelled throughout England between London, the north, Cambridge and Wisbech, for a year, forging an alliance between the Society's opponents despite their own differences. In light of Fisher's activities and his success, and his subsequent admission that he was not the first to initiate contact among the three groups, Penelope Renold opined that the stirs of 1595 were most probably an attempt by Bagshaw and his allies "to establish a recognisable anti-Jesuit party in England, parallel to those in Flanders and in Rome."[62] Whether such a desire was at the root of the stirs may be debated; that it was a consequence, is without doubt. Arnold Pritchard astutely observed that a major reason for the failure to conclude another agreement at Wisbech after the collapse of the accord of November was the realization that friction there was not isolated incident but one of a series of conflicts involving the Society of Jesus. Issues were more complicated than a common daily order at Wisbech and they affected the future of Catholicism in England.[63]

"in caves, in secret and unfrequented places": Jesuit Life in Scotland without the Catholic Earls

"This yeere [1596] is a remarkable yeere to the Kirk of Scotland, bothe for the beginning and for the end of it," asserted David Calderwood:

> The Kirk of Scotland was now come to her perfectioun, and the greatest puritie that ever she atteaned unto, both in doctrine and discipline, so that her beautie was admirable to forraine kirks. The assemblies of the sancts were never so glorious, nor profitable to everie one of the true members thereof, than in the beginning of this yeere. There was good appearance of further reformation of abuses and corruptions, which were espied, when the covenant with God was renued first in the Generall Assemblie, then in particular synods and presbyteries.[64]

Despite perfection, the Kirk still encountered problems that she thought threatened its survival. The Kirk feared that "the craft and policie of politicians and dissembled Papists" would aid the return from exile

---

[62] Renold, *Wisbech Stirs*, p. xvii.

[63] Arnold Pritchard, *Catholic Loyalism in Elizabethan England* (London, 1979), pp. 93–94.

[64] Thomas Thomson, (ed.), *Calderwood's History of the Kirk of Scotland* (8 vols, Edinburgh 1842–1849), vol. 5, pp. 387–88. Again unless specifically noted, I follow his (vol. 5, pp. 387–535) and Andrew Lang's narratives and *A History of Scotland from the Roman Occupation* (4 vols, Edinburgh/London, 1900–1907), vol. 2, pp. 401–24).

of George Gordon, Earl of Huntly, and Francis Hay, Earl of Erroll. Presbyterian vigilance was even more required after a royal proclamation of January 2 broadcast a Spanish threat without mentioning the role of the earls. According to the proclamation, Philip II continued pursuing a policy directed towards the conquest of England and the acquisition of its crown. The implications of that policy for Scotland were obvious:

> And now, what perell this his pretended conqueist, incace it succeeded, (as God forbid), might carie with it to the estate of our countrie, we leave to the consideratioum of anie Scotish man that is not blinded with his buddes, how so great and ambitious a monarch, of nature ever givin to conquering, professing, yea, the onlie patron of that tyrannick and bloodie religioun, which is directlie opposite to that truthe which, in the great merceis of God, we professe, can become our neerest nighbour, undivided by seas or anie other impediment, without the eminent hazard of our utter thraldome both in soule and bodie, the subversioun of our crowne and estat, and the redacting of this whole natioun (so long free) in a perpetuall slaverie, the accustomed fortune of all the countreis that are by force brought under his dominioun.[65]

To prevent any Spanish aggression, James urged his countrymen to be ready for battle. To prevent Spain from taking advantage of any internal problems, James sought to restore order and a respect for law by punishing "the horners, and all other contemners therof, as by giving order for taking away, and pulling put by the root, the whole disordered deidlie feeds and bloodie inimiteis within our realme."[66] Moreover, because in the past Spain encouraged border skirmishes to strain Scottish relations with England, James exhorted all subjects along the border "not onlie to desist and ceasse from all violence and hostilitie against the opposite borders of England, but farther, to mainteane and increasse, by their loving and courteous behaviour toward them, that happie amitie inviolablie continued betuixt us, the two princes, during the whole space of both our raignes, as the nearenesse of blood betuixt our two persons, the uniformitie in the true religioun, (the greatest bond of amitie that can bind true Christians,) and the likenesse in language and maners, most justly do require."[67] Such language may have appeased Elizabeth but she did not display her gratitude

---

[65] Thomson, *Calderwood*, vol. 5, p. 390.
[66] Thomson, *Calderwood*, vol. 5, p. 390.
[67] Thomson, *Calderwood*, vol. 5, p. 392. See also Susan Doran, "Loving and Affectionate Cousins? The Relationship between Elizabeth I and James VI of Scotland 1586–1603," in *Tudor England and its Neighbours*, (eds.) Susan Doran and Glenn Richardson (Basingstoke, 2005), pp. 203–34.

by furnishing promised financial assistance. The king needed money: if Spain provided some, few doubted that James would alter his stance.

In the beginning of 1596 James and his council appointed eight commissioners, nicknamed "Octavians," to supervise royal revenue and expenditure: Alexander Seton, Lord President of the Court of Session; William Stewart, Prior of Blantyre; David Carnegie, Laird of Colluthie; John Lindsay of Baccaras; James Elphinstone of Innernaughty; Thomas Hamilton of Drumcairn; John Skene of Curriehall; and Peter Young, James's old tutor. All were respected legalists; many were understandably suspected of Catholic leanings: Elphinstone had a Jesuit brother who arrived in Scotland in late 1595 and Alexander Seton was educated by Jesuits at Rome's German College.[68]

On March 25 James addressed the General Assembly in Edinburgh. To resist the common enemy of the true faith, James requested contributions to the national defense. If the kingdom was in need, Andrew Melville replied, the king should appropriate monies and lands from the exiled earls. On the eve of their exile, James had promised the earls that their wives and children would continue to enjoy their estates in their absence. Thus James could not confiscate anything. The assembly refused to capitulate, and continued to agitate for a more aggressive treatment of the earls' families and heirs. The elimination of Catholicism was but one aspect of the assembly's proposals for a radical reform of religious abuses and unwarranted practices within the kingdom. One grievance named Jesuits Robert Abercrombie and Alexander MacQuhirrie, who was no longer in Scotland, as being "interteaned within the countrie, deteaning suche as they have perverted in their errours, and enducing others in the same corruptioun, and holding them in hope of the returning of the Popish lords, with assistance of strangers."[69] To remedy this problem the assembly wanted James to seek and apprehend them along with other well-known Catholics.

Four Jesuits remained in Scotland after James Gordon's departure for the continent: Abercrombie, William Murdoch, George Christie, and George Elphinstone.[70] Gordon was the mission's superior. Claudio

---

[68] William Forbes-Leith, S.J., *Narratives of Scottish Catholics under Mary Stuart and James VI* (Edinburgh, 1885), p. 279; Maurice Lee, Jr., "King James's Popish Chancellor," in *The Renaissance and Reformation in Scotland: Essays in Honour of Gordon Donaldson*, (eds.) Ian B. Cowan and Duncan Shaw (Edinburgh, 1983), p. 170.

[69] Thomson, *Calderwood*, vol. 5, p. 416.

[70] Elphinstone left Scotland sometime in late 1596 on some unspecified business with Acquaviva and William Chisholm, Bishop of Vaison. He returned around June of 1597. See Acquaviva to Bishop of Vaison, Rome, November 16, 1596, ARSI, Lugd. 1, fols 251ʳ⁻ᵛ; same to Elphinstone, Rome November 16, 1596, ARSI, Lugd. 1, fol. 251ᵛ; same to Crichton, Rome January 25, 1597, ARSI, Fl. Belg. 1/II, pp. 633–34; same to Gordon, Rome March 8, 1597,

Acquaviva and James Tyrie designated Abercrombie vice-superior because they believed Gordon's continental sojourn would be brief. Abercrombie's long experience on the mission qualified him for the position.[71] Without the earls, conditions were considerably less favorable to Jesuits. Lacking sufficient funds, they could not afford books and liturgical items. Unable to afford anything new, they mended and repaired the secular clothing they wore to avoid recognition. Recent edicts threatened with loss of life and possessions all who offered hospitality to Jesuits. Consequently Jesuits hesitated turning to Catholics for aid lest they endangered their benefactors.[72] According to Abercrombie, Jesuits lived "in caves, in secret and unfrequented places, perpetually moving from place to place, like the gipsies, and ... never lodge[d] two nights in the same locality, for fear of falling into the hands of the enemy. Spies and officers are posted at all inns, and in every parish, to discover our whereabouts, and give us up to the authorities." He claimed that Robert Bowes, English ambassador to Scotland, offered 10,000 Scottish pounds for his apprehension but "I have hitherto escaped, for it would be unfair that I should be sold for more than my dearest Lord was." Indeed Bowes asserted that the elimination of Abercrombie, William Douglas, Earl of Angus, and James Wood, Laird of Boniton,[73] would ensure Protestant victory. Catholic fervor persisted despite the temporary destruction of their cause:

> I sometimes go to an inn, and indeed, more than one, where the master of the house is a Catholic, but his wife and the rest of the family are heretics. I am lodged in an inner room, where the Catholic friends of my host cannot come to see me by the door-way, for fear of being observed; so they put up long ladders at the back of the house, and come in and leave by the window. Persons over sixty years of age will sometimes visit us in this way during the night, but the inmates of the house cannot imagine who they are, since no one is seen entering the house.[74]

Perhaps such devotion was a partial explanation why Alexander MacQuhirrie was anxious to return to Scotland despite threats and

---

ARSI, Fl. Belg. 1/II, p. 637; same to Elphinstone, Rome April 3, 1597, ARSI, Lugd. 1, fols 258ᵛ–259ʳ; same to Bishop of Vaison, Rome June 20, 1597, ARSI, Lugd. 1, fols 260ᵛ–261ʳ.

[71] Acquaviva to William Crichton, Rome January 13, 1596, ARSI, Fl. Belg. 1/I, p. 588.

[72] "Instructio pro Missione Scotica," n.d. [c. 1596], ARSI, Angl. 42, fol. 44ʳ.

[73] On Wood see Francis Shearman, "James Wood of Boniton," *The Innes Review*, 5 (1954): pp. 28–32.

[74] Abercrombie to [Acquaviva or Tyrie], Scotland June 7, 1596, ARSI, Angl. 42, fols 97ʳ⁻ᵛ. Much of the letter was published in Forbes-Leith, *Narratives of Scottish Catholics*, pp. 226–29.

deprivation.[75] James Gordon was also ready to return in early May. The Belgian provincial George Duras, however, delayed Gordon's departure because he doubted the time was ripe. In late October Gordon was still waiting in Belgium for Duras's decision. Acquaviva finally asked Duras to lift the restriction and allow Gordon to return whenever his nephew, the earl of Huntly, agreed. The general recommended the earl discuss the prospect with Abercrombie and reminded Gordon that they must consider the common good and not simply their personal preferences.[76]

In Scotland there were hints that Catholic prospects were improving by the summer. The earls negotiated their return to Scotland as James's agents discussed papal subsidies with Pope Clement VIII. Henrietta, Countess Huntly used her influence at court to intercede for her husband. Indeed Anne of Denmark's continued preference for Catholics occasioned rumors about her conversion. The Jesuit George Christie, betrayed sometime in the spring, was brought before the king. About the meeting we know nothing, but William Forbes-Leith, S.J., contended that James treated him kindly before telling him to leave the kingdom.[77] By 1597 Christie was serving as a military chaplain in Belgium.[78]

In August the Estates General convened in Falkland. On the 12th the earls of Huntly and Erroll requested permission to return home from their exile. The Kirk strongly opposed their request. James liked Huntly and believed that his exile had taught him a lesson. Moreover Huntly was useful in obtaining Catholic support for James's succession to the English throne. Alexander Seton urged that they be allowed to return lest "lyke Coriolanus the Roman, or Themistocles the Athenian, they sould joyne with the enemeis, and creat an unresistable danger to the estat of the countrie."[79] Melville protested that their return threatened the kingdom and the Kirk, and he accused of treason all who supported the motion. The estates concluded that if the king and the Kirk were satisfied, the earls should be allowed to return. Any return, therefore, was conditional. On October 19 Countess Huntly proposed acceptable conditions to the Synod of Moray at Elgin. Her husband was willing to submit to a trial and to accept the court's decision. Moreover he promised to provide guarantees that he would not attempt to subvert the established religion of

---

[75] Acquaviva to MacQuhirrie, Rome March 2, 1596, ARSI, Fl. Belg. 1/I, p. 595.

[76] Acquaviva to Gordon, Rome May 11, 1596, ARSI, Fl. Belg. 1/I, p. 608a; same to same, Rome October 28, 1596, ARSI, Fl. Belg. 1/II, p. 626.

[77] Acquaviva to John Hay, Rome July 6, 1596, ARSI, Fl. Belg. 1/I, p. 613; Forbes-Leith, *Narratives of Scottish Catholics*, pp. 261–62.

[78] ARSI, Fl. Belg. 43, fol. 23ʳ.

[79] Thomson, *Calderwood*, vol. 5, p. 438. See also Lee, "King James's Popish Chancellor," p. 174.

the kingdom and even "banish and eject from his companie and societie all Jesuits, Seminarie preests, excommunicated persons, and notorious knowne Papists."[80] Freed from such pernicious influence, Huntly would listen to the theological arguments of orthodox ministers, support a minister in his own house, and conform to Protestant discipline. In return he asked that his excommunication be lifted so that he could remain in Scotland undisturbed, and that he be given a reasonable amount of time in order to decide between churches. The ministers agreed and the earls were permitted to return until May of 1597 in the hope that they would conform. Both apparently were in Scotland before the decision was made: Huntly was in northern Scotland by the beginning of August and Erroll returned by October.[81]

The Kirk remained apprehensive. Commissioners of the General Assembly and synods protested the return of the earls at their meeting in Edinburgh on 20 October. They doubted their sincerity "so of necessitie, as yitt, seing there remaines in them the same dispositioun and ground of caus, wherupon their whole mischeefes have proceeded, the same effects must follow their credit, peace, and advancement, to the subversioun of religioun, wracke of the countrie, hazard of his Majestie's estat and person, and of the estat and lives of all good men within the land."[82] The commissioners proclaimed a national day of fasting on the first Sunday of December and ordered the excommunication of the earls to be broadcast through the kingdom the following Sunday. They summoned Seton to appear before the Synod of Lothian on 2 November because of his actions in favor of Huntly. To restore harmonious relations between king and Kirk, the commissioners sent a delegation to explain the issues that offended them: favorable treatment of the earls; Countess Huntly's privileged position at court and her presence at the baptism of James's daughter Elizabeth; the appointment of Eleanor, Lady Livingstone, the earl of Erroll's sister and "a professed Papist, and at the point of excommunicatioun," as Elizabeth's governess; and James's attacks on the ministers and their theology.[83] In

---

[80] Thomson, *Calderwood*, vol. 5, p. 442.

[81] Helen Georgia Stafford, *James VI of Scotland and the Throne of England* (New York/London, 1940), p. 172. See also Michael Graham, *The Uses of Reform. 'Godly Discipline' and Popular Behaviour in Scotland and Beyond, 1560–1610* (Leiden, 1996), pp. 261–65. Graham notes how royal pressure prevented the Kirk from fully implementing the penalties of excommunication.

[82] Thomson, *Calderwood*, vol. 5, pp. 445–46.

[83] Thomson, *Calderwood*, vol. 5, p. 451. Princess Margaret was placed with her older sister at the Livingstones shortly after her birth on December 24, 1598. She remained there until her death in 1600. See Maureen M. Meikle, "A meddlesome princess: Anna of Denmark and Scottish court politics, 1589–1603," in *The Reign of James VI*, (eds.) Julian Goodare and Michael Lynch (Edinburgh, 2008), p. 138.

the ensuing controversy the Kirk expressed concern about the religion of Queen Anne. Tempers rose as king and Kirk defined their positions. In early November James learned that David Black had attacked him and Queen Elizabeth in sermons in St Andrews. As James moved against him, the commissioners initiated proceedings against Countess Huntly and Lady Livingstone. More important they denied that Black was accountable to the king and proclaimed their own jurisdiction. The Privy Council retaliated by declaring the work of the commissioners illegal and ordering them to return to their flocks. James vacillated until a religious riot in Edinburgh on December 17 provided him with a perfect opportunity to act. The court withdrew to Linlithgrow on the 18th. James denounced the ministers for their treasonous sermons and introduced new measures to restrict their power and influence in Edinburgh. Henceforth no assemblies would convene in Edinburgh and ministers were forbidden to live together. James reasserted his jurisdiction over preachers. Surprisingly the ministers capitulated: some were imprisoned while others fled to England.[84] James returned to his capital on January 1, 1597. The year that began so auspiciously for David Calderwood ended badly:

> In a word, the end of this yeere beganne that dooleful decay and declynning of this kirk, which has continued to this houre, proceeding from worse to worse; so that now we see such corruptioun as we thought not to have seene in our dayes.[85]

Yes, despite Calderwood's pessimistic conclusion, the commissioners notched up one victory: James concluded that the "Octavians," especially Alexander Seton, were more a liability than an asset and transferred their authority to the Protestant William Stewart, Lord Treasurer.

For "Christ's Catholic Religion": Planning for a New Mission to Ireland

A cease-fire signed in Ireland on January 26, 1596 was scheduled to last until April 1 with a possible extension until May 1. May was also the *terminus ad quem* recommended to Philip II by Hugh Roe O'Donnell and Hugh O'Neill, Earl of Tyrone, for any effective Spanish support. The Irish confederates believed that the cities would support their cause as soon as Spanish soldiers arrived. Spain was already assured of support

---

[84] Acquaviva congratulated Crichton on the wonderful developments for the restoration of Catholicism in Scotland. There were excellent reasons for hope and he wished King James health and peace (Acquaviva to Crichton, Rome January 28, 1597, ARSI, Fl. Belg. 1/II, pp. 633–34). Presumably Crichton had written about James's actions against the Kirk.

[85] Thomson, *Calderwood*, vol. 5, p. 388.

in Waterford, Kinsale, Cork and Limerick. In May, three Spanish ships arrived separately. The first sailed from Santander under Ensign Alonso Cobos; the second from Lisbon under Captains Cisneros and Medinilla and the third, from La Coruña, under Ensigns Montero and Jimenez. Philip sent the three ships to ensure that one would arrive. Arriving first, Cobos reminded O'Neill, O'Donnell and their associates of the Iberian roots of the Gaelic inhabitants of Ireland, and of Pope Adrian IV's gift of Ireland to England. Because of Elizabeth's subsequent deviation from the Catholic faith, Cobos claimed that Philip would help their struggle against her. The Irish agreed to abandon attempts to negotiate a settlement with Elizabeth, even though, they claimed, they had been offered peaceful occupation and freedom of worship, and to accept Philip's sovereignty. In return they were promised military assistance and the possibility of having as their monarch Archduke Albert.[86]

Barely had Cobos departed when Cisneros and Medinilla arrived. Unlike Cobos, the second ship carried munitions to be divided among the confederates. O'Neill and O'Donnell discussed specific landing sites for a future armada; they recommended Galway and Limerick as most suitable, and the possibility of naming the archduke as king of Ireland. Confident that negotiations with the first two ships were sufficient, O'Neill and O'Donnell did not meet with Montero and Jimenez, leaders of the third expedition. Having committed themselves to a Spanish alliance, O'Neill and O'Donnell abandoned negotiations with the English in the late spring of 1596 and awaited Spanish aid. Any chance that it would arrive in 1596 ended when an ill wind destroyed much of the fleet in October. Meanwhile circulars exhorted Irish to join O'Neill and O'Donnell in defending "Christ's Catholic religion."[87] More and more O'Neill portrayed his cause as a Catholic crusade. On November 23, trader's reports claimed that

---

[86] Cobos also carried a letter to Philip II from Seán MacGrath, O.F.M., superior of the Franciscan friary in Donegal. See Benignus Millet, O.F.M., "The Guardian of Donegal Friary Appeals to Philip II of Spain, 1596," *Collectanea Hibernica*, 27–28 (1985–1986): pp. 7–10; Henry A. Jefferies, *The Irish Church and the Tudor Reformations* (Dublin, 2010), p. 268.

[87] In 1596 O'Neill began to imitate James FitzMaurice FitzGerald in the formation of a "faith and fatherland" ideology. See Hiram Morgan, "Hugh O'Neill and the Nine Years War in Tudor Ireland," *Historical Journal*, 36 (1993): pp. 21–37; *idem*, "Faith and Fatherland or Queen and Country? An Unpublished Exchange between O'Neill and the State at he Height of the Nine Years War," *Journal of the O'Neill Country Historical Society*, 9 (1994): pp. 9–65; *idem*,"'Faith & Fatherland' in Sixteenth-Century Ireland," *History Ireland*, 3/2 (1995): pp. 13–20; "'Never any Realm Worse Governed': Queen Elizabeth and Ireland," *Transactions of the Royal Historical Society*, 14 (2004): pp. 295–308. Around this time continental publications began extolling O'Neill's victories and successes. See Hiram Morgan, "Policy and Propaganda in Hugh O'Neill's Connection with Europe," in *The Ulster Earls and Baroque Europe. Refashioning Irish Identities, 1600–1800*, (eds.) Thomas O'Connor and Mary Ann Lyons (Dublin, 2010), pp. 18–20.

O'Neill had rejected Elizabeth's offer of a pardon and had expelled all public heretics and had commissioned ecclesiastical authorities to examine others for heresy.[88]

The situation in Ireland remained volatile in early 1597 as Sir William Russell awaited his replacement Thomas, Lord Burgh as lord deputy. On May 22, 1597 Burgh pronounced the oath and received the sword of office with strict instructions to resolve all problems. With 2,500 troops sent to strengthen English forces, the lord deputy planned an aggressive solution to the problem of O'Neill. But after a few minor initial successes, Lord Burgh retreated to Newry in August of 1597, and left O'Neill unchallenged in the north. On October 13, Lord Burgh died unexpectedly from typhus; Sir John Norris, his logical successor, had died the previous month. The Elizabethan government lost two leaders and desertion soon depleted its forces. The Privy Council instructed the earl of Ormond, Thomas Butler, now military commander of the English forces in Ireland, to negotiate with O'Neill. In December of 1597, O'Neill laid down his conditions: in return for a truce of two months and withdrawal from Leinster, he demanded a pardon for himself and for all involved in the Leinster rebellion, liberty of conscience, and withdrawal of all English garrisons from Ulster and other Gaelic areas. Moreover he refused to hand over his son as a hostage. Agreement was not immediate but a truce was declared as the two sides discussed the other conditions.[89]

Sometime in 1596 Irish exiles on the continent petitioned Pope Clement VIII to authorize a Jesuit mission to Ireland:

> Most Holy Father, there is a good seed that through the mercy of God has been preserved to us, namely some of our countrymen, who are priests of the Society of Jesus, men fit to bring forth the greatest fruit in our fatherland. We, therefore, humbly beseech your Holiness, that some of these priests be sent by your orders and under your auspices to Ireland, where the crop is ripe for harvesting, in the same way as similar missions have been dispatched to

---

[88] Printed in J. Hagan, "Miscellanea Vaticano-Hibernica, 1580–1631 (Vatican Archives: Borghese Collection)," *Archivium Hibernicum*, 3 (1914): p. 234. Throughout 1595 and 1596 significant Irish successes were reported in newsletters to papal officials. Reports of the arrival of Spanish troops to support the Irish were also common. One visitor to Brussels in May of 1595 testified that "the queen never feared anything so much as the present disturbance in Ireland." See the different reports in Cathaldus Giblin, O.F.M., "Catalogue of Material of Irish Interest in the Collection *Nunziatura di Fiandra*, Vatican Archives: Part 1, vols 1–50," *Collectanea Hibernica*, 1 (1958): pp. 47–51.

[89] I follow the basic narrative in Cyril Falls, *Elizabeth's Irish Wars* (London, 1996), pp. 193–210; Steven G. Ellis, *Tudor Ireland: Crown, Community and the Conflict of Cultures 1470–1603* (London, 1985), pp. 302–304; Hiram Morgan, *Tyrone's Rebellion* (Woodbridge, 1993), pp. 199–213.

other countries to reclaim them from heresy or preserve them in the Catholic religion.[90]

Perhaps as a reply to their request, James Archer arrived in Ireland by October. There is no evidence that Acquaviva authorized Archer's journey. As we saw in the last chapter, Acquaviva left all decisions about Archer's trips to solicit alms for the Irish College to González Dávila and Francisco de Porres, provincial of Toledo. Perhaps they approved a trip to Ireland without consulting Acquaviva since finding support for the college was one of Archer's aims. He planned too to examine conditions in Ireland in hope of launching a new Jesuit mission. On October 2, 1596 Lord Deputy Sir William Russell reported that Archer and "divers other Jesuits" had landed at Waterford, forerunners of a Spanish invasion. He was, however, the only Jesuit. Fearful of Archer's influence, the government proclaimed him a traitor and offered a substantial reward for his capture or murder. However Archer did not openly commit himself to the cause of O'Neill and O'Donnell until 1598.[91]

Acquaviva obviously had decided to send Jesuits to Ireland because he contacted different Irishmen whom he wanted for the mission. In April, he told Lorenzo Maggio, Jesuit provincial of Venice, to send Christopher Holywood to Rome. Six weeks later, Acquaviva allowed the provincial to postpone Holywood's departure lest his sudden withdrawal inconvenience the college in Padua where he was lecturing on scholastic theology. Holywood, unaware that he was destined for the Irish mission, did not wish to come to Rome, thus forcing Acquaviva to reconsider the assignment. By June Acquaviva still wanted Holywood for the mission despite his unwillingness and advised Maggio to be prepared for his sudden departure. Meanwhile Maggio was to warn Holywood of this so that he could reflect on this possible mission as he made a retreat in preparation for final vows. In the autumn Acquaviva transferred Holywood from Padua to Milan to lecture on theology: he was more needed there and his eventual departure for Ireland would be less a burden.[92]

---

[90] "Articuli quidam cum supplicatione Suae Sanctitati nomine Ibernorum exulum proponendi," IJA, MS B.21 (published in Edmund Hogan S.J., *Ibernia Ignatiana* [Dublin, 1880], pp. 35–37). I use the translation in Samantha A. Meigs, *The Reformations in Ireland: Tradition and Confessionalism, 1400–1690* (London/New York, 1997), p. 100.

[91] Thomas Morrissey, S.J., "The Irish Student Diaspora in the Sixteenth Century and the Early Years of the Irish College at Salamanca," *Recusant History*, 14 (1978): p. 254; Thomas Morrissey, S.J., *James Archer of Kilkenny: An Elizabethan Jesuit* (Dublin, 1979), pp. 17–18. See also Fergus M. O'Donoghue, S.J., "The Jesuit Mission in Ireland 1598–1651" (unpublished Ph.D. thesis, Catholic University of America, 1981) pp. 21–22.

[92] Acquaviva to Maggio, Rome April 27, 1596, ARSI, Venet. 4/I, fol. 169^r; same to same, Rome June 1, 1596, ARSI, Venet. 4/I, fol. 174^v; same to same, July 29, 1596, ARSI,

Acquaviva selected John Gerrott, a professor of controversial theology at the Jesuit college in Vienna, for the mission. The Austrian provincial Ferdinand Alber, reluctant to relinquish much needed men, protested. Acquaviva, consequently, allowed Gerrott to remain temporarily but argued that other Jesuits could assume his place on the Viennese faculty but a mission to Ireland was a work for the Irish.[93] Gerrott stayed in Austria. Despite Acquaviva's failure to extract Gerrott and Holywood's unwillingness to leave Padua, the general emphasized the mission's importance to Dr Peter Lombard, later O'Neill's agent in Rome and archbishop of Armagh. He promoted it as zealously as he could because he believed that he was failing to employ Jesuits properly if he did not send them there where they could do great work for God's service.[94]

Jesuit interest in Ireland waned in early 1597 probably as a result of the death of Acquaviva's assistant James Tyrie on March 20.[95] An undated memo drafted for a meeting to discuss the Irish mission some time after Tyrie's death but before the arrival of Parsons (he arrived at the end of the month), told of Oliver Mannaerts's willingness to send two Jesuits in his province to Ireland: Henry FitzSimon for reasons of health, and Walter Talbot, a secular priest who had entered the Society in Tournai on May 10, 1595. The Belgian, taking as much interest in a mission to Ireland as he had taken about the initiation of a mission to England in 1579, recommended that Irish Jesuits obtain faculties similar to those held by Jesuits in England. Acquaviva promised to request these from Girolamo Mattei, Cardinal Protector. At the meeting, Acquaviva and Parsons decided that Archer should be the mission's superior as long as he wrote frequently to Rome and did not leave Ireland without Acquaviva's permission.[96] On the other hand, on March 14, 1598 Acquaviva, complaining that he had heard nothing from Archer since his departure for Ireland, claimed that he would not make any decision about a new Jesuit mission until he received some information on the conditions within Ireland.[97]

Venet. 4/I, fol. 183ᵛ; same to same, Rome March 8, 1597, ARSI, Venet. 4/I, fol. 226ʳ; same to same, Rome June 28, 1597, ARSI, Venet. 4/II, fols 247ʳ–248ᵛ; same to same, Rome July 19, 1597, ARSI, Venet. 4/II, fol. 250ʳ; same to same, Rome October 11, 1597, ARSI, Venet. 4/II, fols 263ᵛ–265ʳ; same to Giovanni Francesco Vipera, Rome November 8, 1597, ARSI, Med. 22/I, fol. 109ᵛ.

[93] Acquaviva to Alber, Rome November 16, 1596, ARSI, Austr. 1/II, p. 745.
[94] Acquaviva to Lombard, Rome November 16, 1596, ARSI, Fl. Belg. 1/II, p. 628.
[95] Acquaviva to Maggio, Rome June 28, 1597, ARSI, Ven. 4/II, fols 247ʳ–248ᵛ.
[96] ARSI, Angl. 31/II, fol. 703ᵛ.
[97] ARSI, Fl. Belg. 1/II, p. 671. See also Acquaviva to Mannaerts, Rome March 14, 1598, ARSI, Fl. Belg. 1/II, pp. 670–71.

Ottavio Mirto Frangipani, Nuncio at Brussels, kept Rome informed of all military and political developments in Ireland.[98] News was favorable as Irish leaders anticipated Spanish and, perhaps Scottish aid.[99] Ominously for Elizabeth, King James and the earl of Tyrone were in correspondence throughout 1597.[100] Indeed, on December 22 James accepted O'Neill's offer of service but postponed using it until "it shall please God to call our Sister the Queen of England by death." Expecting Parliament, then in session, to discuss the succession, and James's right to it, he hesitated doing anything that would jeopardize his position.[101]

From Lisbon John Howling relayed less reliable information from Irish merchants and "trustworthy" Irish clerics. All proclaimed Irish victories, each one of which led to the reconciliation of more heretics. Some related atrocities committed by the English. It was claimed that shortly before his death, Sir John Norris martyred "many Irish nobles" because they had sheltered Roman Catholic priests. Because of the reconciliation of so many, there was a greater need for more bishops and Jesuits. Howling assured Acquaviva that Irish Jesuits in Portugal were ready to depart for the mission as soon as the general approved. Reconciliation of so many nobles raised the persistent problem of the rightful ownership of the ecclesiastical property which they had appropriated. Forfeiture of ecclesiastical property by any Irish noble was a public declaration of his Catholicism that could result in confiscation of said property and in loss of the noble's life. Bishops could grant necessary dispensations and Howling recommended specific Irishmen for such faculties. Finally he suggested that the nobles be permitted to retain their property and revenues for the time being on the condition that they devoted a specified sum annually to support the poor in Ireland and seminarians at the Irish College in Lisbon.[102] For unexplained reasons, this concession was not one of the faculties obtained by Cardinal Mattei in May.[103]

---

[98] As nuncio in Cologne, Frangipani exercised jurisdiction over Flanders. He was named nuncio upon the establishment of a nunciature in Brussels in the spring of 1596. He assumed residence in September. He also exercised some authority over the Catholic Church in England: Frangipani claimed that he held the title of "vice protector" of England (*Correspondance d'Ottavio Mirto Frangipani, Premier Nonce de Flandre (1596–1606)*, (eds.) Leon Van der Essen and Armand Louant (4 vols, Rome/Bruxelles/Paris, 1924–1942), vol. 1, pp. l, lviii).

[99] Giblin, "Catalogue of material of Irish interest," pp. 51–52.

[100] See Doran, "Loving and Affectionate Cousins," pp. 216–18.

[101] Stafford, *James VI of Scotland*, pp. 187–90. James's letter to O'Neill written from Holyroddhouse on 22 December 1597, can be found in *CSP Scotland* (1597–1603), p. 1138.

[102] Howling to Acquaviva, Lisbon October 25, 1597, ARSI, Angl. 31/II, pp. 699–702.

[103] O'Donoghue, "The Jesuit Mission in Ireland," p. 23.

Sowing Discontent and Seeking Ecclesiastical Order

Controversies involving English Jesuits on the continent affected work on the English mission. In 1596 Garnet defended himself and his men against accusations whispered against the Society. But, as 1597 began, Garnet's concerns were more immediate and more personal. John Gerard remained a prisoner in the Clink where he carried out his priestly mission with relative ease and with considerable satisfaction: "everything [was] so arranged that I was able to perform there all the tasks of a Jesuit priest, and provided only I could have stayed on in this prison, I should never have wanted to have any liberty again in England."[104] In early April, a secular priest William Atkinson betrayed Gerard.[105] Although Gerard had arranged accommodation for him upon his arrival in England and had been kind to him, the Jesuit suspected "he was a little unsteady and seemed rather too anxious to be free again."[106] Thus Gerard avoided confidences. Perhaps in an attempt to gain his liberty, Atkinson told the authorities that he had seen Gerard pass a packet of letters from Rome and Brussels to "Little John" (Nicholas Owen) for delivery to Garnet. Moreover this was but the most recent of many such transactions. Without warning, a justice of the peace and two pursuivants entered Gerard's cell with the chief warder. With Gerard were two boys whom he was instructing in preparation for their departure for the continent. They searched his cell but found nothing. Nonetheless Gerard was transferred to the Tower of London on April 12. Ralph Emerson, who knew where Gerard hid everything, collected Gerard's possessions and money from their holes and conveyed everything to Garnet. Locked in a cell in the Salt Tower, Gerard slept on a small amount of straw provided by the warder. The following morning he realized that he was in Henry Walpole's former cell when he saw Walpole's name chiselled on the wall. The next day the warder moved him to a more comfortable cell on the floor above despite Gerard's insistence that he preferred to remain where he was. He explained his motives to the warder who then allowed him to return to Walpole's cell occasionally to pray. The warder also offered to collect a bed from any of Gerard's friends willing to provide one. Gerard sent him to his friends in the Clink and the warder returned with the type of bed Gerard liked, "a simple mattress stuffed with wool and feathers in the Italian style" along

---

[104] Caraman, *John Gerard*, p. 78.

[105] On Atkinson see Anstruther, *Seminary Priests*, vol. 1, p. 13 and Patrick McGrath, "Apostate and Naughty Priests in England under Elizabeth I," in *Opening the Scrolls: Essays in Catholic History in Honour of Godfrey Anstruther*, (ed.) Dominic Aidan Bellenger, O.S.B. (Bath, 1987), pp. 61–62.

[106] Caraman, *John Gerard*, p. 102.

with a coat and some linen.[107] On the 14th the warden returned with the sad news that Sir Richard Berkeley, Lieutenant of the Tower, Sir Edward Coke, Attorney General, Sir Thomas Fleming, Solicitor General, Francis Bacon, and Sir William Waad, Secretary of the Privy Council, waited to examine him in the lieutenant's house in the Tower. The questions treated political matters.[108]

As Spanish forces besieged Calais and England prepared to attack the Spanish coast, the interrogators questioned Gerard about letters he received from Antwerp. He refused to explain how the packets and letters were conveyed and to whom he forwarded them. He denied knowing from whom the letters usually came and claimed that he did not read letters for others enclosed with them. He received other letters "from the parts beyond the seas" but explained that they generally dealt with students at St Omers and financial matters. He simply forwarded letters which "came to him because he had more opportunity to receive them and to convey them over." Again he refused to divulge who sent them or how they were conveyed. Asked specifically about Garnet, Gerard refused to mention any name. When pressed, he explained: "I refuse not for any disloyal mind I protest as I look to be saved but for that I take these things not to have concerned any matter of State with which I would not have dealt nor any other but matters of devotion as before."[109] Gerard repudiated Coke's accusation that Garnet was an enemy of the state with the claim that Gerard was "certain that if he [Garnet] were given the opportunity to lay down his life for his Queen and country, he would be glad to do it."[110] Gerard did not know where Garnet lived but even if he did, he would not tell. The examiners authorized use of torture to obtain the desired information. For nearly a day Gerard was suspended by his hands. As the guards led him back to his cell, they passed prisoners who had the run of the Tower. Hoping that they would relay what they overheard, Gerard loudly protested to the guards that he could never disclose the location of Father Garnet because to do so was to betray an innocent man. The following day Waad again demanded to know Garnet's location. Claiming that both Elizabeth and Sir Robert Cecil believed Garnet to be a meddler in politics and a danger to the state, Waad promised that the "Master of Torture" would torture Gerard twice daily until he revealed his superior's

---

[107] Caraman, *John Gerard*, p. 105.
[108] Caraman, *John Gerard*, pp. 102–106.
[109] TNA, SP 12/262/123 (published in John Morris, S.J., *The Life of Father John Gerard, of the Society of Jesus*, 3rd edn. [London, 1881], pp. 235–38).
[110] Caraman, *John Gerard*, p. 107.

location. But Gerard was tortured only once that day. That was the final time.[111]

Presumably by means of the prisoners who overhead Gerard's comments, news was quickly transmitted to Garnet. By April 23, Garnet knew about Gerard's torture in an attempt to discover information about letters from Spain. On May 7 he told Acquaviva that Gerard:

> hath been twice hanged up by the hands, with great cruelty of others, and not less suffering of his own. The inquisitors here say that he is very obstinate, and that he has a great alliance with God or the devil, as they cannot draw the least word out of his mouth, except that in torment he cried "Jesus." They took him lately to the rack, and the torturers and examiners were there already; but he suddenly, when he entered the place, knelt down and with a loud voice prayed to our Lord that, as He had given grace and strength to some of His saints to bear with Christian patience being torn to pieces for His love, so He would be pleased to give him grace and courage, rather to be dragged into a thousand pieces than to say anything that might injure any person or the Divine glory. And so they left him without tormenting him, seeing him so resolved.[112]

Accurate and speedy information kept Garnet informed of Gerard's treatment.

Garnet's sources told him that Gerard would be tried and condemned and thus he duly warned his subject to expect his interrogators to return. On May 13 Gerard was again examined. No longer interested in Gerard's correspondence or Garnet's location, Attorney General Coke addressed specific questions about his priesthood, his return to England, and his attempts to win converts from the Established Church to Roman Catholicism. Gerard admitted he was a Jesuit and had returned to England to reconcile as many as he could to Catholicism, but he refused to say more. Asked to name those with whom he plotted against the government, Gerard denied involvement in any plot or conspiracy. How could he, the examiners wondered, work for the conversion of England and, at the same time, refrain from political involvement? Gerard made his position very clear:

---

[111] Caraman, *John Gerard*, pp. 107–15.

[112] Garnet to Acquaviva, May 7, 1597, ABSI, Anglia II, 27 (published in Morris, *John Gerard*, pp. 248–49). See also Garnet to Parsons, April 23, 1597, ABSI, Coll P II 547 (published in Morris, *John Gerard*, p. 248). Interestingly Verstegan's sources were not as well informed. On April 18 Verstegan relayed word to Roger Baynes that Gerard was dangerously ill; on May 23 he reported that Gerard was still in the Tower and had been tortured two or three times (ARSI, Angl. 38/II, fols 201^{r-v} [published in Petti, *Verstegan Papers*, pp. 253, 254]).

I will speak my mind plainly in this matter of conversion and politics, so that you will be left in no doubt and have no need to question me further. I call on God and His Angels to bear me out—I am not lying. I am hiding nothing from you that I have at heart. If I could have fulfilled all that I wish and desire, I would want the whole of England to return to Rome and the Catholic faith: the Queen, her Council, and yourselves also, and all the magistrates of this realm; yet so, my Lords, that neither the Queen, nor you, nor any officer of state forfeit the honour or right he now enjoys; so that not a single hair of your head perish; but simply that you may be happy both in this present life and in the life to come. But do not think that I want this conversion for any selfish reason of my own—that I may be freed and may enjoy the good things of life. I call on Almighty God to witness: I would gladly go out to-morrow morning to be hanged just as I stand before you now. These are my thoughts, my aspirations. I am not at enmity with the Queen nor with you, nor have I ever been.[113]

Coke ended the silence that followed Gerard's statement by asking the Jesuit to name Catholics: Gerard refused. Finally the attorney general introduced the dangerous subject of equivocation. Like Southwell and Garnet, Gerard argued there was a difference between equivocation and lying: "in equivocation the intention was not to deceive, which was the essence of a lie, but simply to withhold the truth in cases where the questioned party is not bound to reveal it."[114] Gerard explained the conditions restricting use of equivocation, and cited Scriptural precedents. Although Coke took extensive notes as if for a trial, the law term passed without Gerard's indictment.[115] Gerard's behavior gained him the respect of many. It was even reported that the earl of Essex proclaimed that Gerard should be honored for his constancy. Garnet was also reliably informed that the queen did not desire his execution.[116] Gerard, meanwhile, spent four or five hours a day in meditation as he made the Ignatian Spiritual Exercises during his recovery. At the end of the third week, Gerard could move his fingers, hold a knife, and feed himself.[117]

New recruits and new arrivals augmented Jesuit numbers. Ralph Bickley, imprisoned at Wisbech with William Weston, and Richard Banks still sought admission into the Society and Garnet recommended each

---

[113] Caraman, *John Gerard*, pp. 124–25.

[114] Caraman, *John Gerard*, pp. 125–26.

[115] Caraman, *John Gerard*, pp. 123–27.

[116] Garnet to Parsons, January [sic–June] 10, 1597, ABSI, Coll P II 548; same to Acquaviva, June 11, 1597, ABSI, Anglia II, 29.

[117] Garnet to Parsons, May 28, 1597, ABSI, Coll P II 548; Caraman, *John Gerard*, p. 116.

highly.[118] Thomas Fech and two unnamed men "famous in the University of Cambridge" left for Rome in February. Fech intended to apply for the Society; the other two planned to study at their own expense. For some reason, Garnet tried unsuccessfully to dissuade them from their journey. He hoped they would be no trouble and recommended that they be greeted warmly.[119] Joseph Pullen arrived in England in early February. His travelling companion, Richard Collins, remained in Flanders until late April.[120] Unfortunately one Jesuit Garnet did not expect to see, Thomas Lister, also returned to England.

Garnet thought he had solved the problem of Lister by sending him to Belgium but Lister "after undergoing all the perils of the journey, just outside the port of Antwerp, changed plans dangerously and suddenly, and unexpectedly returned to England." His reappearance troubled Garnet who did not know what to do with him. Lister's difficulties in England stemmed "not so much from disease of the brain as from perturbation and fickleness of mind." Garnet dared not send him to Rome as Acquaviva recommended, but instead asked the general to allow him to settle the problem. William Baldwin, who was in Rome by early February, related the full story to Acquaviva.[121] Robert Parsons, perhaps unaware of Baldwin's mission, summoned Garnet to Rome to report on the work of Jesuits under his care in light of the accusations levelled against English Jesuits, and because of crises developing now on three fronts. If Parsons still desired Garnet's presence despite Baldwin's mission in Rome, Garnet would, of course, obey but he wanted clarification. Other Jesuits in England advised him against going and Garnet himself was not eager to go because he thought his absence would harm the mission. But if he did leave England,

---

[118] Garnet to Parsons, April 15, 1597, ABSI, Coll P II 537; same to same, April 23, 1597, ABSI, Coll P II 547; same to same, May 28, 1597, ABSI, Coll P II 548. Garnet considered sending Banks to Rome because "it will be a source of edification for the malcontents to see him, since he is said to be on their side, but this is quite untrue for he is very well behaved and quiet" (Garnet to Acquaviva, May 7, 1597, ABSI, Anglia II, 27).

[119] Garnet to Acquaviva, February 11, 1597, ARSI, Fondo Gesuitico 651/640; same to same, February 11, 1597, ABSI, Anglia II, 23; same to same, May 7, 1597, ABSI, Anglia II, 27. Fech did join the Society but not until 1601 (McCoog, *Monumenta Angliae*, vol. 2, p. 305). On May 7 Garnet sought Acquaviva's permission to apply Fech's pension to the use of the mission as soon as he entered the Society. Presumably the money was not touched immediately.

[120] Garnet to Acquaviva, February 11, 1597, ARSI, Fondo Gesuitico 651/640; same to same, February 11, 1597, ABSI, Anglia II, 23; same to same, May 7, 1597, ABSI, Anglia II, 27. On Pullen and Collins see McCoog, *Monumenta Angliae*, vol. 2, pp. 277, 440–41.

[121] Garnet to Acquaviva, February 11, 1597, ARSI, Fondo Gesuitico 651/640; same to same, February 11, 1597, ABSI, Anglia II, 23; same to same, May 7, 1597, ABSI, Anglia II, 27.

Lister would accompany him to Belgium. By April, Garnet learned to his relief that Parsons no longer considered Garnet's journey necessary.[122]

Garnet greeted the arrival of each new secular priest with trepidation. Would he bring reports of new quarrels in Rome that would exacerbate current tension in England? Would continental problems continue to infect secular-Jesuit relations in England? To Garnet's relief, two priests openly proclaimed how well they had been welcomed by Jesuits in England, contrary to what they had expected.[123] Robert Fisher, however, was not as complimentary. Fisher claimed that he had been sent to England "to observe how ... [Jesuits] tyrannize" but Garnet doubted that Fisher would discover anything incriminating. Despite the lack of evidence, the Society's foes would continue to lie and pretend that many "men of good will" opposed the Society whereas such Catholics, and indeed many not overly fond of Jesuits, avoided him. Fisher's activities threatened the mission as a wolf dressed in sheep's clothing and not trustworthy. Fearful that Fisher would betray any knowledge, Garnet refused to disclose the location of different Jesuits. Because there was always the possibility that some Catholic would inadvertently tell Fisher their dwelling places, Garnet worried about the consequences.[124]

Robert Fisher persevered in his efforts to turn many against the Jesuits. Attempts to disturb the troubled peace at Wisbech failed to the delight even of some of Weston's opponents. Returning to London after travelling around the kingdom, he teamed up with a former crony from Rome, the Dominican and future apostate John Sacheverell.[125] Together they disseminated lies about Jesuits at the English College. According to them, the rector, Girolamo Fioravanti, not only diverted and alienated the college's revenues to the Society of Jesus but, in an unexplained way, was responsible for the death of some seminarians. More outrageous was their claim that he had accepted a hermaphrodite into the college. A doctor discovered this as he tried to give him/her an enema. A student confirmed the doctor's evaluation. Finally the rector enticed many students to join religious orders to the detriment of the mission. Because of such incompetence and so many abuses, Fisher contended Clement VIII had

---

[122] Garnet to Acquaviva, February 11, 1597, ABSI, Anglia II, 23; Garnet to Parsons, April 1597, ABSI, Coll P II 595.

[123] Sylvester Norris and Richard Button were the two priests. On them see Anstruther, *Seminary Priests*, vol. 1, pp. 60, 255–57. Norris later joined the Jesuits. See McCoog, *Monumenta Angliae*, vol. 2, p. 420. They were sent to England to aid the formation of a party hostile to Spain and to the Society (Parsons to Juan de Idiáquez, Rome July 12, 1597, ABSI, 46/12/3, pp. 687–89).

[124] Garnet to Acquaviva, February 11, 1597, ABSI, Anglia II, 23; Garnet to Acquaviva, May 7, 1597, ABSI, Anglia II, 27.

[125] On Sacheverell see McGrath, "Apostate and Naughty Priests," pp. 64–65.

decided to remove Jesuits from the college's government and would have already done so if Parsons had not urged Philip II to intervene in their defense. The pope, realizing that Jesuits were not qualified to govern seminaries, had removed from their control 15 colleges and seminaries within the archdiocese of Milan over the past year. Fisher hoped to determine whether Jesuits dominated and tyrannized the English mission as they did elsewhere. William Holt was especially guilty of flaunting and abusing his authority. According to Fisher, when Holt sought testimonies in his defense, only two secular priests supported him.[126] Fisher's stories, Garnet believed, were too incredible to cause much damage. Nonetheless, if Acquaviva desired evidence to refute Fisher's allegations, Garnet could easily obtain testimonials from principal Catholic laity and especially secular priests. Garnet did, however, notice that the government welcomed Fisher and other "raisers of the fires of sedition of this sort" and did not subject them to persecution.[127] With such unofficial protection from the government, Garnet worried that Jesuits would be targeted. Many suspected that someone betrayed Gerard "not that this matters greatly, if God in His mercy is with us."[128] Those suspicions were justified.

In the Tower of London John Gerard completed the Spiritual Exercises and recovered the use of his hands. An incident involving Francis Page in early May threatened further examinations with potentially fatal consequences.[129] Page met Gerard in the Clink through the Catholic woman Page intended to marry. As a result Page became first a Catholic, then a priest, and finally before his martyrdom on April 20, 1602, a Jesuit. In the late spring of 1597, Page resided with Gerard's former host, William Wiseman, recently released from prison. Out of devotion to Gerard, Page daily visited the Tower, stood some distance from Gerard's cell, and watched the window in hope of a glimpse of the Jesuit. Finally Gerard recognized him and gave him his blessing from the window. His daily attendance and odd behavior attracted the attention of authorities who seized and examined him. Questioned about Gerard, he revealed nothing but he was retained in the Tower pending further investigations. Once authorities learned with whom he resided, they suspected him of communicating with Gerard via signs. Gerard too was

---

[126] We shall return to charges against Holt in Chapter 6.

[127] Fisher complained that the Jesuits spread stories that he was a spy and only pretended to be a Catholic. As a result he now feared Jesuits more than he did heretics. See Fisher to Christopher Bagshaw, May 16, [1597], IT, Petyt MSS. 538, vol. 38, fol. 376 (printed in Renold, *Wisbech Stirs*, pp. 219–24).

[128] Garnet to Acquaviva, London May 14, 1597, ABSI, Anglia II, 28 (I use the translation published in Renold, *Wisbech Stirs*, pp. 212–18).

[129] On Page see Anstruther, *Seminary Priests*, vol. 1, p. 265; McCoog, *Monumenta Angliae*, vol. 2, p. 425.

questioned but he denied knowing Page and ignored him as they passed in the corridor. On Gerard's return from the examination, he addressed a group of young men, one of whom was Page, and demanded to know if anyone was this Page and why he insisted on claiming that they were friends. A prisoner from May 14 to October 13, Page eventually purchased his liberty and departed for the continent.

Denied visitors, Gerard could not develop a ministry comparable to that in the Clink. But, having obtained a quill to pick his teeth, he fashioned it into a pen and initiated secret correspondence with friends, written in the juice of oranges. From prison he was able to arrange with friends to purchase John Lillie's release from Bridewell. During the summer of 1597 he acquired some books and began to study. On July 31, the anniversary of the death of Ignatius Loyola, during meditation, Gerard wondered whether it would be possible to celebrate Mass in the cell of a Catholic prisoner in the tower opposite Gerard's cell. John Arden[130] was allowed to walk on the roof of the Cradle Tower for exercise. From there he greeted Gerard and asked for his blessing. Arden's wife periodically visited him. She, Gerard concluded, would be able to smuggle all that was needed for Mass. But first Gerard needed the warden's approval for a visit. Exchanging letters in invisible orange juice, Gerard and Arden concocted their plan. Through arguments and bribes, Gerard secured the warden's consent. With the assistance of Lillie, Mrs. Arden conveyed all that was necessary for Mass to the Tower. On September 7, the eve of the feast of the Nativity of the Blessed Virgin (and the birthday of Queen Elizabeth), Gerard crossed to Arden's cell where he spent the night. The following morning, they celebrated Mass together. Afterwards as they chatted, Gerard noted how it would be possible to arrange an escape from that tower. Slowly Gerard made the necessary arrangements after he had obtained Garnet's approval, a necessary precaution because of Acquaviva's disapproval of escapes. William Wiseman was warned to make plans for his arrival and concealment. John Lillie and Richard Fulwood were ready to take the risk. The first attempt on October 3 failed and nearly ended in disaster for Lillie and Fulwood. The following night Arden and Gerard slipped down a rope and escaped by boat with Lillie and Fulwood. Upon landing Lillie accompanied Arden to Gerard's house run by Anne Line. Fulwood and Gerard went to Garnet's house in Spitalfields where Nicholas Owen waited with horses. They immediately departed for Uxbridge where they dined with Garnet.[131]

---

[130] This John Arden had been condemned in 1587 for his alleged involvement in the Babington Plot (Caraman, *John Gerard*, p. 239–40 n).

[131] Caraman, *John Gerard*, pp. 116–23, 128–39. Garnet relayed the news to Parsons on October 8 (ABSI, Coll P II 548). By November 7 Verstegan knew of the escape (Verstegan to Baynes, Antwerp November 7, 1597, ARSI, Angl. 38/II, fol. 201ʳ [published in Petti,

Gerard remained with Garnet a few days "to get my strength back and allow time for the talk about my escape to die down."[132] He then returned to a house owned by the Wisemans near the Clink. Fearful of bringing down even more wrath upon his hosts, he allowed only a few visitors to enter and he ventured forth only at night. He did visit his own house where Anne Line was in charge. In late 1597 Gerard sheltered William Alabaster, poet and former chaplain to the earl of Essex on his expedition against Spain. Alabaster was received into the Roman Church sometime in the autumn of 1597 as a result of his theological studies and disputations with the former Jesuit Thomas Wright.[133] Gerard directed Alabaster through the Spiritual Exercises. A fruit of the retreat was a desire to enter the Society. When Gerard asked him why he chose the Jesuits, he replied:

> There are three principal things ... that have induced me to make this decision. First, the fact that heretics and all enemies of God hold the Society in far greater detestation than any other body. I presume this must be because it has the Spirit of God which the devil cannot abide; and because in God's providence, it is destined to destroy heresy and combat sin of every kind. The second is this. The Society will not allow its members to accept ecclesiastical preferment. Ambition therefore is less likely to affect them, and as their best men are not drawn off they are better able to maintain a tradition of holiness and learning. And thirdly, it has a special regard for obedience. And this is a virtue which I place first in order, both for itself and for the good it can do to people's souls. And, besides, all will be in order with a body of men, if they are united in purpose under the direction of God.[134]

Gerard sent Alabaster to William Holt in Belgium to obtain 300 florins for his expenses. He proceeded to Rome where he entered the English College.[135] Garnet believed that Alabaster had a vocation to the Society.[136]

Verstegan Papers, p. 261]). Richard Blount twice escaped pursuivants at Scotney Castle, Sussex, in 1597/98. For accounts see Henry Foley, S.J., *Records of the English Province of the Society of Jesus* (7 vols in 8 parts, Roehampton/London, 1877–1884) vol. 3, pp. 482–88; Morris, *Troubles of Our Catholic Forefathers*, vol. 1, pp. 187–215.

[132] Caraman, *John Gerard*, p. 140.

[133] Garnet to Parsons, October 8, 1597, ABSI, Coll P II 549; Verstegan to Baynes, Antwerp October 24, 1597, ARSI, Angl. 38/II, fol. 201ʳ (published in Petti, *Verstegan Papers*, p. 259).

[134] Caraman, *John Gerard*, p. 141.

[135] He arrived at the English College on November 30, 1598 (Wilfrid Kelly, (ed.), *Liber Ruber Venerabilis Collegii Anglorum de Urbe* [London, 1940], pp. 112–13). See Alabaster's response to the official questionnaire in Anthony Kenny, (ed.), *The Responsa Scholarum of the English College, Rome* (London, 1962), pp. 1–4. Surprisingly he said nothing of the Spiritual Exercises and Gerard. See also Molly Murray, "'Nowe I am a Catholoque': William Alabaster and the Early Modern Catholic Conversion Narrative," in *Catholic Culture in Early Modern England*, (eds.) Ronald Corthell, Frances E. Dolan, Christopher Highley and Arthur F. Marotti (Notre Dame, Indiana, 2007), pp. 189–215.

[136] Garnet to Parsons, May 6, 1598, ABSI, Coll P II 552.

Gerard directed others through the Spiritual Exercises including the secular priest Lionel Woodward. According to Gerard, Woodward intended to enter the Jesuits and crossed to Belgium for that reason. However, he began to work as a military chaplain and died before he could act on his intention.[137] William Atkinson was released from the Clink shortly after Gerard's escape. Because he knew the location of Gerard's house, the Jesuit feared that Atkinson would betray him again by informing the authorities. A sudden raid threatened many. Consequently Gerard abandoned it before the end of the year and found another residence where Anne Line "could continue her good work."[138]

Perhaps as a result of Fisher's tour of England, secular clergy initiated an informal quasi-ecclesiastical structure in late 1596. By February there were "sodalities" in London and in the north.[139] These voluntary associations would elect their own superiors, manage alms, settle disputes, and provide mutual assistance. Their rules regulated the method whereby priests were placed in Catholic households and even proposed clerical boycotts of households that did not abide by the rules.[140] The promulgators were John Mush and John Colleton[141] but not every secular priest was as enthusiastic

---

[137] On Woodward see Anstruther, *Seminary Priests*, vol. 1, pp. 385–86. Woodward lived much longer than Gerard's account suggested. There was plenty of time between the completion of his retreat and his death for him to have entered the Society. Either Gerard misjudged Woodward's intentions or he changed his mind.

[138] Caraman, *John Gerard*, pp. 140–42. Gerard claimed that he retained this house "for a short time" after his escape. That short period of time must have been at least three months because of Alabaster's stay.

[139] Garnet to [?], February 23, 1597, ABSI, Coll P II 548. Copies of the rules can be found in ABSI, Anglia II, 32; AAW, VI, 77 and a copy marked "Mr Swyfte's house in Yorkshire" and dated November 21, 1596 in Scargill-Bird, *Salisbury*, vol. 6, pp. 483–84. Penelope Renold suggested a sinister connection between these sodalities and similar organizations proposed in 1591 by John Cecil when he suggested to William Cecil that, through such an association, seminary priests could be converted to Cecil's service. This remains an hypothesis because, as Renold noted, "connections between John Cecil and Bagshaw's party cannot be shown in 1596–97, but with regard to the 1596 proposals it is difficult to see how a priest so long experienced in the conditions of persecution in England as Mush, could have believed it possible that so detailed a scheme as the above could be worked in secret. He seems, indeed, to have been aware of the construction which would be put in his attempts" (*Wisbech Stirs*, p. 207 introductory note). Parsons suspected something similar. In a letter to Juan de Idiáquez on July 12, 1597 (ABSI, 46/12/4, p. 688), he explained that Catholics in England were setting up two associations, one in London and the other in Lancashire: "the reports assert that among their own aims is that of expelling the Jesuits, as being partisans of the Spanish faction; following the example, they say, of the doctors of the Sorbonne who also expelled the Jesuits as being a party that supported Spain."

[140] Pritchard, *Catholic Loyalism*, pp. 120–21.

[141] On Colleton see Anstruther, *Seminary Priests*, I, pp. 82–85.

as they.¹⁴² Even less enthusiastic was Garnet who questioned the motivation of the founders. It was strange, he mused, that secular priests most opposed to the introduction of any rules at Wisbech were the strongest proponents of the sodalities "as though men that live scattered abroad ought more to live in rules than those which are continually in tumults in one house." He warned Parsons in May that under the pretence of good, these organizations would further dissension and attacks against the Society.¹⁴³ Whether Parsons agreed with Garnet's evaluation of the founders' motives is not known but he did not approve of the associations. Parsons thought they were impractical without judicial authority and, most important, he feared their implementation would lead to the exclusion of secular clergy from the houses of the gentry because of the threat of a boycott.¹⁴⁴ Jesuit opposition alienated Mush. Once interested in entering the Jesuits, Mush now denounced "the foule dealyng of the Jesuits wch bend them selves thus mightely against our association." Having dismissed earlier warnings about the Jesuits, he was obliged to admit their accuracy because of Jesuit accusations:

> charging me to be the author & beginner of them [the problems at the English College, Rome] (whereas before god I was as fre from them as any of you that knewe not of them) & that I am the head of a faction against them, to expell them the realme, &c., &c., you would be more incredulous than I have bene. for y^t is so farr from all not religious & charitable, but honest conceipts also, that no man I thinke can believe them w^{t}out his own experience.¹⁴⁵

By September 10, 1597, the association in the north collapsed for unknown reasons but perhaps related to Jesuit opposition.¹⁴⁶

On August 13, 1597 Robert Parsons, who had returned to Rome at the end of March, presented to Pope Clement VIII a petition for the

---

[142] Alban Dolman opposed the sodalities. See his letter to Bagshaw, January 16, [1597] in Renold, *Wisbech Stirs*, pp. 207–209. For other opponents see p. 211 n. 10.

[143] Garnet to Parsons, May 28, 1597, ABSI, Coll P II 548. In his confessions, Fisher testified that Mush and Richard Dudley opposed a public denunciation of Jesuits "partly because it was difficult to support them with legal proofs, and partly lest it might appear that the associations or fellowships, which they were at the time seeking to promote among the clergy, were inspired, not by zeal for religion, but by jealousy of the Fathers" (published in Renold, *Wisbech Stirs*, pp. 250–51).

[144] The copies of the rules in ABSI, Anglia II, 32 and AAW, VI, 77 contain Parsons's animadversions. See Mark Tierney, *Dodd's Church History of England* (5 vols, London, 1839–1843), vol. 3, pp. 45–47 n. 1 for a criticism of Parsons's objections.

[145] Mush to Bagshaw, June 8, 1597, in Thomas Graves Law, (ed.), *The Archpriest Controversy* (2 vols, London, 1896–1898), vol. 1, p. 2.

[146] Garnet to Parsons, September 10, 1597, ABSI, Coll P II 596.

establishment of "some sort of hierarchy in the priesthood," perhaps a belated acknowledgment of the reality of Mercurian's initial fear. Something must be done as soon as possible for the sake of the English mission. Parsons argued the importance of absolute secrecy to prevent the English government from foiling any plans until the decision was made.[147] And the hierarchy that Parsons proposed, was the traditional episcopacy and nothing novel.[148] Earlier that summer Parsons discussed the possibility with Francisco de Peña, an official of the Rota, and Pietro, Cardinal Aldobrandini. To them he confided another motive for the appointment of bishops: only bishops could exclude seditious students from the English College from working on the mission.[149]

Parsons proposed the appointment of two bishops in order to avoid disagreements resulting from the absence of a hierarchical structure, and in order to remove divisions already present within the English Catholic community.[150] One bishop would reside in England, the other in Belgium. The bishop within the realm would confirm Catholics and ordain clergy, and carry out other duties associated with his office. He would encourage, counsel, and exhort Catholics, eliminate rivalries dividing the clergy, and assign secular clergy to specific areas or households. In so doing, he would relieve Jesuits of a burden carried not *ex officio* but out of charity, that had aroused the ire of some priests. Seven or eight archpriests or archdeacons would be named to assist him. To those dispersed throughout the realm, the bishop could delegate many duties. Equally important was a bishop in Belgium because the threat of persecution would prevent his episcopal colleague in England from exercising jurisdiction in the external forum. The bishop in Belgium could exercise this jurisdiction by summoning from England, and punishing if necessary, whomever the bishop within the realm

---

[147] Parsons to Pope Clement VIII, Rome August 13, 1597, ABSI, Coll P II 355.

[148] On his earlier attempts to have a bishop appointed for England, see Peter Norris, "Robert Parsons, S.J., (1546–1610) and the Counter Reformation in England: A Study of His Actions within the Context of the Political and Religious Situation of the Times" (unpublished Ph.D. thesis: University of Notre Dame, 1984), pp. 172–76. Parsons's proposal, "Rationes pro Episcopis duobus Anglicanis," can be found in Tierney/Dodd, *Church History*, vol. 3, pp. cxvii–cxix. Without advancing any evidence, Tierney claimed that Parsons resurrected his old scheme for bishops to counter-act the associations advanced by secular clergy (vol. 3, p. 47 n. 1).

[149] Parsons to de Peña, Rome, n.d. [August 1597], ABSI, 46/12/4 p. 701; same to Aldobrandini, n.d. [August 1597], Archivio segretto vaticano, Borghese, serie III.124.g.2, fols 25^{r-v}. See also Francis Edwards, S.J., *Robert Persons: The Biography of an Elizabethan Jesuit, 1546–1610* (St. Louis, 1995), pp. 208–10.

[150] Of the many requests made by Parsons, only new restrictions on the taking of doctoral degrees was granted on 19 September 1597. The papal brief can be found in Tierney/Dodd, *Church History*, vol. 3, pp. cii–civ. See also Arnold Oskar Meyer, *England and the Catholic Church under Queen Elizabeth* (London, 1916), pp. 409–11.

would not dare to chastise. Furthermore he could funnel all information from England to Rome, examine all priests and students returning to their native land, and impart faculties to them if they performed well in the examinations. He too should have six archpriests as assistants. If episcopal government were established, Parsons suggested that both bishops be *in partibus* lest an English title intensify the persecution. Both should have universal jurisdiction in England and, for subordination's sake, one, perhaps the bishop in Belgium, should be an archbishop. Both bishops should be ordained as soon as possible, as secretly as possible, and by one bishop and an apostolic brief to prevent the news from becoming even more public.

Either Parsons himself or a Roman official solicited William Holt's views on the subject.[151] Holt surveyed the survival of Catholicism in England after the accession of the "pretended" queen in 1558 as a preface to his recommendation and stressed the suffering endured, the importance of seminaries and priests for the continuation of Catholicism, and the role of Cardinal Allen. Since his death, no one had held comparable authority and influence. As a result there had been tension and conflict. To restore harmony, Holt argued, a mature, trustworthy English cleric should reside in Rome to serve as the cardinal protector's vicar for all matters pertaining to England. A hierarchy, whose head would be subordinate to the vicar in Rome, should also be established in England. Both vicar and superior should be bishops. If anyone should ask why England now needed bishops, Holt replied "the greater their need, the longer the faithful have been deprived without them."[152] The promotion of the mission demanded good government in the seminaries and care must be taken that troublesome students were dismissed. Finally, because of the number of Englishmen there, and because of its accessibility to England, a priest should reside in Belgium as a link between the vicar and the superior. Another cleric could play a similar role in Spain.

Apparently Enrico Caetani, Cardinal Protector of England, asked Garnet to survey clergy in England about a possible episcopacy. Unfortunately Garnet's reply is not extant, but we do know from a cover-letter to Parsons his and others' reactions to the proposal. For the office, the priests surveyed judged George Blackwell or Nicholas Tyrwhit were best qualified.[153] Nonetheless Tyrwhit himself, John Bavant (or Bavand), and William Weston had some hesitations about the proposals. They argued

---

[151] Printed in Thomas Francis Knox, (ed.), *The First and Second Diaries of the English College, Douay* (London, 1878), pp. 376–84 with an English translation in Foley, *Records*, vol. 7/2, pp. 1238–45.

[152] Foley, *Records*, vol. 7/2, p. 1243.

[153] See Anstruther, *Seminary Priests*, vol. 1, p. 365.

that problems with such an arrangement would too great. The principal difficulties anticipated were the possible discovery of his residence and his arrest, and his inability to punish disobedient clergy within the kingdom. If a bishop was appointed, despite potential problems, all three promised to submit to him. Regarding their objections, Garnet thought the first could be remedied if few knew where he lived and had access to him, and if he transacted all business through substitutes or correspondence, annual meetings, and periodic visits to London and the counties. Mild government, on the one hand, and strong support from the many priests throughout the kingdom who would support him could remedy the second anticipated problem. Assuming that a priest already within England would be appointed, Garnet recommended that he be allowed to confirm and to exercise jurisdiction immediately. When it was convenient, he could cross to the continent for consecration.[154]

Jesuits disagreed over the establishment of a hierarchy for England. Parsons, Holt, and Garnet argued in its favor; Weston was less than enthusiastic. Parsons's and Holt's proposals agreed on the importance of a hierarchy for the future of the mission, and both advocated two bishops. Parsons's plan was more detailed and recommended the creation of archpriests or archdeacons to exercise delegated authority throughout the realm. The obvious difference between the two proposals was the location of the second bishop: Parsons and Holt placed him in Flanders and Rome with clerical assistants in Flanders and Spain. Neither plan was accepted,[155] but Holt's bears such similarities to the administrative structure of the English Jesuit mission established in 1598 that one wonders whether the prefecture was modelled on it.[156]

Regardless of whatever type of hierarchy was introduced for the secular clergy, the Society's missionary organization functioned. The 13 Jesuits[157] on the mission met around the feasts of the Exaltation of the Holy Cross (September 14), St Luke (October 18), and the Presentation of the Blessed Virgin (November 21). Rarely did anyone miss these reunions. Despite storms developing on the continent, Garnet did not think that there was

---

[154] Garnet to Parsons, October 8, 1597, ABSI, Coll P II 548–49. See Caraman, *Henry Garnet*, pp. 238–39.

[155] According to Meyer, Roman officials feared that any priest appointed to reside in England as bishop, would either be martyred upon landing in the kingdom, or find himself residing in less than episcopal style (*England and the Catholic Church*, p. 409).

[156] See Thomas M. McCoog, S.J., "The Establishment of the English Province of the Society of Jesus," *Recusant History*, 17 (1984): pp. 121–39.

[157] By my count there should be 15: Garnet, Holtby, Oldcorne, Lister, Gerard, Jones, Bennet, Pullen, Collins, Stanney, Percy, the novice Blount who entered the Society in England in September of 1596, and Weston, Pounde, and Emerson in prison. Garnet must only have counted priests.

any "openly malicious" person in England. What malice there was, had passed and Garnet paid little attention to it. Jesuits on the mission worked diligently and provided no reason for any complaints.[158]

Garnet may have believed there were no grounds for criticism but Robert Fisher continued to look for them. There may not have been open malice but opposition to the Society of Jesus, and its perceived domination of the mission, grew. Fisher returned to Flanders during the summer of 1597. In September, he composed a long attack on the Jesuits, an attack that we shall consider in more detail in the next chapter. Here a few illustrations are sufficient. The work was the fruit of his canvassing of any complaints and criticisms about the Society. An abbreviated version, "An Abstract of the Memorial [of Robert Fisher] and of sundry Letters against the Jesuits." circulated more widely.[159] Both are divided into two sections: the charges levelled against the universal Society of Jesus and English Jesuits working in Rome; and the accusations directed specifically against Jesuits on the English mission. Overweening ambition was the Society's major flaw and it, William Gifford urged, must be destroyed "by laying the axe to the root." If the Society was allowed to continue in England, it would duplicate the damage done there throughout the world. Before God and his angels, Gifford swore "that the largest part of the nobility and clergy of England, both at home and abroad, bewail with groans and tears their most wretched state: they suffer more grievously under these new Jesuit tyrants than from the ordinary persecutors." Unless one had received "the mark of the beast" [that is, a supporter of the Jesuits], he would be subject to constant harassment by the Society, harassment that continued beyond the grave with vilification. The only English seminary outside their control was the college in Douai and Jesuits were determined that it would not elude them much longer. The abstract questioned the fidelity of Jesuits to Rome: 8 of 20 Jesuits in England, it claimed, defected

---

[158] Garnet to [William Baldwin? Robert Parsons?], November 25, 1597, ARSI, Angl. 38/II, fol. 173r.

[159] There are two copies of the abstract among the Petyt MSS. 538, vol. 38, fols 344, 345–46 in the Inner Temple. Another copy can be found in AAW, VI, 58 with Parsons's marginal comments. The "Abstract" was published in Law, *Archpriest Controversy*, vol. 1, pp. 7–15. Richard Hansard reported the dispute to Sir Robert Cecil from Venice on March 14, 1597 and listed many of the charges leveled in the abstract (TNA, SP 12/262/66). On Gifford see Anstruther, *Seminary Priests*, vol. 1, pp. 132–33. Law believed that the Jesuits compiled and circulated the "Abstract" in "hope of putting their adversaries to shame by the extravagance of the charges contained in it" (vol. 1, p. 7 n. a). Surely there would have been better defenses than publication and distribution of the charges regardless of their extravagance.

whereas only 7 of 300 secular priests abandoned their faith.[160] Within England, Jesuits were divided into two factions centered on Garnet and Weston.[161] Nonetheless they controlled the assignment of secular clergy and retained the more comfortable places for themselves and their cronies. On monies collected for imprisoned Catholics or seminaries, Jesuits lived extravagantly and spent on themselves enough money for the support of 20 priests.[162] In Belgium Father Holt accumulated great wealth from the sale of dispensations. Indeed it was estimated that he had more than £50,000! Finally, "there are very many things in the actions of these fathers which offend good men: contempt for the nobility; dismissal of all scholars from Douai; attempts to reduce the once most flourishing and ancient realm of England into a province; the plundering of Catholics in England under the appearance of pious usage by intolerable contributions; continual dealing with heretics and persons of suspect loyalty." The Society of Jesus was the only reason for clerical discord in England and harmony would only be restored with their expulsion from the mission. Pietro, Cardinal

---

[160] This accusation is verifiably false. Thomas H. Clancy, S.J., calculated that there were four Jesuit apostates from 166 Jesuits in the sixteenth century (2.4%) and 32 secular priests apostates from 613 during the same period (5.2%). See "Priestly Perseverance in the Old Society of Jesus," *Recusant History*, 19 (1989): p. 291. McGrath calculated that there were thirty apostate priests out of 471 sent to England ("Apostate and Naughty Priests," p. 67).

[161] More details about an alleged split between Garnet and Weston can be found in Nicholas Bonaert's letter to Robert Parsons, Brussels September 27, 1597, AAW, VI, 59. Bonaert was superior of a Jesuit house in Brussels. Charles Paget told the nuncio, Ottavio Mirto Frangipani, about the split. The nuncio consulted Belgian Jesuits about the affair and asked them to investigate it. Garnet and Weston differed on sixteen issues including equivocation. Bonaert relayed the information to Parsons. According to Paget Weston caused the division at Wisbech and, when ordered by Garnet to repair the breach, he replied that "he would do no such thing, that he was senior to Fr. Garnet, that Fr. Garnet had no business to tell him what to do" (translation from Renold, *Wisbech Stirs*, p. 303 n. 26). If the two did in fact disagree, it is doubtful that Weston would have advanced such an argument because he was not Garnet's senior. At this stage neither had pronounced final vows and Garnet entered the Society a few months before Weston. Weston, however, was ordained before Garnet and was sent to England before him, but seniority in religion was determined by date of entrance or date of final vows.

[162] Interestingly before William Weston entered the Jesuits, he had studied at the English College in Douai. To this college he left his legacy and other monies. Now such benefactions by those entering religious life were deemed null and void by the Council of Trent. Garnet judged it lawful to accept to obtain this money and to put it to Jesuit uses. However, Luis de Molina, S.J., argued that the conciliar decree did not concern alienation of property carried out by candidates before their admission into the Society. Nonetheless Garnet requested some clarification on Molina's evaluation. See Garnet to Acquaviva, June 11, 1597, ABSI, Anglia II, 29. Molina, better known for his teaching on grace and free will, treated personal and economic morality in *De iustitia et iure*, three volumes of which were published before his death in 1600. Four more volumes appeared posthumously.

Aldobrandini, the papal secretary of state, instructed the nuncio Ottavio Mirto Frangipani to control and eventually extinguish the flames of discontent before the mission was permanently damaged.[163]

Fisher's return to the continent altered the strategy of his supporters in Wisbech. After his appearance, according to John Hungerford Pollen, S.J., the controversy at Wisbech was:

> no longer the old personal quarrels, sometimes very loud, though not so very profound. Henceforth the debate begins to turn on politics, on the government of the mission, on rivalries between the secular and regular clergy. The importation of these new quarrels, caused fresh excitement, more vehement than the old remedies could cope with.[164]

Weston's attempt to moderate the dispute by appealing to the former agreement only antagonized his opponents further. John Norden snatched the concord from his hands and refused to return it. Norden's death shortly thereafter was interpreted providentially.[165] The few remaining members of Christopher Bagshaw's faction withdrew to Bluet's room where they took their meals. Now they decided to send an envoy to Rome to inform the pope of the true designs and schemes of the Jesuits. This proposal, originally made by William Gifford, was intended to counteract reports then circulating of peaceful relations between Jesuits and secular clergy in England. Gifford warned Bagshaw that some false brethren were seriously working for the creation of a hierarchy within England, whose head would either be a Jesuit or "one att theare direction." To stop this, Rome must be informed of the true state of affairs in England and he recommended that someone from Bagshaw's party be sent there.[166] Jesuits threatened proper church order. But lurking behind such a concern "for

---

[163] Aldobrandini to Frangipani, Rome October 11, 1597 in Van der Essen, *Correspondance d' Frangipani*, vol. 1, pp. 102–104. Frangipani confessed that he did not know how to handle the problem. He searched but in vain for the truth amidst the many charges and counter-charges (Brussels November 8, 1597, *Correspondance d'Frangipani*, vol. 2, pp. 251–54).

[164] *The Institution of the Archpriest Blackwell* (London, 1916), pp. 19–20.

[165] See Anstruther, *Seminary Priests*, vol. 1, pp. 252–54. Garnet was a little more circumspect in his letter to Parsons: "D. Norden is strangely dead in the beginning of a new tragedy at Wisbech (wherein he only was the speaker, with impudent modesty molesting everywhere his quiet neighbors, so that the Keeper himself was ashamed thereat) suddenly, as many men term it, tongue-tied, a dead lethargy surprising him and taking from him almost his memory also, whereof after many days he died" (August 20, 1597, ABSI, Coll P II 548).

[166] September 20, 1597, IT, Petyt MSS 538, vol. 38, fol. 378 (printed in Renold, *Wisbech Stirs*, pp. 225–29). Apparently Robert Charnock was chosen for the mission. See Garnet to Parsons, September 10, 1597, ABSI, Coll P II 596. On Charnock see Anstruther, *Seminary Priests*, vol. 1, pp. 73–75.

the sanctity of church order," was, as Arnold Pritchard pointed out, "an increasingly open willingness to say and do things that implied recognition of the legitimacy of English temporal authority."[167] More and more anti-Jesuit Catholics resembled the "patriots" described in the *State of English Fugitives*.

Riding to the Rescue: The Return of James Gordon, S.J.

In February of 1597, an extraordinary General Assembly at Perth appointed ministers to discuss religious matters with the earl of Huntly. Their goal was his full participation in the Scottish Church and acceptance of its discipline. As a sign of his sincerity, they insisted that Huntly promise to banish all "Jesuits, preests, and excommunicated persons" from his presence. Finally he must accept the "Confession of Faith." As a result of the earl of Erroll's petition, the assembly authorized the ministers to include him. Elizabeth Douglas, Countess of Angus, requested similar treatment for her husband to resolve his doubts about embracing publicly the reformed religion. By the end of March the three earls expressed their willingness to conform. In May, the earls had to choose: embrace Protestantism and remain in Scotland with full honors restored, or be exiled forever. On June 29 they subscribed to the "Confession of Faith."[168] Huntly expressly promised to avoid further contact "with Jesuits, preests, or excommunicated persons, except with suche as are dealing with the kirk, so to keepe in all tyme comming; and that he sall banishe out of his companie and bounds all Jesuits, preests, and sall expell therefra all excommunicated Papists, except suche as sall have licence of the kirk and king's Majestie. And, finallie, none sall have recept in his bounds that are professed enemeis to the kirk, by his knowledge."[169] Because of their submission, the assembly absolved them and lifted their excommunication as soon as they swore the "Confession of Faith," and promised in writing to banish all Jesuits from their company.[170] In the beginning of August all penalties were lifted and the earls were proclaimed the king's free lieges.

---

[167] Pritchard, *Catholic Loyalism*, p. 97.

[168] Thomson, *Calderwood*, vol. 5, pp. 606–73; Lang, *History of Scotland*, vol. 2, pp. pp. 425–36; Forbes-Leith, *Narratives of Scottish Catholics*, pp. 229–32. It must have taken some time for the news of their capitulation to reach Rome. Acquaviva expressed his sorrow in a letter to Alexander MacQuhirrie on March 10, 1602, ARSI, Franc. 1/II, fol. 464^r.

[169] Thomson, *Calderwood*, vol. 5, p. 636.

[170] Thomson, *Calderwood*, vol. 5, pp. 638–40.

The Jesuit James Gordon returned to Scotland a few days before the capitulation of the earls.[171] Their desertion led to the renunciation of Catholicism by other Catholic lords and nobles. Now without noble protection, the three Jesuits in the kingdom (William Murdoch, Robert Abercrombie, and Alexander MacQuhirrie) were obliged to conceal themselves wherever they could. Because the earl of Huntly had promised to apprehend any Jesuit with his protectors and patrons, he did not welcome his uncle's return. Kinship and friendship may have militated against his taking the Jesuit prisoner but he feared royal wrath, the rage of the ministers, and the loss of his 20,000 Scottish pounds security if he turned a blind eye. Consequently Gordon left for another part of the country, somewhere in the Highlands where there were many Catholics. There his friends welcomed him to the alarm of the Presbyterian ministers. So afraid were the ministers of the influence of one Jesuit, they obtained a royal proclamation forbidding anyone to receive Gordon, to offer him food and drink, or to encourage his work under penalty of high treason. Moreover a reward of 1,000 gold pieces was offered to anyone who captured Gordon or, if he resisted, put him to death. The earl of Huntly used his influence with King James to have a second proclamation promulgated in early July. This proclamation allowed anyone to receive the Jesuit, furnish him material assistance and speak with him without fear as long as they had obtained the earl's permission first. A condition of the second proclamation was the Jesuit's departure from Scotland before August 11. Gordon accepted the condition because it bound him only to leave Scotland and said nothing about his return. For one month Gordon could work openly and freely without risk to anyone. He consoled Catholics devastated by the defection of the nobles. He met Murdoch and MacQuhirrie, and sent messages to Abercrombie who was sick in a distant part of the country. After a consultation with Murdoch, MacQuhirrie and, possibly, an elderly secular priest, James Seton,[172] Gordon decided to challenge all ministers in Scotland to a free public disputation on any and all controverted points. He insisted that said discussion "be held in the presence of the King, of the principal nobility, and above all of the three noblemen who had lately changed their faith." Gordon did not mention

---

[171] A full account of Gordon's trip can be found in his letter to Acquaviva, Hersens September 1, 1597, ARSI, Angl. 42, fols 100 ^{r}–103^v (translated in Forbes-Leith, *Narratives of Scottish Catholics*, pp. 232–42).

[172] According to Gordon, Seton worked closely with Jesuits since his arrival from Pont-à-Mousson ten years ago. He wanted to enter the Society but Gordon dissuaded him because "he is advanced in years and somewhat infirm." Acquaviva was willing to accept him into the Society but he left the decision to Crichton who knew whether it would be more beneficial to the mission if he remained a secular priest (Acquaviva to Crichton, Rome November 17, 1597, ARSI, Fl. Belg. 1/II, p. 661).

Edmund Campion's similar challenge in 1580 but he must have been aware of the precedent. Some Protestants acknowledged that Gordon's challenge was understandable and fair and swore an oath that they would abandon the Established Church if its ministers did not accept the challenge. Nonetheless the ministers hesitated. Gordon then committed his challenge to a broadsheet for distribution throughout the kingdom "to let everyone see how weak and unfounded the heretical cause must be, since its own adherents and teachers did not dare to defend it publicly."[173] He also wrote to the king. Still the ministers did nothing, arguing that they could not accept a challenge without authorization from the General Assembly. Gordon prepared to place his challenge before the assembly as soon as it opened. Because "our armour is spiritual, not carnal, and our sword is the word of God, by means of which Christ our Lord is accustomed to rout and overthrow the armies of Satan," Gordon was confident of success.[174] As the date of his departure approached, Gordon proceeded to Aberdeen where he was to board the ship. There he spoke almost daily with Murdoch who visited him secretly. David Cunningham, Protestant Bishop of Aberdeen, and other ministers called out of respect because he was the earl of Huntly's uncle, but not to discuss religion. With them Gordon pressed his offer to debate. Still unwilling to accept the challenge without permission from the General Assembly, these ministers, however, did allow Gordon to preach to them not in a church but in the grand hall of the local lord with whom Gordon was staying. The ministers promised free access to anyone who wished to attend. Gordon selected the text "The Church is the pillar and ground of the truth" (1 Timothy 3:15). Noting that the ministers disapproved of this text, Gordon allowed them to select the passage. Choosing John 10, "My sheep hear my voice," they insisted that Gordon not discuss tradition but the word of God alone. The Jesuit accepted the condition and on the 11th, the date on which Gordon was scheduled to depart, they scheduled the sermon for August 16.[175] Gordon wanted the date announced five days in advance so that the news could be carried far and wide: with the approval of the Established Church, a Jesuit was allowed to preach in public! So widely anticipated was the event and so many came to Aberdeen to listen to Gordon that the ministers revoked their earlier promise of free access and restricted attendance to ministers. Exclusion angered Catholics and Protestants. "People in the streets" Catholics proclaimed that the "ministers had

---

[173] Gordon to Acquaviva, Hersens September 1, 1597, ARSI, Angl. 42, fols 100ʳ–103ᵛ (translated in Forbes-Leith, *Narratives of Scottish Catholics*, p. 237).

[174] Gordon to Acquaviva, Hersens September 1, 1597, ARSI, Angl. 42, fols 100ʳ–103ᵛ (translated in Forbes-Leith, *Narratives of Scottish Catholics*, p. 238).

[175] He must have obtained an extension to stay in Scotland for the sermon.

proved the falsehood and weakness of their own cause" by prohibiting entrance.[176] Gordon abbreviated his sermon to leave time for replies and objections. Gordon argued that "the voice of Christ addressed us not in the letter alone of the written word, but rather in the true exposition of its meaning; and that this is not to be found in private interpretation, but to be gathered from the sense and consent of the ancient Fathers and Councils."[177] Because the ministers agreed, Gordon asked which fathers and councils they acknowledged. Those of the first 500 or 600 years, they replied. Once the General Assembly granted Gordon's request for a debate, he promised to defend all Catholic doctrines and to refute their heretical ones from the conciliar decrees and patristic writings from that period. At the end the ministers requested that Gordon write a summary of what he had said for their future consultation. He did so immediately and asked them to put into writing their acceptance of the fathers and councils of the first five centuries. This Gordon did not receive until he had boarded ship for departure. He left Aberdeen on August 18 and arrived in Norway on the 21st. By the end of the month he was in southern Denmark, preparing to return to Scotland within a fortnight if the weather permitted. Unfortunately weather prevented his immediate return.

Acquaviva commiserated with the sufferings endured by Scottish Catholics. Obviously wishing the situation were better, he reminded Gordon that God often brought success just when all human hope had failed. Despite pledges to the contrary, he doubted the ministers would dispute with Gordon. Nonetheless he promised to send three companions to assist Gordon in the debates. After the disputation, Acquaviva urged Gordon to withdraw from Scotland if his safety was threatened but to do so in such a way so that the mission's work was disrupted as little as possible. Other Jesuits less well known and thus more easily concealed would be more effective. If Gordon did leave Scotland permanently, he should appoint a superior for the Jesuits who remained.[178]

Unfortunately Acquaviva did not name the three assistants he proposed to send to Gordon. From a letter to William Crichton, we know that John Hay was the only Jesuit and the other two were secular priests "carefully screened to ensure their orthodoxy." Perhaps a successful disputation would work to Catholic advantage and restore their fortunes. Worried about the physical condition of Abercrombie, the general recommended to Crichton that he be recalled from Scotland as soon as possible. Once

---

[176] Gordon to Acquaviva, Hersens September 1, 1597, ARSI, Angl. 42, fols 100^r–103^v (translated in Forbes-Leith, *Narratives of Scottish Catholics*, p. 240).

[177] Gordon to Acquaviva, Hersens September 1, 1597, ARSI, Angl. 42, fols 100^r–103^v (translated in Forbes-Leith, *Narratives of Scottish Catholics*, pp. 240–41).

[178] Acquaviva to Gordon, Rome November 15, 1597, ARSI, Fl. Belg. 1/II, p. 660.

he was back on the continent, Acquaviva would re-assign him.[179] By the spring of 1598, Abercrombie was resting in the Polish province but his stay there was not permanent: he returned to Scotland by July of 1598.

Conclusion

In early 1597 Henry IV broke the power of the Catholic League and was advancing against Spanish forces. In Holland, Count Maurice routed Spanish troops at Turnhout on January 14. With Spanish armies on the defensive, the only remaining external threat to England was a seaborne attack. But in its confrontation with Spain, England could not always depend on the weather. An intricate network of intelligencers provided Sir Robert Cecil and the earl of Essex with information about preparations for another armada, but, not being privy to precise details, they could only guess at its destination. But more important was the time required to transmit news to England. In 1596 news reached England that the armada had set sail 10 days after it had returned to port. England's security demanded a more active policy: the destruction of the armada in Spanish ports before it sailed. Thus Elizabeth ignored French pleas for assistance in retaking Calais—she even resisted Henry's probably insincere offer that England could retain the port after it had been recaptured—to launch an offensive strike against the Spanish navy. Elizabeth planned to recall Sir Thomas Baskerville and his forces from France, but on March 1, Juan de Portocarrero, Spanish Governor of Doullens, captured Amiens. Because most of the Spanish forces were in the Netherlands, Portocarrero was unable to follow up this success with a march on Paris only 80 miles away. Under these circumstances, Baskerville could not be withdrawn, but despite more French entreaties, Elizabeth would not provide more assistance. Increased involvement in Ireland because of O'Neill and O'Donnell and careful preparations for an expedition to Spain precluded any more aid but Elizabeth maintained negotiations with the French possibly to discourage Henry from heeding the demands of many subjects to conclude a peace treaty with Spain.

Divided into three squadrons under the direction of Thomas, Lord Howard, Essex, and Sir Walter Raleigh, an English fleet assembled in the Downs in late June. A Dutch squadron joined it on the 25th. Elizabeth's instructions commissioned Essex to destroy the armada being prepared to attack England or Ireland, or to assist Archduke Albert in the Netherlands. If the armada was still in port, he was to destroy by fire or any other means without endangering any ship. If the armada was already at sea, the fleet

---

[179] Acquaviva to Crichton, Rome November 17, 1597, ARSI, Fl. Belg. 1/II, p. 661.

should pursue it and destroy it. Once this objective had been accomplished, Essex was to head for the Azores to intercept the fleet from the Indies. If this fleet sought sanctuary in any port, Essex should attack it by land and sea. The seizure of gold and silver would prevent Philip II from a rapid recovery to the destruction of his armada. On July 12 heavy winds and storms scattered the English fleet. Raleigh returned to Plymouth on the 18th with heavily damaged ships. Essex arrived in Falmouth on the 19th with battered, leaking ships. Four of Howard's ships, three of Essex's, one of Raleigh's, seven Dutch warships, a number of armed merchantmen, and five flyboats with troops rode out the storm. Howard decided to continue to the appointed rendezvous off Cape Finisterre to await the others. On the 28th he received instructions from Essex and headed homeward, arriving in Plymouth on the 31st.[180]

The prayers of the English Church accompanied the fleet. So often in the past the Lord protected the queen and her people from "many dangerous conspiracies, malicious attempts, and wicked designments."[181] Again her faithful subjects turned to the Lord to beg him to strengthen their leaders and to bless their enterprise with notable victories. They reminded the Lord that their cause was just because they waged "war not in pride or ambition of mind, or any other worldly respect, but only for the necessary defence of Religion, our lives, and Country." England was the victim: "they first conspired to root us out, that we might be no more a people of *English* birth; and that then, thou from heaven didst shew theyself, in scattering their proud forces, to be displeased with their attempt, yet notwithstanding by mighty preparations at this moment they seek our ruin still"[182] Despite their many frustrations, England's enemies troubled her still. Open their eyes, the congregations prayed, "Make them to see that their plots and designments are against thee, who for us fightest against them, drowning their ships, and casting down their strong-holds in which they do trust; that thy Name may be glorified in the day of their conversion."[183]

England's second attempt to take the offensive against Spain in 1597 began inauspiciously. The expedition left Plymouth on August 17, but contrary winds forced it into the Bay of Biscay. Damaged by strong winds, many vessels were not able to rendezvous off Cape Finisterre. Essex decided to move farther south to attack the Indian fleet because of reports from prisoners that the armada would not sail that year. He made a more drastic decision on the 30th of August. Raleigh sent word to Essex that

---

[180] Wernham, *Return of the Armadas*, pp. 144–69.
[181] Clay, *Liturgical Services*, p. 672.
[182] Clay, *Liturgical Services*, pp. 673–74.
[183] Clay, *Liturgical Services*, p. 677.

the armada had left Ferrol on the 4th for the Azores to escort the Indian fleet and treasure home. Essex ordered the ships under his direction to proceed to the Azores. There he found no armada but Essex decided to wait in the Azores for the Indian fleet. Upon its arrival the fleet was so well-protected that an attack was impossible. With little to show for their efforts, the English ships left the Azores on October 9, the very day the armada left Ferrol. Reliably informed that Essex's departure for the Azores left England unprotected, Spanish commanders hastened their departure instead of waiting for more ships and Italian troops on their way from San Lucar and Lisbon. They also modified their objectives. According to the original plan, troops would land at Falmouth, take the city and, if possible, prevent the fleet from using Plymouth as its base. Once the troops were secure, the fleet would return to Ferrol for the winter. In the spring, ships would carry supplies and reinforcements. The revised plan still centered on Falmouth. It, or at least the fortresses protecting the harbor, would be seized. The Spanish fleet would then hide in the Scilly Isles in wait for the return of Essex's fleet. On October 12, the Spanish fleet was approaching the Lizard. Only then did the commander reveal the change in plans to his officers. But a day that began with so much hope ended miserably for the Spanish. Yet another gale wreaked so much havoc on the ships that the fleet was forced to turn around and return to Spain. By November 11, 108 of the original 136 ships were back in Spanish ports. Elizabeth received word of the Spanish fleet off the Lizard on October 26, two days after she had opened Parliament.[184]

In 1593 Parliament granted Elizabeth three subsidies, the last of which was due in February of 1597. The expense of a naval expedition and the cost of preparations for a possible Spanish invasion left the government with little choice but to summon another Parliament for the autumn. Christopher Yelverton, named speaker when Parliament convened on October 24, 1597, matched his predecessors in rhetoric and eloquence in his address to the queen on the 27th. His praise of Elizabeth was effusive. She had faced a task much more difficult than any of the labors of Hercules: the destruction of Popish superstition and the establishment of true religion. She had not only succeeded, but she had emerged triumphant despite efforts of neighboring nations to prevent it. Thus, he concluded:

> You behold other kingdomes distracted into factions, distressed with warres, swarming with rebellions, and embrued with bloud; yours (almost only yours) remaineth calme without tempest, and quiet without dissention, notwithstanding all the desperate and devillishe devises of the Romishe crue, and Jesuites, whose unnaturall affections, bloudy hands, and most cruell harts

---

[184] Wernham, *Return of the Armadas*, pp. 171–90.

do too-too evidentlie bewray there irreligion to be a bottomeles and an endlesse sea of all mischeifes. They seeke to seduce the simple and to allure the ignorant to hearken to the Pope's bull, but not so much for the favour of there religion, as to the alarum bell of all disloiall, and dangerouse treason. But it is strange that this old forewarne folly, banished so many yeares since out of the realme, and for the which so many notable lawes have beene provided, and against the which the comon lawe it self is so penall, should dare to shewe it self, so fond and so furious in this time. But God, the most mightie and all sufficient God, in whose zeale you doe so constantlie persevere, and whose service you doe so effectually preferre, maugre all there despites, doth (and long and long may he) preserve you.[185]

Shortly after Yelverton's panegyric, the tranquility that he had so praised was in jeopardy. Parliament was adjourned for nine days because of news of the approach of the armada. Seizing on the continuing threat of a Spanish invasion, Francis Bacon explained that four events endangered the realm: "First the French kinge's revolt. 2. Callis taken by the Spaniardes. 3. The bleeding ulcer of Ireland. 4. The invasion of the Spaniardes and provokation of sea matters."[186] Without hesitation Parliament voted the queen a threefold subsidy to be collected over three years. In his closing speech Yelverton returned to earlier themes:

What barbarous invasions Spaine hath of long time prepared against this famous and most flourishing land, and what proud and bloudy attemptes the kinge there hath plotted by the provocation of that preist of Rome, both against this, and that your other realme of Ireland, the simplest doth see them: and the wise cannot but with eternall admiration of your Majestie's most high and wonderfull wisedome (in diverting them) in there judgmentes confesse them: for the pride of Rome and the ambition of Spaine have been the two whirwindes of all the mischeifes in Christendome.[187]

No English king had spent money more wisely for the defense of the realm. More money was needed to continue a defense against England's malicious enemies. Because every subject benefited from the defense, every subject should contribute to its maintenance through the subsidies. Elizabeth gained the financial support she needed. Parliament completed its work and closed on February 9, 1598.

---

[185] Yelverton's speech can be found in can be found in T.E. Hartley, (ed.), *Proceedings in the Parliaments of Elizabeth I* (3 vols, Leicester, 1981–1995), vol. 3, pp. 189–93 (quotation from pp. 192–93). For an account of this Parliament see J.E. Neale, *Elizabeth I and Her Parliaments* (2 vols, London, 1953–1957), vol. 2, pp. 325–67.

[186] Hartley, *Proceedings*, vol. 3, p. 232.

[187] Hartley, *Proceedings*, vol. 3, p. 201.

Parliament passed no new legislation against recusants. Indeed there would be no further legislation until the reign of James I. Once measures were introduced to make implementation more efficient, current legislation was sufficient. During the final years of Elizabeth's reign, recusants were regarded as a source of income; their fines and forfeited property became part of the patronage system. At times recusants were also obliged to contribute money to the government. In 1598 a levy of £30 was imposed on all recusants to support the enlarged English forces sent to Ireland to prevent a Spanish invasion.[188]

Bacon's apprehensions about France were justified. Pope Clement VIII continued to apply pressure on Spain and France to conclude a peace. Negotiations intensified in the summer of 1597. Initially Henry IV hesitated because he worried that he would not get fair terms as long as Amiens remained in Spanish hands. The French recaptured Amiens on September 9. In an attempt to relieve the French siege, Archduke Albert lost all the Netherlands north of the Rhine and Waal. On September 24, Pope Clement VIII's mediator Bonaventura Secusi di Calatagirona, Father General of the Franciscans, met with French and Spanish representatives at Arras. Bound by treaty not to make a separate peace without consulting his allies, Henry informed them that Spain was prepared to agree to peace on reasonable terms, and that he could not prolong the war unless the Dutch and the English were prepared to launch a major unified attack aimed at the expulsion of Spanish forces from the Netherlands and Brittany. Caught between Scylla and Charybdis, Elizabeth procrastinated: she could subsidize a major military expedition to expel Spain but, on the other hand, she doubted Spain's sincerity and would not abandon the Dutch. French ministers, however, believed that England had already initiated secret negotiations with Spain through Catholic exiles in Flanders. In the summer of 1597 Thomas Phelippes sent Thomas Barnes to visit Charles Paget. Under Phelippes's direction the two had corresponded for nearly a decade. Barnes claimed that he wanted to sound out the archduke about the possibility of peace. At the time Elizabeth was preparing her fleet for its expedition to Spain and Archduke Albert was organizing his relief of Amiens. Many suspected that Barnes's real assignment was to spy on Spanish preparations and not make overtures for peace. By the end of the

---

[188] Collection of levies such as this was not always easy. See John LaRocca, S.J., "English Catholics and the Recusancy Laws 1558–1625: A Study in Religion and Politics," (unpublished Ph.D. thesis, Rutgers University, 1977), pp. 163–69. On July 16 Garnet reported that the persecution had intensified: "in a single country from which the Queen used to reap only £1000 now £11000 sterling is paid" (ARSI, Angl. 38/II, fol. 177ᵛ).

year Archduke Albert commissioned Paget to write to Sir Robert Cecil: he was now willing to discuss peace with England.[189]

Since the early 1590s the earl of Essex supported some form of toleration for loyal, anti-Spanish Catholics perhaps in an attempt to gain their support. Lewknor singled Essex out for praise in his *State of English Fugitives*. Through his intercession, Sir Thomas Tresham was briefly released from prison in 1593. Essex protected the ex-Jesuit Thomas Wright in 1595 and established contact with exiles such as Charles Paget.[190] Perhaps as part of a general peace, England would grant tolerance to Catholics—or at least those Catholics who had demonstrated their loyalty.

---

[189] Wernham, *Return of the Armadas*, pp. 195–213.

[190] Paul E.J. Hammer, *The Polarisation of Elizabethan Politics: The Political Career of Robert Devereux, 2nd Earl of Essex, 1585–1597* (Cambridge, 1999), pp. 162, 174–78.

CHAPTER 6
"Leagues of Unquiet and Subversive Spirits": Continental Struggles, 1596–1597

Introduction

On April 4, 1591, Robert Parsons expounded on the important role that recently converted English galley-slaves could play in advancing Spanish policy. Convinced that their conversion was sincere and not simply a ploy to gain liberation, the Jesuit marvelled that Spanish authorities treated them so coolly. Once ransomed, these converts would be allowed to return to England. "There is one thing very certain," he continued, "that to imagine that we can prevail in England without having a party within the realm is a very great illusion; and to imagine that we can have this party without establishing it and fostering it is no less an illusion ... "[1] Few would deny the importance of having a party within England, but the suggestion that Spain had not already established one, would have struck many as ludicrous. An increasing number of English clergy and laity were becoming disenchanted with the patently pro-Spanish sympathies then prevalent among Catholic exiles. The conspiracies, plots and threats of invasion involving Spanish sympathizers not only increased the persecution endured by Catholics in England but dulled their protests of allegiance. The aggressive Counter-Reformation policies of Spain, whether on the battlefields, the high seas, or the genealogical charts of royal lineage, were becoming too identified with Roman Catholicism. Elizabeth was their royal sovereign *"rebus sic stantibus"* as Pope Gregory XIII explained to Edmund Campion and Robert Parsons in 1580.[2] Spanish policies undermined that allegiance. Spain was not only England's enemy but she consistently failed to fulfill

---

[1] Parsons to Don Juan de Idiáquez, Seville April 4, 1591, ABSI, Coll P II 249 (printed in Thomas Francis Knox, (ed.), *The Letters and Memorials of William Cardinal Allen (1532–1594)* [London, 1882], pp. 330–32).

[2] Two years earlier Gregory had threatened with excommunication any Dutch Catholic who aided or participated in the rebellion against Spain. See Charles H. Parker, *Faith on the Margins. Catholics and Catholicism in the Dutch Golden Age* (Cambridge, Mass., 2008), p. 194. He was more conciliatory with his treatment of an excommunicated queen.

her promises to the Catholics. The preservation of Catholicism in England, more and more believed, should not depend on Spanish military triumphs.

Sir Thomas Tresham, an English gentleman who had petitioned Elizabeth for tolerance in 1585, was an interesting and important figure who consistently sought to reconcile allegiance to Queen Elizabeth with profession of the Roman Catholic faith.[3] Having conformed to the Established Church in his youth, he returned to Catholicism in 1580 apparently because of the persuasive ability of Robert Parsons, with whom he would later disagree. Tresham craved his role in society as his birthright, from which his religion excluded him. He lamented that he was not allowed to serve the queen against the Spanish forces which he was as eager as anyone to repulse. He was convinced that God was the cause of the Armada's failure: "The Spanish forces no sooner appeared on our coasts, but by the mighty hand of God were discomfited and marvellously dispersed to the unspeakable joy of the whole realm and principally to us."[4] This was not the sentiment of the predominant Allen/Parsons party nor would it remain the voice of one crying in the wilderness.

The Problematic Paget and Morgan, and the Opposition to William Holt, S.J.

Leo Hicks, S.J., entitled his monograph on Charles Paget and Thomas Morgan *An Elizabethan Problem*.[5] They do in fact present a problem

---

[3] On Tresham, see Arnold Pritchard, *Catholic Loyalism in Elizabethan England* (London, 1979), pp. 49–56; Peter Holmes, *Resistance and Compromise: The Political Thought of the English Catholics* (Cambridge, 1982), pp. 177–79; and Sandeep Kaushik, "Resistance, Loyalty and Recusant Politics: Sir Thomas Tresham and the Elizabethan State," *Midland History*, 21 (1996): pp. 37–79.

[4] Reginald Lane Poole et al. (eds.), *Various Collections* (8 vols, London, 1901–1914), vol. 3, pp. 52, 54. The third chapter of Pritchard's book, "Loyalist Sentiment before 1595," *Catholic Loyalism*, pp. 37–72 is a good exposition of attempts by Catholic lay gentry to make their peace with the Elizabethan government.

[5] Leo Hicks, S.J., *An Elizabethan Problem* (London, 1964). The subtitle reveals the thesis of the book: "Some Aspects of the Careers of Two Exile-Adventurers." It is unfortunate that the only study of these two figures should be such a tendentious investigation aimed at the exoneration of Parsons from all charges levelled against him by Paget and Morgan. Could the root of their disagreement have been tactics? It is clear that Paget and Morgan consistently opposed the pro-Spanish policies of William Allen and Parsons. In their dedication to Mary Stuart, did they fear that the Spanish party would result in the triumph of a Spanish candidate and the exclusion of the Stuarts from the English throne? Were they committed to the Stuarts and did they attempt to gain official recognition of the Stuart claims through negotiations with the Elizabethan government? These men, and perhaps their roles as precursors of the appellant clergy, deserve fuller study.

but one not restricted to Elizabethans. To Hicks, Paget and Morgan were double agents, troublemakers, agents of the Elizabethan government, seeking the destruction of English Catholicism by fostering dissension among its leaders because of resentment at their exclusion from the inner circle. That Paget and Morgan did create trouble cannot be denied, but were their motives as base as Hicks suggested? Disagreement over policies, accommodation with the Elizabethan government, and succession to the English throne slowly destroyed the united front that Catholic exiles sought to present to the world. On January 30, 1590, William, Cardinal Allen lamented a breach among the exiles in a letter to Thomas, Lord Paget, Charles's brother, without specifying the cause. The cardinal promised to do all he could to end the division and to address all complaints without prejudice.[6] A year later, Allen's complaint to Charles Paget added details about the nature of the dispute. Because Allen was the acknowledged leader of the English exiles, responsible for the restoration of Catholicism, he thus argued:

> it followeth that all those that seditiously conspire my disgrace ... [and] band themselves directly and traiterously against the good of their countrey and against the service of the highest Princes in Christendom, by whome only we expect succour and releefe for our so unfortunate state; and when I name preists and religious yow must not straight wayes inferre (as yow seeme to do in your letter) that the preists band themselves against the nobility, as though all the nobility in banishment or at home were of Morgans faction, or that preists were not divers of them of as good nobility as most of those few that be addicted to Morgan.[7]

Writing to Thomas Throckmorton on the same day, Allen dismissed Morgan's suggestions which "maketh me a cruell man and of [Thomas, Cardinal] Wolsies inclination." He was not, he continued, ambitious or vindicative, but sincerely concerned with the "defence of the common cause." In his attachment to this cause, he never was partial to any section of the kingdom: "I never put difference betwixte Englishe and Welshe nor any one province of our countrye and another, being readye to serve the whole and everye part and parcell therof with all the faculties of minde and bodye and with my life also when occasion shall be offered." Throckmorton's friend Morgan had initiated disturbances that now

---

[6] Knox, *Letters of Allen*, pp. 315–16.

[7] Rome January 4, 1591, Knox, *Letters of Allen*, p. 319. For some reason, Knox published only a part of the letter. The full text can be found in Penelope Renold, (ed.), *Letters of William Allen and Richard Barret 1572-1598* [London, 1967], pp. 201-204.

disrupted peaceful relations between King Philip II and Catholic exiles and could result in the termination of any more royal assistance.[8]

Assuming that Throckmorton had not received his letter, Allen wrote again on February 20. He repeated his charges that Morgan and his faction were damaging "the common cause and the service of God, the churche and our countrie" by stirring up opposition between "me and the cleargy on thoneside and nobillite and layety on thotherside." He pleaded with Throckmorton:

> to followe in that kinde the maine streame and the principall of your nation with so many of the best and greatest (without comparison) of the nobillite, cleargy and religious, and not to caste yourself in the creekes of a fewe and veary fewe discontented persons; who are not yet so many nor of suche credit ether at home or with other Princes abrode as to countervale the numbers of those that mislike the dealings of thies left handed men, nether yet enow to give the name unto a faction of a whole nation, as thoughe the Englishe were indifferently devided amongst themselves about thies matters; which ys alltogether untrue and in a manner also unpossible, thoughe som of folly may give out so or of simplicite may beleave yt.[9]

"Left handed men" discredited abroad and at home, were claiming a role disproportionate to their number and to their ability. Allen urged Throckmorton to follow the "best and greatest," the "principall of your nation" and avoid the discontented few.

Details about the division emerge from Allen's letters. Allen believed that "Morgans faction" "conspired" against him and accused him of partiality and ambition. Presumably they compared him with Cardinal Wolsey because of his relations with Philip II. This faction worked "traiterously," in some unexplained way, against the good of England and the kingdom best able to assist England, that is, Spain. The faction opposed, again for unexplained reasons, Spanish involvement in English affairs and Spanish proposals to invade England. Allen's letters suggested that this faction fostered conflict between clerics and nobles. Finally, and less important, Morgan hinted at some antagonism between Welsh and English (perhaps a continuation of the disputes that led to the Society's involvement in the English College, Rome in 1579) or, given the role of the

---

[8] Rome January 4, 1591, ABSI, Anglia I, 55, 56 (printed in Knox, *Letters of Allen*, pp. 320–24).

[9] ABSI, Anglia I, 57 (printed in Knox, *Letters of Allen*, pp. 325–29).

Scot William Chisholm, Bishop of Dunblane and, after 1584, Carthusian monk, between Celts (Welsh and Scots) and English.[10]

William Holt was another target. In the above-cited letter to Charles Paget on January 4, 1591, Allen defended Holt. After his arrival in the Low Countries in 1588, Holt became an influential figure at court in Brussels with a significant role in the distribution of Spanish pensions. According to Allen, Paget's charges were "foule and shameful matter and such as you doe not put in paper," but because the accusations were not specific, Allen could not evaluate them and respond properly. If the accusations were as serious as Paget claimed, Allen instructed him to present them fully to Allen or Claudio Acquaviva so that Acquaviva could authorize a thorough examination of the charges.[11] Presumably Paget sent a list of these charges to neither because, when the investigation was conducted, it was carried out by secular authorities.

In May of 1591, as we saw in Chapter 1, the secular priest John Cecil was arrested at Dover. Cecil explained that he had come to England to ascertain whether he could live there and peacefully exercise his religion. Regarding his religion, he was resolute and begged William Cecil, Lord Burghley, not to urge him to do something that violated his conscience. With the exception of religion, he pledged his allegiance to the Elizabethan government and repudiated any seditious plots and conspiracies directed against it. He proposed to Burghley that he abandon oppressive policies designed to force Catholics to conform and, instead, seek to devise some means whereby "Catholiques shoulde have any indulte in matters of conscyence givinge securitye of theyre fydelitye, as they have in Germany & fraunce."[12] This, of course, assumed that Burghley sincerely did not seek the eradication of Catholicism but desired only the political loyalty of Catholics. He advised Burghley to add "one stringe moore to your bowe" by imitating Henry IV, King of France, and using Catholics to

---

[10] Allen complained to Charles Paget on January 4, 1592 [*vere* 1591] that Chisholm meddled too much in "our affaires" for a Carthusian (ABSI, Coll M 129 [printed in Renold, *Letters of Allen and Barret*, p. 202]). See also p. 204 n. 4 regarding attempts to elevate Chisholm to the cardinalate as a counterbalance to Allen.

[11] ABSI, Coll M 129 (printed in Renold, *Letters of Allen and Barret*, pp. 201–204). In an undated letter [c. 1590], Morgan had explained to William Chisholm that many had complained to Holt's superiors of the dirty games he was playing (*CSP Scotland* [1589–1593], pp. 229–37). Around the same time Robert Bowes reported to William Cecil, Lord Burghley that different rumors circulated regarding Holt's involvement in the another enterprise organized by Alessandro Farnese, Duke of Parma, against England (Edinburgh October 3, 1591, *CSP Scotland* [1589–1593], pp. 575–77).

[12] Attempts were made to draft an acceptable oath after the Armada in 1588. Sir Thomas Tresham seems to have been responsible for Catholic versions. See Thomas M. McCoog, S.J., *The Society of Jesus in Ireland, Scotland, and England 1541–1588: "Our Way of Proceeding?"* (Leiden, 1996), p. 257.

work against invasions and disturbances. To achieve this Burghley should encourage exiles discontented with the policies of Allen and Parsons in order to eliminate Allen's influence in English affairs and to dissolve the seminaries. Cecil was confident that "libertye in religion maye with such qualifycation be given to Catholiques that bothe they may have occasion to love yow & al your posteritye, & your Lordship never repente yow of so clemente & charitable an action." Moreover, the clergy in England "in habite conformable to theyre vocation, & take some othe not to heare or suffer any practise of treason, or deale in matter of state, or with suche that deale with foren princes in matters of state, & to have some one ruler amongest them that shoulde be wholy dependente uppon your Lordship ... "[13]

To his detailed replies, Cecil appended the names of numerous English exiles and into which faction they fell. Among those who adhered closely to Allen and Parsons and, thus, were favorers of a Spanish policy were numerous Jesuits including Henry Garnet, Robert Southwell, Joseph Creswell, Edward Oldcorne, William Holt, the future Jesuit Richard Walpole[14] along with Richard Barret, Sir Francis Englefield, Sir William Stanley, and Hugh Owen. Opposed to Spanish policies but, according to Cecil, unable to reveal their displeasure because they could propose no other remedy, were Thomas Stapleton,[15] William Gifford,[16] Christopher Bagshaw, Owen Lewis, Bishop of Cassano, future Jesuits Richard Blount and William Warford along with William Tresham, Ralph [*vere* John?] Stonor, Throckmorton, Morgan, Paget, Nicholas Fitzherbert, William Griffiths, and Roger Baynes.[17]

In his history of the English Jesuits, Henry More, S.J., placed the blame for the division squarely on Morgan and Paget.[18] The split, according to More, began with proposals regarding the liberation of Mary, Queen of Scots. Allen and Parsons argued that any plan should be "entrusted to the discretion of the Catholic King, the Pope and the Duke of Guise." Morgan and Paget disagreed. After Mary's execution, Morgan and Paget were

---

[13] The questions addressed to Cecil can be found in TNA, SP 12/238/165. His reply is SP 12/238/167, 168.

[14] Interestingly Henry Walpole is not named.

[15] Because many believed that Stapleton disliked a pro-Spanish policy, Parsons, as we noted in Chapter 4, questioned him about his allegiance in 1597.

[16] Pietro, Cardinal Aldobrandini first mentioned the conflict between Gifford and Holt to Ottavio Mirto Frangipani on 14 October 1596. See *Correspondance d'Ottavio Mirto Frangipani, Premier Nonce de Flandre (1596–1606)*, (eds.) Leon Van der Essen and Armand Louant (4 vols, Rome/Bruxelles/Paris, 1924–1942), vol. 1, p. 6.

[17] TNA, SP 12/238/181.

[18] Henry More, S.J., *The Elizabethan Jesuits*, (ed.) Francis Edwards, S.J (London, 1981), pp. 340–41.

blamed. During the ensuing argument, Holt received Paget and Morgan in Brussels in a warm manner despite their continual attacks on Allen and Parsons. Shortly thereafter, letters were found in Morgan's rooms and in Morgan's hand that attacked the duke of Parma, the king of Spain, and Allen. As a result, Spanish authorities expelled Morgan from Philip's dominions. He and Paget blamed Holt for the discovery and the sentence.[19] By mid-1593, as we noted in Chapter 4, Holt was depressed because of the tension and eager to leave Belgium. Only the intervention of secretary Esteban de Ibarra prevented Holt's transfer to Spain and Joseph Creswell's move to Belgium. In 1595 the attacks became more acrimonious.

Thomas Covert, formerly Allen's agent in Paris, protested to Acquaviva that William Holt was damaging his good name and reputation. Covert explained that he and Holt had been friends until early August of 1595 when Holt defamed and insulted him:

> ... [he claimed] that I am a very envious person, and malicious; that I have a perpetually hardened conscience, as he fears; that I have at length spewed forth this detestable vice of envy and spite which has secretly been nurtured like a monster's offspring in my heart for seven whole years, against the good name and honor of a certain English nobleman [Hugh Owen], whose defence ... this good father has undertaken very passionately.

Covert approached Holt later to discuss the accusations. Instead of receiving an apology, Covert was subjected to new insults including the charge that Covert was the cause of all of Owen's problems. Covert pressed Holt whether he knew this of his own experience or had heard it from others. Holt replied that he had heard it in the confessional. Covert advised him to be more prudent, but Holt simply repeated that Covert was factious and associated with ambitious people, eager to destroy an innocent man. Distressed by Holt's accusations, Covert suggested that they visit Jean d'Heur, rector of the Jesuit college in Antwerp, who knew Covert well. Holt retorted that he was not his superior and he had nothing

---

[19] When the duke of Parma sent the dossier on Morgan to King Philip, he added that Morgan "attempts to sow cockle and intrigues and undo everything that Cardinal Allen and Father Persons and other good Catholics are doing ... both within and without the kingdom" (cited in Albert J. Loomie, S.J., *The Spanish Elizabethans: The English Exiles at the Court of Philip II* [New York, 1963], p. 115). Morgan went first to Rome and then to Savoy. In the spring of 1593, he urged Anne Dormer Hungerford, an English exile for reasons more scandalous than religious, to persuade her sister Jane Dormer, Duchess of Feria, to move from Spain to Brussels. Morgan and Anne Hungerford were eager that the duchess assume a prominent role in the affairs of the English Catholics, a role that she would exercise under their guidance. On the machinations and proposals, see Loomie, *Spanish Elizabethans*, pp. 113–28.

to do with him especially since he could judge these matters as prudently as he. According to Holt, his only religious superior was the Jesuit general but, Covert added, he may have also mentioned Parsons. In that case, Covert threatened to complain to Acquaviva, an action he took reluctantly because he had always considered himself a devoted friend of the Jesuits. So Covert begged:

> for right and justice against a father whom I have up to now, loved, respected and venerated; such a father, I say, whom I continually defended against his rivals and undertook the defense of his name with all my might ... If silence is not imposed upon him as quickly as possible, he will completely estrange the favor of many from himself and from the Society of Jesus. Indeed, to express what I feel, unless silence is imposed upon him and he is removed from here ... you will perhaps receive complaints a little more weightly against him.

Covert had informed Parsons of his actions and assured Acquaviva that James Tyrie, a Scottish Jesuit who worked on the general's staff, would vouch for him and add more details.[20]

Sometime in 1597, William Crichton drafted a long memorial on the origin and nature of the disturbances among the English in Brussels because many believed him to be responsible for the conflict.[21] He named as the two culprits the Scotsman Robert Bruce and the "Englishman" (*vere* Welshman) Hugh Owen. Bruce, earlier considered an honorable man by Crichton, disputed with most of his fellow Scots and eventually alienated them all. At the same time, he became friendly with Owen.[22] For reasons unexplained, at least by Crichton, Bruce calumniated the chief Scottish Catholic nobles, and especially James Gordon and Crichton himself. Crichton enclosed a copies of the charges levelled against Gordon by the nobles.[23] Bruce also provided "misleading" information to the papal agent Innocenzo Malvasia and, more important, to the king's secretary, Esteban de Ibarra, which he, in turn, forwarded to Philip II. The information Bruce relayed to Malvasia and Ibarra, resulted in considerable harm to the Catholic cause and to various noblemen in Rome and Madrid. So

---

[20] Covert to Acquaviva, Antwerp August 11, 1595, ARSI, Germ. 175, fols 72^r–73^v.

[21] Thomas M. McCoog, S.J., "Harmony Disrupted: Robert Parsons, S.J., William Crichton, S.J., and the Question of Queen Elizabeth's Successor, 1581–1603," *AHSI*, 73 (2004): pp. 170–74.

[22] Owen had organized a network of spies within England to keep Spain informed of important developments. See Loomie, *Spanish Elizabethans*, pp. 52–93.

[23] The "Capita criminum quorum reus agitur Robertus Brusius Scotus inpraesentiarum custodiae mancipatus Bruxellis" may be Crichton's list (*CSP Scotland* [1597–1603], pp. 591–609, 609–10 [French summary]).

frequently did he rant against these Scottish nobles and Scottish Jesuits that someone began spreading tales about him. He was suspected of corresponding secretly with officials in the government of Queen Elizabeth.

At the same time, "certain Englishmen" complained to Crichton about Owen. "Trusting in Father Holt's friendship and familiarity," Crichton discussed these complaints with him, even going so far as to name Owen's critics. To Crichton's shock, Holt repeated everything, names included, to Owen who then directed his anger at Crichton and his known critics. If the truth be known, Crichton opined, many of Owen's critics had long-standing grudges against him. Some English and Scottish exiles with connections at court, suspected Bruce and Owen of clandestine associations with Queen Elizabeth's government and of opposition to Philip II. During the governorship of Don Pedro Enríquez de Azevedo, Count of Fuentes, "a certain courtier" persuaded the governor to initiate secret hearings on the rumored conduct of Owen and Bruce. After depositions had been taken against Bruce, he was arrested and thrown into prison where he remained for more than a year. Regardless of the secrecy of the proceedings, with a network as extensive as Owen's, word about Bruce's fate quickly reached Owen. Relying either on his innocence or on the influence Father Holt had at court, Owen defended himself by attacking maliciously anyone examined during the investigation, accusing them of being both his initial accusers and subsequent witnesses to their own lies. This, according to Crichton, was the beginning of the disturbances. Holt supported Owen throughout. Because Owen thought that the original committee favored his accusers, he insisted that the case be heard in the presence of the royal Privy Council. The Cardinal Archduke Albert, aware of the true nature of the case and hoping that it could be settled amicably, referred the case to a commission comprised of the Jesuit Oliver Mannaerts and Don Juan Bautista de Tassis. He instructed them to listen to all complainants, take depositions, and report to the archduke who would then pass a decision.

In Crichton's evaluation, neither side was without some culpability. Owen's and Holt's suspicion that some nobles delated Owen for ignoble reasons, lacked foundation. Crichton knew that the investigation was launched not by complaints from any English or Scottish noble. In fact, the "certain courtier" was Belgian who had recommended secret hearings to see if there were any evidence for rumors about Owen's and Bruce's involvement with the English authorities. Revenge did not motivate this Belgian; he simply wanted to uncover the truth. Because the hearings would be in secret, no aspersions would have been cast on the reputations of anyone if the commissioners did not unearth any evidence. The nobles were summoned to appear; some refused so the judges travelled to Louvain to examine them. Everything would have passed quietly if Holt and Owen had not made their accusations and publicized the events. Despite their innocence, the unnamed nobles were obliged to defend themselves in the presence of the Privy Council. Not only did they retract nothing, they defended themselves through counter-charges and counter-accusations. Although Holt now considered Crichton an opponent, the Scot insisted that he always defended the Englishman. Now Crichton pleaded with Acquaviva that he attempt to resolve the problem. These nobles did not oppose the Society of Jesus. Indeed, Crichton asserted, they should be numbered among the Society's friends. They complained about one specific Jesuit, William Holt, and indirectly about Robert Parsons because he had acquired this authority for Holt. If rumors accusing English Jesuits of tyrannizing Catholic noblemen eventually reached Rome, Crichton wanted to make it clear that these nobles were not the originators.[24] Those responsible for this indictment were either "malcontent priests sent away from Rome or others who disliked Owen and Holt." They may, in fact, have been friends with these nobles but the nobles themselves were not responsible for the charges. Now they were vexed that father general may consider them the Society's enemies. As evidence that these nobles were "friends who should be cherished and should they be estranged, they ought to be reconciled," he named them and described their previous support for the English Jesuits.

Charles Nevill, Earl of Westmorland, had long been friendly with the Society despite the fact that he had not been a very "good-living man." He was of royal blood and remained a powerful magnate in England even though he was attainted for treason for his role in the Northern Rebellion of 1569. Charles Paget, "of whom I say nothing," had many friends, family, and benefactors in England, who were generous and friendly to the Society. Sir William Tresham had consistently demonstrated his friendship towards the Society. Many relatives in England were Jesuit benefactors and suffered for Catholicism and for their devotion to the Society. John Stonor once accompanied Edmund Campion and Parsons. He was arrested at his father's house with Parsons's printing press and baggage. The paternal uncles of Charles Browne were Jesuit benefactors. The household of Mr. Gage was very Catholic and devoted to the Society. Both Sir Timothy Mohet and Ralph Ligons claimed that no one could be any opponent of the Society unless he was "a heretic, impious or of evil life." Mr. Pansford, until his death in Brussels last July, favored the Society and

---

[24] James Younger reported to William Gifford on November 12, 1596 that "We hear by Dr Worthington that certain, who term themselves chief and principal of our nation, have written unto the pope, that they are tyrannized by an English jesuit here in Flanders, with like tyranny they have complained to be used by the jesuits in England against our seminary priests" (published in M.A. Tierney, (ed.), *Dodd's Church History of England* [5 vols, London: 1839–1843], vol. 3, pp. xc–xci).

in England was always hospitable to Jesuits and the secular priests who supported them. Finally, the secular priest Thomas Covert depended on the Society for 25 years as Parsons could attest. Francis, Lord Dacre and Dr William Gifford agreed with them. It was claimed that the latter wrote and spoke against the Society. If he could be believed, he claimed that he owed the Society much and wanted nothing more than to be at peace with it. Crichton concluded that their reconciliation with Holt and Owen was almost impossible but pleaded with Acquaviva that he not regard these men as enemies of the Society. If good relations were restored, they and their relatives in England could assist the Society's work tremendously; if not, they could obstruct it.[25]

In an undated letter written around the same time, Crichton explained that he had heard from Parsons who now considered Crichton Holt's enemy and a supporter of the Society's opponents. Crichton denied it. He simply was not ready to defend Owen, and he found these English nobles more moderate and eager for peace than either Owen or Holt. Crichton feared the consequences of this dispute: "I see that out of those charges both against these nobles and against the king of Scotland so many enemies to the Society are being created that if the king of Scotland should prevail, there would be a danger that the Society would be expelled from his realms, and for that reason I am anxious that these contentions and charges be resolved."[26]

Spanish pensions may not have been the primary cause of the conflicts amongst English exiles, but money did play a role. Most Catholic exiles applied for a Spanish pension upon arrival in Belgium. Once a pension had been granted, the exile would receive a monthly allowance. System of payment was cumbersome and there were frequent demands for its reformation. In March of 1596, Hugh Owen, Sir William Stanley, and William Holt, in conjunction with Archduke Albert, forwarded a proposal for the system's total revision to King Philip II. Owen, Stanley, and Holt had evaluated all English pensioners and their contributions to the Spanish cause, and distinguished troublesome pensioners designated by the letter B for *bulliciosos* from the others. The report suggested that the troublesome should be transferred to some other part of the Spanish empire or, if more drastic actions were required, deprived of their pensions altogether.[27]

---

[25] ARSI, Angl. 42, fols 46ʳ–47ᵛ.

[26] Crichton to Acquaviva, n.d., ARSI, Germ. 178, fol. 55ʳ.

[27] Presumably an exile whose pension was threatened wrote the anonymous letter to Lord Burghley from Liège on August 24, 1597. The author admitted that he had been a Catholic since birth and that he had fled the kingdom for religious reasons, but had never conspired against Queen Elizabeth. He had sought a pension from Philip II but because Parsons and Holt controlled the purse strings, he did not receive it. He now proposed to

In the future, Spain should only allow English pensioners useful to the Spanish cause to reside in Belgium. The report recommended that the earl of Westmorland, Sir William Tresham, Charles Paget, Oliver Eustace, Ralph Ligons, John Stonor, James Chambers, John Petit, Charles Browne, and William Gifford be either deprived of their pensions, transferred elsewhere, or be paid by other sources. Although no action was taken, the "troublesome" heard that their pensions were in jeopardy.[28] Because most extant sources lack dates, we cannot establish a definite chronology, but it seems that the English nobles were testifying to a commission about Owen at the same time that Owen and Holt were evaluating their pensions. It cannot be a coincidence that one finds practically the same names on both lists.

Letters to Acquaviva protested Holt's involvement in these secular matters, perhaps suggesting that such activity violated recent congregational decrees. Acquaviva reported to Mannaerts that Charles Paget and other English nobles had written to him about Holt and requested his transfer. Acquaviva advised each complainant to discuss the matter with Mannaerts who was in the midst of an official visitation of the province.[29] To Holt, Acquaviva complained about the dissension tearing apart the community of exiles, "which is said to exist and to arise out of the fact that everyone is eager to promote the honors and the business of his own nation." This was a blemish of human weakness. Excessive nationalism was not appropriate for religious "since they all have the same purpose: to take care of God's honor as well as to carry out the one rule of charity." Above all, religious prefer peace and sincere unity; Acquaviva exhorted Holt to do all he could to promote the bond of religious unity.[30] In another context Acquaviva confided to Parsons that "the other blessed father [Crichton] is a little excessive in his zeal for his country."[31]

---

return to England if he and his family were granted liberty of conscience. Meanwhile England was in great danger if it did not grant some toleration to the Catholics (S.R. Scargill-Bird, et al. *Calendar of the Manuscripts of the Most Hon. the Marquis of Salisbury* [24 vols, London, 1883–1976], vol. 7, pp. 363–65). Intentionally or not, the author demonstrated the accuracy of *State of English Fugitives under the King of Spaine and his ministers*.

[28] See Loomie, *Spanish Elizabethans*, pp. 27–37 for more detail on the need for reform and this proposal.

[29] Acquaviva to Crichton, Rome March 2, 1596, ARSI, Fl. Belg. 1/I, p. 595; same to Oliver Mannaerts, Rome March 23, 1596, ARSI, Fl. Belg. 1/I, p. 603; same to Lord Paget, Rome March 23, 1596, ARSI, Fl. Belg. 1/I, p. 603. A few months later Acquaviva explained to Creswell that he had asked Mannaerts to arbitrate a conflict between Crichton and Holt (Rome August 26, 1596, ARSI, Tolet. 5/II, fol. 454ᵛ).

[30] Acquaviva to Holt, Rome March 23, 1596, ARSI, Fl. Belg. 1/I, p. 602.

[31] Rome February 11, 1596, ARSI, Cast. 6, fols 237ʳ–38ʳ.

By early April Holt's supporters were rallying to his defense.[32] Sir Francis Englefield instructed Roger Baynes to warn Acquaviva verbally of the possible consequences of Holt's transfer:

> ... if Fa. Holte should be removed from thence whose travailes and service in the Court cannot be supplied by anie of ours or other nacion, that neither knoweth the differences and particulars of persons, or is so well known by the governors and esteamed by the officers of that Courte. And above all things youe must not forgeate to inculck well unto his Fatherhode, what and who they be which labor the removing of the good father, by securing the Visitors, Provincials and Rectors of those Lowe countries with fraudulent reasons and false allegacions, which they being straungers can never comme to comprehend, nor to discover the false partes of those sedicious and factiouse ...[33]

These letters only reinforced father general's desire to get to the bottom of it.[34]

While others wrote to Acquaviva, William Gifford contacted one of the "malcontents" at the English College. Gifford explained that he had already asked Francisco, Cardinal Toledo (to whom we shall return later in this chapter) to do something about the insolent Holt and his accusations regarding Gifford himself. Holt accused Gifford of supporting James VI's right to the English throne and of approving the absolution of Henry IV of France. Moreover, according to Holt, Gifford had complained about the publication of the *Book of Succession* to the nuncio in Brussels. Gifford asked his correspondent to confirm this account so that Toledo would use his influence to have Holt "the fyrebrande of all sedition and division" transferred, and to find another pension for Charles Paget.[35] Toledo's premature death in September of 1596 prevented him from providing any significant assistance to Gifford and his associates.

Henry More briefly explained the proceedings. Thirty-six specific accusations were made against Holt and presented to the archduke. Among them was the charge "of threatening the reputations, property, liberty, and even life of certain people: neither was he suitably loyal to the King."

---

[32] Acquaviva to Sir William Stanley, Rome April 6, 1596, ARSI, Fl. Belg. 1/I, p. 604.

[33] Madrid February 24, 1596, AAW, V, 39. Englefield stressed the importance of both Parsons and Holt for the survival of the English colleges in Belgium and Spain, and the proofs offered regarding the "suffycientie, integrity, and dexteritie" of both Jesuits. See the testimonies gathered by Dr Thomas Worthington in Holt's favor in Tierney/Dodd, *Church History*, vol. 3, pp. lxxxix–xc. An anonymous memorial that we shall discuss later in this chapter argued that Spain risked losing many friends if the king did not protect and support Holt and Owen.

[34] Acquaviva to Mannaerts, Rome April 6, 1596, ARSI, Fl. Belg. 1/I, p. 604

[35] Gifford to [Robert Markham?], August 8, 1596, AAW, V, 64.

As one of the examiners appointed by the archduke, Mannaerts, fearful that the Society's reputation would be damaged by the affair, showed the charges to Holt. "Grieved that so much could be believed of him before he was heard, and that prejudice of this sort could be entertained by a man of Manare's [Mannaerts's] calibre," Holt promised to reply and to demonstrate that he had done nothing to bring ill repute on the Society's good name. He was ready to reply to each accusation but Tassis, pointing out the 10 major ones, said that replies to these would be sufficient. After Holt had answered the 10, he wanted to be heard on the others, but the commissioners claimed he had done enough to satisfy every issue. Tassis judged that "certain gentlemen felt that the Society, and those who favored it, had too much influence with his Highness and the rest of the Flemish administration. The Jesuits should wield that influence with discretion." Holt gave assurances that he was innocent and would remain so. He assured them that "he had been friendly to all and helpful—even to those who, from the nature of the objections, he could guess to be the authors of this accusation."[36]

Given the extent and the bitterness of the controversy, the issues, as delineated in Holt's explanation, seem almost inconsequential.[37] Contrary to Covert's insistence, Holt did not demand that he revoke his deposition against Owen. He had spoken with Covert, who had visited him in Antwerp to seek his advice, but not about the deposition. Moreover, he had not provided any information to any commissioners that would have obstructed Covert's ordination. Everything that Holt did via-à-vis Covert, was in hope of restoring amiable relations between him and Owen.[38] Other charges related to individuals. He had not accused Walter Pitts, Prior of the English Carthusians, of favoring the king's rebels. Nor had he been involved in the financial affairs of John Pansford. Moreover he had worked—albeit unsuccessfully—for Michael Modye's liberation from prison in Belgium and was not responsible for the harsh conditions that caused the death of Godfrey Fuljambe. Holt's explanation satisfied Tassis and Mannaerts and who judged that Holt "had on many counts been the victim of partisan zeal rather than the object of reasonable doubt." The investigation ended on December 19, 1596 with Holt's vindication.[39]

Holt's acquittal concluded one battle but the war continued. Before the judicial process was initiated, Mannaerts had suggested to Parsons and

---

[36] More, *Elizabethan Jesuits*, pp. 341–42.

[37] Holt's undated reply can be found in AAW, V, 107.

[38] Parsons later intervened in an attempt to restore amiable relations between Holt and Covert. He hoped that the passions had quieted down and that they could resolve their problems as Christians (Rome May 31, 1597, AAW, VI, 37).

[39] More, *Elizabethan Jesuits*, pp. 340–43.

Creswell that Holt's temporary transfer would, to some extent, settle the disputes in Belgium. More than once Parsons considered an exchange, but external forces always prevented it. Now it was proposed that Creswell leave Spain, stop in Rome to correct the problems at the English College and then replace Holt in Brussels. The decision whether the proposal would be implemented, Acquaviva left to Parsons.[40] In January of 1597, Parsons definitively replied to Mannaerts's recommendation. Parsons confessed that he himself had considered an exchange for nearly two years for various reasons: Holt had requested it; Holt's assistance was needed in Spain; and Creswell, "not lacking that tactfulness which your Reverence misses in Fr. Holt," would be more pleasing and acceptable to the English in Belgium. But Parsons eventually concluded that Holt's transfer would not satisfy his critics because they attacked not him but the Society. They would find other targets, perhaps Creswell, once Holt was removed. As evidence, he cited recent events at the English College whose students demanded the removal of Edmund Harewood and promised complete peace once he was gone. Harewood was transferred, but the disturbance continued. Now Parsons was obliged to go to Rome to settle the disturbances—something that he hoped could be done swiftly because he wanted to return to Spain. Although he would discuss the possibility of Holt's transfer with Acquaviva, he did not consider it possible at this time. Before their departure for Spain, Lorenzo Suárez de Figueroa, Duke of Feria, and Esteban de Ibarra, left instructions from Philip II for the archduke. They stressed how useful and important the Society of Jesus was for the king's business "and that therefore it was advisable to promote its interests in every way." Regarding England, the archduke should give preference to Holt's advice because of his experience and trustworthiness. Thus, Parsons's explained, Holt's transfer at this time would not please Philip II. Another reason for postponing his departure was a recent letter to Pope Clement VIII from Holt's critics. The authors attacked not just Holt, but all Jesuits working on the English mission. Jesuits, they claimed, were "lording it over the rest of the clergy, nay that they are issuing tyrannical commands on all sides (and they make this assertion expressly too about Fr Holt) and they say that for this reason they ought all to be withdrawn." A transfer now would be interpreted as an acknowledgment of the accuracy of these accusations.

Because of the poverty, stress and national loyalties of the exiles, to say nothing of the role of spies, Parsons did not think that dissension and conflict should have surprised Mannaerts. Both factions advanced arguments for their position, but the prudent, guided by reason and not

---

[40] Acquaviva to Parsons, Rome February 11, 1596, ARSI, Cast. 6, fols 237^v–238^r; same to same, Rome April 8, 1596, ARSI, Cast. 6, fols 242^v–243^r.

passion, could readily see which party was right. The Society's opponents, because of their inability to emerge victorious from any head-to-head battle with English Jesuits and their supporters, had presented their case to Jesuits of other nations, Jesuits unfamiliar with English affairs and English temperament. They succeeded in winning the sympathy of many. Parsons hoped that the clamor and complaints raised by Holt's critics would not be heeded by Belgian Jesuits "more readily than reason and justice demand, and without hearing the other side. If this is done, great harm and scandal as well will eventually follow." Regarding Holt himself and his personal failings, if Mannaerts considered him too brusque, Parsons advised him to exercise his authority and admonish Holt. Parsons had no doubt that Holt would quickly reform "in view of the respect he has for your Reverence [Mannaerts]."[41]

The duke of Feria thought that Holt's opponents consciously furthered the interests of King James VI and, presumably for that reason, he considered them hostile to Spanish interests. He recommended to King Philip that some pensioners, for example Paget and Tresham, should be transferred to Sicily. Others, for example Westmorland and Stonor, should be strongly reprimanded and warned that a second offense would result in the loss of their pensions. Furthermore, he advised that the king urge Acquaviva to find some excuse for transferring Crichton from Belgium because Crichton "is not only an avowed advocate of the king of Scots, but who has also frequently spoken to me, with the most passionate feeling, on the subject of the monarch's affairs." James Gordon, "a quiet and dispassionate person, divested of his own prepossessions in favour of his own sovereign, and agreeing with those among the English, who are proceeding in the right road," would be the ideal replacement.[42]

Parsons arrived in Rome a few months after Acquaviva learned of Holt's acquittal. Acquaviva had already decided how to proceed: he wrote to Mannaerts and Holt. To Mannaerts, Acquaviva explained that he wanted to raise a personal matter with Holt now that the proceedings had ended: "he should now strive to temper and mitigate his *modus agendi*, which some think too harsh, and by becoming more agreeable and, thus demonstrating the charity which he feels towards everyone, will not give any occasion for similar problems in the future." In response to Mannaerts's suggestion that Holt be transferred, Acquaviva decided that the time was not ripe: a transfer now, even if the archduke permitted it, would seem to

---

[41] Parsons to Mannaerts, Barcelona January 10, 1597, AAW, VI, 4 (partially printed in Tierney/Dodd, *Church History*, vol. 3, pp. lxxxiv–lxxxvi and partially translated in More, *Elizabethan Jesuits*, pp. 343–44).

[42] Duke of Feria to Philip II, Barcelona January 3, 1597, in Tierney/Dodd, *Church History*, vol. 3, pp. liii–lvii.

undermine his innocence. In no way did Acquaviva want to appear to be gratifying Holt's opponents or granting any of their requests. Apparently Parsons had convinced Acquaviva that, despite Crichton's defense of Holt's foes, they were "not so devoted to the Society as they would like to seem but, on the contrary, we must beware of their attacking the Society itself under the pretext of attacking one Jesuit, and of their looking for a lack of unity within the Society." Moreover, although Acquaviva did not wish to reproach any non-English Jesuit involved ever so remotely in this dispute, he argued that English Jesuits, especially when they agreed unanimously on a given subject (as they did on this), were much better informed about the affairs of their country. Finally, Acquaviva requested an official public document attesting to Holt's innocence, and two letters from the archduke, one for the pope and the other for himself, to the same effect. Each would be available to demonstrate Holt's innocence, if needed.[43] On the same day Acquaviva congratulated Holt on his vindication. Since the judicial decision imposed silence on Holt's critics, Acquaviva hoped the matter would end. But, in case anyone raised similar suspicions in the future, Acquaviva recommended that Holt collect testimonies of his innocence from the archduke, perhaps copies of the letters that had been sent to Rome. Since even Holt agreed that the one complaint that was not totally groundless, specifically his brusque nature, Acquviva urged him to be more patient and tolerant.[44]

Acquaviva's third letter on the Holt affair was addressed to Crichton. Because he had written full details about his evaluation of the affair to Mannaerts, Acquaviva was not going to repeat them but instructed Crichton to consult the Belgian Jesuit. He reminded Crichton that "union and harmony of minds is especially necessary among ours, particularly when we must fear that the enemy is craftily trying through others to threaten and destroy that union." Aside from a final comment regarding the importance of this unity for the missions, Acquaviva wanted to add nothing more on the matter.[45]

On the same day, Parsons wrote to Mannaerts. Hoping that Mannaerts would yet live "to see that college in London which we once planned together," an allusion to Mannaerts's role in the foundation of the Jesuit mission to England, Parsons stressed how they had once agreed on everything. Now he worried that Mannaerts's defense of Holt's critics would disrupt their relations and disturb the unity of minds so praised

---

[43] Acquaviva to Mannaerts, Rome April 12, 1597, ARSI, Fl. Belg. 1/II, pp. 640–41 (published in Tierney/Dodd, *Church History*, vol. 3, pp. xciii–xciv).

[44] Acquaviva to Holt, Rome April 12, 1597, ARSI, Fl. Belg. 1/II, pp. 641–42. Other copies can be found in AAW, VI, 25, 26.

[45] Acquaviva to Crichton, Rome April 12, 1597, ARSI, Fl. Belg. 1/II, pp. 642–43.

by Ignatius Loyola. Parsons, obviously, agreed with some of Mannaert's observations, that is, men should not be alienated by injuries or abuse. If Hugh Owen has wronged them, he should cease and give satisfaction. The same was true for Holt, Parsons himself, or anyone. But even if Owen was blameworthy, should others be held responsible because he was their friend? Was it fair to ask Holt to sever relations with him because of the wrath of others? More specifically, Parsons pointed out to Mannaerts that he consistently described Holt's opponents as "nobles" and his supporters as "Owen and his following." Many of Holt's friends deduced from this that Mannaerts considered them to be "of mean birth" whereas, with the exception of the earl of Westmorland, who, incidentally explained to his friends that he had no quarrel with Holt but only with Owen, they were "themselves of far better birth than the other party or, at any rate, of equally good birth." Parsons cited as examples the late Sir Francis Englefield, Thomas Fitzherbert, Sir William Stanley and his brothers, and James Hill. These men have been "loyal to the common cause and most friendly to our Society, which can not be said of the others, at any rate as regards our Society." Mannaerts found it most difficult to believe that Holt's opponents were antagonistic towards the Society *in se*. Parsons agreed that many associated themselves with Paget for a variety of motives: poverty, dislike of Owen, preferences for James VI, and so on, and not hatred of the Society. Nonetheless, he contended, the primary intention of the Paget/Morgan faction for the past 15 years had been its opposition to the Society. Many had witnessed it; Parsons and others had clear proof of it from Richard Barret, Cardinal Allen, Garnet, Creswell. Like Mannaerts, the duke of Feria once believed that anti-Jesuitism did not motivate the faction but, upon examination, he changed his mind as he had informed Parsons during their recent meeting in Barcelona. With all due respect, Parsons suggested that Mannaerts had been deceived. If the Belgian demanded proof, Parsons would provide it. He would show how this faction has spoken disparagingly of the Society; how they had estranged many important men from the Society; how they had signed memorials and had written books against the Society. Now they had begun to boast that they had gained the support of many important Jesuits and have caused a schism in the Society itself. The repercussions of Mannaerts's new friendship with this group spread throughout Belgium and Rome. Parsons cautioned Mannaerts lest he be "carried away by this sentiment of kindliness and by a desire for peace, which will be difficult to attain with me disposed as these are, and from incurring a contrary inconvenience, which, to a certain extent, I see you already have, viz. of giving offence to old friends and failing to attain a firm friendship with these new ones, at any rate towards the Society."[46]

Parsons's letter did not have the desired effect. In a letter to George Duras, a fellow Belgian and currently the assistant to the Jesuit superior general for Germany, Mannaerts continued to lobby for Holt's withdrawal as a way of achieving reconciliation with an important and influential body of English exiles. Mannaerts sympathized with some complaints. He found Holt a secretive man who disclosed little to his superiors and who generally displayed a lack of trust. Contrary to instructions, Holt, and other English Jesuits, sent and received letters from each other without submitting them to the approval of their local superiors as was the rule within the Society. Holt consistently defended his actions while ignoring the advice of his superiors. To make matters worse, Holt considered Owen's enemies his enemies and instead of trying to reconcile the two factions, Holt's letters and comments only deepened the divide. Tassis and Mannaerts sought private resolution, but Owen and Holt insisted that the issue be resolved publicly. Mannaerts thought that Holt's tactics would harm the Society because his opponents had many friends and relatives in England who protected and supported the Jesuits. The attempt to portray Holt's foes as enemies of the Society, Mannaerts dismissed. He was certain that many loved the Society and had, indeed, suffered on its account. Parsons's arguments to the contrary saddened Mannaerts because it made him aware how some English Jesuits conspired against Holt's foes instead of seeking reconciliation with them.[47]

To Acquaviva, Mannaerts admitted that he was sure of Holt's innocence and integrity and, perhaps more important for the matter at hand, that he was ignorant of the deeper issues involved in the dissensions. Nonetheless he concluded that reconciliation was impossible as long as the Jesuits involved were so partisan. Even though Holt and Owen emerged victorious, many attributed their victory to the influence of a few Jesuits with secular authorities. As long as Jesuits obstinately adhered to one side and strove to crush the other, they made the name of the Society hateful to many. The price of their victory would be many enemies. Holt's vindication, Mannaerts thought, was based on insufficient evidence. Holt had been more amenable since the judgment, but his subsequent decisions regarding the Spanish pensions, decisions that would throw some English exiles into debtor's prison and increase the pensions of others, has not allowed the controversy to die.

---

[46] Parsons to Mannaerts, Rome April 12, 1597, AAW, VI, 24 (printed in Tierney/Dodd, *Church History*, vol. 3, pp. lxxxvi–lxxxix).

[47] Mannaerts to George Duras, Brussels July 12, 1597, ARSI, Germ. 177, fols 192^r–193^v.

Mannaerts informed Acquaviva of Parsons's recent admonition that non-English Jesuits were being deceived. Mannaerts remained adamant that, contrary to the efforts of Parsons and Holt to convince everyone that the latter's opponents hated the Society and sought its ruin, many of that group actually loved the Society.[48] Even if some did hate the Society, Jesuits should not respond by attacking them by word and in print, but by attempts to restore peace and harmony. Mannaerts wanted to exonerate Holt and the Society from all jealousy and suspicion. He reminded Acquaviva that he had had no contact with Paget before Acquaviva's request that he examine the matter. Nor had he sought out any role in the official investigation. Indeed he rejected the invitation four times before eventually accepting it. Now he believed it was dangerous to accept Parsons's and Holt's judgment about the quarrel. In fact, he believed that the Society should support neither side but work for reconciliation. Parsons claimed that he has letters proving that these men were responsible for the disturbances at the English College, Rome. Perhaps, but their existence would not alter Mannaert's judgment: he attributed it to human infirmity and passion. We should not be surprised if they lashed out at those whom they suspected of harming them. They were men of the world, soldiers and not religious. But religious should be much more tolerant as they tried to heal wounds.[49]

Mannaerts's remarks annoyed both Duras and Acquaviva. In another letter to Duras, Mannaerts stressed that, regardless of the actions of others, Jesuits must behave as good religious "for if we continue so to behave and to indulge our animosity against others, even though they have caused us trouble, we will turn the spirits of many against us; and since the matter is so unclear that the truth does not shine forth brightly, I do not see how it is safe to cling (except perhaps in affection) more to one side than to the other." Having read Parsons's account of the origins of the dispute which he traced to Paget's and Morgan's exclusion from a meeting in Paris, Mannaerts believed that Parsons could easily be mistaken because the Belgian did not see how such widespread opposition could rest on such a weak foundation. He had seen William Gifford's letter attacking the Society and he condemned it. Some indubitably have been too vitriolic, but the entire group should not be condemned because of them. Mannaerts considered Paget to be extremely able and prudent. If Holt had treated him courteously, he could have been won over to the side of the Society. Instead first Parsons and then Holt treated him with suspicion. Someone, either Owen or another, denounced him publicly to the duke of Parma.

---

[48] Later in 1597, Acquaviva commented that "there may be some friends of the Society amongst the noblemen, but there are also many who seek to denigrate it in various ways" (Acquaviva to Crichton, Rome November 1, 1597, ARSI, Fl. Belg. I/II, pp. 657–58).

[49] Mannaerts to Acquaviva, Brussels August 2, 1597, ARSI, Germ. 177, fols 216^r–17^v.

He was acquitted. Unlike Owen, Paget was accused publicly but he did not respond by stirring up trouble and making accusations. Owen, on the contrary, raised such a storm, and blamed William Crichton and various English nobles for everything. Now, instead of winning their good will, Holt, armed with letters of acquittal, was proclaiming his total lack of disinterest in his opponents' affairs. Mannaerts again stressed that Holt's actions would backfire on the Society. Having prayed about the matter, Mannaerts recommended that Acquaviva transfer Holt, and then insist that Parsons, perhaps by visiting Belgium, actively strive for peace even though Mannaerts doubted that was any longer possible. Parsons was the key to ending the controversy "for being English, being a prudent man, and knowing what has been done in Spain and in Rome, he was known to the cardinal-archduke as a man not driven by any passion."[50] Mannaerts repeated his plea a month later. He worried that the imminent arrival of students expelled from the English College, Rome, would aggravate the bitterness and division. As different nobles, for example Lord Dacre and George More, departed they blame Holt and Owen directly and Parsons indirectly for their misfortunes.[51] Tresham showed a recent letter from Parsons in which the Jesuit asserted that the archduke's exoneration of Holt demonstrated that all charges against him were lies, and his accusers calumniators and slanderers. Mannaerts worried that in their zeal to vindicate a Jesuit brother, Holt's friends assailed the very men whom they should be assuaging. Moreover he feared that Parsons's use of the archduke's letter would anger him: he did not ponder the testimonies of both sides of the dispute in any quasi-judicial way, but simply accepted the report of Mannaerts and Tassis. They had evaluated all charges and decided some were unfounded, others unimportant, others doubtful, and the rest Holt could explain. Mannaerts admitted that he relied more "on the Society's innocence and the presumption of Father Holt's goodness than upon his answers to the articles." The archduke reluctantly wrote the letter of vindication. Now that copies of this letter are being distributed as proof of Holt's innocence, his opponents complained that the hearing was not fair because they were not summoned to testify. They intended to appeal to the archduke. Comments such as this, Mannaerts realized, would confirm Parsons's and perhaps Duras's suspicions that he sympathized with Holt's foes. These fears lacked foundation. Yet he

---

[50] Mannaerts to Duras, Courtrai September 18, 1597 (printed in Tierney/Dodd, *Church History*, vol. 3, pp. xciv–xcviii).

[51] According to Oliver Mannaerts, many English nobles left the service of Philip II, some for Liège, others for Germany. Lord Dacre went to Scotland where he was lavishly received by James VI. Formerly friends of the Society, most were now alienated. See Mannaerts to Acquaviva, Brussels February 13, 1598, ARSI, Germ. 178, fols 51^r–52^v.

opposed an indiscriminate attack on Holt's foes and the successful plot to have them evicted from Flanders. Mannaerts was still convinced that this type of revenge was neither appropriate for religious nor opportune for the success of the Society's work in England. A reduction in the amount of alms collected by Jesuits for priests in English prisons, as but one sign of the increasing opposition to the Society. Personally Mannaerts always found the English noblemen "very courteous even when I had to admonish or blame them in some matter," but from his experience, he found Owen and his associates "very bitter, passionate, haughty, given to threats and to abusive talk about others." Yet Parsons contended Mannaerts was deceived by men who injured and insulted the Society. Mannaerts claimed that he never evaded or avoided any Englishman, but he was always anxious when he met Owen and his associates because of their anger and scurrilous talk. He subtly reminded Duras that he too had complained confidentially to Mannaerts about the same time.

The only possible remedy was an immediate visit by Parsons. He could discuss the matter with the archduke and arrange for the recall of the English nobles and restoration of their previous honors. Parsons should immediately inform Mannaerts of the identities of the exiles "who have persecuted and who are persecuting the Society so that we may not continue to walk in the dark as we now are." Parsons aroused Mannaerts's suspicions about Paget but the Belgian would like to know why. He knew that Gifford has opposed the Society for years, but he believed that Parsons's and Holt's actions were transforming old friends such as Tresham into enemies. About whom should he be on guard? Or, as Mannaerts preferred to express it, whom "must we take greater care to win over and bind to ourselves by our good offices"?[52] But Parsons did not travel to Belgium. Even if Mannaerts had been correct in his evaluation and Parsons had made the trip, the division had become so great that he probably would not have been able to bridge it. Relations deteriorated ever further and the accusations became ever more acrimonious.

Parsons the Arbitrator

The troubles at the English College were the proximate cause of Richard Barret's journey to Rome in early 1596.[53] He feared that Claudio

---

[52] Mannaerts to Duras, Courtrai October 12, 1597 (printed in Tierney/Dodd, *Church History*, vol. 3, pp. xcviii–cii). See Francis Edwards, S.J., *Robert Persons: The Biography of an Elizabethan Jesuit 1546–1610* (St Louis, 1995), pp. 217–19 for his interpretation of Mannaerts's opposition.

[53] Again I follow Anthony Kenny, "The Inglorious Revolution 1594–1597," *The Venerabile*, 17 (1955): pp. 77–94 and Michael E. Williams's shorter account in *The Venerable*

Acquaviva would relinquish the administration of the college, and authorize the withdrawal of the Society from the English mission. He also worried about the financial effect of these decisions on the English College in Douai. A further concern was Filippo, Cardinal Sega's suggestion that the administration of the English College in Douai needed reform. Barret supported the Society, but was not obsequious in his devotion. Thus he was observant enough to realize that responsibility for the disturbances in Rome must be shared by the students and the staff. On April 10, 1596 he wrote to Parsons from Rome:

> Well father theire must needs be a Rector that is skilfull in the affaires of England and such a one as can and will gyve correspondence to the Colleges and your frends abrod and besides he must be a man of gravitie, of countenance and authoritie and such as deale for matters of England and for the Colleges in Flanders must concurre with your frends at Dowaye otherwise yt is not in me to helpe nor in all your frends theare.[54]

To prevent further problems the administration must be improved.

In early April, as we have seen, Enrico Caetani, Cardinal Protector of England, departed for Poland as papal legate. Because Cardinal Sega, the vice-protector, was dying, Pope Clement VIII nominated the Jesuit Francisco, Cardinal Toledo as his successor.[55] Initially, Toledo exercised his authority well. With honesty and kindness, he exhorted the leaders of the opposition to obedience. Impressed with his frankness and hopeful in his support, they concurred, and life slowly returned to normal. On May 17, after a delay of a few months because of the dissension, two students, Sylvester Norris and Richard Button, departed for England. On the same day, Toledo replaced the college's rector Girolamo Fioravanti with Alfonso Agazzari, who had retained his interest in the English mission after the conclusion of his first term as rector in 1586. A few days later, the two controversial, hired prefects were removed, and two student *ripetitori* and one Jesuit restored. Edward Bennett, the leader of the dissidents, met weekly with the cardinal. At these meetings and through his influence, Bennett succeeded in reversing Fioravanti's unpopular decisions. In late May, Toledo decided that he would provide letters of recommendation

---

English College (London, 1979), pp. 16–21.

[54] Barret to Parsons, Rome April 10, 1596, AAW, V, 48 (printed in Penelope Renold, (ed.), *Letters of William Allen and Richard Barret 1572–1598* [London, 1967], p. 251). Barret also defended Holt during his papal audience.

[55] Sega's illness and Caetani's departure troubled Acquaviva. Without their active assistance, he doubted the troubles could be remedied. Even though the arrival of Barret delighted Acquaviva and raised his hopes, he was not very optimistic (Acquaviva to Parsons, Rome April 8, 1596, ARSI, Cast. 6, fols 242ᵛ–243ʳ).

for any student who wished to leave the college. Moreover Pope Clement VIII would pay their expenses. Some dissidents left the college on their own accord. Three leading dissidents recommended that Robert Fisher take this opportunity to depart in order to return to England to encourage anti-Jesuit sentiment.[56]

Toledo introduced a major administrative change. On June 8, 1596, he secured a *motu proprio*, *Cum tu qui absenti*, from Clement whereby the Jesuits at the English College were withdrawn from the jurisdiction of father general and placed directly under Toledo.[57] He thus eliminated any influence that Acquaviva might have had in the college and assumed complete control. Despite these administrative changes, Agazzari lamented to Creswell on July 28, 1596: "We have gained nothing so far but an external appearance of peace and quiet, just enough to avoid scandal and offence to others."[58] Without a choice, Acquaviva acquiesced. Toledo attended to the college's financial problems by obtaining a papal grant of 1,000 scudi and by persuading the dean of the Papal Grooms to abandon his claims to the college's vineyard at S. Maria alle Fornaci. On August 8, with the assistance of Agazzari, Toledo obtained all the faculties and privileges regarding the English mission that had formerly been held by Cardinal Allen.

One source of friction that occasionally surfaced still remained: hostility to Spain. This hostility was not restricted to the group of dissidents. Agazzari complained to Parsons that a student refused to read the *Book of Succession* in the refectory and that students:

> speak often & bitterly about the Book of the Succession to the English Crown, and against its author, that is, as they believe, Fr. Persons, whose name they can scarcely bear to hear. They all rejoice at the disasters which happen to the Spaniards, as recently at Cadiz; they grieve about their successes, as recently at Calais. I do not know whether they hate the Society because of the Spaniards, or the Spaniards because of the Society, or both because of the Scot or the Frenchman or something worse.[59]

One wonders how Toledo reacted when the students refused to salute Gonzalo Fernández de Córdoba, Duke of Sessa, Spain's ambassador to the Papal States and one of Toledo's allies in his campaign against Acquaviva. Whether Toledo would have been able to defuse the anti-

---

[56] In Chapter 5, we discussed his activities after his arrival in England.

[57] ARSI, Rom. 156/II, fols 180ʳ–82ᵛ.

[58] Cited in Kenny, "Inglorious Revolution," p. 83.

[59] Rome August 27, 1596, in Tierney/Dodd, *Church History*, vol. 3, p. lxxv. I use the translation in Kenny, "Inglorious Revolution," pp. 84–85.

Spanish sentiment, we shall never know because he died in September after a brief illness. Agazzari, despite his mistrust, kept a prayerful vigil at the cardinal's bedside. Parsons noted Toledo's death in his "An observation of certayne aparent iudgments of almightye God, againste suche as have beene seditious in the Englishe Catholique cause for these nine or ten yeares past" written in December of 1598:

> And within the same yeare dyed also Cardinall Tollet, who upon evill information, and preoccupatioun by the factiouse, that hadd promised him among other matters to withdraw all Inglish dependantes from Spaine, whereto at that tyme hee was nothinge devoted, was theire only star and pillar of the tumultuouse for a time, thoughe hee was so weaire of them in the ende, as hee told dyverse that if hee lived, hee would punish them severely.[60]

Surprisingly lenient in his evaluation, Parsons, nonetheless, included Toledo in his litany.

Rumors about the disturbances in Rome and the Society's reconsideration of its role in the governance of the English College, reached England. So worried was he by these that Garnet asked Acquaviva "But why, dearest father, are you deserting us now?" In Spain Parsons and Creswell rallied their friends to defend the English Jesuits. But Acquaviva was unconvinced. Taking advantage of Toledo's death, Acquaviva again suggested the Society's withdrawal as a possibility. Richard Barret pleaded with Clement VIII at an audience on September 22 that he not allow the Society to withdraw from the college's administration. Papal approval of their departure, he argued, would mark the end of the English mission. At the end of the meeting, Clement promised that the new vice-protector would be either Cesare, Cardinal Baronio or Camillo, Cardinal Borghese. But no matter who was chosen, he would be instructed to tell the students that the Society was to remain in charge of the college.[61]

Clement met with Acquaviva and Agazzari after his conference with Barret, presumably to inform them of his decision that the Society would retain control of the college. Despite protestations of some students that Cardinal Caetani was, de facto, no longer the college's protector and their desire to nominate the anti-Spanish and anti-Jesuit Antonio Maria, Cardinal Salviati for that office, Clement affirmed that Caetani was still cardinal protector and appointed Cardinal Borghese his vicar. Shortly

---

[60] "The Memoirs of Father Robert Persons," (ed.) John H. Pollen, S.J., in *Miscellanea II* (London, 1906), p. 208.

[61] Barret to Parsons, Rome September 28, 1596, published in Thomas Francis Knox, (ed.), *The First and Second Diaries of the English College, Douay* (London, 1878), pp. 384–86.

thereafter, Barret returned to Flanders. Before his departure, he convinced Thomas Hesketh and some other English laymen to support the Society. After Hugh Griffin (or Griffeth) left Rome to take up his office as provost in Cambrai, leadership of the English colony in Rome passed to Hesketh. No longer supported by the English in Rome, the rebellious students looked even more to the anti-Jesuit faction in Flanders, especially William Gifford whose attacks on the Society became increasingly more virulent.

Throughout the first nine months of 1596, rumors circulated that an English Jesuit, either Parsons or Creswell, would be dispatched to Rome to help mediate the struggle. In letters to the papal-nephew secretary of state, Pietro, Cardinal Aldobrandini, and to Pope Clement VIII, Creswell defended the Society against all charges and blamed William Cecil, Lord Burghley, and the English government for fomenting divisions among the exiles. Cecil encouraged and protected the Society's enemies.[62] Creswell was the original choice as mediator, perhaps because of his friendship with Cardinal Aldobrandini. Moreover, Creswell remained very unpopular among Spanish Jesuits and a mission to Rome provided a great excuse to remove him at least temporarily.[63] It was Parsons, however, who, despite his involvement with other matters in Spain, arrived in Rome on March 27, 1597.[64]

Staying with Acquaviva at the professed house, Parsons met with many students, including the ringleader Edward Bennett, tired of disturbances that had sapped their time and energy for over a year.[65] On Easter Saturday, April 2, 1597, Parsons addressed the seminarians at the English College.[66] Citing Scriptural passages, historical precedents, and their common experiences, he explained the reasons for his trip to Rome, his understanding of the recent difficulties at the college, and his proposed remedies. Parsons had been in Spain for nearly nine years. During that period, new English seminaries and residences were established in Spain,

---

[62] See Creswell to Pope Clement VIII, Madrid April 20, 1596, AAW, V, 50.

[63] Acquaviva to Parsons, Rome January 15, 1596, ARSI, Baet. 3/I, p. 251; same to same, Rome February 11, 1596, ARSI, Cast. 6, fols 237^v–238^r; same to same, Rome April 8, 1596, ARSI, Cast. 6, fols 242^v–243^r; same to same, Rome August 28, 1596, ARSI, Hisp. 75, fol. 49^r.

[64] Parsons departed for Rome by early October. Philip II's secretary Juan de Idiáquez explained that Parsons was leaving Philip's court to go to Rome to treat various matters important for the English Catholics in general and the English colleges specifically (Philip II to Acquaviva, Madrid October 10, 1596, ARSI, Epp. Ext. 29, fols 250^r–51^v [a copy can be found in AAW, V, 77]).

[65] Edward's brother John had accompanied Parsons to Rome (Godfrey Anstruther, O.P., *The Seminary Priests* (4 vols, Ware/Durham/Great Wakering, 1968–1977), vol. 1, p. 31).

[66] The full English text may be found in ABSI, Coll. N II 125–157.

Portugal and Flanders. Each was in reasonably good financial state; yet there were certain problems regarding their governance and direction as well as their privileges, faculties and so on. The primary reason for his visit to Rome was an opportunity to discuss these matters with Pope Clement VIII and Acquaviva. The second motive for the journey "was to see wether by my beinge heare I myght doe any good office for the comforth and benefyt of thys howse and companye in particular after so longe tyme of trowble and discomforth which hath growne to them selves and to there frendes, by that which hath passed in thys place."[67] The disagreements and discord destroying the tranquility and union of the college, he attributed to Satan had sowed darnel among the good seed. Satan has numerous goals in mind. He has destroyed the peace of mind of the students at the college. He has damaged the institution's reputation. He has provided so many distractions that the students were unable to acquire the necessary knowledge. Parsons lingered on the fourth goal: disruption of good relations with the Society of Jesus. Two or three individuals might have outraged or disgusted other English Catholics, but the Society has been the most steadfast friend the mission has:

> I may avouch that, in thys place without offence I hope of anye, that all the world knoweth to be trew, which ys that if any one sorte of poore frendes which our cause and nation hath hadde in thys long affliction, these men have been the most redieste and willinge in all contryes to helpe us: there howses have bene our howses, there frindes our frendes, there credyt our credyt: there woorde always redye to commend us, there handes to helpe us, there labours to assiste us: in all kinde of businesses or necessityes, that have fallen upon us.[68]

In addition to establishing friction with the Society of Jesus, Satan has soured relations with Spain, the major supporter and benefactor of English exiles, and relations between the English College in Rome and other English seminaries and residences. This hostility, of course, delighted the Elizabethan government and horrified Catholics in England.

Having searched the Bible, Parsons recommended that all reflect on certain passages with marked resemblance to the current state of the college: Israel wandering in the desert, Israel exiled in Babylon, and the early church in Corinth. There were difficulties; there was resentment; there were factions. Cardinal Allen "who was in deede our Moyses, our Esdras, our Nehemias, and as I may saye in a certayne sort our first and cheefe Apostle in thys affayre,"[69] had competently coordinated activities

---

[67] ABSI, Coll N II 133.
[68] ABSI, Coll N II 140.
[69] ABSI, Coll N II 151.

performed by the "two hands."[70] From the start there was tension between nationalities, between social classes, and so on. But the situation has deteriorated. Parsons avoided mentioning any name but he informed his audience "that these twoo handes are now manifestlye knowen to the world."[71] What were the differences between the two hands? They were apparent: "for first yt ys evident that there was before thother which ys the difference noted before by our Saviour in the Gospell betweene the twoo seedes, good and badde: and betweene the twoo sowers hym self and hys enimye; to wytte that th'one sowed first and th'other came after and oversprinkled the same."[72] The good hand has worked for the benefit of England from the start. It included "our late good Cardinal Doctor Sanders, Sir franncys Inglefield and the rest of that ranke now deade, and there frindes and comparteners yet alive of the learnedest and gravest of our nacion: And with them have jeoned ever all the fathers of the Societye, all the Seiminaryes, all the preists within and withowt Ingland. All the Catholikes in prison and other abrode withowt exception."[73] By their fruits, the member of the right hand will be known: the martyrs, the confessors, the benefactors and founders of seminaries, colleges and residences. And the left hand? What have they done? Among their accomplishments were:

> ... the overthro of the poore quene of Scots, that otherwyse myght yett have lyved manye a fayre yeare, with the ruyne of those fourteene Inglische Gentilmen that dyed with hyr and for hyr, in trapped by the rashe and undiscrete treatie of [John] Ballarde,[74] wherin I can assure yow, the right hand had nether part nor knowledge. The fall in lyke maner of Gylbert Gifford[75] and hys treatye with the enime were by thys hand; as also the twoo bookes wytten by hym and hys compagnion, The one againste our Cardinals epistle for the deliverye of Deventrye,[76] and the other against the ffathers of the Societye, which were so fondlye and malitiously written as Walsingham hym self was assahaymed to lett them be printed.[77]

---

[70] Did Parsons know of Allen's letter to Thomas Throckmorton on February 20, 1591? At this point his discourse seems to be following it.

[71] ABSI, Coll N II 153.

[72] ABSI, Coll N II 153, 154.

[73] ABSI, Coll N II 154.

[74] John Ballard and thirteen others were executed at Tyburn in 1586 for the Babington Plot. See Anstruther, *Seminary Priests*, vol. 1, pp. 19–20.

[75] See Anstruther, *Seminary Priests*, vol. 1, p. 132.

[76] This is Allen's *The copie of a letter written by M. Doctor Allen: concerning the yeelding up, of the citie of Daventrie* (Antwerp, 1587), *ARCR*, vol. 2, num. 8, *STC* 370. See also McCoog, *Society of Jesus*, pp. 230–33.

[77] ABSI, Coll N II 155.

The left hand fostered the dissension then plaguing the exiles. Parsons wanted to end all disputes:

> Wherefore lettinge passe and bringinge under foote all that ys gone, let us for Gods sayke and for our countryes sayke, and for our owne saykes, utterlye mayke an ende of thys tumulte and returne to our old comforth and quietnes agayne, wherin I off my self to laboure most willinglye withall the vaynes of my harte; and perhappes I may be no evyll meane therin beinge on thon syde an Inglishman and therbye bownde to you to seeke your good every way. And on th'other syde of the Societye, and therby not unfytt to deale with them yf any difficultye showld be of that parte, as I hope there wylbe none, for I know they love bothe yow and our countyre intierlye and for God which ys the surest fundation of love in the worlde.[78]

Parsons informed them that he was there to help.

Sometime in April Parsons had an audience with Pope Clement VIII. Also present were the cardinal-nephews Pietro and Cinzio Passeri Aldobrandini. The *Book of Succession* preoccupied them because they believed it was written not as an objective examination but as an endorsement of Spanish pretensions. Most likely Monsignor Malvasia provided Rome with this interpretation. Understandably because of recent events in France, specifically papal absolution of Henry IV, the papal court found the stories credible. Parsons corrected the misunderstanding and submitted a Latin translation, with a new chapter on the pope's right to settle the succession issue, as evidence.[79] Discussion then turned to the English College where prevalent hostility wearied the pope and the cardinal-nephews pushed Acquaviva to the brink of withdrawal, and scandalized clerical Rome. Parsons recalled a remark of Cardinal Baronio: "or youthes bragged muche of martirdome, but they were Refractarii [stubborn, unmangeable] (that was his word) and had no parte of martirs spirite, wch was in humilitie and obedience." Clement himself, according to Parsons, was "never so vexed with any nacion in the world, ffor one the on syde they pretended zeale and piety and one thother shewed the very spirite of the divell in pryde contumacy and contradiccon ... " Some simply claimed that the English were "*Indiavolati*," possessed by the devil. Clement knew not how to handle the problem "for one theone side to punishe them openly wold be a scandall by reason of the hereticks, and

---

[78] ABSI, Coll N II 157–58.

[79] Parsons to Juan de Idiáquez, Rome May 1, 1597, ABSI, Anglia II, 26. Most likely the translation is Archivio segreto vaticano, Borghese, serie IV. 103. See Peter Holmes, "The Authorship and Early Reception of *A Conference about the Next Succession to the Crown of England*," *Historical Journal*, 23 (1980): p. 423.

yf he should cast them forth of Rome some had told hym that they wold have become hereticks."⁸⁰ At the pope's command, Parsons abandoned the professed house for the English College on April the 9th or 10th and immediately began negotiations with the discontented students. To the consternation of all, reason reigned during the days of discussion. Each side listened to the motives and grievances of their opponents; each side recognized the other had valid points. Parsons the ogre became Parsons the arbitrator. Even Edward Bennett confessed that "he whom we most feared, and whom we accounted for our greatest enemy, hath been our greatest friend; yea, and the only man that hath satisfied us, and put an end to these troubles."⁸¹ Parsons had succeeded in gaining the students' confidence. Several elected delegates, including Bennett, nicknamed "The Tribune" by Parsons, and Parsons met, discussed the issues and reached an agreement. Bennett resigned as confessor. Henceforth the college's confessor would be a Jesuit but there would also be another priest selected by the rector from the students, to whom the students could go for the sacrament. The Jesuit confessor would not encourage any student to enter religious life, but would advise all students in good faith. If a student did decide to enter a religious community and was accepted by that community, he was not to remain any longer in the college. Henceforth superiors would select *ripetitori* from the students, if possible, or from the Jesuits, if necessary. There were to be no appeals over the rector's head to cardinals protector and all clandestine gatherings were forbidden. Superiors should "forgive and forget." The traditional collegiate rules were to be preserved. The remaining articles concerned the college's vineyard and theological examinations.⁸² The vice-protector Camillo, Cardinal Borghese approved the articles. On the feast of the Ascension, May 15, he presided at festivities celebrating the end of the disputes and the reconciliation of the factions.⁸³ On the same day Parsons and Bennett wrote to two friends. Parsons's letter to William Holt began:

> This letter shall be you, I hope in God, of great comfort, to understand thereby of the happy end, which his divine goodness hath given at length to these troubles and disagreements here in Rome; which, in truth, as I found to be greater and more deeply rooted than ever I could imagine (though I had heard

---

⁸⁰ Parsons to Henry Garnet, Naples July 12/13, 1598, ABSI Coll P 438 (published in Thomas Graves Law, (ed.), *The Archpriest Controversy* [2 vols, London, 1896–1898], vol. 1, p. 29).

⁸¹ Bennett to Hugh Griffin, Rome May 16, 1597, in Tierney/Dodd, *Church History*, vol. 3, pp. lxxx–lxxxi.

⁸² Kenny, "Inglorious Revolution," pp. 92–93.

⁸³ The "Articles of Concord" can be found in AAW, VI, 39.

much), so are we more bound to Almighty God for the remedy, which I believe verily to be found, and from the root; as you would also think, if you saw that which I do see: and so do many more besides me, that had far less hope of the redress than ever I had.[84]

In his letter to Griffin on May 16, Bennett's joy was no less real:

> And, to tell you, as my old friend, I did never think that father Persons could ever have gotten that love of the scholars, as he hath gotten: so that, now we have ended all our troubles, the scholars confidently go to confession to the fathers. The pope's holiness is wonderfully pleased with it, as much as he was displeased with our troubles ... Here hereafter there is no place left for the complaints of the Low-Countries, especially seeing we have here united ourselves, whose disagreements before were the occasion that many men were heard, which now shall not. You know what you have best to do: but if you mean to do any good for our country, you must unite with the jesuits; for the common cause hereafter is like to lie altogether with them. I have been much exhorted by the protector to join with father Persons, which I have done; and if you do the like, truly I think you shall be able to do more good in the common cause.[85]

On the 17th, six of the leaders thanked Acquaviva for calling Parsons to Rome and asked that he be named rector.[86] Good news, alas, never spread as rapidly and effectively as bad and the reconciliation of Ascension Day did not establish a precedent to be followed in Flanders and England. Neither did it establish a lasting peace in Rome.

The College of St Omers and William Holt, S.J.

Difficulties were not limited to the English College in Rome. The college in St Omers needed more money to accommodate a larger number of students. To meet this need Parsons asked Philip II to double his pension. On April 24, 1596 Philip instructed his agents in Brussels to examine the request, but the pension was not doubled until 1600. Until then the college relied on alms.[87] With the increase in students, the college outgrew its accommodations. The procurator, William Flack, proposed the purchase

---

[84] Rome May 5 [sic], 1597, AAW, VI, 106 (printed in Tierney/Dodd, *Church History*, vol. 3, p. lxxviii).

[85] Printed in Tierney/Dodd, *Church History*, vol. 3, p. lxxxii. See also Edward Tempest's letter to his brother Robert, Rome May 17, 1597, AAW, VI, 45.

[86] ARSI, Fondo Gesuitico 651/613. See Acquaviva's reply, Naples May 30, 1597, ARSI, Franc. 1/II, fol. 419^r.

[87] Hubert Chadwick, S.J., *St Omers to Stonyhurst* (London, 1962), p. 28.

of a larger house, the Hôtel de Licques, in the Rue St Bertin. Municipal authorities had opposed earlier attempts to acquire the property because they feared the college was becoming too large. But Flack, supported by Parsons and Oliver Mannaerts, persisted. However, during the delay, the house, garden and farm were sold to Louis de Bersacques, Dean of the Cathedral Chapter, but he was willing to sell the house and garden to Flack if he obtained the necessary permission. Steady pressure from both the Spanish court and Jean de Vernois, Bishop of St Omers, induced civic approval. They finally approved in October of 1594 and the college moved to its new location in February of 1595.[88]

Besides constant dangers because of the continuing war between Spain and France, another persistent worry was the plague. In late summer of 1596, it was especially devastating. With the approval of Flack, the rector Jean Foucart, sent some students to safety in Courtrai. Thinking that the plague had passed, Foucart summoned them back to St Omers in the spring of 1597. But it had not; indeed, it intensified after their return. Miraculously no student fell victim to it.[89]

Relations between the English college and the Belgian college, and, indeed, the Belgian province itself remained a source of friction. The regulations formulated by Mannaerts and George Duras in 1594, did not produce the desired harmony so they were revised on June 16, 1597 to the distinct disadvantage of the English. Mannaerts feared discord and rivalry if the rector of the English College was totally independent of the Belgian rector. Instead, he preferred that both colleges followed a common policy. This implied a certain amount of subordination that Mannaerts seemed reluctant to explicate. Thus in certain small matters, for example regarding sick students, the rector of the English college did not have the authority to exempt them from classes without the permission of the prefect of studies of the Belgian college. In case of an emergency, the reasons must be forwarded to the prefect immediately. Permission of the rector and/or prefect of studies was also required for the students to preach and hold discussions in the English College. To the petition that there be some type of communal celebration on the national feasts of St Gregory and St Thomas of Canterbury, Mannaerts replied that these feasts be commemorated piously and quietly without a banquet unless there were important extenuating circumstances. For the time being at least,

---

[88] Leo Hicks, S.J., "The Foundation of the College of St Omers," *AHSI*, 19 (1950): pp. 168–72; Chadwick, *St Omers to Stonyhurst*, pp. 33–34.

[89] Nicholas Smith to Acquaviva, St Omers January 22, 1597, ARSI, Germ. 177, fols 64ʳ–65ᵛ; Jean Foucart to Acquaviva, St Omers July 26, 1597, ARSI, Germ. 177, fols 205ʳ–206ᵛ; Chadwick, *St Omers to Stonyhurst*, p. 36.

Mannaerts argued against a public chapel.[90] Not surprisingly, a month later, Jean Foucart complained that he remained subject not only to the rector of the Belgian college but also its prefect of studies in the everyday administration of the students. Moreover, he objected to the jurisdiction that William Holt exercised within the college. Holt, for example, had the authority to accept students and to decide who should be sent to the colleges in Spain and in Rome. Between the Belgian rector and prefect of studies and the English procurator, the rector had little real authority.[91]

As Mannaerts restricted the rector's power, William Holt sought to expand his own. The Englishman reminded Mannaerts that he had agreed earlier that the English College in St Omers would be governed as the English colleges in Spain and Rome, that is, independent of the local Jesuit college. This, according to Holt, was also father general's wish.[92] Foucart was caught between the two. The problem became more complex over the subject of discipline. Both Flack and Holt reprimanded the rector over an incident that resulted in the public disciplining of four boys. This was the final straw. Frustrated by the arrangement, Foucart asked to be relieved of the burden of office in December of 1597. Rarely, he explained to Jean d'Heur, did he and Father Flack agree on anything: "I have not always had, and I have not now, the same ideas or the same opinions as Fr. Flack. But we both agree on one point: his judgement and desire that the rector of this seminary be changed."[93] On his official visitation, Mannaerts noted that it was the only college under his jurisdiction that lacked "peace and harmony." He specifically blamed Flack and his constant running to Holt and Parsons without saying a word to the provincial George Duras. Now he boasted that Foucart's departure was imminent. Mannaerts preferred that Flack be sent away and suggested that at least two English Jesuits, Simon Swinburne and Nicholas Smith, agreed with him.[94] Probably as a result of his visitation and the continuing problems, Mannaerts changed his mind about the college's administration. In 1598 he too protested that, contrary to the earlier agreement, the rector of the English college should be subordinate to the rector of the Belgian college. Because of his general frustration with Holt, Mannaerts joined Foucart in complaining about the

---

[90] ARSI, Germ. 177, fols 314^{r-v}; Chadwick, *St Omers to Stonyhurst*, p. 37.

[91] Foucart to Acquaviva, St Omers July 26, 1597, ARSI, Germ. 177, fols 205^{r}–206^{v}; same to George Duras, St Omers July 26, 1597, ARSI, Germ. 177, fols 207^{r-v}.

[92] Foucart to Acquaviva, St Omers August 8, 1597, ARSI, Germ. 177, fols 224^{r-v}; same to Duras, St Omers December 4, 1597, ARSI, Germ. 177, fols 304^{r}–305^{v}.

[93] St Omers December 6, 1597, ARSI, Germ. 177, fols 306^{r-v} (translated in Chadwick, *St Omers to Stonyhurst*, p. 38). See also pp. 37–38 and Hicks, "St Omers," pp. 175–77.

[94] Mannaerts to Acquaviva, St Omers November 5, 1597, ARSI, Germ. 177, fols 293^{r-v} same to same, Courtrai December 22, 1597, ARSI, Germ. 177, fols 319^{r}–20^{v}.

Englishman's interference.⁹⁵ Once again Holt was the culprit. Now, for different reasons, Belgian Jesuits opposed Holt almost as strenuously as the English "nobles." Complaints about Holt's interference in the English College were so common in 1596 that Parsons feared the Belgians would eventually forbid Holt's involvement with the college. Father Acquaviva promised that he would not permit a drastic reorganization of the college. With Acquaviva's firm support, the English college retained its own rector, with nebulous and restricted authority, and Holt continued to have a voice in the affairs of the college. Acquaviva did, however, restrict the solicitation of alms.⁹⁶ Problems with Holt persisted. Foucart complained about his interference. Mannaerts questioned Holt's authority to transfer English Jesuits to other positions within Belgium. Indeed, he was annoyed that Holt had summoned Edward Walpole and reassigned him without first discussing it either with Walpole's rector or the vice-provincial, that is, himself. In so doing Holt exceeded his authority and Mannaerts demanded that this authority be more precisely defined.⁹⁷

Preparing for James's Conversion

Sometime in 1595 or 1596, Monsignor Innocenzo Malvasia drafted a memorial for Pietro, Cardinal Aldobrandini, Secretary of State, on the current condition of Catholics in Scotland. Interestingly Philip II complained to Rome about Malvasia's anti-Spanish sentiments and asked that he be withdrawn. The cardinal secretary insisted that Malvasia leave Flanders as soon as possible. He was back in Italy by the end of November of 1595. Most likely he drafted this report after his departure from Brussels. During his sojourn in Flanders, Malvasia clearly favored Scottish interests and was inclined to believe the worse of the English Jesuits.⁹⁸ His report, as he explained, was divided into two parts: the story of the 10,000 scudi given to the Jesuit James Gordon at Pope Clement VIII's orders in

---

⁹⁵ Mannaerts to Duras, Brussels February 13, 1598, ARSI, Germ. 178, fols 53ʳ–54ᵛ. On Mannaerts's change see Hicks, "St Omers," pp. 175–76.

⁹⁶ Acquaviva to Parsons, Rome April 8, 1596, ARSI, Cast. 6, fols 242ᵛ–243ʳ.

⁹⁷ Mannaerts to Acquaviva, Courtrai December 22, 1597, ARSI, Germ. 177, fols 319ʳ–20ᵛ.

⁹⁸ In fact Malvasia recommended Charles Paget and William Gifford to Mirto Frangipani who took them under his protection. See Frangipani to Malvasia, Brussels November 14, 1596, in Van der Essen, *Correspondance d'Francipani*, vol. 1, pp. 259–60.

1594; and possible methods for the successful restoration of Catholicism in Scotland.[99] We shall treat the second first.

Malvasia argued that a policy focused on James's conversion or on improvement of conditions for Catholics, would be more effective than the use of force. The latter would only compel James to defend himself by forging closer ties with the Kirk and his "heretical" subjects and, perhaps, by seeking more aid from England. Increased persecution of Catholics would most likely be a consequence. Moreover, even with Spanish assistance, the pope did not have the financial and military resources necessary for an invasion that could eventually involve English, Danish, Dutch, and French intervention on the side of Scotland. The pope could not even depend on the majority of Scottish nobles who favored Catholicism. These "tepid Catholics" attended heretical services and would "never take up arms against the king, but they will always remain at his absolute command." Only William Douglas, Earl of Angus; Francis Hay, Earl of Erroll; and George Gordon, Earl of Huntly were reliable but the first was currently in disgrace and the other two, in exile. Even if they were restored to favor, as everyone expected, their assistance would not be sufficient.

Conciliation and "conducting matters with judgment and tact" were surer routes. The king manifested a consistently favorable disposition towards Catholics. He could relatively easily have eradicated Catholicism within his kingdom but he refused to do so. He tolerated them and willingly discussed religious matters with them. Never did he allow the laws to be strenuously enforced against them. He had also entrusted major offices and positions of confidence to Catholics, albeit "tepid" ones, and had even allowed Queen Anne of Denmark to do the same with her ladies in waiting. Malvasia claimed that King James always permitted the earl of Huntly to have a Mass said in his chambers whenever he stayed at a royal palace. Even though the doors were closed, anyone who wished, could attend. Ludovic Stuart, Duke of Lennox and a "tepid" Catholic, often attended these Masses. For political reasons, James could not act too boldly. Nonetheless, even stronger political reasons obliged James to favor Catholics. If he hoped to ascend the English throne, he needed their support. Unless James actively solicited Catholic support, they would favor the Spanish claimant. James, of course, would not cultivate English

---

[99] Biblioteca Apostolica Vaticana, Ottob. lat. 2510, fols 270ʳ–76ᵛ. This report, inexplicably without the first part, was published in Alphons Bellesheim, *History of the Catholic Church of Scotland* (4 vols, Edinburgh/London, 1887–1890), vol. 3, pp. 460–73. A different version can be found in *CSP Scotland* (1595–1597), pp. 104–11. See note 2 in Bellesheim for information regarding other manuscript copies.

Protestants because of their treatment of his mother.[100] To encourage James in this movement towards Catholicism, Malvasia suggested that Rome approach the earls of Huntly and Erroll, who would soon be recalled from exile, and the duke of Lennox. With their assistance, toleration of Catholics and permission for Catholic worship in private may be granted especially if the king were offered annual assistance of 10,000–12,000 scudi.[101]

Almost as an aside, Malvasia explained that something must be done to educate more Scottish clergy. The Scots College in Louvain could not support more than six or eight students. William Crichton, nonetheless, did marvellous work with negligible financial resources. Malvasia thus suggested that the papacy assign some source of income to the college and that, until there were enough Scots, the English Colleges in Douai and Rome be asked to send a few English priests north of the border.[102] The papal agent considered the presence of Father Gordon in Scotland extremely important not only because of his learning and piety, but because of his relations with his nephew the earl of Huntly. Malvasia believed that Gordon might be able to win over to Catholicism John Erskine, Earl of Mar, and hereditary custodian of Stirling Castle.[103] As for the religious views of James, the papal agent argued that the king never demonstrated any sincere admiration for the Calvinism in which he was raised. Quite capable of theological debate, he often disagreed with Calvinist doctrines as he evaluated their religious claims. If a Catholic scholar were given the opportunity to discuss religious matters with him, Malvasia believed that he could win over James in no time. Perhaps, Malvasia suggested, Rome should act on the earl of Huntly's advice. Someone should be sent to Scotland to negotiate tolerance and liberty of conscience. In the discussions, the envoy could let it be known that the pope was prepared to excommunicate James unless he made some concessions. It would be safer if the envoy appeared to be from the king's relative Charles (II),

---

[100] Rumors frequently circulated that explained James's flirtation with Catholicism and his clandestine anti-English diplomacy as a desire to avenge both his mother's death and Elizabeth's many broken promises (Scargill-Bird, *Salisbury MSS*, vol. 5, pp. 72–74).

[101] On January 29, 1597, Frangipani reported James's desire to forge a closer alliance with Scottish Catholics to seek revenge against various Protestant conspirators (Van der Essen, *Correspondance d'Frangipani*, vol. 2, p. 36).

[102] Crichton complained to James Tyrie that there were enough suitable people to come to the seminary but that they could not be maintained: "It were death to be sent to live on hope, contract debts, and languish in sustaining themselves. We have 12 here this year. If we had the means of supporting them we might have 20 or 30" (Antwerp June 18, 1595, *CSP Scotland* [1593–1595], pp. 612, 614).

[103] John Ogilvie, Laird of Pury, claimed that Mar was a Catholic and willing to hand over castles and James's son to the Spanish. Malvasia introduced Ogilvie to the pope. See above, Chapter 4.

Duke of Lorraine, who visited from time to time. Under the pretext of some other mission, the envoy could discuss the issues. Malvasia strongly recommended that Jesuits not be employed in this role because James had "little confidence [in Jesuits], looking on them with suspicion as dependants of the king of Spain."

Malvasia concluded his memorial with reflections on the English Jesuits. He did not mention any one specifically but he asserted that "it would be an excellent thing if, both in Scotland and also in England, they would abstain from interfering in State matters and the affairs of princes, and would attend solely to gaining souls and the advancement of religion." If Jesuits refrained from such interference, they would dispel "the suspicion which prevails in those countries, that under the veil of piety and devotion, they are concealing various worldly ideas." They would then receive the esteem and admiration they were due. He reduced the current conflict between many Jesuits and secular clergy, a conflict that threatened the interests of England and Scotland, to one issue, forcible restoration of Catholicism: "for the Jesuits hold it as an axiom established among them, and confirmed by the authority of Father Parsons, that only by force of arms can the Catholic religion be restored to its former state." The only kingdom capable of mounting an invasion was Spain. The Society's opponents, "naturally attached to their country," opposed any invasion to impose a foreign monarch. They were more inclined to the king of Scotland as Elizabeth's successor and anticipated the union of England and Scotland under one monarch. Finally, perhaps through the intercession of King Henry IV, Elizabeth should be dissuaded from the persecution of Catholics and encouraged to follow the example of others and allow the return of Catholic exiles and the practice of Catholic worship quietly at home. To entice the queen, the monsignor suggested that the papacy offer to recall the Jesuits from England "as objects of great suspicion to her majesty" and to assure the queen that severe penalties—even excommunication—would be levied by the Church against any Catholic plotting against the crown or mixing in political matters.

Regarding the money offered by Pope Clement VIII to James VI, William Crichton, along with James Gordon, and Monsignor Malvasia, had considered different ways of transmitting the sum to the king. As we saw in Chapter 3, the money was finally entrusted to a Giovanni Sapiretti with the strict order not to surrender any of it to the king until James had publicly declared himself a Catholic. When the Catholic earls demanded the money to supply their forces, Sapiretti argued that, despite the changes and the necessities, he did not have the authority to alter the instructions given by the pope. Meanwhile the army led by Archibald Campbell, Earl of Argyll, approached. The impasse was resolved when all concerned, the Catholic earls and the Jesuits, took full responsibility for the decision to spend the money to avert a disaster with a promise to make full restitution later. Sapiretti departed for the continent shortly thereafter. Recently, Malvasia continued, Gordon had returned to the continent and explained that Catholicism could be restored in Scotland if more money were available. Although the money had not yet been repaid, Gordon asserted that it was well used for the advancement of Catholicism.[104]

In late summer of 1596, someone informed Enrico, Cardinal Caetani, Cardinal Protector of Scotland, on previous, post-Reformation contact between popes and Scottish rulers. Like Malvasia, the author urged Rome to send another agent to Scotland. Because of the precarious health of Queen Elizabeth, James should now declare publicly his Catholicism so that he would gain Catholic support for his succession. With papal assistance, James would have the courage to take this step and to resist English heretics. If Pope Clement VIII clearly demonstrated his preference for James, Philip II would not usurp Scottish claims as he clearly seemed poised to do. The author suggested that the Guises or Fernando I de Medici, Duke of Florence, be the means for establishing contact with James. The Guises were relatives and confidantes but, as a result of the religious wars in France, they lacked money. Moreover the Guises would not be able to act without Henry IV's knowledge. Thus, the duke of Florence would be better. Through his agency, the pope could inform James that he would facilitate his accession to the English throne as he had earlier facilitated Henry's to the French. Finally, the author recommended that the agent be a non-foreigner and a prelate. Only one person, therefore, fulfilled the requirements: William Chisholm (III), Bishop of Vaison.[105]

In 1596, the Scottish College moved to Louvain. Despite persistent financial difficulties, as Monsignor Malvasia commented, William Crichton did an admirable job. On March 1, 1597, Jean Dilenus, rector of the University of Louvain, granted the petition of the Scots to have a residence at the university. The residence would be capable of accommodating 40 even though there were only 16 students at the current time. Having completed philosophical and theological studies, the students would return to "their sorely afflicted country ... currently tyrannically oppressed by heretics but, as we hope, emerging into better times."[106] Shortly after

---

[104] On December 10/20, 1594, Archduke Ernst wrote to Philip II from Brussels that he believed reports that the only reason why the king had not declared himself a Catholic, was the lack of forces to resist the aid provided to the Protestants by England (Scargill-Bird, *Salisbury MSS*, vol. 5, pp. 34–35).

[105] ARSI, Angl. 42, fols 83^r–86^v. In late 1596 and early 1597, the Jesuit George Elphinstone left Scotland to negotiate with the bishop of Vaison. Is there any connection between his mysterious work and this memorial?

[106] ARSI, Germ. 177, fols 120^r–21^v.

the transfer to Louvain, Clement VIII approved rules and regulations for the college. Upon admission, each student was to make a profession of faith according to the formula of Pope Pius IV as prescribed by the Council of Trent. Each resident student promised to direct his studies for the advantage of his homeland and to accept ordination:

> I, N.N., Scot have been admitted to the Scottish ecclesiastical Seminary with this purpose in mind that, as far as lies in me, I shall strive to help the churches in Scotland progress in their ecclesiastical works. To this end, I intend and promise to direct my studies; I will not allow other studies to deflect or impede this purpose. When the seminary superiors may judge it opportune for my ordination, I will freely accept these orders for the good of my country. I also promise that I will obey the seminary superiors and all its rules, discipline and directions, and to this end, in faith and witness, I now sign on my own hand what I have promised.

Within the college, the prefect of studies directed the programs of the students. The college itself had been entrusted to the Society of Jesus by Clement VIII and father general delegated his authority to the Belgian provincial and the rector. Thus they should be obeyed. Only students capable of serious study of theology should be admitted. Moreover, "no one is to be admitted to the seminary, assuming he comes from a well-to-do family, unless he is properly dressed and has been supplied with books and clothes." Disputations or some similar exercises were held twice a week. In order to do liturgy well, all students should at least learn Gregorian chant.[107]

In April of 1597, someone, presumably William Crichton, described the new house and garden in a report on the college's successful transfer. There were 20 students in the seminary and he expected two more within the next few days. Twelve others were on their way from Scotland, summoned to attend the college on the instructions of Cardinal Caetani. Inadequate finances remained a problem. Cardinal Caetani sought further aid from Pope Clement with the promise that the college would be named "Clementinum" if he would provide sustenance for the students. At the moment the only guaranteed income was 600 crowns, adequate for the support of 12 students. Once more students arrived from Scotland, the college would experience serious financial problems unless other sources of income were found.[108] In other letters and memorials, Crichton proposed approaching rich cardinals for pensions and donations,

---

[107] "Regulae Seminarii Ecclesiastici Scotorum," ARSI, Angl. 39, fols 117r–v.

[108] "Informatio pro Seminario Scotorum Lovaniensi," April 19, 1597, ARSI, Angl. 42, fols 98r–99v.

seeking letters of commendations from illustrious ecclesiastics for use in the solicitation of alms, and sending Scottish Jesuits to conduct begging tours in Spain.[109] Crichton also sought Jesuit members of staff, but his request for George Turnbull and Peter Grene[110] was rejected by Acquaviva. As long as a non-Jesuit governed the college, Acquaviva did not think that Jesuits should serve on his staff. That would change once the Society assumed its administration. Interestingly in the same letter of August 9, 1597, Acquaviva announced the appointment of Andrew Lalo as rector of the Scottish College. Only poor health prevented his entrance into the Society.[111]

Crichton carefully tracked Scottish vocations to the Society. Claudio Acquaviva decided that no Scottish convert could be admitted into Society until he had been a member of the Roman Church for at least five years.[112] Two Scots, John Robb[113] and Andrew Crichton,[114] were novices in Rome. David Seton had entered but for reasons of health, he did not remain. Patrick Anderson[115] entered in Rome in 1597. Besides finding places in the Roman novitiate for Scottish candidates, Acquaviva also placed Scots in the Roman College and the Roman Seminary, for example Francis Douglas, brother of William, Earl of Angus, and Robert Hill.[116] Others might have been sent to Rome as students for a proposed second Scottish college.

The possibility of rehabilitating the old Scottish hospice and converting it into a college had been discussed for more than 20 years. The proposals became more serious as the perceived chances of James becoming a Catholic increased. James Tyrie had labored strenuously for the establishment until his death on March 20, 1597.[117] Shortly thereafter, Cardinal Caetani took the matter in hand. In the autumn of 1597 the cardinal informed Crichton

---

[109] "Instructio pro Seminario Ecclesiastico Scotorum Lovanii," n.d., ARSI, Angl. 42, fols 44ʳ⁻ᵛ; Acquaviva to Crichton, Rome November 15, 1597, ARSI, Fl. Belg. 1/II, p. 661.

[110] See Thomas M. McCoog, S.J., "'Pray to the Lord of the Harvest': Jesuit Missions to Scotland in the Sixteenth Century," *The Innes Review*, 53 (2002): pp. 171–72.

[111] Acquaviva to Crichton, Rome August 9, 1597, ARSI, Fl. Belg. 1/II, pp. 649–50; same to same, Rome August 9, 1597, ARSI, Fl. Belg. 1/II, p. 650.

[112] Acquaviva to Crichton, Rome July 20, 1596, ARSI, Fl. Belg. I/1, p. 615.

[113] See McCoog, "'Pray to the Lord of the Harvest,'" pp. 182–83.

[114] See McCoog, "'Pray to the Lord of the Harvest,'" pp. 165–66.

[115] See McCoog, "'Pray to the Lord of the Harvest,'" p. 163.

[116] Acquaviva to Crichton, Rome November 16, 1596, ARSI, Fl. Belg. I/1I, p. 628; same to same, Rome August 9, 1597, ARSI, Fl. Belg. 1/II, pp. 649–50; same to same, Rome November 15, 1597, ARSI, Fl. Belg. 1/II, p. 661; same to same, Rome December 20, 1597, ARSI, Fl. Belg. 1/II, p. 662.

[117] See Mark Dilworth, O.S.B., "Beginnings 1600–1707," in *The Scots College Rome 1600–2000*, (ed.) Raymond McCluskey (Edinburgh, 2000), pp. 19–20.

of his intention to open a college. He proposed to use some of the money allotted by the pope for the Scottish College in Louvain to launch the project. Initially Crichton, perhaps fearing the possible consequences of the new college on the already precarious financial state of his beloved college in Louvain, was skeptical because of climate, distance, and so on. He reminded Acquaviva that three Scottish secular priests and an equal number of Jesuits died in Rome.[118] By November he was more enthusiastic and had dispatched some unnamed persons to Rome to assist in the college's foundation. The speed of Crichton's response startled Acquaviva who would have "preferred less haste." He reminded Crichton "it is one thing for his eminence to promise a seminary in the city, and another to have everything ready to have those who are to be admitted." Acquaviva worried that the haste would have unfortunate effects on the students and the Jesuits working for the foundation. Therefore he warned Crichton not to send any more students until he had heard from Acquaviva or Caetani that the building was ready.[119]

Discussing Earthly Kingdoms: Crichton vs. Parsons

Crichton's association with Parsons's foes in the Low Countries, his opposition to William Holt, and his preference for the Stuart candidate to the English throne, accelerated his drift from Parsons.[120] The last issue assumed prominence after the publication of *A conference about the next succession to the crowne of Ingland*.[121] More than a year after its appearance, after Parsons had resolved Acquaviva's doubts about the volume's expediency,[122] Crichton situated the volume in the context of tensions and difficulties generated by the English Jesuit. In a letter of December 19, 1595, no longer extant, Crichton complained to Acquaviva about a recent book on the succession to the English throne. He believed that Parsons was the author.[123] Acquaviva replied that Parsons's authorship

---

[118] "Informatio pro Seminario Scotorum Lovaniensi," April 19, 1597, ARSI, Angl. 42, fols 98ʳ–99ᵛ. See also William James Anderson, (ed.), "Abbe Paul MacPherson's History of the Scots College, Rome," *The Innes Review*, 12 (1961): pp. 12–13.

[119] Acquaviva to Crichton, Rome November 1, 1597, ARSI, Fl. Belg. 1/II, pp. 657–58.

[120] Crichton's and Parsons's disagreements were reported to the English government. John Petit explained that Crichton, Tyrie, Westmorland, Dacre, Paget, Tresham, Stonor and Gifford comprised the Scottish faction, and Parsons, Holt, Hugh Owen, Sir William Stanley the Spanish faction (*CSP Scotland* [1595–1597], p. 321).

[121] (n.p. [Antwerp], 1594) *ARCR*, vol. 2, num. 167, *STC* 19398.

[122] See Chapter 4 above on this.

[123] See Victor Houliston, "The Hare and the Drum: Robert Persons's Writings on the English Succession, 1593–96," *Renaissance Quarterly*, 14 (2000): pp. 235–50, *Catholic*

"has not been established as far as I can see; only common rumor claimed it." Whoever did write the book, and it might have been Parsons (*"fieri autem potest"*), had good intentions but failed to achieve his purpose. Once all things were considered, the book should stand as a warning to Catholics lest their quarrels and conflicts over a successor result in the accession of a less worthy candidate. Suspected involvement of a Jesuit would only aggravate the situation. Acquaviva advised Crichton to stay out of the affair and to pray that everything worked out for the best.[124] In a second letter, again no longer extant, on January 20, 1596, Crichton asked Parsons directly about the book. Parsons replied on May 10.[125]

Crichton had asked Parsons to assist the struggling Scots College, perhaps by interceding with Philip II on its behalf, or by serving as the college's agent at the Spanish court. In his reply, Parsons suggested that Crichton had missed a golden opportunity to seek assistance during his sojourn in Spain. If he had done so then, he would most likely have been successful by now. But, without anyone to remind the court continuously of the needs of the Scots College, it would be harder to find benefactions. He recommended that Crichton ask "his eminence the cardinal" (presumably Cardinal Caetani) to intercede. Parsons promised to do what he could, but the needs of the English seminaries in Spain demanded even more than he could provide.[126] If he were not so occupied with English colleges, he would devote his energies to Scottish matters.[127] To alleviate some of Crichton's burdens, he offered to take six Scots "of good character, who are suitable to take the course of philosophy, and who do not disdain to live with Englishmen." If this worked out well for all concerned, Parsons was willing to accept a few more. Most of the letter, however, concerned the question of succession to the English throne. Parsons confessed that he did not know how to answer Crichton's questions—or, indeed, whether they should be answered. Indeed, he preferred to discuss the kingdom of

---

Resistance in Elizabethan England. Robert Persons's Jesuit Polemic, 1580–1610 (Aldershot/Rome, 2007), pp. 71–92, and McCoog, "Harmony Disrupted," pp. 165–70.

[124] Acquaviva to Crichton, Rome, March 2, 1596, ARSI, Fl. Belg. 1/I, p. 595.

[125] Parsons to Crichton, Seville May 10, 1596, ABSI, Coll P I 316 (published with a few omissions in Knox, *Letters of Allen*, pp. 381–83). Copies of the same letter but dated June 30/ July 10 can be found in Scargill-Bird, *Salisbury MSS*, vol. 6, pp. 233–35. See also John H. Pollen, S.J., "The Question of Queen Elizabeth's Successor," *The Month*, 101 (1903): pp. 528–30.

[126] Not all English exiles in Spain were as eager to help the Scots College. Later in this chapter we shall examine an anonymous memorial, written most likely by Sir Francis Englefield or Joseph Creswell, that asserted the king's assistance to this college was not in Spain's interests.

[127] Parsons had assured Acquaviva of the same thing a year earlier. See Parsons to Acquaviva, Valladolid September 7, 1594, ARSI, Hisp. 137, fols 164^{r-v}.

heaven rather than any earthly kingdom, but "the iniquity of the times and the severe misfortunes that have befallen our countries" demanded that they consider the question of a Catholic successor to Elizabeth if they were concerned with the restoration of true religion. Therefore Parsons revealed his understanding of the situation.

After his arrival in England in 1580, Parsons had studied "the interests of the king of Scotland" and, at his own expense, sent the secular priest William Watts to Scotland. Later he sent William Holt. Because of initial success, Parsons had written to Acquaviva to request some Scottish Jesuits for the mission.[128] In Rouen Parsons provided every assistance to Crichton and gave up his only companion, presumably Ralph Emerson, to accompany him. After Crichton's return, Parsons embarked on three journeys, to Lisbon, Flanders and Rome, at considerable risk. He did all this "to pleasure after God the king of Scotland and his mother; and though my assistance did not avail to procure the end we desired, still on two occasions I obtained money for their use: 24000 gold pieces from the king of Spain and 4000 from the supreme pontiff." He knew of no one else who had performed similar services for James and Mary. He stressed this to refute critics who claimed Parsons was hostile to James. He added, perhaps snidely, that Crichton was the most competent witness to refute these critics because he knew of Parsons's activities. After the death of Mary, Queen of Scots, James continued "pursuing his course in heresy." Both William Allen and Parsons did not try to conceal their reluctance to promote the claims of a heretical king. Even Crichton said in 1586 (more or less), as Parsons now reminded him, "that nothing ought to be definitely decided until we had some reliable proof of the king's state of mind." To obtain this proof, Crichton departed for Scotland. As Crichton embarked:

> we willingly awaited your reverence's return, and when this took place some years later, all our hope of the king's conversion was destroyed; for your Reverence declared in the most emphatic terms both here in Spain very frequently and elsewhere—and it was confirmed also by other pious and prudent men of your nation—that there were no grounds for anyone to expect the conversion of the king to the Catholic faith; and subsequent events have very strongly confirmed this view.

Since then, neither Allen nor Parsons gave much consideration to the king of Scotland. Both preferred a claimant "most likely to be helpful in restoring and establishing the Catholic religion and the worship of God in our country." There were many claimants and many considerations, as the recent volume on the succession made clear. Once religion was introduced

---

[128] See McCoog, *Society of Jesus*, pp. 178–87.

into the discussion, could one with a "good conscience support a claimant who is a heretic, or at least a probable one, and whose claim itself is also doubtful, when there were Catholic claimants?"

Parsons repeated his preference for more spiritual discussions and wished that "matters concerning earthly kingdoms were outside the sphere of our interests." But he echoed sentiments earlier expressed to Acquaviva:[129] "the interests of the state and of religion are so mixed up and intertwined that one cannot treat of the restoration of the one without the other, nor of the restoration of the Catholic religion except by means of a Catholic prince." Therefore, as Parsons had frequently said to Crichton face-to-face:

> that the one thing above all else that I have regard to in our future prince is that he should be a true Catholic. For the rest, let him be of any nation, any race any tongue under heaven. And if he have not this qualification, or if there be any doubt about it, I make no account of the nation to which he belongs nor of his personal qualities, nor otherwise of any kind of hereditary right which he may put forward; for this ought not to be admitted if it conflicts with the cause of God, even though in other respects it is entirely well founded.

The earlier-mentioned volume on the succession demonstrated the weakness of the king of Scotland's claim to the English throne. Certainly, as Crichton himself once argued, James's claim was not superior to the other claimants. But Crichton had changed his position. Previously he had unconditionally eliminated James from any consideration; now he asserted that he would not exclude him prematurely. Because of changes in the king, Crichton, according to Parsons, reconsidered his position. That there had been some change in the king's attitude did not surprise Parsons, but the Englishman did not consider it significant. Now Crichton believed that James would side with the Catholics if their forces were stronger, that he would ally himself with the Scottish earls if they proved more powerful. But, Parsons asked, how did Crichton know this with certainty? Obviously prudence and necessity dictated that James ally himself with the stronger forces.[130] Even if he did ally himself, even Crichton admitted that it was uncertain whether he would favor the Catholic religion. Given this uncertainty, "foolish then and wretched we should surely be if after

---

[129] Parsons to Acquaviva, Marchena May 12, 1595, ARSI, Hisp. 136, fols 318^r–319^v.

[130] Verstegan had written to Parsons in early June of 1593 that James "is a man lyke to condescend to any thing whereby he may please our State or procure himself mony: a man irresolute in any thing, mutable in his favours, of no religion but for advantage" (ABSI, Coll B 109 [published in Anthony G. Petti, (ed.), *The Letters and Dispatches of Richard Verstegan (c. 1550–1640)* (London, 1959), p. 165]).

sustaining so many labors, encountering so many dangers and enduring so many martyrdoms we were again to hand over all our interests and those of God and of the state to an heretical king or to one who is suspected to be such."

Crichton admitted the accuracy of Parsons's comments about James and Scotland in his reply of August 20. Nonetheless, turning to the *Book of Succession*, he considered its publication premature and damaging to their common cause. Citing a French proverb that one does not catch hares by a drum, Crichton claimed that he knew of no benefits that followed the book's appearance. Indeed, ministers in both England and Scotland ranted against it.[131]

Colonel William Semple delivered Crichton's letter to Parsons by hand on November 1. The following day Parsons replied. Given the differences in their perspectives and sympathies, Parsons did not think an ongoing discussion of the *Book of Succession* by letter would bear any fruit. If, however, they had a chance to discuss the matter personally, Parsons was sure that they would reach the same conclusion. Regarding the French proverb and Crichton's contention that the volume's publication was premature, Parsons countered different Englishmen, "as prudent as were to be found in Spain, Italy, Belgium, and possibly in England too," read the manuscript and concluded that "the book was not premature but overdue, and very much needed, and very suited to the times." The book surely was a drum but not intended to catch hares but to frighten off the wolf. Because English law threatened anyone who wrote on the succession with a charge of high treason, there was no discussion about the rights of each claimant within the kingdom. Thus "heretics," taking advantage of general ignorance, could foist a Protestant successor on English Catholics. The noise of the drum would prevent this from happening. Moreover, the drum has stirred Christian and Catholic princes to examine their rights. The drum also provided the pope with useful and necessary information so that he might evaluate all claims and rights before resolving the difficult dispute about the succession. Finally the book has aroused English Catholics so that they could now plan how they would react "when necessity forces them to take one side or the other." So, Parsons concluded, "if this book is to be called a drum, it would seem not to be inopportune or an ill-sounding one, as it has so much general usefulness."

Contrary to Crichton's assertion that the volume's appearance had had no beneficial but only harmful consequences, Parsons could produce testimonies from English witnesses vouching for its value. As for an increase in persecution, Catholics were treated more mildly in England. In Scotland

---

[131] Crichton to Parsons, August 20, 1596, ABSI, Coll P I 318 (printed in Knox, *Letters and Memorials of Allen*, p. 384).

since the book's appearance, James had set free two Jesuits and treated others kindly.[132] Before the book's appearance, James had David Graham, the Laird of Fintry, beheaded because of his Catholicism;[133] no one had been executed after the book's publication. Parsons could not imagine why James would be less humane on account of the volume. Parsons feared that Catholics in England would repeat the mistake made at the death of Mary Tudor. They preferred an English woman of doubtful faith to the Catholic Mary "because Scotland was her native land." Meanwhile, Parsons argued "we should put no trust in any blandishments nor in anyone of doubtful expectations" but demand a "true Catholic prince of proven faith." If there was disagreement regarding the most suitable Catholic candidate, Parsons argued that the pope's judgment should be binding on all Catholics.[134]

Preparing for Spanish Intervention

Robert Parsons, meanwhile, worked assiduously with more than his customary optimism for the one claimant to the English throne capable of pressing his title successfully. Sometime in late 1595 after a private audience with the King Philip II, Parsons drafted the first of many memoranda on the succession and on another armada. With Ireland and Scotland distracting the Elizabethan government, Spain should launch its attack. Moreover, Henry IV of France could do nothing, Parsons argued, because of continuing strife within his kingdom. With two of her finest naval captains, Sir John Hawkins and Sir Francis Drake absent, and with Sir John Norris in Ireland, England was especially vulnerable. If Philip planned to attack England directly, he could land either in Kent, the most direct but most dangerous site for a march on London, or at the safer Milford Haven. Other possibilities were Scotland whose ports would be opened by Philip's supporters to Spanish ships, or Ireland. Concerning the succession, although there were some malcontents who disparaged Spanish claims, fostered division among the exiles, and hostility towards Jesuits, the overwhelming majority of English exiles accepted as given Philip's right to name England's king or queen. Nonetheless, Parsons advised that nothing be said about the succession until the Spanish

---

[132] The Cecils were very eager that James see the *Book of Succession* to demonstrate Spanish hostility to him. Copies of the book were also forwarded to him by agents in Flanders (Holmes, "Authorship and Early Reception," p. 426).

[133] On the laird's execution, see Chapter 1 above.

[134] Parsons to Crichton, Madrid November 2, 1596, ABSI, Coll P I 318 (printed in Knox, *Letters and Memorials of Allen*, pp. 384–86).

had landed successfully. Instead the commander of the Spanish forces must speak of nothing but the restoration of Catholicism. At a hastily convened Parliament of Catholic gentlemen, the commander could present the credentials and claims of each pretender as outlined in the *Book of Succession*. In gratitude, the assembly would confer upon Philip the resolution of the succession, and the appointment of the first bishops. Philip would then convene a full Parliament to confirm everything. He recommended that Philip coordinate the invasion with major diversions generated by the Catholic earls in Scotland, and the earl of Westmorland and Lord Dacre in northern England, and an expeditionary force under Colonel (Sir) William Stanley. Equally important was papal cooperation.[135]

Parsons's optimism did not seem misplaced. In July of 1595 a small Spanish squadron demonstrated England's vulnerability by attacking a few villages along the Cornish coast as reprisals for the activities of Sir Francis Drake and Sir John Hawkins in the Caribbean. In the April of 1596 when Calais capitulated to Archduke Albert, Spain acquired what it had so desperately needed in 1588: a deep water port. Fearing the implications of the fall of Calais, the English retaliated with an attack on Cadiz in June. Now Philip sought revenge. But even before the sack of Cadiz, Parsons, Joseph Creswell, and Sir Francis Englefield were exhorting Philip II to take action.[136] Gathering information from letters received from England during March, April and May, they claimed that the success of the seminaries in Spain and the appearance of the *Book of Succession* had opened the eyes of many English Catholics. English Catholics now knew that they had to support a Catholic claimant to the throne and not passively accept either a heretic or a claimant with uncertain religious views. King James, too, was aware that if he hoped to succeed, he had to demonstrate his Catholicism. Having read the book, many now believed that the Spanish infanta, preferably married to the Archduke Albert, was the most sure way of securing Catholicism's restoration. Parsons repeated how James sought to win support among English Catholics by writing personal letters to the earl of Westmorland, Charles Paget and others. Over and over he claimed that he would imitate Henry IV and become Roman Catholic. His representatives travelled around Italy, seeking to

---

[135] ABSI, 46/12/3.

[136] Rumors had long circulated that Spain was planning another armada (see e.g. letters from November 12 and 28, 1595, Scargill-Bird, *Salisbury MSS*, vol. 5, pp. 450–52, 461). In a letter to the earl of Essex, Sir Edward Norreys wrote that the cardinal archduke claimed that Spain had prepared 40,000 men in Spain and Portugal, besides the army in Flanders, for an attack (Ostend February 4, 1596, Scargill-Bird, *Salisbury MSS*, vol. 6, p. 47). A few months later, however, Giacomo Guicciardini wrote to Essex from Florence that Philip had neither the vessels nor the means for an invasion (April 24/May 4, 1596, Scargill-Bird, *Salisbury MSS*, vol. 6, pp. 154–56).

rally princes and prelates, not always eager to further Spanish interests, to James's candidacy. They had convinced important cardinals in the Roman curia, who, in turn, represented James's cause to Pope Clement VIII. They objected only to James's religion. They argued that most English Catholics preferred James and would declare in his favor as soon as he accepted Catholicism. Thus, Parsons argued, immediate action was the only remedy to the possible loss of the kingdom. Once Philip occupied the kingdom, Rome would recognize the *fait d'accompli* and he could dispose of it as he wished. Now he should act. Spain has supporters in England; Ireland was in rebellion; the Catholic earls were negotiating their return to Scotland; Calais was but one of the archduke's military successes. Moreover, the pro-Scottish faction currently being organized in Flanders and Rome would gather momentum over time.[137]

A few months earlier, someone, perhaps Parsons but more likely Englefield or Creswell, forwarded a "Discourse to His Majesty on English Affairs" to Don Juan de Idiáquez with an enclosure for Philip II.[138] To the former, the author delineated specific motives for immediate action "to console and augment the number of those sincerely attached to his service and interests, and to restrain and repress the impudent doings of his opponents." Unless Philip intervened militarily soon, his support would seep away due to the "extraordinary efforts" of his opponents. The author cited the current attack on Holt and Owen as an illustration. Spanish officials must protect and support them; if they did not, few English pensioners would dare to defy the faction. The author predicted that the king of Scotland would make overtures to English Catholics and to the pope in the hope of gaining their support. France and Scotland "have a habit of acting on parallel lines" so James would imitate Henry. Nonetheless, the author was certain that there:

> was no greater hope of the extirpation of heresies and the reformation of the evil government in England than we witness in France in what, owing to the absolution of Henry, has already begun and will, it is to be presumed, continue; but before this toleration for political reasons of all religions takes effect in the irremediable corruption of these two realms, I beg your Majesty ... to take these matters therefore into consideration.

The author recommended the creation of an English cardinal devoted to Spanish interests. Without Spanish assistance, he repeated the now familiar refrain: there was no hope for the restoration of Catholicism and the reformation of evil government. If there was no hope for England, there was

---

[137] n.d. [June? 1596], ABSI, 46/12/3.
[138] Valladolid, Archivum Collegium Sancti Albani, series II, vol. 1, num. 25.

even less for France, Flanders, Scotland and Ireland. Without a cardinal, factions formed. Dissension and hostility increased significantly after Allen's death. The original faction of Morgan and Paget had found allies in a group supporting the Scottish claimant and dissident students in Rome. This faction was now so large and powerful that they obtained, in some surreptitious manner, the original manuscript of the *Book of Succession* before its publication.[139] They even relayed information about its contents to England and to Rome through the papal agent Malvasia. They claimed that Philip aspired to be monarch of the world and disparaged the book because it presented Philip's credentials among those of other pretenders. They had received active support from French cardinals and Italian nobles, and sympathy from Elizabeth and her government. In Rome this faction agitated for an English cardinal and proposed "Pool, Hesketh, and other similar young men who are quite incapable and unfitted for the dignity of that office."[140] Here again they received support and encouragement from certain French cardinals, Italian nobles, and the English government. They wanted a cardinal, and a king nominated by the pope and not one recommended by the king of Spain. The English government cooperated in order to sow hostility between English Jesuits and English secular priests. Their goal was the exclusion of Jesuits from the mission and from colleges on the continent. Their collaborators in the government tolerated or exiled captured secular clergy, but the author continued with considerable exaggeration, "no father of the Society can escape martyrdom" if captured "because most of the said fathers happen to be in favor of your Majesty's title and claim to that crown." The author urged the king to authorize the confiscation of the papers and ciphers of Paget and William Gifford so that everyone could see the extent of the disloyalty of numerous English exiles who received Spanish pensions. Finally, the author suggested that Philip consider "how little profit you and your royal line are going to reap from the foundation of the Scots College in Louvain, or from the alms and subsidies your Majesty is giving to men of that nation and to those Englishmen in the Low Countries who belong to their party and faction."[141]

An invasion of Ireland was the final recommendation. To restrain Elizabeth's forces, Philip should dispatch a sufficient force to occupy the

---

[139] See above Chapter 4.

[140] Hesketh is most likely Thomas Hesketh, a member of Allen's household at his death. Pole is most likely Geoffrey Pole, whose father was Reginald, Cardinal Pole's nephew. See Anstruther, *Seminary Priests*, vol. 1, pp. 162, 279–80.

[141] A reason against Parsons's authorship of this memorial is this opposition to the Scots College in Louvain. That, of course, assumes that Parsons was sincere in his earlier letter to Crichton.

ports and cities of the island. This venture would repay Elizabeth for her bellicose activities and, at the same time, serve as an inducement to English nobles to accept his candidate for the throne. But, he cautioned, Philip must be prudent in his choice of Irish allies: "for the hatred and ill will between the educated and savage elements of this race is no less great than that which both bear to the English; with the result that if your Majesty directs your forces so as to combine with the savage and uncouth elements (which alone have taken up arms against the queen), your Majesty would be liable to lose thereby the good will and support of all the cities and large towns." Whether or not the author included Hugh O'Neill, Earl of Tyrone, among the "savage and uncouth" was unclear. But the author advised that Philip could not allow him to follow the example of the Scottish earls and be suppressed and compelled to make peace because promised assistance never materialized. Among the Spanish forces there should be some English ecclesiastical and secular leaders, for example the secular priest Richard Haydock ("entirely devoted to your Majesty's service") and Sir William Stanley. The memorial ended with a petition that Philip name two Englishmen bishops of Cambrai and Tournai. No name was suggested for the former but simply an allusion "whom I have already suggested to your Majesty to be the English cardinal." He recommended Stapleton for Tournai. These appointments would demonstrate that he did not seek to dominate the world and was "pleased to give preferment and advancement in ... [his] own dominions to such men of our nation whose lives and capabilities deserve[d] it until the time and opportunity comes to give them benefices in their own country."

Parsons continued to send his own memoranda. In "Principal Points to Facilitate the English Enterprise,"[142] he detailed how Philip II should proceed against England.[143] Because of the immense difficulties involved, Philip, like kings of old, should make a special vow to God whereby he promised to restore the former liberties and privileges of the English Church so abruptly curtailed and suppressed by Henry VIII upon the

---

[142] The calendar claims the memorial was given to Martin de Idiáquez, Juan's brother, but offers no proof.

[143] *CSP Simancas* (1587–1603), pp. 628–33. Parsons's memorial is similar in content to a letter written by Sir Francis Englefield to Philip II from Madrid on September 8, 1596, a letter to be delivered after Englefield's death which came soon afterwards. For the final time, Englefield exhorted the king to take action for "without the support and the troops of Spain, it is scarcely probable that the catholic religion will ever be restored and established in that country. Even the seminaries, powerful as they are in preparing men's minds for a change, must fail to complete their object without the aid of temporal force ... " He too urged that the infanta be put forward as the Catholic candidate, that the leaders of the Scottish faction in Flanders be exiled or restrained, and that a conference be held in Flanders on English affairs (Tierney/Dodd, *Church History*, vol. 3, pp. xlviii–liii).

enterprise's success. Especially important was the restitution of confiscated ecclesiastical property. Of assistance in this regard, Parsons recommended a small book that Don Juan de Idiáquez had already seen.[144] Catholic gentlemen with whom Parsons had discussed the matter, believed promises such as these would please God who would then bless the undertaking. Furthermore, to allay suspicions aroused by many opponents to the Spanish claim, Philip should commission the publication of a tract, perhaps written by Sir Francis Englefield, to espouse the candidacy of the Spanish infanta.[145] Once translated into Latin, a copy could be presented to the pope whose consent was absolutely necessary.[146] Many, fearful that England would be annexed to the Spanish crown, were prepared to resist Philip's attempts. Assurances that Philip was acting for the good of the Catholic faith and not for his own self-aggrandizement, would prevent such opposition. Obviously Philip should seize every opportunity to weaken his foes and to strengthen his supporters. Thus he should encourage the Catholic earls in Scotland and the "savages" in Ireland. Some aid should also be provided to English exiles in Flanders so that they could assemble a fleet of small ships to harass the English coast. To foster greater unity among English exiles, Philip should banish from the Flemish court James's supporters. Philip should make overtures to various English nobles and gentlemen serving among the queen's forces in Holland for their assistance to secure the throne upon the death of an elderly queen. The special board for English affairs, which, as we shall see, Parsons also proposed, could handle these matters.

Any fleet sent to England should include a high-ranking English ecclesiastic, for example Thomas Stapleton, as nuncio or simply a cardinal, with authority from the pope and from Philip to settle any problem and to assure the English of the king's good intentions. Any expedition without an ecclesiastic would confirm suspicions that Philip acted only in his own interests. The pope should also renew the queen's excommunication. The proclamations and booklets written by William Allen for the Armada of 1588 along with new ones should be printed for distribution upon arrival.[147] Other clerics should accompany the cardinal/nuncio with appointments

---

[144] We shall return to this volume later in the chapter.

[145] An address of leading English Catholic exiles in favor of the infanta can be found in *CSP Simancas* (1587–1603), pp. 636–37. Detailed reasons for English Catholic espousal of her cause can be found in AAW, VI, 81.

[146] It will be recalled that Parsons had presented a Latin translation of the *Book of Succession* to the pope but he believed that to be an impartial investigation.

[147] Suggestions for the topics to be treated can be found in *CSP Simancas* (1587–1603), p. 635. Joseph Creswell's letter to the king (Madrid September 12, 1598) in which he explained the importance of the edict and the necessity of keeping the religious question in the forefront can be found on pp. 635–36.

to a few English sees, if the armada was heading for England, or to the archbishopric of Dublin if the destination was Ireland. Good arguments could be advanced in face of both England and Ireland as destinations but, regardless of destination, the enterprise must be launched soon so that the king could recover some of the prestige lost as a result of the recent English attack on Cadiz. Again, regardless of destination, Philip should encourage the Catholic earls in Scotland. They would divert the queen's attention and force her to keep an army along the border. With financial assistance, the earl of Huntly would field an army in the north of Scotland, and the earl of Angus in the west. The subsequent turmoil could force James to declare his support for Catholicism as his agent had promised. Finally an effective means of coordinating information must be established. Henry Garnet claimed that trustworthy men could be found in London who would provide information obtained in the queen's council and that they would provide correspondents in the principal ports.

Parsons developed his proposal for a special committee in Flanders in a separate memorandum.[148] Because of its proximity, England had significant influence on Spain's relations with its domains in Flanders. Out of hostility England has been aiding the rebels. Unless England was pacified, Spain would never resolve the problems in Flanders. Thus Parsons proposed a board or committee "for the method of dealing with these affairs by way of memorials is a protracted business and leaves much to be desired; the affairs can not be submitted to examination and they are of such a nature and so numerous that they are outside the range of this method and can not be expedited by it alone." In England more and more realized that the age of the queen meant the issue of succession could not be postponed any longer. If Philip provided an appropriate channel, discreet Englishmen loyal to Spain could initiate negotiations with them. Philip must guarantee secrecy, and promise to implement the fruits of the negotiations. English military leaders in Flanders who served at the whim of the queen and her council might also find it advantageous to discuss these matters with Philip via an appropriate channel.

The committee could effect more solid union among exiles under its jurisdiction, union at least "on all matters that touch the common good of their country and the service of his Majesty." The absence of a recognized ecclesiastical leader with due subordination has resulted in tremendous dissension. One vociferous faction with much ample funds worked against the interests of Spain and England and purchased support. Indeed, in the face of this disunion some of the king's ministers doubted whom they should trust. Confusion and inefficiency resulted. The board

---

[148] *CSP Simancas* (1587–1603), p. 628. I have used a transcript of the entire document in ABSI, 46/12/3.

could galvanize support for a common candidate for the English throne, namely the infanta. Doleman's *Book of Succession* clearly expounded her credentials. But the "unquiet spirits," Paget, Gifford, William Tresham and others in Flanders, and Hugh Griffin, Hesketh, Nicholas Fitzherbert and others in Rome, pursued a contrary policy. The committee could provide Philip with information regarding the character and merits of English exiles. It would provide employment for exiles according to their position and talents. The committee would discredit Elizabeth's cause and keep her anxious and confused. The committee could authorize forays into Flanders, encourage the Catholic earls in Scotland, and the rebels in Ireland. It could initiate negotiations with England and secure the services of sources in the queen's council. Equally important the committee would "run to earth" the different spies dispatched by England into Flanders. In fine, "the committee would be a countermine against all the machinations of the English council, a castle strong enough to withstand all the broadsides of the heretics, an altar raised against altar. It would attract very great numbers to the service of his Majesty against Elizabeth: she would be wearied by it." Spaniards and English should serve on the committee. Since there is no acknowledged leader among the English to select representatives, Parsons recommended exiles whose devotion was known to Philip: Stanley, Owen, Gabriel Traherne, Thomas Worthington and William Percy[149] along with William Holt. If Parsons's memorial had been acted on, Holt and Owen would have been more than vindicated: they would have had a judicial, political post from which they could seek any desired revenge.

Parsons advocated the candidacy of the Spanish infanta even more strongly in a letter to Don Juan de Idiáquez on September 2, 1596.[150] Occupied with the business affairs of the college in Valladolid and with the Latin translation of the *Book of Succession* so that Pope Clement VIII and a committee could examine it, he found time to forward a memorial in favor of the infanta by the duchess of Feria and other exiles. If he had to go to Rome as he anticipated, he would carry it with him. The infanta's succession posed no problem. Indeed, Parsons argued, it would "be a source of infinite advantage to Christendom, and a means of bringing about a general peace everywhere." If the pope planned an active role in the matter, as he would most likely do, he must be informed of her credentials. France, Parsons contended, would prefer the infanta to govern

---

[149] See Anstruther, *Seminary Priests*, vol. 1, p. 272.

[150] Valladolid September 2, 1596, ABSI, 46/12/3. For some reason much of the letter was not included in *CSP Simancas* (1587–1603), pp. 633–34. On internal evidence, i.e. references to the arrival of an anticipated letter, it seems that this letter was written before the above memoranda.

England rather than James, but would be even happier if the infanta renounced her claims to Brittany, Aquitaine, Anjou, Normandy, and so on, and also traditional English claims to the French crown.

Although Parsons had heard nothing definite, he assumed that Don Martin de Padilla's expedition was directed towards Ireland. With the hope that they could play a role in the enterprise, Parsons had sent the Jesuit Charles Tancard[151] and six other priests from Valladolid and Seville to Lisbon to join this armada.[152] Because the seminaries were so debt-ridden, he had to borrow money to pay for their travels. Nonetheless, it was worth it because, once the armies landed, the priests would "be worth their weight in gold." Finally he had left with Creswell principal points that should be included in any proclamation issued after the arrival of the armada, equally appropriate for England, Scotland or Ireland. Because the purpose of the armada was the "restoration of Catholic religion and worship," Parsons instructed the chaplains to prepare for the apostolic work "by humility, by frequent meditation, by mortifying the passions, by desire for suffering and above all, by fervent love of God and their neighbors and a firm confidence that God would assist the undertakings that were intended for his glory." This was a "holy war." A spirit of piety should thus animate it and a sense of justice permeate it. Theft, robbery and any oppression of the poor were to be shunned. God punished such crimes with military defeat. Moreover Catholics in the three kingdoms had suffered so much for their faith that God would not allow any more indignities inflicted upon them. Wherever the armies disembarked, the chaplains were to edify through their conduct and explain to the inhabitants that the armies came to help the downtrodden, and to restore Catholicism. They should promise that possible harm would come only to resisters. Any defectors to the Spanish camp must be received humanely but, on the other hand, the chaplains must be circumspect since spies might seek to permeate Spanish ranks in this way. Once they had landed, they should establish contact with the

---

[151] Tancard had earlier been assigned to travel to Rome with Joseph Creswell to assist in the resolution of the problems at the English College (Acquaviva to Parsons, Rome April 8, 1596, ARSI, Cast. 6, fols 242ᵛ–243ʳ).

[152] Apparently there had been a request for greater Jesuit involvement. Circa February 11, 1596 Acquaviva was planning to write to the Spanish provincials to tell them not to provide many men for the expedition even if they were asked to do so. The general did not think that any more priests were needed than the number usually required to provide spiritual assistance during the expedition. More would be provided if the armada were successful (Acquaviva to Parsons, Rome February 11, 1596, ARSI, Cast. 6, fols 237ᵛ–238ʳ). John Blackfan claimed that two Jesuits and two "priests-alumni" were sent to the royal fleet. Only one embarked with the fleet and he died at sea. Although unnamed in Blackfan, he must be the "John English" mentioned below. See *Annales Collegii S. Albani in oppido Valesoleti*, (ed.) John H. Pollen, S.J. (Roehampton, 1899), p. 53; Peter E.B. Harris, (ed.), *The Blackfan Annals. Los Anales de Blackfan* (Valladolid, 2008), p. 52.

Jesuit superior in England, or Jesuits already in Scotland or Ireland.[153] In all they did, they should preserve and strengthen union and concord.[154] In all likelihood these chaplains did not sail with the fleet: Philip II had issued very clear instructions not to include many English and Scots out of fear of spies. Ireland was the destination but if that should prove impossible, the fleet was to head for Milford Haven. Philip's yearning for revenge was again frustrated. The fleet sailed from Ferrol on October 13, 1596 but was forced to return to port a few days later after a great storm north of Finisterre.[155] The enterprise was again postponed.

Of the many memorials Parsons wrote in 1596, without question the most significant was later published by Edward Gee as *The Jesuit's Memorial, for the Intended Reformation of England, Under their first Popish Prince* to demonstrate how the Glorious Revolution of William of Orange had saved Ireland and the British Isles.[156] More clearly than the other memoranda, this memorial revealed Parsons's vision of a radical reformation of all aspects of English society after a successful Spanish invasion. He doubted not that God would bless the imminent invasion with success. But its goal was not simply the restitution of Catholicism but the establishment of England and Ireland as "the Spectacle of all the World, and an Example of Perfection to all other Catholic Countries and Churches round about it."[157] After full reconciliation with the Church of Rome, the new rulers should nominate for important positions Catholics who had suffered during Elizabeth's regime. Schismatics might also be so employed, but not heretics who would be stripped of their prestige and offices. However, Parsons granted them a certain liberty of conscience for a specified short period of time. Perhaps fearful of driving them into open rebellion ("considering the present State of the Realm and how generally and deeply it is, and has been plunged in all kind of Heresies"), Parsons recommended that the government should not "press any Man's

---

[153] At the moment there was no Jesuit in Ireland; James Archer did not arrive until October of 1596.

[154] "Instructiones pro Patre Carolo Tancardo," August 30, 1596, ABSI, 46/12/3.

[155] See Albert J. Loomie, S.J., "The Armadas and the Catholics of England," *Catholic Historical Review*, 59 (1973): pp. 394–98. Among the Jesuits who died in this armada was a brother known simply as John English. To our knowledge he was the only English Jesuit directly involved. See Francisco de Borja de Medina, S.J., "Jesuitas en la Armada contra Inglaterra (1588)," *AHSI*, 58 (1989): p. 40.

[156] Robert Parsons, *The Jesuit's Memorial, for the Intended Reformation of England, under their first Popish Prince*, (ed.) Edward Gee (London, 1690). See also Alexandra Walsham, "Translating Trent? English Catholicism and the Counter Reformation," *Historical Research*, 78 (2005): pp. 288–310.

[157] "Preface," A 4ᵛ.

Conscience in the beginning for matters of Religion for some few Years."[158] Only "heretics" willing to live quietly and promising to accept proper religious instruction, would be granted tolerance as long as they refrained from teaching, preaching or seeking to promulgate their erroneous notions. Parsons was not arguing for any type of permanent tolerance because "I think no one thing to be so dangerous, dishonourable, or more offensive to Almighty God in the World, than that any Prince should permit the Ark of Israel and Dagon, God and the Devil, to stand and be honoured together, within his Realm or Countrey."[159] Disputations would be the principal means for convincing them of Protestantism's errors. Protestants refused to grant disputations to Catholics because they knew that the weight of the truth of Catholicism would destroy their weak arguments. For the same reason, Catholics had nothing to fear of offering these opportunities to Protestants. With a comment about Protestant treatment of Campion during his disputations in the Tower of London in September of 1581, Parsons wanted books and ample time for preparation to be provided to the Protestant theologians for "full, free, equal, and liberal Disputation."[160] So that England might hope for God's mercy, Parsons insisted that the complex issue of confiscated monastic estates be resolved. Their immediate general restitution to the Church was neither possible nor expedient. Instead, heretics must restore them immediately, but Catholics and those seeking reconciliation with the Church could compound for their lands by paying an annual rent to a central, nation fund. The "Council of Reformation" would direct the fund and use the monies for seminaries, colleges, hospitals, and new religious houses.

Because the name "Inquisition may be somewhat odious and offensive at the beginning," the "Council of Reformation" would be comprised of the archbishop of Canterbury and other clerics. The council would supervise the economic matters of the Church, appoint clerics to all vacancies, license foreign clerics, establish "junior" seminaries in every diocese and major seminaries at the universities, consider the foundation of new military orders, invite exemplary members of religious orders to re-found their houses, draft a new national liturgical calendar, visit the Inns of Court and the universities, debate the feasibility of erecting a third archbishopric and a third university, and authorize publication of books. It would send its ministers into the shires every now and then to ascertain religious and ecclesiastical needs. Once the council had completed its work and been disbanded, it should be succeeded by some manner of Inquisition, perhaps with a different name, modelled more on Roman

---

[158] Parsons, *Jesuit's Memorial*, p. 32.
[159] Parsons, *Jesuit's Memorial*, p. 33.
[160] Parsons, *Jesuit's Memorial*, p. 36.

than Spanish or Italian lines. Parliament would immediately repeal all anti-Catholic legislation. Each member must swear to defend the Catholic faith. Henceforth the introduction of heresy would be considered treason. Parsons even suggested that clergy be allowed to sit as members of the lower house.

The formation and education of good, moral ecclesiastics was essential. Parsons envisioned a church whose archbishops and bishops were vigilant pastors who lived without pomp in their concern for the poor, weak, sick, and so on. They would enforce the decrees of the Council of Trent, and convene frequent synods. They would establish seminaries for the education of foreign clergy of Protestant countries, who would return to their homeland to work among the Catholics. All candidates for ordination must make the Ignatian Spiritual Exercises. Similar exhortations were directed at the nobility and gentry whose activities would be scrutinized by a commission to prevent oppression and injustice. Presiding over everything was a "good Catholick Prince."[161]

Unlike the other, shorter, less idealized memoranda, this was never implemented. It remains, however, more than a testimony to Parsons's powers of observation and reflection. Parsons produced, according to Professor Scarisbrick, "a grand design for a theocracy—blatantly clerical, triumphalist and ultramontane, but something new, and something beyond any previous order." It detailed the creation of "a restored, model Catholicism."[162] But it also threatened Catholics who demanded little more than the pre-Henrician status quo. Parsons did not seek to re-establish "a world we have lost," or an ecclesiastical Jurassic Park, but a godly commonwealth that had more in common with Puritan aspirations than late medieval realities. Anti-Catholic and anti-Jesuit forces seized upon Parsons's *Memorial* as a portent of what to expect if Catholicism were

---

[161] For more extensive summaries see Thomas H. Clancy, S.J., "Notes on Persons's 'Memorial for the Reformation of England'," *Recusant History*, 5 (1959): pp. 17–34; and J.J. Scarisbrick, "Robert Persons's Plans for the 'true' Reformation of England" in *Historical Perspectives: Studies in English Thought and Society*, (ed.) Neil Mc Kendrick (London, 1974), pp. 19–42, and Michael L. Carrafiello, "The *Memorial for the Reformation of England*" and "Parsons's *Memorial*," chapters 4 and 5 of his *Robert Parsons and English Catholicism, 1580–1610* (Selinsgrove/London, 1998), pp. 56–87. John Bossy considers the memorial "a respectable attempt to square the circle" (*The English Catholic Community 1570–1850* [New York, 1976], p. 24). Parsons recommended Pedro de Ribadeneira's *The Christian Prince* (*Tratado de la religion y virtudes que debe tener el príncipe cristiano para gobernar y conservar sus estados, contra lo que Nicolas Maquiavelo y los políticos deste tiempo enseñan*) to learn how to govern properly and thus avoid natural disasters. Incidentally Ribadeneira contended that Mary, Queen of Scots, lost her kingdom as divine punishment for tolerating heretics. See Robert Bireley, S.J., *The Counter-Reformation Prince. Anti-Machiavellianism or Catholic Statecraft in Early Modern Europe* (Chapel Hill/London, 1990), pp. 116, 119.

[162] Scarisbrick, "Persons's Plans," p. 39.

ever restored in England, or if the Society of Jesus were not excluded from the English mission. Parsons's foes circulated copies, and perhaps even summaries,[163] of his *Memorial* in their campaign against the Jesuits. During the subsequent appellant controversy, secular priests attacked Parsons's ideas. Parsons published his rejoinder, *A manifestation of the great folly and bad spirit of certayne in England calling themselves secular priestes*.[164] But the controversy ended with the peaceful accession of James VI and I, only to be revived after the overthrow of his grandson James II/VII.

Quelling the Storms

In Genoa on March 15, 1597, Robert Parsons expounded to William Holt reasons for his journey to Rome. Primarily, he wanted "to settle with his holiness and with father general of the Society all those points that seem necessary to enable us to support our seminaries in Spain, Flanders and Italy, and the mission to England of the fathers of the Society." This was no small task because it included precarious finances, confusing administrative structures, and ecclesiastical faculties and privileges. With such a troublesome agenda, one wonders now how Parsons could have expected to complete just this one task in a short period so that he could return to Spain. The second reason was a desire to settle once and for all the disturbances at the English College. A third reason was the issue of the English crown. Parsons was eager to present the true state of English affairs to the pope with a plea that serious consideration be given to the succession now so as to prevent further damage in the future. To Holt, Parsons repeated his claim that he was not adverse to James VI *in se* and detailed his past support for James's cause. Now, however, he had no hope of James's ever becoming a Catholic. And Catholicism remained the principal consideration in the selection of Elizabeth's successor. At the same time, Parsons added, he had consistently advised Philip against claiming the throne for himself. The king had promised that he would not do so. Thus, according to Parsons, the pope and the king must reach an agreement on a candidate acceptable to them, to the kings of France and Denmark, and to the Catholics of England and Scotland. Of the candidates, Parsons preferred the Spanish infanta married to the cardinal archduke.[165]

---

[163] See, for example, "Discourse of the Providence necessary to be had for the setting upp the Catholick Faith," TNA, SP 12/275/877. The document was endorsed "A Project of Jesuits."

[164] (n.p. [Antwerp], 1602), *ARCR*, vol. 2, num. 631.

[165] Parsons happily reported to Juan de Idiáquez that Clement had informed the Jesuit during a long audience that he was "as ready and eager in the matter of the lady infanta as

But if Holt or any of his friends in Belgium had other suggestions, Parsons was willing to listen.[166]

Over the next few months, Parsons threw himself into the three interrelated projects. Fortunately because of a series of memoranda drafted for various individuals, we know very well how Parsons understood the problems at the English College and, indeed, all the difficulties then facing the English mission. At times Parsons's preoccupation with the Paget/Morgan faction approached obsession. Letters, confidential and confiscated, testified to their involvement in all aspects of opposition to Spain and to the Society of Jesus. He frequently dismissed the pair as insignificant and unimportant but, on the other hand, he insisted that they be stopped for the good of the mission. On May 22, 1597, Parsons explained the origins and progress of the disturbances at the English College apparently to Don Juan de Idiáquez. After Cardinal Allen's death in 1594, Owen Lewis, Bishop of Cassano, requested that the authority to give faculties to priests departing for England formerly vested in Allen should be granted to him as the principal ecclesiastic of English [sic] nationality. With the approval of Girolamo Fioravanti, rector of the college, several students petitioned in Cassano's favor. But Pope Clement VIII would not grant the authority to Cassano but only to the cardinal protector, Enrico Caetani. They focused their anger and disappointment on Caetani and the Society of Jesus who sought to dissuade them from further involvement in ecclesiastical politics. Their protest attracted others opposed to the Society of Jesus and/or Spain. English laymen in Rome and Flanders encouraged them to persist with claims that many other exiles supported them. The appointment of Francisco, Cardinal Toledo as vice-protector gave temporary victory to the discontented students. According to Parsons, he "promised to give them complete satisfaction and that he would change the method of government in the English College in Rome as well as that in Reims, and would act in the same way in regard to matters within England and that he would remove the fathers of the Society."[167] The involvement of "outside agitators," the usual suspects Charles Paget, William Gifford and their supporters, prolonged the dispute. Some leaders of this faction declared that they were ready "to collaborate with the English heretics" in opposition to

---

could be wished" (Rome July 3, 1597, AAW, VI, 42).

[166] AAW, VI, 17 (printed in Tierney/Dodd, *Church History*, vol. 3, pp. lvii–lix). There is another copy in ABSI, Anglia II, 24. Parsons's letter was intercepted. As an appendix to the Italian copy are a number of "calumnious" annotations by William Percy with rejoinders. The appellants later exploited the contents of this letter in their attacks on Parsons and the Society of Jesus.

[167] ABSI, 46/12/4, pp. 629–44 (here p. 631).

Spain, the Society of Jesus, and any cleric involved in politics.[168] They wanted to do everything they could to defend and preserve Elizabeth's temporal authority as long as it did not compromise their Catholic faith. In Rome, Thomas Throckmorton, Nicholas Fitzherbert, Hugh Griffin, and William Sacheverell, O.P., gained the favor of Monsignor Bernadino Morra, sometime visitor, and the Irishman Andrew Wyse, so-called Grand Prior of England. The Flemish branch of the faction had secured the aid of Monsignor Malvasia. The disturbances ended because "God who has care for the interests of the English Catholics who have suffered so greatly in His cause, would not permit them to be brought to ruin by such violent means as these; and so He out forth His hand in a wonderful way and made a marvellous intervention in the cause of peace, which has now been negotiated and concluded." One sign of God's marvellous intervention was the sudden death:

> of the bishop of Cassano and Thomas Throckmorton, who were the chief originators of the whole business. Then Cardinal Toledo died who was the leading spirit in it. Fr. Tyrie also died, the assistant of the Society of Jesus, a Scot who, though a good religious and opposed to the sedition of the rebels, yet resembled them and their abettors in the matter of favoring the King of Scotland and giving up dependence on Spain.[169]

Others were disgraced: Sacheverell fled and later apostatized after he had been caught in a brothel; something similar prompted Griffin's departure from Rome.[170] Nicholas Fitzherbert was sent to Spain under the pretext of business.[171] Without them feeding the students false hopes with misleading information, Parsons found it much easier to discuss different issues; for example, there were fewer members in this faction than they were led to believe, and there was no guarantee that Thomas Stapleton, even if he was offered the red hat, would support their positions. Now that Monsignor Morra and Monsignor Malvasia were aware of the true circumstances,

---

[168] On July 3, Parsons admitted how difficult it would be to uproot some of the strange notions placed in the minds of the students by Paget, e.g. that Jesuits and Spaniards intended to reduce England to a Spanish province (Parsons to Juan de Idiáquez, Rome July 3, 1597, AAW, VI, 42).

[169] ABSI, 46/12/4, p. 638.

[170] See also Parsons to Juan de Idiáquez, Rome 3 July 1597, AAW, VI, 42. There he added a second Dominican, Henry Clitherow, nephew to Paget's friend and adviser William Clitherow. On William, see Anstruther, *Seminary Priests*, vol. 1, p. 81. William Clitherow may have been the author of a treatise in favor of occasional conformity. See Ginevra Crosignani, Thomas M. McCoog, S.J. and Michael Questier, (eds.), with the assistance of Peter Holmes, *Recusancy and Conformity in Early Modern England* (Toronto/Rome, 2010), pp. 116–17.

[171] Parsons to Francesco de Peña, Rome August 16, 1597, ABSI, 46/12/4.

Parsons doubted the college would have to endure similar storms in the future.[172]

Parsons's most detailed analysis of the origins of the tension between the "mainstream" English exiles and the Morgan/Paget faction appeared in another, longer memorial to Juan de Idíaquez, designed to prove that this group "has been and is very harmful to the interests of his Majesty in English affairs."[173] Spain consistently underestimated the damage they did. He repeated his familiar explanation that the disagreement began in 1582 with Paget's and Morgan's exclusion from a meeting to discuss the conversions of England and Scotland. The participants decided that Spanish support was essential and dispatched Parsons to Lisbon and William Crichton to Rome. Because of their exclusion, Paget and Morgan used their influence with Mary, Queen of Scots, to turn her against the project. Later they sought Mary's liberation and succession to the English throne through Henry, Duke of Guise, and Mary's French friends without any aid from Spain. Consistent efforts by Allen and Parsons to win them over were greeted with indifference and acts of treachery that resulted in the deaths of many, for example the Parry and Ballard plots to assassinate Elizabeth. They adamantly opposed anyone who sought Spanish involvement in English affairs. Most recently the faction's opposition to Spain was seen most clearly in their attack on the *Book of Succession*. They sought to discredit the book and to create a party to advance the claims of the king of Scotland. Now they were playing a role in the problems at the English College and striving to stir up anti-Jesuit sentiment among Catholics within the realm. To end their destruction, Parsons urged Philip II to examine carefully "this league of unquiet and subversive spirits" and make an example of some ringleaders by removing them from Flanders and/or publicly depriving them of their pensions.[174]

---

[172] Parsons had earlier written to Juan de Idiáquez on the same matters but with a greater stress on the motives behind the *Book of Succession*, and the attempts by the Morgan/Paget faction to misrepresent the volume to the Roman Curia (Rome May 1, 1597, ABSI, Anglia II, 26).

[173] Rome June 30, 1597, AAW, VI, 41 (printed partially in Tierney/Dodd, *Church History*, vol. 3, pp. lix–lxvii; and fully in Knox, *Letters of Allen*, pp. 386–91).

[174] Parsons returned to this theme a few days later after he had seen letters written by William Gifford and Hugh Griffin to encourage the dissidents to continue their rebellion. Their task was the repudiation of Spanish claims to England and the exclusion of the Society of Jesus from that mission. The work of this faction has been so successful so that "the seed that had been sown in the minds of the young men here, of some sort of captivity intended for our country by the Spaniards and the fathers of the Society in their service, cannot be so easily withdrawn from their minds." Again Parsons pleaded that it was necessary "to put an axe to the root of the tree" (Parsons to Idíaquez, Rome July 3, 1597, AAW, VI, 42).

Unless this or something comparable was done, the group would continue to disrupt Spain's plans.[175]

The euphoria that resulted from Parsons's settlement of the disputes at the English College did not endure.[176] An incident at a tavern in August reignited the affair. One student, having overeaten and overdrunk, returned to the college, sick and vomiting. The significance of this incident was not immediately obvious and life at the college continued without any evident change. On September 3, six students departing for England, accompanied by Parsons and Cardinal Caetani, visited Pope Clement VIII to receive his farewell blessing. In addition to the customary blessing, Clement reprimanded the students for their roles in the disturbances and exhorted them to work peacefully with the Jesuits in England. Shortly thereafter, in an apparently unrelated move, the pope ordered the police to keep a close eye on Roman taverns because of rumors that students from the German College were frequenting them. Bernardino Luzzi, rector of the German College and Lodovico Madrucci, cardinal protector, were so annoyed by the rumor that they sought confirmation. Their inquiry revealed that the offenders were, in fact, students from the English College. Cardinal Madrucci complained to Cardinal Caetani of the damage done to the reputation of his college, and asked Caetani to control the behavior of students of the college entrusted to him.[177] Madrucci's letter was delivered on the September 28, a few minutes before the arrival of the police who had just apprehended some English students.[178]

As the controversy was about to break, Parsons compared his role at the English College to that of a physician "curing a long festered and greevous wound." The procedure progressed through three stages. First, he sought to "appease the present paine" by discussing all matters with the discontented students and attempting to restore domestic peace. Second, he wanted "to divert the influence and concourse of evil humors." Thus he kept the pope, the cardinal protector, the vice-protector and all major ecclesiastical and secular officials informed of the real causes and

---

[175] Parsons argued against Philip II seeking to win the support of all English Catholics. If Philip distributed his favors to all, he encouraged the growth of the Morgan/Paget faction. Now it was simply a few disgruntled men. See Parsons to Juan de Idíaquez, Rome July 12, 1597, ABSI, 46/12/4, p. 689.

[176] I follow Kenny's account in "Inglorious Revolution," pp. 136–55. Parsons's report can be found in ABSI, Coll P I 307 ff. and Coll P II 352 ff.

[177] Madrucci to Caetani, [Rome] September 28, 1597, AAW, VI, 60.

[178] See Caetani's letter to Muzio Vitelleschi, rector of the English College, Rome September 28, 1597, AAW, VI, 61. The students arrested were Henry Percy [?], Robert Middleton, Francis Robinson, Cuthbert Trollop, Bannister [?] (Parsons to [John Bennett], Rome October 18, 1597, ABSI, 46/12/4, pp. 750–51). On the students see Anstruther, *Seminary Priests*, vol. 1, pp. 230, 293, 363.

nature of the dispute while, at the same time, striving to eliminate the negative influence of Englishmen outside the college, eager to exploit student discontent. Finally, the physician must let blood to cure and heal the wound. He began by "gentle sending" away of some of the most troublesome priests. Now he planned to follow that with "a purgation of some more evil humours remayning, which wil not be don perchance with such sweetnesse as the former."[179]

Clement appointed Cardinals Caetani and Camillo Borghese to investigate the accusations. Parsons insisted that a reprimand was useless; more drastic action was demanded. Father Vitelleschi lamented that he no longer could give community exhortations because certain students mocked everything that resembled spirituality and virtue. If Pope Clement wished to resolve the problems definitively, Parsons recommended that he take an axe to the tree "that produces the thorns, and brambles, and poisonous growths." If Clement authorized the transfer of a dozen students to Douai, they themselves would profit from new surroundings and the remaining students at the English College would be freed from their influence.[180] A new investigation, to be conducted by Don Acarizio Squarcione with Parsons's assistance, was announced to the students. Refusal of some of the students to answer the examiners's questions ended when Squarcione received papal permission to use torture. The investigation disclosed that the practice of frequenting taverns was a long-standing one at the English College. On October 14, six offenders were transferred to Douai.[181] Three days later, three seminarians were sent to Spain; four days later, four more were sent to Douai. Three of the greatest offenders, Edward Tempest, Thomas Hill, and Robert Benson, were among the priests lectured by the pope before their departure.[182] On October 10, Caetani instructed Monsignor Ottavio Mirto Frangipani, nuncio in Flanders, to detain the three and revoke their faculties while their case was pending in Rome.[183] But the three had travelled together only as far as Basle. Tempest continued on to Flanders; Benson travelled through France and Hill went through Germany. Thus only Tempest was in Belgium when Frangipani received

---

[179] Parsons to [Thomas Fitzherbert?], Rome September 26, 1597, ABSI, Coll P I 315.

[180] Parsons to Clement VIII, Rome September 28, 1597, ABSI, Coll P II 358.

[181] The letters patent from Cardinals Borghese and Caetani can be found in AAW, VI, 63 with copies in ABSI, Coll P 361 and Anglia II, 31. See also their letter to Muzio Vitelleschi, Rome October 14, 1597, AAW, VI, 64. The six students were George Askew, Francis Foster, John Jackson, Jasper Lothbury, Cuthbert Trollop, George Wolly. See Anstruther, *Seminary Priests*, vol. 1, pp. 12, 122, 186, 213–14, 363, 384.

[182] On them see Anstruther, *Seminary Priests*, vol. 1, pp. 32–33, 167–68, 348–49.

[183] AAW, VI, 66. See also Squarcione to Frangipani, Rome October 30, 1597, AAW, VI, 65; and Caetani to Frangipani, Rome November 1, 1597, AAW, VI, 67.

the letter. Tempest decided to remain with his brother Robert in Douai until he could clear his name.[184] Because Frangipani heard no more about the affair from Rome, he announced the suspension of the three priests on December 29.[185] Tempest was eventually tried at the nuncio's court and punished. He finally crossed to England in early January of 1599 and was captured on the 5th, betrayed by his former ally, now apostate, Friar Sacheverell.[186] At the same court William Gifford was tried for his slanders against the Jesuits.[187] By June of 1598, Hill was in prison in Holland and Benson in the Clink.[188]

The incidents with the taverns resulted in a radical revision in the rules of the English College.[189] Taverns were expressly forbidden; visitors to the college were carefully controlled; all letters and money were to be turned over to the authorities; and students were not to leave the college except in groups of four unless there was a dire emergency.[190] The incidents also destroyed any chance that Parsons would return to Spain as he had hoped: he was appointed rector of the college on December 13, 1597.[191]

Anthony Kenny concluded his historical account of the troubles at the English College with a judicious evaluation of the possible causes.[192] He reasoned that friction was a constant possibility whenever a religious order governed a secular seminary. That possibility was increased tremendously when, as was the case in the English College, the seminarians were not incardinated in any diocese or subject to any bishop. Perhaps Parsons reached the same conclusion and his agitation for the appointment of an

---

[184] See Anstruther, *Seminary Priests*, vol. 1, pp. 349–50.

[185] The letter can be found in Law, *Archpriest Controversy*, vol. 1, pp. 5–6.

[186] See Tempest's letter to Blackwell[?], [late 1598], IT, Petyt MSS 538, vol. 47, fols 270^{r-v} and same to same, Clink 15 January 1599, ABSI, Anglia II, 48.

[187] For the charges against him, his defence and Parsons's comments on his defense, see AAW, VI, 57.

[188] Garnet informed Parsons about both on June 10, 1598 but said nothing about the dates of their capture (ABSI, Anglia II, 37). On October 21, Garnet reported that Benson was now in the Counter and his companion Thomas [Hill?] in the Clink (ABSI, Coll P II 545).

[189] At the congregation of the Roman province (October 9–13, 1597), the troubles of the English College were discussed. The congregation drafted a *postulatum*. It appeared that the Society was unable to govern the college with the current regulations without periodic disturbances. The *postulatum* asked that the pope be petitioned for greater authority in order to strengthen discipline. In the reply, father general promised that, even though the situation seemed to have improved, he would do something to insure its permanence (ARSI, Congr. 47, fols 81^r, 82^r, 91^r).

[190] For a description of life after the transfers, see Parsons's letter to Creswell, Rome November 12, 1597, Valladolid, Archivum Collegium Sancti Albani, series II, vol. 1, num. 29.

[191] ARSI, Angl. 37, fol. 142^v.

[192] Kenny, "Inglorious Revolution," pp. 143–55.

English bishop was partially a response to the disturbances at the English College.

The Armada of 1597

Despite the near disaster of 1596, Philip II had not abandoned plans for another armada, possibly directed towards Ireland where he hoped to aid the insurrection of Hugh O'Neill, Earl of Tyrone. Throughout the early months of 1597, Spanish officials consulted different exiles and proposed various strategies. At least one suggested an alternate strategy: rapprochement with James. An informant, most likely Crichton or someone within his circle, argued that James intended to follow the example of Henry IV and become a Catholic if that was necessary to gain the English throne. As the closest blood heir, James was building up a body of Protestant and Catholic supporters within England. Philip, on the other hand, had no support among the English Catholics with the exception of these dependent on the Jesuits. Moreover James had wide foreign support. Scotland had formed alliances with Holland, certain German princes, and Denmark, and James was a blood relative of the dukes of Lorraine, of Florence, and of Bavaria. Even Henry IV, not a great admirer of James, was more concerned with curbing Spanish power. Thus, the author concluded, Spain should not proceed with the proposed armada but, instead, reach an accord with James. In so doing, Philip could make James a Catholic dependent on him for his accession to the English throne.[193]

Such opponents were a minority. The questions preoccupying the majority concerned where and how. Philip had submitted a proposal to Archduke Albert in Brussels that called for the creation of a diversion in the north of England whenever the armada finally sailed. The king suggested that a small force of 3,000 soldiers land along the Humber River for an attack on Hartlepool. Presumably, the many Catholics in the area would support the invaders.[194] They should be armed in order to prevent any Scottish force from heading south to assist Elizabeth. In Brussels careful consideration was given to sending Sir William Stanley's regiment but the

---

[193] "Considerations addressed to the Spanish minister, Pegna, on the subject of invading England, 1597," in Tierney/Dodd, *Church History*, vol. 3, pp. lxvii–lxx.

[194] This conviction supports Michael Questier's argument that official fear that many northern Catholics would support an invasion, preferably Scottish, underlay the repressive tactics employed by the Council of the North in the 1590s. See his "Practical Antipapistry during the Reign of Elizabeth I," *Journal of British Studies*, 36 (1997): pp. 371–96.

archduke decided against it because of his need for this regiment in his campaign.[195]

Pedro López de Soto, a subordinate captain of the Adelantado, argued that the armada should sail for the deep water port Milford Haven.[196] He too envisioned a diversion north of London instigated by Stanley, and argued in favor of "sowing cockle" in Scotland in order to occupy James. The issue of how much support could be expected from the English Catholics was realistically handled. Pedro López de Soto did not think that the Spanish should rely on the English at all. Even if they favored the Spaniards, they remained fearful of a backlash if they displayed their sympathies prematurely. Thus they would not publicly support an invading army until its success was well established. Nonetheless a proclamation was prepared that would explain the reasons for the invasion. According to it, Philip, prompted by the "universal outcry of the oppressed Catholics," undertook the armada to enforce "ecclesiastical censures" imposed by the popes. Not surprisingly, as Parsons had recommended, the proclamation said nothing explicit about the deposition of the queen and the naming of a successor. Although a reward was offered for the capture of William Cecil, no one was to "use violence against the person of the Queen in order to do her harm, save to deprive those who abuse her name and authority." All Protestant councillors were to be removed. Once that had been done, Parliament and those with legitimate authority would decide the successor most suitable "for the preservation of the Catholic religion and the tranquillity of the same nations by lightening the burden of the oppressed subjects and establishing peace and concord with the rest of the states and princes of Christianity."[197]

Final preparations were accelerated so that the armada could intercept the earl of Essex on his return from the Azores. Once that had been accomplished, the commander was given considerable freedom to decide the armada's destination either in England or in Ireland according to the opportunities that presented themselves, but the preferred site was Falmouth in Cornwall, where the Spaniards hoped to establish a base for a march on Plymouth.[198] The fleet sailed from Ferrol in mid October of 1597. Three English priests served as chaplains: one Jesuit Charles Tancard and

---

[195] Loomie, "Armadas," pp. 398–99.

[196] See Albert J. Loomie, S.J., "An Armada Pilot's Survey of the English Coastline, October 1597," *The Mariner's Mirror*, 49 (1963): pp. 288–300, for an analysis of possible landing sites.

[197] Albert J. Loomie, S.J., "Philip II's Armada Proclamation of 1597," *Recusant History*, 12 (1974): pp. 216–25; Loomie, "Armadas," pp. 399–400.

[198] Graham Darby, "The Spanish Armada of … 1597?," *The Historian*, 55 (1997): p. 15.

two secular priests, John Smithson and Thomas Stillington.[199] In late 1597, intelligence reports relayed stories of Jesuit preparations for an armada and especially of Parsons's exhortations to seminarians at Valladolid and Seville that they assist Philip's recovery of England from heresy with their prayers.[200] Once again storms off the coast of Brittany spared England a Spanish invasion. Twice in approximately a year, storms had destroyed Spanish ships. After the second, Don Martin de Padilla advised Philip: "If Your Majesty decides to continue an attempt on England, take care to make preparations in good time and in good quantity, and if not then it is better to make peace."[201]

Conclusion

In March of 1597, Parsons explained to Holt that he went to Rome to discuss with Claudio Acquaviva and Pope Clement VIII issues necessary for the successful running of the English mission in general, the Jesuit mission in particular, and the English seminaries on the continent. Issues ranged from the disturbances in Rome to the anti-Holt hostility in Belgium, from petitions for the establishment of a hierarchy in England to the question of the succession. The issues, albeit not intrinsically interrelated, generally defined the same factions. And the factions threatened the mission itself. Parsons lobbied for two English bishops, preferably loyal to Philip, capable of restoring order and discipline within the ranks of the secular clergy, and among Catholics within England. He urged that they be approved and consecrated soon to prevent the widening of divisions among Catholics and to sabotage the formation of clerical associations within England, associations that Parsons feared would hide anti-Spanish, anti-Jesuit cabals.

Within the Society, Parsons faced comparable problems due to division and lack of well-defined administrative structures. Spanish rectors and provincials complained about Joseph Creswell and the type of work he did for the English mission. They feared the loss of benefactions and alms after the foundation of English colleges within their cities or provinces. Indeed, triangular conflicts involved Spanish, Irish and English Jesuits as each sought to protect its preferred benefactors. Colleges needed

---

[199] Loomie, "Armadas," p. 400 n. 62. At least one, Smithson, died at sea, but Anstruther gives the year as 1596. According to the same source, Stillington died in San Lucar in 1597. See *Seminary Priests*, vol. 1, pp. 324, 335.
[200] TNA, SP 12/262/50.
[201] Cited in Henry Kamen, *Philip of Spain* (New Haven, 1997), p. 309.

monies for libraries,[202] new accommodations, and so on. As the student population increased so did the expenses. Spanish rectors were not always ideal. Some, not understanding fully the conditions in England and the nature of preparation for a mission there, made life extremely difficult for seminarians. In Belgium, Holt's style of governance antagonized Oliver Mannaerts and others. Mannaerts consequently questioned English practices and preferred restrictions on Holt's and Parsons's roles in the administration of the English College in St Omers, and that the college itself depend on the Belgian college for major decisions. In Rome persistent strife nearly resulted in the Society's withdrawal from the English College. Mannaerts had fallen under the spell of Parsons's enemies who, according to Sir Francis Englefield, secured "the Visitors, Provincials and Rectors of those Lowe countries with fraudulent reasons and false allegacions, which they being straungers can never comme to comprehend nor to discover the false partes of these sedicious and factiouse." He instructed Roger Baynes to explain *viva voce* the importance of Acquaviva's regularizing "the creadite and auctorytie of Fa. Parsons here [Madrid], and of Fa. Holte in Flanders, that their orders and ordinances in governing the persons or affaires of our nacion, be not encountred, altered, nor disssolved by anie Superior Father that be of straunge nacions, withoute the expresse commandement of his Fatherhoode ... "[203] On November 29, 1596, Camillo Caetani, Patriarch of Alexandria and nuncio in Madrid, appointed Parsons superior of the English residences in Lisbon and St Lucar, but that appointment did not resolve any of the problems within the Society.

The death of James Tyrie on March 20, 1597 deprived Irish and Scottish Jesuits of a Roman agent, a role now played by Parsons for the English mission. Acquaviva had rejected James Archer's request for a Roman agent in 1595 with the explanation that Tyrie would serve in that role as far as was necessary. Two days after Tyrie's death, Acquaviva asked Crichton whether someone else should be sent to Rome to supervise Scottish affairs.[204] Moreover, someone was also needed in Rome to supervise the foundation of the Scots College.[205] Crichton recommended John Myrton, but Acquaviva hesitated. Besides his many other problems, Myrton

---

[202] On August 10, 1597, Richard Walpole mentioned to Richard Verstegan how much the English College in Seville needed a better library (TNA, SP 12/264/79).

[203] Englefield to Roger Baynes, Madrid February 24, 1596, AAW, V, 39.

[204] Acquaviva to Crichton, Rome March 22, 1597, ARSI, Fl. Belg. 1/II, p. 638.

[205] Crichton initially opposed the foundation of another Scots College because of the precarious finances of the first (See Dilworth, "Beginnings 1600–1707," p. 20). Later, perhaps reluctantly, he supported it. Acquaviva emphasized that the Society, now that it has assumed the burden, must see it through (Acquaviva to Crichton, Rome, February 19, 1598, ARSI, Fl. Belg. 1/II, pp. 667–68).

consistently questioned the direction of the Scottish mission.[206] After Myrton turned up in Rome, Crichton denied responsibility by declaring that he had received the first letter granting permission but not the second. Regardless, Crichton did not have authority over Myrton and, thus, could not send him anywhere. Despite the confusion, Crichton still thought that "there was no one among us Scots better able to handle Scottish affairs in Rome; Myrton spoke the language, knew the right people, was a strong apostle, and a skilful beggar of funds. On the other hand he certainly has his faults and problems but very few are comprised totally of talents."[207]

Parsons addressed his last extant letter of 1597 to Charles Paget.[208] Apparently Paget had congratulated Parsons for restoring tranquility at the English College through "modest and discreet dealinge." Unfortunately, since the departure of Paget's informant Edward Bennett, Parsons replied, there had been new unpleasant incidents with which the pope dealt severely. Parsons quickly passed to Paget's complaint that each day he heard about more "sundry discourses, libells, letters & speaches divulged agaynste you [Paget], & other noble & gentlemen in Rome Spayne and there in Flanders, & delivered to his holinesse, & to the kinge of Spayne & his ministers to disgrace and defame you throughout the world." Paget had blamed Parsons's accomplices, Holt, Englefield, Owen, Richard Verstegan, and so on, for the dissemination of these lies. But Parsons concluded that he himself was not above suspicion of involvement in this campaign. Until these libels were publicly disowned with reparation, Paget did not foresee any concord between the two factions. Parsons insisted that Paget's case was distinct and must be separated from those of other "offended" parties. Even before the advent of Holt and Owen, when Parsons first dealt with Paget in Rouen about 14 years earlier, he showed himself "no lesse disgusted then now." Paget then complained about priests in general and against William Allen in particular. He and Thomas Morgan disliked priests meddling in "publique matters," the more appropriate domain of Catholic gentlemen then residing in France. But as Parsons reminded Paget, no other Catholic gentleman, with the exception of Morgan, shared his view. Parsons recalled his original rejoinder: "if priests besides ther breviaries or with ther breviaries or by ther creditt in catholike Princes courts, where

---

[206] Acquaviva to Crichton, Rome August 9, 1597, ARSI, Fl. Belg. 1/II, pp. 649–50; same to same, Rome September 20, 1597, ARSI, Fl. Belg. 1/II, pp. 653–54; same to Myrton, Rome September 20, 1597, ARSI, Fl. Belg. 1/II, p. 654. On the problems concerning Myrton, see McCoog, "'Pray to the Lord of the Harvest,'" pp. 151–52.

[207] Crichton to George Duras, Louvain February 7, 1598, ARSI, Germ. 178, fols 44ʳ–45ᵛ.

[208] Parsons to Paget, Rome December 20, 1597, ABSI, Coll P II 452 (partially published in Knox, *Letters of Allen*, pp. 391–94).

breviarie men were esteemed, could holpe and assiste and serve you gentlemen also towards the reduction of our countrey, why should not you be content to use ther labours to your and the publique commoditie without emulation?" Allen and Parsons then sought to improve relations with Paget and his brother, Thomas, Lord Paget, by visiting them in Paris and "impartinge all our affares and secretts with you." And how did Paget then proceed? He commissioned "the secrett sendinge of D. [William] Parry into England without our knowledge" with its dire consequences. Again Parsons and Allen sought reconciliation which was again destroyed by Paget's treachery after which an invasion planned to liberate Mary, Queen of Scots, was cancelled. William Watts, the secular priest sent by Parsons into Scotland in 1581, swore to Henry, Duke of Guise, and his Jesuit confessor Claude Matthieu, both of whom repeated the account to Allen and Parsons, that on the beach immediately before Paget's departure for England, he told Watts that in England, he intended "to overthrowe all our endeavours, and so the effect shewed." Shortly before Parsons and Allen departed for Rome together in September of 1585, they made a third approach. During their absence, Paget conspired with dubious characters such as Gilbert Gifford, Solomon Aldred, and John Ballard "without our privities or ever wrytinge one sillable therof unto us." Opposition to Allen and Parsons remained. More recently, "the chief blowinge of these coals [the troubles at the English College] came from Flaunders." In September of 1597, Paget's associates delivered a new memorial to the nuncio Ottavio Mirto Frangipani in Brussels "agaynst both our poore fathers in England (who daylie and howerlie adventure their lives for Gods cause whilest others live wastelinge and wranglinge heare) & agaynst the rest of the Societie, to whom yett you professe yourselfe a great friend whyle you impugne them."[209] Ironically Paget refused any new attempt at concord because of memorials written against him. They would surely stop, Parsons argued, as soon as Paget amended his behavior and "joyne agayne with the bodie of all good catholike Inglishe both at home and abroad, & to runne unitedlie one, & the self same course with them for the reduction of our countrey." If Paget did that, Parsons was willing to forgive and forget all past offences.

Despite the fears of Crichton and others, the publication of the *Book of Succession* did not intensify persecution in England or Scotland. For the

---

[209] Nicholas Bonaert informed Parsons that William Gifford and Paget had given a copy to the nuncio Mirto Frangipani with the request that he forward it to Cardinal Aldobrandini with a recommendation that the cardinal inform Clement VIII of the contents. Frangipani did send the memorial on but without the commendatory cover-letter. Instead he suggested that an enquiry be made into the truth of the accusations. See Bonaert to Robert Parsons, Brussels September 27, 1597, AAW, VI, 59.

final years of the century, English Catholics—and to a certain extent Scottish Catholics—were troubled more by bitter feuding among themselves than by persecution. Disagreements had been common among English Catholics, for example the dispute between Robert Parsons and Jasper Heywood, and the ongoing controversy about occasional conformity. These conflicts, however, had been domestic and private. Now they became more public and divisive as they challenged each other over ecclesiastical government, candidates for the English throne, administration of seminaries, and access to the Spanish purse. To the glee of the English government, each side acrimoniously labelled the other schismatic or self-seeking. Even within the Society, relations between certain English Jesuits, their foreign colleagues, Belgian visitors, and Spanish provincials were tense. As France and Spain explored peace overtures, wars involving English Jesuits escalated.

CONCLUSION

"Good Newes from Fraunce"

Jesuits Robert Parsons, Edmund Campion and Ralph Emerson left Rome in April of 1580 as members of a larger party that included three secular priests, two seminarians, and four elderly Marian priests. A few days before their departure, as Parsons recounted in his unfinished life of Campion, Pope Gregory XIII, "not without tears," imparted his apostolic blessing. In Parsons's account, it "seemed to Fr. Campian [sic] that God had joined this number together unlooked for of our parts he was wonderfully comforted with the number of twelve, desiring God that seeing it was an apostolical number and cause that they might have also apostolical grace to stand and persevere in the same."[1] Most Englishmen in Rome accompanied the party from the Flaminian Gate to Ponte Molle.[2] The much heralded Jesuit mission to England was launched.

As Christ sent his apostles on missions, his vicar on earth now dispatched another band. Parsons may have airbrushed away tensions between Welsh and English students at the college, and the disagreements over the nature and purpose of the same institution, as he fashioned a touching portrait of a united English Catholic community. Marian priests, seminary priests and Jesuits set forth together with considerable hope and high expectations. They were but the first of many who would return to their homeland upon the successful conclusion of negotiations for a French marriage with its consequent relief and toleration for Catholics. Their hopes had not simply faded; their dreams had become nightmares by the time Parsons had written his account nearly 15 years later. No longer were the missioners expectant home-comers, but now resolute martyrs and confessors of the faith. In late 1594 Parsons may well have reflected back to the April procession to England as a halcyon time of hope and unity. Cracks within the Catholic community visible only to a few in 1580, became more divisive and more apparent.

Disagreements plagued the English College, Rome, from its foundation in 1579. Initially invited to the college to calm nerves, smooth ruffled feathers, and provide a missionary zeal, Jesuits were later accused of siphoning off vocations and fostering division. They themselves blamed outside agitators and Elizabethan spies. Within England the Society of Jesus provided the only semblance of ecclesiastical structure. The Jesuit

---

[1] Parsons, "Of the Life and Martyrdom of Father Edmond Campian," *Letters and Notices*, 11 (1877): p. 336.

[2] See E.E. Reynolds, *Campion and Parsons* (London, 1980), p. 62.

superior had no *de iure* jurisdiction over any secular priest, but ordinarily he was the person contacted upon the arrival of a secular priest; he was the person that arranged living accommodations; he held the common purse. In England Jesuits, despite slight disagreements on the nature of the crime, adamantly adhered to a hard line on recusancy, and disputed anyone advancing any argument in favor of occasional conformity. Some secular clergy associated themselves closely with Jesuit spirituality; many of them eventually entered the Jesuits. Any resentment against the Jesuits would have been discreet out of necessity.

The execution of Mary, Queen of Scots shook the English Catholic community. One could argue that her death divided Catholics into factions. During her lifetime, Catholics had a legitimate heir to Elizabeth, or an acceptable replacement. The coalitions of the early/mid 1580s centered on her. The participants varied but the goal remained the same: the liberation of Mary and her accession to the English throne. After her death as internal religious wars preoccupied France, Spain emerged as the only power capable of restoring Catholicism and exacting vengeance. The Spanish court attracted interested Catholic parties from the three kingdoms. Spain may have been England's greatest enemy, the powerful ally of the Roman Antichrist, but she was also Catholicism's most generous benefactor with a king who identified his cause with that of the Church. Philip II remained committed to another armada. William, Cardinal Allen remained in Rome, and Parsons worked at the Spanish court on English and Jesuit causes. Through Parsons's intercession, Philip endowed and/or contributed to English colleges in Douai/Reims, Valladolid, Seville, and St Omers, and Irish colleges in Salamanca and Lisbon. William Crichton blamed Parsons for the former's failure to obtain Spanish money for a Scots college. Interestingly Philip did not endow any colleges/seminaries for the Spanish Jesuits. The king also provided generous pensions to numerous English, Scots and Irish exiles in Belgium and Spain, some of whom accepted Spanish gold but contested Spanish influence.

Robert Parsons blamed the infamous duo Thomas Morgan and Charles Paget for dividing the community because they resented their exclusion from the Allen/Parsons inner circle. Parsons insisted that their disloyalty and collaboration with the crown resulted in their marginalization. They and their associates, among whom were former Jesuits and former Jesuit benefactors, insisted, in the summary of the first historian of the English Jesuits, Henry More:

> ... [that] things would go better with the Catholics in England if Allen and Parsons abstained from writing, and from any other dealing in English affairs. It would be best of all if any Jesuits still in England were recalled, and no longer sent there in the future. Next – a thing hard to believe as coming from

Catholics – they used every endeavour to persuade authority that it was cruel to send innocent priests to most certain slaughter in England with only very slight prospect of achieving anything. Papal money would be better spent on helping liberally certain private individuals than by giving it to theological colleges, which were weak and insecure helps to the faith. Finally, pouring slander over the discipline of the Roman College, they said that it was more adapted to boys than to form men; especially those men who had passed their youth at the universities, and were obviously adequate to exercise discipline over themselves.[3]

More recently Leo Hicks repeated the charges and accusations initially made by Parsons. He dismissed Morgan and Paget as resentful Quislings adhering to positions incredible to Catholics. What intelligent Catholic urged benefactors to abandon the seminaries and colleges in favor of unnamed private individuals? Did any intelligent Catholic want the supply of clergy disrupted? The absurdity of these positions validated Parsons's evaluation. Unfortunately only Hicks has studied the two, and he was predisposed to their condemnation. Thus he fails to acknowledge and explicate the pro-Stuart, anti-Spanish roots of their opposition.[4] Because of the Armada and persistent fear of another Spanish attack, Catholics in England experienced a "winter of the soul." Robert Southwell prayed that flowers would return in the spring. Meanwhile English hatred for Spain was aimed at Catholics at home who suffered because of the machinations of Catholics abroad. Henry Garnet cried: "It is we who are hauled before the magistrates, we who are subject to questioning, we who are tortured and torn apart, we who are not plotting but hiding at home, giving ourselves to prayer and devotions, we who are beaten about the head unless we swear that we will support the queen in a war, however unjust, unless we affirm that there is no authority in the pope to excommunicate or depose the queen, and that in any case we will take up arms against him."[5] Even Henry Walpole, S.J., considered the possibility of a Spanish invasion as "the wofull ruine of the commonwealth and my dearest country."[6]

Spanish hegemony cast a long, dark shadow over English Catholicism. Sir Christopher Hatton denounced King Philip II at the opening of Parliament on November 12, 1588 as "an insatiable tyrant" and named Allen as the most villainous traitor ever bred and raised in England. English polemical literature in 1593/1594 denounced Philip by name for

---

[3] Henry More, S.J., *The Elizabethan Jesuits*, (ed.) Francis Edwards, S.J. (London, 1981), p. 179.

[4] See Hicks, *An Elizabethan Problem* (London, 1964).

[5] Garnet to Acquaviva, May 25 1590, ARSI, Fondo Gesuitico 651/624.

[6] *Unpublished Documents Relating to the English Martyrs (1584–1603)*, (ed.) John Hungerford Pollen, S.J. (London, 1908), p. 256.

his involvement in plots to assassinate Elizabeth. Sir Thomas Tresham and other Catholic nobles protested their allegiance and distanced themselves from the Spanish policies of the Allen/Parsons party. The ex-Jesuit Thomas Wright resolved a case of conscience whether Catholics could bear arms to defend Elizabeth and England against a Spanish invasion: he concluded they could.

In May of 1591 two secular priests, John Fixer and John Cecil, justified their approach to William Cecil, Lord Burghley, because of their disdain for these policies. Cecil recommended that Burghley add "one stringe moore" to his bow by courting moderate, that is, anti-Spanish Catholics, advice Burghley apparently followed because in the same year Richard Verstegan raised the alarm against false Catholics, "divers foxes in lambes's skins," who were protected by the secretary. John Cecil cited France's King Henry IV as a model. Immediately after the Armada, under the assumed name of Richard Leigh, a Catholic martyr, Cecil tried to wean Catholic sentiment from a dependence on Spain and reliance on force in favor of virtuous examples and sound teaching. Greater care therefore should be exercised regarding the type of priest sent into England: moderate and learned priests, which was barely coded language for non-Jesuits.[7] In *State of English Fugitives under the King of Spaine and his ministers* (London, 1595, 1596) Sir Lewis Lewkner distinguished between Jesuits and their supporters totally devoted to Spain, from Catholic "patriots" disagreeing with Elizabeth only on the religious issue. Subsequent historians such as Joel Hurstfield rightly consider the publication an ingenious tactic to separate the Society of Jesus from the main body of the Catholic community.[8] The 1591 proclamation condemned the colleges founded by Philip II for "dissolute young men" where they will "be instructed in school points of sedition ... to move, stir up, and persuade as many of our subjects as they dare deal withal to renounce their natural allegiance due to us and our crown." Spanish educated priests used oaths, sacraments and indulgences to create a party of Spanish sympathizers.[9] Ten students delivered short orations on the opening verse of Psalm 72, "God, give your justice to the king, your own righteousness to the royal son" in Hebrew, Greek, Latin, English, Scots, Welsh, Spanish, French, Italian, and Flemish, during Philip II's ceremonious royal visit in 1592. Rhetoric tends to hyperbole on such

---

[7] William Cecil, *The copie of a letter sent out of England to don Bernardin Mendoza* (London, 1588), *STC* 15412.

[8] Joel Hurstfield, "Church and State, 1558–1612: The Task of the Cecils," in *Studies in Church History II*, (ed.) G.J. Cuming (London, 1965), p. 135.

[9] Paul L. Hughes and James F. Larkin, C.S.V., (eds.), *Tudor Royal Proclamations* (3 vols, New Haven, 1964–1969), vol. 3, 86–93.

occasions, but the students were most likely expected to demonstrate their appreciation of Philip's benevolence upon their return to England,

The government increased post-Armada surveillance and periodic intense persecution, especially in northern England suspected of persistent pro-Scottish sentiment after Mary's execution. Even after the English government had purchased King James VI's compliance, it maintained careful scrutiny of the borderlands because of the presence of the power and influence of the Catholic earls George Gordon, Earl of Huntly; David Lindsay, Earl of Crawford; Francis Hay, Earl of Erroll; and John Maxwell, Earl of Morton, occasionally in alliance with the maverick Francis Stuart, Earl of Bothwell, usually in correspondence with Spain, generally through the agency of Jesuits such as James Gordon and William Crichton.

Any doubts Acquaviva may have had in the 1580s about the continuation of the Jesuit mission dissipated. The mission explored ways of adapting Jesuit life to hostile conditions. Different Jesuits acknowledged the importance of the semi-annual three-day retreats for prayer, discussion, and perhaps general camaraderie, for their spiritual health and apostolic effectiveness. Despite the risks the practice continued with some modifications until the number of Jesuits made it impossible. The near-capture of most Jesuits at Baddesley Clinton in 1591 and the apprehension of Robert Southwell in 1592 demonstrated the precariousness of the situation.

The mission's expansion required new vocations and better sources of income. Placing English candidates in foreign novitiates remained a problem. Few novitiates had the space and the mission had not the money to pay for their upkeep. Moreover, since these candidates entered the novitiate of the Belgian province for example, they fell under the jurisdiction of the Belgian provincial and not of Parsons who exercised jurisdiction over Jesuits in England, and English Jesuits serving as chaplains in the Spanish army. Their eventual return to England had to be carefully negotiated. Henry Garnet proceeded cautiously with vocations and finances because he feared a reaction among the secular clergy. Garnet visited Jesuits and secular clergy in Wisbech, a prison described by Michael Questier and Peter Lake as a "clerical lodging house" in November of 1593. He lauded what he found as a "college of venerable confessors" and concluded his visit with a solemn High Mass. Beneath the facade, cracks developed. Garnet became more and more preoccupied of how unnamed secular clergy perceived Jesuit activity. To them Garnet seemed more concerned with restrictions on seminary priests than with Jesuits; his collection of funds from candidates for the Society seemed to benefit said Society and not the mission; his withdrawal of secular clergy candidates to send them to novitiates deprived the mission of needed priests. Such complaints whispered in the early 1590s were stridently proclaimed within a few years.

Many English subjects watched in horror as Spain intervened directly in the French religious wars. Spanish assistance and Spanish forces tilted the battle in favor of the Catholic League, but the death of "King Charles X," Charles, Cardinal Bourbon, in May of 1590 left the League without an alternative to the Protestant Henry IV. Philip II proposed his daughter the Infanta Isabella Clara Eugenia as the Catholic claimant once the French Estates-General had abandoned the Salic tradition. English fears of a Spaniard on the French throne and French coastal cities in Spanish hands motivated the government to provide overt assistance to the Protestant contender. In June of 1593 Henry IV publicly repudiated Protestantism. In September of 1595 Pope Clement VIII absolved Henry from excommunication. The dynastic struggle in France could have been a preview of what many feared would happen after Elizabeth's death. Then Spain could again exploit the confusion for dynastic aggrandizement under the guise of a religious crusade. Clement's treatment of Henry also provided a possible template for James VI's reconciliation with Rome. Even William Crichton jumped on the Stuart bandwagon by the summer of 1593 despite his earlier repudiation of Scottish claims.

Many provincial congregations drafted *postulata* about Jesuit involvement in activities considered inappropriate for priests and religious. Interestingly no Spanish Jesuit province touched the issue. The Fifth General Congregation forbade "all of Ours to involve themselves in public affairs of this nature on any grounds, even if invited or enticed, or to deviate from our institute upon pleas or persuasions."[10] The decree alarmed not only Parsons. The Italian Jesuit Antonio Possevino, who had been employed on various papal diplomatic missions,[11] complained about a decree that forbade any involvement in "*cose di stato,*" matters of state, that interpreted "as a "cause of state" everything pertaining to the spiritual direction of magistrates, military officials and court officials" [*che interpreti per cosa di stato tutto ciò che appartiene all'indirecto dell'anime et on assime di magrati, di capitani, et di cortigiani*]. Such a prohibition impeded attempts at conversion, hearing confessions, and preaching. Possevino recalled numerous missions of different Jesuits, including himself, and wondered whether comparable missions would be permitted in the future. Did Ignatius Loyola[12] involve himself in matters of state on his papal

---

[10] John W. Padberg, S.J., Martin D. O'Keefe, S.J., and John L. McCarthy, S.J., (eds.), *For Matters of Greater Moment: The First Thirty Jesuit General Congregations* (St Louis, 1994), p. 201.

[11] See John Patrick Donnelly, S.J., "Antonio Possevino: From Secretary to Papal Legate," in *The Mercurian Project: Forming Jesuit Culture 1573–1580*, (ed.) Thomas M. McCoog, S.J. (Rome/St Louis, 2004), pp. 323–49.

[12] The memorial does not specify Loyola: it simply refers to "N.P.," *nostro padre*.

mission to negotiate peace between Mantua and Parma?[13] Likewise was it a matter of state when Lorenzo Maggio was sent to reconcile the king and queen of Poland? Do Jesuits, if consulted, enter dangerous waters when they discuss as a case of conscience conditions for a just war? Possevino himself testified to the specific missions that he had received from the pope. James Tyrie, a Scottish Jesuit in Rome, Possevino explained in language similar to Parsons's, treated Scottish matters; others treated English affairs "where religious maters are intermixed with affairs of state." How could they obey the decree? Possevino claimed that the *fine*, the goal, the purpose of the mission determined whether the mission itself violated the decree. Acceptable goals included not simply matters of import for Catholicism, but less grand matters regarding colleges, seminaries, publications, and so on. At the end he referred to Robert Bellarmine, Thomas Aquinas, and others. As it stood the decree prevented Jesuits from resisting the most pernicious influence of Niccolò Machiavelli.[14]

Post hoc or *propter hoc* the complaints of Parsons and Possevino, Acquaviva nuanced the congregational restrictions. As the two Jesuits argued, Acquaviva agreed that they could touch on political matters but as long as their goals were supernatural and not natural, spiritual and not temporal, his activities. Possevino cited Bellarmine, who at the time was struggling to give definitive expression to the theory of the indirect power of the pope in temporal affairs,[15] Claudio Acquaviva and other Jesuits implicitly implemented the same theory in their decisions regarding the direction and governance of the Society. Just as many papalists complained that Bellarmine had reduced and restricted the power and authority of the pope so too many Jesuits lamented the extension of spiritual borders to include apparent political activity. In 1616 the Jesuit theologian Giovanni Argenti argued:

---

[13] This is a perplexing reference. In 1545 Paul III created the dukedom of Parma and Piacenza for his son, Pier Luigi Farnese. When Pier Luigi excluded the noble families of Piacenza from government, they plotted against him with the support of the Spanish viceroy in Milan, Ferrante Gonzaga, uncle of Francesco II Gonzaga, Duke of Mantua. When some Piacenza nobles assassinated Pier Luigi Farnese in 1547, Spanish troops immediately occupied the city. Relations were very bad between the Farnese and Gonzaga, and Loyola presumably was asked to intervene in order to prevent war between them. Although war did not break out, I can find no evidence of Loyola's involvement in his correspondence. Possevino, a Mantuan close to the Gonzaga family, may have had insider knowledge. I thank Dr Paul Grendler for this information.

[14] ARSI, Congr. 20b, fols 342^r–344^v.

[15] See John Courtney Murray, S.J., "St. Robert Bellarmine on the Indirect Power," *Theological Studies*, 9 (1948): pp. 491–535.

A religious is not deemed "political" when he, within the limits of his state, has discussions with the prince and government officials, or when he explains from a higher perspective things that concern the foundations of the state. He makes suggestions on his own, or, if asked, advises the prince so that he has before his eyes the King of kings and he reveres justice as the bond of the state. The Jesuit prompts the prince to have no fears and to base everything on the guidance of reason and prudence. He is to look upon himself as defender of the oppressed, the protector of children, the patron of widows. He is to guide the state no longer as a master, but as a father. He should conduct himself in a dignified way and act uprightly ... Who, I ask, would criticize these steps toward encouraging virtue, increasing piety, taking due responsibility? These steps do not pertain to the political sphere, but to the divine, and for that reason they are peculiar to religious and ought not to be blamed in any way, but even are to be highly praised.[16]

Parsons, Crichton and Archer would have argued similarly.

The English Jesuits administered for the English church seminaries in Rome, Valladolid, and Seville. Cardinal Allen oversaw the seminaries; Parsons was his delegate. Each had a Jesuit rector. The English College of St Omers, owned and administered by the Society of Jesus, proved more problematic. The Belgian provincial had jurisdiction over the institution, and he preferred that the English college be subject to the rector of the Belgian college. Parsons had no canonical authority with consequent clashes between his assistant in Brussels, William Holt, and the Belgian provincial. The Belgian Oliver Mannaerts, who had argued in favor of a Jesuit mission to England in 1579/80, partially as a result of this conflict, fell under the spell of Parsons's enemies whom he defended. Similarly Spanish rectors and provincials complained about Joseph Creswell and the type of work he did for the English mission. Clearer regulations were needed.

The death of Cardinal Allen in 1594 unleashed barely concealed resentment at the pro-Spanish policies of the Allen/Parsons party. Charles Paget and Thomas Morgan found more allies and supporters, united especially in their fear that Parsons would be named a cardinal, and thus the principal agent for English Catholics. As the English government denounced Spain for overt and covert, real and pretended, aggression, more English Catholics distanced themselves from Philip II, and deflected now traditional anti-Catholic rhetoric to the Jesuits. They distinguished loyal Catholics from traitorous Jesuits who colluded with the enemy, and sought to establish a breach between the beloved Allen and the perfidious

---

[16] Cited in Sabina Pavona, *The Wily Jesuits and the Monita Secreta. The Forged Secret Instructions of the Jesuits. Myth and Reality* (St. Louis, 2005), pp. 51–52. The original source is *Apologeticus pro Societate Iesu* (Cologne, 1616).

Parsons. Allen finally saw through Parsons, they asserted, and turned against him. Each side claimed Allen. Developments in France provided disgruntled English Catholics with a guidebook.

The Society of Jesus developed from a group of friends at the University of Paris, friends motivated and inspired by Ignatius Loyola and his Spiritual Exercises. The early Jesuits based their educational principles, the *Ratio studiorum*, on Parisian pedagogy.[17] Nonetheless the *parlement* of Paris, and the Faculty of Theology at the university resisted establishment of Jesuit institutions and indeed the presence of Jesuits as threats to the kingdom's Gallican traditions.[18] During the religious wars, Parisian jurists associated with the *parlement* employed new humanistic techniques to argue that the Gallican tradition offered the greatest possibility for the re-establishment of peace and security. In his monograph on Henry IV and French Jesuits, Eric Nelson labels these jurists "erudite Gallicans."[19] Erudite Gallicanism went hand in hand with anti-Jesuitism: Etienne Pasquier and Antoine Arnauld were the Society's most vocal opponents in France. Their anti-Jesuits treatises were translated into English for use in the campaign against the Society. As the Catholic League collapsed and more and more French nobles made their peace with Henry IV, polemicists found a perfect scapegoat for the league's worst excesses: the Society of Jesus.

Arnauld's opposition to the Society evolved gradually. His *The coppie of the Anti-Spaniard*, as the title suggests, an anti-Spanish diatribe, mentions Jesuits only once: they collected and destroyed histories of Spanish atrocities in the New World.[20] A few years later, in an anonymous pamphlet commonly attributed to him, Arnauld blamed the Society for the prevalence of Spanish influence and the promotion of the league itself:

[Philip] sent the Jesuites, very Spanish Colonies, who hath shed forth the poyson of their consperacy under the shadow of holiness, and under the colour of confession (O wonderfull policie:) have abused the devotion of the french nation, whom by secret othes they have bound to their loeague. Who also in lieu of instructing our people in the Catholike religion, are become trumpets of warre, firebrands of sedition, protectors and defenders of murther and robbery, to be brief, who are waren forein levine to sower the domme of our France and

---

[17] See Gabriel Codina Mir, S.J., *Aux sources de la pédagogie des Jésuites; le "Modus Parisiensis"* (Rome, 1968).

[18] For the early conflicts see Philippe Lécrivain, S.J., "The Struggle for Paris: Juan Maldonado in France," in McCoog, *The Mercurian Project*, pp. 295–321.

[19] Eric Nelson, *The Jesuits and the Monarchy. Catholic Reform and Political Authority in France (1590–1615)* (Aldershot/Rome, 2005), pp. 15–16. My analysis follows Nelson's first chapter (pp. 11–55). Henceforth I shall footnote only specific citations.

[20] Antoine Arnauld, *The coppie of the Anti-Spaniard* (London, 1590), STC 684, p. 9.

to alter the fedility into trechery and rebellion, so cunningly conducting their masters affaires that they have filed this realme, before flourishing, with fire and blood ...[21]

A year later Arnauld claimed that Jesuits acknowledged the king of Spain as their master. Pedro de Ribadeneira admitted as much in his biography of Ignatius Loyola: "their institution hath no other end but the advancement of the affayres of Spaine." Jesuits pray for Philip and either publicly or secretly make their vows to him. As the French had evicted the Spaniards (that is the Spanish-sponsored league) from Paris, Arnauld recommended that Jesuits, responsible for the introduction of the Spanish, be likewise expelled.[22] Professor Nelson astutely observes: "By placing the blame for the League exclusively on the Jesuits and their Spanish patrons, Arnauld constructed an acceptable theoretical framework for the reintegration of former leaguers into French society in a way in which the king might have desired. At the same time, Arnauld provided a scapegoat for a section of French society that was patently guilty of participation in the League."[23] Because of their loyalty to the king of Spain and devotion to the pope of Rome, Jesuits, Arnauld argued, could never be integrated properly into French society. For the benefit and protection of the kingdom, they should therefore be expelled. Rehabilitation was impossible; expulsion, the only remedy. He and others recited the problems and woes that followed the arrival of the Jesuits who were agents of the Spanish monarch, France's traditional enemy. Jesuits fostered instability within France. Pierre Barrière was arrested on August 27, 1593 and executed four days later because of an alleged plot to assassinate Henry. Barrière had been a soldier for the league. In the subsequent propaganda, Pasquier advanced a connection between the assassin and the Jesuits. A few months earlier, the Jesuit Jacques Commolet had advocated Henry's assassination in a sermon in Paris, a not uncommon theme during the wars.

On May 15, 1594 the rector of the University of Paris, Jacob Amboise, lodged a formal complaint with the *parlement* of Paris that the Jesuits "showed ... [themselves] wholly partial to and promoter of the Spanish faction to the desolation of this kingdom not only in the whole city of Paris but throughout the whole kingdom of France and beyond."[24] According to Amboise Jesuits abused their influence, especially through the sacraments, to denigrate the secular clergy and to advance Spanish influence and power. Etienne Pasquier sided with the university and

---

[21] Antoine Arnauld, *The Flower de Luce* (n.p. [London], 1593), STC 11088.

[22] Antoine Arnauld, *The arrainement of the whole societie of Jesuites in Fraunce* (London, 1594), STC 779. fols 2ᵛ, 5ᵛ, 28ᵛ.

[23] Nelson, *Jesuits and Monarchy*, p. 33.

[24] Cited in Nelson, *Jesuits and Monarchy*, p. 27.

demanded the expulsion of Jesuits. Ignatius Loyola, Pasquier contended, was as dangerous as Martin Luther: the latter abrogated Roman authority, the former augmented it. The continual presence of Jesuits within the kingdom threatened to divide the Church "betweene the Papist that is the Iesuite and the true *French* Catholike," that is the Gallican.[25]

Erudite Gallicans held Jesuits responsible for all the ills of the kingdom "as leaders of the League, minions of Spain and seducers of the people."[26] The attempted assassination of Henry IV on December 27, 1594 provided all the proof the anti-Jesuit *parlementaires* could have desired. The would-be assassin's attendance at the Jesuit College of Clermont in Paris for more than two years illustrated the Society's perfidy. There, the erudite Gallicans contended, Jean Chastel learned all about tyrannicide as espoused by Jesuits. Within hours of Chastel's capture, *parlement* ordered the arrest of all Jesuits in Paris. In January of 1595 Jesuits were expelled from Paris and regions under the jurisdiction of the Parisian *parlement*. The Society remained strong in southern France because the *parlements* of Toulouse and Bordeaux refused to register its banishment.

In her excellent monograph, Lisa Ferraro Parmelee investigates the rapid translation of seminal works by erudite Gallicans for polemical use in England.[27] She argues that William Cecil, Lord Burghley, orchestrated their publication and dissemination. What the English feared most was unfolding in France: religious warfare regarding succession to the throne with Spanish military intervention. France served as a warning. But for some English Catholics unhappy with the role and tactics of the Society of Jesus, France was also a model. The polemics of Arnauld and Pasquier published under Burghley's auspices to discredit Catholics, provided a road map for Jesuit opponents. By distinguishing loyal Catholics from Jesuits, secular clergy redirected customary official invective from Catholics in general to Jesuits in particular. Jesuits were devoted to Spain, involved in plots and conspiracies, and determined to refashion English Catholicism in their image. English Catholicism's only hope lay in their expulsion from the mission. The Elizabethan government collaborated with the secular clergy who believed Burghley and others sincerely sought a *modus vivendi* after appropriate assurances of Catholic loyalty. Burghley had indeed added one more string to his bow. But was the government misleading the seculars, preying upon their hopes simply to divide and destroy English Catholicism? This unholy alliance threatened the English

---

[25] Etienne Pasquier, *The Jesuite displayed* (London, 1594), STC 19448, fols [D4ʳ], Fʳ.
[26] Nelson, *Jesuits and Monarchy*, p. 31.
[27] Lisa Ferraro Parmelee, *Good Newes from Fraunce: French Anti-League Propaganda in Late Elizabethan England* (Woodbridge, 1996).

Jesuits. Declared traitors by the crown, denounced by secular clergy, and derided by continental Jesuit colleagues, the English Jesuit mission was beleaguered by the late 1590s.

Bibliography

Manuscripts

Archives of the Archdiocese of Westminster, London

V.	Miscellaneous documents, 1595–1596.
VI.	Miscellaneous documents, 1597–1600.
Anglia IX.	Miscellaneous papers from the collection of Christopher Bagshaw, and the archives of the Roman agent of the secular clergy. Formerly at Stonyhurst, this codex passed to the Westminster Archives in an exchange in 1921.

Archivio segreto vaticano, Vatican City

Borghese, serie II.448.a–b.	Jesuitica.
Borghese, serie III.124.c.	Inghilterra Varia; Missioni di Scozia e di Irland.
Borghese, serie III.124.g.2.	Inghilterra. Lettere di Personio e Creswello, 1594–1597.
Borghese, serie IV.103.	*De regiae successionis apud Anglos.*
Segreteria di Stato, Spagna 38.	Lettere di Spagna, 1586–1591.
Segreteria di Stato, Spagna 40.	Lettere di Spagna, 1592–1593.

Archivum Collegium Sancti Albani, Valladolid

Series II, Vol. 1.	Miscellanea, 1589–1600.

Archivum Romanum Societatis Iesu, Rome

Angl. 30/I–II.	Anglia Historia I 1550–1589.
Angl. 31/I–II.	Anglia Historia II 1590–1615.
Angl. 37.	Anglia Historia VIII 1579–1624.
Angl. 38/I–II.	Anglia Historia IX 1568–1664.
Angl. 39.	Anglia Fundationes Collegiorum.
Angl. 41.	Hibernia Historia 1566, 1591–1692.
Angl. 42.	Scotia Historia 1566–1634.
Aquit. 1/I–II.	Epistolae Generalium a 1571 ad 1612.

Aquit. 9/I–II.	Catalogi personarum et officiorum prov. Aquitaniae 1556–1649.
Austr. 1/I–II.	Epistolae Generalium a 1573 ad 1600.
Baet. 2.	Epistolae Generalium a 1584 ad 1591.
Baet. 3/I–II.	Epistolae Generalium a 1591 ad 1609.
Baet. 8.	Catalogi informationum prov. Baeticae 1583–1622.
Cast. 6.	Epistolae Generalium a 1588 ad 1603.
Congr. 20b.	De rebus congregationum generalium I–V.
Congr. 45.	Acta Congr. Provinc. 1592–1593 I.
Congr. 46.	Acta Congr. Provinc. 1592–1593 II.
Congr. 47.	Acta Congr. Provinc. 1597.
Fondo Gesuitico 651.	Epistolae selectae ex Anglia. Fasciculi 593–661.
Fondo Gesuitico 678/21.	Acta quaedam de administratione et disciplina S.I Opuscula apologetica de eadem Societate. 21 Cifraria S.I. saec. XVI–XVII
Fl. Belg. 1/I–II.	Epistolae Generalium a 1573 ad 1576, a 1583 ad 1610.
Fl. Belg. 2.	Epistolae Generalium a 1576 ad 1582.
Fl. Belg. 43.	Catalogi personarum et officiorum prov. Flandro-Belgicae 1577–1615.
Franc. 1/I–II.	Epistolae Generalium a 1573 ad 1604.
Gal. 44.	Registrum secretum epistolarum. Generalium a 1583 ad 1602.
Gal. 93.	Epistolae Galliae 1589–1601.
Germ. 170.	Epistolae ass. Germaniae 1592.
Germ. 171.	Epistolae ass. Germaniae 1593.
Germ. 172.	Epistolae ass. Germaniae 1594.
Germ. 173.	Epistolae ass. Germaniae 1594.
Germ. 174.	Epistolae ass. Germaniae 1595 3 ian.–27 iul.
Germ 175.	Epistolae ass. Germaniae 1595.
Germ. 177.	Epistolae ass. Germaniae 1597.
Germ. 178.	Epistolae ass. Germaniae 1598–1599.
Hisp. 74.	Epistolae Generalium soli 1585–1599.
Hisp. 76.	Epistolae Generalium soli 1586–1610.
Hisp 134.	Epistolae ass. Hisp. oct.1587–1592.
Hisp. 135.	Epistolae ass. Hisp. 1593.
Hisp. 136.	Epistolae ass. Hisp. aug.1593–1594 iun.
Hisp. 137.	Epistolae ass. Hisp. 1594.

Hisp. 138.   Epistolae ass. Hisp. 1594–1595.
Hisp. 139.   Epistolae ass. Hisp. 1595–1596.
Hist. Soc. 42.   Catalogus defunctorum S.I. 1557–1623.
Hist. Soc. 54.   Catalogus dimissorum Societatis Iesu 1573–1640.
Hist. Soc. 61.   Litterae patentes 1573–1601.
Instit. 40.   Originale Ordinationum communium omnibus Provinciis.
Lugd. 1.   Epistolae Generalium a 1583 ad 1599.
Lus. 44/I–II.   Catalogi officiorum prov. Lusitaniae 1587–1645.
Lus. 72.   Epistolae ass. Lusitaniae 1593–1594.
Med. 20.   Epistolae Generalium a 1586 ad 1598.
Med. 21/I–II.   Epistolae Generalium a 1583 ad 1595.
Med. 22/I–II.   Epistolae Generalium a 1583 ad 1595.
Rh. Inf. 3.   Epistolae Generalium a 1590 ad 1600.
Rom. 156/I–II.   Romana Historia Collegiorum Anglorum, Scotorum et Hibernicorum 1579–1783.
Rom. 169.   Registrum novitiorum prov. Romanae 1556–1668.
Rom. 171A.   Liber novitiorum prov. Romanae 1569–1594.
Tolet. 4.   Epistolae Generalium a 1586 ad 1594.
Tolet. 5/I–II.   Epistolae Generalium a 1588 ad 1600.
Tolet. 37a.   Historia 1547–1610.
Venet. 4/I–II.   Epistolae Generalium a 1593 ad 1599.

Archivum Britannicum Societatis Iesu, London

Anglia I.   Collected Manuscripts, 1554–1594. Formerly at Stonyhurst College.
Anglia II.   Collected Manuscripts, 1595–1600. Formerly at Stonyhurst College.
Coll B.   Christopher Grene's 17th century collection of manuscripts and transcripts, section B. Formerly at Stonyhurst College.
Coll M.   Christopher Grene's 17th century collection of manuscripts and transcripts, section M. Formerly at Stonyhurst College.
Coll N I/II.   Christopher Grene's 17th century collection of manuscripts and transcripts, section N. Formerly at Stonyhurst College.

Coll P I/II.	Christopher Grene's 17th century collection of manuscripts and transcripts, section P in two parts. Formerly at Stonyhurst College.
A.II.3	De Rebus Scoticis (1610–1734). Formerly at Stonyhurst College.
A.V.9.	Joseph Creswell, S.J., *Responsio ad Calumnias*. Formerly at Stonyhurst College.
46/4/10.	Transcripts of documents relating to Jesuits in Scotland and Scottish Jesuits, 1596–1606.
46/5A/1–2.	John Hungerford Pollen's manuscript history of Jesuits in Elizabethan England.
46/12/1–6.	Transcripts of the Correspondence of Robert Parsons, S.J.
46/23/8.	MacErlean Transcripts (Dublin) 16th – 17th Century.
100/967/1–4.	Francis Edwards's proposed edition of documents relating to English affairs, 1595–1610, in the Archivio secreto vaticano.

Biblioteca Apostolica Vaticana, Vatican City

Ottob. lat. 2510.	Miscellanea.

British Library, London

Add. MSS 39, 828.	Tresham Papers.
Lans. 71.	Burghley Papers, Varia, c. 1592
Lans. 96.	Burghley Papers, Religious documents, c. 1556–1597

Inner Temple, London

Petyt MS. 538, vol. 38.	Tracts etc. Sixteenth and Seventeenth Centuries.
Petyt MS. 538, vol. 47.	Original papers concerning Ecclesiastical Matters and Jesuits.

Irish Jesuit Archives, Dublin

MS. B. Miscellaneous original documents, 1576–1698.

The National Archive, Kew

SP 12.	State Papers Domestic, Elizabeth.
SP 78.	State Papers Foreign, France.

Published Primary Sources

Anderson, William James (ed.), "Abbe Paul MacPherson's History of the Scots College, Rome," *The Innes Review*, 12 (1961): 3–172.
Bain, Joseph et al. (eds.), *Calendar of the State Papers relating to Scotland, and Mary, Queen of Scots, 1547–1603* ... (13 vols in 14 parts, London: His Majesty's Stationery Office, 1898–1969).
[Blackfan, John, S.J.], *Annales Collegii S. Albani in oppido Valesoleti*, John Hungerford Pollen, S.J. (ed.) (Roehampton: Manresa Press, 1899).
Bruce, John (ed.), *Letters of Queen Elizabeth and King James VI of Scotland*, Camden Society, 46 (London: Camden Society, 1849).
Cano Echevarría, Berta and Ana Sáez Hidalgo (eds.), *The Fruits of Exile. Los Frutos del Exilio* (Valladolid: Royal English College, 2009).
Caraman, Philip, S.J. (ed.), *John Gerard: The Autobiography of an Elizabethan* (London: Longmans, Green and Co., 1951).
——, *William Weston: The Autobiography of an Elizabethan* (London: Longmans, Green and Co., 1955).
Carayon, Auguste, S.J. (ed.), *Documents Inédits Concernant la Compagnie de Jésus* (23 parts in 14 vols, Poitiers: Henri Oudin, 1863–1886).
Castelli, Giovanni Battista, *Correspondsnce du Nonce en France Giovanni Battista Castelli (1581–1583)*, Robert Toupin, S.J. (ed.), Acta Nuntiaturae Gallicae, 7 (Rome/Paris: Gregorian University/E. de Boccard, 1967).
Chadwick, Hubert, S.J., "Father William Creichton S.J., and a Recently Discovered Letter (1589)," *AHSI*, 6 (1937): 259–86.
——, "A Memoir of Fr. Edmund Hay S.I.," *AHSI*, 8 (1939): 66–85.
Clay, William Keatinge Clay (ed.), *Liturgical Services. Liturgies and Occasional Forms of Prayers set forth in the Reign of Queen Elizabeth*, Parker Society, 30 (Cambridge: Cambridge University Press, 1847).
Crosignani, Ginevra, Thomas M. McCoog, S.J. and Michael Questier (eds.), with the assistance of Peter Holmes, *Recusancy and Conformity in Early Modern England*, Studies and Texts, 170/MHSI, n.s., 7 (Toronto/Rome: Pontifical Institute of Medieval Studies/Institutum Historicum Societatis Iesu, 2010).
[Foley, Henry, S.J., ed.], "Two Conferences in the Prison at York with Father Walpole, S.J., An. Dom. 1594. Related by Himself," *Letters and Notices*, 9 (1873): 46–63.
Forbes-Leith, William, S.J. (ed.), *Narratives of Scottish Catholics under Mary Stuart and James VI* (Edinburgh: William Patterson, 1885).
Frangipani, Ottavio Mirto, *Correspondance d'Ottavio Mirto Frangipani, Premier Nonce de Flandre (1596–1606)*, Leon Van der Essen and Armand Louant (eds.), Analecta Vaticano-Belgica, 2e Série: Nonciature

de Flandre (3 vols in 4 parts, Rome/Bruxelles/Paris: Institut Historique Belge/P. Imbrechts/H. Champion, 1924–1942).

Garnet, Henry, S.J., *A Treatise of Equivocation*, David Jardine (ed.) (London: Longmans and Co., 1851).

Hagan, J., "Some Papers Relating to the Nine Years' War," *Archivium Hibernicum*, 2 (1913): 274–320.

——, "Miscellanea Vaticano-Hibernica, 1580–1631 (Vatican Archives: Borghese Collection)," *Archivium Hibernicum*, 3 (1914): 227–365.

Harris, Peter E.B. (ed.), *The Blackfan Annals. Los Annales de Blackfan* (Valladolid: Royal English College, 2008).

Hartley, T.E. (ed.), *Proceedings in the Parliaments of Elizabeth I* (3 vols, Leicester: University of Leicester, 1981–1995).

Henson, Edwin (ed.), *Registers of the English College at Valladolid, 1589–1862*, CRS, 30 (London: Catholic Record Society, 1930).

Hicks, Leo, S.J. (ed.), *Letters and Memorials of Father Robert Persons, S.J.*, CRS, 39 (London: Catholic Record Society, 1942).

Hogan, Edmund, S.J. (ed.), *Ibernia Ignatiana* (Dublin: The Society of Jesus, 1880).

Holmes, Peter (ed.), *Elizabethan Casuistry*, CRS, 67 (London: Catholic Record Society, 1981).

Huarte, Amalio, "Petitions of Irish Students in the University of Salamanca, 1574–1591," *Archivium Hibernicum*, 4 (1915): 96–130.

Hughes, Paul L. and James F. Larkin, C.S.V. (eds.), *Tudor Royal Proclamations* (3 vols, New Haven: Yale University, 1964–1969).

Hume, Martin A.S. (eds.), *Calendar of letters and papers ... preserved principally in the archives of Simancas* (4 vols, London: His Majesty's Stationery Office, 1892–1899).

Ignatius Loyola, *Saint Ignatius Loyola: Letters to Women*, Hugo Rahner, S.J. (ed.) (Freiburg/London: Herder/Nelson, 1960).

Jessop, Augustus (ed.), *Letters of Fa. Henry Walpole, S.J.* (Norwich: Miller and Leavins, 1873).

Kelly, Wilfrid (ed.), *Liber Ruber Venerabilis Collegii Anglorum de Urbe*, CRS, 37 (Rome: Catholic Record Society, 1940).

Kenny, Anthony (ed.), *The Responsa Scholarum of the English College, Rome*, CRS, 54 (London: Catholic Record Society, 1962).

Kingsford, Charles Lethbridge et al. (ed.), *Report on the Manuscripts of Lord D'Isle and Dudley Preserved at Penshurst Place*, HMC, 77 (6 vols, London: His Majesty's Stationery Office, 1925–1966).

Knox, Thomas Francis (ed.), *The First and Second Diaries of the English College, Douay*, Records of the English Catholics Under the Penal Laws, I (London: David Nutt, 1878).

——, *The Letters and Memorials of William Cardinal Allen (1532–1594)*, Records of the English Catholics Under the Penal Laws, II (London: David Nutt, 1882).

Law, Thomas Graves (ed.), *A Historical Sketch of the Conflicts between Jesuits and Seculars in the Reign of Queen Elizabeth* (London: David Nutt, 1889).

——, "Documents Illustrating Catholic Policy in the Reign of James VI," in *Miscellany of the Scottish History Society. Vol. I*, Scottish History Society, 15 (Edinburgh: University of Edinburgh Press, 1893), pp. 1–70.

——, *The Archpriest Controversy*, Camden Society n.s., 56, 58 (2 vols London: Camden Society, 1896–1898).

Lemon, Robert et al. (eds.), *Calendar of State Papers, Domestic Series of the Reigns of Edward VI …* (12 vols, London: His Majesty's Stationery Office, 1857–1872).

McCoog, Thomas M., S.J. (ed.) *Monumenta Angliae*, MHSI, 142, 143 (2 vols, Rome: Institutum Historicum Societatis Iesu, 1992).

——, *English and Welsh Jesuits 1555–1650*, CRS, 74, 75. (1 vol. in 2 parts, London: Catholic Record Society, 1994–1995).

——, "The Letters of Robert Southwell, S.J.," *AHSI*, 63 (1994): 101–24.

—— and László Lukács, S.J. (eds.), *Monumenta Angliae III*, MHSI, 151 (Rome: Institutum Historicum Societatis Iesu, 2000).

Morris, John, S.J. (ed.), *The Condition of Catholics under James I: Father Gerard's Narrative of the Gunpowder Plot* (London: Longmans, Green and Co., 1871).

—— (ed.), *Troubles of Our Catholic Ancestors as Related by Themselves* (3 vols, London: Burns and Oates, 1872–1877).

—— (ed.), *The Life of John Gerard, of the Society of Jesus*, 3rd edn. (London: Burns and Oates, 1881).

Murphy, Martin (ed.), *St Gregory's College, Seville, 1592–1767*, CRS, 73 (London: Catholic Record Society, 1992).

O'Doherty, Denis J., "Students of the Irish College Salamanca (1595–1619)," *Archivium Hibernicum*, 2 (1913): 1–26.

Palmer, Martin E., S.J. (ed.), *On Giving the Spiritual Exercises: The Early Jesuit Manuscript Directories and the Official Directory of 1599* (St Louis: The Institute of Jesuit Sources, 1996).

Parsons, Robert, S.J., "Of the Life and Martyrdom of Father Edmond Campian," *Letters and Notices*, 11 (1877): 219–42; 308–39; 12 (1878): 1–68.

Petti, Anthony G. (ed.), *The Letters and Dispatches of Richard Verstegan (c. 1550–1640)*, CRS, 52 (London: Catholic Record Society, 1959).

Pollen, John Hungerford, S.J. (ed.), "The Memoirs of Father Robert Persons," in *Miscellanea II*, CRS, 2 (London: Catholic Record Society, 1906), pp. 12–218.

———, *Unpublished Documents Relating to the English Martyrs (1584–1603)*, CRS, 5 (London: Catholic Record Society, 1908).

———, "Fr. Robert Persons, S.J.–Annals of the English College at Seville, with Accounts of other Foundations at Valladolid, St Lucar, Lisbon and St Omers," in *Miscellanea IX*, CRS, 14 (London: Catholic Record Society, 1914), pp. 1–24.

Poole, Reginald Lane et al. (ed.), *Various Collections*, HMC, 55 (8 vol., London: His Majesty's Stationery Office, 1901–1914).

Prothero, G.W. (ed.), *Select Statutes and Other Constitutional Documents Illustrative of the Reigns of Elizabeth and James I*, 4th edn. (Oxford: Clarendon Press, 1946).

Renold, Penelope (ed.), *The Wisbech Stirs (1595–1598)*, CRS, 51 (London: Catholic Record Society, 1958).

———, *Letters of William Allen and Richard Barret 1572–1598*, CRS, 58 (London: Catholic Record Society, 1967).

Scargill-Bird, S.R. et al. (eds.), *Calendar of the Manuscripts of the Most Hon. the Marquis of Salisbury*, HMC, 9 (24 vols, London: His Majesty's Stationery Office, 1883–1976).

Southwell, Robert, S.J., *Two Letters and Short Rules of a Good Life*, (ed.) Nancy Pollard Brown (Charlottsville: University Press of Virginia for the Folger Library, 1973).

Stevenson, Joseph et al. (eds.), *Calendar of State Papers Foreign Series of the Reign of Elizabeth* (23 vols in 26 parts, London: His Majesty's Stationery Office, 1863–1950).

Strype, John, *Annals of the Reformation and Establishment of Religion*, 2nd edn. (4 vols, London: Thomas Edlin, 1725–1731).

———, *Annals of the Reformation and Establishment of Religion* (4 vols in 7 parts, Oxford: Clarendon Press, 1824–1840).

Wernham, Richard B. *List and Analysis of State Papers Foreign Series: Elizabeth I* (7 vols, London: His Majesty's Stationery Office, 1964–2000).

Primary Sources

Allen, William, *The copie of a letter written by M. Doctor Allen: concerning the yeelding up, of the citie of Daventrie* (Antwerp, 1587), ARCR, vol. 2, num. 8, STC 370.

———, *An admonition to the nobility and people of England and Ireland* (Antwerp, 1588), ARCR, vol. 2, num. 5, STC 368.

———, *A declaration of the sentence and deposition of Elizabeth, the usurper and pretensed queen of Englande* (Antwerp, 1588), ARCR, vol. 2, num. 10, STC 23617.5.

Arnauld, Antoine, *The coppie of the Anti-Spaniard* (London, 1590), *STC* 684.
——, *The Flower de Luce* (n.p. [London], 1593), *STC* 11088.
——, *The arrainement of the whole societie of Jesuites in Fraunce* (London, 1594), *STC* 779.
[Arundel, Charles], *The copie of a leter, wryten by a master of arts of Cambridge, to his friend in London* [*Leicester's Commonwealth*] (n.p. [Paris?], 1584), *ARCR*, vol. 2, num. 31, *STC* 5742.9. *Leicester's Commonwealth: The Copy of a Letter Written by a Master of Art of Cambridge (1584) and Related Documents*, (ed.) Dwight C. Peck (Athens, Ohio/London: Ohio University Press, 1985).
Bagshaw, Christopher, *A true relation of the faction begun at Wisbich* (n.p. [London], 1601), *ARCR*, vol. 2, num. 39, *STC* 1188. Thomas Graves Law (ed.) in *A Historical Sketch of the Conflicts between Jesuits and Seculars in the Reign of Queen Elizabeth* (London: David Nutt, 1889).
——, *A sparing discoverie of our English Iesuits* (n.p. [London], 1601), *ARCR*, vol. 2, num. 38, *STC* 25126.
Canisius, Peter, S.J., *A summe of Christian doctrine* (n.p., n.d. [London, 1592–1596]), *ARCR*, vol. 2, num. 333.
Cecil, John, *A discoverye of the errors committed and iniures done to his Ma. off Scotlande*, (n.p., n.d. [Paris, 1599]), *ARCR*, vol. 2, num. 129, *STC* 4894.
Cecil, William, *The execution of justice in England* (London, 1583), *STC* 4902, 4903.
——, *The copie of a letter sent out of England to don Bernardin Mendoza* (London, 1588), *STC* 15412.
Creswell, Joseph, S.J., *Exemplar literarum, missarum, e Germania, ad D. Guilielmum Cecilum, consiliarium regium* (n.p. [Rome], 1592), *ARCR*, vol. 1, num. 275.
Discours veritable de diverses conspirations contre la vie de la roine (London, 1594), *STC* 7580.
Doleman, R., *A conference about the next succession to the crowne of Ingland* (n.p., n.d. [Antwerp, 1594]), *ARCR*, vol. 2, num. 167, *STC* 19398.
Durie, John, S.J., *Confutatio responsionis Gulielmi Whitakeri ...* (Paris, 1582), *ARCR*, vol. 1, num. 334.
Garnet, Henry, S.J., *The Societie of the Rosary* (n.p., n.d. [London, 1593–1594]), *ARCR*, vol. 2, num. 319, *STC* 11617.4. New edn., *ARCR*, vol. 2, num. 320, *STC* 11617.5.
——, *An apology against the defence of schisme* (n.p, n.d. [London, 1593]), *ARCR*, vol. 2, num. 318, *STC* 11617.2.
——, *A treatise of Christian renunciation* (n.p., n.d. [London, 1593]), *ARCR*, vol. 2, num. 322, *STC* 11617.8.

Ignatius Loyola, *The Spiritual Exercises of St Ignatius*, (ed.) Louis J. Puhl, S.J. (Chicago: Loyola University Press, 1951).

——, *The Constitutions of the Society of Jesus*, (ed.) George E. Ganss, S.J. (St Louis: The Institute of Jesuit Sources, 1970).

——, *Saint Ignatius Loyola: Letters to Women*, (ed.) Hugo Rahner, S.J. (Freiburg/London: Herder, 1960).

[Leslie, John]. *A treatise of treasons against Q. Elizabeth, and the crowne of England* (n.p. [Louvain], 1572), ARCR, vol. 2, num. 502, STC 7601.

[Lewkner, Sir Lewis?], *State of English Fugitives under the King of Spaine and his ministers* (London, 1595, 1596), STC 15562–65.

More, Henry, S.J., *Historia Provinciae Anglicanae Societatis Iesu* (St Omers, 1660).

——, *The Elizabethan Jesuits*, (ed.) Francis Edwards, S.J. (London: Phillimore, 1981).

Padberg, John W., S.J. Martin D. O'Keefe, S.J. and John L. McCarthy, S.J. (eds.), *For Matters of Greater Moment: The First Thirty Jesuit General Congregations* (St Louis: The Institute of Jesuit Sources, 1994).

Parsons, Robert, S.J., *A brief discours contayning certayne reasons why Catholiques refuse to goe to church* (Douai [vere East Ham], 1580), ARCR, vol. 2, num. 613; STC 19394.

——, *Elizabethae Angliae Reginae haeresim Calvinianum propugnantis saevissimum in Catholicos sui regni edictum* (Augsburg [vere Antwerp], 1592), ARCR, vol. 1, num. 885. See nos. 886–892 for other editions.

——, *A relation of the King of Spaines receiving in Valladolid, and in the Inglish College of the same towne, in August last part of this yere. 1592* (n.p. [Valladolid?], 1592), ARCR, vol. 2, num. 634; STC 19412.5. See ARCR, I, num. 899 for a Spanish translation. Facsimile editions of both can be found in Berta Cano Echevarría and Ana Sáez Hidalgo (ed.), *The Fruits of Exile. Los Frutos del Exilio* (Valladolid: Royal English College, 2009).

——, *Newes from Spayne and Holland* (n.p. [Antwerp], 1593), ARCR, vol. 2, num. 632, STC 22994.

——, *The Jesuit's Memorial, for the Intended Reformation of England, under their first Popish Prince*, (ed.) Edward Gee (London, 1690).

——, *A manifestation of the great folly and bad spirit of certayne in England calling themselves secular priestes* (n.p. [Antwerp], 1602), ARCR, vol. 2, num. 631.

Pasquier, Etienne, *The Jesuite displayed* (London, 1594), STC 19448.

Rainolds, William, *De iusta reipub. Christianae in rrges [sic] impios et haereticos authoritate* (Paris, 1590), ARCR, vol. 1, num. 931.

Southwell, Robert, S.J., *An humble supplication to her Maiestie* (n.p. [London], 1595 [vere 1600/1601]), ARCR, vol. 2, num. 717, STC

22949.5. (ed.) R.C. Bald (Cambridge: Cambridge University Press, 1953).

——, *A short rule of good life* (n.p, n.d. [London?, 1596–1597]), *ARCR*, vol. 2, num. 721, *STC* 22968.5.

Stapleton, Thomas, *Apologia pro Rege Catholico Philippo II* (Constance [*vere* Antwerp?], 1592), *ARCR*, vol. 1, num. 1141.

Thomson, George (pseudo?), *De antiquitate Christianae religionis apud Scotos* (Rome, 1594), *ARCR*, vol. 1, num. 1251. (ed.) Henry D.G. Law as "The Antiquity of the Christian Religion Among the Scots, 1594," in *Miscellany of the Scottish History Society, Vol. II*, Scottish History Society, 44 (Edinburgh: University of Edinburgh Press, 1904), pp. 117–32.

Thomson, Thomas (ed.), *Calderwood's History of the Kirk of Scotland* (8 vols, Edinburgh: Wodrow Society, 1842–1849).

A true report of sundry horrible conspiracies to have taken away the life of the queenes maiestie (London, 1594), *STC* 7603.

Verstegan, Richard, *The copy of a letter lately written by a Spanishe gentleman* (n.p. [Antwerp], 1589), *ARCR*, vol. 2, num. 759, *STC* 1038.

——, *A declaration of the true causes of the great troubles* (n.p. [Antwerp?], 1592), *ARCR*, vol. 2, num. 760, *STC* 10005.

——, *An advertisement written to a secretarie of my L. Treasurers* (n.p. [Antwerp?], 1592), *ARCR*, vol. 2, num. 757, *STC* 19885.

Wentworth, Peter, *A pithie exhortation to her maiestie for establishing her successor* (Edinburgh, 1598), *STC* 25245.

Secondary Sources

Alford, Stephen, *The Early Elizabethan Polity: William Cecil and the British Succession Crisis, 1558–1569* (Cambridge: Cambridge University Press, 1998).

Allison, Anthony F. and David M. Rogers, (eds.), *The Contemporary Printed Literature of the English Counter-Reformation between 1558 and 1640* (2 vols, Aldershot: Scolar Press, 1989–1994).

Anstruther, Godfrey, O.P., *The Seminary Priests* (4 vols, Ware/Durham/Great Wakering: St Edmund's College/Ushaw College/Mayhew-McCrimmon, 1968–1977).

——, "The Sega Report," *The Venerabile*, 20 (1961): 208–23.

——, "Owen Lewis," *The Venerabile*, 21 (1962): 274–94.

Arblaster, Paul, *Antwerp & the World: Richard Verstegan and the International Culture of Catholic Reformation* (Leuven/Louvain: Leuven University Press, 2004).

Bangert, William V., S.J., *A History of the Society of Jesus*, revised edn. (St Louis: The Institute of Jesuit Sources, 1986).
Baxter, J.H., "The Scots College at Douai," *Scottish Historical Review*, 24 (1927): 251–57.
Baumgartner, Frederic J., *Radical Reactionaries: The Political Thought of the French Catholic League* (Geneva: Librairie Droz, 1975).
——, "Renaud de Beaune, Politique Prelate," *Sixteenth Century Journal*, 9 (1978): 99–114.
Bellesheim, Alphons, *History of the Catholic Church of Scotland* (4 vols, Edinburgh/London, 1887–1890).
Bireley, Robert, S.J., *The Counter-Reformation Prince. Anti-Machiavellianism or Catholic Statecraft in Early Modern Europe* (Chapel Hill: University of North Carolina Press, 1990).
——, *The Jesuits and the Thirty Years War. Kings, Courts, and Confessors* (Cambridge: Cambridge University Press, 2003).
Black, Joseph, "The Rhetoric of Reaction: The Martin Marprelate Tracts (1588–89), Anti-Martinism, and the Uses of Print in Early Modern England," *Sixteenth Century Journal*, 28 (1997): 707–25.
Bossy, John, "Rome and the Elizabethan Catholics: A Question of Geography," *Historical Journal*, 7 (1964): 135–42.
——, *The English Catholic Community 1570–1850* (New York: Oxford University Press, 1976).
Brown, Nancy Pollard, "Paperchase: The Dissemination of Catholic Texts in Elizabethan England," in *English Manuscript Studies*, (ed.) Peter Beal and Jeremy Griffiths (vol. 1. Oxford: Oxford University Press, 1989), pp. 120–43.
——, "Robert Southwell: The Mission of the Written Word," in *The Reckoned Expense: Edmund Campion and the Early English Jesuits. Essays in Celebration of the First Centenary of Campion Hall, Oxford (1896–1996)*, (ed.) Thomas M. McCoog, S.J. (Woodbridge: Boydell and Brewer 1996), pp. 193–214. 2nd edn. BIHSI, 60 (Rome: Institutum Historicum Societatis Iesu, 2007), pp. 251–75.
Buisseret, David, *Henry IV* (London: Allen and Unwin, 1984).
Burgaleta, Claudio, S.J., *José de Acosta, S.J. (1540–1600): His Life and Thought* (Chicago: Jesuit Way, 1999).
Burke, Peter, "The Black Legend of the Jesuits: An Essay in the History of Social Stereotypes," in *Christianity and Community in the West. Essays for John Bossy*, (ed.) Simon Ditchfield (Aldershot: Ashgate, 2001), pp. 165–82.
Burrieza Sánchez, Javier, *Valladlid, tierras y caminos de jesuitas. Presencia de la Compañía de Jesús en la provincia de Valladolid, 1545–1767* (Valladolid: Diputación de Valladolid, 2007).

Camm, Bede, O.S.B., "The Adventures of Some Church Students in Elizabethan Days," *The Month*, 91 (1898): 375–85.
Caraman, Philip, S.J., *Henry Garnet (1555–1606) and the Gunpowder Plot* (London: Longmans, 1964).
——, *A Study in Friendship* (Anand: Gujarat Sahitya Prakash, 1991).
Carlson, Leland H., *Martin Marprelate, Gentleman: Master Job Throckmorton Laid Open in His Colors* (San Marino, California: Huntington Library, 1981).
Carrafiello, Michael L., "Robert Parsons and Equivocation, 1606–1610," *Catholic Historical Review*, 79 (1993): 671–80.
——, *Robert Parsons and English Catholicism, 1580–1610* (Selinsgrove: Susquehanna University Press, 1998).
Carroll, Stuart, *Martyrs and Murderers. The Guise Family and the Making of Europe* (Oxford: Oxford University Press, 2009).
Castro Santamaria, Ana and Nieves Rupérez Almajano, "The Real Colegio de San Patricio de Nobles Irlandeses of Salamanca: Its Buildings and Properties, 1592–1768," in *The Ulster Earls and Baroque Europe. Refashioning Irish Identities, 1600–1800*, (eds.) Thomas O'Connor and Mary Ann Lyons (Dublin: Four Courts Press, 2010), pp. 223–41.
Cesareo, Francesco C., "The Jesuit Colleges in Rome under Everard Mercurian," in *The Mercurian Project: Forming Jesuit Culture 1573–1580*, (ed.) Thomas M. McCoog, S.J., BIHSI, 55 (Rome/St Louis: Institutum Historicum Societatis Iesu/The Institute of Jesuit Sources, 2004), pp. 607–44.
Chadwick, Hubert, S.J., "The Scots College, Douai, 1580–1613," *English Historical Review*, 56 (1941): 571–85.
——, "Crypto-Catholicism, English and Scottish," *The Month*, 178 (1942): 388–401.
——, *St Omers to Stonyhurst* (London: Burns and Oates, 1962).
Clancy, Thomas H., S.J., "Notes on Persons's 'Memorial for the Reformation of England,'" *Recusant History*, 5 (1959): 17–34.
——, "English Catholics and the Papal Deposing Power, 1570–1640," *Recusant History*, 6 (1960–1961): 114–60, 205–27; 7 (1963–1964): 2–10.
——, "A Political Pamphlet: *The Treatise of Treasons* (1572)," in *Loyola Studies in the Humanities*, (ed.) G. Eberle (New Orleans: Loyola University of New Orleans Press, 1962), pp. 15–30.
——, *Papist Pamphleteers: The Allen-Persons Party and the Political Thought of the Counter-Reformation in England 1572–1615* (Chicago: Loyola University Press, 1964).
——, "Priestly Perseverance in the Old Society of Jesus," *Recusant History*, 19 (1989): 286–312.

Codina Mir, Gabriel, S.J., *Aux sources de la pédagogie des Jésuites; le "Modus Parisiensis"*, BIHSI, 28 (Rome: Institutum Historicum Societatis Iesu, 1968).

Collinson, Patrick, *The Elizabethan Puritan Movement* (London: Jonathan Cape, 1967).

——, "Ecclesiastical Vitriol: Religious Satire in the 1590s and the Invention of Puritanism," in *The Reign of Elizabeth I: Court and Culture in the Last Decade*, (ed.) John Guy (Cambridge: Cambridge University Press, 1995), pp. 150–70.

Connolly, S.J., *Contested Island: Ireland 1460–1630* (Oxford: Oxford University Press, 2007).

Crosignani, Ginevra, *"De adeundis ecclesiis protestantium": Thomas Wright, Robert Parsons, S.J., e il dibattito sul conformismo occasione nell'Inghilterra dell'età moderna*, BIHSI, 56 (Rome: Institutum Historicum Societatis Iesu, 2004).

Darby, Graham, "The Spanish Armada of ... 1597?," *The Historian*, 55, (1997): 14–16.

Descimon, Robert, "Chastel's Attempted Regicide (27 December 1594) and its Subsequent Transformation into an 'Affair,'" in *Politics and Religion in Early Bourbon France*, (eds.) Alison Forrestal and Eric Nelson (Basingstoke: Palgrave Macmillan, 2009), pp. 86–104.

Devlin, Christopher, S.J., *The Life of Robert Southwell Poet and Martyr* (London: Longmans, Green and Co., 1956).

——, "The Earl and the Alchemist," in *Hamlet's Divinity* (London: Rupert Hart-Davis, 1963), pp. 74–114.

Dillon, Anne, "Praying by Number: The Confraternity of the Rosary and the English Catholic Community, c. 1580–1700," *History*, 88 (2003): 451–71.

Dilworth, Mark, O.S.B., "Beginnings 1600–1707," in *The Scots College Rome 1600–2000*, (ed.) Raymond McCluskey (Edinburgh: John Donald, 2000), pp. 19–42.

Donnelly, John Patrick, S.J., "Antonio Possevino: From Secretary to Papal Legate," in *The Mercurian Project: Forming Jesuit Culture 1573–1580*, (ed.) Thomas M. McCoog, S.J., BIHSI, 55 (Rome/St Louis: Institutum Historicum Societatis Iesu/The Institute of Jesuit Sources, 2004), pp. 323–49.

Doran, Susan, "Loving and Affectionate Cousins? The Relationship between Elizabeth I and James VI of Scotland 1586–1603," in *Tudor England and its Neighbours*, (eds.) Susan Doran and Glenn Richardson (Basingstoke: Palgrave Macmillan, 2005), pp. 203–34.

Duffy, Eamon, *The Stripping of the Altars: Traditional Religion in England 1400–1580* (New Haven/London: Yale University Press, 1992).

——, "William, Cardinal Allen, 1532–1594," *Recusant History*, 22 (1995): 265–90.

Durkan, John, "William Murdoch and the Early Jesuit Mission in Scotland," *The Innes Review*, 35 (1984): 3–11.

Edwards, David, "Securing the Jacobean Succession: The Secret Career of James Fullerton of Trinity College, Dublin," in *The World of the Galloglass. Kings, Warlords and Warriors in Ireland and Scotland, 1200–1600*, (ed.) Seán Duffy (Dublin: Four Courts Press, 2007), pp. 188–219.

Edwards, Francis, S.J., *Robert Persons: The Biography of an Elizabethan Jesuit (1546–1610)* (St Louis: The Institute of Jesuit Sources, 1995).

——, *Plots and Plotters in the Reign of Elizabeth I* (Dublin: Four Courts Press, 2002).

Edwards, Robert Dudley, *Church and State in Tudor Ireland* (London: Longmans, Green, and Co., 1935).

Ellis, Steven G., *Tudor Ireland: Crown, Community and the Conflict of Cultures 1470–1603* (London: Longman, 1985).

Endean, Philip, S.J., "'The Strange Style of Prayer': Mercurian, Cordeses, and Álvarez," in *The Mercurian Project: Forming Jesuit Culture, 1573–1580*, (ed.) Thomas M. McCoog, S.J., BIHSI (Rome/St Louis: Institutum Historicum Societatis Iesu/The Institute of Jesuit Sources, 2004), pp. 351–97.

——, "'The Original Line of Our Father Ignatius': Mercurian and the Spirituality of the Exercises," in *The Mercurian Project: Forming Jesuit Culture 1573–1580*, (ed.) Thomas M. McCoog, S.J., BIHSI, 55 (Rome/St Louis: Institutum Historicum Societatis Iesu/The Institute of Jesuit Sources, 2004), pp. 35–48.

Falls, Cyril, *Elizabeth's Irish Wars* (London: Constable, 1996).

FitzGibbon, Basil, S.J., "Addition to the Biography of Thomas Wright," *Biographical Studies* (later *Recusant History*), 1 (1952): 261–62.

Flynn, Dennis, *John Donne & the Ancient Catholic Nobility* (Bloomington, Indiana: Indiana University Press, 1995).

——, "Jasper Heywood and the German Usury Controversy," in *The Mercurian Project: Forming Jesuit Culture 1573–1580*, (ed.) Thomas M. McCoog, S.J., BIHSI, 55 (Rome/St Louis: Institutum Historicum Societatis Iesu/The Institute of Jesuit Sources, 2004), pp. 183–211.

Foley, Henry, S.J., *Records of the English Province of the Society of Jesus* (7 vols in 8 parts, Roehampton/London: Manresa/Burns and Oates, 1877–1884).

Frye, Susan, "The Myth of Elizabeth at Tilbury," *Sixteenth Century Journal*, 23 (1992): 95–114.

Garstein, Oskar, *Rome and the Counter-Reformation in Scandinavia Jesuit Educational Strategy 1553–1622* (Leiden: E.J. Brill, 1992).

Giblin, Cathaldus, O.F.M., "Catalogue of Material of Irish Interest in the Collection *Nunziatura di Fiandra*, Vatican Archives: Part 1, vols. 1–50," *Collectanea Hibernica*, 1 (1958): 7–134.

Gleason, Elizabeth G., "Who Was the First Counter-Reformation Pope?," *Catholic Historical Review*, 81 (1995): 173–84.

Goodare, Julian, "James VI's English subsidy," in *The Reign of James VI*, (eds.) Julian Goodare and Michael Lynch (Edinburgh: John Donald, 2008), pp. 110–25.

Graham, Michael F., *The Uses of Reform: "Godly Discipline" and Popular Behaviour in Scotland and Beyond, 1560–1610* (Leiden: E.J. Brill, 1996).

Grant, Ruth, "The Brig o' Dee Affair, the sixth earl of Huntly and the politics of the Counter-Reformation," in *The Reign of James VI*, (eds.) Julian Goodare and Michael Lynch (Edinburgh: John Donald, 2008), pp. 93–109.

Graves, Michael A.R., *Burghley: William Cecil, Lord Burghley* (London: Longman, 1998).

Green, Janet M., "'I My Self': Queen Elizabeth I's Oration at Tilbury Camp," *Sixteenth Century Journal*, 28 (1997): 421–45.

Gregory, Brad S., *Salvation at Stake. Christian Martyrdom in Early Modern Europe* (Cambridge, Mass./London: Harvard University Press, 1999).

———, "Can We 'See Things Their Way'? Should We Try," in *Seeing Things Their Way: Intellectual History and the Return of Religion*, (eds.) Alister Chapman, John Coffey, and Brad S. Gregory (Notre Dame: University of Notre Dame Press, 2009), pp. 24–45.

Haigh, Christopher, *Elizabeth I* (London: Longman, 1988).

Hammer, Paul, "An Elizabethan Spy Who Came in from the Cold: The Return of Anthony Standen to England in 1593," *Historical Research*, 65 (1992): 277–95.

———, "New Light on the Cadiz Expedition of 1596," *Historical Research*, 70 (1997): 182–202.

———, *The Polarisation of Elizabethan Politics: The Political Career of Robert Devereux, 2nd Earl of Essex, 1585–1597* (Cambridge: Cambridge University Press, 1999).

Henry, Gráinne, "The Emerging Identity of an Irish Military Group in the Spanish Netherlands, 1586–1610," in *Religion, Conflict and Coexistence in Ireland: Essays Presented to Monsignor Patrick J. Corish*, (eds.) R.V. Comerford, Mary Cullen, Jacqueline R. Hill, and Colm Lennon (Dublin: Gill and Macmillan, 1990), pp. 53–77.

Hicks, Leo, S.J., "Father Persons, S.J., and the Seminaries in Spain," *The Month*, 157 (1931): 193–204, 410–17, 497–506; 158 (1931): 26–35, 143–52.

——, "Cardinal Allen and the Society," *The Month*, 160 (1932): 342–53, 434–43, 528–36.

——, "The English College, Rome and Vocations to the Society of Jesus, March, 1579–July, 1595," *AHSI*, 3 (1934): 1–36.

——, "The Foundation of the College of St Omers," *AHSI*, 19 (1950): 146–80.

——, "Father Robert Persons, S.J. and *The Book of Succession*," *Recusant History*, 4 (1957): 104–37.

——, *An Elizabethan Problem* (London: Burns and Oates, 1964).

Hodgetts, Michael, *Secret Hiding Holes* (Dublin: Veritas Publications, 1989).

——, "The Owens of Oxford," *Recusant History*, 24 (1999): 415–30.

——, "Owen, Nicholas," in *The Oxford Dictionary of National Biography*, (eds.) H.C.G. Matthew and Brian Harrison (60 vols Oxford: Oxford University Press, 2004), XLII, pp. 241–42.

Höpfl, Harro, *Jesuit Political Thought. The Society of Jesus and the State. c. 1540–1630* (Cambridge: Cambridge University Press, 2004).

Hogge, Alice, "Closing the Circle: Nicholas Owen and Walter Owen of Oxford," *Recusant History*, 26 (2002): 291–300.

Holmes, Peter. J., "The Authorship and Early Reception of *A Conference about the Next Succession to the Crown of England*," *Historical Journal*, 23 (1980): 415–29.

——, *Resistance and Compromise: The Political Thought of the English Catholics* (Cambridge: Cambridge University Press, 1982).

——, "Robert Persons and an Unknown Political Pamphlet of 1593," *Recusant History*, 17 (1985): 341–47.

Holt, Mark, *The French Wars of Religion 1562–1629* (Cambridge: Cambridge University Press, 1995).

Houliston, Victor, "The Hare and the Drum: Robert Persons's Writings on the English Succession, 1593–6," *Renaissance Studies*, 14 (2000): 235–50.

——, "The Lord Treasurer and the Jesuit: Robert Persons's Satirical *Responsio* to the 1591 Proclamation," *Sixteenth Century Journal*, 32 (2001): 383–401.

——, *Catholic Resistance in Elizabethan England. Robert Persons's Jesuit Polemic, 1580–1610*, BIHSI, 63 (Aldershot/Rome: Ashgate/Institutum Historicum Societatis Iesu, 2007).

Hufton, Olwen, "Every Tub on its Own Bottom: Funding a Jesuit College in Early Modern Europe," in *The Jesuits II, Cultures, Sciences, and the Arts, 1540–1773*, (eds.) John W. O'Malley, S.J., Gauvin Alexander Bailey, Steven J. Harris, and T. Frank Kennedy, S.J. (Toronto: University of Toronto Press, 2006), pp. 5–23.

Hume, Martin A.S., *Treason and Plot: Struggles for Catholic Supremacy in the Last Years of Queen Elizabeth* (London: James Nisbet and Co., 1901).

Hurstfield, Joel, "Church and State, 1558–1612: The Task of the Cecils," in *Studies in Church History II*, (ed.) G.J. Cuming (London: Nelson, 1965), pp. 119–40.

Hutton, Ronald, *The Rise and Fall of Merry England: The Ritual Year 1400–1700* (Oxford: Oxford University Press, 1994).

Jefferies, Henry A., *The Irish Church and the Tudor Reformations* (Dublin: Four Courts Press, 2010).

Jessop, Augustus, *One Generation of a Norfolk House: A Contribution to Elizabethan History*, 3rd edn., revised (London: T. Fisher Unwin, 1913).

Jonsen, Albert R. and Stephen Toulmin, *The Abuse of Casuistry: A History of Moral Reasoning* (Berkeley: University of California Press, 1988).

Kamen, Henry, *Inquisition and Society in Spain in the Sixteenth and Seventeenth Centuries* (London: Weidenfeld & Nicholson, 1985).

——, *The Spanish Inquisition: An Historical Revision* (London: Weidenfeld & Nicholson, 1997).

——, *Philip of Spain* (New Haven/London: Yale University Press, 1997).

Kaplan, Benjamin J., *Divided by Faith. Religious Conflict and the Practice of Toleration in Early Modern Europe* (Cambridge, Mass.: Belknap Press of Harvard University Press, 2007).

——, Bob Moore, Henk van Nierop and Judith Pollmann (eds.), *Catholic Communities in Protestant States. Britain and the Netherlands c. 1570–1720* (Manchester: Manchester University Press, 2009).

Katz, David S., *The Jews in the History of England 1485–1850* (Oxford: Clarendon Press, 1994).

Kaushik, Sandeep, "Resistance, Loyalty and Recusant Politics: Sir Thomas Tresham and the Elizabethan State," *Midland History*, 21 (1996): 37–79.

Kelly, John N.D., *The Oxford Dictionary of Popes* (Oxford: Oxford University Press, 1986).

Kelsey, Harry, *Sir Francis Drake: The Queen's Pirate* (New Haven/London: Yale University Press, 1998).

Kenny, Anthony, "The Inglorious Revolution 1594–1597," *The Venerabile*, 16 (1954): 240–58; 17 (1955): 7–25; 77–94; 136–55.

Kilroy, Gerard, "Paper, Inke and Penne: The Literary *Memoria* of the Recusant Community," *The Downside Review*, 119 (2001): 95–124.

Knecht, Robert J., *The French Wars of Religion 1559–1598* (London: Longman, 1989).

Lake, Peter and Michael Questier, "Prisons, Priests and People," in *England's Long Reformation 1500–1800*, (ed.) Nicholas Tyacke (London: University College, London Press, 1998), pp. 195–233.

——, "Puritans, Papists, and the 'Public Sphere' in Early Modern England: The Edmund Campion Affair in Context," *Journal of Modern History*, 72 (2000): 587–627.

——, "Discourses of Vice and Discourses of Virtue: 'Counter-Martyrology' and the Conduct of Intra-Catholic Dispute," in *The Antichrist's Lewd Hat: Protestants, Papists and Players in Post-Reformation England*, Peter Lake with Michael Questier (New Haven: Yale University Press, 2002), pp. 281–314.

Lang, Andrew, *A History of Scotland from the Roman Occupation* (4 vols, Edinburgh/London: W. Blackwood and Co., 1900–1907).

Law, Thomas Graves, "The Spanish Blanks and Catholic Earls, 1592–94," in *Collected Essays and Reviews*, (ed.) P. Hume Brown (Edinburgh: T. and A. Constable, 1904), pp. 244–76.

Lécrivain, Philippe, S.J., "The Struggle for Paris: Juan Maldonado in France," in *The Mercurian Project: Forming Jesuit Culture 1573–1580*, (ed.) Thomas M. McCoog, S.J., BIHSI 55, (Rome/St Louis: Institutum Historicum Societatis Iesu/The Institute of Jesuit Sources, 2004), pp. 295–321.

Lee, Maurice, Jr., "King James's Popish Chancellor," in *The Renaissance and Reformation in Scotland: Essays in Honour of Gordon Donaldson*, (eds.) Ian B. Cowan and Duncan Shaw (Edinburgh: Scottish Academic Press, 1983), pp. 170–82.

Lennon, Colm, *Sixteenth Century Ireland: The Incomplete Conquest*, New Gill History of Ireland, 2 (Dublin: Gill and Macmillan, 1994).

Lewy, Guenter, "The Struggle for Constitutional Government in the Early Years of the Society of Jesus," *Church History*, 29 (1960): 141–60.

Limm, Peter, *The Dutch Revolt 1559–1648* (London: Longman, 1989).

Loomie, Albert J., S.J., *The Spanish Elizabethans: The English Exiles at the Court of Philip II* (New York: Fordham University Press, 1963).

——, "An Armada Pilot's Survey of the English Coastline, October 1597," *The Mariner's Mirror*, 49 (1963): 288–300 (reprinted in Albert J. Loomie, S.J. (ed.), *Spain and the Early Stuarts, 1585–1655* [Aldershot: Ashgate, 1996], Article III).

——, "Religion and Elizabethan Commerce with Spain," *Catholic Historical Review*, 50 (1964): 27–51 (reprinted in Loomie, *Spain and the Early Stuarts*, Article I).

——, "Richard Stanyhurst in Spain: Two Unknown Letters of August 1593," *Huntington Library Quarterly*, 28 (1965): 145–55.

——, "King James I's Catholic Consort," *Huntington Library Quarterly*, 34 (1971): 303–16 (reprinted in Loomie, *Spain and the Early Stuarts*, Article XII).

——, "The Armadas and the Catholics of England," *Catholic Historical Review*, 59 (1973): 390–91 (reprinted in Loomie, *Spain and the Early Stuarts*, Article V).

——, "Philip II's Armada Proclamation of 1597," *Recusant History*, 12 (1974): 216–25 (reprinted in Loomie, *Spain and the Early Stuarts*, Article IV).

——, "Fr. Joseph Creswell's *Información* for Philip II and the Archduke Ernest, ca. August 1594," *Recusant History*, 22 (1995): 465–81.

Lowe, Ben, "Religious Wars and the 'Common Peace': Anglican Anti-War Sentiment in Elizabethan England," *Albion*, 28 (1996): 415–35.

Lukács, Ladislaus, S.J., "De graduum diversitate inter sacerdotes in Societate Iesu," *AHSI*, 37 (1968): 237–316. (English summary in Ignatius Loyola, *The Constitutions of the Society of Jesus* (ed.) George E. Ganss, S.J. [St Louis: The Institute of Jesuit Sources, 1970], pp. 349–56).

Lynch, John, *Spain 1516–1598: From Nation State to World Empire*, A History of Spain (Oxford: Blackwell, 1991).

MacCaffrey, Wallace T., *Elizabeth I: War and Politics 1588–1603* (Princeton: Princeton University Press, 1992).

McClain, Lisa, *Lest We Be Damned. Practical Innovation and Lived Experience among Catholics in Protestant England, 1559–1642* (New York/London: Routledge, 2004).

——, "Without Church, Cathedral, or Shrine: The Search for Religious Space among Catholics in England, 1559–1625," *Sixteenth Century Journal*, 33 (2002): 381–99.

McCoog, Thomas M., S.J., "The Finances of the English Province of the Society of Jesus in the Seventeenth Century: Introduction," *Recusant History*, 18 (1986): 14–33.

——, "'The Slightest Suspicion of Avarice': The Finances of the English Jesuit Mission," *Recusant History*, 19 (1988): 103–23.

——, "'The Flower of Oxford': The Role of Edmund Campion in Early Recusant Polemics," *Sixteenth Century Journal*, 24 (1993): 899–913.

——, "Ignatius Loyola and Reginald Pole: A Reconsideration," *Journal of Ecclesiastical History*, 47 (1996): 257–74.

——, *The Society of Jesus in Ireland, Scotland, and England 1541–1588: 'Our Way of Proceeding?'* (Leiden: E.J. Brill, 1996).

——, "'Playing the Champion': The Role of Disputation in the Jesuit Mission," in *The Reckoned Expense: Edmund Campion and the English Jesuits. Essays in Celebration of the First Centenary of Campion Hall, Oxford (1896–1996)*, (ed.) Thomas M. McCoog, S.J. (Woodbridge:

Boydell and Brewer, 1996), pp. 119–39. 2nd edn. BIHSI, 60 (Rome: Institutum Historicum Societatis Iesu, 2007), pp. 139–63.

——, "The Society of Jesus in Wales; The Welsh in the Society of Jesus: 1561–1625," *The Journal of Welsh Religious History*, 5 (1997): 1–29.

——, "The English Jesuit Mission and the French Match, 1579–1581," *Catholic Historical Review*, 87 (2001): 185–213.

——, "'Pray to the Lord of the Harvest': Jesuit Missions to Scotland in the Sixteenth Century," *The Innes Review*, 53 (2002): 127–88.

——, "'Sparrows on the Rooftop': 'How We Live Where We Live' in Elizabethan England," in *Spirit, Style, Story: Essays Honoring John W. Padberg, S.J.*, (ed.) Thomas M. Lucas, S.J. (Chicago: Jesuit Way, 2003), pp. 327–64.

——, "'Striking Fear in Heretical Hearts': Mercurian and British Religious Exiles," in *The Mercurian Project: Forming Jesuit Culture 1573–1580*, (ed.) Thomas M. McCoog, S.J., BIHSI, 55 (Rome/St Louis: Institutum Historicum Societatis Iesu/The Institute of Jesuit Sources, 2004), pp. 645–73.

——, "Harmony Disrupted: Robert Parsons, S.J., William Crichton, S.J., and the Question of Queen Elizabeth's Successor, 1581–1603," *AHSI*, 73 (2004): 149–220.

——, "'Replant the Uprooted Trunk of the Tree of Faith': The Society of Jesus and Continental Colleges for Religious Exiles," forthcoming.

—— and Peter Davidson, "Father Robert's Convert: The Private Catholicism of Anne of Denmark," *Times Literary Supplement* (24 November 2000): 16–17.

MacCuarta, Brian, S.J., *Catholic Revival in the North of Ireland 1603–41* (Dublin: Four Courts Press, 2007).

MacDonald, Alan R., *The Jacobean Kirk, 1567–1625: Sovereignty, Polity and Liturgy* (Aldershot: Ashgate, 1998).

McGettigan, Darren, *Red Hugh O'Donnell and the Nine Years War* (Dublin: Four Courts Press, 2005).

McGrath, Patrick, "Apostate and Naughty Priests in England under Elizabeth I," in *Opening the Scrolls: Essays in Honour of Godfrey Anstruther*, (ed.) Dominic Aidan Bellenger, O.S.B. (Bath: Downside Abbey, 1987), pp. 50–85.

——, "The Bloody Questions Reconsidered," *Recusant History*, 20 (1991): 305–19.

—— and Joy Rowe, "Anstruther Analysed: The Elizabethan Seminary Priests," *Recusant History*, 18 (1986): 1–13.

Maltby, William S., *The Black Legend in England: The Development of anti-Spanish Sentiment, 1558–1660* (Durham, N.C.: Duke University Press, 1971).

Mancia, Anita. "La controversia con i protestanti e i programmi degli studi teologici nella Compagnia di Gesù 1547–1599," *AHSI*, 54 (1985): 3–43, 209–66.

Marshall, Peter, "Papist as Heretic: The Burning of John Forest, 1538," *Historical Journal*, 41 (1998): 351–74.

Maryks, Robert A., *The Jesuit Order as a 'Synagogue of Jews': Jesuits of Jewish Ancestry and Purity-of-Blood Laws in the Early Society of Jesus* (Leiden: E.J. Brill, 2009).

——, "The Jesuit Order as a 'Synagogue of Jews': Discrimination against Jesuits of Jewish Ancestry in the Early History of the Society of Jesus," *AHSI*, 78 (2009): 339–416.

Mears, Natalie, "*Regnum Cecilianum*? A Cecilian Perspective of the Court," in *The Reign of Elizabeth I: Court and Culture in the Last Decade*, (ed.) John Guy (Cambridge, 1995), pp. 46–64.

Medina, Francisco de Borja, S.J. "Jesuitas en la Armada contra Inglaterra (1588)," *AHSI*, 58 (1989): 3–42.

——, "Ignacio de Loyola y la '*limpieza de sangre*,'" in *Ignacio de Loyola y Su Tiempo*, (ed.) Juan Plazaola, S.J. (Bilbao: Mensajero, n.d. [1992]), pp. 579–615.

——, "Intrigues of a Scottish Jesuit at the Spanish Court: Unpublished Letters of William Crichton to Claudio Acquaviva (Madrid 1590–1592)," in *The Reckoned Expense: Edmund Campion and the Early English Jesuits. Essays in Celebration of the First Centenary of Campion Hall, Oxford*, (ed.) Thomas M. McCoog, S.J. (Woodbridge: Boydell and Brewer, 1996), pp. 217–19. 2nd edn. "Intrigues of a Scottish Jesuit at the Spanish Court: William Crichton's Mission to Madrid (1590–1592)," BIHSI, 60 (Rome: Institutum Historicum Societatis Iesu, 2007), pp. 277–325.

——, "Escocia en la Estrategia de la Empresa de Inglaterra: La Misión del P. William Crichton cerca de Felipe II (1590–1592)," *Revista de Historia Naval*, 17 (1999): 53–110.

——, "El Colegio Inglés de San Gregorio Magno de Sevilla (Notas y comentarios)," *Archivo Teológico Granadino*, 62 (1999): 77–105.

——, "Everard Mercurian and Spain: Some Burning Issues," in *The Mercurian Project: Forming Jesuit Culture, 1573–1580*, (ed.) Thomas M. McCoog, S.J. BIHSI, 55 (Rome/St Louis: Institutum Historicum Societatis Iesu/The Institute of Jesuit Sources, 2004), pp. 945–66.

Meigs, Samantha A., *The Reformations in Ireland: Tradition and Confessionalism, 1400–1690* (London/New York: Macmillan, 1997).

Meikle, Maureen M., "A meddlesome princess: Anna of Denmark and Scottish court politics, 1589–1603," in *The Reign of James VI*, (eds.) Julian Goodare and Michael Lynch (Edinburgh: John Donald, 2008), pp. 126–40.

Meyer, Arnold Oskar, *England and the Catholic Church under Queen Elizabeth* (London: Kegan, Paul, Trench, Trübner, & Co., 1916).
Millet, Benignus, O.F.M., "The Guardian of Donegal Friary Appeals to Philip II of Spain, 1596," *Collectanea Hibernica*, 27–28 (1985–1986): 7–10.
Milward, Peter, S.J., *Religious Controversies of the Elizabethan Age: A Survey of Printed Sources* (London: Scolar Press, 1977).
Morley, Adrian, *The Catholic Subjects of Elizabeth I* (London: Allen and Unwin, 1978), p. 125.
Morgan, Hiram, *Tyrone's Rebellion* (Woodbridge: Boydell Press for the Royal Historical Society, 1993).
——, "Hugh O'Neill and the Nine Years War in Tudor Ireland," *Historical Journal*, 36 (1993): 21–37.
——, "Faith and Fatherland or Queen and Country? An Unpublished Exchange between O'Neill and the State at the Height of the Nine Years War," *Journal of the O'Neill Country Historical Society*, 9 (1994): 9–65.
——, "'Faith & Fatherland' in Sixteenth-Century Ireland," *History Ireland*, 3/2 (1995): 13–20.
——, "'Never any Realm Worse Governed': Queen Elizabeth and Ireland," *Transactions of the Royal Historical Society*, 14 (2004): 295–308.
——, "'Slán Dé fút go hoiche': Hugh O'Neill's Murders," in *Age of Atrocity: Violence and Political Conflict in Early Modern Ireland*, (eds.) David Edwards, Pádriag Lenihan and Clodagh Tait (Dublin: Four Courts Press, 2007), pp. 95–118.
——, "Policy and Propaganda in Hugh O'Neill's Connection with Europe," in *The Ulster Earls and Baroque Europe. Refashioning Irish Identities, 1600–1800*, (eds.) Thomas O'Connor and Mary Ann Lyons (Dublin: Four Courts Press, 2010), pp. 18–52.
Morrissey, Thomas, S.J., *James Archer of Kilkenny: An Elizabethan Jesuit* (Dublin: Studies "Special Publications," 1979).
——, "The Irish Student Diaspora in the Sixteenth Century and the Early Years of the Irish College at Salamanca," *Recusant History*, 14 (1978): 242–60.
Mousnier, Roland, *The Assassination of Henry IV: The Tyrannicide Problem and the Consolidation of the French Absolute Monarchy in the Early 17th Century* (London: Faber and Faber, 1973).
Murray, John Courtney, S.J., "St Robert Bellarmine on the Indirect Power," *Theological Studies*, 9 (1948): 491–535.
Murray, Molly, "'Nowe I am a Catholoque': William Alabaster and the Early Modern Catholic Conversion Narrative," in *Catholic Culture in Early Modern England*, (eds.) Ronald Corthell, Frances E. Dolan,

Christopher Highley and Arthur F. Marotti (Notre Dame: University of Notre Dame, 2007), pp. 189–215.

Neale, John E., *Elizabeth I and Her Parliaments* (2 vols, London: Jonathan Cape, 1953–1957).

Nelson, Eric, *The Jesuits and the Monarchy: Catholic Reform and Political Authority in France (1590-1615)*, BIHSI, 58 (Aldershot/Rome: Ashgate/Institutum Historicum Societatis Iesu, 2005).

Nenner, Howard, *The Right to be King: The Succession to the Crown of England, 1603–1714* (London: Macmillan, 1995).

O'Connell, Patricia, *The Irish College at Lisbon 1590–1834* (Dublin: Four Courts Press, 2001).

——, "The Early-Modern Irish College Network in Iberia, 1590–1800," in *The Irish in Europe, 1580–1815*, (ed.) Thomas O'Connor (Dublin: Four Courts Press, 2001), pp. 49–64.

Ó Fionnagáin, Prionsias, S.J., *The Jesuit Missions to Ireland in the Sixteenth Century* (n.p., n.d. [privately printed]),

——, *Irish Jesuits 1598–1773* (n.p., n.d. [privately printed]).

O'Malley, John W., S.J., *The First Jesuits* (Cambridge, Mass.: Harvard University Press, 1993).

——, *Trent and All That. Renaming Catholicism in the Early Modern Era* (Cambridge, Mass.: Harvard University Press, 2000).

——, Gauvin Alexander Bailey, Steven J. Harris and T. Frank Kennedy, S.J. (eds.), *The Jesuits II, Cultures, Sciences, and the Arts, 1540–1773* (Toronto: University of Toronto Press, 2006).

Padberg, John W., S.J., "The General Congregations of the Society of Jesus: A Brief Survey of Their History," *Studies in the Spirituality of Jesuits*, 6/1–2 (1974).

——, "Ignatius, the Popes, and Realistic Reverence," *Studies in the Spirituality of Jesuits*, 25/3 (1993): 1–38.

Palmer, William, *The Problem of Ireland in Tudor Foreign Policy 1485–1603* (Woodbridge: Boydell Press, 1994).

Parker, Charles H., *Faith on the Margins: Catholics and Catholicism in the Dutch Golden Age* (Cambridge, Mass.: Harvard University Press, 2008).

Parker, Geoffrey, *The Dutch Revolt* (London: Allen Lane, 1977).

——, *The Grand Strategy of Philip II* (New Haven/London: Yale University Press, 1998).

——, "The Place of Tudor England in the Messianic Vision of Philip II of Spain," *Transactions of the Royal Historical Society*, 6th series, 12 (2002): 167–221.

Parmelee, Lisa Ferraro, *Good Newes from Fraunce: French Anti-League Propaganda in Late Elizabethan England* (Rochester, N.Y.: University of Rochester Press, 1996).

Pavone, Sabina, *The Wily Jesuits and the Monita Secreta. The Forged Secret Instructions of the Jesuits. Myth and Reality* (St Louis: The Institute of Jesuit Sources, 2005).

Pettegree, Andrew, "Nicodemism and the English Reformation," in *Marian Protestantism: Six Studies* (Aldershot: Ashgate, 1996), pp. 86–117.

Pollard, A.W. and G.R. Redgrave (eds.), A *Short Title Catalogue of Books Printed in England, Scotland, and Ireland and of English Books Printed Abroad, 1475–1640*. 2nd edn. Revised and enlarged W.A. Jackson, F.S. Ferguson and Katherine F. Pantzer (3 vols, London: The Bibliographical Society, 1986–1991).

Pollen, John Hungerford, S.J., *The Counter-Reformation in Scotland* (London: Sands & Co., 1921).

———, "The Question of Queen Elizabeth's Successor," *The Month*, 101 (1903): 517–32.

———, "The Accession of King James I," *The Month*, 101 (1903): 572–85.

———, "The Origin of the Appellant Controversy, 1598," *The Month*, 125 (1915): 461–75.

———, "The Institution of the Archpriest," Blackwell (London: Longmans, Green, and Co., 1916).

Pritchard, Arnold, *Catholic Loyalism in Elizabethan England* (London: Scolar Press, 1979).

Questier, Michael C., "Practical Antipapistry during the Reign of Elizabeth I," *Journal of British Studies*, 36 (1997): 371–96.

———, "The Politics of Religious Conformity and the Accession of James I," *Historical Research*, 71 (1998): 14–30.

———, "Loyal to a Fault: Viscount Montague Explains Himself," *Historical Research*, 77 (2004): 225–53.

———, *Catholicism and Community in Early Modern England. Politics, Aristocratic Patronage and Religion, c. 1550–1640* (Cambridge: Cambridge University Press, 2006).

Rea, W.F., S.J., "Self-Accusations of Political Prisoners: An Incident in the Reign of Queen Elizabeth," *The Month*, 6 (n.s.) (1951): 269–79.

———, "The Authorship of 'News from Spayne and Holland' and its Bearing on the Genuineness of the Confessions of the Blessed Henry Walpole, S.J.," *Biographical Studies* (later *Recusant History*), 1 (1951–1952): 220–30.

Redworth, Glyn, "Between Four Kingdoms. International Catholicism and Colonel William Semple," in *Irlanda y la Monarquía Hispánica: Kinsale 1601–2001. Guerra, Política, Exilio y Religión*, (eds.) Enrique García Hernán, Miguel Ángel de Bunes, Óscar Recio Morales, and Bernardo J. García García (Madrid: Universidad de Alcalá/Consejo Superior de Investigaciones Científicas, 2002), pp. 255–64.

Reites, James W., S.J., "St Ignatius of Loyola and the Jews," *Studies in the Spirituality of Jesuits*, 13/4 (1981).

Reynolds, Ernest E., *Campion and Parsons* (London: Sheed and Ward, 1980).

Rogers, David M., "A Bibliography of the Published Works of Thomas Wright (1561–1623)," *Biographical Studies* (later *Recusant History*), 1 (1952): 262–80.

Rose, Elliot, *Cases of Conscience: Alternatives Open to Recusants and Puritans under Elizabeth I and James I* (Cambridge: Cambridge University Press, 1975).

Rose, Paul Lawrence, "Bodin and the Bourbon Succession to the French Throne, 1583–1594," *Sixteenth Century Journal*, 9 (1978): 75–98.

Scarisbrick, J.J., "Robert Persons's Plans for the 'true' Reformation of England," in *Historical Perspectives: Studies in English Thought and Society*, (ed.) Neil McKendrick (London: Europa, 1974), pp. 19–42.

Schineller, Peter, S.J., "From an Ascetical Spirituality of the *Exercises* to the Apostolic Spirituality of the *Constitutions*: Laborers in the Lord's Vineyard," in *Ite inflammate omnia*, (ed.) Thomas M. McCoog, S.J., BIHSI, 72 (Rome: Institutum Historicum Societatis Iesu, 2010), pp. 85–108.

Schmitt, Robert F., S.J., "The Christ-Experience and Relationship Fostered in the Spiritual Exercises of St Ignatius of Loyola," *Studies in the Spirituality of Jesuits*, 6/5 (1974).

Schneider, Burkhart, S.J., "Der Konflikt zwischen Claudius Aquaviva und Paul Hoffaeus," *AHSI*, 26 (1957): 3–56, 27 (1958): 279–306.

Scully, Robert E., S.J., "'In the Confident Hope of a Miracle': The Spanish Armada and Religious Mentalities in the Late Sixteenth Century," *Catholic Historical Review*, 89 (2003): 643–70.

Shagan, Ethan (ed.), *Catholics and the "Protestant Nation," Religious Politics and Identity in Early Modern England* (Manchester: Manchester University Press, 2005).

Shearman, Francis, "The Spanish Blanks," *The Innes Review*, 3 (1952): 81–103; 4 (1953): 60.

——, "James Wood of Boniton," *The Innes Review*, 5 (1954): 28–32.

——, "Father Alexander McQuhirrie, S.J.," *The Innes Review*, 6 (1955): 22–45.

Sommerville, Johann P., "The 'New Art of Lying': Equivocation, Mental Reservation, and Casuistry," in *Conscience and Casuistry in Early Modern Europe*, (ed.) Edmund Leites (Cambridge: Cambridge University Press, 1988), pp. 159–84.

Stafford, Helen Georgia, *James VI of Scotland and the Throne of England* (New York/London: Appleton Century, 1940).

Stroud, Theodore A., "Father Thomas Wright: A Test Study for Toleration," *Biographical Studies* (later *Recusant History*), 1 (1952): 189–219.

Taillon, Alain, "Henri IV and the Papacy after the League," in *Politics and Religion in Early Bourbon France*, (eds.) Alison Forrestal and Eric Nelson (Basingstoke: Palgrave Macmillan, 2009), pp. 21–41.

Tait, Clodagh, "'The Vengeance of God': Reporting the Violent Deaths of Persecutors in Early Modern Ireland," in *Age of Atrocity: Violence and Political Conflict in Early Modern Ireland*, (eds.) David Edwards, Pádriag Lenihan and Clodagh Tait (Dublin: Four Courts Press, 2007), pp. 130–53.

Thomas, Keith, "Cases of Conscience in Seventeenth-Century England," in *Public Duty and Private Conscience in Seventeenth-Century England: Essays Presented to G.E. Aylmer*, (eds.) John Morrill, Paul Slack, and Daniel Woolfe (Oxford: Clarendon Press, 1993), pp. 29–56.

Thurston, Herbert, S.J., "Confraternity of the Holy Rosary," in *Catholic Encyclopedia* (16 vols, New York: Robert Appleton, 1907–14), Vol. XIII, pp. 188–89.

Tierney, M.A. (ed.), *Dodd's Church History of England* (5 vols, London: Charles Dolman, 1839–1843).

Trevor-Roper, Hugh, "Twice-Martyred: The English Jesuits and Their Historians," in *Historical Essays* (London, 1957), pp. 113–18.

Tutino, Stefania, "Between Nicodemism and 'Honest' Dissimulation: The Society of Jesus in England," *Historical Research*, 79 (2006): 534–53.

——, "Nothing But the Truth? Hermeneutics and Morality in the Doctrines of Equivocation and Mental Reservation in Early Modern Europe," *Renaissance Quarterly*, 64 (2011): 127–28.

Villoslada, Riccardo G, S.J., *Storia del Collegio Romano dal suo inizio (1551) alla soppressione della Compagnia di Gesù (1773)* (Rome: Gregorian University, 1954).

Wabuda, Susan, "Equivocation and Recantation During the English Reformation: The 'Subtle Shadows' of Dr Edward Crome," *Journal of Ecclesiastical History*, 44 (1993): 224–42.

Walsham, Alexandra, *Church Papists: Catholicism, Conformity, and Confessional Polemic in Early Modern England*, Royal Historical Society Studies in History, 68 (Woodbridge: Boydell Press for the Royal Historical Society, 1993).

——, *Providence in Early Modern England* (Oxford: Oxford University Press, 1999).

——, "'Yielding to the Extremity of the Time': Conformity, Orthodoxy and the Post-Reformation Catholic Community," in *Conformity and Orthodoxy in the English Church, c. 1560–1660*, (eds.) Peter Lake and Michael Questier (Woodbridge: Boydell and Brewer, 2000), pp. 211–36.

——, "Translating Trent? English Catholicism and the Counter Reformation," *Historical Research*, 78 (2005): 288–310.

——, "'This Newe Army of Satan': The Jesuit Mission and the Formation of Public opinion in Elizabethan England," in *Modern Panics, the Media and the Law in Early Modern England*, (eds.) David Lemmings and Clare Walker (Basingstoke: Palgrave Macmillan, 2009), pp. 41–62.

Wernham, Richard B., *After the Armada: Elizabethan England and the Struggle for Western Europe 1588–1595* (Oxford: Clarendon Press, 1984).

——, *The Return of the Armadas: The Last Years of the Elizabethan War against Spain 1595–1603* (Oxford: Clarendon Press, 1994).

——, "Queen Elizabeth I, the Emperor Rudolph II, and Archduke Ernest, 1593–94," in *Politics and Society in Reformation Europe: Essays for Sir Geoffrey Elton on his Sixty-Fifth Birthday*, (eds.) E.I. Kouri and Tom Scott (New York: Macmillan, 1987), pp. 437–51.

Whitehead, Bertrand T., *Brags and Boasts: Propaganda in the Year of the Armada* (Stroud: Sutton, 1994).

Wiener, Carol Z., "The Beleaguered Isle. A Study of Elizabethan and Early Jacobean Anti-Catholicism," *Past and Present*, 51 (1971): 27–62.

Williams, Michael E., *The Venerable English College* (London: Associated Catholic Publishers, 1979).

——, *St Alban's College, Valladolid* (London: C. Hurst & Company, 1986).

——, "The Ascetic Tradition and the English College at Valladolid," in *Monks, Hermits and the Ascetic Tradition*, (ed.) W.J. Sheils, Studies in Church History, 22 (Oxford: Basil Blackwell, 1985), pp. 275–83.

——, "The Origins of the English College, Lisbon," *Recusant History*, 20 (1991): 478–92

——, "Campion and the English Continental Seminaries," in *The Reckoned Expense: Edmund Campion and the Early English Jesuits. Essays in celebration of the First Centenary of Campion Hall, Oxford (1896–1996)*, (ed.) Thomas M. McCoog, S.J. (Woodbridge: Boydell and Brewer, 1996), pp. 285–99. 2nd edn. BIHSI, 60 (Rome: Institutum Historicum Societatis Iesu, 2007), pp. 371–87.

Williams, Penry, *The Later Tudors: England 1547–1603*, The New Oxford History of England (Oxford: Oxford University Press, 1995).

Woolfson, Jonathan, *Padua and the Tudors: English Students in Italy 1485–1603* (Cambridge: James Clarke & Co., 1998).

Wright, Jonathan, "The World's Worst Worm: Conscience and Conformity during the English Reformation," *Sixteenth Century Journal*, 30 (1999): 113–33.

——, "Marian Exiles and the Legitimacy of Flight from Persecution," *Journal of Ecclesiastical History*, 52 (2001): 220–43.

Yellowlees, Michael, *"So strange a monster as a Jesuite"*: *The Society of Jesus in Sixteenth-Century Scotland* (Isle of Colonsay: House of Lochar, 2003).

Zagorin, Perez, *Ways of Lying: Dissimulation, Persecution, and Conformity in Early Modern Europe* (Cambridge, Mass.: Harvard University Press, 1990).

Unpublished Doctoral Theses

Gifford, J.V., "The Controversy over the Oath of Allegiance of 1606," Oxford University, 1971.

LaRocca, John, S.J., "English Catholics and the Recusancy Laws 1558–1625: A Study in Religion and Politics," Rutgers University, 1977.

Norris, Peter, "Robert Parsons, S.J. (1546–1610) and the Counter Reformation in England: A Study of His Actions within the Context of the Political and Religious Situation of the Times," University of Notre Dame, 1984.

O'Donoghue, Fergus, S.J., "The Jesuit Mission in Ireland 1598–1651," Catholic University of America, 1981.

Richardson, William, "The Religious Policy of the Cecils 1588–1598," Oxford University, 1994.

Sommerville, Johann P., "Jacobean Political Thought and the Controversy over the Oath of Allegiance," Cambridge University, 1981.

Index

Abercrombie, Robert, S.J. 52, 58, 80, 176, 298–300, 326, 328–329
Abercrombie, Thomas, S.J. 128
Abreo, Don Francisco de, S.J. 135
Acosta, José de, S.J. 97–99, 105, 106n 38, 119n 93, 135–136, 211–212, 229–232
Acquaviva, Claudio, S.J.
 authority over English mission 7, 18, 35, 37, 44, 46, 47, 49–51, 72–74, 77–78, 91, 92, 97, 139n 162, 154, 167, 169, 179, 190, 192, 202, 224, 228, 241, 243, 248–249, 254–256, 283–286, 288–291, 293, 299–300, 305–306, 312, 314–315, 339, 341–342, 344–347, 349–351, 353–355, 376–378, 401–402, 411
 colleges and seminaries 105, 108–109, 114–117, 129–130, 132, 138, 211, 214, 216–223, 225–226, 235–239, 263–266, 268, 270, 272–274, 295, 357–361, 363, 365, 368, 374–375
 conformity 66, 68–69
 fear of scandal 50–51
 impresa against England 1, 141, 158
 Inquisition 98–99
 Irish mission 87, 89–90, 105, 120, 307
 persecution and martyrdom 47, 50, 162–163, 168, 183, 310
 political involvement 8, 9, 64–65, 143, 205, 245, 413
 role as general superior 209–210, 212, 229–234, 250, 261
 Scottish mission 52, 56, 58, 121–123, 126, 140, 171, 302n 84, 325n 168, 328–329
 Sodality of the Blessed Virgin 42
 Stuart dynasty in England 124
 tension between the Society and Philip II 135–136, 138
 Wisbech stirs 195–196, 200, 287, 294
Adrian IV, Pope 303
Agazzari, Alfonso, S.J. 76n 249, 201, 250, 265, 270, 357
d'Aguila, Juan 101
Alabaster, William 316, 317n 138
Alarcón, García de, S.J. 212
Alber, Ferdinand, S.J. 306
Albert, Archduke of Austria 105, 208, 276, 303, 329, 333–334, 343, 345, 381, 399
Aldobrandini, Cinzio Passeri, Cardinal 363
Aldobrandini, Pietro, Cardinal 250n 138, 319, 363
Aldred, Solomon 404
Allen, Thomas (alias Hesketh) 202–203n 203, 360, 383, 387
Allen, William, Cardinal
 allegations against 19, 28, 409
 colleges 108, 111–112, 114, 116, 131n 133, 138–139, 193, 226, 273, 358, 361, 393, 414
 conformity 30n 58, 68–69, 294
 English mission 5, 12, 18, 23, 141, 195, 200–201, 203, 248, 261, 272, 320, 339–340, 383, 408
 overthrow of the queen 6, 7, 11, 26, 32, 33n 69, 141, 274, 385
 political role 97, 336, 403, 410
 relationship with Catholics 34, 145, 147, 245–247, 260, 337–338, 341, 352, 395, 404, 415
 relationship with Parsons 202, 254, 256, 258
 religious toleration 144, 146
 Scotland 123, 377

Allison, Antony 161, 256
Alonso, Gaspar, S.J. 210, 219
Amboise, Jacob 416
Anderson, Patrick, S.J. 374
Anne of Brittany 126
Anne of Denmark, Queen of Scotland and England 56–57, 82n 271, 128, 300, 302, 369
Anjou, Duke of *see* Valois, François de
Archer, James, S.J. 87, 105, 117, 119–120, 139, 178–179, 237–239, 305–306, 389n 153, 402, 414
Arcos, Duke of *see* Ponce de Léon, Rodrigo, Duke of Arcos
Arden, John 27n 44, 143–146, 315
Arden, Robert, ex S.J. 27n 44, 143–144
Argenti, Giovanni, S.J. 413
Argyll, Earl of *see* Campbell, Archibald, Earl of Argyll
Armada
    (1588) 7, 12, 18–20, 24, 35, 55, 58, 63, 85–86, 89–90, 95–97, 99, 101, 125, 140, 336, 385, 409–411
    later armadas 88, 126, 172, 253, 275, 277, 279–280, 303, 329–332, 380, 381n 136, 386, 388, 389n 155
    (1597) 399–401, 408
Arnauld, Antoine 167, 205, 415–417
    Work
    The coppie of the Anti-Spaniard 415
Arundel, Countess of *see* Howard, Anne Dacre
Arundel, Earl of *see* Howard, Philip, Earl of Arundel
Arundel, Anne 167
Arundel, Charles 253
    Work
    Leicester's Commonwealth 253
Arundel family 74
Arundel, Sir John 167
Ashton, Roger 33
Askew, George 397n 181
Atkinson, William 308, 317

Auchindoun, Laird of *see* Gordon, Patrick, Laird of Auchindoun
Avellaneda, Diego de, S.J. 99
Avila, Gonzalo de, S.J. 138
Ayamonte, Marquis of *see* Guzmán y Sotomayor, Antonio de, Marquis of Ayamonte
Azevedo, Don Pedro Enríquez de, Count of Fuentes 104, 208, 343

Babington Plot 37, 181, 315n 130, 362n 74
Babthorpe, Grace 60
Bacon, Anthony 65
Bacon, Francis 309, 332–333
Bacon, Nicholas 253
Baddesley Clinton 36, 46n 131, 62, 73, 91, 169, 411
Bagenal, Sir Henry 89, 177–178
Bagshaw, Christopher 12, 192n 161, 193–194, 196–198, 201n 199, 295–296, 317n 139, 324, 340
Baldwin, William, S.J. (alias Ottaviano Fuscincelli) 77n 255, 133n 142, 191–192, 196, 216n 31, 292–293, 312
Ballard, John 362, 395, 404
Bancroft, Richard, Archbishop of Canterbury 17
Banks, Richard, S.J. 293, 311, 312n 118
Barclay, Hugh 243
Barnes, Thomas 333
Baronio, Cesare, Cardinal 359, 363
Barret, Richard 106–107, 200, 247, 261, 270–271, 288, 340, 352, 356–357, 359–360
Barrière, Pierre 151, 416
Barton, Edward 147–148
Baskerville, Sir Thomas 208, 275, 329
Bavant, John 197, 320
Baynes, Roger 33, 49n 141, 148n 16, 163, 167n 84, 215, 249n 133, 254n 154, 266, 273n 228, 310n 112, 340, 347, 402
Beaton, James, Archbishop of Glasgow 52, 122, 125, 129, 172

INDEX

Beaumont, Francis 184
Béjar, Duke of *see* Zuñiga y Sttomayor, Francisco de, Duke of Béjar
Bell, Thomas 66–71, 91, 154, 203
Bellamy, Anne 48, 181, 188
Bellamy family 179
Bellamy, Mary 49
Bellamy, Richard 48
Bellamy, Thomas 48
Bellarmine, Robert, S.J., Cardinal 156, 413
Bennet, John, S.J. 41, 46–47, 321n 157
Bennet, John, Dr 154
Bennett, Edward 263, 357, 360, 364–365, 403
Bennett, John 360n 65
Benson, Robert 397
Berkeley, Sir Richard 309
Bernal, Pedro, S.J. 220, 222
Bersacques, Louis de, Dean 366
Bertie, Peregrine, Baron Willoughby d'Eresby 22n 23, 100
Berwick, Treaty of 52, 62, 86
Bickley, Ralph, S.J. 41, 293, 311
Bird, Henry 261, 263n 193
Black, David 302
Blackfan, John, S.J. 106, 155n 40, 388n 152
Blackness Castle 79
Blackwell, George 320, 398n 186
Bleuse, Jean, S.J. 129
Blount, Charles, Lord Mountjoy 183
Blount, Sir Michael 179
Blount, Richard, S.J. 190n 156, 315n 131, 321n 157, 340
Bluet, Thomas 193, 194n 169, 197, 324
Bolt, John 164
Bonaert, Nicholas, S.J. 323n 161, 404n 209
Boniton, Laird of *see* Wood, James, Laird of Boniton
Borghese, Camillo, Cardinal *see* Paul V, Pope
Bossy, John 3
Boste, John 163
Bosville, John 106

Bothwell, Earl of *see* Stuart, Francis, Earl of Bothwell
Bourbon, Charles, Cardinal 101, 412
Bourbon, Catherine de 56
Bowes, Robert 299
Brakenbury, William, S.J. 138
Broët, Paschase, S.J. 4
Brooksby, Eleanor Vaux 46, 184n 140, 285
Browne, Anthony, Viscount Montague 26n 40, 31n 61
Browne, Charles 344, 346
Browne, William 244n 110
Broy, Henry, S.J. 132, 289n 41
Bruce, Robert 55, 121, 240, 245, 342–343
Brushford, John 61
Burgaleta, Claudio, S.J. 229
Burgh, Thomas, Lord 304
Burghley, Lord *see* Cecil, William, Lord Burghley
Burke, McWilliam 86, 88
Butler, Thomas, Earl of Ormond 304
Button, Richard 262, 313n 123, 357
Byrd, James 61

Cabredo, Rodrigo de, S.J. 112, 209–210, 212–213, 217, 219, 222
Cadiz 113, 115n 80, 276–278, 358, 381, 386
Caetani, Camillo, Patriarch of Alexandria, Nuncio 250
Caetani, Enrico, Cardinal 236, 247, 250, 261–264, 267, 270, 289n 42, 320, 357, 359, 372–373, 375–376, 393, 396–397, 402
Cahill, Hugh 62, 63n 190
Calderwood, David 54, 81, 84, 296, 302
Camillo, Paolo, Cardinal Sfondrata 140
Campbell, Archibald, Earl of Argyll 170, 173–174, 371
Campion, Edmund, S.J.
  martyrdom 168, 185

mission to England 5–7, 18, 58, 67, 92, 140, 185, 197n 177, 222n 46, 335, 344, 390, 407
Works
"Brag" 6, 17, 327
Rationes decem 17
Canisius, Peter, S.J.
Work
A summe of Christian doctrine 288
Carrafiello, Michael 256
Caraman, Philip, S.J. 32, 48
Carnegie, David, Laird of Colluthie 298
Castelli, Giovani Battista, Bishop of Rimini, Nuncio 129
Castro, Melchior de, S.J. 213
Castro, Rodrigo de, Cardinal Archbishop of Seville 115
Catharina, Princess 126
Catholic League 22, 75, 100–104, 111n 61, 127, 152, 205–206, 257n 165, 329, 412, 415–417
Cecil, John
  and Burghley 22–24, 317n 139, 339, 410
  and colleges 106–107, 113–114, 213n 18, 215
  and Scotland 81, 83n 275, 240n 96, 242–243
  and Spain 250n 139, 266
  succession 123, 149
Cecil, Sir Robert 64–66, 148–149, 152, 179–180, 219n 38, 276, 309, 322n 159, 329, 334, 380n 132
Cecil, William, Lord Burghley
  Bloody Question 26–28
  Catholic colleges 109n 54, 410
  espionage 143
  exiles 360
  military invasion 84, 242n 104, 400
  penal legislation 64–66, 86, 107, 131
  persecution 20, 22–24, 29, 271, 283, 291, 317n 139, 339–340
  plots against the queen 152
  and Spain 147, 276
  succession 149, 252n 143, 253, 380n 132, 417
Works
A Declaration of the causes moving the Queen's Majesty to prepare and send a Navy to the seas for Defence of her Realms against the King of Spain's Forces 276
The copie of a letter sent out of England to don Bernardin Mendoza 24
Chambers, James 346
Champney, Anthony 263
Charles II, Duke of Lorraine 126–127, 370, 371, 399
Charles IX, King of France 171
Charles Emmanuel, Duke of Savoy 103
Chastel, Jean 206, 417
Cheyne, James 235
Chideock Castle 38, 74, 78, 167
Chisholm, James 82
Chisholm, William, Bishop of Dunblane 53
Chisholm, William, Bishop of Vaison 173n 104, 241, 298n 70, 339, 372
Cholmeley, Lady, of Whitby 60
Cholmeley, Ursula 60
Christie, George, S.J. 176, 298, 300
Cisneros, Captain 303
Clancy, Thomas H., S.J. 274
Clement VII, Pope 238n 91
Clement VIII, Pope
  and William Allen 246
  candidates for cardinal 250, 261
  conformity 68, 294
  colleges 111, 115, 136, 235, 238, 263–264, 267–268, 270–271, 313, 357–361, 373, 393, 396–397
  English mission 318, 349, 401
  and France 104, 146, 206, 333, 412
  mission to Ireland 304

and Scotland 84, 127, 173, 241, 300, 368, 371–372, 382
and the Society of Jesus 229–230, 294
Spain 172, 276, 333
succession 144, 255, 363, 387, 404n 209
Clemént, Jacques 99
Clibburn, Gerard 106–107
Clifton, Thomas 61
Clitherow, Henry 394
Clitherow, William 394
Cobos, Alonso 303
Coke, Sir Edward 181–182, 188, 309–311
Colleton, John 317
Collins, Richard, S.J. 312, 321n 157
Collinson, Patrick 95
Commolet, Jacques, S.J. 416
Como, Cardinal of *see* Galli, Tolomeo, Cardinal of Como
Como, Fabricio, S.J. 97, 216, 220
Confraternity of the Rosary 41–42, 51, 72
Constable, Henry 60, 153
Constable, Lady of Everingham 60
Constable, Margaret 60
Cordeses, Antonio, S.J. 213
Cornelius, John, S.J. 41, 74, 78, 167
Corti, Paolo de, C.R. 268n 209
Coton, Pierre, S.J. 206
Cottam, Thomas, S.J. 168
Coughton Court 36
Covert, Thomas 341–342, 345, 348
Cowling, Richard, S.J. 266n 202, 268n 212
Cowling, William 106–107
Crawford, Earl of *see* Lindsay, David, Earl of Crawford
Creswell, Joseph, S.J.
   on candidates for cardinal 247, 250
   colleges 108, 111n 62, 115–117, 212n 18, 213, 217, 219, 221, 223–224, 259, 264, 266n 202, 273n 228, 293, 349, 358–361, 376n 126

issues of conformity 154n 36
English mission 35, 77, 138, 169, 190n 156, 401, 414
enterprise to restore Catholicism 141, 146, 340, 381–382, 388
as Parsons's assistant 234, 239
tension among priests 341, 346n 29
tension with exiles 352
Work
   Historia de la vida y martyrio que padecio en Inglaterra, este año de 1595. P. Henrique Valpopo ... el primer martyr de los seminarios de España 221
Crichton, Andrew, S.J. 374
Crichton, Robert, Lord Sanquhar 240
Crichton, William, S.J.
   Armada (1588) 58
   Armada (1597) 399
   Catholicism of James VI 82n 271
   deposition of Elizabeth I 7
   enterprise 81, 141
   English mission 52, 75n 242
   France 205n 1
   Scots College 138–140, 235–241, 243–245, 370–379, 383n 141, 408, 411–412, 414
   Scottish invasion 53, 55–56, 242n 106
   Scottish mission 59, 92, 120–130, 171–172, 173n 104, 175n 113, 302n 84, 326n 172, 328, 402–404
   Spanish Blanks affair 84–85
   successor to Elizabeth I 259, 274
   tension among priests and with exiles 342–346, 350–351, 355, 395
Crome, Edward, Dr 187
Cunningham, David, Protestant Bishop of Aberdeen 327
Curry, John, S.J. 37–38, 46–47, 291

Dacre, Anne *see* Howard, Dacre, Anne
Dacre, Francis, Lord 62, 122, 124–125, 345

Dacre, Leonard, Lord 122–123, 125, 355, 381
Dalmer, Christian, S.J. 227
Davidson, John 82, 84, 171
Dawson, Miles 220n 29
Delapré, François, S.J. 235
Derby, Earl of *see* Ferdinando Stanley, Lord Strange, Earl of Derby, and Stanley, Henry, Earl of Derby
Devereux, Robert, Earl of Essex 65–66, 148–149, 151–152, 207, 258n 174, 276–278, 311, 316, 329–331, 334, 381, 400
Dilenus, Jean 372
Docking, John Baptist, ex S.J. 289n 41
Dolman, Alban 197, 318n 142
Doleman, R.
   Works
      A conference about the next succession to the crowne of Ingland 209, 243, 245, 254–259, 274, 375–376, 379–381, 387
Doran, Susan 93
Dormer, Jane, Duchess of Feria 108, 341n 19
Douglas, Elizabeth, Countess of Angus 325
Douglas, Francis, Lord 374
Douglas, James, Earl of Morton 258
Douglas, William, Earl of Angus 53, 81–82, 170, 173, 174n 111, 175–176, 299, 369, 374, 386
Douglas, William, Earl of Morton 174
Douai
   English College 12, 73, 106–107, 111, 128, 130, 131n 133, 138, 226, 228, 235, 247, 260, 269–270, 322–323, 357, 370, 397–398, 408
   Scottish College 123, 140, 235, 236n 86, 238, 244
Drake, Sir Francis 107, 207–208, 275, 380–381
Drury, Henry, S.J. 35, 50, 75n 243
Dudley, Richard 198, 318n 143

Dudley, Robert, Earl of Leicester 253–254
Duffy, Eamon 13, 144n 3, 201
Duke, Sir Henry 177
Duras, George, S.J. 216, 227, 235, 300, 353–356, 366
Durie, George, ex S.J. 58
Durie, John, S.J. 58

Edinburgh Castle 57, 125, 173
Edwards, Francis, S.J. 26
Effingham, Lord Howard of *see* Howard, Charles, Lord of Effingham
Egerton, Sir Thomas 165
Egerton, Thomas 215
Elizabeth I, Queen of England
   Bloody Question 166
   excommunication 5, 67, 141, 335
   foreign policy 75, 104, 146–147, 203, 207, 329, 412
   and Ireland 88, 177, 303–304, 307, 383–384
   military invasion against 26, 96, 169, 275–277, 279, 331–333, 399, 410
   overthrow, plots against 6–7, 11, 13, 18, 52, 62–63, 81, 127–128, 148–151, 153, 158, 162–163, 395, 410
   penal laws and proclamations 24–25, 131
   and Philip II 101, 122, 143–144
   and recusancy 66, 333
   relationship with Jesuits 29, 105, 166, 281,
   relationship with subjects 15, 145, 280, 282–283, 337, 345, 383, 394, 410
   religious settlement 13, 188
   religious toleration 19, 278, 336, 371
   and Scotland 53, 56, 80, 82–86, 93, 125, 174n 109, 176, 242, 297, 302, 343, 370n 100
   succession 23, 28, 126, 186, 244, 251–253, 258–259, 274,

371–372, 377, 387, 389, 392, 408
Elphinstone, George, S.J. 176, 298, 372n 105
Elphinstone, James 298
Ely, Humphrey 260
Emerson, Ralph, S.J. 5, 18, 34, 43–44, 50, 165, 308, 321n 157, 377, 407
Englefield, Sir Francis 108, 118, 158, 160, 249, 255n 155, 256, 273n 228, 340, 347, 352, 376n 126, 381–382, 384n 143, 385, 402–403
English, John, S.J. 388n 152, 389n 155
Ernst, Archduke of Austria 103–104, 126, 145–147, 150–151, 180, 207–208, 227, 240, 246, 248, 372n 104
Erroll, Earl of *see* Hay, Francis, Earl of Erroll
Erskine, John, Earl of Mar 242, 370
Essex, Earl of *see* Devereux, Robert
Eu
   English College 106, 131
Eustace, Oliver 346
Everard, Thomas, S.J. 36, 74n 240, 289n 41

Farnese, Alessandro, Duke of Parma 35, 55, 97, 101–105, 117, 127, 234, 258, 339n 11, 341, 354
Farnese, Pier Luigi, Duke of Parma 413n 13
Farnese, Ranuccio, Prince of Parma 28n 49, 123, 147, 158, 172
Favour, John, Dr 154
Fech, Thomas, S.J. 312
Fenwick, John 60
Ferdinand, Duke of Florence 127
Ferdinand, King of Spain 4
Feria, Duchess of *see* Dormer, Jane, Duchess of Feria
Feria, Duke of *see* Figueroa, Lorenzo Suárez de, Duke of Feria

Fernández de Córdoba, Gonzalo, Duke of Sessa 229, 231, 242, 246, 265, 358
Fernández de Córdoba y Cardona, Antonio, Duke of Sessa 28n 49, 112n 67, 115, 145–146
Fernández de Córdoba y Figueroa, Pedro, Marquis of Priego 115, 213
Ferrera da Gama, Estevan 148
Fife, Synod of 82, 170
Figueroa, Lorenzo Suárez de, Duke of Feria 103, 248, 349
Fintry, Laird of *see* Graham, David, Laaird of Fintry
Fioravanti, Girolamo, S.J. 259–262, 264n 195, 270, 313, 357, 393
Fisher, John *see* Percy, John
Fisher, Robert 268, 295–296, 313–314, 317, 318n 143, 322, 324, 358
FitzGerald, James FitzMaurice, 303n 87
FitzGerald, Maurice 87–88
FitzGerald, Thomas, Viscount Baltinglas 87
Fitzherbert, Nicholas 340, 387, 394
Fitzherbert, Thomas, S.J. 352
FitzSimon, Henry, S.J. 306
Fitzwilliam, William, Lord Deputy of Ireland 86, 177
Fixer, John 22–24, 106, 410
Flack, William, S.J. 108, 110, 112, 132–133, 228, 365–367
Fleming, Sir Thomas 309
Floyd, Henry, S.J. 106
Folch y Cardona, Don Antonio, Duke of Sessa *see* Fernández de Córdoba y Cardona, Antonio, Duke of Sessa
Fonseca, Pedro, S.J. 105, 118
Forbes-Leith, William, S.J. 300
Forest, John 187–188
Foucart, Jean, S.J. 132, 139, 228, 272–273, 366–368
Fosler, Emerich, S.J. 90
Foster, Francis 397n 181

Fowler, Francis 261
Fox, Nicholas 33
Frangipani, Ottavio Mirto, Nuncio 250n 138, 307, 323n 161, 324, 340n 16, 368n 98, 370n 101, 397–398, 404
Frank, John 164–165
French, Walter 118
Fuentes, Count of *see* Azevedo, Don Pedro Enríquez de, Count of Fuentes
Fuljambe, Godfrey 348
Fulwood, Richard, S.J. 164, 292, 315
Fuscincelli, Ottaviano *see* Baldwin, William

Gage, Mr. 344
Galli, Tolomeo, Cardinal of Como 129
Galloway, Patrick 57, 78, 170
García, Juan, S.J. 223–224
Gardiner, Sir Robert 177
Garnet, Helen 162
Garnet, Henry, S.J.
   colleges 226, 228, 359
   conformity 67–72, 203
   effect of Spanish Armada 16, 18
   equivocation 39, 187–189, 311
   lay Catholics 45, 62, 66
   raids and hiding 46–49, 91, 159, 164, 309, 398n 188
   mission to England 7, 32, 35–45, 73–78, 92, 153–154, 162–163, 167, 169, 179, 188–189, 192–198, 200, 277, 291–292, 312–316
   penal legislation against recusants 64–65
   persecution and martyrdom 21, 50–51, 59–62, 155–156, 183, 285, 293, 310, 333n 188, 409
   political concerns 64, 340, 386
   tension among priests 199, 201, 283–284, 286–290, 294–295, 308, 318, 320–323, 324n 165, 352, 411
   Works
      A treatise of Christian renunciation 71, 288
      An Apology against the defence of schisme 70
      "The Declaration of the Fathers of the Councell of Trent" 72
      The Societie of the Rosary 42
Garnet, Margaret 162
Gazi, Giovanni Hieronimo, S.J. 129
Gee, Edward 389
Gennings, Edmund 33
Gerard, John, S.J. 35–38, 40, 43, 46–47, 50n 145, 96, 106, 161, 163–167, 169, 186, 189, 190n 155, 191, 199, 275, 283, 289, 291n 48, 292, 308–311, 314–317, 321n 157
Gerrott, John, S.J. 306
Gibbons, Richard, S.J. 108, 110, 118, 199, 217–219
Gifford, Gilbert 362, 404
Gifford, William, Dr
   attacks on Society of Jesus 360, 383, 398, 404n 209
   candidates for cardinal 261
   colleges 271, 295
   English mission 322, 340, 345–346, 354, 356, 368n 98
   overthrow of, plots against the queen 150, 387, 393, 395n 174
   Scottish mission 241–242, 375n 120
   succession 257n 165, 258n 170, 259, 347
   tension among priests 324, 344n 24
Gillibrand, John 106
Goldwell, Thomas, Bishop of St Asaph 6
Gonzaga, Ferrante 413n 13
González Dávila, Gil, S.J. 105, 121n 101, 135, 224–225, 230, 239, 305
Good, William, S.J. 5
Goodwin, William 154
Gordon, George, Earl of Huntly 53–55, 56n 163, 59, 79–83,

93, 170, 173, 174n 109 and 111, 175–176, 239, 245, 297, 300–302, 325–327, 369–370, 386, 411
Gordon, Henrietta, Countess Huntly 300–301
Gordon, James, S.J. 52, 57, 59, 80, 83, 92, 171–175, 176n 121, 185–186, 239–241, 245, 298–300, 325–328, 342, 350, 368, 370–372, 411
Gordon, Patrick, Laird of Auchindoun 81–82, 170, 173
Gouda, Nicolas da, S.J. 5
Graham, David, Laird of Fintry 81, 122, 380
Grene, Christopher, S.J. 213n 18, 254n 154, 278n 6
Grene, Peter, S.J. 374
Gregory XIII, Pope 5, 52, 116, 129, 335, 407
Gregory XIV, Pope 24, 28, 102, 111–112, 140–141, 209n 10, 229
Gregory XV, Pope 268n 209
Gregory, Brad S. 10
Greenwich, Treaty of 276
Grey, Henry, Lord 65
Grey, Robert 33
Griffin, Hugh 265, 360, 365, 387, 394, 395n 174
Griffiths, William 340
Guicciardini, Giacomo 381n 136
Guise, Charles, Cardinal of Lorraine 129
Guise, Charles, Duke of Mayenne 100, 102–103
Guise, Henry, Duke of Guise 6, 100, 106–107, 340, 395, 404
Guise, Louis, Cardinal 100
Guzmán, Enrique de, Count of Olivares 1, 97, 246, 255
Guzmán, Pedro de, S.J. 110
Guzmán y Sotomayor, Antonio de, Marquis of Ayamonte 115

Habington, Edward 37
Habington, Dorothy 36–37
Habington, Thomas 36
Hamilton, Claude, Lord 54–55, 82n 271
Hamilton, Thomas 298
Hammer, Paul 148, 152n 31, 241n 100, 276n 2
Hardesty, William 154
Harewood, Edmund, S.J. 261–263, 265, 292, 349
Harrington, William 163
Harvey, Thomas, S.J. (alias Stanney) 41–42, 46–47, 321n 157
Hastings, Henry, Earl of Huntingdon 59–62, 69, 85, 123, 153–154, 156–157, 184–185, 254
Hatton, Sir Christopher 19, 409
Hawkins, Sir John 207, 380–381
Hay, Edmund, S.J. 52, 55–58, 92, 121n 101, 122n 102
Hay, Francis, Earl of Erroll 53, 55–57, 81–82, 170, 173, 175–176, 239, 297, 300–301, 325, 369–370, 411
Hay, George 59
Hay, John, S.J. 173n 107, 176n 121, 328
Haydock, Richard 266, 384
Heneage, Sir Thomas 143–144
Henry III, King of France 11, 100–101, 103, 205
Henry IV, King of France 21–22, 23, 63, 75, 100–104, 126–127, 128, 141, 143, 146, 151, 174, 185, 205–206, 242, 271, 275, 329, 333, 339, 347, 363, 371–372, 380–381, 399, 410, 412, 415–417
Henry VIII, King of England 4, 187, 253, 384
Henry of Navarre *see* Henry IV, King of France
Henshaw, Thomas 177
Herbert, Edward 177
Hernandez, Sebastian, S.J. 225
Herries, Lord *see* Maxwell, William, Lord Herries
Hesketh Plot 149–150

Hesketh, Richard 149, 181, 186
Hesketh, Thomas *see* Allen, Thomas
d'Heur, Jean, S.J. 130, 132–134, 205n 1, 227, 341, 367
Heywood, Jasper, S.J. 405
Hicks, Leo, S.J. 83, 47, 109, 131, 202, 249, 256, 258n 170, 336–337, 409
Higgins, Anthony 183
Hill, James 352
Hill, Robert 374
Hill, Thomas 262, 268, 289, 397–398
Holmes, Peter 32–33, 256, 282–283n 25
Holt, Mark P. 103
Holt, William, S.J.
  as dangerous to monarchy 162, 184–185
  Catholic ecclesiastical hierarchy 320–321
  colleges 116n 82, 117, 132–133, 139n 162, 190–191, 228, 271, 274, 314, 364, 367–368, 392–393, 402, 414
  dissension among exiles 285, 403
  English mission 35, 62n 188, 202, 234–235, 273n 228, 283, 289n 41, 316, 323, 401
  enterprise 52
  overthrow of the queen 146, 150, 160, 203, 387
  recusancy 92n 304
  and Scotland 241, 243, 244n 110, 245, 375, 377, 382
  secular tensions 339–357
  succession 149
Holtby, Lady 60
Holtby, Richard, S.J. 37, 46–47, 59–61, 154–156, 293, 321n 157
Holywood, Christopher, S.J. 305–306
Höpfl, Harro 8, 256n 161
Hopkins, Richard 144–145
Houliston, Victor 257
Howard, Anne Dacre, Countess of Arundel 38–39, 43, 165
Howard, Charles, Lord of Effingham 191, 276

Howard, Philip, Earl of Arundel 21n 21
Howard, Thomas, Lord 276, 329–330
Howling, John, S.J. 118, 120, 307
Hume, Alexander, Lord 80, 82, 170
Hume, Sir James 125, 175
Hume, Martin A.S. 149
Hungerford, Anne Dormer, Lady 147, 341n 19
Huntingdon, Earl of *see* Hastings, Henry, Earl of Huntingdon
Huntly, Countess of *see* Gordon, Henrietta, Countess of Huntly
Huntly, Earl of *see* Gordon, George, Earl of Huntly
Hurstfield, Joel 24, 410

Ibarra, Esteban de 234–235, 241–242, 341–342, 349
Idiáquez, Don Juan de 89, 113n 74, 123, 125, 140, 223, 231, 255, 265, 317n 139, 360n 64, 382, 384–385, 387, 392n 165, 393, 395
Idiáquez, Martin de 384
Ingleby, Catherine 60
Ingram, John 163
Innocent IX, Pope 111, 209n 10
Inverness Castle 173
Isabella Clara Eugenia, Infanta 101–103, 112, 126, 144, 258, 381, 384n 143, 385, 387–388, 392, 412

Jackson, John 268, 397n 181
James V, King of Scotland 4
James VI and I, King of Scotland and King of England
  anti-Catholic legislation 79
  Armada (1597) 399–400
  and Catholic earls 54–55, 82–83, 93, 169–176, 300–302
  colleges 271
  and Ireland 307
  marriage to Anne 56–57

question of his Catholicism 52,
    239, 242–243, 256n 161,
    369–370, 372, 374, 381
  loyalty to 12, 355n 51
  penal legislation 333
  plots to kidnap and overthrow him
    78, 80–81
  relationship with Jesuits 5, 35,
    57–59, 241, 326, 352, 371, 377
  relationship with Philip II 240,
    350, 385
  Spain-Scotland alliance against
    England 53
  Spanish invasion of Scotland
    84–85, 123–129, 297–298, 386
  succession to English throne 245,
    251, 253, 255, 258–259,
    347, 378–380, 382, 388, 392,
    411–412
James VII and II, King of Scotland and
    King of England 392
Jessop, Augustus 159–160
Jimenez, Ensign 303
Jones, Anne Bellamy *see* Bellamy, Anne
Jones, John 284n 27
Jones, Nicholas 48
Jones, Robert, S.J. 174, 190, 196,
    321n 157
Julius III, Pope 1

Kaplan, Benjamin J. 10
Katz, David S. 152
Kelly, J.N.D. 24n 34, 102
Kenny, Anthony 259, 269, 398
Kerr, George 80–82, 84
Keynes, George, S.J. 75
Killingale, Anne 60
King, Mr. 154
King, Thomas, S.J. 5
Knox, Andrew 80
Knox, Thomas Francis 201, 203

Laínez, Diego, S.J. 3
Lake, Peter 76, 293n 54, 411
Lalo, Andrew 374
Lampton, John 61
Langdale, Alban 67, 69

Langdale, Thomas, ex S.J. 287n 35
LaRocca, John, S.J. 26
Law, Thomas Graves 84, 194
Lawson, Mrs. 60
Lennox, Duke of *see* Stuart, Esmé,
    Sieur d'Aubigny and Duke of
    Lennox, and Stuart, Ludovic,
    Duke of Lennox
Leslie, John, Bishop of Ross 44n 119,
    129, 253
  Work
  A treatise of treasons against Q.
    Elizabeth, and the crowne of
    England 253
Leunis, Jan, S.J. 42
Lewkner, Lewis 282, 410
  Work
  State of English Fugitives under
    the King of Spaine and his
    ministers 279, 334, 410
Lewknor, Samuel 282–283, 334
Lewis, Owen, Bishop of Cassano 147,
    241, 247, 249–250, 260–263,
    265, 267, 270, 340, 393
Ligi, Ambroglio, S.J. 216
Ligons, Ralph 147, 344, 346
Lillie, John, S.J. 165, 315
Lindsay, David, Earl of Crawford 53,
    55, 58, 298, 411
Lindsay, John 298
Lindsay, Sir Walter 243
Line, Anne 166, 292, 315–317
Lingham, Edward 153
Lisbon
  Irish College 120, 138, 236, 307,
    408
Lister, Thomas, S.J. 199, 284, 292,
    312–313, 321n 157
Livingstone, Eleanor 301–302
Lockwood, Francis 106–107
Loftus, Adam, Archbishop of Dublin
    177
Lombard, Peter, Dr 306
Loomie, Albert J., S.J. 146, 282
Lopez Plot 104n 30, 148, 150, 152
Lopez, Rodrigo 148–149, 152
López de Manzano, Juan, S.J. 110

López de Soto, Pedro 400
Lothbury, Jasper 397n 181
Lothian, Synod of 301
Lovelace, Thomas 106
Loyola, Ignatius, S.J. 1, 3–4, 35,
    78, 315, 352, 412, 413n 13,
    415–417
  Works
    Spiritual Exercises 2, 35, 39,
      43, 165–166, 237, 311, 314,
      316–317, 391, 415
Ludovisi, Alessandro *see* Gregory XV,
    Pope
Lugo 135
Luzzi, Bernardino, S.J. 396

MacGauran, Edmund, Archbishop of
    Armagh 87, 105, 177
MacQuhirrie, Alexander, S.J. 53, 92n
    305, 176n 121, 298–299, 325n
    168, 326
Madrucci, Lodovico, Cardinal 396
Maggio, Lorenzo, S.J. 305, 413
Magrath, Miler, Archbishop of Cashel
    86n 285, 88
Maguire, Hugh 87–89, 177–178
Maitland, Sir John 55–56, 79, 173
Malvasia, Innocenza, Nuncio 174n
    108, 175, 240–242, 250n 139,
    259, 342, 363, 368–372, 383,
    394
Mannaerts, Oliver, S.J. 43, 45n 125,
    52, 73–75, 128n 116, 130,
    132–134, 216n 31, 226–228,
    247–249, 292n 51, 306, 343,
    346, 348–356, 366–368, 402,
    414
Mansfelt, Count of *see* Peter Ernest,
    Count of Mansfelt
Marcén, Antonio, S.J. 98
Maria, Dowager Empress 246
Marshall, Peter 188
Martinez, Fr, S.J. 209–210
Martin Marprelate tracts 16–17
Mary I, Queen of England 4–5, 30, 95,
    187, 380

Mary, Queen of Scots 5–6, 18, 52–53,
    79, 122, 126, 129, 252–254,
    258, 336n 5, 340, 377, 391n
    161, 395, 404, 408, 411
Masi, Cosme 234
Mattei, Girolamo, Cardinal 236,
    306–307
Matthew, David 3
Matthieu, Claude, S.J. 404
Maurice of Nassau, Count 151, 329
Maxwell, John, Earl of Morton 53–54,
    57–58, 411
Maxwell, William, Lord Herries 58
Mayenne, Duke of *see* Guise, Charles,
    Duke of Mayenne
Medeley, William 192
Medina, Francisco de Borja, S.J. 84,
    125
Medinilla, Captain 303
Melville, Andrew 298, 300
Méndez, Cristobal, S.J. 215
Mendoza, Don Alfonso de, O.S.B. 109
Mendoza, Francisco Sarmiento de,
    Bishop of Jaen 211
Mercoeur, Duke of *see* Philippe
    Emmanuel, Duke of Mercoeur
Mercurian, Everard, S.J. 2, 5–8, 18,
    40, 52, 97, 116, 132, 193n
    162, 200, 319
Metham, Catherine 60
Metham, Thomas, S.J. 34, 50,
    192–193, 194–195n 169
Middleton, Robert 396n 178
Millino, Pietro, Bishop, Nuncio 84,
    127n 115
Modye, Michael 348
Mohet, Timothy 344
Molina, Luis de, S.J. 211, 323n 162
Mompesson, Laurence 26
Monaghan Castle 178
Montague, Viscount *see* Browne,
    Anthony, Viscount Montague
Montero, Ensign 303
Moray, Earl of *see* Stuart, James, Earl
    of Moray
Moray, Synod of 300
More, George 355

INDEX

More, Henry, S.J. 38n 95, 106, 194, 340, 347, 408
Morgan, Thomas 147, 243, 267, 274, 336–338, 339n 11, 340–341, 352, 354, 383, 393, 395, 396n 175, 403, 408–409, 414
Morra, Bernadino 263, 266, 268, 394
Morrissey, Thomas, S.J. 119, 179, 237n 89
Morton, Earl of *see* Douglas, James, Earl of Morton, Douglas, William, Earl of Morton, and Maxwell, John, Earl of Morton
Morton, Thomas 189n 153
Munnez, Juan de, S.J. 115
Murdoch, William, S.J. 58, 173–174, 176, 298, 326–327
Murphy, Martin 221
Mush, John 41, 198, 200, 290, 317–318
Myrton, John, S.J. 81n 267, 174–176, 190n 156, 240–241, 402–403

Neale, Sir J.E. 64
Nelson, Eric 415–416
Nelson, John, S.J. 41, 46–47, 60, 291
Nevill, Charles, Earl of Westmorland 62, 124, 344, 346, 350, 352, 375n 120, 381
Norden, John 193, 324
Norreys, Sir Edward 381n 136
Norris, Sir John 104, 107, 304, 307, 380
Norris, Sylvester 357
Northumberland, Earl of *see* Percy, Thomas, Earl of Northumberland

Ogilvie, John, Laird of Pury 84, 240–243, 245, 370n 103
Ogilvie, William, S.J. 58, 83, 129
Ogle 60
Óg O'Rourke, Brian 87–88
Oldcorne, Edward, S.J. 35–38, 45–47, 321n 157, 340
O'Hely, James, Archbishop of Tuam 87–89

O'Donnell, MacManus, Hugh 87
O'Donnell, Hugh Roe 87–89, 177–178, 277, 302–303, 305, 329
O'Malley, John W., S.J. 3
O'Mulrian, Cornelius, Bishop of Killaloe 88
O'Neill, Cormac 177–178
O'Neill, Hugh, Earl of Tyrone 8, 12, 86–89, 177–179, 277, 302–304, 306–307, 329, 384, 399
O'Neill, Turlough Luineach 178
O'Neill, Art MacBaron 178
Ormond, Earl of *see* Butler, Thomas, Earl of Ormond
O'Rourke, Brian 87–88
Owen, Hugh 146, 150, 172, 202, 340–346, 347n 33, 348, 352–356, 375n 120, 382, 387, 403
Owen, John 288n 39
Owen, Nicholas, S.J. 164–165, 288, 308, 315
Owen, Walter 288n 39

Padilla, Antonio de, S.J. 209–212
Padilla, Don Martin de 388, 401
Page, Francis, S.J. 314–315
Paget, Charles
  on candidates for cardinal 261
  English mission 323n 161
  and Jesuits 344, 354–356, 368n 98, 393, 394n 168
  as troublesome exile, opposed to Allen 147, 336–337, 339–341, 352, 403–404, 408–409, 414
  peace in England 158, 333–334
  plots against Elizabeth 150
  and Scotland 241–243, 375n 120
  and seminaries 295
  and Spain 346–347, 350, 395, 396n 175
  Stuart marriage talks 28n 49
  succession 259, 274, 381, 383, 387
Paget, Thomas, Lord 337, 404
Pansford, John 344, 348
Parker, Charles H. 9
Parker, Geoffrey 95

Parma, Duke of *see* Farnese, Alessandro, Duke of Parma, and Farnese Pier Luigi, Duke of Parma
Parma, Prince of *see* Farnese, Ranuccio, Prince of Parma
Parmelee, Lisa Ferraro 417
Parsons, Christina 163
Parsons, John 163
Parsons, Robert, SJ
 campaign against persecution 11–13, 19, 22–23, 26, 28–29, 33
 candidacy for cardinal 247–251
 colleges 73n 233, 75n 242, 106–114, 117, 119, 132–133, 138–139, 201, 208–228, 235, 237–239, 264–268, 271–274, 340, 347n 33, 357–359, 364–368, 383n 141, 392, 394–398, 402–403, 408–409
 conformity 6–7, 9, 67
 and Ireland 306
 mission to England 5–9, 18, 76n 249, 77, 91–92, 95–97, 116, 137, 140, 158, 168–169, 171, 185, 188, 194, 199, 234, 275, 283, 293, 312–314, 317n 139, 318–321, 336, 341–342, 344–346, 348–356, 360–363, 393, 404–405, 407, 411–412, 415
 overthrow of Elizabeth 62, 85, 141, 162, 202–203, 371, 381, 384–389, 391, 400–401, 410
 religious toleration 146, 390
 and Scotland 52, 83, 123–124, 241, 243–246, 413–414
 and Philip II 98–99, 105–106, 116, 130, 135, 229–233, 335, 382
 succession 254–260, 375–381, 387, 392
 Works
  A brief discours contayning certayne reasons why Catholiques refuse to goe to church 29, 67

  A manifestation of the great folly and bad spirit of certayne in England calling themselves secular priestes 392
  De persecutione Anglicana 221
  Elizabethae Angliae Reginae haeresim Calvinianam propugnantis 160
  Newes from Spayne and Holland 160–161, 254
  The Jesuit's Memorial, for the Intended Reformation of England, Under their first Popish Prince 389
Pasquier, Etienne 415–417
Pattenson, William 33
Paul V, Pope 271, 359, 364, 397
Pavone, Sabina 8
Peck, Dwight C. 258
Pembroke, Richard, S.J. 89–90, 178
Peña, Francisco de 319, 394n 171
Peralta, Francesco de, S.J. 115, 210, 213–214, 216, 222
Percy, Henry 396n 178
Percy, John, S.J. (alias Fisher) 291–292, 293n 54, 321n 157
Percy, Thomas, Earl of Northumberland 36
Percy, William, Dr 269–270, 387, 393n 166
Perez, Bartolomé, S.J. 114, 225
Perkins (or Parkins), Christopher, ex S.J. 75n 245, 101n 20, 147, 287n 35
Peter Ernest, Count of Mansfelt 104
Petit, John 241n 101, 346, 375n 120
Phelippes, Thomas 333
Philip II, King of Spain
 colleges 25n 36, 106–107, 111–112, 114–115, 117, 119, 130–131, 133, 136, 226, 238, 265–266, 314, 365, 376, 395, 411
 and English exiles 338, 341, 345, 350, 355n 51, 396n 175
 France 21, 101–104, 143, 206, 208, 224–225

Inquisition 98, 136
Scotland 4, 54, 56, 81n 267, 85–88, 89n 294 and 296, 121–127, 169, 178, 223, 240–244, 297, 302–303, 342–343, 368, 372
 and Parsons 12, 116, 231, 234, 249, 255, 380, 414
 Society of Jesus 99, 105, 135, 138, 167, 209, 229–230, 246, 248, 349
 overthrow of Elizabeth 1, 4–5, 7–8, 19, 24, 27n 46, 28, 53n 152, 63, 95–97, 110, 140, 150, 172, 207, 258, 260, 277–280, 297, 330, 380–387, 389, 392, 399–401, 408–410, 412
 peace with Elizabeth 143–149, 151
 Spanish cruelty 281, 415–416
Philip, Prince (later King Philip III) 225
Philippe Emmanuel, Duke of Mercoeur 206–207
Pigenat, Odo, S.J. 56n 163, 126
Pitts, John 247
Pitts, Walter 348
Pius IV, Pope 5, 373
Pius V, Pope
 Regnans in Excelsis 5, 30n 58, 67, 126
Pole, Reginald, Cardinal 4
Pollard, A.W. 282
Pollard, Henry (alias Sharpe, James) 286n 34
Pollen, John Hungerford, S.J. 11, 24, 157, 159, 161, 202, 245, 256n 164, 324
Ponce de Léon, Rodrigo, Duke of Arcos 115
Pont-à-Mousson
 Scottish-Irish College 129–130
Popham, Sir John 181–182
Porres, Francisco de, S.J. 239, 305
Portmort, Thomas 61
Portocarrero, Juan de 329
Possevino, Antonio, S.J. 412–413
Pounde, Thomas, S.J. 34, 50, 192, 321n 157

Priego, Marquis of *see* Fernández de Córdoba y Figueroa, Pedro, Marquis of Priego
Pritchard, Arnold 296, 325
Puckering, Sir John 63–64
Puente, Luis de la, S.J. 210
Pullen, Joseph, S.J. 77n 258, 312, 321n 157
Pury (or Purie), Laird of *see* Ogilvie, John, Laird of Pury

Questier, Michael 3, 61, 76, 162, 411
Quiñones, Don Alfonso de 107–108, 111
Quiñones, Juan Vigil de 109
Quiroga, Gaspar, Cardinal de 98, 238

Radford, John, S.J. 73, 77n 258
Raleigh, Sir Walter 276, 329–330
Rawlins, Alexander 185
Rea, W.F., S.J. 160–161
Redgrave, G.R. 282
Reims
 English College 38n 96, 44n 121, 106–107, 111, 131n 133, 193, 221, 226, 264, 393, 408
Renichon, Michel 151
Renold, Penelope 196, 202, 296
Reynosa, Don Francisco de 108, 111
Ribadeneira, Pedro de, S.J. 5, 95–96, 137n 156, 225, 391n 161, 416
 Work
  The Christian Prince (*Tratado de la religion y virtudes que debe tener el príncipe cristiano para gobernar y conservar sus estados, contra lo que Nicolas Maquiavelo y los políticos deste tiempo enseñan*) 391n 161
Richardson, William 65–66
Río, Gonzalo del, S.J. 210–212
Robb, John, S.J. 374
Robinson, Francis 396n 178
Rogers, David 161, 256
Rome
 English College 5, 35, 106, 108–109, 111–112, 116–118,

138, 193, 201, 203, 251, 273, 284, 361, 365, 370, 393
Ross, John 170
Rouen, Edict of 206
Row, William 80
Rudolph II, Holy Roman Emperor 75, 147
Russell, Sir William 86, 177, 304–305
Rutherford, Thomas 60

St Leger, Sir Anthony 177
St Omer
　English College 92, 130–134, 138–139, 155, 158, 166, 168, 216, 226, 228, 235, 238, 244, 272–273, 283, 309, 365–367, 402, 408, 414
St Paul's Cathedral (London) 16–17
Sacheverell, John (Fr. William) 268, 313, 394, 398
Sagan, Ethan 3
Salamanca
　Irish College 117, 119–120, 138–139, 178, 236–239, 408
Salmerón, Alfonso, S.J. 4
Salviati, Antonio Maria, Cardinal 359
Sánchez, Alonso, S.J. 136, 230
Sander 183
Sanquhar, Lord see Crichton, Robert
Sapiretti, Giovanni 173–174, 371–372
Saville, Sir John 184
Scudmore, John 62, 63n 188 and 189, 68n 209
Secusi di Calatagirona, Bonaventura 333
Sega, Filippo, Cardinal 268–270, 357
Semple, Colonel William 53, 123n 106, 243, 379
Sessa, Duke of see Fernández de Córdoba, Gonzalo, Duke of Sessa, and Fernández de Córdoba y Cardona, Antonio, Duke of Sessa
Seton, Alexander 173, 298, 300–302
Seton, David, ex S.J. 374
Seton, George, Lord 173
Seton, James 326

Seville
　College of San Hermenegild 213, 222
　English College 113–115, 117, 131, 191, 211, 213–216, 220, 222, 248, 264, 402n 202, 408, 414
Shankly, Bill 9
Sharpe, James see Pollard, Henry
Shearman, Francis 83
Sheldon, Hugh, S.J. 45–46
Sherrat, Henry 106
Sicilia, Bartolomé de, S.J. 110, 114
Sieur d'Aubigny see Stuart, Esmé
Sigüenza, Juan de 230
Sixtus V, Pope 19, 97–98, 100–102, 127, 129, 135, 229
Skene, John 298
Smith, Nicholas, S.J. 132, 216n 31, 228, 367
Smithson, John 401
Sodality of the Blessed Virgin 41–42
Southwark, Synod of 67
Southwell, Robert, S.J.
　apostolic mission 7, 20–21, 31, 35, 37–38, 40, 43, 68, 77, 92, 153, 288, 340
　Armada of 1588 16, 18–19, 409
　capture, imprisonment, and torture 33, 49, 50n 146, 51, 91, 155, 161–162, 165, 167–169, 179–181, 192, 411
　equivocation 39, 181–182, 186–188, 189n 153, 311
　literary mission 7, 27n 46, 29, 31–32, 39, 90
　martyrdom 183, 185–186, 283
　raids and hiding 38, 45–48
　Works
　　An Humble supplication 29, 31n 61, 32, 39, 186
　　A Short Rule of Good Life 39
Southworth, Christopher 41
Squarcione, Acarizio 397
Stafford, Helen Georgia 57
Standen, Sir Anthony 258
Stanihurst, Richard 255n 155

Stanley, Ferdinando, Lord Strange, Earl of Derby 23, 123, 149–150, 158, 171, 244
Stanley, Henry, 4th Earl of Derby 149, 171
Stanley, William 149
Stanley, Sir William 86, 101n 19, 149–150, 153n 35, 158, 162, 186, 202, 279, 340, 345, 352, 375n 120, 381, 384, 387, 399, 400
Stanney, Thomas see Harvey, Thomas
Stapleton, Thomas, ex S.J. 156, 247, 250–251, 340, 384–385, 394
Stewart, William, Prior of Blantyre 298, 302
Stillington, Thomas 106, 114, 401
Stirling Castle 83, 370
Stonor, John 147, 340, 344, 346, 350, 375n 120
Stonyhurst
   English College 132
Strange, Lord see Stanley, Ferdinando, Lord
Strange, Earl of Derby 14
Stuart, Arabella 28, 123, 147, 158
Stuart, Elizabeth, Princess 301
Stuart, Esmé, Sieur d'Aubigny and Duke of Lennox 52
Stuart, Francis, Earl of Bothwell 53, 55, 57, 78–82, 84–85, 127, 170, 174–176, 411
Stuart, Henry Frederick, Prince of Wales 83, 173
Stuart, Hercules 174
Stuart, James, Earl of Moray 79, 170
Stuart, James see James VI, King of Scotland, and James VII, King of Scotland
Stuart, Ludovic, Duke of Lennox 369–370
Stuart, Margaret, Princess 301n 83
Stuart, Mary see Mary, Queen of Scots
Suárez, Francisco, S.J. 211
Suffield, William 164
Swinburne, Simon, S.J. 191n 158, 216, 367

Sydney, Sir Robert 244n 110

Talbot, Walter, S.J. 306
Tancard, Charles, S.J. 108, 115, 210, 213, 216–219, 388, 400
Tarbuck, John 164
Tassis, Don Juan Bautista de 343, 348, 353, 355
Tempest, Edward 261, 263, 268, 365n 85, 397
Tempest, Robert 398
Tesimond, Oswald, S.J. 139n 162, 215–216
Tierney, Mark, Canon 256
Tinoco, Emmanuel Luis 148
Thomas, John 61
Thomson, George 236n 84
Throckmorton, Nicholas 36
Throckmorton Plot 6
Throckmorton, Thomas 147, 150, 202–203, 265, 267, 337–338, 340, 362n 70, 394
Toledo, Francisco, S.J, Cardinal 201, 229, 247n 126, 270–271, 347, 357–359, 393–394
Topcliffe, Richard 48–49, 90, 154–155, 157, 163, 165–166, 179, 181, 185, 291
Torrentius, Laevinus, Bishop of Antwerp 246
Traherne, Gabriel 387
Trent, Council of 72, 80, 206, 323n 162, 373, 391
Tresham, Sir Thomas 20, 31n 63, 164n 73, 334, 336, 339n 12, 410
Tresham, William 147, 340, 344, 346, 350, 355–356, 375n 120, 387
Trevor-Roper, Hugh 4
Trinity College (Dublin) 87, 120, 238n 91
Trollop, Cuthbert 396n 178, 397n 181
Trollope, John 38, 60
Turnbull, George, S.J. 218, 374
Tyrie, James, S.J. 56n 163, 68n 209, 81n 267, 90, 126–127, 128n 116, 129–130, 169, 172, 175, 235, 236n 86, 239, 270, 299,

306, 342, 370n 102, 374, 375n 120, 394, 402,
Tyrie, Thomas 175
Tyrone, Earl of *see* O'Neill, Hugh, Earl of Tyrone
Tyrwhit, Nicholas 320

Urban VII, Pope 102, 209n 10

Vair, Guillaume du 103
Valladolid
  College of San Ambrosio 110, 209–210
  English College 98, 106–115, 116n 82, 118–120, 131, 136, 138, 139n 162, 192n 160, 209, 211–213, 216–218, 222, 225, 230, 232, 237, 264, 387–388, 401, 408, 414
Valois, François de, Duke of Anjou 5–6, 253
Vargas, Don Alonso de 126
Vaux, Anne 46–47, 184n 140, 285
Vaux, Eleanor *see* Brooksby, Eleanor
Vaux family 7
Vaux, Henry, S.J. 184n 140, 285
Vaux, William, Lord 38, 92n 304, 184n 140
Vernois, Jean de, Bishop of St Omer 226, 244, 366
Verstegan, Richard 26–29, 32–33, 49, 62n 185, 64n 194, 70, 75, 82n 271, 88n 290, 89n 296–297, 96, 147n 14, 148n 16, 161, 163, 167n 84, 176n 118, 177n 23, 254, 256, 259, 292n 49, 310n 112, 315n 131, 378n 130, 402n 202, 403, 410
  Works
  A declaration of the true causes of the great troubles 27
  An advertisement written to a secretarie of my L. Treasurers 27–28, 160–161
  The copy of a letter lately written by a Spanishe gentleman 96
Visconti, Lazario, S.J. 129

Vitelleschi, Muzio, S.J. 117, 135, 259, 397

Waad, Sir William 309
Waller, Robert 215
Walpole, Edward, S.J. 73, 75, 278n 6, 289n 41, 368
Walpole, Henry, S.J. 43n 117, 77, 91, 105, 117, 119–120, 133, 153–164, 167–169, 183–186, 191n 158, 215, 283, 308, 340, 409
Walpole, Richard, S.J. 402n 202 15
Walpole, Thomas 153, 155n 38
Walsham, Alexandra 10–11, 95
Walsingham, Sir Francis 86, 362
Warford, William, S.J. 47n 132, 73–74, 77n 258, 113, 340
Watts, William 52, 377, 404
Wells, John 44n 119
Wells, Swithun 33
Wentworth, Peter 253
  Works
  A pithie exhortation to her maiestie for establishing her successor 253n 146
  "Booke of the heir apparent to the Throne" 253
Wernham, R.B. 85, 100, 143, 152, 152
Westmorland, Earl of *see* Nevil, Charles, Earl of Westmorland
Weston, William, S.J. 7, 18, 34, 43–44, 50, 76–77, 92, 167–169, 186, 189, 192–199, 283, 290–291, 293, 295, 311, 313, 320–321, 323–324
Whitaker, William, Dr 58
White, Eustace 43n 116
White, Thomas, S.J. 119
Whitgift, John, Archbishop of Canterbury 48, 67, 191, 277
Wilkes, Sir Thomas 146, 150, 169, 180
William V, Duke of Bavaria 236
Williams, Penry 152
Williams, Richard 61, 149–150, 181
Wisbech Castle 34, 76, 192–193, 200

Wiseman, Jane 164–166
Wiseman, John, S.J. 36, 43, 51
Wiseman, Thomas, S.J. 36, 43, 51, 92
Wiseman, William 163–166, 314–315
Wolfe, David, S.J. 5, 8
Wolly, George 397n 181
Wolsey, Thomas, Cardinal 337–338
Wood, James, Laird of Boniton 299
Woodroff, Elizabeth 36
Woodhouse, Thomas, S.J. 5
Woodward, Lionel 317
Worthington, Thomas, Dr 150, 184, 269–270, 344n 24, 347n 33, 387
Worthington, William 192n 160
Wright, Thomas, ex S.J. 217–219, 220n 38, 277–278, 316, 334, 410
Wyse, Andrew 265, 394

Ximenes, António Fernandez 118

Yelverton, Christopher 331–332
Yelverton, Edward 35
Yepes, Diego de
  Work
  Historia particular de la persecucion de Inglaterra y de los martirios que en ella ha aiudo desde el año del señor, 1570 221
Yorke, Edmund 149–150, 181
Yorke Plot 149–150, 181
Yorke, Rowland 149, 279
Young, Henry 149–150
Young, Peter 298
Young, Richard 48
Younger, James 45–46, 63n 189, 73, 344n 24

Zuñiga y Sotomayor, Francisco de, Duke of Béjar 115

Made in United States
North Haven, CT
22 January 2022